Thailand's
Islands & Beaches

Andrew Burke
Celeste Brash, Austin Bush,
Brandon Presser, Adam Skolnick

BANGKOK (p64)
The City of Angels mixes temples, galleries, markets and rooftop bars into Southeast Asia's most vibrant and beguiling capital

KAENG KRACHAN NATIONAL PARK (p172)
Thailand's largest national park is an unending expanse of jungle embellished with rare birds and the Pala-U waterfall

KO CHANG ARCHIPELAGO (p148)
Choose resort luxury or backpacker basics as you island hop through this less-touristed chain of verdant islands

KO TAO (p233)
Be a small fish while diving in a big tank with mighty whale sharks from this coral-fringed island

SIMILAN (p295) & SURIN ISLANDS (p289)
Go Cousteau on a live-aboard dive or snorkelling safari around these fantasy coral islands

AO PHANG-NGA (p297)
Kayak around this scenic bay filled with limestone towers such as 'James Bond Island'

PHUKET TOWN (p308)
A hotchpotch of cultural, historical and culinary influences makes this old town a perfect break from the beach

RAILAY (p346)
A stunning beach and limestone cliffs rising out of the sea make this about the best rock-climbing spot on earth

KO PHI-PHI (p351)
Possibly the most beautiful place you (and thousands of others) will ever see

TRANG BEACHES (p371)
A bleach-blonde coast of undeveloped beaches and islands perfect for escaping the masses

KO TARUTAO MARINE NATIONAL PARK (p383)
Remote islands and uninhabited beaches where you can live out your *Survivor* fantasies

KO PHA-NGAN (p216)
Steaming jungle, all-around beaches and a beach-bum, laid-back vibe, except at Hat Rin where the beach parties come loud and often

On the Road

ANDREW BURKE Coordinating Author
There are plenty of reasons not to take a Bangkok túk-túk (see p426), but when the heavens opened after a long day of researching I had little choice. Once I'd established that I didn't want to be taken to a tailor, gem shop or strip show, the flat-to-the-floor-or-not-at-all ride was a fun reminder that, for all its faults, the túk-túk is a uniquely Thai experience.

CELESTE BRASH One thing I love about Thais is that they can be very silly. Here I had forgotten my friend had painted my face with mud as I posed with this harmless snake caught in the jungle on Ko Chang (p275). Everyone laughed: beware of mad guidebook authors loose in the forest!

BRANDON PRESSER There are few things I like more than diving, and there are few places I like to do it more than Ko Tao (p233). Scubaphiles are quick to point out that tiny Tao's sites aren't the world's best – it's all about the lifestyle here: powder-soft beaches, positive vibes and great friends to hang out with after a long day with the fishes. I can never seem to tear myself away. Travellers beware, you're gonna get stuck here too!

AUSTIN BUSH Food is understandably one of the main reasons to visit Thailand, but not all of it's amazing; this disturbingly technicolour spread was encountered at an old-school food hall on Th Dinso, in Bangkok's Banglamphu district.

ADAM SKOLNICK Emerald Cave (p373) in high season usually draws a crowd, so we got up at dawn, hopped in our long-tail boat from Hat Faràng and arrived before anyone else. We swam through pitch blackness, which eventually faded into pale morning light streaming into this magnificent *hôrng*. Not a bad way to begin my birthday.

For full author biographies see p451.

Thailand's Islands & Beaches Highlights

The stunning, palm-lined beaches of Thailand's coasts and islands are the highlight of many journeys to the land of smiles. But as Lonely Planet staff and readers note here, there is plenty more to see and experience on your Thai beach holiday. You can discover a reef adorned with colourful coral or a serene shrine amid the Phuket hustle. Spend lazy, guiltless days in hammocks and on massage beds, and sip cocktails into the night as the sea laps at your feet. Or drink up Thai culture during a memorable festival. Or all of the above… Whatever it is that floats your boat, tell us about it at on the Thorn Tree forum at lonelyplanet.com.

KRAIG LIEB

1 SONGKRAN: NEW YEAR IN APRIL

Mobs of wet, smiling children take control of the streets to drench passing vehicles and pedestrians with water. Roaming pick-up trucks carry kids armed with water guns and buckets looking to soak anyone who has miraculously managed to stay dry. Trying to walk down the street is like trying to walk on water – you're going to end up wet (see p20).

Michael Rossi, Traveller, Australia

JOHN BORTHWICK

2 MASSAGE OR MASOCHISM?

Nothing beats lying on a Thai beach with fresh pineapple juice and book in hand. Nothing, that is, apart from a beachside massage (surely?). I was at Hat Thian on Ko Pha-Ngan and feeling full of adventure, so I stepped onto the beachside platform for a traditional Thai massage (p395). More extreme workout than relaxing massage, I found myself bent over 'mama' as she grabbed my shoulders, placed her feet in my back and rolled me into a backwards arch. Boy, I felt good afterwards.

Katie Lynch, Lonely Planet Staff

ERNEST MANE

3 SIMILAN ISLANDS

Best reached from Phuket via a live-aboard, these lovely islands (p295) harbour prolific marine life, gorgeous soft corals and even the occasional whale shark. Undersea boulders provide both a sense of scale as well as a home for all sorts of critters.

SirVerity, Traveller

SHRINE OF THE SERENE LIGHT, PHUKET

Hidden down a narrow alleyway in Phuket Town is the tiny Shrine of the Serene Light (p309). Surrounded by buildings, this little oasis is free from traffic noise and large throngs of tourists. A great place to find some peace and serenity.

Renée Barker, Traveller, Australia

INGO JEZIERSKI / ALAMY

KO SAMUI

Where lazy is accepted and bored is unheard of, Ko Samui (p195) is an escape of indulgence. I will never bore of the ocean over my feet at dinner, nor the flowing cocktails from sunrise to sunset.

Lisa Downs, Traveller, Australia

AUSTIN BUSH

RICHARD NEBESKY

KO TAO

Learning from its big brother Ko Pha-Ngan (epicentre of Thailand's full-moon debauch), 'Turtle Island' (p233) knows a thing or two about nightlife. Most spend their days in the blue waters chasing fish; evenings are spent drinking like them.

Alexander L Cross, Traveller, USA

CHATUCHAK WEEKEND MARKET, BANGKOK

Countless stalls line the dozens of dimly lit aisles where everything from reels of bright fabrics to exotic animals are sold (p109). Cries of *'sà·wàt·dee kâ'* echo while noodles fry and incense burns – an exhilarating day. Are your haggling skills top-notch?

Nick Boulos, Traveller, UK

NOT FOR THE SQUEAMISH: VEGETARIAN FESTIVAL, PHUKET

If you're lucky enough to be in Phuket in September/October, take a deep breath because it's time for the annual Vegetarian Festival (p312). Buddhist mediums expressing the presence of deities flood the streets while inserting sharp objects through their faces. Though in their trance they may feel no pain, for many onlookers it's excruciating to watch.

Christine Murray, Traveller, USA

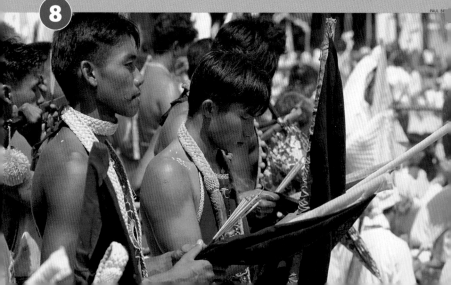

Contents

Regional Map Contents

BANGKOK
pp70–1

EASTERN GULF COAST p117

NORTHWESTERN GULF COAST p167

NORTHERN ANDAMAN COAST p272

SOUTHWESTERN GULF COAST p194

SOUTHERN ANDAMAN COAST p335

Destination Thailand's Islands & Beaches

Sweeping white-sand beaches, hammocks swinging lazily between palm trees and dramatic limestone karsts emerging from sun-kissed bays are the sort of images that populate our dreams of a tropical paradise. On the islands and along the coasts of southern Thailand, the dream becomes reality. That you can enjoy Thailand's islands and beaches whichever way you choose only adds to the allure. If it's solitude you seek, there are islands where the footprints in the sand can be yours alone. Feeling more social? Stomp the sand with thousands of others at a heaving full-moon party. You can choose a beachside hut or a resort with its own spa, go scuba diving or snorkelling, take out a sea kayak or climb those karst formations. Or just lay in a hammock – still a perfectly respectable way to experience Thailand.

Thailand's islands and beaches might be the stuff of dreams, but keep in mind that the wave of faràng (foreigners of European descent) seeking a slice of paradise has impacts on the local population. Tourism brings plenty of money and for that most Thais are thankful. It is also accompanied by rapid improvements to roads, schools and health centres. But tourists, and those who cater to their tastes, have also brought some less-desirable changes. Problems with drugs and organised prostitution are among the most notable, but less-obvious issues, such as the cultural changes mass tourism brings and how it affects local youth, are also a concern. Speak to locals, however, and you'll probably hear strikingly familiar concerns differing only in their 'tropical paradise' setting: having and keeping a job, physical security and access to reliable health care and useful education for themselves and their families.

Economically, vast numbers of people in southern Thailand rely on tourism. Just look around any beach resort to see how many people are employed there, and how many more survive on the money spent by holidaying visitors. It's these people who have been most affected by the country's ongoing political trouble.

Many Thais are divided along colour lines: yellow shirts represent the establishment based in Bangkok and red shirts the mainly rural supporters of ex-prime minister Thaksin Shinawatra. When yellow shirts occupied Bangkok's airports for a week, the fallout was greatest in the south. Countless people cancelled their holidays and the tourism industry – having recovered so well from the horrors of the 2004 tsunami – was brought to its knees. Hundreds of thousands of people were laid off.

Anyone in Thailand at the time could see the actual dangers were minimal. However, the same can't be said for the deep south, where the military's hardline attitude to the majority Islamic population continues to drive young men into the separatist movement. More than 3000 people have died in this conflict, which shows little sign of resolution.

It is important to be aware of the stories behind the places you visit and some knowledge of the local situation will be greatly appreciated by the locals you meet. That said, for most travellers Thailand's islands and beaches will seem a million miles away from the whatever-it-was you flew here to escape. Thais seem almost pathologically good-natured and even when times are bad they maintain an admirable ability to see the fun side of life. Given that most times are not that bad at all, expect the waters to be as blue, the sands as white and the smiles as warm as you dreamed them to be.

The unrest in Thailand's deep south should not deter tourism in other parts of the peninsula, but travellers should monitor the situation through Thailand's English-language media at www.bangkokpost.com, and seek feedback from other travellers on the Thorn Tree bulletin board at lonelyplanet.com. For more on the south, see the boxed texts on p28 and p265.

FAST FACTS

Population: 64,632,000

Religion: Buddhist 94.6%, Muslim 4.6%

GDP per capita (PPP): US$8400

Minimum daily wage: 148–203B depending on province

Inflation: 5.8%

Number of attempted coups d'etat since 1932: 19

Coastline: 3219km

Number of yellow shirts worn on Mondays: about 15 million

Number of 7-Elevens: almost 5250, and rising

Getting Started

Thailand is a traveller's paradise and it's easy and cheap to eat, sleep and get around. If you're a bit flexible and it's not the busiest period around Christmas and New Year, you can pretty much just turn up and make all your decisions as you go. Of course, if you have your heart set on staying at a particular place, book it online. No immunisations are required, visas are easy to obtain and seats on discount flights, comfortable long-distance buses and trains keep most of Thailand within easy reach for not much money. Food and accommodation are plentiful; the beauty of Thailand is that, even on a shoestring, you can see everything and still have money for a shopping binge before you head home.

WHEN TO GO

The best time to visit coastal Thailand is during the tourist high season between November and April. Accommodation prices are at their highest but almost everything in the country is open, the weather is mainly dry and temperatures are reasonable. The mid-December to late-January period is busiest (and priciest). Local festivals (see p20) also cause spikes throughout the year, notably for a week either side of Songkran (Thai New Year; 13–15 April).

The rest of the year (May to October) is the rainy season, when the southwest monsoon drenches the country and tourists stay away – for tourism-related businesses this is low season. Prices for accommodation plummet and as competition hots up deals can be found on everything from transport to food, activities, tailoring and even massage. During this time some smaller or harder-to-reach resorts and islands shut down completely, and the ferries that service them either stop or run less frequently. Stormy seas can also play havoc with schedules. Divers should note that in the rainy season visibility drops dramatically.

It's not known as the rainy season for nothing, but in southern Thailand not all rain is equal. Often there will be a couple of days without rain or the only rain will be a short, dramatic downpour in the mid-afternoon, which is not enough to ruin the trip. But it all depends on where you are. For example, in September Phuket has about 200mm less rain that Ko Chang, but three times more than Ko Samui. The various permeatations are too numerous to explain here, but see the Travelfish weather map

If the weather sounds confusing, see the Climate Charts, p396, or check out the innovative weather map at Travelfish (www.travelfish .org/weather_fish.php), which has stats on average rainfall and the number of rainy days per month so you can work out where the driest beach will be before you arrive.

DON'T LEAVE HOME WITHOUT...

- Checking the visa situation (p411) – travellers of many nationalities can get an entry permit on arrival, but make sure you're one of them
- A copy of your travel insurance policy details (p404)
- Looking online for hotel deals (p390)
- Long-sleeved and leg-covering clothes for showy dinners, visiting temples and air-con buses and trains
- A mix of credit cards and cash, packed separately for extra security (p406)
- Unpacking all the useless things that make your bag weigh a tonne; lighten your load physically and mentally
- Your sense of humour: you're on holiday, enjoy it

(www.travelfish.org/eather_fish.php) for detail. Southern Thailand also receives rain from the northwest monsoon from November to January. To maximise your chances of sunny days, visit between December and March and prioritise the gulf coast over the Andaman coast, which gets more of the northwest monsoon and is generally wetter year-round.

Temperatures from November to March hover between 22°C and 30°C throughout Thailand, though they're usually nearer to 30°C. They rise from March to May, when they almost always peak above 30°C. The south is usually a few degrees cooler during the monsoon.

COSTS

Thailand is cheap by Western standards and it's possible to get by on 1000B (US$30) a day and still live reasonably comfortably. If you're disciplined and stay only in budget guesthouses, eat at street stalls or local restaurants and travel by train or government buses, you can get by on less, but even the smallest appetite for beer will put serious pressure on your budget. Guesthouse accommodation ranges from about 350B to 1000B a day on most beaches.

For a little more pampering (air-conditioned bungalows, flights in and out, romantic dinners, boat tours and motorbike rental on the islands), raise your daily budget to about 1700B (US$50).

Style costs more but it's possible to get a quality room with character for between about 1700B and 3400B, depending on the season. The upper midrange and associated lifestyle (think mud masks, diving, cocktails) is expanding fast, and you're looking at about 3400B (US$100) a day minimum. At the top end, the sky (actually, the outer atmosphere) is the limit. Luxury resorts start at about 5000B and attached restaurants, bars and spa facilities soon blow that out; though you can always pop out for a 40B green curry. To all these prices add about 20% to 30% in Bangkok.

Children can usually stay free in their parents' room. Discounts for children are available at museums and on internal flights, trains and some tours and activities.

HOW MUCH?

Restaurant dinner
80-1000B

Beachfront room
300-30,000B

Open Water dive
certification course
9800-20,000B

Boat trip between Surat
Thani and Ko Samui 200B

2nd-class air-con sleeper
train from Bangkok to
Surat Thani 758B

TRAVELLING RESPONSIBLY

The key to responsible travel in Thailand, like anywhere, is to be considerate. Consider what impact your actions will have before you act and you'll likely do the right thing by yourself and the country and people of Thailand.

Environmental considerations include the obvious, such as littering above and below the surface of the water, not having your towels washed every day and reusing water bottles and the like to avoid excess consumption, but are also impacted by the companies you choose to use for activities such as diving, trekking and climbing; for green businesses, see p463.

You can also act responsibly in other ways. When shopping, try to buy souvenirs from the producer if possible, and avoid coral and animal products. When bargaining, by all means start low but do keep it in context and remember a good deal is good for you and the vendor (see the boxed text, p408).

Perhaps the most satisfying, sustainable and memorable responsible travel is by using homestay accommodation, which is available on many islands, and particularly the smaller, less commercial islands. Not only do you bring money directly into the community, but you get to experience the oft-talked about but seldom found 'real Thailand'.

TRAVEL READING

Most English-language books about Thailand, be they fiction or nonfiction, focus on Bangkok, but a few do take trips to the south.

TOP PICKS

FILMS

Get into the mood for exotic Thailand with these flicks. For more on Thailand's home-grown cinema, see p41.

- *Krung Thep Antara* (Bangkok Dangerous, 1999) – The Pang brothers' stylish, award-winning story of a deaf hit man who has a crisis of confidence after unexpectedly finding love. A not-so-hot Nicolas Cage remake was released in 2008.

- *OK Baytong* (2003) – A monk enters the modern world to care for his orphaned niece; set in southern Thailand, the story touches on the violence between Thais and Muslims.

- *The Man with the Golden Gun* (1973) – James Bond thwarts the usual plot for world domination via a long-tail boat chase in Bangkok and a showdown in the villain's evil-yet-idyllic island lair (now visited as 'James Bond Island', p299).

- *Ploy* (2007) – Psycho-drama about a Thai couple who return to Bangkok after years in America and face a relationship acid test when a young woman moves into their room.

- *The Beach* (2000) – A big and beautiful Hollywood spectacle based on the Alex Garland novel and often credited for turning Thailand's beach scene from backpacker to flashpacker. Mostly filmed on Ko Phi-Phi Leh (p358).

RESORT HOTELS

Thailand's resort hotels come in all shapes, sizes and price ranges. For destination-specific recommendations, see our picks for Phuket (p330), Ko Samui (p203), Ko Phi-Phi (p357) and Hua Hin (p180).

- **Jungle retreat** – Anantara (p207) on Ko Samui, and Golden Buddha Beach Resort (p290) on Ko Phra Thong.

- **Arty chic** – Library (p204) and Zazen (p207) on Ko Samui, Putahracsa (p180) in Hua Hin and Sala Phuket (p331) on Phuket.

- **Modern luxury** – Zeavola (p357) on Ko Phi-Phi, Vijitt (p316) or Amanpuri Resort (p329) on Phuket, and Sala Samui (p205) on Ko Samui.

- **Private beach** – Four Seasons Koh Samui (p208) or Sila Evason Hideaway (p206) on Ko Samui, Chedi (p328) on Phuket, The Paradise Ko Yao (p300) on Ko Yao Noi and Ko Jum Resort (p366).

- **High style, low price** – Ko Kood Beach Resort (p162) on Ko Kood, Jungle Club (p202) or L'Hacienda (p206) on Ko Samui, and Casa 104 (p311) in Phuket Town.

ADVENTURE EXPERIENCES

Roll out of the hammock and you'll find plenty of adventure activities to get the blood pumping.

- **Rock climbing** – The awesome limestone walls at Railay (p346).

- **Diving** – Coral? Wrecks? Whale sharks? Take your pick of some of Asia's best diving (see the boxed text, p282).

- **Hiking** – Stride into one of the oldest rainforests in the world at Khao Sok National Park (p290).

- **Sea kayaking** – Paddle through the limestone cliffs, hidden lagoons and peach-coloured beaches of Ang Thong Marine National Park's 42 islands (p248).

- **Snorkelling** – The Gulf of Thailand and Andaman Sea are like one vast snorkelling possibility, but it's hard to beat the reefs around Ko Phi-Phi (p353).

The Beach, Alex Garland's account of a backpacker's discovery of a beach Eden that is spoiled somewhat by drug lords and sharks, is a highly appropriate Thai beach read. Emily Barr's *Backpack* is the chick-lit equivalent. It follows a young British woman's attempt to rediscover herself, against a backdrop of holiday romances and backpacker murders.

John Burdett's cop dramas are also great beach reads. In *Bangkok 8* and *Bangkok Tattoo,* hard-boiled Sonchai, a Bangkok police investigator, cracks open several page-turning mysteries.

Jasmine Nights, by Thai champion-of-the-arts SP Somtow, uses the fictional 1960s friendship between a 12-year-old Thai boy and an African-American boy to closely examine Thai culture.

On the nonfiction shelf *Very Thai: Everyday Popular Culture,* by Philip Cornwel-Smith, colourfully explains all manner of Thai oddities, from why taxis have dashboard shrines to why Thais put salt in their fruit drinks. *Travelers' Tales Thailand: True Stories* features travel essays by Charles Nicholls, Pico Iyer and others, with some savvy travel tips sprinkled throughout the text.

INTERNET RESOURCES

The Web is awash with websites about Thailand and Thai culture. Useful sites include the following:

2Bangkok.com (www.2bangkok.com) English translations from the Thai press, ongoing monitoring of the situation in the south and other news.

Lonely Planet (www.lonelyplanet.com) General information, long reviews of hotels and resorts with a booking function and, of course, the Thorn Tree traveller forum.

Tezza (tezza-thailandbeachesandislands.blogspot.com) Tezza blogs on his travels to a huge variety of islands, with timely comments and links.

Thai Visa (www.thaivisa.com) An expat message board dealing with visa issues and FAQs; good info but lots of drivel, too.

Tourism Thailand (www.tourismthailand.org) Tourist Authority of Thailand's website.

Travelfish (www.travelfish.org) The best independent travel site for backpackers coming to Thailand.

Itineraries
CLASSIC ROUTES

FIRST-TIMER ISLAND HOPPING Two to Three Weeks / Bangkok to Bangkok
Spend some time in **Bangkok** (p64), before bussing south to **Chumphon** (p189), the jumping-off point for diving or snorkelling in **Ko Tao** (p233) and full-mooning in **Ko Pha-Ngan** (p216). These islands are supremely chilled with a dash (you say when) of hedonism thrown in. Ko Pha-Ngan is one of the most diverse islands in the Gulf: 20-somethings go for trance-crazed **Hat Rin** (p218), 30s-and-beyond burrow further north, maybe peeping into the party for old-time's sake, and families dig the toddler-friendly bays.

When you tire of your hammock head via air or Surat Thani to the beautiful Andaman coast, decorated with the iconic limestone sea cliffs that have made Thailand's beaches famous. From **Krabi** (p336) squeeze into a minivan to explore the surrounding beaches or go to **Railay** (p346) to climb the world-famous seaside karst cliffs. For more beaches, check out **Ko Lanta** (p358) before returning to Krabi via **Ko Phi-Phi** (p351) to see what all the fuss is about.

Drag yourself off the sand for some jungle trekking in **Khao Sok National Park** (p290) or **Khao Sam Roi Yot National Park** (p183), closer to Bangkok. Then head back to Bangkok for a wrap up of souvenir shopping and city pampering.

Join the classic beach-hunters' trail by leap-frogging across the peninsula and dipping your toes into both the Gulf of Thailand and the Andaman Sea (1400km round trip).

HAMMOCK TOUR EXTRAORDINAIRE   One Month / Bangkok to Bangkok

A month, you say? There are thousands of perfectly good itineraries to think up but, well, why not consider a hammock tour extraordinaire. Not just any old beach trip, this is enough time to really get to know southern Thailand's islands, beaches, jungle parks and cuisine – you'll eat a lot of *kà·nŏm jeen* (a southern noodle dish). On your way south from **Bangkok** (p64) stop in at **Cha-am** (p172) for a brief taste of beach culture Thai style (nary a faràng to be seen). Continue south via Chumphon out to the odd-couple island twins of **Ko Tao** (p233) and **Ko Pha-Ngan** (p216).

With a bit of experience under your (dive) belt it's time to leave the pack behind for some real travelling along the beaches between **Surat Thani** (p249) and **Nakhon Si Thammarat** (p254). Continue to **Hat Yai** (p260), the gateway to the 'deep south', and then west to the sleepy Muslim town of **Satun** (p378), the jumping-off point to the wildly beautiful natural islands of **Ko Tarutao Marine National Park** (p383).

Turning north, head up to **Trang** (p367) and pop over to the beaches of Hat Chao Mai National Park, including delightful **Ko Kradan** (p374), or the wild mangroves of **Ko Libong** (p375), home to endangered dugongs and exotic birds. Hopscotch through a series of beach resorts: quickly morphing **Ko Lanta** (p358), backwater **Ko Jum** (p366) and **Ko Phi-Phi** (p351), which can be crowded but is also stunningly beautiful. Don't forget the beaches around **Krabi** (p336) for real sand credibility. Then hightail it to **Phuket** (p302), Thailand's most powerful tourist tractor beam, and push on north to idyllic **Hat Khao Lak** (p292). From here, sail out on a live-aboard dive or snorkelling safari into the **Similan Islands** (p295) or the **Surin Islands** (p289). Back on dry land, get yourself back to Bangkok to catch up on some shopping and partying to round out the trip.

Take your time exploring the beauty of a broad range of Thailand's beaches, islands and national parks – above and below the water (1800km round trip).

EAST COAST POP-IN   Seven to 10 Days...Maybe More / Bangkok to Bangkok

Thailand's southern islands might draw the big crowds, but if you're pushed for time or heading into Cambodia this route along the eastern gulf coast is both easier to get to and relatively less touristed. From **Bangkok** (p64) head directly to **Ban Phe** (p138), the transfer point for trips to rustic **Ko Samet National Park** (p139), where Bangkokians kick off their flip-flops.

Continue along the coast to sleepy **Trat** (p145) or just go direct to Laem Ngop for the boat into the Ko Chang Archipelago, where you can choose your level of comfort and isolation from a host of islands. Jungle-topped **Ko Chang** (p150) is the largest and most developed island, with diversions ranging from **elephant trekking** (p154) and guided **hikes** (p154) of the rugged interior to diving into the underworld. To get further off the beaten beach, jump on a boat to more secluded **Ko Mak** (p162) or jungle-clad **Ko Kood** (p160). For most travellers these will be well and truly unspoilt enough. If, however, you've decided you won't be making it back to work/real life on time and fancy yourself as an explorer (do email your mum to warn her you're disappearing off the face of the earth...but will be returning) head for ultra simple **Ko Kham** or **Ko Rayang** (p165) for some stunning coral, or to the national park at **Ko Rang** (p165) for a genuine *Survivor* experience, sans pesky host, cameramen and tribal councils.

If and when you're heading back to Bangkok, consider a stop in (brace yourself) **Pattaya** (p120), where you might be surprised at how much there is to do that doesn't involve sleaze (though there's certainly plenty of that!).

Pressed for time or tied to the capital? You can deposit your beach towel on silky sand within a half-day's journey of Bangkok, or go a couple of hours further to the relatively less-visited Ko Chang Archipelago (500–600km round trip).

TAILORED TRIPS

HONEYMOON DREAMING

Wedding = stress. Honeymoon = romance. With just a week, touch down for a night in a boutique hotel in **Bangkok** (p93) then fly direct to **Ko Samui** (p195) or **Phuket** (p302) to minimise your travelling time. These islands have long, voluptuous beaches and amenities developed for package tourists, but they also have quiet corners for down-to-earth relaxing.

Skip Samui's rowdier beaches for less beautiful but more romantic **Bo Phut** (p206). Drop into a **spa resort** (p200) for a well-earned chance to be rubbed and revitalised while just laying back and thinking of…anything except seating plans. Suitably de-stressed, join a tour to the wilderness of nearby **Ang Thong Marine National Park** (p248).

Phuket is Thailand's most famous island but there's more to it than gaudy high-rises and supercommercial Patong. Stay at a romantic, out-of-the-way beach, such as **Hat Mai Khao** (p331). Once settled, soak up some culture in **Phuket Town** (p308), a spice trade-era port town with mixed Chinese, Indian and Portuguese influences and some fine restaurants. For a little more action dive or snorkel in the Andaman Sea (p304) or explore the beaches of **Sirinat National Park** (p330).

With two weeks, you can split your affections between two islands. Motor from Phuket over to stunning **Ko Phi-Phi** (p351). Too much civilisation? Then embrace your inner Tarzan and Jane and go 'native' on napping **Ko Jum** (p366).

THE ANTI-HAMMOCK

If you prefer climbing limestone rock faces to climbing into your hammock, diving into the unknown realm to diving into the infinity pool, then you've come to the right part of the world. While **Ko Tao** (p233) is a good place to get your dive licence, Thailand's best diving, snorkelling and climbing is spread along the remarkable Andaman coast. Fly south from **Bangkok** (p64) to **Trang** (p367) and kick on to lesser-known but stunning beaches and islands such as **Ko Kradan** (p374). The waters near Kradan are a favourite hangout for turtles and lionfish, while the island itself has a lush tangle of jungle. Take a boat up to **Ko Phi-Phi** (p351) for a change of scene, both above and below the surface.

Time to trade your flippers for carabiners so head to **Krabi** (p336) and around to pretty **Railay** (p346), where you can ascend the karst limestone walls in Thailand's most-renowned rock-climbing region and sneak in a little hammock time. But we're not done yet. The cliffs conquered, it's time to strap on the tanks or snorkelling gear again for the *coup de grâce*. Meet up with your live-aboard yacht in **Phuket** (p304) or **Hat Khao Lak** (p293) – yes, invite your new dive friends to share the cost – and set sail for the tropical archipelago of the **Similan Islands** (p295). With enough time and money, finish the trip in the **Surin Islands** (p289), where you might meet some of Jacques Cousteau's old manta mates at Richelieu Rock.

Events Calendar

Thailand has some cracking festivals and events. Many are religious, with festivities revolving around the local wát or mosque, but a growing number of others are secular, ranging from celebrations of jazz to underwater weddings. Exact dates for most festivals vary from year to year; for more information, see p402.

JANUARY

NEW YEAR'S DAY   30 Dec-1 Jan
This is the first of Thailand's three New Year's celebrations and features Western-style revelry.

FEBRUARY–MARCH

CHINESE NEW YEAR   3-5 Feb 2011, 23-25 Jan 2012
Thailand's large Thai-Chinese population celebrate *drùd jeen* (lunar new year) with a week of house cleaning, lion dances and fireworks. The most impressive festivities are in Bangkok's Chinatown and Phuket Town's Old Town.

PHRA NAKHON KHIRI FAIR   early Feb
Notable temple festival in Phetchaburi with classical dance and dramatic performances and a beauty contest for local widows; see p171.

TRANG UNDERWATER WEDDING   14 Feb
On Valentine's Day lovers with Scuba fetishes take their vows under the waters off Ko Kradan, in Trang province. The ceremony has become a big deal in Trang, which now markets the 'Season of Love'. Locals and foreigners are welcome; see p376.

PHUKET GAY PRIDE
This four-day weekend party event has been running for years, though the dates are notoriously changeable (usually sometime between February and April); see p326.

MAGHA PUJA (MAH·KÁ BOO·CHAH)
                              18 Feb 2011, 8 Mar 2012
The full moon of the third lunar month is celebrated countrywide to commemorate the Buddha's spontaneous, unannounced preaching to 1250 enlightened monks, who came to hear him 'without prior summons'. The festival culminates in a candle-lit walk around the main chapel at every wát.

BANGKOK JAZZ FESTIVAL   Mar
Formerly a December event in Dusit Park, this major festival of international and Thai musicians has (for now) moved to March and the Central World shopping mall; see www.bangkokjazz festival.com.

APRIL

CHAKRI DAY   6 Apr
Across the country, celebrations are held for the founding of the Chakri royal dynasty.

SONGKRAN   13-15 Apr
The celebration of the Thai New Year is the major festival on the Thai calendar. Many people head home on holiday to observe traditional rites such as Buddha images being 'bathed' and monks and elders receiving the respect of younger Thais through the sprinkling of water over their hands. Tourists are not exempt: most travellers tend to become thoroughly immersed in one mega-waterfight or another, so dress to be soaked! Organised 'shows' are held in Bangkok at Th Khao San and Patpong, where you can arm yourself with a high-calibre water gun and go berserk. Elsewhere you're just as likely to get saturated (it's very uncool to get angry at someone throwing water on you), so don't carry anything you don't want to get wet.

MAY–JUNE

SAILBOAT REGATTA   early May
Hat Chao Mai (p371), near Trang, holds an annual regatta for traditional wooden sailboats, accompanied by music and theatre.

VISAKHA PUJA (WÍ·SÄH·KÀ BOO·CHAH)
                              17 May 2011, 4 Jun 2012
The full moon of the sixth lunar month commemorates the Buddha's birth, enlightenment and *parinibbana* (passing away). Activities are centred on the wát, with candle-lit processions, chanting and sermons.

HUA HIN JAZZ FESTIVAL   mid-Jun
This annual event in Hua Hin is Thailand's best jazz festival; see p179.

JULY–AUGUST

ASALHA PUJA (AH·SĂHN·HÀ BOO·CHAH)
26 Jul 2010, 15 Jul 2011, 2 Aug 2012

This Buddhist festival, on the full moon of the eighth lunar month, commemorates the day the Buddha preached his first sermon after attaining enlightenment and is marked at Theravada Buddhist temples with a candle-lit procession at night.

KHAO PHANSA (KÔW PAN·SĂH)
27 Jul 2010, 16 Jul 2011, 3 Aug 2012

The day after Asalah Puja marks the beginning of the Buddhist 'lent' and rains retreat. Young men traditionally enter the monkhood for the rainy season, and all monks sequester themselves in a monastery for three months. It's a good time to observe a Buddhist ordination.

SEPTEMBER–OCTOBER

VEGETARIAN FESTIVAL

For nine days at the start of the ninth lunar month (usually in September or October), devout Chinese Buddhists give up meat and engage in stomach-turning acts of self-mutilation. It's celebrated with special vigour in Phuket, Trang and Bangkok, while Krabi and Phang-Nga partake on a smaller scale; see p312.

BANGKOK INTERNATIONAL FILM FESTIVAL
late Sep

Dates and venues are notoriously fickle for Bangkok's two film festivals; this one usually runs for 10 days and most recently was held in late September. About 150 films are shown, with an emphasis on Asian cinema, ending with the awarding of the festival's Golden Kinnaree; see www.bangkokfilm.org.

OK PHANSA
23 Oct 2010, 12 Oct 2011, 29 Oct 2012

The end of Buddhist 'lent' on the full moon of the 11th lunar month sets off a national party. It celebrates the Buddha's three-month retreat to heaven to talk to his mother.

NOVEMBER

BANGKOK PRIDE
mid-Nov

Usually held in mid-November, this week-long festival of parades, parties, awards, sequins and feather boas is organised by city businesses and organisations for Bangkok's gay, lesbian, bisexual and transgender community. Don't miss the opening 'Pink in the Park' fair in Lumphini Park; see www.bangkokpride.org.

LOI KRATHONG
21 Nov 2010, 10 Nov 2011, 28 Nov 2012

On the night of the full moon of the 12th lunar month, small lotus-shaped gràtong (baskets or boats made of a section of banana trunk for flotation, banana leaves, flowers, incense, candles and a coin – don't use the Styrofoam versions) are floated down Mae Nam Chao Phraya in Bangkok and rivers, lakes and canals across Thailand. The ceremony, which originated in Sukhothai, is both an offering to the water spirits and a symbolic cleansing of bad luck.

DECEMBER

KING'S BIRTHDAY
5 Dec

Across the country, formal processions and cultural displays take place. It's huge in Bangkok, where festivities centre on the Grand Palace and the Dusit palace district.

CONCERT IN THE PARK
mid-Dec–mid-Feb

The Bangkok Symphony Orchestra performs free concerts in Bangkok's Lumphini Park every Sunday evening (from 5.30pm) between mid-December and mid-February; see www.bangkoksymphony .org/concertinpark.html.

History

EARLY CULTURES

Little evidence remains of the cultures that existed in Thailand before the middle of the 1st millennium AD, partly due to the destructive effects of the tropical climate and encroaching jungle. What is known about these civilisations comes from a handful of archaeological sites in the northeast and far south of the country, most notably Ban Chiang in Udon Thani Province and the area around Krabi in the south. These early peoples buried their dead with complex rituals and left mysterious cave paintings throughout the south and northeast of Thailand, including the caves of Tharnbok Korannee National Park (p341) near Krabi.

Evidence of hunter-gatherer peoples from up to 180,000 years ago has been found in caves in northern Thailand.

EMERGING EMPIRES

From the 3rd century BC Indian traders began visiting the Gulf of Thailand, introducing the peoples of the region to Hinduism, which rapidly became the principal faith in the area. By 230 BC, when Chinese traders began visiting these shores, large parts of Thailand had been incorporated into the kingdom of Funan, the first state in Southeast Asia. The name Funan means 'king of the mountain', a reference to Mt Meru, the home of the Hindu gods. Funan established its main port at Oc Eo at the mouth of the Mekong River in Vietnam, and traded as far afield as India and possibly even Europe. At its peak, the state included large parts of Thailand, Laos, Cambodia and Vietnam and had active trade with the agrarian communities along the Malay Peninsula as far south as modern-day Pattani and Yala. A factory producing trade beads for the Funan empire was recently discovered at Khlong Thom near Krabi.

Khmer influence on early Thai society was so strong that, even as late as the 15th century, public documents tended to be written both in Thai and Khmer.

During the first few centuries AD, and possibly even much earlier, it is thought that present-day Thailand began to be populated by Tai peoples moving south from China (see the boxed text, opposite).

After the peak of the Funan Kingdom, around AD 600, a new star was rising in Southeast Asia, the kingdom of the Khmer, from modern-day Cambodia. This Hindu kingdom became famous for its extravagant sculpture and temple building; Khmer styles of art and design – as featured on the magnificent Hindu temples at Angkor Wat in Cambodia – had a profound effect on the art, language and religion of the Thais. Many Thai men became mercenaries for the Khmer armies and are clearly depicted in the bas-relief carvings in the Angkor compound.

Thailand is 543 years ahead of the West, at least according to its calendar, which measures the beginning of the modern era from the birth of Buddha instead of Christ.

During this period, much of central Thailand was still dominated by the dark-skinned indigenous peoples of the Malay Peninsula, known today as Negritos. A few small pockets of tribal Negrito people still survive in the

TIMELINE

3rd Century BC	1–300 AD	2nd–13th Century
Hinduism is thought to have arrived in Southeast Asia from India, and remains the dominant religion in the region for the next thousand years.	Increasingly displaced by the spreading Han in China, the Tai people begin to arrive in the fertile river valleys of mainland Southeast Asia.	Based in present-day Sumatra, the Srivijaya kingdom comes to dominate much of Indonesia and the Malay Peninsula, eventually extending as far as Madagascar.

central forests of southern Thailand. Increasingly, the fertile river basins of central Thailand became inhabited by groups of Tai-speaking people moving south who formed various independent city-states known as *meu-ang*. These people, the forerunners of modern Thais, would eventually refer to their territory as Syam or Sayam, later transliterated to 'Siam' by the English trader James Lancaster in 1592.

As the power of the Khmer grew, another culture began to have an influence on Thailand – the Mon people of current-day Myanmar (Burma), who had been converted to Buddhism by the missionaries of the Indian king Asoka. The Mon dominated western and upper-southwestern Thailand from the 3rd to 6th centuries, spreading Buddhism and building Thailand's first Buddhist stupa at Nakhon Pathom, west of Bangkok. The conversion of Nakhon Pathom, then capital of the Dvaravati kingdom, was recorded in the 5th century in the Mahavamsa (the sacred chronicle of Sri Lankan Buddhism). The Mon were later driven back into Myanmar by the Khmer and subsequent Thai kingdoms, but vestiges of Mon culture can still be seen on Ko Kret in north Bangkok.

Thai script is based on southern Indian writing systems adopted and adapted by the Mon and Khmer; the first examples date back to the 13th century.

KINGDOMS OF THE MALAY PENINSULA

Two distinct spheres of power existed within the region by the 12th century: the Khmer kingdom and minor Thai city-states dominated central Southeast Asia, while the Srivijaya kingdom of Sumatra and smaller entities dominated the Indonesian archipelago and Malay Peninsula, including parts of modern-day Thailand.

Of the series of city-states that grew to prominence along the Malay Peninsula, Tambralinga established its capital on the site of present-day Nakhon Si Thammarat. Tambralinga eventually became part of the Srivijaya kingdom, a confederation of maritime states that ruled southern Thailand and Malaysia from the 7th to 13th centuries. The Srivijaya became hugely wealthy from tolls extracted from traffic through the Strait of Malacca.

THE TAIS THAT BIND

The Tai, an ethno-linguistic group that includes modern-day Thais, the Lao, the Shan and other smaller groups, range in area from Hainan Island in China to Assam in northeastern India. Although it was long assumed that modern-day Thais originally separated from Tai groups in southern China in the first few centuries AD and moved south, remains found in northeastern Thailand may suggest that Tais have been living in present-day Thailand much longer than previously thought. The evidence, some of it dating back to 2500 BC, suggests that the people living there were among the earliest farming societies in the world, as well as some of the first metalworkers. The Tai may have even introduced the concept of tone to the languages of China and Southeast Asia, and today China, not Southeast Asia, is home to the greatest diversity of Tai ethnic groups.

5th Century	7th–11th Century	1238
Introduced by the Mon people, Theravada Buddhism gains a foothold in present-day Thailand. The religion initially mixes with and eventually replaces Hinduism as the dominant religion in the region.	The Angkor kingdom extends its control from present-day Cambodia into northeastern and central Thailand, dominating the culture of much of mainland Southeast Asia for more than 500 years.	Phor Khun Si Intharathit forms the first Thai kingdom at Sukhothai, which also sees the emergence of art, architecture and design that today are regarded as classically 'Thai'.

Remains of the Srivijaya culture can be seen around Chaiya near modern-day Surat Thani, and in Nakhon Si Thammarat, which has relics from Srivijaya times in its museum. Many art forms of the Srivijaya kingdom, such as Thai *năng dà·lung* (shadow theatre) and *lá·kon* (classical dance-drama), were developed in Nakhon Si Thammarat and incorporated into modern Thai culture. Also in Nakhon Si Thammarat is the ancient monastery of Wat Phra Mahathat, reputedly founded at the height of the Srivijaya kingdom. (For more information on the historic attractions of Nakhon Si Thammarat, see p254.)

> It is thought that Thai boxing may have its origins in unarmed warfare during the Ayuthaya period.

Although Buddhism is thought to have been introduced to the Chao Phraya Basin by the Mon as early as the 5th century, it was not until the 13th century that trade between Sri Lanka and various Thai kingdoms resulted in the spread of Theravada Buddhism. The southern port city of Trang was a gateway for much of this exchange, which also saw the introduction of influential ideas in science, law, medicine and literature.

THE FIRST THAI KINGDOM & THE RISE OF ISLAM

> For an epic modern take on Thai history, seek out *The Legend of Suriyothai* (2003), the most expensive film ever made in Thailand.

During the 13th century, several Tai principalities in the Mekong Valley united and wrested control of central Thailand from the Khmer, making their new capital at Sukhothai (Rising of Happiness). Many Thais consider Sukhothai to have been the first true Thai kingdom. Under King Phor Khun Si Intharathit, Sukhothai declared its independence from the Khmer empire in 1238 and expanded its sphere of influence, taking over many parts of the Srivijaya kingdom in the south.

In its prime, the Sukhothai kingdom extended as far as Nakhon Si Thammarat in the south, to the upper Mekong River Valley in Laos and to Bago (Pegu) in southern Myanmar, an area larger than present-day Thailand.

Roughly in this same period, Islam was introduced to southern Thailand via Malaysia during the reign of Sultan Iskandar, reaching Pattani by 1387 and spreading as far north as Songkhla. The Malay dialect of Yawi became the main language of the deep south and Islam came to replace Buddhism through that region. Even many of the seminomadic *chow lair* (sea gypsies) who migrated up and down the coast were eventually converted. Although no great monuments from this time survive today, the culture of the deep south is still predominantly Malay, and Yawi is still widely spoken.

> Inscriptions written in Thai, Khmer, Chinese and Arabic have been found inside temples in Ayuthaya, showing just how cosmopolitan this early Thai kingdom was.

Another early Malay kingdom was Pattani, which evolved in the 15th century into a prosperous trading port on the gulf-coast side of the peninsula. Ancient Pattani included parts of modern-day Malaysia as well as the Thai provinces of Pattani, Yala, Narathiwat, Songkhla and Satun. After the decline of the Srivijaya kingdom in the 14th century and the rise of the Thai kingdoms, Pattani struggled with its northern neighbour for more than 100 years until it was successfully invaded in the late 18th century by Rama I.

13th Century	1350	1511
Islam begins to gain a foothold in mainland Southeast Asia, having been introduced by Muslim traders from India up to 500 years previously.	Under the leadership of U Thong, also known as Ramathibodi I, Ayuthaya usurps power from Sukhothai and begins building a regional empire that will last 400 years.	The Portuguese are the first European visitors to Ayuthaya, eventually establishing a consulate and forming a cultural and economic relationship that will last 150 years.

THE RISE & FALL OF AYUTHAYA

The Thai kings of Ayuthaya extended their influence deep into Khmer territory, conquering Angkor in 1431. To this day, some Thais still regard Angkor as part of Thailand, a cause of frequent diplomatic rows between Thailand and Cambodia. Ayuthaya became one of the greatest and wealthiest cities in Asia, far larger and more powerful than most European capitals at that time, attracting trade and visitors from across the world. The kingdom sustained an unbroken monarchical succession through 34 reigns, from King U Thong (r1350–69) to King Ekathat (r1758–67).

By the early 16th century Ayuthaya was receiving European visitors, and a Portuguese embassy was established in 1511. The Portuguese were followed by the Dutch in 1604, the English in 1612, the Danes in 1621 and the French in 1662. In the mid-16th century, Ayuthaya and the independent kingdom of Lanna came under the control of the Burmese, but the Thais took back control of both by the end of the century.

The Burmese besieged Ayuthaya again in 1765 and conquered it two years later. The Burmese were determined to eliminate the rival capital, and proceeded to destroy not only the town itself, but all remnants of its cultural and intellectual life as well. Thai resentment ran high, and Phraya Taksin, a charismatic half-Chinese, half-Thai general, declared himself king of the Thais in 1769, ruling from a new capital at Thonburi on the banks of the Chao Phraya River, opposite present-day central Bangkok. Over time, Taksin's inner circle began to fear his power and claims of divinity, and the king was executed in the custom reserved for royalty: he was beaten to death with sandalwood clubs while enveloped in a velvet sack so that no royal blood would touch the ground.

BANGKOK RULE

Bangkok first appeared as a power in 1782, under another general, Chao Phaya Chakri – crowned as Phraphutthayotfa Chulalok. He moved the royal capital directly across the river to Bangkok and assumed a new hereditary title system, taking the name 'Rama I' for himself. The Chakri dynasty continues as the ruling family of Thailand to this day.

Rama I was successful in centralising power and employing the military to expand the borders of his kingdom, which eventually extended east into modern-day Laos and Cambodia, north into Chiang Mai (which, since the 16th century had been part of Myanmar) and as far south as the modern-day Malaysian states of Kedah and Terengganu.

Rama IV (King Mongkut; r 1851–68), was one of the more interesting and innovative of the early Chakri kings. After being passed over as heir to the throne for 27 years – during which time he was a Buddhist monk and became adept in Sanskrit, Pali, Latin and English, and studied Western sciences – the new king expertly courted ties with European nations. Rama IV

During the Ayuthaya period, the upper classes flaunted their wealth by brandishing elaborate silver betel nut boxes.

The dominance of the central Thai dialect as the country's standard language didn't occur until centralisation of the education system under the reign of Rama V.

Thailand's first printed periodical was the *Bangkok Recorder*, a monthly newspaper founded in 1844 by American missionary Dr Dan Beach Bradley.

1765	1769	1782
The Burmese sack Ayuthaya, essentially rendering the city to rubble and making it necessary to relocate the capital. The city is virtually abandoned until the early 20th century.	Under the leadership of Taksin the Great, Siam expands its territory into the Malay Peninsula, northern Thailand and present-day Laos. By 1778 Cambodia is under the loose control of Siam.	King Phraphutthayotfa Chulalok, now known as Rama I, reestablishes the Siamese court across the river from Thonburi, resulting in both the current Thai capital and the beginning of the Chakri dynasty.

became famous in Europe due to the largely fictitious memoirs of his English governess, Anna Leonowens. The stories spawned a Rogers and Hammerstein play and several movies; the most recent, *Anna & the King*, was banned in Thailand for some glaring historical inaccuracies.

The relationship between Rama IV and Anna Leonowens was given the full Hollywood treatment in *The King & I* (1956).

Like his father, Rama V (King Chulalongkorn; r 1868–1910) was regarded as a skilful diplomat and is credited for successfully playing European powers off against one another to avoid colonisation. However, in exchange for this independence, Thailand was forced to cede much of the territory originally gained by Rama I, and present-day Laos and Cambodia were ceded to French Indochina between 1893 and 1907. In 1902 the former Pattani kingdom was ceded to the British, who were then in control of Malaysia, but it reverted to Thailand five years later. Many from this region continue to consider it to be occupied by the Thai government (see the boxed text, p28).

REVOLUTION

In the early 20th century, the Thai military began to take an active interest in governing the kingdom, staging an unsuccessful coup in 1912. Thai students educated in France staged another bloodless coup in 1932, which led to the end of absolute monarchy in Siam. Thailand adopted a constitutional monarchy along British lines, with a mixed military-civilian group in power. King Rama VII (King Prajadhipok; r 1925–35) abdicated in 1935 and retired to Britain. The king's nine-year-old nephew Ananda Mahidol was later

Male literacy rates in parts of Thailand during the 1890s were higher than those of Europe or America.

ALL THE KINGS' WOMEN

Until polygamy was outlawed by Rama VI (King Vajiravudh; r 1910–25), it was expected of Thai monarchs to maintain a harem, consisting of numerous 'major' and 'minor' wives, and the children of these relationships. This led to some truly 'extended' families: Rama I (King Phraphutthayotfa Chulalok; r 1782–1809) had 42 children by 28 mothers; Rama II (King Phraphutthaloetla; r 1809–24), 73 children by 40 mothers; Rama III (King Phranangklao; r 1824–51), 51 children by 37 mothers (he would eventually accumulate a total of 242 wives and consorts); Rama IV (King Mongkut; r 1851–68), 82 children by 35 mothers; and Rama V (King Chulalongkorn; r 1868–1910), 77 children by 40 mothers. In the case of Rama V, his seven 'major' wives were all half-sisters or first cousins, a conscious effort to maintain the purity of the bloodline of the Chakri dynasty. Other consorts or 'minor' wives were often the daughters of families wishing to gain greater ties with the royal family.

In contrast to the precedence set by his predecessors, Rama VI had one wife and one child, a girl born only a few hours before his death. As a result, his brother, Rama VII (King Prajadhipok; r 1925–35), was appointed as his successor. Rama VII also had only one wife and failed to produce any heirs. After abdicating in 1935, he did not exercise his right to appoint a successor, and once again, lines were drawn back to Rama V, and the grandson of one of his remaining 'major' wives, nine-year-old Ananda Mahidol, was chosen to be the next king.

1851–1910	1893	1909
The modernisation of Thailand occurs during the reigns of Rama IV and Rama V, which see the introduction of Western culture and technology, reform of the role of the monarchy, and increased infrastructure.	After a minor territory dispute, France sends gunboats to threaten Bangkok, forcing Siam to give up most of its territory east of the Mekong River. Siam takes on much of its modern boundaries.	The Anglo-Siamese Treaty allows Siam to keep Yala, Pattani, Narathiwat and Songkhla, while relinquishing control of Kedah, Kelantan, Perlis and Terengganu to Britain.

crowned Rama VIII, but power really remained with Phibul Songkhram, one of the military masterminds of the 1932 coup. Under the influence of Phibul's government, the country's name was officially changed in 1939 from Siam to Thailand.

Ananda Mahidol ascended the throne in 1935, but was shot dead in his bedroom under mysterious circumstances in 1946 and to this day his death remains a taboo subject in Thailand. In the same year, his brother, Bhumibol Adulyadej (pronounced Poo·mí·pon À·dun·yá·dèt), was appointed Rama IX, the ninth king of the Chakri dynasty. He continues to reign today, and you'll see his image everywhere, including at the cinema before the movie starts (see the boxed text, p31).

WWII & THE COUP ERA

Thailand's rulers collaborated with the Japanese during WWII, allowing troops access to the Gulf of Thailand, which helped in the annexation of the Malay Peninsula. In the process, the Japanese troops occupied a portion of Thailand, and Phibul went so far as to declare war on the USA and Great Britain in 1942. His ambassador in Washington, Seni Pramoj, refused to deliver the declaration, and Phibul later resigned under pressure from growing underground resistance to his rule.

After V-J Day (marking the Allied victory over Japan in WWII) in 1945, Seni Pramoj became prime minister. Thus began a political chess game in which one leader after another was displaced by popular uprisings, elections and military coups. First to go was Seni, who was unseated in a general election in 1946. A democratic civilian government took over under the leadership of Pridi Phanomyong, a law professor who had been instrumental in the 1932 revolution. Thailand reverted to its old name of 'Siam' for about a year, until Phibul returned to power and suspended the constitution, reinstating 'Thailand' as the country's official name. Phibul's political rivals and dissidents were sent to the prison island of Ko Tarutao (p383), off the coast of Satun. Under Phibul the government took an extreme anticommunist stance and became a loyal supporter of French and US foreign policy in Southeast Asia. This had profound implications for Thailand's role during the Vietnam War.

Phibul lost his post again in 1951 to another general, Sarit Thanarat, though he retained the title of prime minister until 1957 when Sarit finally had him exiled. That same year, Sarit was voted out in the elections and went abroad for 'medical treatment', returning in 1958 and seizing control in another coup. He promptly abolished the constitution, dissolved the parliament and banned all political parties, maintaining effective power until he died of cirrhosis in 1963.

Meanwhile, in the south of the country, long-held Muslim resentments against the ruling Buddhist government began to boil over (see p28).

During the first three decades of the 20th century more than half of Bangkok's population was Chinese.

At its peak in the late 1930s, Thailand's Opium Monopoly accounted for nearly 20% of the country's national budget.

During WWII, much of southern Thailand's railway system was disassembled and relocated by the Japanese in order to build the 'Death Railway' into Burma.

1914	1917	1932
Don Muang, Thailand's first international airport, officially opens; it remains the country's main domestic and international airport until the opening of Suvarnabhumi in 2006.	In a move meant to assert its sovereignty and gain favour with France and Britain, Siam joins the allied side in a mostly token role in Europe during WWI.	A bloodless coup transforms Siam from absolute to constitutional monarchy. The disposed king, Rama VII, by most accounts a willing accessory, continues to remain on the throne until resigning three years later.

CONFLICT IN THE SOUTH

Long before being incorporated into Thailand in 1902, the three border provinces of Pattani, Narathiwat and Yala previously formed a Malay kingdom known as Pattani. The majority of inhabitants of these provinces continue to be ethic Malay Muslims, and speak a Malay dialect called Yawi. During the 1930s, the Phibul government tried to impose Thai language and culture on the region, and proceeded to shut down religious schools and Islamic courts. This led to growing dissatisfaction with the central government, which eventually manifested itself as a desire for more autonomy and, in some cases, separatism. In 1948, in what is regarded as the beginning of the modern insurgency, Haji Sulong Tomina, a prominent religious leader, proposed that the people of the border provinces should be led by a locally born governor. He was charged with treason, prompting an uprising in the southernmost provinces that led to the death of hundreds. In 1954 Haji Sulong mysteriously disappeared, ostensibly executed by the authorities.

Throughout the latter part of the 20th century, despite an official government policy of religious tolerance, the people of the region continued to be largely left out of state affairs, and their religious beliefs and language were viewed with scepticism by officials in Bangkok. In 1968 the Pattani United Liberation Organisation (PULO) was created with the goal of creating a separate Muslim state. Unrest flared again in the 1970s and 1980s, but the issues raised by PULO were largely resolved by negotiation.

The most recent phase of the insurgency began in earnest in 2004 when a raid on an army depot in the province of Narathiwat led to the death of four soldiers and the theft of hundreds of weapons. A brutal form of marshal law was immediately imposed on the three border provinces. In April of that year, after simultaneous attacks on several police outposts, 32 suspected militants hiding out in Pattani's Krue Sae Mosque were killed by the Thai military after a tense standoff. In October of the same year in the town of Tak Bai, Narathiwat, 78 Muslim protesters suffocated to death after being arrested and packed into military vehicles. In both cases the Thaksin government showed little remorse, claiming in the case of the Tak Bai incident that the deaths were due to the fact that the protesters were already weak from fasting during the month of Ramadan.

Since the 2006 military coup, led by the Thai army's first Muslim commander, Sonthi Boonyaratglin, and despite a doubling of police and military presence since 2007, there has been only a slight lull in the virtually daily murders and bombings, which have moved as far north as Hat Yai in Songkhla Province. And despite having resulted in nearly 4000 deaths since 2004, the conflict has received scant international attention.

In 2009 the administration of Abhisit Vejjajiva launched a US$1 billion-plus economic stimulus plan for the country's deep south, and in early 2010 the prime minister even proclaimed his willingness to enact an amnesty. Yet with the identity and exact aims of the insurgents still largely unknown, and a population skeptical of the central government and scornful of the massive military presence, a quick solution to southern Thailand's violence appears an unlikely event.

1939	1946	1946
Military dictator and 1932 coup leader Phibul Songkhram renames Siam as Thailand, a nationalistic gesture meant to imply the unity of all Tai people.	Bhumibol Adulyadej, Thailand's current king, is crowned after the death of his brother. This ushers in a period of revived interest in the monarchy, an institution that had been waning since the reign of Rama V.	Pridi Phanomyong, an architect of the 1932 coup, becomes Thailand's first democratically elected prime minister. After a military coup the following year, Pridi flees Thailand, returning only briefly once in his life.

From 1964 to 1973, Thailand was governed by the army officers Thanom Kittikachorn and Praphat Charusathien, who negotiated a package of economic deals with the USA in exchange for allowing the US to develop military bases in Thailand to support the war in Vietnam. Thailand found itself flooded with American GIs, who pumped US dollars into the Thai economy and created a culture of financial dependency on foreign investment that continues to be a problem in Thailand. Another effect of the American presence was the massive expansion of the sex industry. Although prostitution and extramarital affairs were culturally accepted, Thailand's relationship with US troops as an R & R destination developed its lasting reputation as a destination for sex tourism.

Despite the effects of the US presence, most Thais were more worried about military rule. Reacting to political repression, 10,000 students publicly demanded reinstatement of the constitution in June 1973. In October that year, the military brutally suppressed a large demonstration at Thammasat University in Bangkok, killing 77 and wounding over 800. Rama IX stepped in, forcing Thanom and Praphat to leave Thailand. Oxford-educated Kukrit Pramoj took charge of a 14-party coalition, creating a leftist government that introduced a national minimum wage, repealed anticommunist laws and ordered the departure of US forces from Thailand.

Constitutional government lasted until October 1976 when students demonstrated again, this time protesting against Thanom's return to Thailand as a monk. Thammasat University again became a battlefield as the Border Patrol Police, along with right-wing, paramilitary civilian groups, assaulted a group of 2000 students holding a sit-in. Officially, 46 people died in the incident (the actual number may be much higher), and more than 1000 were arrested.

The breakdown of order gave the military the perfect excuse to step in and reinstall a right-wing military government, this time with Thanin Kraivichien as prime minister. After this, many Thai students and intellectuals joined the People's Liberation Army of Thailand (PLAT) – a group of armed communist insurgents, based in the hills of northern and southern Thailand.

The military subsequently appointed Prem Tinsulanonda in 1980, who set about dismantling the PLAT insurgency, banning the Communist Party of Thailand, launching military offensives against PLAT and granting amnesty to members who surrendered. Simultaneously, Prem created political and economic stability, removing the primary motivation for the armed uprisings.

In 1988 Prem was replaced in elections by Chatichai Choonhavan, who created a government dominated by business executives and who set about transforming Thailand into an 'Asian Tiger' economy. Thailand seemed to be entering a new era during which the country's economic boom coincided with increasing democratisation. Yet, by the end of the 1980s, some high-ranking military officers had become increasingly dissatisfied, complaining that Thailand was being governed by a plutocracy.

For one of the more readable 20th-century histories of Thailand, David Wyatt's *Thailand: A Short History* is still the definitive guide.

Four Reigns, a novel by Kukrit Pramoj, describes the changes in Thai society from absolute monarchy to the modern era as seen through the eyes of a fictitious noblewoman.

1957	1965	1967
Muslim separatists dissatisfied with unjust treatment from Bangkok initiate a guerrilla war with the aim of creating a separate Muslim state in southern Thailand.	Communist insurgency begins with the Communist Party of Thailand (CPT) officially announcing an armed struggle. Thousands of university-age Thais take refuge in remote corners of the country.	Association of Southeast Asian Nations (Asean) is formed by five core members: the Philippines, Indonesia, Malaysia, Singapore, and Thailand. Other Southeast Asian states join throughout the 1980s and 1990s.

THE MODERN ERA

After a brief period of peace, the army seized power again in February 1991, handing power to the newly formed National Peace-Keeping Council (NPKC), led by General Suchinda Kraprayoon. It was Thailand's 18th coup attempt and one of 10 successful coups since 1932. Once again, the Thai constitution was abolished and parliament was dissolved.

In May 1992 Bangkok was once again rocked by demonstrations, this time led by charismatic Bangkok governor, Chamlong Srimuang. After street confrontations between protesters and the military near Bangkok's Democracy Monument resulted in nearly 50 deaths and hundreds of injuries, Chamlong and Suchinda were publicly scolded by Rama IX, and Suchinda resigned after less than six weeks as prime minister. The military-backed government also agreed to institute a constitutional amendment – Thailand's 15th – requiring that Thailand's prime minister come from the ranks of elected parliamentarians. Civilian Anand Panyarachun was reinstated as interim prime minister for a four-month term.

The September 1992 elections squeezed in veteran Democrat Party leader Chuan Leekpai with a five-seat majority. A food vendor's son and native of Trang Province, the new prime minister was well regarded for his honesty and high morals, but didn't really achieve much that the Thai people could take home with them.

Chuan did not complete his four-year term, and was replaced by 63-year-old billionaire Banharn Silapa-archa, whom the Thai press called a 'walking ATM'. Banharn wasn't very popular with the Thai media, who immediately attacked his tendency to fill senior government positions with cronies known to be heavily involved in money politics. In September 1996 the Banharn government collapsed amid a spate of corruption scandals and a crisis of confidence. However, the Thai economy continued to grow and Thailand appeared to be on the verge of joining its neighbours South Korea, Taiwan, Hong Kong and Singapore as an Asian Tiger economy.

THE CRISIS & THE PEOPLE'S CONSTITUTION

Banharn was replaced that November by former deputy prime minister and army commander, Chavalit Yongchaiyudh, of the New Aspiration Party, in an election marked by violence and accusations of vote buying. Like his predecessor – and most other political leaders in Asia and around the world for that matter – Chavalit failed to see that the Asian economic bubble was about to burst. In mid-1997, the Thai currency fell into a deflationary tailspin, losing 40% of its value, and the economy crashed to a virtual halt.

On 27 September 1997, the Thai parliament voted in a new constitution, Thailand's 16th since 1932 and the first to be decreed by a civilian government. Known as *rát·tam·má·noon 'brà·chah·chon* (people's constitution) it put new mechanisms in place to monitor the conduct of elected officials and

The History of the Malay Kingdom of Patani, by Ibrahim Syukri, is a nationalistic history of the southern provinces from the Muslim perspective.

A History of Thailand, by Chris Baker and Pasuk Phongpaichit, is a good source of information regarding the significant events of Thailand's modern era.

1970s	1973	1975
A period of insurgency begins in Thailand's southernmost provinces. The unrest continues until the 1990s, when the government agrees to provide more representation and funding.	Large-scale student protests in Bangkok lead to violent military suppression. The 1971 coup leader Thanom Kittikachorn is ordered into exile by Rama IX.	US troops depart from Thailand after 14 years of using the country as an operating base for the Vietnam War. The US presence has a large and lasting impact on Thai culture and economy.

THE KING

If you see a yellow Rolls Royce flashing by along city avenues, accompanied by a police escort, you've probably just caught a glimpse of Thailand's longest-reigning monarch – and the longest-reigning living monarch in the world – King Bhumibol Adulyadej. Also known in English as Rama IX (the ninth king of the Chakri dynasty), the king was born in the USA in 1927, while his father Prince Mahidol was studying medicine at Harvard University.

Fluent in English, French, German and Thai, His Majesty ascended the throne in 1946 following the death of his brother Rama VIII (King Ananda Mahidol), who reigned for 11 years before being shot in mysterious circumstances.

An ardent jazz composer and saxophonist when he was younger, King Bhumibol has hosted jam sessions with the likes of jazz greats Woody Herman and Benny Goodman. His compositions are often played on Thai radio.

His Majesty administers royal duties from Chitralada Palace in the Bangkok's Dusit precinct, north of Ko Ratanakosin. As protector of both nation and religion, King Bhumibol traditionally presides over several important Buddhist and Brahmanist ceremonies during the year. Among the more colourful are the seasonal robe-changing of the Emerald Buddha in Wat Phra Kaew and the annual Royal Ploughing Ceremony, during which ceremonial rice is sown to ensure a robust economy for the coming year, at Sanam Luang.

The king and Queen Sirikit have four children: Princess Ubol Ratana (born 1951), Crown Prince Maha Vajiralongkorn (1952), Princess Mahachakri Sirindhorn (1955) and Princess Chulabhorn (1957).

After over 60 years in power, Rama IX is preparing for his succession. For the last few years the Crown Prince has performed most of the royal ceremonies the King would normally perform, such as presiding over the Royal Ploughing Ceremony, changing the attire on the Emerald Buddha and handing out academic degrees at university commencements.

Though Thailand's political system is officially classified as a constitutional monarchy, the constitution stipulates that the king be 'enthroned in a position of revered worship' and must not be exposed 'to any sort of accusation or action'. With or without legal writ, the vast majority of Thai citizens regard Rama IX as a sort of demigod, partly in deference to tradition but also because of his impressive efforts to promote public works.

political candidates and to protect civil rights, achieving many of the aims of the prodemocracy movement. This wasn't enough to save the Chavalit government, which was judged on its failure to deal effectively with the economic disaster. Chavalit was forced to resign in November 1997.

An election brought Chuan Leekpai back into office, just as many banks and finance companies went into total collapse. The International Monetary Fund (IMF) stepped in with US$17.2 billion in loans, with the stipulation that the Thai government follow the IMF's prescriptions for recapitalisation and restructuring. The IMF medicine seemed to work, and after shrinking 10% in 1998, the Thai economy grew nearly 5% in both 1999 and 2000, allowing Thailand to take an 'early out' from the IMF's loan package in 2000.

In 2005 the government of Thaksin Shinawatra became the first elected civilian administration to complete a four-year term.

1976	**1980**	**1985**
Former coup leader Thanom returns to Thailand as a monk. Protests at Thammasat University are put down by the military, leading to the deaths of 46 students.	Prime Minister Prem Tinsulanonda successfully negotiates peace with the country's communist insurgents by following a dual policy of urging cadres to defect and offering amnesty.	Chamlong Srimuang is elected mayor of Bangkok. Three years later, after forming his own largely Buddhist-based political party, the Palang Dharma Party, he is elected mayor again.

THE THAKSIN ERA

Economic survival wasn't enough to save Chuan, who was replaced in January 2001 by Thaksin Shinawatra, a billionaire telecommunications tycoon from Chiang Mai. Thaksin was able to capitalise on rural discontent by promising a suspension of farmers' debt payments and a million baht in development funds for each and every village in Thailand, and overwhelmingly defeated Chuan in the general elections. Thaksin was generally able to deliver on his populist promises and won another sweeping victory in 2005, making him the first Thai leader in history to be re-elected to a consecutive second term.

However, soon after his second victory, the Thaksin era began to be filled with political high drama. First there were the troubles in southern Thailand (see p28), public discontent with Thaksin's desire to privatise certain state agencies, and even allegations of Thaksin's perceived ambitions to take on roles associated with the monarchy. The final nail in Thaksin's coffin occurred when members of his family sold their family-owned Shin Corporation shares to the Singaporean government for a tax-free profit of 73 billion baht (US$1.88 billion), thanks to newly introduced telecommunications legislation that exempted individuals from capital gains tax. Thaksin responded to the growing displeasure by dissolving parliament and calling for re-elections in a month's time, promising to step down if his party did not win a majority.

In the lead-up to the 2006 re-elections, many of Thaksin's most highly placed supporters had turned against him and had organised a series of massive anti-Thaksin rallies in Bangkok. Nonetheless, with just a month to organise and campaign, the opposition realised the task was monumental and chose to boycott the election. When the ballots were tallied, Thaksin proclaimed victory. However, just one day later, after a private council with the king, Thaksin announced that for the sake of national unity he would not accept the position of prime minister.

THE BLOODLESS COUP

On the evening of 19 September 2006, while Thaksin was attending a UN conference in New York, the Thai military led by General Sonthi Boonyaratglin took power in a bloodless coup. Calling themselves the Council for Democratic Reform under the Constitutional Monarch, the junta cited the Thai Rak Thai (TRT) government's alleged violation of lèse majesté laws, corruption, interference with state agencies and creation of social divisions as justification for the coup. The public initially overwhelmingly supported the coup, and scenes of tourists and Thai families posing in front of tanks remain the defining images of the event. Thaksin quickly flew to London, where he lived in exile and busied himself by buying the Manchester City football club.

In January 2007, an Assets Examination Committee put together by the junta found Thaksin guilty of concealing assets to avoid paying taxes. Two

The 2006 coup leader, General Sonthi Boonyaratglin, was the first Muslim to head the Buddhist kingdom's army.

One of the only sources of information during the 2006 coup, www.2Bangkok.com features background and perspective on local news with summaries of the Thai-language press updated on a daily basis.

1992	1997	1997
Street protests led by Chamlong Srimuang against 1991 coup leader Suchinda Kraprayoon leads to violent confrontations. Both Chamlong and Suchinda are publicly scolded by Rama IX, leading to Suchinda's resignation.	A civilian government introduces Thailand's first constitution drafted by an elected assembly. The document emphasises human rights, advances political reform, and empowers and protects citizens.	In July Thailand devalues its currency, the baht, heralding the Asian economic crisis; massive unemployment and personal debt, and a significant crash of the Thai stock market.

months later, Thaksin's wife and brother-in-law were also charged with conspiracy to evade taxes. In late May, a court established by the military government found TRT guilty of breaking election laws. The court dissolved the party and banned its executive members from public service for five years.

Under a new a military-drafted constitution, long-awaited elections were finally conducted in late 2007. The newly formed People Power Party, of which Thaksin has an advisory role, won a significant number of seats in parliament, but failed to win an outright majority. After forming a loose coalition with several other parties, parliament chose the veteran politician and close Thaksin ally, Samak Sundaravej, as prime minister.

Not surprisingly, Samak was regarded as little more than a proxy of Thaksin by his opponents, and shortly after taking office became the target

> Thailand has had 19 coups since 1932, of which 10 resulted in a change of government.

COBRA SWAMP

If you arrived in Bangkok by air, bear in mind that the sleek glass and steel terminal you most likely pulled into was nearly 40 years in the making. Suvarnabhumi (pronounced sù·wan·ná·poom), Sanskrit for 'Golden Land', could hardly be a more apt name for Thailand's new airport, particularly for the politicians and investors involved.

Originally begun in 1973, the location chosen for Thailand's new international airport was an unremarkable marshy area with the slightly less illustrious working title of Nong Ngu Hao, Thai for 'Cobra Swamp'. Despite the seemingly disadvantageous setting, over the years the flat marshland was eagerly bought and sold by politicians and developers hoping to make a quick profit.

It wasn't until the self-styled CEO administration of Thaksin Shinawatra that work on the airport began in earnest. Thaksin harboured desires to make Bangkok a 'transportation hub' to rival Hong Kong and Singapore, and went on a virtual spending spree, commissioning construction of the world's tallest flight control tower, as well as the world's largest terminal building.

The construction of Suvarnabhumi was rife with allegations of corruption, including the use of faulty building materials and substandard, insufficient runways. Undoubtedly the most embarrassing single scandal associated with the airport was the suspect purchase of 20 CTX security scanners from a US company.

On 29 September 2005, Thaksin presided over a much-criticised 'soft' opening ceremony. The event was essentially little more than a face-saving measure considering that the airport was still far from operational. Suvarnabhumi eventually began flights a year later, on 28 September 2006. In an ironic twist of fate, Thaksin, the main catalyst behind the project, was in exile in England, having been ousted in a military coup the week before, the junta citing corruption and shoddy construction of the airport among its justifications for the takeover.

Despite being the largest airport in Southeast Asia, and among the largest in the world, in March 2007, many domestic flights were relocated back to the old Don Muang Airport, with officials citing overcrowding of runways and safety concerns as reasons for the move. With little foresight, a train link to the distant airport was only begun after its opening, and did not begin operations until 2010.

2001

Thaksin Shinawatra, Thailand's richest man, is elected prime minister on a populist platform.

2004

The modern phase of southern Thailand's Muslim insurgency begins in January when militants raid an army base in Narathiwat, killing four guards and stealing hundreds of weapons.

2004

An earthquake-triggered tsunami on Boxing Day (26 December) damages much of Thailand's Andaman coast, causing more than 5000 deaths and destroying much tourist-industry infrastructure.

of a series of large-scale protests held by the People's Alliance for Democracy (PAD), the same group of yellow-shirted, mostly Bangkok-based royalists who called for Thaksin's resignation in the lead up to the 2006 coup. In August 2008, several thousand PAD protesters took over Government House in Bangkok. The takeover was followed by sporadic violent clashes between the PAD and the United Front for Democracy against Dictatorship (UDD), a loose association of red-shirted Thaksin supporters who had set up camp nearby at Sanam Luang.

In September 2008 the Thai Supreme Court unanimously ruled that Samak's paid appearances as the host of a television cookery program constituted a conflict of interest, and he was forced to step down. In the remaining months of 2008, Samak was succeeded by no fewer than three prime ministers.

The PAD continued to hold Government House for nearly four months, when on 25 November, a group of armed PAD protesters stormed Bangkok's Suvarnabhumi and Don Muang Airports, entering the passenger terminals and seizing control of the control towers. Thousands of additional PAD sympathisers eventually flooded Suvarnabhumi, leading to the cancellation of all flights and leaving as many as 230,000 domestic and international passengers stranded. The standoff lasted until 2 December, when the Supreme Court banned Samak's successor from politics and ordered his political party and two coalition parties dissolved.

The airport siege took place during the height of Thailand's tourist season and the impact wounded the industry profoundly, with the Bank of Thailand estimating that the incident cost the country 210 billion baht (over US$5 billion). The events of 2008 also effectively succeeded in polarising much of Thailand between the predominately middle- and upper class, urban-based PAD and the largely working-class, rural UDD.

In December 2008, after a great deal of political wrangling, a tenuous new coalition was formed, led by Oxford-educated Abhisit Vejjajiva, leader of the Democrat Party. Despite being young, photogenic and allegedly untainted by corruption, Abhisit's perceived association with the PAD has done little to placate the UDD. Subsequent violent clashes between the UDD 'red shirts' and Thai military in 2009, not to mention Abhisit's inability to dominate the popular vote, unite parliament and gain favour with influential national institutions such as the police and military suggest that his days in power are limited.

In February 2010, in a long-awaited ruling, the Thai Supreme Court seized 46.37 billion baht (US$1.4 billion) worth of former premier Thaksin Shinawatra's frozen assets, claiming that the money was gained illegally through conflicts of interest during Thaksin's tenure as prime minister. As this left Thaksin with nearly half of his fortune, the decision was regarded as an effort to appease antigovernment protesters, an illustration of Thaksin's ongoing influence and popularity despite the fact that, at the time of writing, he still remained in exile.

Global Terrorism Analysis (www.jamestown.org /terrorism) publishes online articles about the southern Thai insurgency as well as other international hot spots.

Thailand's King Bhumibol Adulyadej, also known as Rama IX, and who marked the 60th anniversary of his accession to the throne in 2006, is the world's longest-reigning monarch.

2006	**2008**	**2010**
In September a bloodless coup sees the Thai military take power from Prime Minister Thaksin Shinawatra while he is at a UN meeting in New York.	In November, thousands of yellow-shirted anti-Thaksin protesters calling themselves the Peoples' Alliance for Democracy (PAD) take over both of Bangkok's airports, impacting tourism severely.	In February the Thai Supreme Court seizes 46.37 billion baht (US$1.4 billion) worth of assets belonging to former premier Thaksin Shinawatra, claiming that the money was gained illegally when Thaksin was prime minister.

The Culture

REGIONAL IDENTITY

Religion, royalty and tradition are the defining characteristics of Thai society. That Thailand is the only country in Southeast Asia never colonised by a foreign power has led to a profound sense of pride in these elements. However, the country is not homogenous, and in the south, a strong cultural identity prevails that is more in tune with the Islamic culture of nearby Malaysia.

Before modern political boundaries divided the Malay peninsula into two countries, the city states, sultanates and villages were part of an Indonesian-based Srivijaya empire, sharing intermingled customs and language, all vying for local control over shipping routes. Many southern Thai towns and geographic names bear the hallmark of the Bahasa language, and some village traditions would be instantly recognized by a Sumatran but not by a northern Thai. Chinese culture is also prominent in southern Thailand, as seen in the numerous temples and clan houses, and it is this intermingling of domestic and 'foreign' culture that defines the south.

> Instead of a handshake, the traditional Thai greeting is the *wâi* – a prayerlike gesture with the palms placed together.

Saving Face & Having Fun

An important Thai concept across all religions is the idea of 'saving face', that is, avoiding confrontation and trying not to embarrass yourself or other people. For this reason, Thais shy away from negative topics in everyday conversation and generally won't interfere with others unless someone complains or asks for their help. This is one of the sources of the Thai smile – it's the best possible face to put on in almost any situation. Arguing over prices or getting angry while haggling causes everyone involved to lose face and should be avoided. The only time you'll see Thais failing to show due respect is when it may be a source of *sà·nùk* (fun). The Thais love to joke and *sà·nùk* plays an important part in saving face.

> There is no universally accepted method of transliterating from Thai to English, so some words and place names are spelled a variety of ways.

LIFESTYLE

The ordinary life of a southern Thai can be divided into two categories: country and city.

Those in rural areas are typically employed with rubber farming or fishing, though rice and livestock farming are also evident. Rubber farmers live in

---

SPEAKING SOUTHERN

The southern dialect of the Thai language, known as *pah·săh đâi*, is famous for its rapid cadence and tendency to clip or omit entire words. There is a wealth of vocabulary specific to southern Thai, and as Thai is a tonal language, the southern dialect relies on its own particular set of tones, making it all but imperceptible even to native speakers of other Thai dialects. Even within southern Thailand there are enough differences in vocabulary and pronunciation that a local can tell if someone is a native of Trang or *kon korn* (a native of Nakhon Si Thammarat).

To help you win some smiles from the locals, we've provided a brief lexicon of the local lingo.

■ *Bái đěe mái*	How are you?		■ *Pan préu/Wăh préu*	What's up?
■ *Mâi préu*	No worries		■ *Mâh dâir*	Come here
■ *Káap káap*	Quickly!		■ *núk*	Fun
■ *rôy jang hóo*	Delicious		■ *ai bŏw*	Man
■ *ai nŏo*	Child			

small, typically inland settlements identified by straight rows of trees and pale sheets of drying latex. Surviving fishing villages are typically as close to the sea as possible, so that their inhabitants can watch the tides and their boats. Traditional Muslim villages are built directly over the water in a series of connected stilt houses. Because the Andaman Sea had a history of tranquil behaviour, there was no fear of the ocean's wrath, a preconception painfully destroyed by the 2004 tsunami.

Within the cities, life looks a lot like the rest of the country (busy and modern), but the presence of Chinese and Indian merchants marks the uniqueness of southern Thai cities. The commercial centres are also the market towns, where the brightly coloured fishing boats ease into the harbour, unloading the catch and filling the marina with the aroma of fish.

Culture Shock Thailand, by Robert and Nanthapa Cooper, is a humorous and helpful introduction to confusing Thai ways.

Family Values

The importance of the family unit in Thai society is immediately apparent to a visitor in the many family-owned and -operated businesses. It is still common to see three generations employed in a family-run guesthouse, or sharing the same house. The elderly are involved in day-to-day life, selling sweets to neighbourhood kids, renting motorcycles to tourists and many other ways. Although tourism has significantly altered the islanders' traditional way of life, the presence of jobs helps to keep many ambitious children from seeking employment on the mainland.

Even the Thai pronouns reflect a strong sense of family. Thais will refer to people in their own generation as an older *(pêe)* or younger *(nórng)* sibling, regardless of bloodline. Sometimes Thais will translate this tribal custom into English, referring to nonfamily members as 'sister' or 'brother', inadvertently amazing foreigners with the vastness of Thai families.

Elaborate wooden bird cages holding cooing doves can be found along the streets of many towns in southern Thailand. Even dove singing contests are held.

ECONOMY

Due to tourism, fishing, prawn farming and rubber, the south is Thailand's wealthiest region. Most rubber tappers are born into it, inheriting the profession of their fathers and mothers. Prawn and fish farming, on the other hand, are relatively new industries, introduced as an economic development program for rural communities losing ground to commercial fishing operations. The venture proved profitable and Thailand is one of the leading exporters of farm-raised prawn. However, fish farms have been largely unregulated until recently, leading to a host of environmental problems, such as water pollution and the destruction of mangrove forests.

Tourism has undoubtedly had the most tangible impact on the economy of the area, transforming many small villages into bilingual enterprises. Women who would otherwise sell products at market have studied Thai traditional massage, and walk up and down the beach beseeching customers. Other do-it-yourself franchises, so prolific in Thai communities, have been tailored to tourists: shops along the beach thoroughfares sell sunscreen and postcards instead of rice whisky and grilled fish, itinerant vendors hawk sarongs and henna tattoos instead of feather dusters and straw brooms, while fishermen sometimes abandon their nets for bigger catches – tourists on snorkelling trips.

In 1913 Rama VI introduced the concept of surnames to Thailand, granting many himself.

Across Thailand, the size of the middle class is growing with successive decades, bridging the gap between rich and poor. Thailand doesn't suffer from poverty of sustenance; even the most destitute Thai citizens can have shelter and food. Rather, the lower rung of Thai society suffers from poverty of material: money isn't available for extensive education, material goods or health care. This is most obvious from an economic perspective: the average Thai income stands at around US$2000 a year, but many in rural provinces earn as little as US$570 a year.

DOS & DON'TS

The Thais are generally very understanding and hospitable, but there are some taboos you should be aware of.

Temple Etiquette

- Always dress neatly and conservatively when visiting temples. No shorts or sleeveless tops for men or women.
- Take your shoes off when you enter any building that contains a Buddha image.
- Women should not touch a monk or a monk's belongings. To avoid an accidental brush, don't sit next to a monk on a public bus and let them pass first on a crowded street.
- Sit with your feet pointed away from any Buddha images: the feet are regarded as the lowest part of the body and pointing your feet towards someone is highly disrespectful.

Everyday Etiquette

- Avoid disparaging remarks about the king, queen or anyone in the royal family.
- Treat objects with a picture or image of the king, including coins and banknotes, with respect.
- Stand with respect for the royal anthem, which is played in movie theatres before the show, and for the national anthem, often played through loudspeakers at 8am and 6pm.
- The rules of returning a *wâi* (palms-together Thai greeting) are quite involved; in general return a *wâi* to an adult but not to children or servers.
- A smile and *'sà·wàt·dee kráp'* (male) or *'sà·wàt·dee kâ'* (female) is the standard all-purpose greeting and is acceptable for all ages.
- Don't show anger or lose your temper; it causes a 'loss of face' for everyone present. Even talking loudly is seen as rude by cultured Thais, whatever the situation.
- The head is regarded as the highest part of the body, so never touch Thais on the head or ruffle their hair. For the same reason, you should never sit on pillows meant for sleeping or put a hat on the floor.
- The feet are considered the lowest part of the body. You should never step over someone, even if they are lying on the floor – squeeze around them or ask them to move instead.
- When handing things to people, use your right hand and place your left hand on your elbow, a sign of good manners.
- Mind your appearance. Thais are fastidious in their appearance and are sometimes displeased by foreigners' unkempt looks. Clean it up if you've got to pay a visit to a government office.
- If invited to a home, bring a small gift, either food or drinks, but not flowers, which are typically reserved for merit-making.

Beach Etiquette

- Avoid public nudity on the beaches. Thais are traditionally very modest and all but the most flamboyant Bangkok Thais will swim fully clothed.
- Men should wear shirts away from the beach unless they want Thai people to think that they are real lowlifes.

POPULATION

Over one third of all Thais live in urban areas and Bangkok is, without doubt, the largest city in the kingdom, with nearly eight million inhabitants – more than 10% of the total population. The four next-most-populated cities are located in the northeast and the northern part of the country. Most of the other towns in Thailand have populations well below 100,000.

About 75% of the citizenry are ethnic Thais, predominantly Buddhist, and are divided into a number of cultural subgroups with their own dialects. People of Chinese ancestry make up 14% of the population and fill the shopkeeper niche in southern Thai society. The second-largest ethnic minority group living in Thailand are Muslims of Malay origin (4%), most of whom reside in the southern provinces of Songkhla, Yala, Pattani and Narathiwat. The remaining 10.5% of the population is made up of smaller non-Thai-speaking groups such as the Vietnamese, Khmer, Mon and Moken (*chow lair,* often spelled as *chao leh,* sea gypsies; see the boxed text, opposite), and small numbers of Europeans and other non-Asians in Bangkok, Phuket and Chiang Mai.

Every Thai person has a nickname, which range from Thai words such as Nóy (small) or Nŏo (mouse), to English words such as 'Chief' or 'Ice'.

RELIGION
Buddhism
Approximately 95% of Thais follow Theravada Buddhism, also known as Hinayana or 'Lesser Vehicle' Buddhism to distinguish it from the Mahayana or 'Great Vehicle' school of Buddhism. The primary difference between the faiths is that Theravada Buddhists believe every individual is responsible for their own enlightenment, while Mahayana Buddhists believe society can work together to achieve enlightenment for all.

One in 10 Thai citizens lives and works in Bangkok.

The ultimate end of all forms of Buddhism is to reach *nibbana* (from Sanskrit, nirvana), which literally means the 'blowing out' or extinction of all desire and thus of all *dukkha* (suffering). Having achieved *nibbana*, an individual is freed from the cycle of rebirths and enters the spiritual plane. In reality, most Thai Buddhists aim for rebirth in a 'better' existence in the next life, rather than striving to attain *nibbana*. To work towards this goal, Buddhists carry out meritorious actions *(tam bun)* such as feeding monks, giving donations to temples and performing regular worship at the local *wát* (temple). The Buddhist theory of karma is well expressed in the Thai proverb *tam dee, dâi dee; tam chôo-a, dâi chôo-a* (do good and receive good; do evil and receive evil).

There is no specific day of worship in Thai Buddhism; instead the faithful go to temple on certain religious holidays, when it is convenient or to commemorate a special family event. Most temple visits occur on *wan prá*

STOPPING CHILD-SEX TOURISM IN THAILAND

Sadly, Thailand has become a destination for a significant number of foreigners seeking to sexually exploit local children. A range of socioeconomic factors renders many children vulnerable to such abuse, and some depraved individuals seem intent to prey upon this vulnerability.

The sexual abuse and exploitation of children has serious, lifelong and even life-threatening consequences. Child-sex tourism is a crime and a violation of the rights of a child. Strong laws exist in Thailand to prosecute offenders. Many countries also have extraterritorial legislation that allows nationals to be prosecuted in their own country for such crimes.

Responsible travellers can help to stop the scourge of child-sex tourism by reporting suspicious behaviour. Don't ignore it! Your actions may be critical in helping to protect children from future abuse and exploitation.

In Thailand, travellers can report on a dedicated hotline number: ☎ 1300. If you know the nationality of the individual, you can report them directly to their embassy.

ECPAT (End Child Prostitution & Trafficking; ☎ in Bangkok 0 2215 3388; www.ecpat.net) is a global network focusing on these issues with more than 70 affiliate organisations around the world. Its head office is located in Bangkok. ECPAT is actively working to combat child-sex tourism in Thailand and around the world.

Child Wise (www.childwise.net) is the Australian member of ECPAT. Child Wise has been involved in providing training to the tourism industry in Thailand to counter child-sex tourism.

(excellent days), which occur every full and new moon. Other activities include offering food to the temple *sangha* (community of monks, nuns and lay residents), meditating, listening to monks chanting *suttas* (discourses of the Buddha) and attending talks on *dhamma* (right behaviour).

MONKS & NUNS

There are about 32,000 monasteries in Thailand and 200,000 monks, many of them ordained for life. Traditionally, every Thai male is expected to spend time as a monk, usually between finishing school and marrying or starting a career. Even his Majesty King Bhumibol served as a novice at Wat Bowonniwet in Banglamphu, Bangkok. Traditionally boys would devote a year or more to monastic life, but these days most people enter the *sangha* for two weeks to three months during *pan·săh* (Buddhist lent), which coincides with the rainy season.

Women can become *mâa chee* (eight-precept nuns) but this is held in slightly lower regard than the status of male monks, as most Thais believe that a woman can only achieve *nibbana* if she is reincarnated as a man. Both monks and nuns shave their heads and wear robes – orange for men, white for women – give up most of their personal belongings and live on charity. Thais donate generously to the local wát, so monks often live quite comfortable lives.

An increasing number of foreigners are coming to Thailand to be ordained as Buddhist monks or nuns. If you want to find out more, see p397 or visit the website **Buddha Net** (www.buddhanet.net).

As long as you dress appropriately and observe the correct etiquette (p37) you will be welcome at most monasteries. However, take care not to disturb monks while they are eating or meditating – nothing breaks the concentration quite like tourists snapping photographs!

Islam

Thailand is home to 1.6 million Muslims (around 4% of Thailand's population), concentrated in the south of the country. Most Thai Muslims are of Malay origin and generally follow a moderate version of the Sunni sect mixed with pre-Islamic animism.

> Thais follow the lunar calendar, with the traditional New Year falling in mid-April.

> After his death, the Buddha's body was supposedly dealt up into 84,000 relics, many of which are claimed to be entombed in various religious structures throughout Thailand.

> Every Thai Buddhist male over the age of 20 is expected to become a monk. This ordination can last as long as several months, or be as brief as a few days.

CHOW LAIR

Southern Thailand is home to one of Thailand's smallest ethnic groups, the *chow lair*, literally, 'people of the sea'. Also known as Moken *(mor·gaan)*, or sea gypsies, the *chow lair* are an ethnic group of Malay origin who span the Andaman coast from Borneo to Myanmar. The remaining traditional bands of *chow lair* are hunter-gatherers, living primarily off the sea. They are recognised as one of the few groups of humans that primarily live at sea, although in recent years many have turned to shantylike settlements on various islands. Perhaps as a result of generations of this marine lifestyle, many *chow lair* can hold their breath for long periods of time and also have an uncanny ability to see underwater. Life at sea has also helped them in other ways; during the 2004 tsunami, virtually no *chow lair* were killed, as folk tales handed down from generation to generation alerted them to the dangers of the quickly receding tide, and they were able to escape to higher ground.

Until recently, the *chow lair* were neglected but mostly ignored until their islands became valuable for tourism. Entrepreneurs bought up large tracts of beachfront land and the *chow lair* moved on to smaller, less valuable islands. With these pressures, it was perhaps inevitable that the *chow lair* culture would slowly disappear. Many sea gypsies now make a living ferrying tourists around the islands or harvesting fish for seafood buffets at tourist resorts. One vestige of traditional *chow lair* life you may see is the biannual 'boat floating' ceremony in May and November, in which an elaborate model boat is set adrift, carrying away bad luck.

MULTICULTURAL THAILAND

Buddhism typically enjoys a worldwide reputation for being peaceful and accommodating, which makes the current tensions (see p28) in the Muslim majority regions of southern Thailand (Narathiwat, Pattani and Yala provinces) perplexing. Why do the cultural and religious beliefs of the Muslim Thais clash with the Buddhist administration?

Firstly, Islam mandates concrete rules for living a good life; a Muslim's day is strictly governed by sacred rituals, from the performance of daily prayers to the preparation of meals and the education of children. But the laws outlined in the Quran aren't represented in the policy-making decisions of the national government, and several well-intentioned economic development schemes have deeply offended Muslim Thais. The government-run lottery, for example, is used to fund need-based scholarships, but gambling is viewed as sinful by Muslims, and clerics have instructed the faithful to reject these much-needed financial opportunities for their children. Interest-based loans for struggling villages also run counter to Islamic beliefs.

Another stumbling block for cross-cultural understanding is the private *pondok* (or *madrasah*) schools, where Muslim children receive religious education. A *pondok* is a village boarding school where male children live a studious and religiously contemplative life before returning to the village with religious leadership skills. The *pondok* custom is viewed as vital to the Islamic way of life but is lacking modern application, and increasingly, many are suspected of imparting a militant Muslim education. In the 1970s the Thai government forced the schools to start teaching secular subjects, a move viewed as distracting and destructive to the Islamic faith.

In recent years, the education ministry has been more sensitive to the importance of the *pondok* tradition while trying to educate its citizens, mainly in Thai language and other subjects that might help relieve the economic hardships of the region. This has been coupled with more conciliatory central government policies, as well as increased representation and funding, but continued scepticism of each other's traditions ensures that the conflict between Buddhists and Muslims is likely to continue.

For more on the conflict in southern Thailand, see the boxed text, p28.

A decade-long revival movement has cultivated more devote Islamic practices and suspicions of outside influences. Under this more strenuous interpretation of Islam, many folk practices have been squeezed out of daily devotions and local people see the mainly Buddhist government and education system as intolerant of their way of life (see the boxed text, above). Schools and infrastructure in the Muslim-majority south are typically underfunded and frustration with the Bangkok government is sometimes defined as a religious rather than political struggle.

Many Muslims from the southernmost regions of Thailand speak Yawi, a dialect of Malay, as their native language.

There are mosques throughout southern Thailand but few are architecturally interesting and most are closed to women. If you do visit a mosque, remember to cover your head and remove your shoes.

Other Religions

Half a percent of the population – primarily hill tribes converted by missionaries and Vietnamese immigrants – is Christian, while half a percent is made up of Confucians, Taoists, Mahayana Buddhists and Hindus. Chinese temples and joss houses are a common sight in the south and in Bangkok's Chinatown, and Bangkok is also home to a large, colourful Hindu temple.

ARTS

Much of Thailand's creative energy has traditionally gone into the production of religious and ceremonial art. Painting, sculpture, music and theatre still play a huge role in the ceremonial life of Thais and religious art is very much a living art form.

Literature

The most pervasive and influential work of classical Thai literature is the Ramakian, based on the Hindu holy book, the Ramayana, which was brought to Southeast Asia by Indian traders and introduced to Thailand by the Khmer about 900 years ago. Although the main theme remains the same, the Thais embroidered the Ramayana by providing much more biographical detail on arch-villain Ravana (*Thótsàkan* in the Ramakian) and his wife Montho. The monkey-god, Hanuman, is also transformed into something of a playboy.

The epic poem, *Phra Aphaimani,* was composed by poet Sunthorn Phu (1786–1855) and is set on the island of Ko Samet. *Phra Aphaimani* is Thailand's most famous classical literary work, and tells a typically epic story of an exiled prince.

Modern Thai literature is usually written in Thai, so it isn't very accessible to non-Thais. Modern authors you may find translated include Seni Saowaphong, whose most famous title *Pisat, Evil Spirits* deals with conflicts between the old and new generations. Former prime minister, Kukrit Pramoj, is another respected author – his collection of short stories, *Lai Chiwit* (*Many Lives*), and the novel *Si Phandin (Four Reigns),* which is set in the Rama V era, have been translated into English.

Celebrated contemporary writer Pira Sudham was born into a poor family in northeastern Thailand. *Monsoon Country,* one of several titles Sudham wrote in English, brilliantly captures the region's struggles against nature and nurture.

Chart Korbjitti is a two-time winner of the Southeast Asian Writers Award (SEA Write): in 1982 for *The Judgement,* the drama of a young village man wrongly accused of a crime; and in 1994 for a 'mixed-media' novel, *Time.*

SP Somtow has been described as 'Thailand's JD Salinger'. *Jasmine Nights,* Somtow's upbeat coming-of-age novel, fuses traditional ideas with modern Thai pop culture. *Jasmine Nights* won acclaim throughout the world.

Writer Sri Daoruang adapted the Ramayana into modern Bangkok in *Married to the Demon King.* Short stories by modern Thai women writers appear in the collection *A Lioness in Bloom,* translated by Susan Kepner.

The leading postmodern writer is Prabda Yoon, whose short-story collection *Probability* won the 2002 SEA Write award. Although his works have yet to be translated, he wrote the screenplay for *Last Life in the Universe* and other Pen-ek Ratanaruang–directed films, and in 2004 was commissioned by Thailand's Ministry of Culture to write a piece on the 2004 tsunami. The result, *Where We Feel: A Tsunami Memoir by an Outsider,* was distributed free along the Andaman coast.

Another name worth looking out for is Siriworn Kaewkan, whose novels *The Murder Case of Tok Imam Storpa Karde* and *A Scattered World* have recently been translated into English by Frenchman Marcel Barang. In fact Barang, who is also working on an updated translation of *Si Phandin (Four Reigns),* is currently the preeminent translator of Thai fiction into English, and several of his translations, including stories by Chart Korbjitti and two-time SEA Write winner Win Lyovarin can be downloaded as e-books at www.thaifiction.com.

Cinema

Thailand has a lively homespun movie industry, producing some very competent films in various genres. The most expensive film ever made in the country, not to mention the highest grossing, was director Prince Chatrichalerm Yukol's epic *Legend of Suriyothai* (2003), which tells the story of a 16th-century warrior princess. But what has propelled Thai viewers to forsake Hollywood imports are generally action flicks such as *Ong*

When speaking with or about royalty, a special vocabulary called *râht-chá-sàp* is used by Thais.

Much of Thai culture and art, particularly literature and dance and a significant amount of language, originally came from India along with Buddhism.

Nine is largely considered a lucky number in Thailand because it sounds similar to the Thai word for progress.

Bak: Thai Warrior and the follow-up *Tom Yum Goong*, directed by Prachya Pinkaew.

Thailand has cropped up in various foreign film festivals over the years, with several critically acclaimed art-house movies. Pen-Ek Ratanaruang's clever and haunting movies, such as *Last Life in the Universe* and *6ixty9ine* have created a buzz on the film-festival circuit. Apichatpong Weerasethakul leads the avant-garde pack with his Cannes-awarded *Tropical Malady* and *Blissfully Yours*.

The Thai government is now actively touting Thailand as a location for foreign film-makers. The most famous film to be made here in recent years was *The Beach* (2000). Based on the Alex Garland novel, it was filmed at Maya Bay on Ko Phi-Phi, Phuket, and several jungle locations near Krabi and Khao Yai National Park. The film caused controversy for allegedly damaging the environment in Maya Bay, which was also a location for the 1995 pirate stinker *Cutthroat Island*. Other famous films made here include the James Bond romp *The Man with the Golden Gun* (1974), which was filmed in Ao Nang Bay, *Good Morning Vietnam* (1987), *The Killing Fields* (1984) and *The Deer Hunter* (1978).

Thailand's third sex, the *gà·teu·i (often spelled kà·thoey;* transgender men), get a starring role in *Iron Ladies,* a movie about the true story of an all-transvestite volleyball team that became the national men's champions.

Music

Traditional Thai music may sound a little strange to visitors, as the eight-note Thai octave is broken in different places to the European octave. Thai scales were first transcribed by Thai-German composer Phra Chen Duriyanga (Peter Feit), who also composed Thailand's national anthem in 1932.

The classical Thai orchestra is called the *Ƀèe·pâht* and can include anything from five to 20 musicians. The most popular stringed instrument is the *ja·kêh*, a slender guitar-like instrument played horizontally on the ground, which probably evolved from the Indian *vina*. Woodwind instruments include the *khlùi*, a simple wooden flute, and the *Ƀèe*, a recorder-like instrument with a reed mouthpiece, based on the Indian *shennai*. You'll hear the *Ƀèe* being played if you go to a Thai boxing match. Other popular instruments include the *saw*, a three-stringed fretless instrument, similar to the Japanese *shamisen,* and the *rá·nâht èhk*, a bamboo-keyed xylophone played with wooden hammers.

THAI CINEMA: A CRITIC'S VIEW *Kong Rithdee*

I wish those grand old stand-alone cinemas that once dotted most streets in Bangkok were still around. Sadly it's not to be. Now we have to be content with the cineplex, which lacks character and vibe. Nowadays cinemas in Thailand aren't generally that much different than those in the West. In fact Thai cineplexes have more comfy seats – and the ticket is certainly much cheaper.

Thai horror films have a global reputation for being inventive and scary; they're obviously made by people who believe in ghosts. At the same time, we have quite a few art-house directors who are well known internationally and who are expanding the horizons of Thai film. I like the films of Apichatpong Weerasethakul, Pen-ek Ratanaruang and Wisit Sasanatieng, and my favourite Thai films are *Black Silk*, by Ratana Pestonji; *Tropical Malady,* by Apichatpong Weerasethakul; and *Monrak Transistor,* by Pen-ek Ratanaruang.

Thai movies released in the cinema come equipped with English subtitles, so check them out. The subtitles are usually accurate. What's more elusive is the Thai humour – the wordplay and cultural allusions – which is harder to grasp for someone who's not familiar with the country.

I wouldn't recommend most foreign films shot in Thailand, as they don't do justice to the city. They tend to exoticise the place and the people, especially films like *The Beach* and *Bangkok Dangerous.*

Kong Rithdee lives in Bangkok and is a film critic for the Bangkok Post.

Perhaps the most familiar Thai instrument is the *kĭm* or hammer dulcimer, responsible for the plinking, plunking music you'll hear in Thai restaurants across the world. The dulcimer resembles a flat harp played with two light bamboo sticks and has an eerie echoing sound. Another unusual Thai instrument is the *kórng wong yài*, a semicircle of tuned gongs arranged in a wooden rack. The double-headed *dà·pohn* drum sets the tempo for the whole ensemble.

The contemporary Thai music scene is strong and diverse. The most popular genre is undoubtedly *lôok tûng*, a style analogous to country and western in the USA that tends to appeal most to working-class Thais. The 1970s ushered in a new style dubbed *pleng pêu·a chee·wít* (literally 'music for life'), inspired by the politically conscious folk rock of the USA and Europe. The three biggest modern Thai music icons are rock staple Carabao, pop star Thongchai 'Bird' MacIntyre, and *lôok tûng* queen, Pumpuang Duangchan, who died tragically in 1995.

See www.thaistudents .com for Thai pop downloads, language tips and culture chat.

Today there are hundreds of youth-oriented Thai bands, from chirpy boy and girl bands to metal rockers, making music that is easy to sing along with and maddeningly hard to get out of your head.

In the 1990s an alternative pop scene – known as *pleng tâi din* (underground music) – grew in Bangkok. Modern Dog, a Britpop-inspired band, is generally credited with bringing independent Thai music into the mainstream, and their success paved the way for more mainstream alternative acts such as Apartmentkunpha, Futon, Chou Chou and Calories Blah Blah. Thai headbangers designed to fill stadiums include perennial favourite Loso, as well as Big Ass, Potato and Bodyslam.

Architecture

Most traditional Thai architecture is religious in nature. Thai temples, like Thai Buddhism, gladly mix and match different foreign influences, from the corn-shaped stupa inherited from the Khmer empire to the bell-shaped stupa of Sri Lanka. Despite the foreign flourishes, all Thai temples' roof lines mimic the shape of the *naga* (mythical serpent) that protected the Buddha during meditation and is viewed as a symbol of life. Green and gold tiles represent scales while the soaring eaves are the head of the creature.

See www.seasite.niu .edu/thai/music for snatches of Thai tunes, from classical music to pop.

Traditional teak homes can be seen throughout northern Thailand, but are also present in the capital. The capital's finest teak building is Vimanmek Mansion (p84), said to be the largest golden-teak building in the world. Teak houses are typically raised on stilts to minimise the damage caused by flooding and provide a space for storage and livestock. The whole structure is held together with wooden pegs and topped by sweeping eaves that rise to distinctive gables at either end of the house. Houses are traditionally roofed with glazed tiles or wooden shingles.

In the south, houses have traditionally been simpler, relying heavily on bamboo poles and woven bamboo fibre. You might also see Malay-style houses, which use high masonry foundations rather than wooden stilts.

Architecture over the last 100 years has been influenced by cultures from all over the world. In the south, you can still see plenty of Sino-Portuguese *hôrng tăa·ou* (shophouses) – plastered Chinese-style masonry houses with shops below and living quarters above. Classic examples of this style can be found in Phuket's main city, Phuket Town (p309). Since WWII the main trend in Thai architecture has been one of function over form, inspired by the European Bauhaus movement. As a result, there are lots of plain buildings that look like egg cartons turned on their sides.

Thais believe it is unlucky to get a haircut on Wednesday, and it is on this day that barbers take their holiday.

Thai architects began experimenting during the building boom of the mid-1980s, resulting in creative designs such as Sumet Jumsai's famous robot-shaped Bank of Asia on Th Sathon Tai in Bangkok, or the Elephant Building off Th Phaholyothin in northern Bangkok.

Painting

Except for the prehistoric and historic cave paintings found in the south of the country, not much ancient formal painting exists in Thailand, partly due to the devastating Burmese invasion of 1767. The vast majority of what exists is religious in nature, and typically takes the form of temple paintings illustrating the various lives of the Buddha.

Since the 1980s boom years, Thai secular sculpture and painting have enjoyed increased international recognition, with a handful of Impressionism-inspired artists among the initial few to have reached this vaunted status. Succeeding this was the 'Fireball' school of artists such as Manit Sriwanichpoom, who specialise in politically motivated, mixed-media art installations. In recent years Thai artists have again moved away from both traditional influences and political commentary and towards contemporary art, focusing on more personal themes, such as those seen in the gender explorative works of Pinaree Sanpitak, or Maitree Siriboon's identity-driven work. For information about visiting Bangkok's galleries and art museums, see p69.

Theatre & Dance

Traditional Thai theatre consists of four main dramatic forms: *kŏhn* is a formal masked dance-drama, traditionally reserved for royalty, depicting scenes from the Ramakian; *lá·kon* is dance-drama performed for common people; *lí·gair* is partly improvised, often bawdy, folk play featuring dancing, comedy, melodrama and music; and *hùn lŏo·ang (lá·kon lék)* is traditional puppet theatre enacting religious legends or folk tales.

Most of these forms can be enjoyed in Bangkok, both at dinner shows for tourists and at formal theatrical performances. There are also some distinctively southern theatrical styles, predating the arrival of Islam on the Malay Peninsula. The most famous is *má·noh·rah*, the oldest surviving Thai dance-drama, which tells the story of Prince Suthon, who sets off to rescue the kidnapped Mánohraa, a *gin·ná·ree* (woman-bird) princess. As in *lí·gair*, performers add extemporaneous, comic rhymed commentary. Trang also has a distinctive form of *lí·gair*, with a storyline depicting Indian merchants taking their Thai wives back to India for a visit.

Another ancient theatrical style in the south is shadow-puppet theatre, which also occurs in Indonesia and Malaysia, in which two-dimensional figures carved from buffalo hide are manipulated against an illuminated cloth screen. The capital of shadow puppetry today is Nakhon Si Thammarat, which has regular performances at its festivals. There are two distinctive shadow-play traditions. *Năng dà·lung* uses delicate puppets manipulated by a single puppet master to tell stories from the Ramakian, while *năng yài* (literally, 'big hide'), uses much larger puppets with several operators, but is sadly a dying art. Both kinds of puppets are popular souvenirs for tourists.

Food & Drink

Eating is one of the highlights of any trip to Thailand, and it doesn't take long to see that the locals are equally enthusiastic about their national cuisine. Thais appear to spend a significant part of their lives snacking and eating, and rightfully so: the spectrum of things to eat in even an average-sized Thai city is mind-boggling, and a visit to Thailand's southern provinces will expand your culinary horizons even further (see the boxed text, p49). Such an abundance of eats would result in waistline problems elsewhere, but Thai food, with its fresh ingredients and emphasis on bold tastes, fills diners with flavour rather than bulk.

The closest thing to being Thai without surrendering your passport is to jump headfirst into this jungle of flavour. To guide you, we've put together a primer of the essential ingredients and dishes you're bound to run into along the way.

You eat rice dishes with a spoon and a fork, treating the spoon like the fork and the fork like a knife. Noodle soups and *pàt tai* are the only dishes eaten with chopsticks.

STAPLES & SPECIALITIES
Rice

Thailand has been a leader in rice exports since the 1960s and the quality of Thai rice, according to many discerning Asians, is considered the best there is. Thailand's *kôw hŏrm málí* (jasmine rice) is so coveted that there is a steady underground business in smuggling bags of the fragrant grain to neighbouring countries.

Rice is so central to Thai food culture that the most common term for 'eat' is *gin kôw* (consume rice) and one of the most common greetings is *'Gin kôw láa·ou rĕu yang?'* (Have you eaten rice yet?). All dishes eaten with rice – whether curries, stir-fries or soups – are simply classified as *gàp kôw* (with rice).

Two dishes that use rice as a principal ingredient are *kôw pàt* (fried rice), which is found all over the country, and *kôw mòk gài* (chicken biryani), typically a Muslim-Malay dish. A sure sign that the staff at your guesthouse are from the northeastern part of the country is if you spot them eating *kôw nĕe·o* (sticky rice), usually eaten with the hands and accompanied by fried chicken and *sô·dam* (spicy green-papaya salad).

Written and photo-graphed by the author of this chapter, Austin Bush's food blog (www.austinbushphotography.com) details food and dining in Thailand and abroad.

Noodles

You'll find four basic kinds of noodle in Thailand. Given the Thai fixation with rice, the overwhelming popularity of *gŏo·ay dĕe·o* (rice noodles) is hardly surprising. They're made from pure rice flour mixed with water to form a paste, which is then steamed to form wide, flat sheets. These are then sliced into noodles of varying sizes.

The king of Thai noodledom, *gŏo·ay dĕe·o* comes as part of many dishes. The simplest, *gŏo·ay dĕe·o nám*, is noodles served in a bowl of meat stock along with bits of meat (usually pork), bean sprouts and *pàk chee* (coriander leaf) as garnish. When you order a bowl of noodle soup from a vendor, you'll need to call your noodle size – *sên lék* (flat, thin rice noodles), *sên yài* (flat, wide rice noodles) or *bà·mèe* (egg noodles) – and the meat of your choice. You then flavour the bowl with the four seasonings that appear on the table – a dash of sugar, dried chillies, fish sauce and vinegar. Foreigners think that curries define the national food consciousness, but the humble noodle dish is more emblematic: Thais eat *gŏo·ay dĕe·o* for breakfast and lunch, and as a predinner snack and hangover cure.

Cookbook writer Kasma Loha-Unchit features recipes and other culinary events on her website www.thaifoodandtravel.com.

A speciality of southern Thailand, *kà·nŏm jeen* is stark white noodles produced by pushing rice-flour paste through a sieve into boiling water. The noodles are topped with spicy fish curry and loaded up with an assortment of pickled and fresh vegetables.

Finally there's *wún·sên,* an almost clear noodle made from mung-bean starch and water. *Wún·sên* (jelly thread) is used for only a few dishes in Thailand: *yam wún·sên,* a hot and tangy salad made with lime juice, fresh sliced *prík kêe nǒo* (mouse-dropping peppers), fresh prawns, ground pork and various seasonings; and *ʼbòo òp wún·sên,* which is bean thread noodles baked in a lidded clay pot with crab and seasonings.

Despite their importance in modern Thai food, chillies are a relatively new addition to the Thai kitchen, and were brought by Portuguese traders more than 400 years ago.

Curries

For many people, *gaang* (curries; it sounds like 'gang') are the definitive Thai dish, but few visitors have ever met the real McCoy. A well-made curry should possess a balance of the four main flavours: salty, fishy, spicy and a little sweet. Usually restaurants with a Western clientele will overdose on coconut milk and sugar to cater to their customers' sweet tooths.

All chilli-based *gaang* start as fresh – not powdered – ingredients that are smashed, pounded and ground in a stone mortar and pestle to form a thick, aromatic and extremely pungent paste. Typical ingredients include dried or

---

BACKPACKER FOOD *Austin Bush*

It all began with an order of Hat Yao fried rice, a bizarre concoction of rice fried with ketchup and chicken, enveloped in a thin omelette. Now, I've eaten lots of Thai dishes in nearly every region of Thailand and have never come across anything quite like Hat Yao fried rice. I'd also never seen a green curry the way it was served the next night: soupy and impotent and laden with carrots, cauliflower and potatoes. In fact, once I sought it out, I discovered an entire repertoire of food on Ko Pha-Ngan's Hat Yao that I'd never encountered previously. This genre of cuisine, characterised by unrecognisable interpretations of local and foreign dishes, dull flavours, a strong vegetarian bias, facsimile menus, mystery ingredients and even more mysterious origins, I called Backpacker Food.

The simple fact that Backpacker Food exists begs the question: Why does one need comfort food when on the road? Isn't the point of travelling to try new things? Admittedly, there are times when a tender tummy might require familiar flavours, and perhaps this is when a queasy Italian would order the spaghetti carbonara, or when a nauseous native of the islands would choose the pork chop Hawaiian. (I'm still not exactly sure who would order Contigi prawn, fried chicken mayonnaise, no name falafel-style chicken or cauliflower cheese.) But the ubiquity of such menu items suggests that they are the norm rather than the exception.

Backpacker breakfasts in particular seemed to have the least in common with the local food. The English, with their 'Full English Breakfast' seemed to dominate this area, while the Swiss, with their muesli, often little more than oatmeal with a few cornflakes thrown in, have also had a palpable, though unpalatable, impact. And the ubiquitous 'American Breakfast' of instant coffee, lighter-than-air white bread, warm hotdogs and oily fried eggs isn't doing much to promote the image of American food abroad, and certainly isn't a good way to start the day.

Even if you do make an effort to go 'local', Thai-style Backpacker Food is often just as bizarre, if not more, than the quasi-Western food. Authentic southern Thai cooking is a vibrant seafood-based cuisine that is among the most full-flavoured in the country, if not the world, but the guesthouse kitchens of Hat Yao put out consistently weak Thai-style salads, limp tasteless stir-fries, barely-there curries, and oddly enough, despite being on an island, very few seafood dishes.

If the lack of authentic Thai food on Ko Yao is getting to you, my suggestion is to keep an eye out for where your guesthouse staff are eating, usually off the main tourist trail. Or you could always order American fried rice – rice fried with ketchup, sliced hotdogs and sweet raisins, and topped with a fried egg. Despite the name, the dish is found throughout Thailand and is particularly popular among Thai children and university students. It was, as far as I could tell, the only truly Thai dish on the restaurant menus of Ko Yao.

fresh chilli, galangal (also known as Thai ginger), lemon grass, kaffir lime zest, shallots, garlic, shrimp paste and salt. Certain curries employ dried spices such as coriander seeds or a touch of cumin.

During cooking, most *gaang* pastes are blended in a heated pan with coconut cream, to which the chef adds the rest of the ingredients. These include watery coconut milk, used to thin and flavour the *gaang*, although some recipes omit coconut milk entirely to produce a particularly fiery *gaang* known as *gaang ḃàh* (jungle curry).

Salads

Standing right alongside *gaang* in terms of Thai-ness are *yam,* the ubiquitous hot and tangy salads combining a blast of lime, chilli and fresh herbs and a choice of seafood, roast vegetables, noodles or meats. Thais prize *yam* dishes so much that they are often eaten on their own, without rice, before the meal has begun. On Thai menus the *yam* section will often be the longest. The usual English menu translation is either 'Thai-style salad' or 'hot and sour salad'.

Lime juice provides the tang, while fresh chillies produce the heat. Other ingredients vary, but there are usually plenty of leafy vegetables and herbs present, including lettuce (often lining the dish) and Chinese celery. Lemon grass, shallots, kaffir lime leaves and mint may also come into play. Most *yam* are served at room temperature or just slightly warmed by any cooked ingredients.

Yam are the spiciest of all Thai dishes, and if you're not so chilli-tolerant, a good *yam* to start off with is *yam wún·sên:* mung bean noodles tossed with prawns, ground pork, coriander leaves, lime juice and fresh sliced chillies.

Stir-Fries & Deep-Fries

The simplest dishes in the Thai culinary repertoire are *pàt* (stir-fries), brought to Thailand by the Chinese, who are famous for being able to stir-fry a whole banquet in a single wok.

The list of Thai dishes that you can *pàt* is seemingly endless. Many are better classified as Chinese, such as *néu·a pàt nám·man hŏy* (beef in oyster sauce). Some are clearly Thai-Chinese hybrids, such as *gài pàt prík kǐng,* in which chicken is stir-fried with ginger, garlic and chillies – ingredients shared by both traditions – but seasoned with fish sauce.

Tôrt (deep-frying in oil) is generally reserved for snacks such as *glôo·ay tôrt* (fried bananas) or *ḃò·ḃée·a* (egg rolls). One exception is *ḃlah tôrt* (crisp fried fish). Only a very few dishes require ingredients to be dipped in batter and then deep-fried, including *gài tôrt* (fried chicken) and *gûng chúp ḃâang tôrt* (batter-fried prawns).

Soups

Thai soups fall into two broad categories – *đôm yam* (also spelt as *tôm yam)* and *gaang jèut* – which are worlds apart in terms of seasonings. *Đôm yam* is almost always made with seafood, though other meats may also be used. It's often translated on English menus as 'hot and sour Thai soup', although this often leads non-Thais to mistakenly relate the dish to Chinese hot-and-sour soup, which is thinner in texture, milder and includes vinegar. *Đôm yam* is meant to be eaten with rice, not alone, and the first swallow often leaves the uninitiated gasping for breath.

In contrast, *gaang jèut* (mild soup with vegetables and pork) is a soothing broth seasoned with little more than soy or fish sauce and black pepper. It isn't a very interesting dish by itself, but provides a nice balance when paired with other spicier dishes. It is also a good option if your tummy is feeling tender.

Curries and soups are generally ladled onto a plate of rice, rather than eaten directly out of the bowl.

Thai Food, by David Thompson, is widely considered the most authoritative book on Thai cooking, and includes authentic recipes from the country's south.

The wok and technique of stir-frying were probably brought to Thailand by Chinese immigrants.

SOMETHING'S FISHY

Westerners might scoff at the all-too-literal name of this condiment, but for much Thai food, fish sauce is more than just another ingredient, it is *the* ingredient.

Essentially the liquid obtained from salted and fermented fish, fish sauce, known in Thai as *nám 'blah*, takes various guises depending on the region. In northeastern Thailand, discerning diners prefer *'blah ráh*, a thick, pasty mash of fermented freshwater fish and sometimes rice. Elsewhere, where people have access to the sea, fish sauce takes the form of a thin liquid extracted from salted anchovies. In both cases the result is highly pungent, generally salty (rather than fishy) in taste, and used in much the same way as the salt shaker is in the West.

Fruit

Thai fruits are so decadent and luscious that some visitors concoct entire meals of the different varieties. Common fruits that are in season all year include *má·prów* (coconut), *fa·ràng* (guava), *kà·nǔn* (jackfruit), *má·kǎhm* (tamarind), *sôm* (orange), *má·lá·gor* (papaya), *sôm oh* (pomelo), *đaang moh* (watermelon) and *sàp·'bà·rót* (pineapple).

Seasonal fruits to look for include: *chom·pôo* (rose apple; April to July), *mang·kút* (mangosteen; April to September), *má·môo·ang* (mango; several varieties and seasons), *ngó* (rambutan; July to September) and *nóy·nàh* (custard apple; July to October).

> Thais are among the most prolific consumers of garlic in the world.

Sweets

Sweets mostly work their way into the daily Thai diet as between-meal snacks and are typically sold by market or street vendors.

Ingredients for many *kŏrng wǎhn* (Thai sweets) include grated coconut, coconut milk, rice flour, cooked sticky rice, tapioca, mung-bean starch, boiled taro and fruits. For added texture and crunch some may also contain fresh corn kernels, sugar-palm kernels, lotus seeds, cooked black beans and chopped water chestnuts. Egg yolks are a popular ingredient in Thai sweets, particularly in the ubiquitous *fŏy torng* ('golden threads' that actually look like strands of gold), a sweet of Portuguese origin.

Thai sweets similar to the European concept of 'sweet pastry' are called *kà·nŏm*. Probably the most popular *kà·nŏm* are bite-sized items wrapped in banana or pandanus leaves, especially *kôw đôm mát*, which consists of sticky rice grains steamed with coconut milk inside a banana-leaf wrapper to form a solid, almost toffeelike, mass.

> Not everything in your bowl of *đôm yam* is edible. Like bay leaves, the ingredients with the texture of bark are only there for flavouring.

DRINKS
Coffee & Tea

Thais are big coffee drinkers, and good-quality arabica and robusta are cultivated in hilly areas of northern and southern Thailand. The traditional filtering system is nothing more than a narrow cloth bag attached to a steel handle. The bag is filled with ground coffee and hot water poured through, producing *gah·faa tǒong* (traditional filtered coffee) or *gah·faa boh·rahn* (traditional coffee).

Black tea, both locally grown and imported varieties, is available at the same places that serve real coffee. *Chah tai* derives its characteristic orange-red colour from ground tamarind seed added after curing. *Chah rórn* (hot tea), like coffee, will almost always be served with condensed milk and sugar, so be sure to specify if you are wanting black tea. Chinese-style tea is *nám chah*. *Chah yen* is a tall glass of Thai iced tea with sugar and condensed milk, while *chah má·now* (lemon tea) comes without milk, and with a squeeze of lime.

> Meals in southern Thailand are often accompanied by a complimentary tray of fresh herbs and vegetables and a fiery shrimp paste–based dipping sauce.

SOUTHERN FLAVOUR

Fans of subtle flavours beware: southern Thai cooking is undoubtedly the spiciest regional cooking style in a country of spicy regional cuisines. The food of Thailand's southern provinces also tends to be very salty, and seafood, not surprisingly, plays an important role, ranging from fresh fish that is grilled or added to soups, to fish or prawns that have been pickled or fermented and served as sauces or condiments. Two of the principal crops in the south are coconuts and cashews, both of which find their way into a variety of dishes. In addition, southern Thais love their greens, and nearly every meal is accompanied by a platter of fresh herbs and vegies and a spicy 'dip' of shrimp paste, chillies, garlic and lime. Specific southern greens to look out for include *sà-đor* (a pungent green beanlike vegetable known also as stink bean), *lôok nee-ang* (a round dark-green bean) and *mét ree-ang* (similar to large, dark-green bean sprouts).

Dishes you are likely to come across include the following:

- *Gaang đai Ъlah* – an intensely spicy and salty fish curry that includes *đai Ъlah* (salted fish stomach); much better than it sounds.
- *Kà-nŏm jeen nám yah* – this dish of fermented rice noodles served with a fiery currylike sauce is always accompanied by a tray of fresh vegetables and herbs.
- *Kôw yam* – this popular breakfast includes rice topped with sliced herbs, bean sprouts, dried prawns, toasted coconut and powdered red chilli served with a sour-sweet fish-based sauce.
- *Gaang sôm* – known as *gaang lĕu-ang* (yellow curry) in central Thailand, this sour-spicy soup gets its hue from the copious use of turmeric, a root commonly used in southern Thai cooking.
- *Ngóp* – something of a grilled curry, this dish takes the form of a coconut milk and herb paste containing seafood that is wrapped in a banana leaf and grilled until firm.
- *Gài tôrt hàht yài* – the famous deep-fried chicken from the town of Hat Yai gets its rich flavour from a marinade containing dried spices.

Fruit Drinks

The all-purpose term for fruit juice is *nám* (water/juice) *pŏn-lá-mái* (fruit). When a blender or extractor is used, you've got *nám kán* (squeezed juice), hence *nám sàp-Ъà-rót kán* is freshly squeezed pineapple juice. *Nám ôy* (sugarcane juice) is a Thai favourite and a very refreshing accompaniment to *gaang* dishes. A similar juice from the sugar palm, *nám-đahn sòt*, is also very good and both are full of vitamins and minerals. Mixed fruit blended with ice is *nám Ъàn* (mixed juice) as in *nám má-lá-gor Ъàn*, a papaya shake.

Beer & Whisky

Advertised with such slogans as *Ъrà-têht row, bee-a row* (Our Land, Our Beer), the Singha label is considered the quintessential 'Thai' beer by *faràng* and locals alike. Pronounced 'sing' (not 'sing-hah'), it claims about half the domestic market, and has an alcohol content of 6%. Singha is sold in bottles and cans, and is also available on tap as *bee-a sòt* (draught beer) in many pubs and restaurants. Dutch-licensed but Thailand-brewed Heineken and Singapore's Tiger brand are also popular selections. You'll find other, even cheaper, Thai beers in supermarkets, but rarely in restaurants.

Rice whisky is a favourite of the working class because it's more affordable than beer. Most rice whiskies are mixed with distilled sugar-cane spirits and have a sharp, sweet taste not unlike rum, and an alcohol content of 35%. More popular nowadays is the slightly more expensive domestic rum, Sang Som.

WHERE TO EAT & DRINK

All restaurants, large and small, are referred to by the single Thai term *ráhn ah-hăhn* ('food shop', the term for restaurants). Decoration may be limited

For the best of Lonely Planet's culinary wisdom, seek out *World Food Thailand,* by Joe Cummings.

COFFEE, SOUTHERN STYLE

In virtually every town or city in southern Thailand you'll find numerous old-world cafes known locally as *ráhn goh·bée*. The shops are almost exclusively owned by Thais of Chinese origin, and often seem suspended in time, typically sporting the same decor and menu for decades. Characteristics of *ráhn goh·bée* include marble-topped tables, antique mugs and dishes, and an almost exclusively male clientele that also seems not to have budged since opening day. Some of the most atmospheric *ráhn goh·bée* in Thailand can be found in the town of Trang (p367).

The beans used at *ráhn goh·bée* are sometimes grown abroad, but are roasted domestically, and although they're as black as the night, the drink typically tends to lack body. This may be due to the brewing method, which involves pouring hot water through a wind-socklike piece of cloth that holds the loose grounds. Typically, *goh·bée* is served over a dollop of sweetened condensed milk and a tablespoon (or more) of sugar in small, handleless glasses. For those lacking a sweet tooth, try *goh·bée or* (black coffee), or just ask them to hold the sugar. All hot coffee drinks are served with a 'chaser' of weak green tea.

Ráhn goh·bée are also a great place for a quick bite. Upon arriving at the more traditional ones, you'll be greeted by a tray of steamed Chinese buns or sweet snacks, such as sticky rice wrapped in banana leaf or baked goods.

to a few beer posters and a small shrine or something more incongruous, such as a faded picture of the Swiss Alps. Fluorescent lighting – cheap and cool – is the norm. Such restaurants typically specialise in a single cuisine, whether local or regional.

At the more generic *ráhn ah·hǎhn đahm sàng* (food-to-order shop), cooks can whip up almost any Thai dish you can name, including any kind of rice or noodle dish as well as more complex multidish meals. Most of the standard Thai dishes are available, including those in the *đôm yam, yam* and *pàt* categories. You can recognise this type of restaurant by the raw ingredients displayed out front.

More upmarket restaurants have printed menus, usually with broken English translations, where you'll find tablecloths, air-con and the Western idea of 'ambience'. Average Thais prefer to order their favourite dishes without referring to a menu at all, so these more expensive restaurants only cater to an upper-class clientele with international tastes.

Check out the international message board at www.chowhound.com, where culinary hobbyists post reviews of Thailand's restaurants.

Quick Eats

One of the simplest, most pleasurable venues for dining out in Thailand is the night market, which can vary from a small cluster of metal tables and chairs alongside the road to more elaborate affairs that take up whole city blocks. What they all have in common is a conglomeration of *rót kĕn* (vendor carts) whose owners have decided that a particular intersection or unused urban lot makes an ideal location to set up their mobile kitchens.

There are two types of night markets: the *đà·làht yen* (evening market) sets up just before sunset and stays open until around 9pm or 10pm – possibly later in large cities. The second type is the *đà·làht đôh rûng* (open until dawn), which begins doing business around 11pm and keeps going until sunrise. Typical places to look for both types of night market include in front of day markets, next to bus or train stations and at busy intersections.

VEGETARIANS & VEGANS

The number of vegetarian restaurants in Thailand is increasing, thanks largely to Bangkok's former governor Chamlong Srimuang, whose strict vegetarianism inspired a nonprofit chain of *ráhn ah·hǎhn mang·sà·wí·rát* (vegetarian restaurants) in Bangkok and several provincial capitals. The food at these restaurants is usually served buffet-style and is very cheap. Dishes are almost always 100% vegan; that is, no meat, poultry, fish, dairy or egg products have been used in their creation.

The phrase 'I'm vegetarian' in Thai is *pŏm gin jair* (for men) or *dì·chăn gin jair* (for women). Loosely translated this means 'I eat only vegetarian food', which includes no eggs and no dairy products – in other words, totally vegan.

HABITS & CUSTOMS

There are no 'typical' times for meals, though the customary noon to 1pm lunch break tends to cluster diners in local restaurants at that hour. Nor are certain genres of food restricted to certain times of day. Practically anything can be eaten first thing in the morning, whether it's sweet, salty or chilli-ridden.

Thais tend to avoid eating alone, especially for the evening meal. When forced to fly solo – such as during a lunch break – a single diner usually sticks to one-plate dishes such as fried rice or curry over rice.

If an opportunity presents itself, dining with a group of Thais will reveal more about Thai culture than watching canned classical dance performances. A big group means everyone has a chance to sample several different kinds of dishes. Traditionally, the party orders a curry, a fish, a stir-fry, a *yam*, a vegetable dish and a soup, taking care to balance cool and hot, sour and sweet, salty and plain.

When serving yourself from a common platter, put no more than one spoonful onto your plate at a time. Sometimes serving spoons are provided. If not, you simply dig in with your own spoon.

The website www.happy cow.net has a searchable index of vegetarian restaurants across the world, including entries for Thailand.

THE MUSLIM INFLUENCE

Muslims are thought to have first visited southern Thailand during the late 14th century. Along with the Quran, they brought with them a meat- and dried-spice-based cuisine from their homelands in India and the Middle East. Nearly 700 years later, the impact of this culinary commerce can still be felt. While some Muslim dishes such as roti, a fried bread similar to the Indian *paratha*, have changed little, if at all, others such as *gaang mát·sà·màn* are a unique blend of Thai and Indian/Middle Eastern cooking styles and ingredients. In more recent years, additional Muslim dishes have arrived via contact with Thailand's neighbour to the south, Malaysia.

Typical Muslim dishes include the following:

■ *Kôw mòk* – biryani, a dish found across the Muslim world, also has a foothold in Thailand. Here the dish is typically made with chicken and is served with a sweet/sour sauce and a bowl of chicken broth.

■ *Sà·đé* (satay) – these grilled skewers of meat probably came to Thailand via Malaysia. The savoury peanut-based dipping sauce is often mistakenly associated with Thai cooking.

■ *Má·đà·bà* – known as *murtabak* in Malaysia and Indonesia, these are roti that have been stuffed with a savoury or sometimes sweet filling and fried until crispy.

■ *Súp hăhng woo·a* – oxtail soup, possibly another Malay contribution, is even richer and often more sour than the 'Buddhist' Thai *đôm yam*.

■ *Sà·làt kàak* – literally 'Muslim salad' (*kàak* is a slightly derogatory word used to describe people or things of Indian and/or Muslim origin), this dish combines iceberg lettuce, chunks of firm tofu, cucumber, hard-boiled egg and tomato, all topped with a slightly sweet peanut sauce.

■ *Gaang mát·sà·màn* – 'Muslim curry' is a rich coconut milk–based dish, which, unlike most Thai curries, gets much of its flavour from dried spices. As with many Thai-Muslim dishes, there is an emphasis on the sweet.

COOKING COURSES

The standard one-day course features a shopping trip to a local market to choose ingredients, followed by preparation of curry pastes, soups, curries, salads and desserts. Some of the better cooking classes in Bangkok and southern Thailand include the following:

It Rains Fishes: Legends, Traditions and the Joys of Thai Cooking, by Kasma Loha-Unchit, is both a cookbook and a charming culinary text.

Baipai Thai Cooking School (p88) Bangkok.
Blue Elephant Cooking School (p88) Bangkok.
Boathouse (p307) Phuket Town, Phuket.
KATI Culinary (p156) Ko Chang.
Khao Cooking School (p88) Bangkok.
Koh Chang Thai Cooking School (p156) Ko Chang.
Krabi Thai Cookery School (p343) Ao Nang, Krabi.
Pum Restaurant & Cooking School (p354) Ko Phi-Phi.
Pum Thai Cooking School (p307) Hat Patong, Phuket.
Samui Institute of Thai Culinary Arts (p201)) Hat Chaweng, Ko Samui.
Sarojin (p292) Hat Bang Sak, Khao Lak.
Silom Thai Cooking School (p88) Bangkok.
Time for Lime (p362) Ko Lanta.

FOOD GLOSSARY

See p443 for some phrases to use when dining out.

Thai Hawker Food, by Kenny Yee and Catherine Gordon, is an illustrated guide to recognising and ordering street food in Thailand.

Menu Decoder

ah·hăhn tá·lair	อาหารทะเล	**seafood**
gûng tôrt	กุ้งทอด	fried prawns
blah jĕe·an	ปลาเจี๋ยน	whole fish cooked in ginger, onions and soy sauce
blah mèuk pàt pèt	ปลาหมึกผัดเผ็ด	spicy fried squid
blah brêe·o wăhn	ปลาเปรี้ยวหวาน	sweet and sour fish
blah tôrt	ปลาทอด	crisp fried fish
gaang	แกง	**curries**
gaang gà·rèe gài	แกงกะหรี่ไก่	mild, Indian-style curry with chicken
gaang kĕe·ow wăhn blah/gài/néu·a	แกงเขียวหวานปลา/ไก่/เนื้อ	green curry with fish/chicken/beef
gaang mát·sà·màn gài/néu·a	แกงมัสมั่นไก่/เนื้อ	Muslim-style curry with chicken/beef and potatoes
gaang pèt gài/ néu·a/mŏo	แกงเผ็ดไก่/เนื้อ/หมู	red curry with chicken/beef/pork
gaang pá·naang	แกงพะแนง	Penang curry (red curry with sweet basil)
kôw	ข้าว	**rice**
kôw man gài	ข้าวมันไก่	boned, sliced Hainan-style chicken with rice
kôw mŏo daang	ข้าวหมูแดง	red pork with rice
kôw nâh gài	ข้าวหน้าไก่	chicken with sauce over rice
kôw nâh bèt	ข้าวหน้าเป็ด	roast duck over rice
kôw pàt mŏo/ gài/gûng	ข้าวผัดหมู/ไก่/กุ้ง	fried rice with pork/chicken/prawns
gŏo·ay dĕe·o/bà·mèe	ก๋วยเตี๋ยว/บะหมี่	**noodles**
bà·mèe nám/hâang	บะหมี่น้ำ/แห้ง	wheat noodles with vegetables and meat in broth/dry

găo·ay đĕe·o nám/hâang	ก๋วยเตี๋ยวน้ำ/แห้ง	rice noodles with vegetables and meat in broth/dry
pàt see·éw	ผัดซีอิ๊ว	fried noodles with soy sauce
pàt tai	ผัดไทย	thin rice noodles fried with tofu, vegetables, egg and peanuts

súp — ซุป — **soups**

gaang jèut	แกงจืด	mild soup with vegetables and pork
kôw đôm ʰblah/gài/gûng	ข้าวต้มปลา/ไก่/กุ้ง	rice soup with fish/chicken/prawns
đôm kàh gài	ต้มข่าไก่	soup with chicken, galangal root and coconut
đôm yam gûng	ต้มยำกุ้ง	prawn and lemon grass soup with mushrooms

ah·hăhn èun — อาหารอื่น — **other dishes**

gài pàt bai gà·prow	ไก่ผัดใบกะเพรา	chicken fried with basil
gài pàt mét má·môo·ang	ไก่ผัดเม็ดมะม่วง	chicken fried with cashews
gài tôrt	ไก่ทอด	fried chicken
gée·o tôrt	เกี๊ยวกรอบ	fried wonton
kài jee·o	ไข่เจียว	plain omelette
kài yát sâi	ไข่ยัดไส้	omelette with vegetables and pork
kà·nŏm jeen nám yah	ขนมจีนน้ำยา	noodles with fish curry
lâhp gài/néu·a	ลาบไก่/เนื้อ	spicy chicken/beef salad
néu·a pàt nám man hŏy	เนื้อผัดน้ำมันหอย	beef in oyster sauce
pàt pàk roo·am	ผัดผักรวม	stir-fried mixed vegetables
sà·đé (satay)	สะเต๊ะ	skewers of barbecued meat
sôm đam	ส้มตำ	spicy green papaya salad
tôrt man ʰblah	ทอดมันปลา	fried fish cakes with cucumber sauce
yam néu·a	ยำเนื้อ	hot and sour, grilled beef salad
yam wún sên	ยำวุ้นเส้น	cellophane noodle salad
ʰbò·ʰbée·a	เปาะเปี๊ยะ	spring rolls

néu·a láa ah·hăhn tá·lair — เนื้อและอาหารทะเล — **meat & seafood**

néu·a	เนื้อ	beef
gài	ไก่	chicken
ʰboo	ปู	crab
bèt	เป็ด	duck
ʰblah	ปลา	fish
mŏo	หมู	pork
ah·hăhn tá·lair	อาหารทะเล	seafood
gûng	กุ้ง	prawn/shrimp
ʰblah mèuk	ปลาหมึก	squid

pàk — ผัก — **vegetables**

má·rá jeen	มะระจีน	bitter melon
gà·làm ʰblee	กะหล่ำปลี	cabbage
dòrk gà·làm	ดอกกะหล่ำ	cauliflower
đaang gwah	แตงกวา	cucumber
má·kĕu·a	มะเขือ	eggplant
grà·tee·am	กระเทียม	garlic
pàk gàht	ผักกาด	lettuce
tòo·a fàk yow	ถั่วฝักยาว	long bean
grà·jée·ap	กระเจี๊ยบ	okra
hŏo·a hŏrm	หัวหอม	onion
tòo·a lí·sŏng	ถั่วลิสง	peanuts

man fà·ràng	มันฝรั่ง	potato
fák torng	ฟักทอง	pumpkin
pèu·ak	เผือก	taro
má·kěu·a têt	มะเขือเทศ	tomato

pŏn·lá·mái	ผลไม้	**fruit**
glôo·ay	กล้วย	banana
má·prów	มะพร้าว	coconut
nóy·nàh	น้อยหน่า	custard apple
tú·ree·an	ทุเรียน	durian
fa·ràng	ฝรั่ง	guava
kà·nŭn	ขนุน	jackfruit
má·now	มะนาว	lime
má·môo·ang	มะม่วง	mango
mang·kút	มังคุด	mangosteen
sôm	ส้ม	orange
má·lá·gor	มะละกอ	papaya
sàp·bà·rót	สับปะรด	pineapple
sôm oh	ส้มโอ	pomelo
ngó	เงาะ	rambutan
má·kăhm	มะขาม	tamarind
đaang moh	แตงโม	watermelon

kŏrng wăhn	ของหวาน	**sweets**
glôo·ay bòo·at chee	กล้วยบวชชี	banana in coconut milk
săng·kà·yăh má·prów	สังขยามะพร้าว	coconut custard
môr gaang	หม้อแกง	egg custard
glôo·ay kàak	กล้วยแขก	fried, Indian-style banana
kŏw nĕe·o daang	ข้าวเหนียวแดง	sticky rice with coconut cream
săng·kà·yăh	สังขยา	Thai custard
đà·gôh	ตะโก้	Thai jelly with coconut cream

krêu·ang dèum	เครื่องดื่ม	**beverages**
bee·a	เบียร์	beer
kòo·at	ขวด	bottle
nám deum	น้ำขวด	bottled drinking water
nám chah	น้ำชา	Chinese tea
gah·faa tŏong (go·bée)	กาแฟถุง(โกปี้)	coffee (traditional filtered)
gah·faa rórn	กาแฟร้อน	coffee with milk and sugar
gâa·ou	แก้ว	glass
nám kăang	น้ำแข็ง	ice
oh·lée·ang	โอเลี้ยง	iced coffee with sugar, no milk
nom jèut	นมจืด	milk
nám blòw	น้ำเปล่า	plain water
nám soh·dah	น้ำโซดา	soda water
chah dam rórn	ชาดำร้อน	tea (black)
chah rórn	ชาร้อน	tea with milk and sugar
wai	ไวน์	wine

Environment

THE LAND

Thailand's odd shape – bulky and wide up north, with a long pendulous arm draping to the south – has often been compared to the head of an elephant. Roughly the size of France, about 517,000 sq km, Thailand stretches an astounding 1650km along a north-south axis and experiences an extremely diverse climate, including monsoons from both the southwest and northwest. The north of the country rises into high forested mountains, while the south consists of a long ridge of limestone hills, covered in tropical rainforest.

Bound to the east by the shallow Gulf of Thailand and to the west by the Andaman Sea, an extension of the Indian Ocean, Thailand possesses one of the most alluring coastlines in the world, with exquisitely carved limestone formations above water and tremendously rich coral reefs below. Hundreds of tropical islands of all shapes and sizes adorn the coast, from flat sand bars covered in mangroves to looming karst massifs licked by azure waters and ringed by white sand beaches. Both coasts have extensive coral reefs, particularly around the granitic Surin Islands (p289) and Similan Islands (p295) in the Andaman Sea. More reefs and Thailand's most dramatic limestone islands sit in Ao Phang-Nga (p297) near Phuket. The west coast is of particular interest to divers because the waters are stunningly clear and extremely rich in marine life.

The famous white sands of Thailand's beaches are actually tiny bits of coral that have been defecated by coral-eating fish.

WILDLIFE

With its diverse climate and topography, it should come as no surprise that Thailand is home to a remarkable diversity of flora and fauna. What is more surprising is that Thailand's environment is still in relatively good shape, particularly considering the relentless development going on all over the country. That said, there are certainly problems; see also p56 on endangered species and p61 on marine environmental issues.

Animals

Animals that live on the coasts and islands of Thailand must adapt to shifting tides and the ever-changing mix of salt and freshwater. Rather than elephants and tigers, keep your eyes open for smaller creatures, like the odd little

---

IT'S ALL CORAL

If there's one thing visitors to Thailand notice right away, it's the dramatically sculpted limestone formations towering over land and water throughout the country. These formations are the fossilised remains of sea shells and coral reefs, and their widespread presence in Thailand demonstrates that much of the region lay underwater more than 200 million years ago. Pushed upward by the crushing forces of two earth plates colliding 30 million years ago, these limestone formations are now exposed to rain and waves that dissolve calcium carbonate in the limestone creating bizarre towers and caves of all sizes. Sometimes the roof of a limestone chamber will collapse, forming a hidden *hôrng* (also spelt *hong*) that lets in sunlight or sea water.

Not only is Thailand the site of a massive fossil reef, it is also one of the best places in the world to see living corals; over 250 species of coral can be found on the Andaman coast alone. Whether old or young, reefs are composed of the skeletal remains of tiny marine organisms that extract calcium carbonate from sea water to build mineral homes. Coral reefs are biologically complex and diverse habitats for countless sea creatures. See p61 for the environmental issues surrounding coral degradation.

mudskipper, a fish that leaves the water and walks around on the mud flats when the tide goes out; or the giant water monitor, a fearsome 350cm-long lizard that climbs and swims effortlessly in its search for small animals.

Without a doubt you will see some of the region's fabulous birdlife – Thailand is home to 10% of the world's bird species – especially sandpipers and plovers on the mud flats, and herons and egrets in the swamps. Look overhead for the sharply attired, chocolate brown and white Brahminy kite, or scan low-lying branches for one of the region's many colourful kingfishers. You are likely to spot a troop of gregarious and noisy crab-eating macaques, but don't be surprised to see these monkeys swimming from shore. With luck you may glimpse a palm civet, a complexly marbled catlike creature, or a serow, the reclusive 'goat-antelope' that bounds fearlessly among inaccessible limestone crags.

The oceans on either side of the Thai peninsula are home to hundreds of species of coral, and the reefs created by these tiny creatures provide the perfect living conditions for countless species of fish, crustaceans and tiny invertebrates. You can find one of the world's smallest fish (the 10mm-long goby) or the largest (a 10m-long whale shark), plus reef denizens such as clownfish, parrotfish, wrasse, angelfish, triggerfish and lionfish. Deeper waters are home to larger species such as groupers, barracudas, sharks, manta rays, marlin and tunas. You might also encounter turtles, whales and dolphins.

ENDANGERED SPECIES

Thailand is a signatory to the UN Convention on International Trade in Endangered Species (Cites) but the enforcement of these trade bans is notoriously lax – just walk around the animal section of Bangkok's Chatuchak Weekend Market (p109) to see how openly the rules are flouted – on one recent day in Bangkok we say a full tiger skin laid out for sale on a roadside near the Grand Palace. Due to habitat loss, pollution and poaching, a depressing number of Thailand's mammals, reptiles, fish and birds are endangered, and even populations of formerly common species are diminishing at an alarming rate. Rare mammals, birds, reptiles, insects, shells and tropical aquarium fish are routinely smuggled out to collectors around the world or killed to make souvenirs for tourists.

Many of Thailand's marine animals are under threat, including whale sharks, although they have been seen more frequently in Thai waters recently, and sea turtles, which are being wiped out by hunting for their eggs, meat and shells. Many other species of shark are being hunted to extinction for their fins, which are used to make shark-fin soup.

The rare dugong (also called manatee or sea cow), once thought extinct in Thailand, is now known to survive in a few small pockets, mostly around Trang in southern Thailand, but is increasingly threatened by habitat loss and the lethal propellers of tourist boats.

The Thai government is slowly recognising the importance of conservation, perhaps due to the efforts and leadership of Queen Sirikit, and many of the kingdom's zoos now have active breeding and conservation programs. Wildlife organisations such as the Phuket Gibbon Rehabilitation Centre (p332) are working to educate the public about native wildlife and have initiated a number of wildlife rescue and rehabilitation projects.

Plants

Southern Thailand is chock-full of luxuriant vegetation, thanks to its two monsoon seasons. The majority of forests away from the coast are evergreen rainforests, while trees at the ocean edge and on limestone formations are stunted due to lack of fresh water and exposure to harsh minerals.

Bird-lovers will definitely want to carry *A Guide to Birds of Southeast Asia* by Craig Robson.

The estuarine crocodile was one of Thailand's most formidable predators, reaching over 6m in length and 1000kg, but they are now thought to be extinct in the kingdom.

The most beautiful shoreline trees are the many species of palm trees occurring in Thailand, including some found nowhere else in the world. All have small tough leaves with characteristic fanlike or featherlike shapes that help dissipate heat and conserve water. Look for the elegant cycad palm on limestone cliffs, where this *lblông* (mountain coconut) grows from cracks in the complete absence of soil. Collected for its beauty, this common ornamental plant is disappearing from its wild habitat.

Thailand is also home to nearly 75 species of salt-tolerant mangroves – small trees highly adapted to living at the edge of salt water. Standing tiptoe-like on clumps of tall roots, mangroves perform a vital ecological function by trapping sediments and nutrients, and by buffering the coast from the fierce erosive power of monsoons. This habitat serves as a secure nursery for the eggs and young of countless marine organisms, yet Thailand has destroyed at least 50% of its mangrove swamps to make way for prawn farms and big hotels.

> Palm trees have been around for over 100 million years, and various types of palm frond are used in traditional housing.

NATIONAL PARKS

National parks in Thailand are a huge draw for beach visitors. The popular island getaways of Ko Chang and Ko Samet sit just off the mainland along the eastern gulf coast. Ko Tarutao Marine National Park is remote and undeveloped for real back-to-nature vacations. Ao Phang Nga, north of Phuket, is endlessly photogenic with its limestone cliffs jutting out of the aquamarine water while knotted mangrove roots cling to thick mud flats. Meanwhile the Similan Islands and Surin Islands National Parks, in the waters of the Andaman Sea, have some of the world's best diving.

Approximately 13% of Thailand is covered by 112 national parks and 44 wildlife sanctuaries, which is a very respectable rate by international standards. Of Thailand's protected areas, 18 parks protect islands and mangrove environments. Thailand's parks and sanctuaries contain more than 850 resident and migratory species of birds and dwindling numbers of tigers, clouded leopards, koupreys, elephants, tapirs, gibbons and Asiatic black bears, among other species.

Despite promises, official designation as a national park or sanctuary does not always guarantee protection for habitats and wildlife. Local farmers, well-moneyed developers, and other business interests will often prevail, either legally or illegally, over environmental protection in Thailand's national parks. Islands that are technically exempt from development often don't adhere to the law and there is little government muscle to enforce regulations. Ko Chang, Ko Samet and Ko Phi-Phi are all curious examples of national parks with development problems.

> If anyone in Thailand comes across a white elephant, it must be reported to the Bureau of the Royal Household, and the King will decide whether it meets the criteria to be a royal white elephant.

For foreigners, parks charge entry fees of 200B per adult and 100B for children under 14 years. In recent years these rates were doubled, then rescinded on a case-by-case basis, so what you pay may differ from park to park. In some cases the **Royal Forestry Department** (Map pp70–1; ☎ 0 2561 4292/3; www.forest .go.th/default_e.asp; 61 Th Phahonyothin, Chatuchak, Bangkok 10900) rents out accommodation; make reservations in advance as this is a popular option for locals. All parks are best visited in the dry season, particularly marine national parks which can have reduced visibility in the water during the monsoon.

ENVIRONMENTAL ISSUES

Thailand is in a different developmental stage than most Western countries and this affects both the environmental problems and how people react to them. Thailand is wealthier, better developed and educated than its regional neighbours, so there is an awareness of environmental issues that barely exists in countries such as Cambodia and Myanmar. But that awareness is

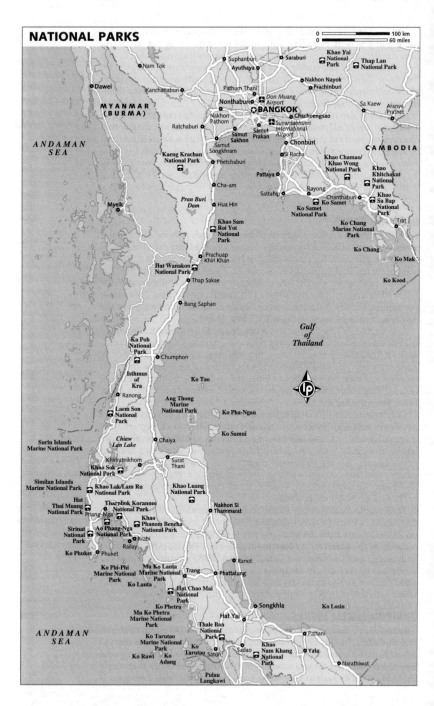

NATIONAL PARKS

often limited in scope and, while this is slowly changing, it rarely develops into the sort of high-profile, widespread movements seen in Europe, North America or Australia.

As such most issues have a very low profile, with only the most visibly obvious problems, such as pollution, overdevelopment and a lack of adequate planning, making it onto a visitor's radar. Look a little deeper and you'll see the environment has often been the victim in Thailand's rapid modernisation, with short-term considerations usually to the fore. Few Thais see any problem with cutting down mangroves to make prawn farms, or powering their development with energy from dams in Laos and dubious natural gas concerns in Myanmar.

So many well-meaning laws have been put on the books that it might seem Thailand is turning the corner towards greater ecological consciousness. But lawyers at a 2008 UN conference revealed that corruption and lack of political resolve have severely hampered efforts to enforce these environmental laws. With the deep split within Thai politics showing no signs of being healed and governments having to make all sorts of undesirable concessions just to stay in power, it seems the political will to enforce these laws remains a way off. Ironically, however, this same lack of political stability has also scared off investors.

> For detailed descriptions of all of Thailand's protected areas, the definitive text is *National Parks and Other Wild Places of Thailand,* by Stephen Elliot. The book has loads of colour pictures and covers conservation projects around the country.

The Land Environment

The main area in which Asia exceeds the West in terms of environmental damage is deforestation, though current estimates are that Thailand still has about 25% of its forests remaining, which stands up favourably against the UK's dismal 5%. The government's National Forest Policy, introduced in 1985, recommended that 40% of the country should be forested, and a complete logging ban in 1989 was a big step in the right direction. By law Thailand must maintain 25% of its land area as 'conservation forests'. But predictably the logging ban simply shifted the need for natural resources elsewhere. Illegal logging persists in Thailand, though on a relatively small scale. In contrast, in neighbouring Cambodia, Laos and particularly Myanmar, the scale has been huge ever since the 1989 ban. A great number of logs are illegally slipped over the border from these countries.

Despite Thailand being a signatory to Cites, all sorts of land species are still smuggled out of Thailand either alive or as body parts for traditional Chinese medicines. Tigers may be protected by Thai law, but the kingdom remains the world's largest exporter of tiger parts to China (tiger penis and bone are believed to have medicinal effects and to increase libido). Other animal species are hunted (often illegally) to make souvenirs for tourists, including elephants, jungle spiders, giant insects and butterflies; and along the coast clams, shells and puffer fish.

> For a colourful and comprehensive overview of Thailand's natural ecosystems check out *Wild Thailand* by Belinda Steward-Cox.

The government has cracked down on restaurants serving *ah·hăhn ʼbàh* (jungle food), which includes endangered wildlife species such as barking deers, bears, pangolins, gibbons, civets and gaurs. A big problem is that national park officials are underpaid and undertrained, yet are expected to confront armed poachers and mercenary armies funded by rich and powerful godfathers.

The widely touted idea that ecotourism can act as a positive force for change has been extensively put to the test in Thailand. In some instances tourism has definitely had positive effects. The expansion of Thailand's national parks has largely been driven by tourism. In Khao Yai National Park, all hotel and golf-course facilities were removed to reduce damage to the park environment. As a result of government and private-sector pressure on the fishing industry, coral dynamiting has been all but eliminated in the Similan and Surin Islands, to preserve the area for tourists.

THAILAND'S NATIONAL PARKS

Park	Features	Activities	Page
Eastern Gulf Coast			
Ko Chang Marine National Park	archipelago marine park with virgin rainforests, waterfalls beaches and coral reefs	snorkelling, diving, elephant trekking, hiking	p148
Ko Samet National Park	marine park with beaches; near-shore coral reefs	snorkelling, diving, boat trips, sailboarding	p139
Northwestern Gulf Coast			
Kaeng Krachan National Park	mainland park with waterfalls and forests; plentiful birdlife and jungle mammals	bird-watching	see boxed text, p172
Khao Sam Roi Yot National Park	coastal park with caves, mountains cliffs and beaches; serow, Irrawaddy dolphins and 300 bird species	cave tours, bird-watching, kayaking	p183
Southwestern Gulf Coast			
Ang Thong Marine National Park	40 scenic tropical islands with coral reefs, lagoons and limestone cliffs	sea kayaking, hiking, snorkelling	p248
Khao Luang National Park	mainland park with forested mountain peaks, streams and waterfalls; jungle mammals, birds and orchids	hiking	see boxed text, p256
Northern Andaman Coast			
Ao Phang-Nga National Park	coastal bay with limestone cliffs, islands and caves; coral reefs and mangroves	sea kayaking, snorkelling, diving	p299
Khao Lak/Lam Ru National Park	coastal park with cliffs and beaches hornbills, monkeys and bears	hiking, boat trips	p292
Khao Sok National Park	mainland park with thick rainforest, waterfalls and rivers; tigers, monkeys, *rafflesia* and 180 bird species	hiking, elephant trekking, tubing	p290
Laem Son National Park	coastal and marine park with 100km of mangroves; jungle and migratory birds	bird-watching, boat trips	p277

When threatened, the lionfish spreads its set of multicoloured fins into an impressive mane, giving fair warning not to touch this poisonous fish.

However, tourism can be a poisoned chalice. Massive developments around and frequently in national parks have ridden roughshod over the local environment in their rush to provide bungalows, luxury hotels, beach-bars and boat services for tourists. Ko Phi-Phi (p351) and Ko Samet (p139) are two national parks where business interests have definitely won out over the environment. In both cases, the development began in areas set aside for *chow lair* (sea gypsies, the semi-nomadic people who migrate up and down the coast; see the boxed text, p39). Ko Lipe in Ko Tarutao Marine National Park (p383) and Ko Muk in Hat Chao Mai National Park (p371) now seem to be heading the same way.

Rubbish and sewage are growing problems in all populated areas, even more so in heavily touristed areas where an influx of visitors overtaxes the local infrastructure. One encouraging development was the passing of the 1992 Environmental Act, which set environmental quality standards, designated conservation and pollution-control areas, and doled out government clean-up funds. Pattaya built its first public wastewater treatment plant in 2000 and conditions have improved ever since.

While Thais generally remain reluctant to engage in broader environmental campaigns, ordinary people are increasingly aware, and particularly so when they will be affected. Local people have campaigned for years against the

Park	Features	Activities	Pag
Northern Andaman Coast (continued)			
Similan Islands Marine National Park	marine park with granite islands; coral reefs and seabirds; underwater caves	snorkelling, diving	p295
Sirinat National Park	coastal park with casuarina-backed beaches; turtles and coral reefs	walking, snorkelling, diving	p330
Surin Islands Marine National Park	granite islands; coral reefs, whale sharks and manta rays	snorkelling, diving	p289
Southern Andaman Coast			
Hat Chao Mai National Park	coastal park with sandy beaches, mangroves, lagoons and coral islands; dugong and mangrove birds	sea kayaking, snorkelling, diving	p371
Khao Phanom Bencha National Park	mainland mountain jungle with tumbling waterfalls; monkeys	hiking	see boxed text, p339
Ko Phi-Phi Marine National Park	archipelago marine park with beaches, lagoons and sea-cliffs; coral reefs and whale sharks	sea kayaking, snorkelling, diving	p351
Ko Tarutao Marine National Park	archipelago marine park with remote jungle islands and tropical beaches; monkeys, jungle mammals and birds	snorkelling, hiking, diving	p383
Mu Ko Lanta Marine National Park	archipelago marine park with scenic beaches; coral reefs and reef sharks	sea kayaking, elephant trekking, hiking, snorkelling, diving	p359
Mu Ko Phetra Marine National Park	rarely visited archipelago marine park; dugong, birds and coral reefs	sea kayaking, snorkelling	see boxed text, p385
Tharnbok Korannee National Park	coastal park with mangrove forests and limestone caves; monkeys, orchids and seabirds	sea kayaking	p341

building of dams, though usually without success. The filming and damage to a favourite beach by the movie *The Beach* in Ko Phi-Phi National Park triggered demonstrations around the country and the filming of the US TV show *Survivor* in Ko Tarutao Marine National Park provoked a similar outcry. The construction of a petroleum pipeline to Songkhla in 2002 created a remarkable level of grass-roots opposition by ordinary village people.

A group of ecologically engaged Buddhist monks, popularly known as Thai Ecology Monks, have courageously set one of the best examples by using their peaceful activism to empower local communities in their fight against monolithic projects. One such project was saving trees around the Elephant Nature Park in Chiang Mai by ordaining them.

For ideas on ecotourism destinations and venues, see www.thailand.com /travel/eco/eco.htm.

The Marine Environment

Thailand's coral reef system, including the Andaman coast from Ranong to northern Phuket and the Surin and Similan Islands, is one of the world's most diverse. Some 600 species of coral reef fish, endangered marine turtles and other rare creatures call this coastline home.

The 2004 tsunami caused high-impact damage to about 13% of the Andaman coral reefs. However, damage from the tsunami was much less than first thought and relatively minor compared to the ongoing environmental

...on that accompanies an industrialised society. It is estimated that ...% of Thailand's coral reefs have died as a result of industrial pol-...d that the annual loss of healthy reefs will continue at a rapid rate. ...ound the dive centre of Phuket, dead coral reefs are visible on the ...n coast. The biggest threat to corals is sedimentation from coastal ...pment: new condos, hotels, roads and houses. High levels of sediment ...water stunts the growth of coral. Other common problems include ...tion from anchored tour boats or other marine activities, rubbish and ...ge dumped directly into the sea, and agricultural and industrial run-off. ...n people urinating in the water as they swim creates by-products that can kill sensitive coral reefs.

The environmental wake-up call from the tsunami emphasised the importance of mangrove forests, which provide a buffer from storm surges. Previously mangroves were considered wastelands and were indiscriminately cut down. It is estimated that about 80% of the mangrove forests lining the gulf coast and 20% on the Andaman coast have been destroyed for conversion into fish and prawn farms, tourist development or to supply the charcoal industry. Prawn farms constitute the biggest threat because Thailand is the world's leading producer of black tiger prawns, and the short-lived, heavily polluting farms are built in pristine mangrove swamps at a terrific environmental and social cost. Prawn farms are big business (annual production in Thailand has soared from 900 tonnes to 277,000 tonnes in the past 10 years), and the large prawn-farming operations are often able to operate unharrassed in spite of environmental protection laws. Protesting voices rarely get much play in the media.

Contributing to the deterioration of the overall health of the ocean are Thailand and its neighbours' large-scale fishing industries, frequently called the 'strip-miners of the sea'. Fish catches have declined by up to 33% in the Asia-Pacific region in the past 25 years and the upper portion of the Gulf of Thailand has almost been fished to death. Most of the commercial catches

...where you can ...
reefs growing on the
edges of limestone cliffs
that were themselves
once coral reefs.

Fragile mud flats are so
full of life that on a low
tide it is common to see
a hundred local villagers
out gathering seafood for
their meals.

RESPONSIBLE TOURISM

What can the average visitor to Thailand do to minimise the impact of tourism on the environment? While many of Thailand's environmental issues are dependent upon the enforcement of environmental regulations, there are small measures you can take that will leave less of a footprint during a visit.

- Reduce your garbage. Buy drinking water in returnable glass bottles, which are available in some restaurants. Alternatively, reuse plastic bottles by refilling them when drinking water is provided from returnable containers.
- Refuse the plastic straws and plastic bags that are provided every time you buy a drink in Thailand.
- Don't toss cigarette butts into the ocean or on the beach; dispose of them in designated receptacles.
- Try to double up with other travellers for snorkelling outings to conserve fuel.
- Avoid restaurants serving exotic wildlife species, including endangered marine life, bird's nest soup and shark-fin soup. Report offending restaurants to the Tourist Authority of Thailand (TAT) or Royal Forest Department.
- On boat trips or visits to islands – including while diving – collect any rubbish you see and dispose of it properly on the mainland.
- Never buy souvenirs made from rare plants or animals, including anything made of ivory, mounted giant insects, sea shells, turtle products and shark teeth.

are sent to overseas markets and rarely see a Thai dinner table. The seafood sold in Thailand is typically from fish farms, another large coastal industry for the country.

Making a Difference

It may seem that the range of environmental issues in Thailand is too overwhelming, but there is actually much that travellers can do to minimise the impact of their visits, or to even leave a positive impact. The way you spend your money has a profound influence on the kingdom's economy and on the pocketbooks of individual businesses. Ask questions up front and take your money elsewhere if you don't like the answers. For instance, a number of large-scale resorts that lack road access transport clients across fragile mud flats on tractors (a wantonly destructive practice), so when booking a room inquire into transport to the hotel. Of the region's countless dive shops, some are diligent about minimising the impact their clients have on the reefs; however, if a dive shop trains and certifies inexperienced divers over living reefs, rather than in a swimming pool, then it is causing irreparable harm to the local ecosystem. As a rule, do not touch or walk on coral, monitor your movements so you avoid accidentally sweeping into coral, and do not harass marine life (any dead puffer fish you see on the beach probably died because a diver poked it until it inflated).

Make a positive impact on Thailand by checking out one of the many environmental and social groups working in the kingdom. If you do some research and make arrangements before arriving, you may connect with an organisation that matches your values, but here are some favourites to start the juices flowing.

The **Wild Animal Rescue Foundation of Thailand** (Map pp70-1; WAR; ☎ 0 2712 9715; www.warthai.org; 65/1 3rd fl, Soi 55, Th Sukhumvit, Bangkok 10110) is one of the leading advocates for nature conservation in Thailand and currently runs four wildlife sanctuaries that use volunteers to rehabilitate and return former pets to the wild.

The **Bird Conservation Society of Thailand** (Map pp70-1; ☎ 0 2691 4816; www.bcst.or.th) provides a plethora of information about the birds of Thailand, offering field trip reports, sightings of rare birds, bird festivals, bird surveys and a birding web board.

Make a big change by checking out the **Sanithirakoses-Nagapateepa Foundation** (www.sulak-sivaraksa.org), which was started by the 1995 Alternative Nobel Prize winner, Sulak Sivaraksa. This umbrella group is associated with numerous environmental and social justice groups in Thailand including the Foundation for Children, Forum of the Poor, the Thai-Tibet Centre, and Pun Pun, an organic farm and sustainable living centre. These groups offer countless opportunities to help empower local communities, and to get involved in issues important to the people of Thailand. They have also started an alternative college called Spirit in Education Movement (SEM) that offers a spiritually based, ecologically sound alternative to mainstream education.

Other groups promoting environmental issues in Thailand include the following:

Thailand Environment Institute (☎ 0 2503 3333; www.tei.or.th)
Wildlife Friends of Thailand (☎ 0 3245 8135; www.wfft.org)
WWF Thailand (☎ 0 2524 6168; www.wwfthai.org)

A grow... of overseas ι... companies now ir... that Thailand's tourism operators have environmental policies in place before doing business with them.

Students at Dulwich International College in Phuket collected 5000kg of garbage from the beach in a single day; help them out by picking up rubbish whenever you can.

Unlike ... usly chilled islands and beaches, there's something about Bangkok that never fails to ge... he blood pumping. This big, crowded, polluted and seemingly chaotic Asian mega-city is many things to many people, but no one calls it boring.

For the visitor, the impact is immediate. Your first move is likely to be joining the cacophonous arteries of metal that pump – just barely – almost eight million people around the region's biggest city. Everywhere you look the streets and waterways are alive with commuters. School kids run without sweating, smiling vendors create mouth-watering food in push-away kitchens, monks rub bare shoulders with fashionistas in air-conditioned malls... Whether it's in one of Bangkok's famous golden temples, riding in the back of a speeding túk-túk or just walking down the street, something odd and inexplicable will happen at the most unexpected time. Hey, was that an elephant with a tail light?

If all you want to do is kick back on a peaceful beach, at first glance Bangkok will seem like a transit burden full of concrete towers instead of palm trees. But once you tire of sea breezes, you'll better appreciate Bangkok's conveniences, sophistication and breakneck pace. With its mix of the historic and contemporary, dangerously appealing shopping and some of the most delicious and best-value eating on earth, the City of Angels is surely one of the most invigorating destinations in Asia.

HIGHLIGHTS

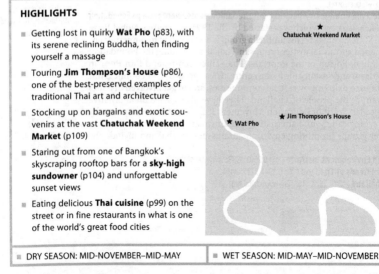

- Getting lost in quirky **Wat Pho** (p83), with its serene reclining Buddha, then finding yourself a massage
- Touring **Jim Thompson's House** (p86), one of the best-preserved examples of traditional Thai art and architecture
- Stocking up on bargains and exotic souvenirs at the vast **Chatuchak Weekend Market** (p109)
- Staring out from one of Bangkok's skyscraping rooftop bars for a **sky-high sundowner** (p104) and unforgettable sunset views
- Eating delicious **Thai cuisine** (p99) on the street or in fine restaurants in what is one of the world's great food cities

★ Chatuchak Weekend Market

★ Jim Thompson's House

★ Wat Pho

■ DRY SEASON: MID-NOVEMBER–MID-MAY ■ WET SEASON: MID-MAY–MID-NOVEMBER

HISTORY

As capital cities go, Bangkok is a fairly recent invention. Following the sacking of Ayuthaya by the Burmese (p25), King Taksin established the Thai capital at Thonburi, on the west bank of Mae Nam Chao Phraya (Chao Phraya River). But in 1782 Rama I (King Phraphutthayotfa Chulalok; r 1782–1809) founded the Chakri dynasty (p25) and promptly moved his capital across the river to the modest village of Bang Makok (current-day Bangkok).

Buddhist relics from Ayuthaya, Thonburi and Sukhothai were re-enshrined in towering new temples and the city expanded rapidly around the royal compound at Ko Ratanakosin. Under Rama IV (King Mongkut; r 1851–68) and his son Rama V (King Chulalongkorn; r 1868–1910), Bangkok and the country began to modernise, adopting and integrating Western customs, styles and architecture. Europeans flocked to the city to negotiate trade contracts and increase their influence in the region.

In 1932 Bangkok saw the end of absolute monarchy and the beginnings of a turbulent political era. From that momentous shift of power until the present day, Bangkok has witnessed 19 attempted coups d'état, half of which half have resulted in a change of government. The latest, in September 2006, saw controversial Prime Minister Thaksin Shinawatra ousted without a shot being fired following months of protests in the capital. However, previous political ructions were not so peaceful and on several occasions mass demonstrations have ended in the military massacring student protesters.

During the 1970s Bangkok became an R and R base for American troops fighting in Vietnam and its reputation as 'sin city' was born. During the 1980s and '90s Thailand's economy and Bangkok's skyline grew rapidly. But when the Bangkok stock market collapsed in 1997 the city, the country and indeed most of the region ground to an economic halt.

After some rocky years, Bangkok is again every bit the modern Asian metropolis, if not quite the 'world city' it so wants to be. Large infrastructure projects, such as the Skytrain and Metro urban railways and Suvarnabhumi International Airport, have all made the city a less-congested and more enjoyable place; construction of Metro and Skytrain lines continues.

> **WHAT'S YOUR NAME AGAIN**
>
> The name Bangkok is derived from Makok, meaning 'Place of Olive Plums', the name of a village that pre-dates the arrival of the capital in 1782. The full official title of the capital is 'Krungthep mahanakhon amon rattanakosin mahintara ayuthaya mahadilok popnopparat ratchathani burirom udomratchaniwet mahasathan amonpiman avatansathit sakkathattiya visnukamprasit'. Not surprisingly, most Thais abbreviate it to Krung Thep (City of Angels). Pretty much the only place you'll find the full name spelt out is on a very wide sign outside City Hall (Map pp74–5); bring your wide-angle lens.

ORIENTATION

Bangkok is a vast sprawling mess of a city and the urban chaos can be pretty intimidating at first. Concrete towers as far as the eye can see make it difficult to discern any real centre. But the capital does have several distinctly different districts. For the sake of simplicity, however, it makes sense to divide the city into two areas: 'old Bangkok', which has most of the royal palaces and historic temples, and 'new Bangkok', which is dominated by towering skyscrapers, shopping malls and a growing number of luxury hotels.

Old Bangkok straddles Mae Nam Chao Phraya, with the original royal centre of Ko Ratanakosin occupying a manmade island on the east bank and the former capital of Thonburi now serving as a suburb on the west bank. To the north of the royal district, still on Ko Ratanakosin, is Banglamphu. This is one of Bangkok's oldest neighbourhoods and was once home to officials and members of the royal court. Today it's the main budget travellers' centre and home to a thriving independent art and bar scene that attracts as many young Bangkokians as travellers. Northeast of Ko Ratanakosin is Dusit, the new royal district. The riverside district south of Ko Ratanakosin is home to the Indian neighbourhood of Phahurat and Bangkok's Chinatown, near the main Hualamphong train station.

Surrounding the old city and stretching for at least 20km in every direction, the rest of Bangkok is a modern creation consisting of quite unfathomable amounts of concrete, divided by massive highways and soaring this part of the main streets. Th from Chinatown Mae Nam Chao n this road are Th d Th Silom, which staurants, shopping ping dose of sleaze, hich adds embassies and consulates el mix.

Head north of the Silom neighbourhood along Th Phayathai or Th Ratchadamri and you'll reach Th Phra Ram I and the Siam Sq and Th Ploenchit shopping districts. East of here, Th Sukhumvit hosts hotels, restaurants and a rather seedy reputation at its start, before becoming more sophisticated and expensive east of Soi 21 (Soi Asoke).

Bangkok's Suvarnabhumi International Airport is about 30km east of the centre, while the old Don Muang airport is about 25km north and has some (but not all) domestic flights to island and beach destinations.

Maps

From the moment you enter Thailand – literally right after you've passed immigration – you'll see your first free maps. Get used to it; Thailand is full of them. Quality varies but unless you're planning to explore off the beaten track they should be good enough.

There are also several maps that are worth your money. One often imitated but never equalled is *Nancy Chandler's Map of Bangkok* (www.nancychandler.net; 250B), a colourful hand-drawn map with useful inset panels for Chinatown, Th Sukhumvit and Chatuchak Weekend Market. To master the city's bus system, purchase Roadway's *Bangkok Bus Map* (150B). If travelling to districts outside central Bangkok, Thinknet's *Bangkok City Atlas* is a wise investment for 250B.

INFORMATION
Bookshops

Bangkok is well stocked with bookshops selling new titles in English and, less often, other languages. Virtually every major mall has branches of **Asia Books** (www.asiabook.com), **Kinokuniya** (www.kinokuniya.com), Bookazine and/or **B2S** (www.b2s.co.th). Tourist areas also have secondhand bookshops, and those on Th Khao San have the most diverse range of titles in the country (though they're not all that cheap). Recommended bookshops include the following:

Asia Books (www.asiabook.com) Soi 15 (Map p82; 221 Th Sukhumvit, Soi 15); Siam Discovery Center (Map pp80-1; 4th fl, Siam Discovery Center, Th Phra Ram I)

Dasa Book Café (Map p82; ☎ 0 2661 2993; btwn Soi 26 & 28, Th Sukhumvit)

Kinokuniya (☎ 0 2255 9834) Emporium (Map p82; 3rd fl, 622 Th Sukhumvit); Siam Paragon (Map pp80-1; 4th fl, Siam Paragon, Th Phra Ram I)

Shaman Bookstore (Map pp74-5; ☎ 0 2629 0418; ground fl, Dang Derm Hotel, 68-70 Th Khao San & Soi Susie) Used books galore.

BANGKOK IN...

Two Days

In two days you can explore Bangkok's famous sights: the **Grand Palace & Wat Phra Kaew** (p69); **Wat Pho** (p83), home to the largest reclining Buddha in Thailand; and missile-shaped **Wat Arun** (p83). If you are jet-lagged on day two, get up early and head to **Lumphini Park** (p86) to see the locals practising t'ai chi. Then chase away the heatstroke with a visit to the shopping centres on Th Phra Ram I and Th Ploenchit. Don't forget to follow the Thai crowds to the busy **Erawan Shrine** (p85). In the afternoon, visit **Jim Thompson's House** (p86) for an introduction to traditional Thai architecture. Take in the sunset from one of the **sky-high bars** (p104), before finding somewhere with better food for dinner.

Four Days

With more time, factor in a visit to the **Museum of Siam** (p83) then the **amulet market** (p89), and take the **Chinatown Walking Tour** (p87). Take a detour up to Dusit to see **Vimanmek Teak Mansion Museum** (p84), built entirely from golden teak, and get out on the river in a long-tail boat or on the ferry. After dark, head to Th Sukhumvit to experience modern Bangkok at one of the fashionable restaurants or clubs, such as **Bed Supperclub** (p105). If you're here on the weekend juggle this plan to fit in the **Chatuchak Weekend Market** (p109).

Emergency

For an ambulance, call one of the hospitals listed under Medical Services (right).

Fire (☎ 199)

Police (☎ 191) Ordinary Thai police don't usually speak English.

Tourist Police (☎ 1155; ⏰ 24hr) An English-speaking unit that handles crime involving tourists, including gem scams. It can also act as a bilingual liaison with the regular police.

Immigration

For visa extensions or applications, visit the **Immigration Bureau office** (Map pp70-1; ☎ 0 2141 9889, Call Center 1178; Bldg B, Government Center, Soi 7, Th Chaeng Watthana, Thung Hong Song, Laksi; ⏰ 8.30am-noon & 1-4.30pm Mon-Fri). Most applications and extensions require two photos. See p412 for details.

Internet Access

Bangkok has literally hundreds of internet cafes and plenty of wi-fi hotspots where you can get online for free (or for the price of a coffee). Internet cafes come and go so we haven't recommended specific places. Rates are generally pretty cheap, and charges are similar within certain neighbourhoods. For example, Th Khao San and around have some of the cheapest rates in town, starting at about 40B an hour; 60B to 120B an hour is common elsewhere. Most internet cafes can also print and upload digital camera files, but fewer have CD-burning capabilities. You'll find independent internet cafes or guesthouse terminals along Th Sukhumvit and Th Silom, and in all the big shopping centres.

Almost every hotel listed in this chapter offers some level of internet access, from in-room wi-fi to a lonely machine in the corner of the lobby. Prices are also diverse, ranging from free (in many midrange places) to outrageous in some top-end places; check rates before you make a booking. Free wi-fi is available in a growing number of cafes, including chains such as Gloria Jeans; look for the 🛜 symbol in our reviews.

Media

Bangkok has well-established English-language media. The *Bangkok Post* (www.bangkokpost.com) is the major daily broadsheet, with local and international news as well as articles on culture, entertainment, dining and events. Friday's edition includes *Guru*, a lifestyle insert with listings for upcoming music and other events. The *Nation* (www.nationmultimedia.com) is now a business paper published in conjunction with a free tabloid called *Daily Xpress*. The *International Herald Tribune* is widely available, as are all major international magazines.

Medical Services

Bangkok is the leading health-care centre in the region and the better hospitals have become major centres of elective 'medical tourism'. They can also handle medical and dental emergencies.

Bangkok Hospital (Map pp70-1; ☎ 0 2310 3000; www.bangkokhospital.com; 2 Soi 47, Th Phetburi Tat Mai, Bangkapi)

BNH Hospital (Map pp78-9; ☎ 0 2686 2700; www.bnhhospital.com; 9 Th Convent, Silom)

Bumrungrad International Hospital (Map p82; ☎ 0 2667 1000; www.bumrungrad.com; 33 Soi 3, Th Sukhumvit)

Samitivej Sukhumvit Hospital (Map pp70-1; ☎ 0 2711 8181; www.samitivej.co.th; 133 Soi 49, Th Sukhumvit)

Money

You won't need a guide to find an ATM in Bangkok – they're everywhere. Bank ATMs accept major international credit cards and many will also cough up cash for accounts linked to the Cirrus and Plus networks. In tourist areas, such as the Siam Sq shopping district and Th Khao San, you'll often find small money-exchange counters outside banks; these can change cash and cheques in major currencies and are typically open from about 9am or 10am to 8pm daily.

Post

Services at the art deco–style **main post office** (Map pp78-9; Th Charoen Krung; ⏰ 8am-8pm Mon-Fri, 8am-1pm Sat & Sun) include poste restante and packaging within the main building. Do not send money or valuables via regular mail. Get here via a walk from Saphan Taksin Skytrain station or a Chao Phraya express boat to Tha Si Phraya.

There are convenient **post office branches** (⏰ 8am-5pm Mon-Fri, 9am-noon Sat) on Th Sipsahm Hang, opposite Wat Bowonniwet (Map pp74–5), and on the alley immediately north of Th Ratchadamnoen Klang, just east of Th Tanao (Map pp74–5).

Telephone

Many Bangkok internet cafes have Skype and this or similar programs are the cheapest way to make international calls; see p409 for more details. Internet cafes often also have their own phones with competitive rates, starting at about 10B a minute to Europe, North America and Australia. The online *Yellow Pages* (www .yellowpages.co.th) can be handy. For information on mobile phones, see p410. If you need a new mobile phone, the 4th floor at MBK (p108) has millions of them. Staff can also 'unlock' phones here. If you must resort to the official carriers (and their rates):

Communications Authority of Thailand (CAT; Map pp78–9; ☎ 0 2614 1000; Th Charoen Krung; ☉ 8am–8pm) Has a small air-conditioned international call centre outside the main post office.

Telephone Organization of Thailand (TOT; Map pp80–1; ☎ 0 2251 1111; Th Ploenchit) For long-distance calls.

Toilets

If you don't want to pee against a tree like the túk-túk (pronounced đúk đúk; three-wheeled motorcycle) drivers, use a public toilet in a shopping centre, hotel or fast-food restaurant. Shopping centres might charge 1B to 2B for a visit; some newer shopping centres have toilets for the disabled. In modern Bangkok squat toilets are positively difficult to find – expect to be greeted by a throne.

Tourist Information

Bangkok has two organisations that handle tourism matters: TAT for countrywide information, and Bangkok Tourist Division for city-specific information. Note that these offices do not make travel arrangements. Also be aware that travel agents near the train station and other tourist centres co-opt T.A.T. as part of their name to lure in commissions. So how can you tell the difference? Apparently it's all in the full stops – 'T.A.T.' means agency, 'TAT' is official.

For new restaurants, current happy hours, band dates and which DJs are in town, there are two good-quality independent publications: the free and irreverent weekly *BK Magazine* (www.bkmagazine.com), and the monthly *Bangkok 101* (www.bangkok101 .com), which has photo features and handy reviews of sights, restaurants, nightclubs and theatres; it costs 100B.

Bangkok Tourist Division (Map pp74–5; ☎ 0 2225 7612–4; www.bangkoktourist.com; 17 Th Phra Athit; ☉ 8am–7pm Mon-Fri, 9am-5pm Sat & Sun) Immediately south of Saphan Phra Pin Klao, it's fantastically well organ-ised with hundreds of brochures and free booklets. Green kiosks around town are less useful, but do have maps. Look for the symbol of a mahout on an elephant.

TAT (☎ for assistance 8am-8pm 1672; www.tourismthai land.org) Banglamphu (Map pp74–5; ☎ 0 2283 1555; cnr Th Ratchadamnoen Nok & Th Chakrapatdipong; ☉ 8.30am-4.30pm); Main Office (Map p82; ☎ 0 2250 5500; 1600 Th Phetchaburi Tat Mai; ☉ 8.30am-4.30pm Mon-Fri); Suvar-nabhumi International Airport (☎ 0 2134 4077; 2nd fl, near Exit Door 1 & Exit Door 10; ☉ 8am-10pm) The Banglamphu branch is opposite the boxing stadium.

Travel Agencies

Travel agents are a dime a dozen in Bangkok, especially in popular tourist areas such as Th Khao San. Heavily discounted plane tickets are often available, though the cheapest fares are usually DIY affairs through Air Asia. Most agents will sell you a ticket or book a trip without any hassle, but sharks are out there, so be careful. Flight tickets will usually be OK, but if the ticket sounds too good to be true it might prove to be a scam; see p401 for more scams information. Generally, it's best to buy long-distance bus and train tickets directly at stations instead of at travel agents.

DANGERS & ANNOYANCES

As you might expect for a city of seven million, Bangkok has its fair share of con artists, many of whom specifically target foreigners. Most of the scams involve touts who try to lure foreigners into jewellery and tailor shops in exchange for a commission, the cost of which will be tacked on to your bill. For details, see opposite.

The most common con artists are the taxi and túk-túk drivers who steer foreigners towards 'gem sales' or promotions at souvenir shops. The offer of a cheap ride with a short stop at a gem shop will always result in a drawn-out attempt to separate you from your money – see p108 for more on buying gems.

Be wary of smartly dressed people who approach you asking where you're from and where you're going. Rather than becoming your new and exotic Thai friend – be they man or woman – they will almost certainly be trying to con you. Popular hunting grounds for scammers include the areas around the Erawan Shrine, the Grand Palace and Wat Pho, and around Siam Sq, Th Khao San and Th Sukhumvit.

JUST SAY NO: BANGKOK SCAMS

If your travel funds are ample, it might seem like a bother to resist the various scams that siphon off negligible sums. But diligence to fair and honest business benefits the travellers who follow in your footsteps. As a gift to future visitors, stop the scam cycle by just saying 'no'. For details of gem scams, see p400.

- Closed today – Ignore any 'friendly' local who tells you that an attraction is closed for a Buddhist holiday or for cleaning. These are set-ups for trips to a bogus gem sale.

- Túk-túk rides for 10B – Say goodbye to your day's itinerary if you climb aboard this ubiquitous scam. These alleged 'tours' bypass all the sights and instead cruise to all the fly-by-night gem and tailor shops that pay commissions. We have, however, heard of some confident travellers scamming the scammers by taking the 10B tour and resisting all sales efforts.

- Flat-fare taxi rides – Flatly refuse any driver who quotes a flat fare (usually between 100B and 150B for in-town destinations), which will usually be three times more expensive than the very reasonable meter rate. Walking beyond the tourist area will usually help in finding an honest driver. If the driver has 'forgotten' to put the meter on, just say 'meter, kráp/kâ'.

- Tourist buses to the south – On the long journey south, well-organised and connected thieves have hours to comb through your bags, breaking into (and later resealing) locked bags, searching through hiding places and stealing credit cards, electronics and even toiletries. This scam has been running for years but is easy to avoid simply by carrying valuables with you on the bus. See p421 for more.

SIGHTS

Thailand's islands and beaches are not particularly well stocked with traditional Thai 'sights', so it's well worth taking in a few while you're in Bangkok. Fortunately, the capital is home to some of the most impressive wát (temples) and palaces in the country. Many are conveniently concentrated on Ko Ratanakosin, Thonburi and nearby Dusit, all of which abut the Banglamphu hotel district. Note that some royal and religious sights – particularly the Grand Palace and palaces in Dusit Park – won't allow you in unless you have covered shoulders and legs; see the boxed text, p37, for details.

Ko Ratanakosin & Thonburi

These two districts are in the old part of Bangkok and are filled with historic wát, atmospheric shophouses and fine views of the river.

WAT PHRA KAEW & GRAND PALACE
วัดพระแก้ว/พระมหาราชวัง

Thailand's most famous attractions are Wat Phra Kaew (Temple of the Emerald Buddha) and the **Grand Palace** (Map pp74-5; ☎ 0 2222 6889; Th Na Phra Lan; admission to both & Dusit Park 350B; ☮ 8.30am-4pm, last entry 3.30pm), occupying the same expansive walled compound south of Sanam Luang. The temple buildings are extravagant, with golden *chedi* (Thai-style stupas), ornate statues of mythical beings and incredible amounts of gold inlay.

Housed in the main *bòht* (chapel), the so-called Emerald Buddha (Phra Kaew) – actually made of nephrite jade – dates back to at least the 15th century. The image is only 66cm high but has repeatedly been a high-profile spoil of war. It spent more than 200 years in Laos before it was won back in 1778; it has been in Bangkok ever since. The image has three sets of robes, which are ceremonially changed by the king (or the crown prince) to mark the changing seasons.

Beyond Wat Phra Kaew the defined tourist path takes you through **Amarindra Hall**, originally a hall of justice but now used for coronation ceremonies, and on to the grand triple-winged **Chakri Mahaprasat** (Grand Palace Hall), which blends Italian Renaissance and traditional Thai architecture, before finishing at the more classically Thai, Ratanakosin-style **Dusit Hall**, which initially served as a venue for royal audiences and later as a royal funerary hall.

Guides can be hired at the ticket kiosk – ignore anyone outside – and there's an audio guide costing 200B for two hours. Wat Phra Kaew and the Grand Palace are best reached either by a short walk south from

(Continued on page 83)

BANGKOK

GREATER BANGKOK

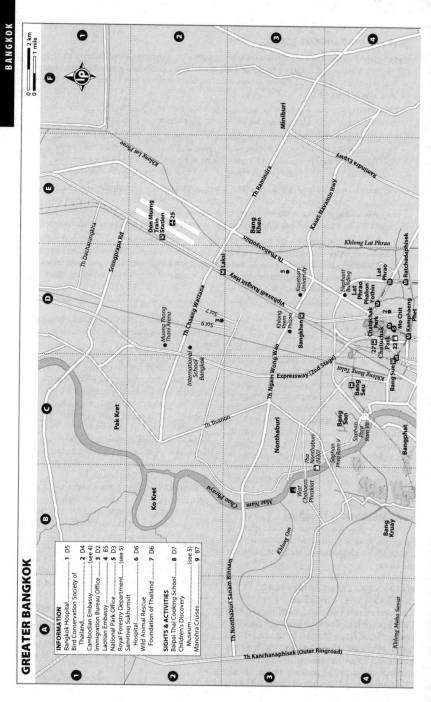

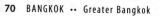

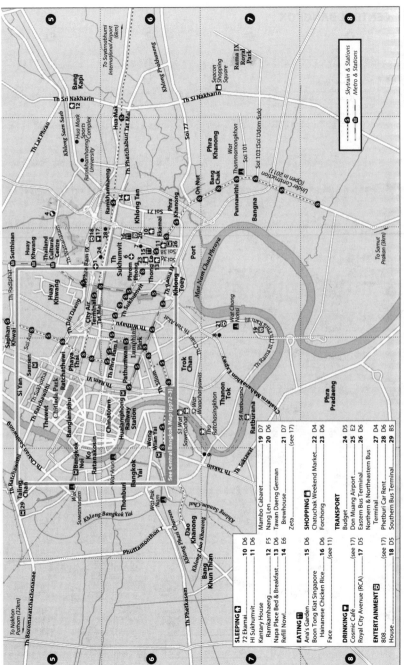

CENTRAL BANGKOK

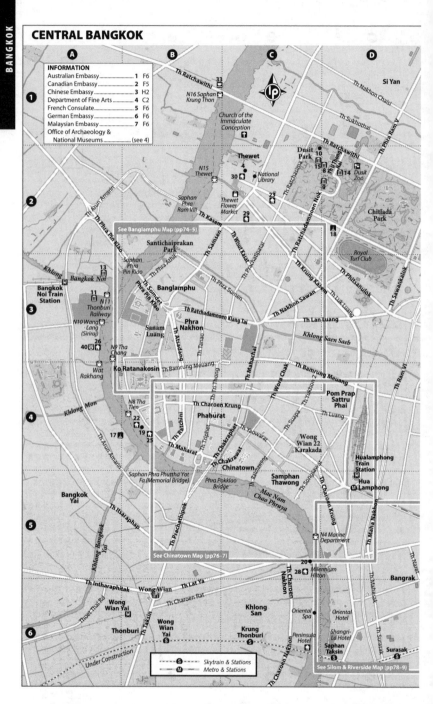

INFORMATION		
Australian Embassy	**1**	F6
Canadian Embassy	**2**	F5
Chinese Embassy	**3**	H2
Department of Fine Arts	**4**	C2
French Consulate	**5**	F6
German Embassy	**6**	F6
Malaysian Embassy	**7**	F6
Office of Archaeology &		
National Museums	(see 4)	

See Banglamphu Map (pp74–5)

See Chinatown Map (pp76–7)

See Silom & Riverside Map (pp78–9)

Skytrain & Stations

Metro & Stations

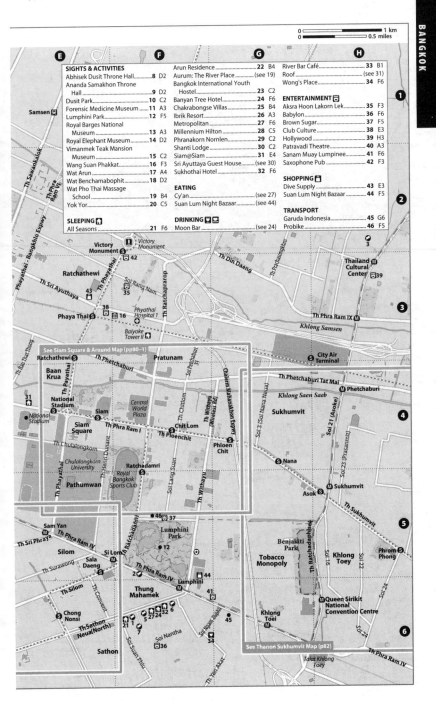

0 _____ 1 km
0 _____ 0.5 miles

SIGHTS & ACTIVITIES
Abhisek Dusit Throne Hall............**8** D2
Ananda Samakhon Throne
   Hall..**9** D2
Dusit Park.......................................**10** C2
Forensic Medicine Museum.......**11** A3
Lumphini Park................................**12** F5
Royal Barges National
   Museum.......................................**13** A3
Royal Elephant Museum............**14** D2
Vimanmek Teak Mansion
   Museum.......................................**15** C2
Wang Suan Phakkat.....................**16** F3
Wat Arun..**17** A4
Wat Benchamabophit..................**18** D2
Wat Pho Thai Massage
   School..**19** B4
Yok Yor...**20** C5

SLEEPING 🛏
All Seasons....................................**21** F6

Arun Residence.............................**22** B4
Aurum: The River Place..........(see 19)
Bangkok International Youth
   Hostel...**23** C2
Banyan Tree Hotel........................**24** F6
Chakrabongse Villas.....................**25** B4
Ibrik Resort....................................**26** A3
Metropolitan..................................**27** F6
Millennium Hilton.........................**28** C5
Phranakorn Nornlen......................**29** C2
Shanti Lodge..................................**30** C2
Siam@Siam....................................**31** E4
Sri Ayuttaya Guest House......(see 30)
Sukhothai Hotel............................**32** F6

EATING
Cy'an..(see 27)
Suan Lum Night Bazaar..........(see 44)

DRINKING 🍷🍸
Moon Bar.................................(see 24)

River Bar Café...............................**33** B1
Roof...(see 31)
Wong's Place.................................**34** F6

ENTERTAINMENT 🎭
Aksra Hoon Lakorn Lek...............**35** F3
Babylon...**36** F6
Brown Sugar..................................**37** F5
Club Culture...................................**38** E3
Hollywood......................................**39** H3
Patravadi Theatre.........................**40** A3
Sanam Muay Lumpinee.................**41** F6
Saxophone Pub.............................**42** F3

SHOPPING 🛍
Dive Supply....................................**43** E3
Suan Lum Night Bazaar...............**44** F5

TRANSPORT
Garuda Indonesia..........................**45** G6
Probike..**46** F5

BANGLAMPHU

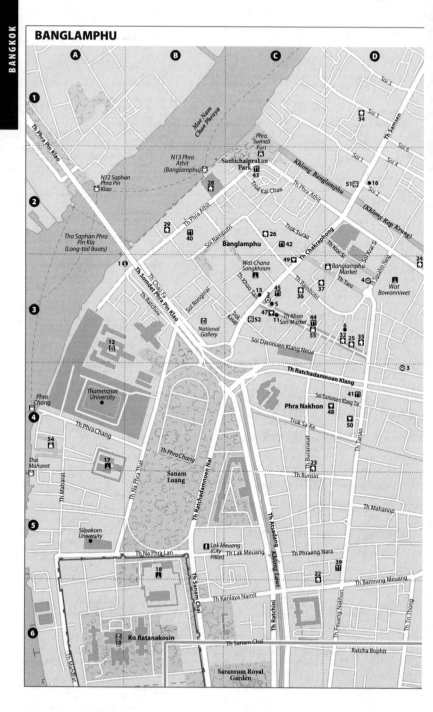

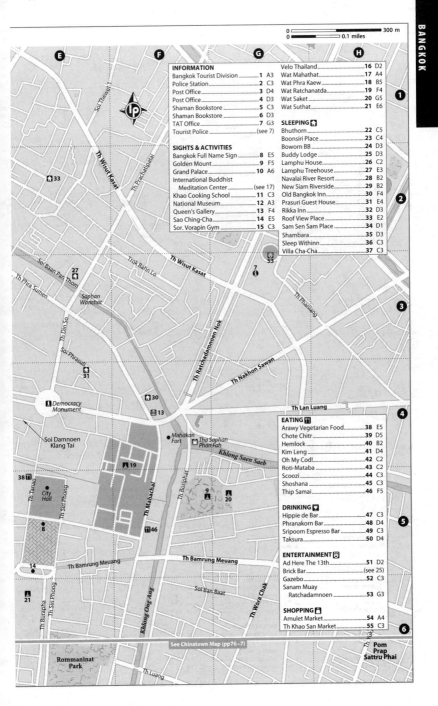

INFORMATION
Bangkok Tourist Division **1** A3
Police Station....................................**2** C3
Post Office **3** D4
Post Office **4** D3
Shaman Bookstore **5** C3
Shaman Bookstore **6** D3
TAT Office **7** G3
Tourist Police ....(see 7)

SIGHTS & ACTIVITIES
Bangkok Full Name Sign **8** E5
Golden Mount **9** F5
Grand Palace **10** A6
International Buddhist
   Meditation Center ....(see 17)
Khao Cooking School **11** C3
National Museum **12** A3
Queen's Gallery **13** F4
Sao Ching-Cha **14** E5
Sor. Vorapin Gym **15** C3

Velo Thailand.................................**16** D2
Wat Mahathat **17** A4
Wat Phra Kaew **18** B5
Wat Ratchanatda...........................**19** F4
Wat Saket...**20** G5
Wat Suthat.......................................**21** E6

SLEEPING
Bhuthorn **22** C5
Boonsiri Place **23** C4
Boworn BB **24** D3
Buddy Lodge **25** D3
Lamphu House................................**26** C2
Lamphu Treehouse **27** E3
Navalai River Resort.....................**28** B2
New Siam Riverside.......................**29** B2
Old Bangkok Inn............................**30** F4
Prasuri Guest House......................**31** E4
Rikka Inn **32** D3
Roof View Place **33** E2
Sam Sen Sam Place.......................**34** D1
Shambara...**35** D3
Sleep Withinn.................................**36** C3
Villa Cha-Cha..................................**37** C3

EATING
Arawy Vegetarian Food..............**38** E5
Chote Chitr **39** D5
Hemlock **40** B2
Kim Leng **41** D4
Oh My Cod!.....................................**42** C2
Roti-Mataba **43** C2
Scoozi...**44** C3
Shoshana **45** C3
Thip Samai......................................**46** F5

DRINKING
Hippie de Bar.................................**47** C3
Phranakorn Bar..............................**48** D4
Sripoom Espresso Bar...................**49** C3
Taksura...**50** D4

ENTERTAINMENT
Ad Here The 13th...........................**51** D2
Brick Bar...................................(see 25)
Gazebo...**52** C3
Sanam Muay
   Ratchadamnoen **53** G3

SHOPPING
Amulet Market **54** A4
Th Khao San Market......................**55** C3

BANGKOK

CHINATOWN

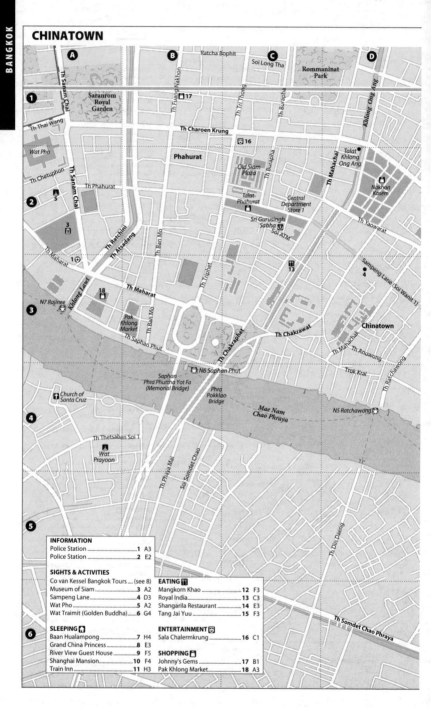

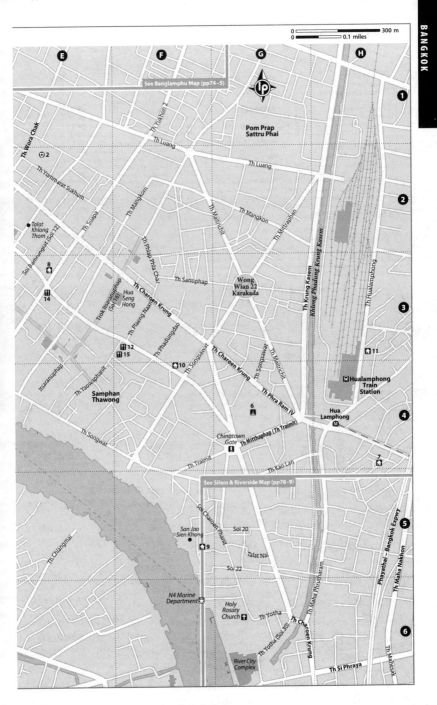

BANGKOK

SILOM & RIVERSIDE

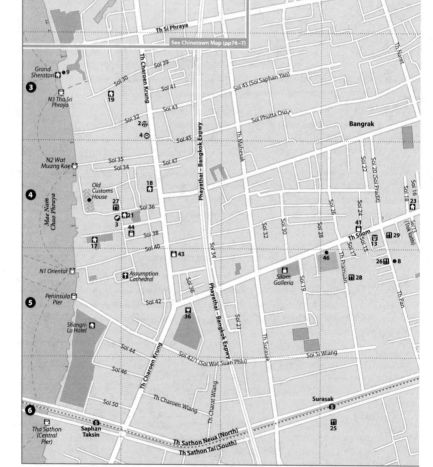

See Chinatown Map (pp76–7)

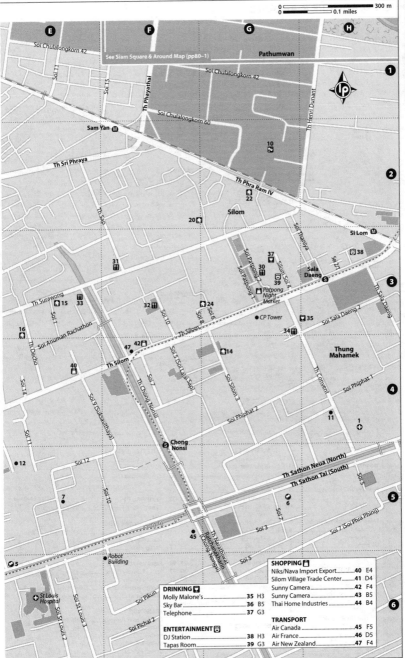

BANGKOK

SIAM SQUARE & AROUND

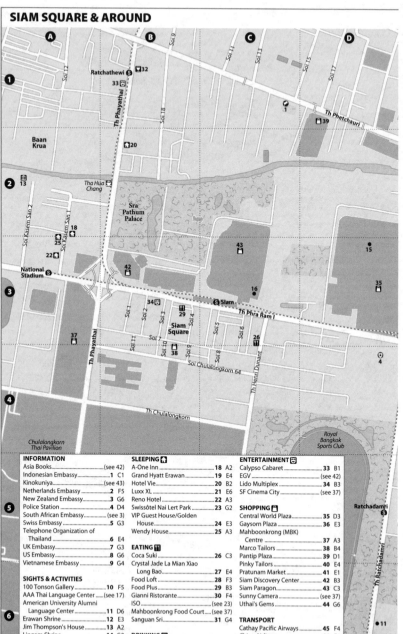

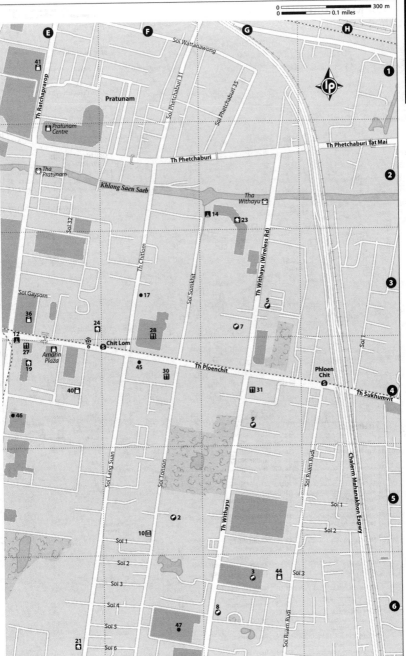

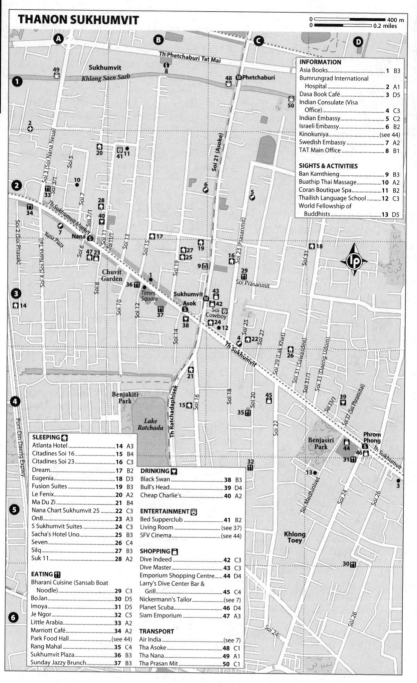

THANON SUKHUMVIT

(Continued from page 69)

Banglamphu, via Sanam Luang, or by Chao Phraya express boat to Tha Chang. From the Siam Sq area (in front of MBK, Th Phra Ram I) take bus 47.

WAT PHO
วัดโพธิ์(วัดพระเชตุพน)

Bangkok's largest and oldest temple, **Wat Pho** (Wat Phra Chetuphon; Map pp76-7; ☎ 0 2622 3533; www .watpho.com; Th Sanam Chai; admission 50B; ☻ 8am-6pm) was founded in the 16th century and is a little quieter than Wat Phra Kaew. The main attraction is the **Reclining Buddha**. Thailand's largest, this 46m-long and 15m-high golden figure includes 3m-high feet bearing fantastic mother-of-pearl inlays.

The surrounding compound has a number of temples with huge golden Buddha images and dozens of colourful mosaic *chedi* (brick stupa). The interior of the main chapel, **Phra Uposatha**, is just as impressive as the Temple of the Emerald Buddha. Towering statues of Chinese mythical heroes guard the doorways within the compound, including figures in European dress said to represent Marco Polo.

Wat Pho is also the national headquarters for the teaching and preservation of traditional Thai medicine, particularly Thai massage. For more information, see p86. The nearest Chao Phraya Express pier is Tha Tien.

NATIONAL MUSEUM
พิพิธภัณฑสถานแห่งชาติ

The **National Museum** (Map pp74-5; ☎ 0 2224 1402; www .thailandmuseum.com; Th Na Phra That; admission 50B; ☻ 9am-4pm Wed-Sun) is one of the largest in Southeast Asia and has a vast collection of Thai antiquities and ceremonial objects. The history wing presents a succinct chronology of events and figures from the prehistoric, Sukhothai, Ayuthaya and Bangkok eras; look for King Ramkamhaeng's inscribed stone pillar (the oldest record of Thai writing), King Taksin's throne and the Rama V section. The museum runs highly recommended free tours in English and French on Wednesday and Thursday, Japanese on Wednesday and German on Thursday; all start from the ticket pavilion at 9.30am.

MUSEUM OF SIAM
สถาบันพิพิธภัณฑ์การเรียนรู้แห่งชาติ

Housed in a European-style 19th-century building that was once the ministry of commerce, the new **Museum of Siam** (Map pp76-7; ☎ 0 2225 2777; www.ndmi.or.th; 4 Th Sanam Chai; admission adult 100B, under 15 free; ☻ 10am-6pm Tue-Sun) looks at the history of Thai culture in an engaging, interactive fashion. Each room has an informative narrated video started by a sensory detector, and features including an Ayuthaya-era battle game, a room full of traditional Thai toys and a street vending cart where you can be photographed pretending to whip up a pan of *pàt tai* will help keep kids interested for at least an hour, adults for longer.

WAT ARUN
วัดอรุณฯ

This striking **wát** (Temple of Dawn; Map pp72-3; ☎ 0 2891 1149; www.watarun.org; Th Arun Amarin; admission 50B; ☻ 8am-6pm) consists of four stupas around an elongated Khmer *brahng* (tower), all covered with Chinese ceramics and seashells. Visit early in the morning or late in the afternoon to avoid the crowds. Cross-river ferries (3B per person) run between Tha Tien (N8) and nearby Tha Thai Wang every few minutes.

ROYAL BARGES NATIONAL MUSEUM
เรือพระที่นั่ง

Over in Thonburi, on the western side of Chao Phraya River, this interesting **museum** (Map pp72-3; ☎ 0 2424 0004; Khlong Bangkok Noi; admission 100B, still/video camera fee 100/200B; ☻ 9.30am-5pm) is the dry dock for Thai royal barges, which are still used by the royal family for important ceremonies of state. The flagship is the ornately decorated *Suphannahong*, or 'Golden Swan', which is more than 200 years old and acts as the king's personal barge. At 45m long and made from a single piece of timber, it is the largest dugout in the world. To get here, take the 3B ferry across the river from Tha Saphan Phra Pin Klao (N12) and follow the signs. Most longtail tours stop here.

Banglamphu & Dusit

Just north of the royal Ko Ratanakosin district, the old residential neighbourhood of Banglamphu has a slow, old-world local feel in parts and the feel of a 24-hour festival around the Th Khao San area of guesthouses, hotels, restaurants and bars. If your trip to Thailand is more about partying than sightseeing, then this is the place for you. Further north, Dusit is the current royal district and has several Victorian-era attractions.

WAT SAKET & GOLDEN MOUNT
วัดสระเกศ

The manmade **Golden Mount** (Map pp74–5; ☎ 0 2621 0576; off Th Boriphat; admission to summit 10B; ☺ 8am-5pm) and adjoining Wat Saket offer fine views over the old city. If you're a sunset buff, a walk up here before it closes will make you fall in love with Bangkok. Wat Saket is walkable from Banglamphu along Th Ratchadamnoen Klang. From eastern parts of the city, take the *klong* (often spelt as *khlong*; canal) boat to its western terminus at Tha Saphan Phan Fah.

WAT RATCHANATDA
วัดราชนัดดา

A mix of every imaginable temple style, **Wat Ratchanatda** (Map pp74–5; ☎ 0 2224 8807; 2 Th Mahachai; admission free; ☺ 8am-5pm) is most stunning at night when the 37 metal spires of the Loha Prasat (Metal Palace) are lit up like a medieval birthday cake. During the day you can climb through the sparsely decorated temple to the top, and investigate the quiet amulet market behind. It's an easy walk from Banglamphu or the Saen Saeb *klong* boat pier at Tha Saphan Phan Fah.

WAT SUTHAT
วัดสุทัศน์

The truly remarkable Buddha image, colourful floor-to-ceiling murals and relative tranquillity make **Wat Suthat** (Map pp74–5; ☎ 0 2224 9845; Th Bamrung Meuang; admission 20B; ☺ 8.30am-4.30pm) arguably the most attractive of Bangkok's Buddhist *wát*. The appeal is in Thailand's largest *wí-hǎhn* (main chapel), which houses the serene 8m-high Phra Si Sakayamuni, Thailand's largest surviving Sukhothai-period bronze. Opposite the north entrance

is **Sao Ching-Cha**, the Giant Swing, a tall, red swing formerly used in a death-defying (or sometimes not) Brahmin religious ritual. Wat Suthat is an easy walk from Banglamphu, or take the *klong* boat to Tha Saphan Phan Fah and walk from there.

DUSIT PARK
สวนดุสิต

Dusit Park (Map pp72–3) is a former palace estate of King Chulalongkorn, who took great inspiration from his turn-of-the-century tour of Europe. The grounds are dominated by **Ananda Samakhon Throne Hall** (admission 150B; ☺ 9am-5pm), built in the early 20th century of Carrara marble in classically European style. It houses an exhibition of expertly produced Thai decorative handicrafts, but the real draws are the East-meets-West frescoes in the ceilings.

Vimanmek Teak Mansion Museum (Phra Thii Nang Wimanmek; ☎ 0 2628 6300-9; Th Ratchawithi; admission 100B, free with Grand Palace ticket; ☺ 9.30am-4pm) is said to be the world's largest golden teak building and is full of royal treasures. It was reportedly built without a single nail, held together by tiny wooden pegs. Compulsory tours (in English) leave every half-hour between 9.30am and 3pm and last about an hour. Free performances of Thai classical dances are staged in a pavilion on the side of the mansion at 10.30am and 2pm.

Nearby is the **Abhisek Dusit Throne Hall** (Phra Thii Nang Aphisek Dusit), a smaller but even more ornate structure with a strong Moorish influence. The facade is amazing, and the museum behind it contains regional handicrafts. Several other buildings have royal treasures on display and the **Royal Elephant Museum**, near the Th U

THANŎN KHAO SAN

Almost 30 years after locals on the Khao San Rd, as it's known, first started converting their homes into guesthouses for smelly backpackers – known jokingly in Thai as faràng *kêe ngók* ('stingy foreigners') – Banglamphu has evolved into a clearing house for travellers unlike anywhere else on earth. At any time of day or night, Th Khao San is mobbed by travellers from across the globe, mingling with beggars, hawkers, transvestites and street performers, and surrounded by stallholders offering hair-braiding, body-piercing, pirated CDs, hippy jewellery, handicrafts, fake brand-name clothes, Thai fast food, cold beers and croaking wooden frogs, among other things. Think of it as a backpacker cabaret in which you are both a spectator and a participant.

Critics claim Th Khao San cocoons travellers from the real Thailand. It's true that many people leave Bangkok having seen just this short stretch of road, but its reputation is not really fair. Today, Banglamphu has become a major entertainment district for young Bangkokians, who add the Thai spice long missing from this dish.

Thong Nai gate, showcases two large stables that once housed three white elephants.

This is royal property so you must dress appropriately; see the boxed text, p37.

WAT BENCHAMABOPHIT
วัดเบญจมบพิตร(วัดเบญจะ)

Built at the same time as the nearby Ananda Samakhan Throne Hall, and of the same shimmering white marble from Carrara in Italy, this renowned **wát** (Marble Temple; Map pp72–3; cnr Th Sri Ayuthaya & Th Phra Ram V; admission 20B; 8.30am-5pm) is a unique blend of classical European and Thai Buddhist styles. The courtyard behind the *bòht* has 53 Buddha images representing every *mudra* (gesture) and style from Thai history, making this the ideal place to compare Buddhist iconography. The surrounding grounds are a pleasant place for a wander.

Chinatown

Bangkok's Chinatown (Map pp76–7) is centred on bustling Th Yaowarat, which is lined with gold shops, herbalists and banquet restaurants, all with loud neon signs in Chinese characters. The whole district is great for aimless wandering through crowded markets, charismatic old soi lined with shophouses and some of the best street food in the city. The old markets along **Sampeng Lane** (Map pp76–7; Soi Wanit, btwn Th Ratchawong and Th Chakrawat) and **Talat Mai** (Trok Itsaranuphap) are the most interesting and congested of all – mornings in Trok Itsaranuphap are like a mosh pit. See the walking tour (p87) for directions. Elsewhere there are dozens of little wát, some of them distinctively Chinese in style, dotted around the backstreets.

WAT TRAIMIT (GOLDEN BUDDHA)
วัดไตรมิตร

This **wát** (Temple of the Golden Buddha; Map pp76–7; 0 2225 9775; Th Traimit (aka Mitthaphap); admission 20B; 8am-5pm) houses an incredible Buddha image made from 5.5 tonnes of solid gold (that was worth a hefty US$190 million at early 2010 prices). The Sukhothai-era image was covered in plaster back in the Ayuthaya period to protect it from Burmese marauders, and its full worth was discovered only in 1955, when the image was accidentally dropped from a crane. Avoid the tour groups by visiting early in the morning or late in the afternoon. It's an easy walk from Hualamphong Metro station, en route to Chinatown proper.

OFF THE BEATEN PATH

There are some lovely, easily reached attractions within the city limits where you'll likely have the whole place to yourself. If you loved Jim Thompson's House, there are at least five other museums in old teak houses, including **Ban Kamthieng** (Map p82; 0 2661 6470; 131 Soi 21 (Asoke); admission 100B; 9am-5pm Tue-Sat) and **Wang Suan Phakkat** (Lettuce Farm Palace; Map pp72–3; 0 2245 4934; Th Sri Ayuthaya; admission 100B; 9am-4pm). Both have collections of Thai artworks and handicrafts and you rarely see a soul, much less a tour bus.

New Bangkok

In the newer part of the city, the religious monuments and museums get crowded out by skyscraping offices, hotels and chic shopping malls the size of small suburbs. There are, however, a few sights that are made more interesting by their juxtaposition amid shiny modern Bangkok.

SRI MARIAMMAN
วัดพระศรีมหาอุมาเทวี

This colourful Hindu **temple** (Map pp78–9; cnr Th Silom & Th Pan; 6am-8pm) is an important place of worship for Bangkok's Indian community as well as for many Thai Buddhists. The temple was built in 1879, and the ornate *gopura* (South Indian tower) is covered in figures from the Mahabharata. You can enter the compound (without your shoes), but photography is prohibited.

ERAWAN SHRINE
ศาลพระพรหม

In spite of all the temples, modern Bangkok might not seem to be a particularly spiritual place, but there are all sorts of interesting shrines hidden away among the skyscrapers. Most famous is this **shrine** (Saan Phra Phrom; Map pp80–1; cnr Th Ploenchit & Th Ratchadamri; 6am-8pm) next to the Erawan Grand Hyatt. When the Erawan Hotel was first built in the 1950s a series of construction disasters occurred. They stopped soon after this shrine to the Hindu god Brahma was erected. The hotel was a huge success and ever since people have come here to pray for luck and fortune. For an idea of just how revered the Erawan shrine is, when a mentally disturbed man attacked it in 2006,

---

EXHIBIT ONE

In recent years Bangkok has seen an explosion in the number of galleries, and the number of people interested in them, meaning you should be able to catch an interesting exhibition at any time. To find out what's on, look for **BAM!** (Bangkok Art Map; www.bangkokartmap.com) from the *Bangkok 101* people, and *Thailand Art & Design Guide* (www.thailandartanddesignguide.com), or check the lifestyle magazines for exhibition opening nights.

Galleries worth looking out for include **Queen's Gallery** (Map pp74-5; ☎ 0 2281 5360; www.queen gallery.com; 101 Th Ratchadamnoen Klang; admission 20B; ☆ 10am-7pm Thu-Tue), for conservative contemporary fare; **100 Tonson Gallery** (Map pp80-1; ☎ 0 2684 1527; www.100tonsongallery.com; 100 Soi Tonson, off Th Ploenchit; ☆ 11am-7pm Thu-Sun), regarded as the city's top commercial gallery; **H Gallery** (Map pp78-9; ☎ 0 2234 7556; www.hgallerybkk.com; 201 Soi 12, Th Sathon; ☆ 10am-6pm Wed-Sun), a private gallery specialising in young Asian artists; and **Kathmandu Photo Gallery** (Map pp78-9; ☎ 0 2234 6700; www.kathmandu-bkk.com; 87 Th Pan, Th Silom; ☆ 11am-7pm Tue-Sun), the city's only truly dedicated photography gallery.

---

bystanders promptly beat him to death. You can see shrine dancers performing traditional *lá-kon gâa bon* dances here. For more on this and other nearby shrines, download the excellent guide *Deities @ Ratchaprasong* from www .heartofbangkok.com.

JIM THOMPSON'S HOUSE
บ้านจิมทอมป์สัน

This complex of traditional **teak buildings** (Map pp80-1; ☎ 0 2216 7368; www.jimthompsonhouse.org; 6 Soi Kasem San 2, Th Phra Ram I; adult/concession (under 25 with ID) 100/50B; ☆ 9am-5pm) is the legacy of the American spy-cum-silk-mogul Jim Thompson. The traditional wooden houses were collected from as far away as northern Thailand and as near as the Muslim village of Baan Krua, just across the *klong* (where silk is still woven today), and reassembled as a private mansion on the edge of Khlong Saen Saep. Guided tours in English, French and Japanese leave every 20 minutes. Photography is prohibited inside the buildings. Jim Thompson's House is a short walk from both the National Stadium Skytrain stop and Hua Chang *klong* boat pier.

LUMPHINI PARK
สวนลุมพินี

Named after Buddha's birthplace in Nepal, Bangkok's largest and most popular public **park** (Map pp72-3; ☆ 5am-8pm) is crisscrossed by walking trails and has tranquil lawns, wooded glades and a large artificial lake with pedalos for hire. It's a great place to watch Bangkokians unwind; practising t'ai chi in the early morning, running, working out, taking part in outdoor aerobics classes or just unleashing their kids on the grass. From mid-

February to April Lumphini is a favourite spot for kite fighting. The main entrance to the park is on Th Phra Ram IV, but there are also entrances on Th Sarasin, Th Withayu and Th Ratchadamri. It's well connected by Metro at Lumphini and Silom and by Skytrain at Sala Daeng and Ratchadamri.

ACTIVITIES
Massage

Bangkokians regard traditional massage as a vital part of preventative health care and they frequent massage parlours more regularly than gyms. There are literally thousands of massage places in Bangkok, ranging from luxury spas to cheap-and-cheerful foot massage joints. Note that a man asking for an 'oil massage' can sometimes lead to techniques that aren't on the curriculum at Wat Pho. If you're not looking for a 'happy ending', avoid parlours where the masseuses are young and wearing short skirts.

In smaller shops a foot massage costs 200B to 300B while a full-body massage is between 300B and 600B. In spas, however, prices are much higher. Recommended massages:

Coran Boutique Spa (Map p82; ☎ 0 2651 1588; www.coranbangkok.com; 27/1-2 Soi 13, Th Sukhumvit; ☆ 11am-10pm; 1hr traditional massage 400B) Top-notch Thai massage by graduates of the adjacent Thai Traditional Medical Services Society (which also offers courses).

Ruen-Nuad Massage & Yoga (Map pp78-9; ☎ 0 2632 2662/3; 42 Th Convent, Th Silom; ☆ 10am-10pm; 1hr traditional massage 350B) In a charming old wooden house the mood is typical of spa facilities, but the prices are very reasonable.

Wat Pho Thai Traditional Massage School (Map pp72-3; ☎ 0 2221 3686; Th Sanamchai; ☆ 8am-6.30pm;

1hr massage 360B) Thailand's primary massage school has two air-conditioned pavilions near the east gate of Wat Pho.

WALKING TOUR

Despite the traffic, the best way to discover much of Bangkok is by foot. And in some cases, such as the claustrophobic alleys of chaotic commerce in Chinatown, it's the only way. We recommend starting this tour after lunch so you can finish with a sunset drink. Remember that the river ferries stop about 7pm.

Starting from the river ferry at Tha Saphan Phut (Memorial Bridge Pier), walk north along Th Chakraphet and into **Phahurat (1)**, aka Little India. Turn right into narrow **Trok Huae Med (2)**, a largely Indian market that extends east into **Sampeng Lane (3)**, signposted as Soi Wanit 1, the original Chinatown market that has been trading since 1782. Today it deals in useful stuff such as bulk Hello Kitty pens or tonnes of stuffed animals.

Turn left on Th Mahachak, walk 30m and turn left again through a covered passage to rows of photogenic, stuccoed yellow **Chinese shophouses (4)**; a peaceful intermission in the market tour. Return to Sampeng Lane and avoid

the trolleys as far east as Th Mangkon, where you'll see two of Bangkok's oldest commercial buildings, the **Bangkok Bank (5)** and **Tang To Kang (6)** gold shop, both more than 100 years old.

Turn left (north) on Th Mangkun and walk up to manic Th Yaowarat, Chinatown's main drag. Turn right past the street's famous gold shops and after about 100m cross Th Yaowarat into super-crowded **Talat Mai (7**; aka Trok Itsaranuphap); you'll know it by the people shuffling into the alley one at a time. About halfway along is **Talat Leng-Buai-Ia (8)**, which was once the city's central vegetable market but today sells mainly Chinese ingredients

WALK FACTS

Start Tha Saphan Phut (Memorial Bridge, river ferry N6)
End Tha Marine Department (river ferry N4) or Hualamphong Metro
Distance 4km
Duration Three hours
Fuel stop Streetside kitchens on Th Plaeng Naam

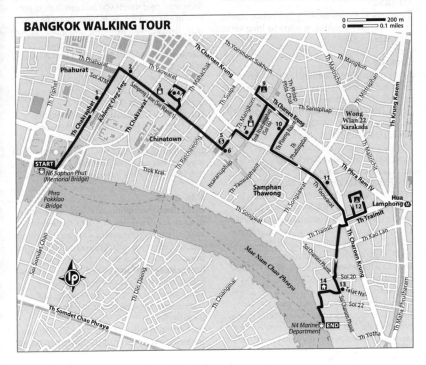

BANGKOK WALKING TOUR

such as fresh cashews, lotus seeds, and shiitake mushrooms. You will, eventually, pop out the far end onto Th Charoen Krung. Cross over a road and on Soi Charoen Krung 21 is **Wat Mangkon Kamalawat (9)**, one of Chinatown's largest and liveliest temples.

Head back to Th Charoen Krung, turn left (east) and then right into **Th Plaeng Naam (10)**. This atmospheric street of shophouses and street food makes a good pit stop, particularly at the two streetside kitchens at the north end. Turn left onto **Th Yaowarat (11)** and after passing a couple of old art deco buildings turn left at the Odeon Circle, with its distinctive Chinese gate, onto Th Traimit (aka Th Mitthaphap) for **Wat Traimit** and the **Golden Buddha (12**; p85). Head back to Odeon Circle, cross and walk past the machine shops of Soi Yaowarat 1 onto Soi Charoen Phanit and the atmospheric **Talat Noi (13)** neighbourhood. You deserve a drink now, so follow the signs to the **River View Guest House (14**; p94), where the 8th-floor restaurant-bar has cheap beer and amazing sunset views. Take either the ferry or the Metro to get your lodgings.

COURSES

There are some interesting courses available, from half-day cooking lessons to long-term language courses.

Cooking

Many of Bangkok's leading luxury hotels offer gourmet Thai cooking courses, and there are several cheaper private schools.

Baipai Thai Cooking School (Map pp70-1; ☎ 0 2294 9029; www.baipai.com; 150/12 Soi Naksuwan, Th Nonsee; 1800B; ✆ lessons 9.30am-1.30pm & 1.30-5.30pm Tue-Sun) Housed in an attractive suburban villa, and taught by a small army of staff, Baipai offers two daily lessons of four dishes each. Transport is available.

Blue Elephant Cooking School (Map pp78-9; ☎ 0 2673 9353; www.blueelephant.com; 233 Th Sathon Tai, Silom; 2800B; ✆ lessons 8.45am-12.30pm & 1.15pm-5pm Mon-Sat) Bangkok's most chichi Thai cooking school offers two lessons daily. The morning class squeezes in a visit to a local market, while the afternoon session includes a detailed introduction to Thai ingredients.

Khao Cooking School (Map pp74-5; ☎ 08 9111 0947; khaocookingschool@gmail.com; D&D Plaza, 68-70 Th Khao San; 1500B; ✆ lessons 8.30am-12.30pm & 2.30-6.30pm Mon-Sat) Although it's located smack-dab in the middle of Khao San, this new cooking school was started up by an authority on Thai food and features instruction on a wide variety of authentic dishes. Located directly behind D&D Inn.

Silom Thai Cooking School (Map pp78-9; ☎ 08 4726 5669; www.bangkokthaicooking.com; 68 Soi 13, Th Silom; 1000B; ✆ lessons 9.30am-1pm & 2-6pm) Although the facilities are basic, Silom crams a visit to a local market and instruction of six dishes into three and a half hours, making it the best bang for your baht. Transport available.

Language

The most intensive language course in Bangkok is held at **American University Alumni Language Center** (Map pp80-1; ☎ 0 2252 8170; www.auathai.com; 179 Th Ratchadamri; per hr 102B), which offers rolling classes from 7am to 8pm Monday to Friday; go whenever you like.

AAA Thai Language Center (Map pp80-1; ☎ 0 2655 5629; www.aaathai.com; 6th fl, 29 Vanissa Bldg, Th Chitlom, Pathumwan) Good-value AAA Thai has a loyal following.

Thailish Language School (Map pp82; ☎ 0 2258 6846; www.thailanguageschool.com; 427 Th Sukhumvit, btwn Sois 21 & 23) This small, personal school has private or small-group classes concentrating on conversation.

Meditation & Massage

Most Buddhist study centres in Bangkok specialise in *vipassana* (insight) meditation. **Dharma Thai** (www.dhammathai.org) has a rundown on several prominent wát and meditation centres, or speak to the **World Fellowship of Buddhists** (WFB; Map p82; ☎ 0 2661 1284; www.wfb-hq.org; 616 Benjasiri Park, Soi Medhinivet, Soi 24, Th Sukhumvit).

International Buddhist Meditation Center (Map pp74-5; ☎ 0 2623 6326; www.mcu.ac.th/IBMC/; Vipassana Section Room 106, Mahachula Bldg, Wat Mahathat, Th Pra Chan) Holds regular lectures on Buddhist topics in English, and meditation classes.

Wat Pho Thai Traditional Massage School (Map pp72-3; ☎ 0 2221 3686; www.watpomassage.com; Soi Phenphat 1, Th Maharat) By far the best place to learn traditional massage. Courses are held at school headquarters across from Wat Pho, just off Th Maharat. A 30-hour course costs 6500/8500B for foot/body massage.

Moo·ay Tai

Many foreigners come to Thailand to study *moo·ay tai* (Thai boxing; also spelled *muay thai*). Training regimens can be *extremely* strict. See www.muaythai.com for more information.

Fairtex Muay Thai Camp (☎ 0 2755 3329; www.muaythaifairtex.com; 99/8 Soi Buthamanuson, Th Theparak, Samut Prakan) Training from 500B a session to 7700B-a-week residence. Samut Prakan is about 25km southeast of central Bangkok.

Sor. Vorapin Gym (Map pp74-5; ☎ 0 2282 3551; www.thaiboxings.com; 13 Trok Krasab, Th Chakraphong) Training

---

FREAKY BANGKOK

Bangkok can be a weird and wonderful place without even trying. But if you need to go beyond the ordinary strangeness, here is a list of its more unusual sights (see p84 for the weirdness of Th Khao San).

The **amulet market** (Map pp74-5; Th Phra Chan) is the commercial side of Thai Buddhism, part animistic and part antiquities. The most common amulets are small ceramic plaques, produced by important Buddhist monasteries, but there are also tiny Buddha images, phallic symbols, bone fragments and other potent objects. If you fancy buying an amulet, several stalls can fit it into a metal pendant case for about 30B.

Perhaps Bangkok's strangest religious site is the **Lingam shrine** (Saan Jao Mae Thap Thim; Map pp80-1; Soi Somkhit, Th Withayu) hidden away behind the Swissôtel Nai Lert Park. Scattered around a spirit house and a 3m-high phallus statue are hundreds of wooden and stone representations of the male organ. Women pray here when they hope to become pregnant (hold on to your daughters).

For a creepy exploration of human mortality, the **Forensic Medicine Museum** (Map pp72-3; ☎ 0 2419 7000; 2nd fl, Forensic Medicine Bldg, Siriraj Hospital; admission 40B; ⊙ 9am-4pm Mon-Sat) features evidence from many of Bangkok's most heinous murder cases, including the preserved body of serial child-killer and cannibal Si Ouey. To get here, take the cross-river ferry from Tha Chang (N9) or Tha Phra Chan to Tha Wang Lang (Siriraj, N10).

---

for foreigners around the corner from Th Khao San. More serious training is held at a second facility outside the city. Half-day/weekly/monthly training costs 500/2500/9000B.

BANGKOK FOR CHILDREN

Bangkok has loads to offer children. Most malls have diverse and appealing attractions for kids of various ages: shopping for the tweens and rides for preschoolers. The website www.bambiweb.org is a useful resource for parents.

Queen Saovabha Memorial Institute (Snake Farm)
สถานเสาวภา

Lovers of things that slither will be fascinated by this working **snake farm** (Map pp78-9; ☎ 0 2252 0161; 1871 Th Phra Ram IV, Lumphini; adult/child 200/50B; ⊙ 9.30am-3.30pm Mon-Fri, 9.30am-1pm Sat & Sun), which provides antivenene for Thai hospitals. You can see deadly snakes being milked for their venom at 11am daily, or have one draped around your neck Monday to Friday at 2.30pm.

Children's Discovery Museum
พิพิธพัณฑ์เด็ก

Bangkok's leading children's **museum** (Map pp70-1; ☎ 0 2618 6509; Queen Sirikit Park, Th Kamphaeng Phet 4; adult/child 70/50B; ⊙ 9am-5pm Tue-Fri, 10am-6pm Sat & Sun) is opposite the sprawling Chatuchak Weekend Market. The displays are fully interactive, and both kids and adults will enjoy pressing the buttons and making giant bubbles with the bubble machine. Follow the signs from the Mo Chit Skytrain station.

Aksra Theatre
โรงละครโจหลุยส

The former Joe Louis Puppet Theatre has moved house and is starting a new life here as the modern **Aksra Hoon Lakorn Lek** (Map pp72-3; ☎ 0 2677 8888 ext 5604; www.aksratheatre.com; King Power Complex, 8/1 Th Rang Nam, Ratchathewi; tickets 800B; ⊙ showtimes 7pm Tue-Fri, 1pm & 7pm Sat & Sun). A variety of performances are held with the highlight being the Ramakian, which requires three puppeteers to strike the humanlike poses.

Siam Ocean World
สยามโอเชี่ยนเวิร์ล

Southeast Asia's largest oceanarium, **Siam Ocean World** (Map pp80-1; ☎ 0 2687 2000; www.siamoceanworld.com; basement, Siam Paragon, Th Phra Ram 1; adult/child 80-120cm 850/650B; ⊙ 10am-8pm) has hundreds of species of fish, crustaceans and even penguins. The main tank is the highlight, with an acrylic tunnel allowing you to walk beneath sharks and rays. Time your trip to coincide with the shark and penguin feedings: sharks at 1pm and 4pm, penguins 12.30pm and 4.30pm.

TOURS

Most tours centre around the big-ticket sights, the river and day trips to Ayuthaya.

Longtail Tours

Longtail boats are Bangkok icons and can be chartered for tours of the Thonburi *klong*, particularly Khlong Bangkok Yai and Khlong Bangkok Noi. You'll find boat drivers at Tha

BANGKOK

GAY & LESBIAN BANGKOK

Is there a gay-friendlier city on the planet? While stepping out of the closet is a gamble for many gays, Bangkok's male-gay nightlife is out and open with bars, discos and gà·teu·i (also spelt kàthoey; ladyboys) cabarets, but night spots for Thai lesbians (torm/dêe) aren't as prominent or as segregated.

Utopia, the well-known gay information provider, publishes the Utopia Guide to Thailand, covering gay-friendly businesses in 18 Thai cities, including Bangkok. More listings and events can be found at www.fridae.com. Both gays and lesbians are well advised to visit Bangkok in mid-November, when the city's small but fun **Pride Festival** (www.bangkokpride.org) is in full swing. Dinners, cruises, clubbing and contests are the order of the week.

Some recommended bars, clubs, discos and saunas:

Babylon (Map pp72-3; ☎ 0 2679 7984; 34 Soi Nantha, off of Soi 1, Th Sathon; cover 260B; ⏰ 10.30am-10.30pm) Bangkok's first luxury sauna remains extremely popular with visitors, many from neighbouring Singapore and Hong Kong.

DJ Station (Map pp78-9; ☎ 0 2266 4029; 8/6-8 Soi 2, Th Silom; admission 200B; ⏰ 10.30pm-late) Massively popular with the younger crowd, and among the most well known gay destinations in town, this place has pounding dance music, flamboyant costume parties and gà·teu·i cabaret at 11pm.

Ratchada Soi 8 (Map pp70-1; ☎ 08 9231 0996; 76/4 Soi 8, Th Ratchadaphisek; ⏰ 8pm-1am) It's packed. The age limit seems to be 25 and there's the usual show with 'coyote boys' (skinny young guys in Speedos and boots).

Telephone (Map pp78-9; ☎ 0 2234 3279; 114/11-13 Soi 4, Th Silom; ⏰ 6pm-1am) Bangkok's oldest gay bar-restaurant is still probably the best place from which to watch the virtual gay pride parade that is Soi 4.

Zeta (Map pp70-1; ☎ 0 2211 1060; 29 Royal City Ave (RCA), off Th Phra Ram IX; ⏰ 8pm-2am) This exceedingly popular lesbian club on the quiet end of RCA is packed to the gills with young torm-dêe on weekends. Women only.

Chang (Map pp74–5), Tha Saphan Phut (Map pp76–7), Tha Oriental (Map pp78–9) and Tha Sri Phraya (Map pp78–9). Rental costs from about 800B an hour (it costs more the closer you are to an expensive hotel); negotiate.

Dinner Cruises

Chao Phraya dinner cruises are hugely popular, with boats ranging from century-old rice barges to neon-clad cruisers taking in the brightly lit riverside sights, passing Wat Arun, the Grand Palace and Saphan Phra Ram IX. Larger vessels often have dance floors and live bands, which might be less romantic than you hoped.

Loy Nava (Map pp78-9; ☎ 0 2437 4932; www.loynava .com; set menu 1766B; ⏰ 6-8pm & 8.10-10pm) offers two daily cruises departing from the pier at River City Shopping Complex aboard a converted rice barge.

The converted rice barge run by **Manohra Cruises** (Map pp70-1; ☎ 0 2477 0770; www.manohracruises .com; Bangkok Marriott Resort & Spa; cocktail cruise 900, dinner cruise 1250-1990B; ⏰ cocktail cruise 6-7pm, dinner cruise 7.30-10pm) departs from the pier at Bangkok Marriott Resort & Spa, but also picks up at Tha Sathon (Map pp78–9), Saphan Taksin and Tha Oriental (Map pp78–9).

Wan Fah Cruises (Map pp78-9; ☎ 0 2222 8679; www .wanfah.in.th; 1200B; ⏰ 7pm-9pm) runs cruises on

a Chinese rice barge leaving from Tha Sri Phraya (the pier near the River City Shopping Complex).

The famous riverside **Yok Yor** (Map pp72-3; ☎ 0 2439 3477; www.yokyor.co.th; dinner 300-550B plus surcharge 140B; ⏰ 8-10pm) restaurant sets out on nightly dinner cruises from Thonburi, across from River City Shopping Complex. Most consider this better value than the hotel rides.

Bicycle Tours

Bangkok's take-no-prisoners traffic and sweat-sapping humidity might not be ideal for cycling. But several operators offer tours that let you discover a side of the city virtually off-limits to four-wheeled transport. Routes include unusual ways around Chinatown and Ko Ratanakosin, but the pick are journeys across the river to Thonburi and, in particular, the 'lungs of Bangkok', **Bang Kachao** (Map pp70–1), an expanse of mangrove, banana and coconut plantations just a few kilometres from the frantic city centre. Recommended companies include the following:

ABC Amazing Bangkok Cyclists (Map p82; ☎ 0 2665 6364; www.realasia.net; 10/5-7 Soi 26, Th Sukhumvit; tours from 1000B)

Bangkok Bike Rides (☎ 0 2712 5305; www.bangkok bikerides.com; tours from 1000B)

Co van Kessel Bangkok Tours (Map pp76-7; ☎ 0 2688 9933; www.covankessel.com; Mezzanine fl, Grand China Princess hotel, 215 Th Yaowarat, Chinatown; tours from 950B; ⏰ 6am-7pm)

Velo Thailand (Map pp74-5; ☎ 08 9201 7782; www .velothailand.com; 88 Soi 2, Th Samsen, Banglamphu; tours from 1000B; ⏰ 10am-9pm)

Other Tours

If you want a custom tour with an expert guide, **Bangkok Private Tours** (www.bangkokprivate tours.com) is earning a reputation for its food tours, among others.

FESTIVALS & EVENTS

As well as the countrywide festivals (see p402), Bangkok has a few celebrations of its own.

Bangkok Jazz Festival (March; www.bangkokjazz festival.com) Features international and Thai performers.

Kite Flying Season (March) Kite fights at Bangkok's public parks and Sanam Luang.

Royal Ploughing Ceremony (May) Ceremonial plough-ing by the king (or more recently the crown prince) at Sanam Luang to forecast the coming rice harvest.

Bangkok International Film Festival (dates vary, but usually sometime July–September; www.bangkokfilm.org) In cinemas across town.

Thailand International Swan-Boat Races (Septem-ber) During the middle of the month on Chao Phraya River, near Saphan Rama IX.

Vegetarian Festival (September/October) Centred on Soi 20, Th Charoen Krung, Chinatown becomes an orgy of veg food.

Fat Festival (November) Popular alternative radio station hosts up-and-coming Thai bands at this annual music event.

SLEEPING

Bangkok boasts more than 400 hotels and guesthouses, ranging from cheap backpacker joints to some of the most luxurious lodgings on earth. They are scattered widely, though hotels of a type tend to congregate in certain neighbourhoods.

Banglamphu and the famous (or should that be infamous?) Th Khao San are a tractor beam for backpackers and few are able to es-cape its pull. This area is conveniently near to the river and the monuments and museums of old Bangkok. A long walk north is Thewet, which is refreshingly laid-back and handy for the palaces in Dusit. It's home to a small cluster of good guesthouses. Further south, Chinatown is a lively but often-overlooked neighbourhood with a couple of decent op-tions, while nearby Hualamphong has some good budget choices near the train station.

The riverside area south of Chinatown boasts several big-name, super-luxurious ho-tels with spectacular views, while Th Silom and more recently Th Sathon are home to

---

BANGKOK ROOMS: WHAT YOUR MONEY WILL BUY

Bangkok suffers from capital-city syndrome and room rates can be considerably higher than elsewhere in Thailand. We have divided rooms into the following three categories:

Budget: under 1000B
Midrange: 1000B–4500B
Top end: over 4500B

These are the walk-in rates we were quoted, but it's well worth noting that big, sometimes huge, discounts can be found by booking online or in advance by phone; see p393 for details.

So what do you get for your money? At the budget end, the days of 50B beds in Banglamphu are over but those on wafer-thin budgets can still get a dorm bed with a shared bathroom for between 150B and 400B. More comfortable and stylish doubles are available for upwards of 800B, with prices rising with size and location.

The midrange is where you will find the biggest discounts for advance bookings. Rooms with a listed rate up to 4500B will often go for somewhere between 2500B and 3000B. More modest properties tend to have more modest rates – modesty seemingly defined by the style of the decor. Thus the older places are often quite cheap, while trendier new places more pricey. If you're on a lower midrange budget, some very nice rooms can be had for between about 1500B and 2500B.

Bangkok's growing array of top-end hotels start at about 4500B per room and climb much higher. In the top tier rooms start at more than 10,000B, but in most of the luxurious design and boutique hotels, and the vast majority of the international brands, you're looking at about 6000B to 9000B, before hefty online discounting.

several new, stylish and well-priced midrange hotels and some chic top-end places. The area around Siam Sq also has several more stately upmarket hotels, plus a handful of budget options. Th Sukhumvit, where you'll find sleaze and class in plentiful supply depending on which soi you're in, is home to a bunch of new boutique and wannabe-boutique places, numerous tour-group oriented midrangers and a smattering of quirky budget and top-end affairs. See p390 for more on accommodation in Thailand.

Ko Ratanakosin & Thonburi

Bangkok's oldest districts make an ideal base for exploring the city's major historic sights. It's best to book well ahead.

Bhuthorn (Map pp74-5; ☎ 0 2622 2270; thebhuthorn .com; 96-98 Th Phraeng Phuthon, San Chao Phor Seua; d from 2800B; 🅿 💻 🛜) In two century-old shophouses on a peaceful village square, the Bhuthorn is a delightfully stylish three-room B&B in old Bangkok with personal service to match. Rooms are fitted with period antiques and modern luxuries; wi-fi is free. Book ahead.

Arun Residence (Map pp72-3; ☎ 0 2221 9158; www.arun residence.com; 36-38 Soi Pratu Nokyang, off Th Maharat, Ko Ratanakosin; d 3500-5500B; 🅿 💻 🛜) Near Wat Pho, this romantic six-room retreat appeals for its location overlooking the river and Wat Arun, its midcentury decor and the Deck restaurant and rooftop bar that are perfect for watching the sun sink over Bangkok. The three rooms with private decks are the pick.

Aurum: The River Place (Map pp72-3; ☎ 0 2622 2248; www.aurum-bangkok.com; Soi Pansuk, off Th Maharat, Ko Ratanakosin; tw/d with breakfast 3600/4100B; 🅿 💻 🛜) At the river end of a row of old Chinese godowns, the attractive and very comfortable faux-Parisian-style Aurum has 12 tastefully furnished rooms with not-wholly-uninterrupted river views.

Ibrik Resort (Map pp72-3; ☎ 0 2848 9220; www.ibrik resort.com; 256 Soi Wat Rakhang, Th Arun Amarin, Thonburi; d 4000B; 🅿) In a white wooden house that's literally right on the river on the Thonburi side, Ibrik has just three romantic rooms with silks and four-poster beds. It's not exactly luxurious, but it's very private. The Moonlight room has no view.

Chakrabongse Villas (Map pp72-3; ☎ 0 2222 1290; www.thaivillas.com; 396 Th Maharat; Ko Ratanakosin; villas 4500-25,000B; 🅿 🛜 🏊) The grounds of Prince Chakrabongse Bhuvanath's 19th-century mansion have been adapted to become one

of the city's classiest, most discrete boutique properties. The mansion remains a private home, but seven villas are set at either end of the garden. The riverside dining pavilion is super-romantic; meals are cooked to order. Delightful.

Banglamphu

The days of Th Khao San (p84) being all about supercheap flophouses are over. As hippies have been replaced by flashpacking couples so the tiny, boxlike fan rooms featured in the movie *The Beach* have been replaced by larger, air-conditioned rooms with private bathrooms starting at about 500B. Most places have attached restaurants serving faràng-oriented food and screening nightly movies.

Calmer guesthouses and a growing number of midrange places have spread in a 1km radius from Th Khao San, and these are where more experienced travellers prefer to stay. From December to February competition for rooms is intense and many places are full by 10am. Advance bookings are possible, though you'll usually need to pay in advance.

Get here by public bus, Chao Phraya River Express to Tha Phra Athit (Tha Banglamphu, N13) or Airport Express bus from Suvarnabhumi.

BUDGET

There are close to 100 guesthouses and hotels in Banglamphu. If one is not listed here, that doesn't mean it's no good – look around and use your own discretion. Remember that most of the best (and cheapest) places are not actually on Th Khao San, and the street can get pretty noisy. Look along Soi Rambutri, which bends around Wat Chana Songkhram west of Th Khao San; in the soi off Th Samsen north of Khlong Banglamphu; and if you're going supercheap the alley running parallel between Th Khao San and Th Ratchadamnoen Klang for old-style wooden guesthouses offering rooms with fan and shared bathroom (250B to 500B) or with fan and private bathroom (400B to 750B).

Shambara (Map pp74-5; ☎ 0 2282 7968; www.shambara bangkok.com; 138 Th Khao San; r 300-600B; 🅿 💻 🛜) Just off Th Khao San, this century-old wooden home has nine tiny rooms that share two clean showers and toilets. Great atmosphere. Book ahead.

Lamphu House (Map pp74-5; ☎ 0 2629 5861; www.lamphu house.com; 75-77 Soi Rambutri, Th Chakraphong; d 400-740B;

⊠ ▣) Lamphu House creates a mellow mood with its hidden, relatively quiet location and clean, smartly decorated rooms. Cheaper rooms with fans and shared bathrooms are also available.

Sam Sen Sam Place (Map pp74–5; ☎ 0 2628 7067; www .samsensam.com; 48 Soi 3, Th Samsen; r 500–2100B; ⊠ ▣) In a quiet location north of Th Khao San, this welcoming, laid-back guesthouse has a palette of fruit-coloured rooms that vary greatly in size, but all have polished floorboards and teak furnishings. The smallest share bathrooms.

Roof View Place (Map pp74–5; ☎ 0 2280 1272; Soi 6, Th Samsen; s 580B, d 680–780B; ⊠ ▣ 🛜) These white, sparsely stylish rooms and a friendly young crew make the Roof View worth the 10-minute walk to Th Khao San. Guests can use the kitchen.

Rikka Inn (Map pp74–5; ☎ 0 2282 7511; www.rikkainn .com; 259 Th Khao San; r 600–950B; ⊠ ▣ 🛋) With a rooftop pool, small but clean rooms and a central Th Khao San location, the Rikka is great value.

Villa Cha-Cha (Map pp74–5; ☎ 0 2280 1025; www .villachacha.com; 36 Th Tani; r 800–2750B; ⊠ ▣ 🛜 🛋) Tucked away off Th Rambutri, the 74-room Villa Cha-Cha is popular for its courtyard pool and après-beach feel. Rooms are big and comfortable enough, though some are a little dark.

Other options:

Prasuri Guest House (Map pp74–5; ☎ 0 2280 1428; prasuri_gh_bkk@hotmail.com; Soi Phrasuli; s 220–380B, d 280–420B; ⊠ ▣ 🛜) Old-style, family-run place with simple, tired rooms.

Boworn BB (Map pp74–5; ☎ 0 2629 1073; www.boworn bb.com; 335 Th Phra Sumen; r 700–800B; ⊠ ▣ 🛜) Boworn has bland but clean rooms but it's the familial atmosphere centred around the cafe-lobby and the garden rooftop that are most attractive.

MIDRANGE

Midrange places are popping up in Banglamphu faster than mushrooms at a Ko Pha-Ngan Full Moon Party.

Sleep Withinn (Map pp74–5; ☎ 0 2280 3070; www.sleep withinn.com; 76 Th Rambutri; r 1100–1800B; ⊠ ▣ 🛜 🛋) This new flashpacker haunt offers Global Zen style in the 50 compact rooms, a rooftop pool and excellent value. Very popular; discounts online.

New Siam Riverside (Map pp74–5; ☎ 0 2629 3535; www .newsiam.net; 21 Th Phra Athit; d with breakfast 1390–2490B; ⊠ ▣ 🛋) The fourth member of the New Siam guesthouse empire, this 104-room hotel

on the riverfront has a pool and vaguely stylish rooms; those with views (from 1890B) are best. The nearby New Siams II and III are also popular.

Boonsiri Place (Map pp74–5; ☎ 0 2622 1551; www .boonsiriplace.com; 55 Th Buranasat; d 1500–1900B; ⊠ ▣) In the historic village area south of Th Khao San, this modern low-rise 48-room hotel is an excellent choice for those looking for style, value and quiet. Rooms are large and are a bargain at these prices.

Lamphu Treehouse (Map pp74–5; ☎ 0 2282 0991; www .lamphutreehotel.com; Soi Baan Pan Thom, 155 Wanchat Bridge, Th Prachatipatai; s/d 1500/2100B; ⊠ ▣ 🛜 🛋) Accessed via a *klong*-side footpath a few minutes northeast of Th Khao San, the Lamphu is no treehouse, but with a pool and 40 colourful, comfortable rooms it's become a flashpacker fave.

our pick **Navalai River Resort** (Map pp74–5; ☎ 0 2280 9955; www.navalai.com; 45/1 Th Phra Athit; d from 2100B; ⊠ ▣ 🛜 🛋) Perched between the banks of Mae Nam Chao Phraya and arty Th Phra Athit, this busy 74-room boutique hotel delivers on style and location. Some of the spacious rooms have sweeping river views, or you can watch the sunset from the rooftop pool or riverside restaurant. 'River Breeze' rooms are worth the extra; book ahead.

Old Bangkok Inn (Map pp74–5; ☎ 0 2629 1787; www.old bangkokinn.com; 609 Th Phra Sumen; d 3190–3990B, f 5590B; ⊠ ▣ 🛜) In several evocatively furnished old shophouses, this 10-room boutique hotel offers both charisma and warm service in a historic setting.

Buddy Lodge (Map pp74-5; ☎ 0 2629 4477; www.buddy lodge.com; 265 Th Khao San; r 4000-5000B; 🅿 🛜 🖵) The leader of Th Khao San's gentrification, Buddy has 76 airy, tropical-manor-style rooms, a rooftop pool, a middle-of-the-action location…and…a Maccas in the lobby. Book online for big discounts.

Thewet & Dusit

North of Banglamphu near the National Library a strip of family-run budget places actually pre-dates Th Khao San but has managed to maintain a genuinely local feel, with no nightclubs and the only fast food coming from the nearby wet market. Thewet appeals particularly to repeat travellers who are 'over' Th Khao San. These places, plus the ecofriendly midrange Phranakorn Nornlen, are a (longish) walk to Th Khao San, Ko Ratanakosin and Dusit, but not that convenient to other areas. To get here, take a Chao Phraya Express boat (get off at Tha Thewet, N15) or public buses 3, 30 and 53 along Th Samsen.

Bangkok International Youth Hostel (Map pp72-3; ☎ 0 2282 0950; www.hihostels.com; 25/2 Th Phitsanulok, Dusit; dm 170B, r 450-1100B; 🅿 🖵 🛜) In a relatively dull location this HI has nonetheless benefited from almost three years of renovations, though older rooms and dorms remain tired. The big selling point is the enthusiastic Thai volunteers who lead free tours for a chance to practise their English. It's 50B cheaper for members. Wi-fi is free.

Shanti Lodge (Map pp72-3; ☎ 0 2281 2497; www.shanti lodge.com; 37 Th Sri Ayuthaya, Thewet; dm 350, s 400-850B, d 500-950B; 🅿 🖵 🛜) Stylish and self-assured, Shanti Lodge has a variety of rooms from simple affairs to the newer concrete wing with artful wall murals and bathrooms. The downstairs cafe and restaurant has a beachside feel with people hanging out, strumming guitars and doing little else. Very chilled.

Sri Ayuttaya Guest House (Map pp72-3; ☎ 0 2282 5942; Th Sri Ayuthaya; s 350B, d 650-750B; 🅿) Not quite as social as the neighbouring Shanti, but still superior to many Th Khao San joints. Rooms are attractive and offer fair value.

ourpick Phranakorn Nornlen (Map pp72-3; ☎ 0 2628 8188-90; www.phranakorn-nornlen.com; 46 Soi Thewet 1, Th Krung Kasem, Thewet; s/d 1800/2200B; 🅿 🖵 🛜) Everyone loves this arty, rustically charming boutique hotel set in a garden and a converted

wooden building. Social and environmental responsibility is atop the agenda. Delicious organic breakfasts are served in the rooftop garden, but the helpful staff will also encourage you to spend your money at local restaurants and markets. Recommended.

Chinatown & Hualamphong

Bangkok's Chinatown is noisy, hectic and full of energy. Most hotels are institutional affairs suffering from the sort of total charisma bypass familiar in hotels in, ahm, China. However, change is coming and some of the budget places around Hualamphong train station, and one trippy boutique hotel, are quite appealing. Most hotels in Chinatown are in the midrange price bracket, and we've listed the best of these.

There are several very rundown dosshouses beside Hualamphong train station, on Th Rong Muang (aka Th Hualamphong), but avoid them and try for one of these options instead.

Baan Hualampong (Map pp76-7; ☎ 0 2639 8054; www.baanhualampong.com; 336/20-21 Soi Charlong Krung, Th Rama IV; dm 220B, s 290B, d 520-900B; 🅿 🖵) Near Mahanakorn Intersection and just a short walk from the station, this old-style wood-and-concrete guesthouse has developed a loyal following among those seeking a mix of family atmosphere and backpacker self-sufficiency. The owner is a font of knowledge.

River View Guest House (Map pp76-7; ☎ 0 2234 5429; www.riverviewbkk.com; 768 Soi Phanurangsi, Th Songwat; r 250-950B; 🅿 🖵) The aptly named River View has some rooms (on upper floors) and a rooftop bar-restaurant with views you'd pay thousands for in nearby hotels. Rooms are big but simple; air-con costs more. It's in a fascinating maze of a local neighbourhood; start at the Maritime Department ferry stop or Hualamphong station, follow our map then look for the signs.

Train Inn (Map pp76-7; ☎ 08 1819 5544; www.thetrain inn.com; 428 Th Hualamphong; r 450-900B; 🅿 🖵) The clean, secure and relatively funky Train Inn is a breath of fresh air. Owner Jana maintains a young, friendly and helpful atmosphere and her 41 rooms are hostel-style compact; ask to see a few.

ourpick Shanghai Mansion (Map pp76-7; ☎ 0 2221 2121; www.shanghaimansion.com; 479 Th Yaowarat; r 3200-6400B; 🅿 🛜) The Shanghai is a genuine boutique hotel that brings a technicolour interpretation of '30s Shanghai to manic Th

Yaowarat. The 55 Chinese-style rooms have four-poster beds, brightly painted walls and as many as 10 hanging silk lights. Chinatown's – and indeed one of Bangkok's – best.

Grand China Princess (Map pp76-7; ☎ 0 2224 9977; www.grandchina.com; 215 Th Yaowarat; r 4200-4800B; ✻ ▢ ▨) A certifiable monstrosity to look at, this hotel in the heart of Chinatown is popular with groups and has nondescript but comfortable rooms buoyed by great views. Big discounts online.

Siam Square & Around

This is Bangkok's retail heart, so if hunting for bargains in half-a-dozen huge air-conditioned malls sounds like a good time to you, look no further. Several big international chains have hotels on or around Th Ploenchit and Th Withayu, and a few midrange places are dotted about. For budgeteers there is Soi Kasem San 1. This area is easily reached by Skytrain, or via a boat along Khlong Saen Saep.

BUDGET & MIDRANGE

If you prefer to spend your baht shopping than sleeping, the places along Soi Kasem San 1 are for you. This dead-end soi is off Th Phra Ram I just before the intersection with Th Phayathai, a five-minute walk to Siam Sq, MBK and Jim Thompson's House.

A-One Inn (Map pp80-1; ☎ 0 2215 3029; www.aoneinn.com; 25/13-15 Soi Kasem San 1, Th Phra Ram I; d 600-700B; ✻ ▢ ▨) This friendly family operation has 25 cosy rooms (with hot showers and TVs) that, as the cheapest place in the area, live up to its billing of value 'in the heart of town'.

Wendy House (Map pp80-1; ☎ 0 2214 1149-50; www.wendyguesthouse.com; Soi Kasem San 1; Th Phra Ram I; s/d/tw 1000/1100/1200B; ✻ ▢ ▨) Wendy is a cheery backpacker joint with 38 small but well-scrubbed rooms and tiled bathrooms; all are nonsmoking. Desk staff are sweet and the well-lit lobby is quietly social. Breakfast and wi-fi are free.

Reno Hotel (Map pp80-1; ☎ 0 2215 0026; www.renohotel.co.th; 40 Soi Kasem San 1, Th Phra Ram I; d 1200-1600B; ✻ ▢ ▨) This Vietnam War veteran has embraced the new millennium with colour and some flair, keeping some attitude with its retro features (check out the monogrammed pool) and funking up the foyer and cafe. The 70 rooms remain fairly simple, the best being those overlooking the pool. Service can be reluctant.

VIP Guest House/Golden House (Map pp80-1; ☎ 0 2252 9535-8; www.goldenhouses.net; 1025/5-9 Th Ploenchit; r from 1650B; ✻ ▨) The 27 clean, quiet and mainly bright rooms make this a good lower-midrange choice in this otherwise pricey part of town.

Luxx XL (Map pp80-1; ☎ 0 2684 1111; staywithluxx.com; 82/3 Soi Lang Suan, Lumphini; d from 2600B; ✻ ▢ ▨) Luxx XL is a new, highly designed boutique place with 50 rooms ranging from 33 sq m studios to suites three times that size. The mode is predominantly teak complemented by flat-screen TVs, DVD players and free wi-fi. The rack rates are extra-large, too – be sure to book online.

Hotel Vie (Map pp80-1; ☎ 0 2309 3939; www.viehotelbangkok.com; 39-40 Th Phayathai; r from 3500B; ✻ ▢ ▨) Billed as a 'world class design hotel', 'uniquely stylish' and 'the new benchmark of the world's hip hotels', this new tower on the block is indeed very appealing. The 154 rooms are huge and well laid out, and the service is professional. It's not quite the 'new benchmark', but it is excellent value for money (except for the 17B-a-minute in-room wi-fi).

TOP END

These and several other top-end hotels gather around this central commercial area.

Swissôtel Nai Lert Park (Map pp80-1; ☎ 0 2253 0123; www.nailertpark.swissotel.com; 2 Th Withayu (Wireless Rd); d from 5600B; ✻ ▢ ▨) An '80s matron who's had some work done, the Nai Lert can fool you into thinking she's younger than she is in all but the standard rooms, which are dated and bad value. The main attraction is really the private garden-park, where a huge tree hangs over the swimming pool. In-room internet is 749B a day.

Siam@Siam (Map pp72-3; ☎ 0 2217 3000; www.siamatsiam.com; 865 Th Phra Ram I; d from 5700B; ✻ ▢ ▨) This world of concrete, rust, copper and railway sleepers, with dashes of orange, takes industrial design to the limit. The 203 rooms occupy the 14th to 25th floors and have city views. Rates include breakfast and wi-fi internet.

Grand Hyatt Erawan (Map pp80-1; ☎ 0 2254 1234; www.bangkok.grand.hyatt.com; 494 Th Ratchadamri; d from 7700B; ✻ ▢ ▨) The Erawan's neoclassical lobby, embellished with mature tropical trees, sets the establishment tone in what is one of Bangkok's most respected hotels. The 320 rooms are relatively big and well-designed. Wi-fi is extra.

Riverside

The riverside area along Th Charoen Krung has several of Bangkok's top hotels, plus a couple of cheaper options. A combination of the Skytrain to Saphan Taksin and either a walk or ferry ride on the complimentary hotel ferries is the way to reach the top-end places. To get to Chinatown and the Ko Ratanakosin sights just take a ferry.

New Road Guesthouse (Map pp78-9; ☎ 0 2630 6994-98; www.jysk-rejsebureau.dk; 1216/1 Th Charoen Krung; dm 130-220B, d 800-1300B, f 2500B; 🅿 💻) This Danish-run guesthouse is the go-to budget lodging in this part of town, with a wide range of rooms, a social communal area and an evenings-only bar. The JYSK tourist office here offers quality tours. Good choice.

Swan Hotel (Map pp78-9; ☎ 0 2235 9271-73; www .swanhotelbkk.com; 31 Soi 36, Th Charoen Krung, Bangrak; s 800-1200B, d 900-2000B; 🅿 💻 🛜 🍽) Hidden among shade trees and quiet riverside lanes, the Swan Hotel has 67 clean, compact and well-equipped rooms with decor that is tasteful if not extravagant. They are set around a central pool and garden, which is the real attraction. It's excellent value for this area.

P&R Residence (Map pp78-9; ☎ 0 2639 6091-93; pandr residence@gmail.com; 34 Soi 30, Th Charoen Krung, Bangrak; r 900-1200B; 🅿) A comfortable, clean and very fairly priced midrange option in an atmospheric old part of town.

Millennium Hilton (Map pp72-3; ☎ 0 2442 2000; bang kok.hilton.com; 123 Th Charoen Nakhon, Klongsan; d from 6500B; 🅿 💻 🛜 🍽) Newer, cheaper and with a less formal atmosphere than its establishment neighbours on the riverside, the Hilton is nonetheless an excellent choice. Its modern Asian design is pleasing and the 543 room all have cinemascopic views. The Beach (sun beds by the pool) and ThreeSixty (jazz, penthouse views) add to the package. A private ferry connects it to River City and Saphan Thaksin Skytrain.

Mandarin Oriental (Map pp78-9; ☎ 0 2659 9000; www .mandarinoriental.com/bangkok; 48 Soi Oriental, Th Charoen Krung; r from US$420; 🅿 💻 🍽) Bangkok's answer to Raffles in Singapore or the Peninsula in Hong Kong, this classic hotel is also one of the finest in Southeast Asia. The original Author's Wing is steeped in colonial-era charm. Since those days, two vast new wings have been added, and there are several fine restaurants, including Le Normandie (p102). The hotel also has a dinner show, a luxury spa and a cooking school.

Silom & Lumphini

Although the infamous Soi Patpong is right on the doorstep, the sleaze is limited to that area and is easy enough to avoid if desired.

BUDGET & MIDRANGE

This area has a growing selection of 'boutique hostels' and plenty of good-value midrange hotels, most of which are family friendly.

Urban Age (Map pp78-9; ☎ 0 2634 2680; www.guest house-bangkok.com; 130/6 Soi 8, Th Silom; dm/d 250/800B; 🅿 💻 🛜) A New Age version of the classic Bangkok budget haunt. Rooms are small but attractive, bathrooms are shared and the women who run the place are friendly. The dorms are six storeys up, all stairs.

Lub*D (Map pp78-9; ☎ 0 2634 7999; www.lubd.com; 4 Th Decho, Th Surawong; dm/d 550/1800B; 🅿 💻 🛜) This popular 'boutique hostel' has four storeys of dorms (including a ladies-only wing) and rooms (with and without bathrooms) in industrial-chic style. It has free internet, tight security and a streetside bar-cum-lobby.

our pick Rose Hotel (Map pp78-9; ☎ 0 2266 8268-72; www.rosehotelbkk.com; 118 Th Surawong, Silom; r from 1950B; 🅿 💻 🛜 🍽) After a much-needed facelift, the veteran Rose has been reborn as one of the best-value hotels in Bangkok. Its 70 spacious, stylish rooms are complemented by a small gym, sauna and Thai restaurant in an old teak house set around an oasis-like pool.

All Seasons (Map pp72-3; ☎ 02343 6333; www.allseasons -sathorn.com; 31 Th Sathon Tai; r 2000-2500B; 🅿 💻 🛜) The 78 spacious, mostly high-ceilinged rooms in this made-over hotel have a contemporary feel and are well equipped, with desk, free wi-fi and cable broadband. Superior and deluxe rooms are best, and are excellent value. Note this is not in All Seasons Place.

La Résidence Hotel (Map pp78-9; ☎ 0 2233 3301; www.laresidencebangkok.com; 173/8-9 Th Surawong; d/ste 2400/3400B; 🅿 🛜) La Résidence is a charming boutique inn with 26 playfully and individually decorated rooms that are both casually sophisticated and fantastic value. The top-floor studio has its own garden and at 3700B is fantastic value. Service is personal and obliging.

Other options:

Take a Nap (Map pp78-9; ☎ 0 2637 0015; www .takeanaphotel.com; 920-926 Phra Ram 4; dm 380-750B, s1000B, d1300-1500B; 🅿 💻 🛜) Small rooms with pop art murals contribute to an an easygoing vibe. Some rooms can be noisy. Wi-fi is patchy.

HQ Hostel (Map pp78-9; ☎ 0 2233 1598; www.hqhostel .com; 5/3-4 Soi 3 (Soi Phiphat), Th Silom; dm 380-750B, d1500B; 🏵 🖳 🛜) Another industrial-style hostel squeezing several four- to 10-bed dorms and a few doubles into a narrow multistorey building just off Silom. Good vibe in the communal areas.

TOP END

Many of Bangkok's finest and most interesting luxury hotels are in this area.

Triple Two Silom (Map pp78-9; ☎ 0 2627 2222; www.triple twosilom.com; 222 Th Silom; r/ste 6000/7000B; 🏵 🖳 🛜) Once a bland shopping mall, this is now a classy, 75-room boutique hotel in a pleasing pan-Asian mode. Rooms are large and well kitted out with both wi-fi and ADSL internet at the desk. Book online for huge savings.

Banyan Tree Hotel (Map pp72-3; ☎ 0 2679 1200; www .banyantree.com; Thai Wah II Bldg, 21/100 Th Sathon Tai; d from 10,500B; 🏵 🖳 🛜 🛋) The hotel in this tall, wafer-thin architectural icon (it's the building with a huge hole through the middle) appeals for its luxury spa, spacious and well-designed rooms and professional management. Then, of course, there is the dreamy Moon Bar and Vertigo grill (p104) on the roof.

Sukhothai Hotel (Map pp72-3; ☎ 0 2344 8888; www.sukhothai.com; 13/3 Th Sathon Tai; r from 12,900B; 🏵 🖳 🛜 🛋) Architect Ed Tuttle's uniquely Thai modernism embraces both classic Thai features – think winged roofs, hardwood floors and gardens full of Sukhothai-style brick stupas – and a modern minimalism that is deeply satisfying. Luxury with a difference.

Other good luxury hotels in this area include the following:

Metropolitan (Map pp72-3; ☎ 0 2625 3322; www .metropolitan.como.bz; 27 Th Sathon Tai; d US$290-360; 🏵 🖳 🛋) Ubercool urban chic; excellent C'yan restaurant (p102); pricey rooms.

Le Meridien Bangkok (Map pp78-9; ☎ 0 2232 8888; www.lemeridien/bangkoksurawong; 40/5 Th Surawong; r from 6500B; 🏵 🖳 🛜 🛋) Bravely setting up shop on the doorstep of sleazy Patpong is this brand new, ultra-designed 24-storey glass tower with 282 rooms and excellent service. Wi-fi is 650B a day.

Thanon Sukhumvit

A 21st-century building boom has made Th Sukhumvit the midrange hotel centre of Bangkok. Many of the new places are boutique and design hotels, mostly in the midrange and top end, though there are a couple of decent budget places scattered about. Intense competition, especially among the newer midrange places, means big discounts can be found online.

BUDGET

HI Sukhumvit (Map pp70-1; ☎ 0 2391 9338; www.hisuk humvit.com; 23 Soi 38, Th Sukhumvit; dm 330B, s 600B, d 900-1150B; 🏵 🖳) Out east near Ekamai bus station, the clean, simple dorms and rooms, and welcoming family owners, make this budget place a real find. The breezy rooftop and nearby night food market add to the appeal.

Nana Chart Sukhumvit 25 (Map p82; ☎ 0 2259 4900; www.thailandhostel.com; Soi 25, Th Sukhumvit; dm/s/d 390/1200/1500B; 🏵 🖳) This place looks a bit institutional and service is a lesson in reluctance, but it's still fair value in this area. The large, clean rooms and dorms are well equipped (though dorms need three people for the air-con to be turned on). Prices are for nonmembers of HI, but sign up for 200B per person and save 100/300/500B on a dorm/single/double.

Suk 11 (Map p82; ☎ 0 2253 5927-28; www.suk11 .com; sub-soi off Soi 11, Th Sukhumvit; s 500-650B, d 700-900B; 🏵 🖳 🛜) Sukhumvit's predominant outpost of backpacker culture, Suk 11 creates an atmosphere of convivial postbeach chill amid the concrete jungle. The small, garden-guarded entrance opens Tardis-like to 80 upstairs rooms along a treehouse-style hallway. Rooms come with and without bathrooms.

Refill Now! (Map pp70-1; ☎ 0 2713 2044; www.refillnow .co.th; 191 Soi Pridi Banhom Yong 42, Soi 71, Th Sukhumvit; dm/s/d 525/1085/1470B; 🏵 🖳 🛋) Refill promises and delivers 'high-style low-cost', with spotless white private rooms and dorms that have flirtatious pull screens between each double-bunk; women-only dorms are also available. It's inconveniently located and pricey for shared bathrooms, but the hip-and-unpretentious vibe has made it hugely popular. It's 20 minutes from the airport by taxi, or 15 minutes by City Link to Ramkamhaeng station, then a 50B taxi. On the Skytrain, get off at Phra Kanong and take a taxi or moto taxi down Soi 71, turn right on Soi 42 and then left; or best of all come by *klong* taxi to Khlorng Tong and walk.

Atlanta Hotel (Map p82; ☎ 0 2252 1650; fax 0 2656 8123; 78 Soi 2, Th Sukhumvit; s 642-800B, d 856-1020B; 🏵 🛋) Sukhumvit's first hotel is like a time capsule of 1950s decor, with old-fashioned writing desks and a grand-entrance staircase sweeping up five floors (there's no lift). The rooms are unadorned yet functional and those on the top floor aren't good at all, but they're all fair value. Note: 'The Atlanta does not welcome sex tourists and does not try to be polite about it.'

BANGKOK

MIDRANGE

See also the boxed text, below, for more choices.

Citadines Soi 23 (Map p82; ☎ 0 2204 4777; www .citadines.com; 37 Soi 23, Th Sukhumvit; d from 1900; ☒ ☐ ☎ ☒) The best of four Citadines 'Apart-Hotels' on Sukhumvit, this one has well-designed studio (28 sq m) and one-bedroom (45 sq m) lodgings in orange and lime flavours. Expect a kitchenette you can actually cook in, a living area and bedroom (separated by a partition in the studio); families will find these unbeatable value. The rooftop pool and a hip Minibar Royal cafe-restaurant add to the package.

Le Fenix (Map p82; ☎ 0 2305 4000; www.lefenix -sukhumvit.com; 33 Soi 11, Th Sukhumvit; r 2500B; ☒ ☐ ☎) Accor's foray into the hip-design, boutique market has 147 rooms at the end of busy Soi 11 and is aimed at young, party-oriented tourists. It is reasonable value, though bear in mind that the small rooms all come with two single mattresses on one base, pushed together or separated by a few inches.

Fusion Suites (Map p82; ☎ 0 2665 2644; www.fusion bangkok.com; 143/61-62 Soi 21, Th Sukhumvit; d 2600-4600B; ☒ ☐ ☎) It's hard to classify what's going on in this seven-storey, 35-room boutique hotel. Dark rooms with polished concrete floors are embellished with Persian carpets, Indian wooden furniture, parlour-room buttoned leather couches, Buddhist iconography and a head-spinning array of high-tech gadgetry – think iPod dock, multimedia control panel, free wi-fi, DVD player and big flat-screen TV. It sounds dizzying, but seems to work. Deluxe rooms are the pick.

72 Ekamai (Map pp70-1; ☎ 0 2714 7327; www.72ekamai .com; 72 Soi 63 (Soi Ekamai), Th Sukhumvit; r from 2750B; ☒ ☐ ☎ ☒) This stylish, sophisticated, retro-sleek hotel fits in perfectly in trendy Ekamai. The studios and one-bedroom suites are huge (from 30 to 62 sq m) and mix Fab Four walking dolls with flat-screen TVs and free wi-fi. Outside, a pool is accompanied by a bar-restaurant serving Thai and Italian food, and live music Monday to Saturday.

Napa Place Bed & Breakfast (Map pp70-1; ☎ 0 2661 5525; www.napaplace.com; 11/3 Yaek 2, Soi 36, Th Sukhumvit; d 2750-4800B; ☒ ☐) Tucked away in a quiet soi seven minutes' walk from Thong Lo Skytrain, the 12-room Napa has a homely B&B atmosphere and appeals to families because it has huge rooms (36 to 67 sq m), plenty of communal space, solid security and free buffet breakfasts. Cable broadband is also free. Superb value.

Seven (Map p82; ☎ 0 2662 0951; www.sleepatseven .com; 3/15 Soi 31, Th Sukhumvit; r 3100-6000B; ☒ ☐ ☎) Six rooms, seven colours. From the designers of London's Ministry of Sound, this boutique hotel applies to its six small rooms and lobby the Thai idea that each day has its own colour (eg Monday is yellow; the king was born on a Monday, hence the yellow shirts on Mondays). Rooms are well appointed with free wi-fi and mobile phones and iPods to use during the stay. Good for hip young singles and couples.

TOP END

Eugenia (Map p82; ☎ 0 2259 9017; www.theeugenia.com; 267 Soi 31, Th Sukhumvit; r 6600-8500B; ☒ ☐ ☎ ☒) This unique 12-room boutique place is

---

MIDRANGE MANIA

Th Sukhumvit is a forest of good-value, wannabe-boutique hotels. Most have embraced the Global Zen style so popular in this range – think faux-wooden floors in smallish rooms, white linen, hanging silks, compact bathrooms with rain showers, flat-screen TVs and earthy colours. Competition is fierce, especially online. Following is a list of those we liked; all opened in 2009.

Citadines Soi 16 (Map p82; ☎ 0 2663 8777; www.citadines.com; 38 Soi 16, Th Sukhumvit; d from 1950B; ☒ ☐ ☎ ☒) Bright, well-equipped rooms and one-bed suites, a pool on the roof and efficient service. Super value.

Silq (Map p82; ☎ 0 2252 6800; www.silqbkk.com; 54 Soi 19, Th Sukhumvit; d from 2500B; ☒ ☐ ☎) Smooth operation with bright rooms that feel larger than they are; good service.

Sacha's Hotel Uno (Map p82; ☎ 0 2651 2180; www.sachas.hotel-uno.com; 28/19 Soi 19, Th Sukhumvit; d from 2500B; ☒ ☐ ☎) Well wired for business; the 'deluxe' rooms in the main building are the best value.

S Sukhumvit Suites (Map p82; ☎ 0 2661 7252; www.ssukhumvitsuites.com; 403 Th Sukhumvit; d 2600-3600B; ☒ ☐ ☎) Very near to the Skytrain; rooms here are not as sharp as others.

On8 (Map p82; ☎ 0 2254 8866; www.on8bangkok.com; 162 Th Sukhumvit; d 2900-3200B; ☒ ☐ ☎) Highly designed place in the Nana area; small comfortable rooms with no views.

AIRPORT ACCOMMODATION

If you have an early departure or late arrival it's worth considering a hotel near Suvarnabhumi International Airport. That said, taxis are cheap and early morning traffic means the trip doesn't take that long.

Refill Now! (p97) Nearest good budget option.

Kantary House Ramkamhaeng (Map pp70-1; ☎ 0 2374 5544; www.kantarygroup.com; 14 Soi 42, Th Ramkamhaeng, Bangkapi; s/tw from 2100/2250B; ❄ ❑ ☎ ☎) Big, new, well-equipped and excellent-value studios and apartments.

Novotel Suvarnabhumi Airport Hotel (☎ 0 2131 1111; www.novotel.com; r from 5000B; ❄ ❑ ☎ ☎) Boasts 600-plus luxurious rooms in the airport; big discounts online.

---

modelled on the colonial mansions of Africa and the Subcontinent. Think Livingston, Hemingway, Indian Raj and rooms packed full of art, books, antique furniture, beaten copper bathtubs and stuffed animals. Rooms aren't huge (the Siam suites are tiny), but it's the ambience you're here for. Ask about the vintage-car airport transfers.

Dream (Map p82; ☎ 0 2254 8500; www.dreambkk .com; 10 Soi 15, Th Sukhumvit; r from US$250; ❄ ❑ ☎) Call it 'boutique' or 'design', but this hotel in two adjacent buildings is a rock-star world of cream leather, mirrors, silver-and-blue motifs and, in the uberchic Flava lounge bar-cum-restaurant, a white tiger (with blue stripes). Blue is the theme, and 195 rooms are blue-lit (for deeper sleep, apparently). Seriously large discounts usually available online.

Ma Du Zi (Map p82; ☎ 0 2615 6400; www.maduzi hotel.com; cnr Th Ratchadaphisek & Sukhumvit Soi 16; r from 8900B; ❄ ❑ ☎) This 41-room luxury hotel is a masterpiece of design. The fittings, restrained but stylish decor and service are all top-notch – everything works. Rooms are huge and come with working desk ideal for business, espresso machine and excellent service. The French restaurant is also top-notch, and the whole place is very discrete; entry by reservation only.

EATING

Nowhere else is the Thai reverence for food more evident than in Bangkok. The city's characteristic body odour is a unique blend of noodle stall and car exhaust, and in certain parts of town, restaurants appear to form the majority of businesses, typically flanked by streetside hawker stalls and mobile snack vendors. To outsiders, the life of an average Bangkokian can appear to be little more than a string of meals and snacks punctuated by the odd job, not the other way around. If you can

adjust your stomach clock to fit this schedule, we're confident your stay in Bangkok will be a happy one indeed.

Despite the global infatuation with Thai food, many visitors go from one mediocre meal to another, mainly at guesthouse kitchens and tourist-oriented restaurants catering more to a Western definition of ambience than food. In order to break the bonds of so-so meals, we strongly urge you to break out of the ghetto mentality and explore the small eateries and street stalls of this great city. Virtually every regional Thai cuisine can be found in Bangkok.

The standard opening hours for restaurants here are approximately 10am to 11pm daily, but many midrange places close from 2.30pm to 6pm.

Banglamphu

Despite encompassing faràng-dominated Th Khao San, Banglamphu is home to some of the city's most legendary Thai eats. The foreign influence has resulted in an abundance of cheap Western-style and vegetarian restaurants.

Arawy Vegetarian Food (Map pp74-5; 152 Th Din So; mains 20-50B) Employing a variety of tasty meat substitutes and sticking to a repertoire of classic Thai dishes, even dedicated flesh-eaters will be happy at this tiny restaurant.

Thip Samai (Map pp74-5; ☎ 0 2221 6280; 313 Th Mahachai; mains 25-120B; ☽ dinner) Less than a five-minute túk-túk drive from Th Khao San is Thip Samai, home to the most legendary pàt tai in town. For something a bit different, try the delicate egg-wrapped version or the pàt tai fried with man gûng (shrimp fat).

Kim Leng (Map pp74-5; ☎ 0 2622 2062; 158-160 Th Tanao; mains 40-80B; ☽ lunch & dinner Mon-Sat) Kim Leng is a true Bangkok eatery and, as with much of the food of the capital, sweet intermingles with spicy. You can't go wrong with the *hòr mòk* (steamed curry) or *nám prík gà·bì* (shrimp paste dip served as a set with vegies and deep-fried fish).

Roti-Mataba (Map pp74-5; ☎ 0 2282 2119; 136 Th Phra Athit; mains 50-90B; ❤ Tue-Sun) This classic eatery serves tasty Thai-Muslim dishes such as roti, *gaang mát·sà·màn* (Muslim curry), a brilliantly sour fish curry, and *má·tà·bà* (a sort of stuffed Indian pancake). An upstairs air-conditioned dining area provides barely enough seating for its loyal fans.

Chote Chitr (Map pp74-5; ☎ 0 2221 4082; 146 Th Phraeng Phuton; mains 60-150B; ❤ lunch & dinner) Combining just six tables and two talented cooks, Chote Chitr (pronounced chôht jìt) puts out delicious, dictionary-definition central Thai fare. The second-generation restaurant is particularly renowned for its *mèe gròrp* (sweet-and-spicy crispy fried noodles), still made the old-school way.

Hemlock (Map pp74-5; ☎ 0 2282 7507; 56 Th Phra Athit; mains 64-140B; ❤ dinner Mon-Sat) Hemlock offers sublime Thai cuisine in stylish surroundings. As well as more familiar dishes such as *gaang pá·naang gài* (Penang curry with chicken), this place serves ancient and unusual dishes you won't find elsewhere, and boasts an expansive vegetarian menu.

Oh My Cod! (Map pp74-5; ☎ 0 2282 6553; 95d, Rambuttri Village Inn, Soi Rambutri; mains 70-200B) Fish and chips fried to perfection, plus all-day breakfast and a sunny courtyard dining area where parched Anglophiles can enjoy a proper cuppa.

Shoshana (Map pp74-5; ☎ 0 2282 9948; 86 Th Chakraphong; mains 90-150B) The 'I heart Shoshana' T-shirts worn by the wait staff may be a hopelessly optimistic description of employee morale, but the gut-filling chips-falafel-and-hummus plates leave nothing to be desired.

Chinatown

There are surprisingly few formal restaurants in Chinatown, and those that exist specialise in shark fin and bird's nest soup and dim sum. At night much of the neighbourhood is taken over by hawkers serving some of Bangkok's finest street food. Seafood is also great value – you can get *gûng pŏw* (grilled prawns) for a fraction of the cost of many Bangkok restaurants.

Chinatown becomes a major culinary destination during the Vegetarian Festival in September or October, when every restaurant in the area turns out special veg dishes.

During the day in nearby Phahurat, heaps of tiny shops serve Indian food including fresh chapattis and Indian-style *chai* (tea), catering to Bangkok's small Indian community.

Mangkorn Khao (Map pp76-7; cnr Th Yaowarat & Th Yaowaphanit; meals 25-40B; ❤ dinner Tue-Sun) Mangkawn Khao (White Dragon), a popular street stall, is a respected vendor of *bà·mèe*,(Chinese-style wheat noodles) and *gée·o* (wontons), both served with generous slices of bacon-like barbecued pork.

Royal India (Map pp76-7; ☎ 0 2221 6565; 392/1 Th Chakraphet; mains 100-250B; ❤ lunch & dinner) This legendary north Indian place continues to draw local foodies despite the lack of aesthetics. Try any of the delicious breads or saucy curries, and finish with a homemade Punjabi sweet.

Tang Jai Yuu (Map pp76-7; ☎ 0 2224 2167; 85-89 Th Yaowaphanit; mains 100-300B; ❤ lunch & dinner) This Chinatown legend specialises in Teo Chew and Chinese-Thai specialities with an emphasis on seafood. You can't go wrong choosing a fresh fish from the tank out front and letting the experts grill it for you.

Shangarila Restaurant (Map pp76-7; ☎ 0 2224 5933; 306 Th Yaowarat; mains 220-500B; ❤ lunch & dinner) Roast duck, red pork and freshly steamed seafood feature prominently on the menu at this popular Chinese banquet restaurant. Chow down on some dim sum at lunchtime or Peking duck in the evening.

Siam Square & Thanon Ploenchit

This shopping area has lots of fast-food-type places that cater to diners on the run, plus a handful of posher options.

Food Plus (Map pp80-1; alleyway btwn Soi 3 & Soi 4, Siam Sq; mains 30-70B; ❤ 6am-6pm) This claustrophobic alleyway is bursting with the wares of several *ráhn kôw gaang* (rice and curry stalls). You'll be hard-pressed to spend more than 100B and the flavours are unanimously authentic and delicious.

Sanguan Sri (Map pp80-1; ☎ 0 2252 7637; 59/1 Th Withayu, Th Ploenchit; mains 60-150B; ❤ lunch Mon-Sat) This restaurant can afford to remain decidedly *cheu·i* (old-fashioned) simply because of its reputation. Follow the lead of the local hungry office staff and try the excellent *gaang pèt bèt yaang* (red curry with grilled duck breast served over snowy white *kà·nŏm jeen* noodles).

Coca Suki (Map pp80-1; ☎ 0 2251 6337; 416/3-8 Th Henri Dunant, Siam Sq; mains 60-200B; ❤ 11am-11pm)

FOOD COURT FRENZY

Every Bangkok mall worth its escalators has some sort of food court. In the recent past these were the abode of working-class Thais: the food was cheap, the settings bland, and you were even expected to serve yourself. In recent years, however, food courts have moved upmarket, and the setting, cuisine and service have risen accordingly. Expect to pay 30B to 150B for a meal at one of these.

Food Loft (Map pp80-1; 7th fl, Central Chidlom, 1027 Th Ploenchit; ☺ lunch & dinner) This new concept in food court serves up fresh Thai, Chinese, Vietnamese, Indian and Italian dishes prepared by staff from some of Bangkok's better restaurants. Upon entering, you'll be given a temporary credit card and will be led to a table. You have to get up again to order, but the dishes will be brought to you. Pay on your way out.

`our pick` **Mahboonkrong Food Court** (Map pp80-1; 6th fl, Mahboonkrong (MBK) Centre, cnr Th Phra Ram I & Th Phayathai; ☺ lunch & dinner) A virtual crash-course in Thai food, MBK's food court offers tens of vendors selling eats from virtually every corner of the country and beyond. Standouts include an excellent vegetarian food stall (stall C8), whose mock-meat mushrooms almost taste better than the real thing, and a very decent Isan food vendor (C22).

Park Food Hall (Map p82; 5th fl, Emporium Shopping Centre, 622 Th Sukhumvit, cnr Soi 24; ☺ lunch & dinner) Park brings together some of the city's most-loved international food vendors. Emporium Food Hall, on the same floor, features cheaper, mostly Chinese/Thai food, and what must be the cheapest meal with a view in town. Pay by buying coupons at the windows in the entrance. Be sure to leave these in your pocket until the next day when it's too late to get a refund; it's an integral part of the food court experience.

Immensely popular with Thai families, *sù-gêe* takes the form of a bubbling hotpot of broth and the raw ingredients to dip therein. Coca is one of the oldest purveyors of the dish, and the Siam Sq branch reflects the brand's efforts to appear more modern.

Crystal Jade La Mian Xiao Long Bao (Map pp80-1; ☎ 0 2250 7990; Urban Kitchen, Basement, Erawan Bangkok, 494 Th Ploenchit; mains 160-400B; ☺ lunch & dinner) The tongue-twistingly long name of this Singaporean chain refers to the restaurant's signature wheat noodles *(la mian)* and Shanghainese steamed dumplings *(xiao long pao)*.

Gianni Ristorante (Map pp80-1; ☎ 0 2252 1619; 34/1 Soi Tonson; mains 330-990B; ☺ lunch & dinner) This classy restaurant nearly single-handedly upped the bracket for Italian dining in Bangkok. Homemade sausages, lobster-stuffed ravioli and braised lamb shank transport taste buds to the Adriatic. Wine lovers rave about the huge and unique selection.

Silom & Lumphini

The business heart of Bangkok has dozens of upmarket restaurants for business lunches and dinners, and fast-food eateries catering to hungry office workers.

Th Charoen Krung and the river end of Th Silom, near Th Charoen Krung, are good places for Indian and Muslim food.

BUDGET

Khrua Aroy Aroy (Map pp78-9; ☎ 0 2635 2365; Th Pan, Silom; mains 30-70B) Prepare yourself for the trip down south at this southern-style curry shack. The richest curries around and interesting daily specials make Khrua Aroy Aroy ('Delicious Delicious Kitchen') live up to its lofty name.

Somtam Convent (Map pp78-9; ☎ 0 2634 2839; 2/4-5 Th Convent, Silom; mains 30-120B; ☺ lunch & dinner) Northeastern-style Thai food is usually relegated to less-than-hygienic stalls perched by the side of the road with no menu or English-speaking staff in sight. A less intimidating introduction to the wonders of *lâhp, sôm·đam* (papaya salad) and other Isan delights can be had at this popular restaurant.

Home Cuisine Islamic Restaurant (Map pp78-9; ☎ 0 2234 7911; 196-198 Soi 36, Th Charoen Krung; mains 45-130B; ☺ lunch & dinner, closed lunch Sun) This bungalowlike restaurant does tasty Thai-Muslim with an endearing Indian accent. Sit out on the patio and try the simultaneously rich and sour fish curry, accompanied by a flaky roti or three.

Chennai Kitchen (Map pp78-9; ☎ 0 2234 1266; 10 Th Pan, Th Silom; mains 50-150B; ☺ lunch & dinner) This thimble-sized restaurant near the Hindu temple puts out solid southern Indian vegetarian nosh. If you're feeling indecisive, go for the banana-leaf thali that seems to incorporate just about everything in the kitchen.

HOTEL BUFFET BONANZA

Sunday brunch is a Bangkok institution, and virtually every large hotel offers decadent buffet-style spreads on weekdays as well. Reservations are generally required.

ISO (Map pp80-1; ☎ 0 2253 0123; Swissôtel Nai Lert Park, 2 Th Withayu; per min 5B; ◷ lunch Mon-Fri) Bangkok's fastest eaters have been raving about the Swissôtel Nai Lert Park's international buffet that costs 5B per minute.

Lord Jim (Map pp78-9; ☎ 0 2655 9900; Mandarin Oriental, Soi 38, Th Charoen Krung; 1500B; ◷ lunch) Even if you can't afford to stay at the Oriental, you should save up for the hotel's riverside seafood buffet.

Marriott Café (Map p82; ☎ 0 2656 7700; ground fl, JW Marriott, 4 Soi 2, Th Sukhumvit; 919B; ◷ lunch) American-style abundance fills the buffet tables with fresh oysters, seafood, pasta and international nibbles at this daily buffet.

Rang Mahal (Map p82; ☎ 0 2261 7100; 26th fl, Rembrandt Hotel, 19 Soi 20, Th Sukhumvit; 848B; ◷ lunch Sun) Couple views from this restaurant's 26th floor with an all-Indian buffet, and you have one of the most popular Sunday destinations for Bangkok's South Asian expat community.

Sunday Jazzy Brunch (Map p82; ☎ 0 2649 8353; 1st fl, Sheraton Grande Sukhumvit, 250 Th Sukhumvit; 1850B; ◷ lunch Sun) The Sheraton's Sunday brunch unites all the hotel's restaurant outlets to a soundtrack of live jazz.

---

our pick **Kalapapruek** (Map pp78-9; ☎ 0 2236 4335; 27 Th Pramuan; dishes 60-120B) This venerable Thai eatery has numerous branches and mall spin-offs around town, but we still fancy the quasi-concealed original branch. The diverse menu spans regional Thai specialities from just about every region, daily specials and, occasionally, seasonal treats as well.

Suan Lum Night Bazaar (Map pp72-3; Th Phra Ram IV; meals 60-120B; ◷ dinner) Find a seat (preferably as far from the tacky stage music as possible if you value your eardrums), order a draught hefeweizen and a dish of deep-fried soft-shell crabs, and settle down for an evening of typically tasty Thai entertainment. There is talk that Suan Lum is slotted for the wrecking ball, but until the bulldozers arrive, we're remaining sceptical.

Several cheap food markets, such as the **Soi 10 food courts** (Map pp78-9; Soi 10, Th Silom), set up along Th Silom at lunchtime to cater to the area's numerous and hungry office staff.

MIDRANGE & TOP END

Scoozi Silom (Map pp78-9; ☎ 0 2234 6999; 174 Th Surawong, Silom; mains 150-350B; ◷ lunch & dinner); Th Khao San (Map pp74-5; ☎ 0 2280 5280; 201 Soi Sunset) At this trendy pizzeria you can witness your pie being skilfully tossed and topped before being blistered in a wood-burning oven from Italy. The Scoozi empire also has a branch on Th Khao San.

Somboon Seafood (Map pp78-9; ☎ 0 2233 3104; cnr Th Surawong & Th Narathiwat Ratchanakharin; mains 150-400B; ◷ dinner) As with all good Thai seafood restaurants, your fish should be enjoyed with as many friends as you can get together, and

an immense platter of *kôw pàt ʿboo* (fried rice with crab).

Le Bouchon (Map pp78-9; ☎ 0 2234 9109; Soi Patpong 2, Th Silom; mains 180-830B; ◷ lunch & dinner) This homey bistro smack-dab in the middle of one of Bangkok's more 'colourful' districts is a capable and fun introduction to French cooking. Choose your dishes from a chalkboard menu of Gallic faves toted about by the cheery wait staff.

Blue Elephant (Map pp78-9; ☎ 0 2673 9353; 233 Th Sathon Tai, Silom; mains 180-880B; ◷ lunch & dinner) If you're going to do upmarket Thai, you can do worse than the Blue Elephant. Set in a stunning Sino-Portuguese colonial building with service fit for royalty, the restaurant also features an impressive cooking school (p88).

Cy'an (Map pp72-3; ☎ 0 2625 3333; Metropolitan Hotel, 27 Th Sathon Tai, Silom; 9-course meal 3100B) Combining vibrant Mediterranean and Moroccan flavours, a healthy obsession with the finest seafood, and a chic yet intimate atmosphere, the result is quite possibly the most faultless fine dining experience in town.

Le Normandie (Map pp78-9; ☎ 0 2236 0400; Mandarin Oriental, Soi 38, Th Charoen Krung; 4-/6-course meals 3800/4400B; ◷ lunch & dinner, closed lunch Sun) This elegant glass case overlooking Chao Phraya River is the epitome of the French culinary tradition. Michelin-starred chefs and decadent ingredients are flown in from all corners of the world, making reservations and formal attire (including jackets) a necessity.

Thanon Sukhumvit

Stretching east all the way to the city limits, Th Sukhumvit attracts equal numbers of business travellers and monkey-business travellers. This is where to go to eat foreign food, as the majority of expats and immigrants claim a Sukhumvit address.

BUDGET

Bharani Cuisine (Sansab Boat Noodle) (Map p82; ☎ 0 2664 4454; Soi 23, Th Sukhumvit; mains 35-200B; ⊙ lunch & dinner) This cozy Thai restaurant dabbles in a bit of everything, from ox tongue stew to rice fried with shrimp paste, but the real reason to come is for the rich, meaty 'boat noodles' – so called because they used be sold from boats plying the *klongs* of Ayuthaya.

Imoya (Map p82; ☎ 0 2663 5185; 3rd fl, Terminal Shop Cabin, 2/17-19 Soi 24, Th Sukhumvit; mains 40-150B; ⊙ dinner) A visit to this well-hidden Japanese restaurant, with its antique advertisements, wood panelling and wall of sake bottles, is like taking a trip in a time machine. Even the prices of the better-than-decent Eastern-style pub grub haven't caught up with modern times.

Boon Tong Kiat Singapore Hainanese Chicken Rice (Map pp70-1; ☎ 0 2390 2508; 440/5 & 396 Soi 55, Th Sukhumvit; mains 60-100B; ⊙ lunch & dinner) The unofficial national dish of Singapore is treated with holy reverence at this humble eatery. After taking in the exceedingly detailed and ambitious chicken rice manifesto written on the walls, order a plate of the restaurant's namesake and witness how a dish can be so simple, yet so delicious.

MIDRANGE

Je Ngor (Map p82; ☎ 0 2258 8008; 68/2 Soi 20, Th Sukhumvit; mains 100-500B; ⊙ lunch & dinner) Je Ngor proffers banquet-sized servings of tasty Thai-Chinese dishes in a banquetlike setting. The relatively brief seafood-heavy menu features rarities such as *sôm·dam ʼboo dorng* (papaya salad with preserved crab), and baked rice with preserved olive.

Sukhumvit Plaza (Map p82; cnr Soi 12 & Th Sukhumvit; ⊙ lunch & dinner) Known around Bangkok as 'Korean Town', this multistorey complex is the city's best destination for authentic 'Seoul' food. Local residents swear by Arirang (☎ 0 2653 0177; dishes 120B to 350B), although there are a few cheaper places in the complex as well.

Ana's Garden (Map pp70-1; ☎ 0 2391 1762; 67 Soi 55, Th Sukhumvit; mains 150-250B; ⊙ dinner) Ana's lush garden of broad-leafed palms and purring fountains will almost make you forget about the urban jungle on the other side. The spicy

yam tòo·a ploo (wing bean salad), on the other hand, will leave no doubts about which city you're in.

Little Arabia (Map p82; Soi 3/1, Th Sukhumvit) Packed full of Middle Eastern restaurants, Little Arabia provides a delicious respite from rice and noodles. *Shishah* (water pipe) smoke perfumes the air while concentrating couples devour sesame-flecked flatbread, creamy hummus and flawless falafels.

TOP END

Face (Map pp70-1; ☎ 0 2713 6048; 29 Soi 38, Th Sukhumvit; mains 280-1750B; ⊙ dinner) This handsome dining complex is essentially three very good restaurants in one: Lan Na Thai does excellent domestic (with an emphasis on regional) Thai dishes, Hazara dabbles in exotic-sounding 'North Indian frontier cuisine', and Misaki does Japanese.

our pick Bo.lan (Map p82; ☎ 0 2260 2962; 42 Soi Rongnarong Phichai Songkhram, Soi 26, Th Sukhumvit; set meals 1500B; ⊙ dinner Tue-Fri, lunch & dinner Sat & Sun) Upmarket Thai is usually not worth the price tag, but this chic new restaurant, started up by two former chefs of London's Michelin-starred Nahm, is the exception. Bo and Dylan (Bo.lan, a play on words that also means 'ancient') take a scholarly approach to Thai cuisine, and expansive set meals featuring full-flavoured regional Thai dishes are the results of this tuition.

DRINKING

Bangkok's girlie-bar scene may still be going just as strong as it has for the last 30 years, but having a good time in the city doesn't have to involve ping-pong balls or bar fines. Just like any other big international city, Bangkok's drinking and partying scene ranges from classy to trashy, and touches on just about everything in between.

Bangkok's nightlife took a serious hit in 2004 when the Thaksin administration decided that the city's residents needed to go to bed at a respectable hour. A gradual moving back to pre-2004 hours was halted by a renewed crackdown in 2008.

The good news is that everything old is new again. Th Khao San, that former outpost of foreigner frugality, has undergone something of an upmarket renaissance, and is now more popular with the locals than ever. And RCA (Royal City Avenue; Map pp70–1), a suburban nightclub zone previously associated with

BANGKOK

gum-snapping Thai teenagers, is drawing in dancers and drinkers of all ages and races.

Cheap Charlie's (Map p82; Soi 11, Th Sukhumvit) An outdoor wooden shack decorated with buffalo skulls and wagon wheels, Charlie's is refreshingly out of place on image-conscious Th Sukhumvit, and draws a staunchly foreign crowd that doesn't mind a bit of kitsch and sweat with their Singha.

Coco Walk (Map pp80-1; 87/70 Th Phayathai) This covered compound is a smorgasbord of pubs, bars and live music popular with Thai university students and other locals.

Cosmic Café (Map pp70-1; ☎ 08 1605 9469; Zone C Royal City Ave (RCA), off Th Phra Ram IX) Cosmic calls itself a cafe and looks like a live-music club but in reality is more of a bar… Despite the slight identity crisis, this is a fun place to drink, rock to live music and meet Thai-style.

Hippie de Bar (Map pp74-5; ☎ 0 2629 3508; 46 Th Khao San; ⏰ 3pm-2am) Another staunchly local holdout on Th Khao San, Hippie boasts a great soundtrack and several levels of fun, both indoor and outdoor.

Phranakorn Bar (Map pp74-5; ☎ 0 2282 7507; 58/2 Soi Damnoen Klang Tai) Students and arty types make Phranakorn Bar a home away from hovel with eclectic decor, gallery exhibits and, the real draw, a rooftop terrace with great views over old Bangkok.

River Bar Café (Map pp72-3; ☎ 0 2879 1747; 405/1 Soi Chao Phraya, Th Rachawithi) Sporting a picture-perfect riverside location, good food, and live music, River Bar Café combines all the essentials of a perfect Bangkok night out.

ourpick Sripoom Espresso Bar (Map pp74-5; ☎ 0 2281 4445; 95 Th Chakraphong) This industrial-themed hole in the wall serves some of the best mixed drinks in the area. There's a diverse soundtrack, and the room upstairs allows you to challenge your drinking mates to a game of Nintendo Wii.

Taksura (Map pp74-5; ☎ 0 2622 0708; 156/1 Th Tanao) There are no signs to lead you to this seemingly abandoned almost 100-year-old mansion in the heart of old Bangkok. Take a seat outside to soak up the breezes, and go Thai and order some spicy nibbles with your drinks.

Wong's Place (Map pp72-3; 27/3 Soi Sri Bumphen, off Soi Ngam Duphli, Th Phra Ram IV) A time warp into the backpacker world of the early 1980s, Wong's works equally well as a destination or a last resort, but don't bother knocking until midnight.

Every expat neighbourhood has an Irish-style pub where the lads can catch the game on a big-screen TV and drink Guinness amid North Atlantic temperatures. On Silom there's **Molly Malone's** (Map pp78-9; ☎ 0 2266 7160; 1/5-6 Th Convent) and on Th Sukhumvit, **Bull's Head** (Map p82; ☎ 0 2259 4444; 595/10-11 Soi 33/1, Th Sukhumvit) and **Black Swan** (Map p82; ☎ 0 2626 0257; 326/8-9 Th Sukhumvit) are two homey places to knock back a pint or three.

ENTERTAINMENT

Bangkok is a mature metropolis with lots of entertainment options for both culture vultures and cosmopolitan clubbers. To get an idea of what's going on, check out the enter-

---

SKY-HIGH SUNDOWNERS

In recent years we've seen Bangkok become the unofficial rooftop bar capital of the world. And we mean rooftop in the most literal sense – often only a waist-high barrier is all that separates you from a surreal Bangkok sunset or the Chao Phraya River, dozens of floors below. Throw in a stiff drink and a stiff breeze, and you have an experience few other cities can match.

Many of the places below also offer food, but the price tags are typically as lofty as the addresses, and we recommend a sunset cocktail or two before heading elsewhere for dinner. Also, keep in mind that most hotel-bound bars vigorously enforce the ubiquitous 'no-shorts, no-flip-flops' dress-code.

Moon Bar (Map pp72-3; ☎ 0 2679 1200; Banyan Tree Hotel, 21/100 Th Sathon Tai) Perched near the clouds on the 61st floor with the roar of Bangkok traffic far below, Moon Bar has a front-row view of virtually the entire city.

RedSky (pp80-1; ☎ 0 2100 1234; 55th fl, Centara Grand, Central World Plaza) Bangkok's most recent rooftop dining venture is probably the most upmarket of the lot, and boasts equally elite views from 55 floors up.

Roof (pp72-3; ☎ 0 2217 3070; 25th fl, Siam@Siam, 865 Th Phra Ram I) In addition to views of central Bangkok, the Roof offers a dedicated personal martini sommelier and an extensive wine and champagne list.

Sky Bar (Map pp78-9; ☎ 0 2624 9555; 63rd fl, State Tower, 1055 Th Silom) A sweeping staircase provides a Hollywood-style entrance to rooftop restaurant Sirocco. The connected Sky Bar is poised on the roof's edge and pours shots of vertigo.

tainment listings in the daily *Bangkok Post* and *Nation* newspapers, the excellent weekly listings rag *BK* (www.bkmagazine.com) and the monthly *Bangkok 101* (www.bangkok101 .com).

Discos & Nightclubs

Fickleness is the reigning characteristic of the Bangkok club scene, and venues that were pulling in thousands a night just last year are often only vague memories today. What used to be a rotating cast of hotspots has slowed to a few standards on the sois off Sukhumvit, Silom, Ratchadapisek and RCA (Royal City Ave), the city's 'entertainment zones' that qualify for the 2am closing time. You'll need an ID prove you're legal (20 years or older); they'll card even the grey hairs. Cover charges run as high as 700B and usually include a drink. Most places don't begin filling up until midnight.

To get an idea of current happenings around town, check out the entertainment press, in particular *BK* and the *Bangkok Post's* Friday supplement, *Guru*, and the *Bangkok Recorder's* online mag (www.bangkokrecorder .com).

808 (Map pp70-1; ☎ 08 4323 9998; www.808bangkok .com; Block C, Royal City Ave (RCA), off Th Phra Ram IX) Named after the infamous beat machine, this club pulls in the big-name DJs and hosts insanely crowded events. Other popular RCA clubs include Slim/Flix and Route 61.

Bed Supperclub (Map p82; ☎ 0 2651 3537; www .bedsupperclub.com; 26 Soi 11, Th Sukhumvit; cover 500-700B) Bed has basked in the limelight for quite a few years now, but has yet to lose any of its futuristic charm. Arrive at a decent hour to squeeze in dinner, or if you've only got dancing on your mind, come on Tuesday for the hugely popular hip-hop night.

Club Culture (Map pp72-3; ☎ 08 9497 8422; www.club -culture-bkk.com; Th Sri Ayutthaya; cover 250B) Housed in a unique 40-year-old Thai-style building and hosting heaps of fun local events, Culture is the Thai-est locale on Bangkok's club scene.

Hollywood (Map pp72-3; Soi 8, Th Ratchadaphisek) Like taking a time machine back to the previous century, Hollywood is a holdover from the days when a night out in Bangkok meant live stage shows, wiggling around the whisky set table, and neon, neon, neon.

Nang Len (Map pp70-1; ☎ 0 2711 6564; 217 Soi 63 (Ekamai), Th Sukhumvit) Nang Len (literally 'Sit Around') is a ridiculously popular sardine

tin of live music and uni students on popular Th Ekamai. Get in before 10pm or you're not getting in at all.

Tapas Room (Map pp78-9; ☎ 0 2234 4737; www.tapas room.net; 114/17-18 Soi 4, Th Silom; cover 100B) Although it sits staunchly at the front of Bangkok's pinkest street, this longstanding box manages to bring in just about everybody. Come Thursday to Saturday, when the combination of DJs and live percussion brings the body count to critical level.

Live Music

Bangkok's live-music scene is fairly diverse: international jazz in the high-end hotels, blues in funky closet pubs, Thai pop in shiny kitchen clubs and Thai folk in cosy art bars.

ourpick **Ad Here The 13th** (Map pp74-5; 13 Th Samsen) Featuring a soulful house band that plays at 9.30pm nightly, Ad Here is one of those places that somehow manages to be both raucous and intimate.

Brick Bar (Map pp74-5; ☎ 0 2629 4477; basement, Buddy Lodge, 265 Th Khao San; cover 100B) This subterranean live-music den features nightly performances of Teddy Ska, one of Bangkok's most energetic live bands.

Brown Sugar (Map pp72-3; ☎ 0 2250 1825; 231/19-20 Th Sarasin) Cosy Brown Sugar mingles jazz musicians and listeners into an intimate embrace of good times and good music. The pub is the longest-running spot along a strip of bars on Th Sarasin, just north of Lumphini Park.

Gazebo (Map pp74-5; ☎ 0 2629 0705; 3rd fl, 44 Th Chakraphong) Like an oasis above Th Khao San, this Middle Eastern–themed pub draws in backpackers and locals alike with fun cover bands and fez-topped *shishah* attendants. Its elevated location also appears to lend it some leniency with the city's strict closing times.

Living Room (Map p82; ☎ 0 2649 8888; Level 1, Sheraton Grande Sukhumvit, 250 Th Sukhumvit) Every night this deceptively bland hotel lounge transforms into one of the city's best venues for live jazz, attracting a dedicated following of regulars. Check ahead of time to see which sax master or hide hitter is currently in town.

Saxophone Pub (Map pp72-3; ☎ 0 2246 5472; 3/8 Th Phayathai) A live-music institution, good old Saxophone is worth the trip from your Banglamphu buffer zone for jazz, blues and beyond.

Tawan Daeng German Brewhouse (Map pp70-1; ☎ 0 2678 1114; 462/61 Th Narathiwat Ratchanakharin, cnr Th Phra Ram III) Despite its hangarlike girth, this

BANGKOK

LIFE IN BANGKOK: A STUDENT'S VIEW

'I am an undergraduate accounting major at Chulalongkorn University. I'd say school here is moderately tough, I really only study for exams. For some classes I have daily exercises, but generally I don't have homework every night.

'Judging from the lives of my exchange friends, I would say that student life in Thailand is quite different. Here, the majority of students still live with their parents. This means we're also financially dependent on our parents, as few students work. Dorms are only popular among people from other provinces, and generally, Thai universities are relatively cheap. Uniforms are another big difference, but I'm okay with wearing one because it makes preparing for school quicker. But I despise the idea of not being able to enter or contact official university centres simply because I am missing my belt.

'During the day, if we don't have class, my friends and I usually hang out in the Siam Sq/ Chitlom area. When we go out at night we usually go clubbing on Ekamai, Thong Lor or RCA, that's where most Chula kids go. We usually go out in groups – Thais are more of a collective society than other countries. Even dating is done in groups, but in the later stage, if a girl's more comfortable, she'll do the one-on-one dating thing.

'After graduation I'll still definitely stay at home, it's Thai culture. We don't usually move out until we get married. I'm happy staying at home; my parents give me more freedom as I get older, and when I get a job, I can finally earn and spend my own money!'

Peach Likhitsuwan is a 21-year-old university student living in Bangkok.

Thai version of a Bavarian beer hall manages to pack 'em in just about every night with live music and fresh beer.

Cabaret

Bangkok is famous with tourists for its *gà·teu·i* (ladyboys) cabarets that are basically lip-syncing dance routines performed by Thailand's third gender.

Calypso Cabaret (Map pp80-1; ☎ 0 2653 3960-2; 1st fl, Asia Hotel, 296 Th Phayathai; tickets 900-1550B; ☺ shows 8.15pm & 9.45pm) Bangkok's most popular *gà·teu·i* cabaret, this place is half Moulin Rouge, half Broadway show.

Mambo Cabaret (Map pp70-1; ☎ 0 2294 7381; www .mambocabaret.com; 59/28 Th Yannawa Tat Mai; tickets 800-1000B; ☺ shows 7.15pm, 8.30pm & 10pm) This is a less flashy operation than at the Calypso, but the show is still entertaining.

Cinemas

You might think that only film fanatics would want to see a movie overseas, but Bangkok's love of excess makes the glitzy cinemas worth a visit in their own right. VIP seats ring in at a mere 500B and include reclining seats (some with electric massage) and seatside service. Most cinemas are housed in the big shopping centres around Th Phra Ram I and Th Ploenchit. Hollywood blockbusters in English and Thai movies (sometimes subtitled in English) are the staples. Many of Bangkok's

cultural centres also screen movies for the benefit of expats, and various annual film festivals ensure going to the movies is a social event.

The royal anthem is played before every screening and you are expected to stand respectfully.

For movie listings and show times, see the *Bangkok Post* or www.movieseer.com; some reviews of Thai movies are available at www .thaicinema.org.

EGV (Map pp80-1; ☎ 0 2129 4635-36; www.egv.com; Siam Discovery Center, cnr Th Phra Ram I & Th Phayathai) Bangkok's poshest cinema shows international and Thai films in English.

SF Cinema City (Map pp80-1; ☎ 0 2268 8888; www .sfcinemacity.com; 7th fl, Mahboonkrong Centre, Th Phra Ram I) This place has comfortable VIP seats and shows international blockbusters in English and Thai films with English subtitles.

Lido Multiplex (Map pp80-1; ☎ 0 2251 1265; Siam Sq, Soi 2) This retro cinema shows some European and art-house films as well as US blockbusters.

SFV (Map p82; ☎ 0 2260 9333; www.sfcinemacity.com; Emporium Shopping Centre, Th Sukhumvit) This is a convenient cinema for the Sukhumvit hotels.

House (Map pp70-1; ☎ 0 2641 5177; www.houserama .com; 3rd fl, UMB Cinema, RCA, Th Phra Ram IX) Arty and avant-garde flicks are on the menu here.

Go-Go Bars

Bangkok is legendary for its go-go bars, and lonely foreign men still flock here in huge numbers to take advantage of Thailand's liberal attitude towards love for sale. For some people this is paradise, for others it's pitiable.

Most visitors to Bangkok put in an appearance at Soi Patpong 1 and Soi Patpong 2, between Th Silom and Th Surawong, for the spectacle, but few stay here for any longer than it takes to buzz around the pirated goods market and sink a cold beer at one of the circuslike 'sex' shows.

These days the serious sex business has mainly shifted to the streets off Th Sukhumvit, particularly Soi Cowboy (Soi 23) and Nana Plaza (Soi 4), and the long strip of vast 'entertainment complexes' along Th Ratchadaphisek, which cater to an Asian clientele.

Sport

MOO·AY TAI

No-holds-barred *moo·ay tai* can be seen at two boxing stadiums in central Bangkok. Admission fees vary according to seating. Ringside seats are the most expensive and where the VIPs usually sit, backpackers usually opt for the 2nd-class seats while die-hard *moo·ay tai* fans bet and cheer from the bleachers in 3rd class. At some programs a ticket Mafia tries to steer every tourist into buying an expensive ringside seat. Don't believe anyone who says that the cheap seats are sold out unless you hear it directly from a window ticket vendor.

Sanam Muay Lumpinee (Map pp72-3; ☎ 0 2252 8765; Th Phra Ram IV; admission 1000-2000B; 🕑 bouts 6.30pm Tue, Fri & Sat) This large, popular stadium is close to Lumphini Park.

Sanam Muay Ratchadamnoen (Map pp74-5; ☎ 0 2281 4205; 1 Th Ratchadamnoen Nok; admission 1000-2000B; 🕑 bouts 6pm Sun, Mon & Wed, 5pm Thu) The best-matched bouts are held here on Thursday nights.

Theatre

Several theatres around town feature both modern and classical Thai theatrical performances, including traditional *lá·kon* and *kŏhn* performances (Thai mask dramas based on stories from the Ramayana) and modern plays. The following theatres are worth a look.

Patravadi Theatre (Map pp72-3; ☎ 0 2412 7287; www .patravaditheatre.com; 69/1 Soi Wat Rakhang, Thonburi; tickets 500B; 🕑 performances vary) Patravadi is Bangkok's

sole modern-dance venue. The theatre is also the primary location for the Bangkok International Fringe Festival, held in January or February.

Sala Chalermkrung (Map pp76-7; ☎ 0 2222 0434; www .salachalermkrung.com; 66 Th Charoen Krung, Chinatown; tickets 1000-1200B; 🕑 shows 7.30pm Fri & Sat) This art deco Bangkok landmark, a former cinema dating back to 1933, is one of the few remaining places to witness *kŏhn*.

SHOPPING

Hope you brought your credit card; hardly a street corner in Bangkok is free from a vendor, hawker or impromptu stall, and the city is also home to one of the world's largest outdoor markets and Southeast Asia's largest mall. There's something here for just about everybody, and often the real and the knock-off live happily side-by-side. Although the tourist brochures tend to tout the upmarket malls, Bangkok still lags slightly behind Singapore and Hong Kong in this area, and the open-air markets are where the best deals and most original items are found.

Cameras & Electronics

Contrary to popular belief, Bangkok is not a good place to invest in electronic gadgetry. Import taxes probably make the prices more than you'd pay at home, and the selection doesn't compare with that of places such as Tokyo or Hong Kong. Where the city does excel is in the grey-market trade of pirated software and DIY recycling of computer peripherals.

Pantip Plaza (Map pp80-1; 604 Th Phetchaburi) The best place to browse for tech gear and software, Pantip has five storeys of computer stores and dozens of stalls selling computers and peripherals (both genuine and openly pirated software). IT City (☎ 0 2656 5030), on the 5th floor of the plaza, is a reliable computer megastore that is used to providing VAT refund forms for tourists.

Niks/Nava Import Export (Map pp78-9; ☎ 0 2235 2929; www.niksthailand.com; 166 Th Silom; 🕑 8.30am-5.30pm Mon-Fri) Thailand's biggest camera importer sells all types of professional equipment, including Nikon, Mamiya and Rollei. It's also the best place to bring your sick Nikon for a check-up.

Sunny Camera Mahboonkrong (Map pp80-1; ☎ 0 2620 9293; 3rd fl, Mahboonkrong Centre); Silom (Map pp78-9; ☎ 0 2236 8365; 144/23 Th Silom; 🕑 10am-6pm Mon-Sat);

Th Charoen Krung (Map pp78-9; ☎ 0 2235 2123; 1267-1267/1 Th Chareon Krung) Dedicated Nikon-heads should go directly to Sunny Camera to satisfy their gear addiction.

Clothing

Once you realise everything you packed completely disagrees with Thailand's tropical heat, you'll need Bangkok's fashion-focused stores to fill the gaps. Clothes and food are typically sold side-by-side in Thai markets, but the sizes are far too petite for most foreigners; Pratunam and Chatuchak Weekend Market (see opposite) are notable exceptions, selling sizes and styles geared towards Westerners.

Bangkok is also a popular destination to get a custom suit tailored, but unfortunately unscrupulous stitchers abound; refer to our boxed text (below) for recommended tailors.

Central World Plaza (Map pp80-1; ☎ 0 2635 1111; cnr Th Phra Ram I & Th Ratchadamri, Ploenchit) Boasting seven floors of unadulterated commercial bliss, we fancy the concrete-floored Section F that features cool domestic brands with barely pronounceable names such as Playground!, MOF, Qconceptstore and Flynow III.

Gaysorn Plaza (Map pp80-1; ☎ 0 2656 1149; cnr Th Ploenchit & Th Ratchadamri) More haute than the catwalk, Gaysorn is a manicured showroom

for vogue fashions. The 2nd-floor 'Urban Street Chic' zone highlights the handiwork of local designers.

Mahboonkrong (MBK) Centre (Map pp80-1; ☎ 0 2620 9111; cnr Th Phra Ram I & Th Phayathai) The energy of a Thai market is in full force in Bangkok's most popular mall. Just about everything is available here, and the 6th floor holds one of the city's best food courts (see p101).

Siam Discovery Center (Map pp80-1; ☎ 0 2658 1000-19; Th Phra Ram I) Clothes, furniture and books round out Siam Discovery's subdued corridors. The mall is also, somewhat incongruously, one of the best places in town to stock up on outdoor gear. Within tent-pitching distance of each other on the 3rd floor are Pro Cam-Fis, Equinox Shop and the North Face.

Gems & Jewellery

Bangkok is a major centre for the gem trade, but amateurs should tread carefully as many gem dealers are notorious for their underhanded sales techniques. Flawed or even glass gems are passed off as top quality, and many stores offer big commissions to túk-túk drivers and other touts who bring in foreigners off the street or offer phoney 'sales' to entice customers (for more information see p400). Above all, beware of the infamous gem scam, where shop-

---

BESPOKE TAILORING: READ THIS FIRST

Clothes can be custom tailored in Bangkok for prices you'd only dream of back home. But it's important to understand the process if you want to avoid disappointment. The Golden Rule is that you get what you pay for. If you sign up for a suit, two pants, two shirts and a tie, with silk sarong thrown in for US$169 (a very popular offer in Bangkok and indeed the islands), the chances are it will look and fit like a sub-US$200 wardrobe.

Have a good idea of what you want before walking into a shop. If it's a suit you're after, should it be single- or double-breasted? How many buttons? What style trousers or skirt? Alternatively, bring a favourite garment from home and have it copied. Set aside a week to get clothes tailored. Shirts and trousers can often be turned around in 48 hours or less, but most reliable tailors will ask for two to five sittings for a suit. Treat any tailor that can sew your order in less than 24 hours with extreme caution.

Reputable tailors include the following:

Forchong (Map pp70-1; ☎ 0 2258 7823; 919 Soi 49, Th Sukhumvit; 🕙 9am-9pm Mon-Sat, 9am-4pm Sun) Longstanding tailor recommended by local residents.

Marco Tailors (Map pp80-1; ☎ 0 2251 7633; 430/33 Soi 7, Siam Sq; 🕙 10am-5pm Mon-Fri) Dealing solely in men's suits, this longstanding and reliable tailor has a wide selection of banker-sensibility wools and cottons.

Nickermann's Tailor (Map p82; ☎ 0 2252 6682; basement, Landmark Hotel, 138 Th Sukhumvit; 🕙 10am-9pm) Corporate ladies rave about Nickermann's power suits that suit curves and busts, and fetching ball gowns.

Pinky Tailors (Map pp80-1; ☎ 0 2252 9680; 888/40 Mahatun Plaza Arcade, Th Ploenchit; 🕙 10am-7.30pm Mon-Sat) Suit jackets have been Mr Pinky's speciality for 35 years. Located behind the Mahatun Building.

Siam Emporium (Map p82; ☎ 0 2251 9617; Soi 8, Th Sukhumvit; 🕙 10am-8.30pm) Another reliable, low-key tailor.

keepers try to persuade customers to buy large quantities of gems to sell at a profit back home. Two longstanding and reputable shops:

Johnny's Gems (Map pp76-7; ☎ 0 2224 4065; 199 Th Fuang Nakhon; ⊙ Mon-Sat) A long-time favourite of Bangkok expats, Johnny's Gems is a reliable name in an unreliable business.

Uthai's Gems (Map pp80-1; ☎ 0 2253 8582; 28/7 Soi Ruam Rudi, Th Ploenchit; ⊙ Mon-Sat) With 40 years in the business, Uthai's fixed prices and good service, including a money-back guarantee, make him a popular choice among expats.

Handicrafts

Handicrafts are excellent value in Bangkok. The best place to start is Chatuchak Weekend Market (below), followed by the Suan Lum Night Bazaar (right), but the street markets on Th Khao San, Th Sukhumvit and Th Silom are also well stocked.

Some reliable shops selling handicrafts:

Silom Village Trade Center (Map pp78-9; ☎ 0 2234 4448; 286 Th Silom) This complex of teak houses has been converted into a handicrafts market, with some decent open-air restaurants as well as nightly dance performances.

Thai Home Industries (Map pp78-9; ☎ 0 2234 1736; 35 Soi Oriental; ⊙ Mon-Sat) A visit to this templelike building is like discovering an abandoned attic of Asian booty. Despite the odd assortment of items and lack of order (not to mention the dust), it's heaps more fun than the typically faceless Bangkok handicraft shop.

Markets

In every tourist area there are day and night markets for almost 24-hour souvenir shopping. Polite bargaining is expected and prices at Th Khao San market (pp74–5) are more reasonable than at those in Patpong, Th Silom and Th Sukhumvit.

Chatuchak Weekend Market (Jatujak Market; Map pp70-1; ☎ 0 2272 4440; Th Phahonyothin; ⊙ 9am-6pm Sat & Sun) This gigantic market is the daddy of all Thai markets, with thousands of vendors selling everything from live rabbits to hilltribe handicrafts.

Around 200,000 people mob the market every Saturday and Sunday. Pickpockets are common so keep an eye on your belongings. Many people make a day of it and eat at one of the many excellent covered restaurants and food stalls around the market. It's easy to get lost along the endless rows of covered booths, so a map can be helpful – *Nancy Chandler's*

BUYING BUDDHAS

The government of Thailand places strict controls on the export of Buddha images and antiquities. Reproductions of antiquities and modern Buddha images can be exported, but only with a permit. You should contact the **Department of Fine Arts** (Map pp72-3; ☎ 0 2221 4443) for more information. If you don't have the appropriate paperwork and a Buddha image is discovered in your bags when you are leaving the country, it will be confiscated.

Map of Bangkok has a good Chatuchak panel. The best way to get to Chatuchak is by taking the Skytrain to Mo Chit or Metro to Chatuchak Park.

Suan Lum Night Bazaar (Map pp72-3; Th Phra Ram IV; ⊙ 7pm-midnight) If you aren't in Bangkok for a weekend, Suan Lum is a fine alternative to Chatuchak. It is a huge government-sponsored night market with thousands of stalls selling slightly pricey modern Thai souvenirs, handicrafts and a few antiques.

Pak Khlong Market (Map pp76-7; off Th Maharat near Tha Saphan Phut (Memorial Bridge); ⊙ 9pm-late) Orchids might not be on your gift-giving list, but Bangkok's wholesale flower market is a fascinating destination for flora lovers and people watchers. Keep an eye out for *poo-ang mah-lai* (flower garlands) that are offered to sacred Buddhas by merit-makers.

Pratunam Market (Map pp80-1; cnr Th Phetchaburi & Th Ratchaprarop) A virtual jungle of predominantly clothing-based markets and shops that extends north from Th Phetchaburi, Pratunam is probably the cheapest place in town to update your wardrobe.

Religious Paraphernalia

Th Bamrung Muang, near Wat Suthat, is lined with dozens of emporia selling massive bronze Buddha statues and other votive objects used in Buddhist rituals. See the boxed text, above, for information about exporting these objects.

To buy traditional Buddhist amulets, visit the amulet markets (see the boxed text, p89), or try at Wat Mahathat (Map pp74–5) and Wat Ratchanatda (p84).

Scuba Diving Supplies

Most of Bangkok's dive shops are located around Th Sukhumvit.

Dive Indeed (Map p82; ☎ 0 2665 7471; www.dive
indeed.com; 14/2 Soi 21, Th Sukhumvit)
Dive Master (Map p82; ☎ 0 2259 3191; www.dive
master.net; 16 Asoke Court, Soi 23, Th Sukhumvit)
Dive Supply (Map pp72-3; ☎ 0 2354 4815; www.dive
supply.com; 457/4 Th Sri Ayuthaya)
Larry's Dive Center, Bar & Grill (Map p82; ☎ 0 2663
4563; www.larrysdive.com; 8 Soi 22, Th Sukhumvit)
Planet Scuba (Map p82; ☎ 0 2261 4412/3; www
.planetscuba.net; 666 Th Sukhumvit)

GETTING THERE & AWAY
Air

Bangkok has two main airports. Opened in
late 2006, **Suvarnabhumi International Airport**
(☎ 0 2132 1888; www2.airportthai.co.th) is the vast
glass-and-concrete construction 30km east
of central Bangkok that acts as the main international airport. Suvarnabhumi (pronounced
sù·wan·ná·poom) works fairly efficiently and
the unofficial www.bangkokairportonline
.com site has real-time details of airport arrivals and departures.

Don Muang Airport (Map pp70-1; ☎ 0 2535 1111; www2
.airportthai.co.th) is 25km north of the city centre
and after being temporarily retired it now
serves domestic routes operated by Nok
Air and One Two Go; all Air Asia and Thai
Airways flights use Suvarnabhumi.

For hotels near Suvarnabhumi, see p99.
For transport details to the airports, see p112.
Many airline offices appear on the various
Bangkok maps in this chapter.

Bus

A vast network of public and private bus
services fans out from Bangkok all over the
kingdom. Buses come in several varieties (see
p421 for details). Ordinary and air-conditioned
public buses are run by Baw Khaw Saw, the
state-run bus company, which has three terminals around Bangkok.

On all buses, and especially on buses catering to tourists and running to the beaches and
islands in the south, keep valuables on your
person or within reach; see p421 for details
of bus scams.

PRIVATE BUS
The best private buses leave from the government bus stations (see right); book tickets at
the terminals themselves, not through a travel
agent. Buses leaving from Banglamphu are
comfortable enough, but don't feel very Thai
and have a higher risk of theft.

See p421 and the regional chapters for more
information about bus travel in Thailand.

PUBLIC BUS
There are three main public bus terminals
in Bangkok:
Eastern Bus Terminal (Ekamai; Map pp70-1; ☎ infor-
mation 0 2391 8097, ☎ booking 0 2931 6846; Soi 40, Th
Sukhumvit) Buses to cities on or near the eastern gulf coast
including Pattaya, Rayong, Chanthaburi and Trat. Ekamai
Skytrain station is right by the terminal.
Northern & Northeastern Bus Terminal (Mo
Chit; Map pp70-1; ☎ northern office 0 2936 2852 ext
311/442, northeastern office 0 2936 2852 ext 611/448; Th
Phahonyothin) North of Chatuchak Park (and the Weekend Market), all buses to the north and northeast leave
from here. From Mo Chit Skytrain station you can take an
ordinary bus 3; alternatively you can catch bus 3 from Th
Phra Athit in Banglamphu.
Southern Bus Terminal (Sai Tai Mai; Map pp70-1; ☎ 0
2435 1200; cnr Th Boromaratchachonanee & Th Phuttamon-
thon 1, Chim Phli) Across Saphan Phra Pinklao in the far
western suburbs, buses leave this well-organised station for
all points south – hello Phuket, Surat Thani, Krabi, Hat Yai –
as well as Kanchanaburi and western Thailand. You can
reach the station by taxi or on bus 503 from Th Phra Athit.

Thai buses come in numerous states of speed
and comfort and the prices listed here and in
the regional chapters reflect this variety. Put
simply, the more you pay the better, faster and
more conveniently timed your bus will be.
Fares listed here are for government-run services from the Southern Bus Terminal that have
air-con. Private companies also offer more
expensive services on most of these routes:

Destination	Price	Duration	Frequency
Chumphon	209-500B	7hr	7 daily
Hat Yai	535-1070B	14hr	9 daily
Hua Hin	99-171B	3½hr	half-hourly 5am-6pm
Ko Samui	330-700B	15hr	6-8 daily
Ko Pha-Ngan	850-1400B	8-12hr	6-8 daily
Krabi	357-700B	12hr	5 daily
Nakhon Si Thammarat	350-700B	12-13hr	7 daily 6-8am & 5.30-10pm
Pattaya	100-140B	2hr	half-hourly
Phetchaburi	86-120B	2-2½hr	every 20min 9.20am-6pm
Phuket	375-1120B	13-15hr	11 daily
Ranong	220-665B	10hr	6 daily
Satun	425-1200B	14hr	6 daily
Songkhla	563-1126B	15hr	3-5 daily
Surat Thani	289-700B	11hr	7 daily
Trang	367-1050B	14hr	6 daily

Places on the eastern gulf coast are served by long-haul buses from the Eastern Bus Terminal. Rayong and Ban Phe are used for connections to Ko Samet and Chanthaburi, and Laem Ngop or Trat for Ko Chang.

Destination	Price	Duration	Frequency
Ban Phe	138-160BB	3hr	hourly 5am-8pm
Chanthaburi	146-200B	4½hr	hourly 4.30am-midnight
Pattaya	90-117B	2hr	every 40min 5am-11pm
Rayong	152B	3½hr	every 30min 5am-11.30pm
Trat	223-300B	5-6hr	hourly 5am-11.30pm

Train

Centrally located just southeast of Chinatown, historic **Hualamphong train station** (Map pp76-7; ☎ 0 2220 4334, information & advance bookings 1690; www.railway.co.th; Th Phra Ram IV) is Bangkok's – and indeed Thailand's – main rail hub and the one you'll use when heading south. Ordinary, rapid and express trains depart for Hua Hin, Surat Thani, Trang, Nakhon Si Thammarat, Hat Yai and then on to Malaysia; see p426.

Infrequent trains to western Thailand (including Kanchanaburi) leave from **Bangkok Noi train station** (Map pp72-3; Thonburi), across the river from Banglamphu.

GETTING AROUND

Bangkok may seem chaotic and impenetrable at first but, regular traffic jams notwithstanding, its transport system is not nearly as dire as legend would have it. The Skytrain, Metro, river and klong ferries and more than 70,000 clean, dirt-cheap taxis make getting to most parts of Bangkok reasonably easy. Not surprisingly, the trains and ferries are fastest during peak hours, while taxis are handy at other times. Rush hours are from about 7.30am to 10am and 5pm to 7.30pm. On Friday nights traffic in Bangkok is an immovable force of nature between about 4.30pm and 9.30pm. The urban railways are continually being extended and, with faster access to more of the city and fewer cars on the roads, the whole system should work better. Well, that's the theory, anyway.

To/From the Airport

For all the ways of getting to and from Suvarnabhumi, see the boxed text, p112. There are fewer services to Don Muang.

DON MUANG AIRPORT

Getting to/from Don Muang you can take a taxi or bus. Taking a taxi is the fastest and most comfortable option, and fares at most times will be a very reasonable 200B to 350B depending on the traffic and how far you're going. Taxis depart from outside the arrivals hall, and there is a 50B airport charge added to the meter fare, plus expressway tolls. There are no longer any express airport buses to/from Don Muang, but regular air-con buses include the following:

Bus 29 Northern Bus Terminal, Victory Monument, Siam Sq and Hualamphong train station.
Bus 510 Victory Monument, Southern Bus Terminal.
Bus 513 Th Sukhumvit, Eastern Bus Terminal.

If you plan to fly into Bangkok and take the first train south, you could take a train from Don Muang station – connected to the airport via skybridge – to Hualamphong station to meet a southbound train.

Boat

Although many of Bangkok's klong have been paved over, there is still plenty of transport along and across Chao Phraya River and up adjoining canals. See p114 for information on river ferries.

TOURIST BOATS

Several tourist boat services operate on the river, the most regular being between Phra Athit and Sathorn every 30 minutes between 9.30am and 3pm. A one-day pass for unlimited travel costs 150B. All this is best illustrated in the small, folding maps that detail routes, prices and times and are sometimes available at ferry piers – ask for one – or on boards at the piers.

There are also dozens of cross-river ferries, which charge 3B and run every few minutes until late at night.

KLONG BOATS

Canal taxi boats run along Khlong Saen Saeb (Banglamphu to Ramkhamhaeng) and are an easy way to get between Banglamphu and Jim Thompson's House, the Siam Sq shopping centres (get off at Th Hua Chang for both), and other points further east along Sukhumvit – after a mandatory change of boat at Tha Pratunam. These boats are mostly used by daily commuters and pull into the piers for just a few seconds – jump straight

BANGKOK

on or you'll be left behind. Fares range from 8B to 18B.

Car

Renting a car just to drive around Bangkok is not a good idea. Parking is impossible, traffic is frustrating, road rules can be mysterious and the alternative – taxis – are cheap and ubiquitous. But if you still want to give it a go, all the big car-hire companies have offices in Bangkok and at Suvarnabhumi airport. Rates start at around 1300B per day for a small car. A passport plus a valid licence from your home country (with English translation if necessary) or an International Driving Permit are required for all rentals. Most places can also provide drivers (from about 600B per day, 8am to 6pm), which gives local drivers a job and means you don't have to navigate, park

or deal with overzealous police. Child seats cost an extra 200B a day.

Reliable car-rental companies:

Avis (Map pp80-1; ☎ 0 2255 5300; www.avisthailand .com; 2/12 Th Withayu)

Budget (Map pp70-1; ☎ 0 2203 9200, 0 2203 0225; www.budget.co.th; 19/23 Bldg A, Royal City Ave, Th Phetburi Tat Mai)

Hertz (Map pp80-1; ☎ 0 2654 1105; www.hertz.com; M Thai Tower, All Seasons Pl, 87 Th Withayu)

Phetburi Car Rent (Map pp70-1; ☎ 0 2318 8888; 2371 Th Petchaburi)

Motorcycle Taxi

Motorcycle taxis serve two purposes in Bangkok. Most commonly and popularly they form part of the public transport network, running from the corner of a main thoroughfare, such as Th Sukhumvit, to the far ends

---

GETTING TO & FROM SUVARNABHUMI

Airport Bus

Airport Express runs four useful routes between Suvarnabhumi and Bangkok city. They operate from 5am to midnight (closer to 7am coming from the city) for a flat 150B fare, meaning a taxi will be a comparable price if there are two people heading to central Bangkok, but more expensive if you're going somewhere further, such as Banglamphu. The Airport Express counter is near entrance 8 on level 1. Routes stop at Skytrain stations, major hotels and other landmarks.

AE-1 to Silom (by expressway) Via Pratunam, Central World, Ratchadamri Skytrain, Lumphini Park, Saladaeng Skytrain, Patpong, Plaza Hotel and others.

AE-2 to Banglamphu (by expressway) Via Th Phetchaburi Soi 30, Amari Watergate Hotel, Democracy Monument, Royal Hotel, Th Phra Athit, Th Phra Sumen, Th Khao San.

AE-3 to Sukhumvit Soi 52, Eastern (Ekamai) Bus Terminal, Thong Lo Skytrain, Sukhumvit Sois 38, 34, 24, 20, 18, Asoke Skytrain/Sukhumvit MRT, Sukhumvit Sois 10 and 6, Central Chidlom, Central World, Soi Nana.

AE-4 to Hualamphong train station Via Victory Monument Skytrain, Phayathai Skytrain, Siam Skytrain, Siam Sq, MBK, Chulalongkorn University.

Local Buses

If you have more time and less money, local buses are the cheapest way into town short of hitching (and no-one hitches). Like the intercity buses that run to Pattaya and further, all local buses depart from the **Public Transportation Center** (☎ 0 2132 1888), which you get to via free shuttle buses that leave 24 hours from level 1 at the airport.

Several air-con local buses serve Suvarnabhumi for fares rising to a maximum of 35B. Departures are every 15 or 20 minutes unless stated. Most useful:

Bus 551 Siam Paragon (☺ 24hr) Via Victory Monument. This is the cheapest way to Th Khao San and Banglamphu; get off at Victory Monument, take bus 59, 503 or 509 and get out at Democracy Monument.

Bus 552 Klong Toei (☺ 24hr) Via Sukumvit 101 and On Nut Skytrain.

Buses 554 & 555 Don Muang Airport (☺ 5am-midnight)

Bus 556 Southern Bus Terminal (☺ hourly 5am-10pm) Via Democracy Monument and Thammasat University.

Intercity buses to places including Pattaya (106B), Rayong (155B) and Trat (248B) also stop at least six times daily at the Public Transportation Centre. Buses to Laem Ngob (250B), for the Ko Chang ferry, depart between 7.10am and 10am. Some Pattaya buses leave directly from airport level 1.

of sois that run off that thoroughfare. Riders wear coloured, numbered vests and gather at either end of their soi, usually charging 10B to 20B for the trip (without a helmet unless you ask).

Their other purpose is as a means of beating the traffic. You tell your rider where you want to go, negotiate a price (from 20B for a short trip up to about 150B going across town), strap on the helmet (they will insist on longer trips) and say a prayer to whichever god you're into. Drivers range from responsible to kamikaze, but the average trip involves some time on the wrong side of the road and several near-death experiences. It's the sort of white-knuckle ride you'd pay good money for at Disneyland, but is all in a day's work for these riders. Comfort yourself with the knowledge that there are good hospitals nearby.

Public Transport

BUS

Bangkok's public buses are a cheap if not always comfortable way to get around the city. They are run by the **Bangkok Mass Transit Authority** (☎ 0 2246 4262; www.bmta.co.th), which has a website with detailed information on bus routes. Air-con fares typically start at 10B or 12B and increase depending on distance. Fares for ordinary (fan-con) buses start at 7B or 8B. Most of the bus lines run between 5am and 10pm or 11pm, except for the 'all-night' buses, which run from 3am or 4am to midmorning.

Bangkok Bus Map, by Roadway, available at Asia Books (p66), is the most up-to-date route map available. Have small change and be careful with your belongings when riding on Bangkok buses. Bag-slashers and pickpockets

Minivan

If you are heading to the airport from Banglamphu, the hotels and guesthouses can book you on air-con minivans. These pick up from hotels and guesthouses and cost about 140B per person.

Suvarnabhumi Airport Rail Link (SARL)

After years of delays, the new SARL (aka City Link) began operation in 2010 from the bottom floor of the airport to a huge new City Air Terminal in central Bangkok, near Soi Asoke (Sukhumvit Soi 21) and Th Phetchaburi. A 'Skytrain' by any other name, it includes an express service (the Pink Line) that takes 15 minutes and costs 150B one-way, and a local service (the Red Line) via five other stations taking about 27 minutes and costing a very reasonable 45B. The express service travels the 28.6km route at 160km/h. Both lines connect to the MRT Blue Line at Phetchaburi and the slower red line continues to Phaya Thai BTS station.

How useful this service is depends on whether you're travelling alone and how far your hotel is from the City Air Terminal. Except during the worst traffic (hello Friday evenings!) a taxi covers the same trip in about 35 minutes for about 250B.

At thet tome of writing, an extremely useful in-town check-in service, like the one in Hong Kong, was scheduled to start operating later in 2010.

Taxi & Limousine

Ignore the annoying touts and all the yellow signs pointing you to 'limousines' (actually cars and 4WDs costing from 600B to 3500B depending on the vehicle and distance) and head outside to the fast-moving public taxi queues outside doors 3 and 10. Cabs booked through these desks should always use their meter, but they often try their luck quoting you an inflated fare; insist by saying 'meter, please'. You must also pay a 50B official airport surcharge and reimburse drivers for any toll charges (up to 60B); drivers will usually ask your permission to use the tollway. Depending on traffic, a taxi to Asoke should cost 200B to 250B, Silom 300B to 350B and Banglamphu 350B to 425B. Fares are per vehicle, not per person. Break big notes before you leave the airport to avoid a 'no change' situation.

Charter taxis also run to Pattaya (1300B), Chonburi (1000B) and Trat (3500B), among many others.

are common on ordinary buses, particularly around Hualamphong train station.

METRO (SUBWAY)

Bangkok's first underground railway line is operated by the **Metropolitan Rapid Transit Authority** (MRTA; www.mrta.co.th) and is known locally as *rót fai dâi din* or 'Metro' – no one understands 'subway'. Metro plans see a series of lines running more than 150km, but for now the 20km Blue Line runs from Hualamphong train station north to Bang Sue and features 18 stations. Fares cost 15B to 40B; child and concession fares can be bought at ticket windows. Trains run every seven minutes from 6am to midnight, more frequently between 6am and 9am and from 4.30pm to 7.30pm.

The Metro is more useful to residents than visitors, unless you're staying in the lower Sukhumvit area. Useful stations (from north to south) include Kamphaeng Phet and Bang Sue for Chatuchak Weekend Market; Thailand Cultural Centre; Sukhumvit, where it links to Asoke Skytrain station; Khlong Toei for the market; Lumphini Park; Silom (with access to Sala Daeng Skytrain station); and Hualamphong train station and Chinatown at its southern end.

RIVER FERRIES

The **Chao Phraya Express Boat Co** (☎ 0 2623 6001; www.chaophrayaboat.co.th) operates the main ferry service along Chao Phraya. The central pier is known as Sathorn, Saphan Taksin or sometimes Central Pier, and connects to the Skytrain's Saphan Taksin station. Each pier is numbered from Sathorn, and ferries run four stops south to Wat Ratchasingkhon (S4), though tourists rarely use these. Much more useful are the services running to and from Nonthaburi (N30) and Pak Kred (N33) in northern Bangkok; the maps in this book show the piers and their numbers. Fares are cheap and differ by distance and service from 9B to 30B. There are four different services, differentiated by the colour of the flags on their roofs. To avoid an unwanted trip halfway to Nonthaburi be sure to keep an eye on those flags.

Green-Yellow Express Nonthaburi express, stopping N3, N5, N10, N12, N15, N22, N24, N30, N32, N33. Every 15 minutes 6.15am to 8.05am, and every 20 minutes 4.05pm to 6.05pm.

Local Line (no flag) The all-stops service, operating every 20 minutes 6.20am to 8.20am and 3pm to 5.30pm.

Orange Express Stops at S3, Sathorn (Central), N1, N3, N4, N5, N6, N8, N9, N10, N12, N13, N15, N18, N21, N22, N24, N30. The most common service, departing every 10 to 20 minutes until 7pm. All journeys 13B.

Yellow Express Stops at S4, Sathorn (Central), N3, N5, N10, N12, N15, N22, N24, N30. Departing every five to 20 minutes depending on the time of day. Last boat 8pm.

SKYTRAIN (BTS)

The **BTS Skytrain** (☎ tourist information 0 2617 7340; www.bts.co.th) allows you to soar above Bangkok's legendary traffic jams in air-con comfort. Known by locals as 'BTS' or *rót fai fáh* (literally 'sky train'), services are fast, efficient and relatively cheap, although rush hour can be a squeeze. Fares range from 15B to 40B, and trains run from 6am to midnight. Ticket machines (when they're working) accept coins and notes, or pick up change at the staffed kiosks. One-day (120B) passes are available, but the rechargeable cards (130B, with 100B travel and 30B card deposit) are more flexible. There are two Skytrain lines, which are well marked on free tourist maps available at most stations.

Si Lom Line

Starting at National Stadium on Th Phra Ram I in central Bangkok, it passes the Siam interchange station and bends around via the eastern section of Th Silom and western end of Th Sathon, crosses Mae Nam Chao Phraya at Saphan Taksin and (since late 2009) finishes at Wongwian Yai. The Saphan Taksin station, on the river near the intersection of Th Charoen Krung and Th Sathon, is super convenient because it connects to the Chao Phraya river ferries (left).

Sukhumvit Line

At the time of writing the southern end of this line was at On Nut. Five new stations were being built and at sometime in 2011 the Sukhumvit Line should extend all the way to Bearing, at distant Soi 107 of Th Sukhumvit. In the meantime it runs north and then west from On Nut along Th Sukhumvit, connecting to the Metro at Asoke. It continues into the shopping and commercial district and the main interchange station at Siam, where it meets the Silom BTS line. From here it turns north up to Mo Chit, near Chatuchak Weekend Market.

Taxi

Bangkok's brightly coloured taxis are some of the best-value cabs on earth. Most are new, air-conditioned Toyota Corollas and have working seatbelts in the front seat, though less often in the back. You can flag them down almost anywhere in central Bangkok. The meter charge is 35B for the first 2km, then 4.50B for each of the next 10km, 5B for each kilometre from 13km to 20km and 5.50B per kilometre for any distance greater than 20km, plus a small standing charge in slow traffic. Freeway tolls – 25B to 70B depending on where you start – must be paid by the passenger.

Taxi Radio (☎ 1681; www.taxiradio.co.th) and other 24-hour 'phone-a-cab' services are available for 20B above the metered fare.

During the morning and afternoon rush hours taxis might refuse to go to certain destinations or, in some touristy areas, refuse to use the meter; if this happens, just try another cab. You can hire a taxi all day for 1500B to 2000B, depending on how much driving is involved. Taxis can also be hired for trips to Pattaya (1500B), Ayuthaya (800B), Hua Hin (2300B) and Phetchaburi (1700B), among others; see www.taxiradio.co.th for fares. If you leave something in a taxi your best chance of getting it back (still pretty slim) is to call ☎ 1644.

Túk-Túk

Bangkok's iconic túk-túk (like motorised rickshaws) are used by Thais for short hops not worth paying the taxi flag fall for. For foreigners, however, these emphysema-inducing machines are part of the Bangkok experience, so despite the fact they overcharge outrageously and you can't see anything due to the low roof, pretty much everyone takes a túk-túk at least once. It's worth knowing, however, that túk-túk are notorious for taking little 'detours' to commission-paying gem and silk shops and massage parlours. En route to 'special' temples, you'll meet 'helpful' locals who will steer you to even more rip-off opportunities. See p401 for more on túk-túk scams, and ignore anyone offering too-good-to-be-true 10B trips.

The vast majority of túk-túk drivers ask too much from tourists (expat faràng never use them). Expect to be quoted a 100B fare, if not more, for even the shortest trip. Try bargaining them down to about 40B for a short trip, preferably at night when the pollution (hopefully) won't be quite so bad. Once you've done it, you'll find taxis are cheaper, cleaner, cooler and quieter.

Eastern Gulf Coast

This is Thailand's wild coast, from its labyrinthine rainforests and uncrowded beaches to infamous Pattaya's high-octane debauchery. If you want glamour and daydreams, head to the Andaman or southern gulf coasts; the eastern gulf is for travellers who want a peek at the real world and to experience some action alongside their beach.

Start in little-visited Ko Si Chang, the closest island to Bangkok, for a lazy stay in a Thai fishing village bobbing in a sea of supertankers. Only a few hours down the road is Pattaya, Ko Si Chang's antitheses, where any hint of wholesome Thailand has been overrun by concrete, tour buses and teetering high heels. There's a feast of sights, safaris and adrenaline-packed sports during the day, while nights offer every variation of neon-lit kinky fantasy. When you want to relax again head to the powder-white sands of ex-pat favourite Ko Samet to party all night at a techno-thumping beach shack or catch up on your reading on a secluded beach.

But the undisputed jewel in the eastern gulf's crown is the Ko Chang Archipelago, where jungle and beach compete for your attention. Trek through the vast rainforests on Ko Chang then island-hop to the friendly sands of Ko Mak or the decadent isolated coves of Ko Kood. For even more isolation, a handful of other spectacular islands quietly wait to be explored. From here you can continue east along pristine coastline to the Cambodian border.

HIGHLIGHTS

- Trekking through buzzing rainforest to find hidden waterfalls and giant spiders in the mountains of **Ko Chang** (p150)

- Gazing across dazzling sands and emerald waters with nary a tourist in sight from your bungalow on **Ko Kood** (p160)

- Watching a transvestite cabaret before hitting the streets of ludicrously wild **Pattaya** (p120) at night

- Beach-hopping by bike on low-lying **Ko Mak** (p162) then popping on a mask and snorkel to cool off

- Not feeling like a tourist while eating roadside noodles in an authentic fishing village on **Ko Si Chang** (p119)

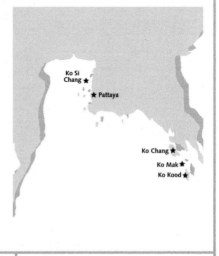

- DRY SEASON: NOVEMBER-APRIL | - WET SEASON: MAY-OCTOBER

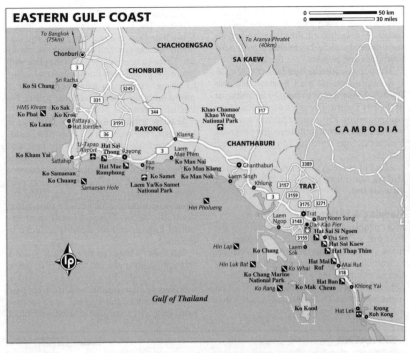

EASTERN GULF COAST

Climate

The eastern gulf coast experiences three seasons, or rather, three variations of hot. November to February are milder months with little rain. The hottest months are March to May, while in mid-May, the temperatures drop a smidgen to welcome the monsoons that last till October. In the height of the monsoon season, the easternmost islands are usually not accessible due to choppy waves.

National Parks

Almost every island in the region is in a national park. Ko Samet (p139) and the surrounding islands belong to Laem Ya/Ko Samet National Park, and further east Ko Chang and its siblings, Ko Mak and Ko Kood, fall within Ko Chang Marine National Park (p148), which also includes many small areas.

SRI RACHA
ศรีราชา
pop 141,400

Sri Racha (also called Si Racha) is easy to pass through without a glance but lingering an hour or so is recommended. Two hours

from Bangkok by bus (or 40 minutes from Suvarnabhumi International Airport), most of the town is dull and modern but behind the concrete hides a veritable floating city on the waterfront – a maze of wooden piers and interconnected stilt buildings housing hotels, restaurants and markets. Though ships waiting to dock at nearby Laem Chabang port stud the horizon, they're far enough away not to spoil the illusion of days gone by.

Information

Ice Net (Th Jermjompol; internet per hr 20B; ⏱ 24hr) A short walk from the pier.
Krung Thai Bank (cnr Th Surasak 1 & Th Jermjompol)
Post office (Th Jermjompol)
Samitivej Sriracha Hospital (☎ 0 3832 4111; Th Jermjompol soi 8)

Sights & Activities

Weeknights at around 6pm a massive group of local aerobicisers gather at the **Health Park** near the jetty to work out as one giant colour-coordinated unit – it's surreal. Other than this and the wobbly waterfront piers, Sri Racha's only other downtown attraction is **Ko Loi**, a small rocky island that is connected to the mainland by a long jetty. A **Chinese Buddhist temple** (☉ dawn-dusk) inhabits the island and is surrounded by a low-key festival atmosphere, food stalls and ponds of sea turtles.

The popular **Sriracha Tiger Zoo** (☎ 0 3829 6556-8; www.tigerzoo.com; 341 Moo 3, Nongkham; adult/child 250/150B; ☉ 8am-6pm) sits about 9km southeast of the city centre. The main attraction is the compound of 250 tigers that are involved with the zoo's remarkable breeding program. Visitors can get up close and personal with the cubs.

Most of the zoo's visitors stay in nearby Pattaya and make the short 20km journey on a day trip.

Sleeping & Eating

Most people stay at Pattaya 27km down the road but Sri Racha has some interesting options. As you'd expect, the town specialises in seafood and several memorable places are tucked within the maze of dangling sea shacks. Other cheap eats are available at the sprawling night market on Th Sri Racha Nakorn 3 that kicks off around 5pm.

Sriwichai Hotel (☎ 0 3832 5024; 37 Th Cheimjomphom; r 250-400B) The best of the stilt village hotels, Sriwichai offers a huge range of rustic, authentic shacks perched over swishing murky sea. There's a near-village feel to the place with its creaky, potted-fern-lined walkways leading to sitting areas and a never-ending slew of rooms with hard beds and squat toilets. No English is spoken.

Seaview Sriratcha Hotel (☎ 0 3831 9000; Th Jermjompol; r 990-1900B; ❄ ☏) This new, modern waterfront place is a comfy nest and sea-facing rooms offer views over the eerie juxtaposition of sea shanties next to a modern concrete sprawl; top-floor rooms offer even more spectacular vistas out to sea. Avoid the street-side rooms, which can be noisy from the traffic below. The perky staff speak excellent English and breakfast is included in the price.

Tam Show (Th Jermjompol; dishes 80-200B; ☉ lunch & dinner; ☏) A great place to watch the sunset as well as the Health Park aerobics aficionados, this place is a five-minute walk from the pier. Try the excellent and original *sôm·dam* fruit salad (a spicy green papaya salad with other

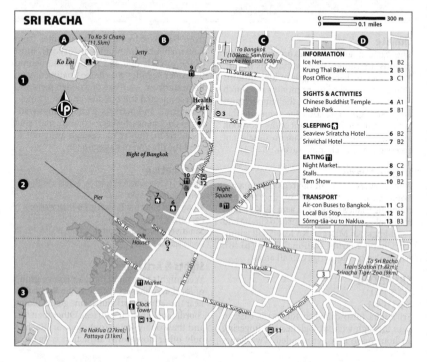

SRI RACHA

0 — 300 m
0 — 0.1 miles

To Ko Si Chang (11.5km)

Jetty

Ko Loi ■ 4

Th Surasak 2

To Bangkok (100km); Samitivej Sriracha Hospital (500m)

Health Park

⊛ 3

Soi 1

Bight of Bangkok

Pier

10 ⊠ 12

7 ⊠ 6

Night Square

8 ⊞

Th Sri Racha Nakorn 3

Soi 16 Soi 10

Stilt Houses ⊠ 2

Soi 18

Th Tessaban 1

Th Tessaban 3

Th Surasak 1

Th Surasak Sunguan

Th Sukhumvit

To Sri Racha Train Station (1.8km); Sriracha Tiger Zoo (9km)

3

■ Market

■ Clock Tower

⊟ 13

To Naklua (27km); Pattaya (31km)

⊟ 11

mixed fruit topped with peanuts) or choose from a wide selection of Thai favourites.

Getting There & Away

Buses bound for Sri Racha (ordinary/air-con 84/106B, two hours) leave every half-hour from Ekamai in Bangkok and five times per day from the bus station at Suvarnabhumi International Airport (76B, 40 minutes). Ordinary direct buses stop near the pier for Ko Si Chang, while through buses and air-con buses stop along Th Sukhumvit (Hwy 3). Túk-túk (pronounced đúk đúk; motorised vehicle) can take you to the pier for 60B.

Sŏrng·tăa·ou (also spelt săwngthăew; small pickup trucks) bound for Naklua (north Pattaya; 40B, 30 minutes) leave from near the clock tower in Sri Racha throughout the day. Once you're in Naklua, you can easily catch another sŏrng·tăa·ou to central Pattaya for 10B to 15B. You can also flag down local buses (30B, 30 minutes) that run to Pattaya along Th Sukhumvit.

KO SI CHANG

เกาะสีชัง

pop 4500

There are a few OK beaches on Ko Si Chang but it's really not a beach destination. Take the wobbly wooden boat from Sri Racha with a crowd of locals who juggle bags of groceries, sleeping babies and scuttling toddlers. Hardly anyone gives you a glance when you arrive at Ko Si Chang's port; find a túk-túk and buzz through the bustling fishing village, dodging dogs and breathing in scents of fish sauce and seafood. Then just about everyone in town tries to rent you a motorbike, probably so you'll leave them to their fishing industry and discover the island's simple pleasures on your own.

The island's sole settlement faces the mainland and doubles as the ferry terminus. Bumpy roads link the village with all the other sights.

Kasikornbank (99/12 Th Atsadang) Has an ATM and currency-exchange facilities.

Tourist Services Centre (☎ 0 3821 6201; Th Atsadang; ☙ 9am-4.30pm Mon-Fri) Opposite Sichang Palace hotel. Ask for the *Island Welcome* brochure.

Sights & Activities

Hat Tha Wang Palace (Th Chakra Pong; admission free; ☙ 9am-5pm) at the western end of the island (2km from the pier) is the island's main draw. The residence was used by a few generations of Thai kings, particularly Rama V (King Chulalongkorn). A palace was under construction but was abandoned when the French briefly occupied the island in 1893. The main throne hall – a magnificent golden teak structure called Vimanmek – was moved to Bangkok in 1910 (see p84).

Today several restored buildings are scattered over manicured gardens and house a few interesting exhibits. You could easily spend two hours here, exploring the grounds up the hill to the old white **Pra Chedi of Wat Asadanghainmit** shaded by a sacred Bodhi tree (taken as a sapling from Buddha Gaya, India) or even further up to the **Khaw Noi View Point** for views over the freighter-dotted sea.

Ko Si Chang's most imposing sight is the ornate **San Jao Phaw Khao Yai Chinese Temple** (☙ dawn-dusk). During Chinese New Year in February, the island is overrun with Chinese visitors from the mainland. This is one of Thailand's most interesting Chinese temples, with shrine caves, multiple levels and a good view of the ocean. It's east of the town, high on a hill overlooking the sea.

Hat Tham Phang (Fallen Cave Beach) in the southwest has simple facilities with deckchair and umbrella rental. A beach area along the coast by Hat Tha Wang Palace (left) is popular with locals, and the island's best swimming is at **Hat Sai Kaew** to the south. Several locals run **snorkelling trips** to Koh Khaang Khao (Bat Island) on Ko Si Chang's southern tip. A boat for 10 people will cost around 2500B.

Recharge at **Si Chang Healing House** (☎ 0 3821 6467; 167 Mu 3 Th Makhaam Thaew; ☙ 9am-6pm Thu-Tue), which offers massage and beauty treatments (400B to 800B) in a garden labyrinth; it's about 50m along the road towards town from Pan & David Restaurant. The lovely owner also has a Zen-like, rustic room for rent here for 300B.

A Buddhist meditation hermitage, **Tham Yai Phrik Vipassana Centre** (☎ 0 3821 6104; ☙ dawn-dusk) surrounds a series of meditation caves filled with Buddha images and swooping bats. Monks from all over Thailand come here to take advantage of the peaceful environment for meditation and faràng (foreigners of European descent) are also welcome; just be sure to phone ahead and be prepared to follow the monastery's strict code of conduct. Whether you visit for an hour or a month, please leave an appropriate donation.

Sleeping & Eating

Most places to stay have food available for guests and nonguests; there are plenty of food stalls in the village serving cheap local grub.

Tiewpai Bungalows (☎ 08 1947 0573; www.tiewpai .com; Th Atsadang; r 200-800B; ⌨) Set back in a quiet glade of trees, this central place might not be the prettiest but it offers the best tourist support in town. The cheapest rooms have shared bathrooms while slightly more expensive rooms have pleasant sitting areas. There's no hot water but everything is clean.

Sichang View Resort (☎ 0 3821 6210; r 600-1400B; ✕ ⌨) You'll need transport to make this your island base, but the plain rooms here are in a fabulously flowery garden perched at the edge of a cliff-side public view point and fishing spot. To get here, follow the road up the hill past the Chinese temple. After 1.5km Sichang View Resort is on your right.

Sichang Palace (☎ 0 3821 6276; www.sichangpalace .com; Th Atsadang 81; r 1200-1400B; ✕ ⌨) The exterior of this place looks like a pink-and-cream birthday cake – inside are comfy tiled rooms all with mini balconies. 'Sea view' rooms offer great panoramas over the boat-clogged pier but you'll get to glimpse the sea even from the standard rooms. Ask for a discount in the low season. The swimming pool is nothing fancy but offers a cool dip.

Pan & David Restaurant (☎ 0 3821 6629; 167 Moo 3, Th Makhaam Thaew; dishes 100-400B; ⏱ breakfast, lunch & dinner Thu-Tue) With free-range chicken, homemade ice cream (try the maple-pecan), French-pressed coffee, a wine list, and excellent Thai dishes, the menu can't go wrong.

Getting There & Around

Boats between Ko Si Chang (60B, 40 minutes) and Sri Racha depart hourly between 7am and 8pm. Once you are on the island, motorcycle taxis can take you anywhere for 20B to 40B. Island tours in a four-seater túk-túk cost 250B for the day. Motorbikes are available to rent from Tiewpai-Park Resort for 250B per day and you can also rent bicycles for around 120B to 150B per day at several places along Th Atsadang.

PATTAYA
พัทยา
pop 117,000

Imagine a several-blocks-long red-light district, add carnival colours, a bright beach and bus-loads of package tourists and you have Pattaya.

PR pundits are working overtime to erase the city's sordid history of slow boats and fast women, but the reputation is firmly implanted and, let's be honest, sex is the motor of this town and it's here to stay. With this thought firmly in mind, a visit to the Disneyland of hedonism can be pretty entertaining, even if you're just showing up as a spectator.

The clientele is decidedly international. On Walking St you can start at an 'Espace Francaphone' cafe then head to the dive shop next door where the sign is entirely in Russian. Eat an authentic Italian pizza, wash it down with a beer at a German or Irish pub then head over to a bar that promises European girls and Chinese food. Indian tailors beckon you in as you brush shoulders with Middle Easterners holding hands with Thai girls. Unlike saucier Patong, Pattaya's southern sister in sin, the visitors here are decidedly older; think over 45 and looking for love on the rebound. In this sense Pattaya has a melancholy that's hard not to notice in the lone, bloated male faces pickled in beer and pretty Thai smiles.

The surprise to Pattaya is that if you wake up early enough there are activities galore to redress your daytime/night-time balance. Hit the dive shops to explore the city's offshore reefs and wrecks, or check out any of the very interesting sights surrounding the city.

Once a lonely fishing village, Pattaya started to morph into its present state during the Vietnam War, when American GIs were looking for female respite on their break from war. Since then, this tourist metropolis has become a living testament to unchecked development.

Orientation
PATTAYA

Curving around Ao Pattaya (Pattaya Bay), Hat Pattaya (Pattaya Beach) is the city's powdery yet skinny showcase stretch of sand. Th Hat Pattaya (known colloquially as Beach Rd) runs along the waterfront and is lined with hotels, shopping centres and go-go bars. At the southern end of Th Hat Pattaya, 'Walking St' is a semi-pedestrianised, in-your-face-sex-for-sale string of restaurants and nightclubs. The alleyways running between Th Hat Pattaya and Th Pattaya 2 each have their own character: Soi 3 is the heart of the gay area, dubbed 'Boyztown,' while Soi 6, also called 'Soi Sex',

(Continued on page 129)

THREE DIMENSIONS OF PARADISE

You'd be excused for being suspicious of terms such as 'beach paradise', 'outrageous sunset' and 'underwater wonder' as being tourist-brochure puffery. But when it comes to the islands and beaches of Thailand, the superlatives are justified. Swaying palms fringing sun-kissed stretches of white sand are at the very heart of our idea of tropical paradise, yet this is only one dimension. Roll out of the hammock and you'll discover national parks protecting everything from enormous flowers to gigantic whale sharks. Or sit down to a local dinner for a chance to redefine Thai spice. Best of all, the experience almost always outdoes the adjectives.

AUSTIN BUSH

Beach Paradises

It isn't fair really – there are over 200 countries around the globe and Thailand has managed to snag a disproportionate number of the world's top beaches. These aren't your average stretches of sand; you're about to uncover perfect powder-soft dunes and dramatic limestone crags that pop straight out of impossibly clear waters. Robinson Crusoe, eat your heart out!

① Hat Phra Nang

This beauty (p347) in Railay will shock and awe. Perfect sand, limestone cliffs and caves, emerald water and colourful long-tail boats make this photographic bliss. It's little more than a cosy nook, and tends to get crowded in high season.

② Hat Khao Lak

On this seemingly endless swath of golden, boulder-studded beach (p292), expect outrageous sunsets and lazy days. The Surin and Similan Islands as well as inland jungle parks are an easy boat or road trip away.

③ Ko Tao

Trying to decide between a slice of lively sand and hermitic retreat? Ko Tao (p233) offers plenty of both. Hit the island's west side for tiki-torched beach bars, and escape to the eastern shores where there is virtually nothing, but it feels like everything you'll ever need.

④ Ko Mak & Ko Kood

Take your pick on quiet Ko Mak (p162): sling your hammock up on a desolate beach or the next one over, which is just as perfect and pristine. Next door, jungly Ko Kood (p160) has an excellent spread of flaxen sand as well.

⑤ Ko Ngai

Cook on the slender, powder-white beach, dip in the sandy-bottomed shallows then slip over the reef for clear water, healthy corals and fish aplenty (p372). Knobby karst islands fill the horizon towards the Krabi mainland in the distance.

⑥ Ao Bang Thao

With over 8km of white sand, expect calm seas in the high season and surfable waves during the low season. Don't let the posh Laguna complex scare you off; this laid-back yet lively beach (p329) has something for everyone.

⑦ Ko Pha-Ngan

Every month, on the night of the full moon, pilgrims pay tribute to the party gods with trancelike dancing and neon body paint. Join the legions of bucket-sippers on the infamous Sunrise Beach for the world's greatest – and biggest – beach party (p218). When you've recovered, retreat to serene beaches on the far side of the island.

Southern Thai Cuisine

You may think you know Thai food, but a trip to Thailand's south is a new stamp in your culinary passport. With palpable influences from China and Malaysia, copious fresh seafood and an obsession with bold flavours, the food of Thailand's beaches and islands is dynamic and diverse, not to mention intense.

❶ Thai-Muslim Food

From satay to biryani, Thailand's Muslim minority makes some mean dishes (see p51). The emphasis is often on meat, but even vegetarians can dig into *sà·làt kàak* (a salad of lettuce, tomato, cucumber and hearty chunks of tofu, all topped with a sweet peanut sauce).

❷ Kôw Yam

Where else is the cheapest dish also among the most delicious? For less than a packet of gum back home you get a dish of *kôw yam*, rice steamed with purple flowers and topped with toasted coconut, shredded herbs and a sweet, spicy fish sauce.

❸ Night Markets

Southern Thailand's night markets are among the best in the country. In particular, the ones in Songkhla (p257), Satun (p378) and Trang (p367) are particularly good places to sample authentic southern Thai dishes such as *kà·nŏm jeen* (noodles served with curry) or local sweets.

❹ Hat Yai–Style Fried Chicken

Legendary across the entire kingdom, Hat Yai's deep-fried bird gets its special flavour from a marinade spiked with dried spices – a rarity in most schools of Thai cooking. A dry texture and a red hue round out the package (p262).

❺ Coffee Shops & Mŏo Yâhng, Trang

The unassuming town of Trang has several atmospheric *ráhn goh·b̄ée* (coffee shops) that haven't changed in decades, a healthy addiction to *mŏo yâhng* (crispy barbecued pork), and to top it off, one of Thailand's tastiest night markets (see p370).

❻ Bang Po Seafood

The native cuisine of Ko Samui can be difficult to find. To truly taste the island, visit Bang Po Seafood (p211), a popular local seaside shack where you can dig into local specialities such as a salad of sea urchin eggs or grilled turmeric-coated flying fish.

❼ Roti

Real roti are nothing like the guesthouse menu cliché. Whether served on the street and drizzled with sweetened condensed milk or paired with a bowl of curry, they're a taste of southern Thailand.

National Parks

Some of southern Thailand's most appealing areas are its out-of-this-world national parks and protected areas. The range is enormous: from far-out islands with virgin corals to little-visited mangrove swamps. The most popular areas are stressed environmentally by the number of visitors they receive each year, so please tread lightly.

1 Surin & Similan Islands Marine National Parks

These tiny islands 60km off-shore, though astoundingly beautiful above water, are known more for their underwater wonders. Whale sharks are elusive but you're sure to see sea turtles, myriad healthy corals and multicoloured fish (see p289 and p295).

2 Ang Thong Marine National Park

The ultimate cache of unspoiled lands, Ang Thong Marine National Park (p248) is a stunning collection of easily anthropomorphised islets stretching along the cerulean waters like an emerald necklace.

3 Ao Phang-Nga National Park

Motor or paddle through a seemingly endless maze of steep, limestone isles (p299) to visit cave paintings, a rickety Muslim fishing village and the hideout of Scaramanga, James Bond's old nemesis. Don't expect to get any of it to yourself, though.

4 Khao Sok National Park

Thought to be the oldest rainforest in the world, Khao Sok (p290) is a dripping, juicy jungle overflowing with lurking beasts, gushing waterfalls and an alien flora, including the largest flower in the world, which measures almost 1m in diameter!

5 Khao Sam Roi Yot National Park

Khao Sam Roi Yot (p183) is known as the 'land of the 300 peaks' for its stunning, seemingly endless expanse of chunky limestone crags. Walk quietly as you trudge between the hidden temples deep within – you may hear the distant rustle of dusky langur monkeys dangling in the trees above.

6 Laem Son National Park

Find the easy pace of yesteryear's Thailand in this mangrove-laden park (p277). Ko Phayam has a groovy, reggae-inspired beach scene while on Ko Chang life moves in slow motion. Snorkelling isn't great, although divers can go on trips to the Surin Islands.

7 Ko Phi-Phi Marine National Park

Phi-Phi (p351) deserves its fame for being one of Thailand's most beautiful protected areas. The fine sand, limestone cliffs and turquoise waters mean excellent diving, climbing and beachside relaxation, but you'll have to share the experience with throngs of other travellers.

Sunset at Big Buddha Beach (p195), Ko Samui
BILL WASSMAN

(Continued from page 120)

is where the sex industry hits its all-time low –
there's no blinking neon just cheap back
rooms and unhealthy-looking prostitutes
dressed like schoolgirls. Things get much
more young, hip and PG-rated northward
from Soi 3 and this area is popular with families. Hat Naklua, a smaller beach 1km north
of Pattaya, is even quieter.

HAT JOMTIEN
Head to Hat Jomtien, a 6km stretch of attractive beach and cleaner water, for a mellower
scene. The lush northern end of the beach,
a shady, pedestrian-only area popular with
gay men (and lots of male masseurs on the

beach), is called 'Dongtan' (no pun intended).
The centre area of Hat Jomtien is the busiest
while further south it gets quite backwater
and sleepy. Hat Jomtien is only 5km south of
Hat Pattaya, or a 20B to 40B sŏrng·tăa·ou ride.
There's still a girlie-bar scene but it's not as
in-your-face as Pattaya.

Information
BOOKSHOPS
Book Corner (Map p129; Soi Post Office; 🕙 10am-
10pm) Decent selection of English-language fiction and
travel guides.
Bookazine (Map p129; 1st fl, Royal Garden Plaza, Th
Hat Pattaya; 🕙 11am-11pm) Has loads of travel books,
literature and magazines. There's also a branch at Hat
Jomtien (Map p131).

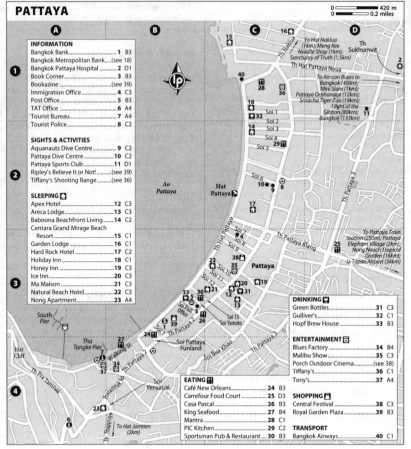

PATTAYA

INFORMATION	
Bangkok Bank	**1** B3
Bangkok Metropolitan Bank	(see 18)
Bangkok Pattaya Hospital	**2** D1
Book Corner	**3** B3
Bookazine	(see 39)
Immigration Office	**4** C3
Post Office	**5** B3
TAT Office	**6** A4
Tourist Bureau	**7** A4
Tourist Police	**8** C2
SIGHTS & ACTIVITIES	
Aquanauts Dive Centre	**9** C2
Pattaya Dive Centre	**10** C2
Pattaya Sports Club	**11** D1
Ripley's Believe It or Not!	(see 39)
Tiffany's Shooting Range	(see 36)
SLEEPING	
Apex Hotel	**12** C3
Areca Lodge	**13** C3
Baboona Beachfront Living	**14** C2
Centara Grand Mirage Beach Resort	**15** C1
Garden Lodge	**16** C1
Hard Rock Hotel	**17** C2
Holiday Inn	**18** C1
Honey Inn	**19** C3
Ice Inn	**20** C3
Ma Maison	**21** C3
Natural Beach Hotel	**22** C3
Nong Apartment	**23** A4

EATING	
Café New Orleans	**24** B3
Carrefour Food Court	**25** D3
Casa Pascal	**26** B3
King Seafood	**27** B4
Mantra	**28** C1
PIC Kitchen	**29** C2
Sportsman Pub & Restaurant	**30** B3
DRINKING	
Green Bottles	**31** C3
Gulliver's	**32** C1
Hopf Brew House	**33** B3
ENTERTAINMENT	
Blues Factory	**34** B4
Malibu Show	**35** C3
Porch Outdoor Cinema	(see 38)
Tiffany's	**36** C1
Tony's	**37** A4
SHOPPING	
Central Festival	**38** C3
Royal Garden Plaza	**39** B3
TRANSPORT	
Bangkok Airways	**40** C1

0 — 420 m
0 — 0.2 miles

To Hat Naklua (1km); Meng Kee Noodle Shop (1km); Sanctuary of Truth (1.5km)

Th Sukhumvit

Th Hat Pattaya Neua

To Air-con Buses to Bangkok (400m); Mini Siam (1km); Pattaya Orphanage (12km); Sriracha Tiger Zoo (19km); Flight of the Gibbon (80km); Bangkok (133km)

Ao Pattaya

Hat Pattaya

Th Hat Pattaya

Th Pattaya Klang

To Pattaya Train Station (250m); Pattaya Elephant Village (2km); Nong Nooch Tropical Garden (16km); U-Tapao Airport (34km)

South Pier

Pattaya

Th Pattaya 3

Soi Post Office

Tha Tangke Pier

Hat Cliff

Walking St

Th Pattaya 2

Soi Pattaya Funland

Soi Bua Khao

Th Pattaya 3

Soi Yensabai

Soi 13
Soi Yamato

Soi Yensabai

Th Phra Tamnak

Th Thapphraya

To Hat Jomtien (2km)

EASTERN GULF COAST

EMERGENCY
Tourist Police (Map p129; ☎ 0 3842 9371, emergency 1155; tourist@police.go.th; Th Pattaya 2) The head office is on Pattaya's busy main artery. There are also police boxes along the Pattaya and Jomtien beaches.

IMMIGRATION
Immigration office (Map p129; ☎ 0 3825 2751; Soi 8, Th Pattaya Klang) Handles visa extensions.

INTERNET ACCESS
There are internet places around Soi Praisani (aka Soi Post Office), at the Royal Garden Plaza and along Th Pattaya 2. At Hat Jomtien, they pop up regularly along Th Hat Jomtien.

INTERNET RESOURCES
Pattaya At Night (www.pattaya-at-night.com)

MEDIA
The weekly *Pattaya Mail* (www.pattayamail .com) publishes articles on political, economic and environmental developments in the area.

MEDICAL SERVICES
Bangkok Pattaya Hospital (Map p129; ☎ 0 3825 9911, emergency 1719; 301 Moo 6, Th Sukhumvit, Naklua; ☼ 24hr) Pattaya's premier health-care provider; has a hyperbaric chamber.

MONEY
Finding an ATM around Pattaya and Hat Jomtien is nearly as easy as finding a date; they're everywhere and most banks have foreign-exchange booths that stay open late (usually to 8pm).
Bangkok Bank (Map p129; ☎ 0 3822 2370; Th Hat Pattaya; ☼ 9.30am-7pm Mon-Fri)

Bangkok Metropolitan Bank (Map p129; ☎ 0 3842 8418; Th Hat Pattaya; ☼ 8.30am-3.30pm Mon-Fri)

POST
Post office (Map p129; ☎ 0 3842 9341; Soi Post Office)

TOURIST INFORMATION
The bimonthly *What's On Pattaya* is a good resource with several maps, articles and a crossword to do while you relax at the beach. In addition to the TAT office, there is a small tourist bureau near the police booth on Walking St.
Pattaya Call Centre (☎ 1337, 0 3841 0393) Provides vital information regarding accommodation, attractions, restaurants and shopping.
Tourism Authority of Thailand (TAT; Map p129; ☎ 1672, 0 3842 8750; tatchon@tat.or.th; 609 Moo 10, Th Pra Tamnak; ☼ 8.30am-4.30pm) Located at the northwestern edge of Rama IX Park. Offers mountains of brochures.

Dangers & Annoyances
Watch out if walking along Hat Pattaya at night as there are some notorious ladyboy muggers who pray on drunk men and the police seem to turn a blind eye. Late-night Pattaya can get a little wild, and though it's not necessarily dangerous, there are sometimes brawls between drunken Westerners. If you find yourself caught in the middle of an uncomfortable situation, get out fast. In these situations, the police are prompt.

Sights
There's so much to do in Pattaya, you might not have time to catch some rays on the beach.

If you're only going to visit one place in Pattaya, make it the **Sanctuary of Truth** (off Map

---

PATTAYA: FUN FOR THE WHOLE FAMILY?

Trudging down Walking St, mum holds hands with her wide-eyed son as dad trudges behind their confused-looking daughter; a scantily dressed ladyboy follows them with her eyes while smoking a cigarette while the numerous bar girls fussing over drunk Western men don't even give them a glance. Is this the holiday destination these people thought they were getting when they booked that tour? Pattaya does have a lot to offer families – from the fun Pattaya Elephant Village (see opposite) and Pattaya Park water park to the Underwater World aquarium – but realise that the sex industry is unavoidable here and if you bring the kids you'll probably have some uncomfortable explaining to do.

If you're set on visiting Pattaya as a family, the best option is either to stay in northern Pattaya or Naklua at a self-contained resort or in Hat Jomtien where the go-go scene is a bit a softer. Otherwise, there are so many other fabulous beach resorts in Thailand, consider your options.

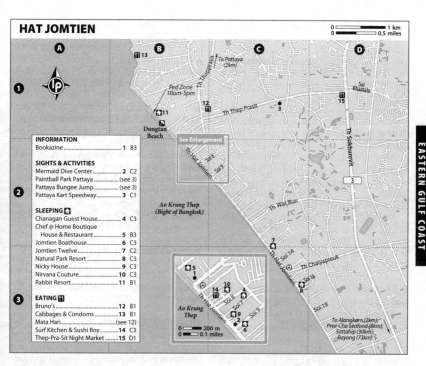

HAT JOMTIEN

p129; ☎ 0 3836 7229; www.sanctuaryoftruth.com; 206/2 Moo 5, Naklua; admission 500B; ☒ 8am-5pm). Although not technically a temple, this stunning teakwood palace details the pan-Eastern school of thought regarding the order of the universe. Visitors will undoubtedly be awestruck when they glimpse this incredible rambling fortress.

The **Nong Nooch Tropical Garden** (off Map p129; ☎ 0 3842 9321; 163 Th Sukhumvit, Sattahip; admission 400B; ☒ 9am-sunset) is located south of Pattaya. The manicured grounds feature four daily elephant and Thai dancing shows (between 9am and 3.45pm).

Just 2.5km out of town, **Pattaya Elephant Village** (off Map p129; ☎ 0 3824 9818; www.elephant -village-pattaya.com; ☒ according to show & trek times) is a nonprofit sanctuary for former working elephants. There's a 2.30pm elephant show (adult/child 500/400B) that demonstrates training techniques, and daily elephant treks (adult/child 2000/1300B).

Many tourists also visit the **Tiger Zoo** in nearby Sri Racha (see p118).

Located at the Royal Garden Plaza mall, **Ripley's Believe It or Not!** (Map p129; ☎ 0 3871 0294;

admission 580B; ☒ 11am-11pm) has a museum of oddities containing bizarre artefacts from all over the world. There's also a 4-D simulator, a tricky maze and a haunted house.

Mini Siam (off Map p129; ☎ 0 3872 7333; 387 Moo 6, Th Sukhumvit; adult/child 250/120B; ☒ 7am-10pm) is – you guessed it – a scaled-down set of replicas of Thailand's ancient and famous sights. It's about 1.5km east of town.

Activities

Pattaya has a huge range of outdoor activities, including but by no means limited to **bowling**, **snooker**, **archery**, **target-shooting**, **softball**, **horse-riding** and **tennis**. Many of these activities are available at the **Pattaya Sports Club** (Map p129; ☎ 0 3836 1167; www.pattayasports.org; 3/197 Th Pattaya 3) or can be organised by most hotels.

You can take target practice at **Tiffany's Shooting Range** (Map p129; ☎ 0 3842 9642; ground fl, Tiffany's, Th Pattaya 2; admission 250B plus ammunition; ☒ 9am-10pm). There's a 56m bungee jump at **Pattaya Bungee Jump** (Map p131; ☎ 0 3830 1209; Soi 9, Th Thep Prasit; jumps 1500B; ☒ 9am-6pm) and the nearby **Paintball Park Pattaya** (Map p131; ☎ 0 3830 0608; www.paintballpark-pattaya.com; 248/10 Moo 12, Th

Thep Prasit; 50 bullets starting at 500B; 10am-6pm) lets you take your anger out on your friends with paint-filled bullets. To gratify your need for speed, drop into the **Pattaya Kart Speedway** (Map p131; ☎ 0 3842 2044; 248/2 Soi 9, Th Thep Prasit; admission from 250B; 9am-6pm), where you can race go-karts around an impressive 1km loop.

A 50-minute drive from Pattaya is the area's newest and arguably most exciting attraction, **Flight of the Gibbon** (off Map p129; ☎ 0 8997 05511; www.treetopasia.com; full-day tours from 2300B). Get shuttled to the largest and highest rainforest adventure course in the world including 3km of zip-lines, a huge safari animal park and a 'Tarzan' swing all in 3000 *rai* (480 hectares) of untouched biodiversity.

There are several islands off the coast of Pattaya that are worth the short boat trip if you need an afternoon away from the city. **Ko Laan**, about 45 minutes away, is a popular choice – many visitors go on glass-bottom boat tours for views of the coral reef. **Ko Sak** and **Ko Phai** have powder sand beaches, and **Ko Krok** is a hot spot for divers. Ferry tickets can be booked at the large pier in South Pattaya. Tickets are around 20B to 85B.

DIVING & SNORKELLING
With 20 dive sites orbiting the coast, Pattaya is a good spot for scuba if you can't make it down the coast to the southern part of Thailand. Diving in the region is split up into three sections: the Near Islands, the Far Islands and Samaesan.

The **Near Islands** have experienced overfishing and heavy boat traffic, so these sites can be barren with poor visibility. Nearby Ko Laan, Ko Sak and Ko Krok are fine for beginners. In most places expect 3m to 9m of visibility under good conditions, or, at more remote sites, 5m to 12m.

The **Far Islands**, located about 90 minutes from town, feature bright coral reefs including the popular artificial reef created by the shipwrecked HMS *Khram*.

Samaesan is a small fishing village south of Pattaya with some of the best diving in the region. The shipwrecked *Petchburi Bremen* and *Hardeep* have created artificial reefs and are interesting dive sites. One of the best dive sites around is an old US Navy ammunition dump called Samaesan Hole. This advanced dive goes down to 87m and has a gentle slope covered thickly with coral where you can see barracuda and large rays. The visibility here

is pretty good, and you can see up to 20m on a good day.

A two-dive excursion costs around 4000B, including the boat, equipment, underwater guide and lunch. Snorkellers may join these day trips for around 1400B. PADI Open Water certification, which takes three to four days, can cost anywhere between 13,000B and 15,000B, including all instruction and equipment. Certification costs are considerably less on Ko Tao (see p235).

There are several dive operators in town, including the following. It's best to organise these by phone, or through your hotel.

Adventure Divers (☎ 0 3836 4453; www.pattayadivers .com; 391/77-78 Th Thappraya)

Aquanauts Dive Centre (Map p129; ☎ 0 3836 1724; www.aquanautsdive.com; Soi 6, Th Pattaya 1) Operates separate snorkelling and boat tours as well.

Mermaid's Dive Center (Map p131; ☎ 0 3830 3333; www.mermaiddive.com; Soi White House, Hat Jomtien)

Pattaya Dive Centre (Map p129; ☎ 0 3871 0918; www.divecentrepattaya.com; 219/3 Moo 10, Soi 6, Th Pattaya 1)

OTHER WATER SPORTS
Pattaya and Hat Jomtien have some of the best water sports facilities in Thailand and operators line the main beach roads competing for your custom. **Water-skiing** costs around 1000B per hour including equipment, boat and driver. **Parasailing** is around 500B a shot (about 10 to 15 minutes). **Game-fishing** is also possible; rental rates for boats, fishing guides and tackle are reasonable. Hat Jomtien is the best spot for **windsurfing** (600B per hour), not least because you're a little less likely to run into people parasailing or jet-skiing.

VOLUNTEERING
At the **Pattaya Orphanage** (☎ 0 3824 1373; volunteer@ redemptorists.or.th) volunteers are needed to care for more than 50 children under the age of three; teach English to older children; and work in a drop-in centre for street kids. The well-run orphanage is an uplifting balance to the Sin City streets of Pattaya. Volunteers are expected to commit to at least six months, but shorter stays are considered on a case-by-case basis. Food and accommodation is provided.

Sleeping
The proximity to Bangkok means that weekends tend to be crowded and prices often rise

---

DETOUR: KHAO CHAMAO/KHAO WONG NATIONAL PARK

อุทยานแห่งชาติเขาชะเมา–เขาวง

Although less than 85 sq km, **Khao Chamao/Khao Wong National Park** (☎ 0 3889 4378; reserve@ dnp.go.th; admission 400B; ☾ 8.30am-4.30pm) is famous for limestone mountains, high cliffs, caves, dense forest and waterfalls. Secreted in the rugged landscape are wild elephants, bears, gaur, gibbons and deer. The park features a few waterfalls and over 80 limestone caves and is a good spot for hiking – there are several trails that wind through it. The park is inland from Ban Phe, 17km north of the Km 274 marker off Hwy 3. To get to here, take a sŏrng·tăa·ou (50B) from Ban Phe to the marker, and another sŏrng·tăa·ou (25B) to the park.

You can stay at a camp site (per person 50B) or rent a two-person bungalow (600B to 1000B). To book, email reserve@dnp.go.th, or phone ☎ 0 2562 0760.

---

accordingly. Stay in Pattaya if you want to party but Hat Jomtien has a much better beach and is more relaxing.

PATTAYA & NAKLUA

Budget

Budget options in Pattaya are all noisy with traffic and well off the beach; better-value choices are found in Hat Jomtien.

Apex Hotel (Map p129; ☎ 0 3842 8281; www.apex hotelpattaya.com; 216/2 Soi 11; r 550-600B; ❄ ☀) Rome wasn't built in a day, but Apex probably was. The cheapest rooms are doled out on a first-come basis, but paying an extra 50B gets you a better room with faux-marble flooring, air-con and cable TV.

Ice Inn (Map p129; ☎ 0 3872 0671; www.iceinnpattaya .com; 528/2-3 Th Pattaya 2; r 580B; ❄ ☐) This is the best budget option in Pattaya, not that that's saying much. Tiled, clean rooms with big fridges all surround a tiered courtyard area. The staff are remarkably laid-back and there's an internet cafe in front.

Honey Inn (Map p129; ☎ 0 3842 9133; 529/2 Soi 11 Th Pattaya 2; r 600-800B; ❄ ☐) Clean, bright rooms with terraces overlooking a slightly seedy street. You're close to good nightlife without being in its lap.

Midrange

Garden Lodge (Map p129; ☎ 0 3842 9109; fax 0 3842 1221; Th Naklua; r 850-1300B; ❄ ☀) Escape the hype and hustle of Pattaya in one of the area's best value midrange options tucked over in Naklua. There's no skimping on the garden atmosphere with fishponds and leafy pavilions, and the tour desk at reception offers a raft of day trips.

Natural Beach Hotel (Map p129; ☎ 0 3842 9239; www.naturalbeach.com; 216 Moo 10, Soi 11; r from 950B; ❄ ☀) The main draw here is that you get a swimming pool without dropping a ton of baht plus you're just across the road from the beach. Rooms are big and clean yet bland but the pool, surrounded by greenery, is a nice place to escape the busy streets just over the gate.

Ma Maison (Map p129; ☎ 0 3871 0433; www.mamaison -hotel.com; 386 Moo 10, Soi 13; r 1200-1500B; ❄ ☀) Ma Maison feels a bit more personal than most of the other lodging options around town – the decor is rife with rows of potted flowers and hanging collectables, such as splayed fans and antique farming equipment. Rooms wind around the central pool, which acts like an oasis attracting weary guests after a long night among buzzing lights. Reservations recommended.

Nong Apartment (Map p129; ☎ 0 3871 3371; www .pattayavacation.com; 373/5-6 Moo 10, Soi Yensabai; apt 1200-2400B; ❄ ☐) Nong is a fantastic deal for small groups, families and those who are looking to stick around town for a while. Apartment-style units are arranged around a long rectangular courtyard stuffed with a vivid assortment of enormous potted plants. Guests can retreat to their private patios, or lounge in the common areas covered with portraits of US naval cruisers.

Areca Lodge (Map p129; ☎ 0 3841 0123; www.areca lodge.com; 198/23 Mu 9, Soi Diana Inn, Tha Pattaya 2; r incl breakfast from 1300B; ❄ ☐ ☀) The stylish rooms with huge windows, excellent service and two swimming pools, mean this ever-expanding, great-value place could pass as high-end but the prices are anything but. It's no secret though and Areca is nearly always full with an over-50 golf-club-toting set and their sporty Thai girlfriends. Prices go up around 50% in December and January.

ourpick Baboona Beachfront Living (Map p129; ☎ 0 3848 8720; www.baboonabeach.com; btwn Soi 3-4,

EASTERN GULF COAST

119/3 Moo 9, Th Hat Pattaya; r 1600-2400B; 🐾 ☐ 🛜)
At the hip and clean northern end of Pattaya right on the beach road, this new place is the chicest midranger in town. Rooms are painted with a trendy mix of bright colours, have black-and-white-chequered tiled floors and are imbibed with a fresh, fruity scent. Higher-priced rooms have excellent views of the water while techno-jazz is pumped through the lobby.

Top End

Pattaya is popular with package tourists and convention-goers, so there are plenty of top-end options. Rooms are often cheaper (sometimes over 50%) when booked through a Bangkok travel agency, or via the internet. Count on paying a 10% service charge and a 7% value-added tax (VAT) for these places.

Holiday Inn (Map p129; ☎ 0 3872 5555; www .holidayinn.com; 463/68 Th Pattaya Soi 1; r from 3600B; 🐾 ☐ 🛜 🏊) Every room has a sea view at this brand-new family-friendly high-rise hotel. A soothing ocean colour scheme of greys and weathered blues blends harmoniously with the aqua vistas out the massive windows. The executive suites have bathtubs right against the windows so you can experience a vertiginous, view-filled soak. There's a great kids' pool plus an adult pool and spa and service is exceptionally friendly.

Hard Rock Hotel (Map p129; ☎ 0 3842 8755; www .hardrockhotels.net/pattaya; 429 Moo 9, Th Hat Pattaya; r 6500-45,000B; 🐾 ☐ 🏊) Hard Rock is fun, friendly and has excellent staff. Funky design details include dangling guitars, giant music-related murals and awesome headboards featuring a Warhol-esque image of a rock legend. Drop the kids off at the Lil' Rock childcare program that takes the tykes to the on-site climbing wall, swimming pool (with floating trampoline), and arts and crafts centre. If you're staying on one of the top floors, you'll have access to the King Club, a private lounge serving up unlimited pre-dinner drinks in the early evening.

our pick Centara Grand Mirage Beach Resort (Map p129; ☎ 0 3830 1234; www.centarahotelsresorts .com; 277 Moo 5, Naklua; r 9000-12,500B, ste 20,000-90,000B; 🐾 ☐ 🛜 🏊) The 'Lost World' theme here is so full-on it's verging on feeling like Disneyland, but ingeniously the fun and fantasy come off as classy. The grounds are a cascade of pools and water slides tumbling past giant tiger and elephant totem poles, suspended rope bridges

and tiki torches; the entrance is a majestic arching thatch roof, the elevators are lined with crocodile-skin-textured tin and even the wall behind reception has a live tangle of jungle plants crawling all over it. Comfortable big rooms have sand sculpture murals on the walls, desks that look like old leather trunks and the colour scheme is an Indiana Jones–ish camel, khaki and orange. All rooms have sea views, there's an excellent stretch of beach out front and service is stellar.

HAT JOMTIEN
Budget

Explore the area around Sois 3 and 4 for good value budget guesthouses.

Chanagan Guest House (Map p131; ☎ 08 9834 3561; Soi 6, Th Hat Jomtien; r 500-600B; 🐾) Peaceful and old-school with more character than any of the other cheapies around town, the basic airy rooms here are painted cheery colours and all have hot water, cable and air-con. There's an interesting mix of locals hanging out in the common area downstairs (one guy was tattooing his own leg when we passed) but everyone is very friendly and there's a resident band of small dogs.

Nicky House (Map p131; ☎ 0 3823 2000; nickyhouse@ hotmail.com; cnr Soi 7 Th Hat Jomtien; d 650-850B, q 1000-1200B; 🐾 ☐) The large tiled, clean rooms here have a hint of Zen style and the sea-view rooms have terraces overlooking the beach. Staff are friendly and there's an internet cafe downstairs.

Midrange

our pick Chef @ Home Boutique House & Restaurant (Map p131; ☎ 0 3823 1986; www.chefathomepattaya.com; 75/10-11 Th Hat Jomtien; r incl breakfast 1000-1200B; 🐾 ☐) It's hard to get past the ground-floor restaurant here – it smells so good that you'll want to take a seat between the plumeria trees for a second lunch. But getting up to the rooms is worth it. Each floor has a signature colour – orange, green or violet – and rooms are decorated with a beautiful mix of eclectic wallpaper, stylish photography and bold paint. All rooms are a little dark but are spotless and cosy. European and Thai mains downstairs cost 100B to 150B and the service all around is smiley and fun.

Nirvana Couture (Map p131; ☎ 0 3823 1926; www .nirvanacouture.com; Th Hat Jomtien Soi 4; r 1100-1500B; 🐾 ☐) Run by the folks of the plush Nirvana resort on Ko Chang (p158), this place is a much more humble affair but still packs a stylish punch. The decor is all about rock 'n' roll with framed photos of Dylan, The White Stripes and Blondie hung between spiky plants coming out of minimalist urns. It's all got a sort of white and black nouveau-1980s appeal. Rooms are windowless but comfortable.

Jomtien Twelve (Map p131; ☎ 0 3875 6865; www .thejomtientwelve.com; 240/13 Moo 12, Th Hat Jomtien; r 1100-1400B; 🐿) Jomtien Twelve is trying to pull off 'boutique chic': the exterior incorporates teak slatting into a contemporary design scheme, and the lobby is dripping with trendy goodness. After that, however, it seems like the designer got lazy – the rooms are well kept (especially the bathrooms), but they're noticeably devoid of that yuppie sensibility set loose downstairs.

Jomtien Boathouse (Map p131; ☎ 0 3875 6143; www.jomtien-boathouse.com; 380/5-6 Th Hat Jomtien; r 1200-1400B; 🐿) The lobby here looks like the abode of a crusty grandad sea captain, with schools of taxidermic fish and models of wooden frigates. On deck, you'll find a terrace and a cosy pub that serves hearty fare. The very ordinary rooms upstairs don't retain the nautical theme, but they're clean. Go for the beachside rooms – the 'Garden View' accommodation has extremely tiny windows.

Natural Park Resort (Map p131; ☎ 0 3823 1561; www.naturalparkresort.com; 412 Th Hat Jomtien; r 2500B, ste from 4000B; 🐿 🖳 🐾) Natural Park changes things up along Jomtien's beach boulevard with its lush jungly property punctuated by mini hotel blocks. The lagoonlike swimming pool has an adorable island smack in the middle with two frizzy palms. Rooms are bedecked in a charming blend of teak beams, wicker lounge chairs and Japanese sliding screens.

Top End

Rabbit Resort (Map p131; ☎ 0 3830 3303; www.rabbit resort.com; Th Hat Dongtan 4; r 4900-6000B; 🐿 🖳 🐾) Situated on a prime slice of northern Hat Jomtien property in the pedestrian-only zone, Rabbit Resort is a refreshing change from the clunky chain hotels nearby. This family-run operation offers forested rooms and villas featuring decadent Thai-style furnishings and handmade, rustic textiles. The separate kids' pool and private beach area are added perks.

Eating

Western food rules the culinary roost, with several noteworthy establishments that have

been around for decades. Pattaya's also the perfect place to step off the beaten path and explore some local haunts. There are some fantastic seafood joints that serve up excellent dishes for less baht than the usual tourist magnets.

PATTAYA

Carrefour Food Court (Map p129; Th Pattaya Klang; 🕒 11am-10pm) In the absence of a decent night market, head to the food court under the Carrefour supermarket. The Thai food is authentically spicy and dishes start from 30B.

Sportsman Pub & Restaurant (Map p129; Soi 13 Th Hat Pattaya; breakfast 70-180B; 🕒 7am-2am) For the best breakfast in town head to this British pub for everything from bacon and eggs and Weetbix to black pudding and bubble and squeak. There are Cornish pasties at lunch and the place packs at night when big sports events are on telly.

King Seafood (Map p129; ☎ 0 3842 9459; king_sea food@hotmail.com; 94 Walking St; dishes 80-300B; 🕒 lunch & dinner) This seafood mothership is a classic Walking St establishment. The tome-like menu is a veritable almanac of edible marine life.

Café New Orleans (Map p129; ☎ 0 3871 0805; www .cafeneworleans.info; Soi Pattaya Funland; dishes 150-750B; 🕒 3pm-midnight) Café New Orleans has perfectly synthesised the unique Bourbon St atmosphere that mixes baroque and bayou charm. A lengthy menu echoes the ambience with juicy steaks and Creole onion soups. It's hard to believe that this romantic setup is just seconds away from Pattaya's other articulations of 'love'.

PIC Kitchen (Map p129; ☎ 0 3842 8374; 10 Soi 5, Th Pattaya 2; dishes 160-550B; 🕒 lunch & dinner) This teaklined place has an intimate atmosphere with open-sided rooms, fluffy cushions and low wooden tables. Sample the Thai menu and sneak upstairs to the Jazz Pit for some post-repast tunes.

Casa Pascal (Map p129; ☎ 0 3872 3660; www.restau rant-pattaya.com; 485/4 Moo 10, Th Pattaya 2; mains 350-1500B; 🕒 lunch & dinner Mon-Sat, lunch Sun) Casa Pascal is an elegant dining experience set under a colonnade of large wooden pillars. Loosen your belt for the never-ending Sunday brunch buffet (899B), complete with a fanfare of napkin sculptures, cooking stations and delicious samplers, such as rock lobster and beef tartare. The regularly changing menu features gourmet French, Italian and Thai dishes.

BUY THE LADY A DRINK

Wandering around Pattaya you might wonder how the seemingly thousands of bar girls manage to make a living off a fluctuating number of male visitors. The truth is that many girls are on a small salary at the bar where they hang out and get paid as long as they bring in around 30 or more 'lady drinks' per month. So, if you're male and sitting at a bar you will often be pestered to buy a girl a drink – this is how these women make part or even all of their living. Depending on what she orders a drink can cost up to 160B but on average it's more like 90B to 100B; some better bars still let guys offer drinks on their own after a girl has been sitting with him but no matter where you are the protocol is to buy – and usually more than one.

---

ourpick Mantra (Map p129; ☎ 0 3842 9591; www .mantra-pattaya.com; Th Hat Pattaya Neua; mains around 1200B; ⓨ dinner daily, brunch Sun; ✻) Creating a fusion between Japanese, Indian, Middle Eastern, Chinese and Western both in decor and cuisine, this is undoubtedly Pattaya's coolest address in town. The interior combines steady bursts of jet black and slick, lipstick red while the restaurant has seven kitchens, each one dedicated to a specific cuisine: there's a sushi counter, Indian ovens and a homemade pasta station, to name just a few. A fabulous several-course discovery menu starting with Peking duck rolls, and finishing with a baked mango parcel with vanilla-infused sticky rice and coconut ice cream, costs 1500B per person.

HAT JOMTIEN

Thep-Pra-Sit Night Market (Map p131; Th Sukhumvit; dishes from 20B; ⓨ 6-10pm Fri-Sun) Low prices and small portions make this popular night market the perfect spot to sample some local faves. While nibbling on your street cuisine, browse stalls of the standard knockoffs. To get here, grab a taxi or sŏrng·tǎa·ou.

Surf Kitchen & Sushi Boy (Map p131; ☎ 0 3823 1710; Th Hat Jomtien; dishes 75-250B; ⓨ breakfast, lunch & dinner) You get two restaurants in one at this mellow and shady sidewalk-side stop. Surf Kitchen's Thai food is authentic while the Western food is awfully tasty as well. Order fresh sushi sets (from 69B) from the separate Sushi Boy menu.

Cabbages & Condoms (Map p131; ☎ 0 3825 0035; www.cabbagesandcondoms.co.th; 366/11 Moo 12, Th Phratamnak 4; mains 100-300B; ⓨ breakfast, lunch & dinner) This saucily named restaurant hides along the secluded beach at the Birds & Bees Resort; this is one of the nicest sea views in the Pattaya area. Charming lamps, crafted from fish traps and coconuts, cast a romantic hue over sated diners. If that gets you in the mood, you'll be happy to know that the standard bin of farewell breath mints has been appropriately replaced with a bucket of prophylactics.

Bruno's (Map p131; ☎ 0 3836 4600; 306/63 Chateau Dale Plaza, Th Thappraya; lunch mains 100-200B, dinner mains 360-390B, pasta dishes 210-280B; ⓨ lunch & dinner) The walk-in wine cellar makes Bruno's the go-to place for those seeking vino with their victuals. Lunchtime is a bargain – the team of gourmet chefs prepares scrumptious steaks and seafood courses for less than 200B.

Mata Hari (Map p131; ☎ 0 3825 9799; 482/57 Moo 12, Th Thappraya; mains 200-600B; ⓨ dinner Tue-Sun) Mata Hari has been a Pattaya staple for over 40 years, serving haute cuisine to visitors and faithful expat patrons. The menu largely focuses on European fare, with a couple of exotic flavours tossed in to tempt the palate.

Drinking

Pattaya is an ever-evolving creature and it's not just go-go bars anymore. Walking St is the heart of Pattaya's nightlife, and it overloads the senses with trance music, gyrating bodies and buzzing neon signs advertising every fetish imaginable. Down the street, the convoluted Sois 1, 2 and 3 are collectively known as 'Pattayaland', and consist of wall-to-wall bars blaring the latest pop tunes. Obviously, most of the establishments in the area cater to the skin trade in some creative way or another.

Hopf Brew House (Map p129; ☎ 0 3871 0650; Th Hat Pattaya 219; ⓨ 3pm-1am Sun-Fri, 4pm-2am Sat; ✻) Moodily authentic in dark wood, the Hopf Brew House offers a very drinkable pilsner and wheat beer that are brewed on site – you can smell the hops when you walk in. Huge wood-fired pizzas and only slightly smaller schnitzels are recommended to soak up the liquid hospitality.

Green Bottles (Map p129; ☎ 0 3842 9675; 216/6-20 Th Pattaya 2) Charmingly cosy and retro (you can even request your favourite songs from the band), Green Bottles has been on the scene since 1988 and is one of Pattaya's more traditional pubs.

Gulliver's (Map p129; ☎ 0 3871 0641; Th Hat Pattaya; 🕐 11.30am-2am) At the northern end of Pattaya, Gulliver's is a classy bar-girl-free zone with pool tables, a big international drinks menu and a spacious outdoor patio right across from the beach.

Entertainment

Trolling Pattaya's streets can turn up everything from all-male synchronized swimming shows to bars made entirely out of ice. It depends what's on and exploring is the best way to discover how crazy things can get.

CLUBS & CABARETS

Missing a transvestite cabaret in Pattaya would be like going to Paris and not visiting the Louvre. OK, not really, but these spectacles really are a work of art and are so much fun to watch.

Malibu Show (Map p129; ☎ 0 3842 8667; Th Pattaya 2, Soi 9-10; 🕐 shows 9.45pm & 11.45pm) If you can't afford a big-venue cabaret show, stop by this hole in the wall for their nightly small stage spectacular. Shows are free if you buy a drink.

Blues Factory (Map p129; ☎ 0 3830 0180; www.the bluesfactorypattaya.com; Soi Lucky Star) Off Walking St, Pattaya's best venue for no-nonsense live music features at least two bands every night and a hassle-free atmosphere just metres from the heavier hype of Walking St.

our pick **Tiffany's** (Map p129; ☎ 0 3842 1700-5; www.tiffany-show.co.th; 464 Moo 9, Th Pattaya 2; VIP seat 800B, standard seat 700B; 🕐 shows 6pm, 7.30pm & 9pm, plus 10.30pm on holidays) The costumes here are the definition of glitz and glam, and every feminine nuance has been practised and perfected. Stick around after the show to take photographs with the lovely 'ladies'.

Tony's (Map p129; ☎ 0 3842 5795; www.tonydisco.com; 139/15 Walking St; admission free; 🕐 8.30pm-2.30am) Run by Tony, this club-conglomerate has it all: a deafeningly loud, neon-lit disco, pool tables and an in-house Thai boxer. Tony also runs a spa, gym, brewery and dog shelter.

OTHER ENTERTAINMENT

Porch Outdoor Cinema (Map p129; top fl, Central Festival, Th Pattaya 2, Soi 9-10; tickets 500B) Settle into a big squishy couch with a cocktail while watching the latest blockbuster. The open terrace has views over Pattaya and the ambience feels decadent. There are four film showings per day and the price includes a drink and a snack.

Alangkarn (off Map p131; ☎ 0 3826 6000; www.alang karnthailand.com; admission 1000B; 🕐 by performance) Located a couple of kilometres southeast of Pattaya, this large theatre features a variety of flashy performances involving elaborate costumes, dancing elephants and pyrotechnics.

Upstairs at the flashy new **Central Festival** (Map p129; Th Pattaya 2, Soi 9-10) shopping mall you'll find a cinema with several screens.

Getting There & Away

AIR

Bangkok Airways (Map p129; ☎ 0 3841 2382; www.bang kokair.com; 179/85-212, Mu 5, North Pattaya Rd; 🕐 8.30am-4.30pm Mon-Fri, to noon Sat) links **U-Taphao Airport** (off Map p129; ☎ 0 3824 5599), about 33km south of Pattaya, with Ko Samui and Phuket (one-way from 2000B, daily).

BUS

There are air-con buses to Pattaya from Bangkok's Eastern (Ekamai; every half-hour from 9.30am to 11pm) and Northern (Mo Chit; every half-hour from 6am to 9pm) bus terminals (100B to 140B, two hours) as well as from the Suvarnabhumi Airport bus terminal (124B, 1½ hours, every two hours from 7am to 9pm). From Pattaya, buses to Ekamai and to Mo Chit run from 4.30pm to 9pm; to the Suvarnabhumi Airport bus terminal buses run from 8am to 8pm. In Pattaya the air-con bus station is on Th Hat Pattaya Neua, near the intersection with Th Sukhumvit. Once you reach the main Pattaya bus terminal, waiting red sŏrng·tǎa·ou will take you to the main beach road for 30B to 40B per person. Note that buses travelling from Ekamai to Hat Jomtien are often 2nd class; it's often faster to take the 1st-class bus to north Pattaya and hop on a sŏrng·tǎa·ou to Hat Jomtien.

Several hotels and travel agencies run minibuses to addresses within Bangkok, or east to Ko Samet and Ko Chang – the fares start at about 200B.

A direct bus service runs from Bangkok's Suvarnabhumi airport arrivals terminal and Pattaya and Hat Jomtien (150B to 250B, two hours).

For Sri Racha (40B, 30 minutes) buses stop near the corner of Th Sukhumvit and Th Pattaya Neua. From here, you can flag down buses to Rayong (60B to 90B, 1½ hours).

You can also catch a white sŏrng·tǎa·ou from the Naklua market to Sri Racha (30B, 30 minutes).

TRAIN

One slow train per day Monday through Friday travels between Pattaya and Bangkok's Hualamphong station (third class 45B, 3¾ hours). Check times at **Pattaya train station** (off Map p129; ☎ 0 3842 9285), off Th Sukhumvit just north of Th Hat Pattaya Neua.

Getting Around

CAR, JEEP & MOTORCYCLE

Jeeps can be hired for around 2500B per day, and car hire generally starts at 1500B, though you can pay as little as 1000B for a 4WD Suzuki in the low season. Motorcycle rentals usually cost between 200B and 350B per day. There are motorcycle rental places along Th Hat Pattaya and Th Pattaya 2.

SŎRNG·TǍA·OU

Sŏrng·tǎa·ou cruise up and down Th Hat Pattaya and Th Pattaya 2 – just hop on and when you get out pay 10B anywhere between Naklua and South Pattaya, or 20B if you take the truck from Pattaya to Jomtien (or vice versa). A chartered sŏrng·tǎa·ou to Jomtien should be no more than 40B.

Readers have complained about having taken the 10B sŏrng·tǎa·ou with local passengers and then having been charged a higher 'charter' price of 20B to 50B. Establish the correct fare in advance. Also don't board a sŏrng·tǎa·ou that is waiting empty at the side of the road, as the driver may insist you have 'chartered' the entire vehicle.

RAYONG & AROUND

อ.เมืองระยอง

pop 106,700

Almost every visitor to Rayong Province, 200km southeast of Bangkok, comes for a beach getaway on sunny Ko Samet (opposite). Travellers will rarely have to stop in the region's capital, as there is a regular bus service from Bangkok to Ban Phe, the ferry port to Ko Samet. We don't want to discourage you from contributing to Rayong town's tourism industry, but with little here besides the bus station and a few barking dogs, your holiday time is better spent elsewhere.

The quaint fishing village of **Ban Phe** has managed to remain small despite its ferry mo-

nopoly. Should you decide to blaze your own tourist trail, this seaside shantytown is also the jumping-off point to several lesser-known beach destinations in the area. The province actually has over 100km of coastline, but the lack of tourist development and transport infrastructure means that most of these beaches have slipped under the tourism radar. From Ban Phe, sŏrng·tǎa·ou can take you along the coast to the 'resort towns' (and we use that term lightly) of **Laem Charoen**, **Laem Mae Phim**, **Hat Sai Thong** and **Hat Mae Ramphung**. Ferries from near Ban Phe go to private resorts on the secluded islands of **Ko Man Klang** and **Ko Man Nok** (see the boxed text, p141); advance bookings are highly recommended.

Information

Krung Thai Bank (Th Sukhumvit 144/53-55) One of several banks along Rayong's main drag, Th Sukhumvit, with exchange services and ATMs.

TAT (☎ 0 3865 5420; tatyong@tat.or.th; 153/4 Th Sukhumvit; ☺ 8.30am-4.30pm) Located 7km east of Rayong on Hwy 3; a worthwhile stop if you have your own transport.

Sleeping & Eating

RAYONG

Should you somehow get stuck in Rayong town, there are a couple of lodging choices within eyeshot of the bus station, but most of the quality options are a short cab ride away. The bus terminal is set within a large market, so there are plenty of food options nearby.

Rayong President Hotel (☎ 0 3862 2771; www .rayongpresident.com; 16/8 Th Phochanakon; r incl breakfast from 550B; ☒) Located halfway between the bus station and Wat Khod Thimtaram, this large, white hotel is a quiet place to catch a couple of 'Z's.

BAN PHE

Christie's Guesthouse (☎ 0 3865 1975; 280/92 Soi 1; r 500B; ☒) Big clean rooms, hot water and even TVs with cable and DVD players make this place (conveniently located across from the pier) a steal. Try the hearty Western breakfast (from 160B), or take your lunch to go for a nibble on the ferry ride. In the evening, the restaurant becomes a popular hang-out for local expat English teachers.

M@c Garden (☎ 0 3865 1150; 280/153 Th Ban Phe Mu 2; r 700B; ☒ ☐) A friendly new hotel that has beautiful teak bungalows (1200B) and smaller rooms that, though plain, are clean and new.

Getting There & Around

See p144 for information regarding ferries from Ban Phe to Ko Samet. If you are heading straight to Ko Samet from Bangkok, take a direct bus to Ban Phe (138B to 160B, three hours, hourly), which depart from Bangkok's Ekamai station between 5am and 8pm. Air-con buses to Rayong (146B, 2½ hours, every 30 minutes) leave from Ekamai between 4am and 10pm and from the Suvarnabhumi Airport bus terminal (155B, two hours, hourly) between 8.30am and 6.30pm. Sŏrng·tăa·ou between Rayong bus station and Ban Phe are 25B. Rayong has comprehensive bus services to destinations further east, such as Chanthaburi and Trat.

Fifty metres west of Ban Phe pier, buses depart four times a day for Bangkok starting at 12.30pm. Slower, but more frequent, buses depart across from Nuan Tip pier, 100m east of Ban Phe pier.

Minivan services connect the pier in Ban Phe to a variety of destinations such as Pattaya (250B), Trat (250B) and Ko Chang (250B, not including boat ticket). These can be booked in Ban Phe or at resorts and travel agencies on Ko Samet.

KO SAMET

เกาะเสม็ด

If Goldilocks were a Bangkokian socialite, she'd probably spend her weekends here – Pattaya's too close and noisy, Ko Chang's too far and rugged, but pretty white-sand Ko Samet is just right. Statistically, this little isle boasts the most days of sunshine out of any beach retreat in the kingdom, which makes everyone living in the vicinity stake-out a beach umbrella here on weekends. On Friday and Saturday nights, the northeast beaches are drowned in duelling, throbbing techno from the bars so if you're planning on sleeping at this time, book a place at the south or on the west coast. During the week the island relaxes and you're more likely to discover the laid-back sandy bliss that has attracted backpackers for decades. If you're willing to venture further south, there are some undeniably gorgeous bays where development is still low-key and which come with a relaxed traveller vibe.

Ostensibly Ko Samet is a national park, but along the developed northeast coast it's hard to see where your 200B park entrance fee is being invested. The island's ecosystem is overtaxed and it is vital visitors play their part by conserving water and being mindful of rubbish.

Orientation

Most of the action on the 8km-long island takes place along the northern half of the eastern shore. Boats arrive at Na Dan, the island's only village, which is linked to the east coast by a built-up ribbon of road replete with a 7-Eleven, internet cafes, noodle stalls and bars. A large gate lies at the end of the street – this is where faràng pay their 200B entrance fee.

Ko Samet's small size makes it a great place to explore on foot. A network of difficult dirt roads connects the western beach and most of the southern bays, while walking trails snake over the boulders and headlands that separate beaches.

Information

Ko Samet is a national park and the entrance fee (adult/child 200/100B) is collected at the main National Parks office – your sŏrng·tăa·ou from the pier will stop at the gates. Hold on to your ticket for later inspections.

There are several ATMs on Ko Samet. One is at the pier and another two are near the National Parks office.

There are internet cafes on the road from Na Dan to Hat Sai Kaew; the best is Miss You Café (p144).

Around the island you can check your email at Jep's Bungalows (p142) and Naga Bungalows (p142) in Ao Hin Hok, and at a couple of spots along Ao Wong Deuan. All charge a steep 2B per minute.

A satellite phone for making international calls is located outside the National Parks office visitor centre.

Ko Samet Health Centre (☎ 0 3861 1123; ⏱ 8.30am-9pm Mon-Fri, to 4.30pm Sat & Sun) On the main road between Na Dan and Hat Sai Kaew. On-call mobile numbers are posted for after-hours emergencies.

National Parks main office (btwn Na Dan & Hat Sai Kaew) Has another office on Ao Wong Deuan.

Police station (☎ 1155) On the main road between Na Dan and Hat Sai Kaew. There's a substation on Ao Wong Deuan.

Post office Naga Bungalows in Ao Hin Khok acts as the island's post office; it also loans and sells secondhand books.

Samed Travel Service (☎ 08 1664 8563; ⏱ 8.30am-5pm) Opposite the ferry terminal; makes transport (including railway) and accommodation bookings.

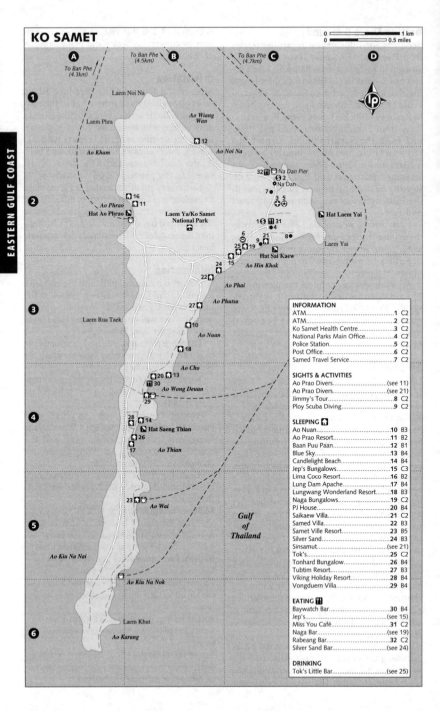

KO SAMET

| | 0 ———— 1 km |
| | 0 ———— 0.5 miles |

To Ban Phe (4.3km)
To Ban Phe (4.5km)
To Ban Phe (4.7km)

Laem Noi Na

Laem Phra

Ao Kham

Ao Phrao
Hat Ao Phrao

Ao Wiang Wan

Ao Noi Na

Laem Ya/Ko Samet National Park

Na Dan Pier
Na Dan

Hat Laem Yai

Laem Yai

Hat Sai Kaew

Ao Hin Khok

Ao Phai

Ao Phutsa

Laem Rua Taek

Ao Nuan

Ao Cho

Ao Wong Deuan

Hat Saeng Thian

Ao Thian

Hat Sai Kaew

Ao Wai

Gulf
of
Thailand

Ao Kiu Na Nai

Ao Kiu Na Nok

Laem Khut

Ao Karang

EASTERN GULF COAST

Dangers & Annoyances

Ko Samet has been malarial in the past, and while the health centre now claims to have the problem under control, the island is infested with mosquitoes. Cover up and use buckets of repellent.

Take care on the road leading away from the beach past Sea Breeze Bungalows in Ao Phai, as travellers have reported being robbed in this area.

We've had reports of boat scams on the mainland, in which travellers are sold a speedboat ticket for around 800B per person. Refer to p144 for prices and timetables, but note that a speedboat going one-way should cost anywhere from 1500B to 2500B *total*, no matter how many passengers.

Sights & Activities

Sailboards, boogie boards, inner tubes and snorkelling equipment can all be rented on the beaches at Hat Sai Kaew, Ao Hin Khok and Ao Phai. The best diving around Ko Samet is at **Hin Pholeung** (Map p117), about halfway between the island and Ko Chang. This isolated spot is well away from destructive boat traffic and has two towering underwater rock pinnacles with excellent visibility (up to 30m) and a great assortment of marine life.

Two reputable dive operations on the island are **Ploy Scuba Diving** (☎ 0 3864 4212; www .ployscuba.com) in Hat Sai Kaew, and **Ao Prao Divers** (☎ 0 3864 4100–3; aopraodivers@hotmail.com), based at the Ao Prao Resort and Saikaew Villa.

Naga Bungalows (p142) offers *moo·ay tai* (also spelled *muay thai;* Thai boxing) lessons in its beachside boxing ring. One program caters specifically to women and is quite popular.

In addition to Ko Samet, there are several other islands that belong to Laem Ya/Ko Samet National Park. They include **Ko Man Klang**, **Ko Man Nok** and **Ko Man Nai**. Like on Ko Samet, this official park status hasn't deterred development. Ko Man Nai is home to the Rayong **Turtle Conservation Centre** (☎ 0 3861 6096; 9am-4pm), which is a breeding place for endangered sea turtles. Ask at Christie's Bar & Restaurant (attached to Christie's Guesthouse; p138) about visiting from Ban Phe, or join one of the many boat tours departing from Ko Samet. You can also volunteer to work at the centre by contacting **Starfish Ventures** (www .starfishventures.co.uk).

Tours

There are tons of low-key tour operators around the island with giggle-worthy names such as 'Happy Fun Safe Tour'. Most excursions are for three hours, and they usually involve snorkelling, eating, some beach-bumming and a visit to the nearby Turtle Conservation Centre (above).

Jimmy's Tours (☎ 08 9832 1617/27) runs a variety of trips around Ko Samet and the neighbouring islands. A six-hour boat tour (10am to 4pm) of the neighbouring islets, including the Turtle Conservation Centre on Ko Man Nai, costs 1500B per person (with a minimum group size of 10 people). Jimmy's Tours has booking offices at both the Ao Phrao and Sai Kaew Beach resorts.

Sleeping

Ko Samet's status as the 'it' weekend getaway spot means that prices skyrocket on Fridays and Saturdays (and go even higher on long

---

KO HABITATION

If you're looking for peace and quiet, and Ko Samet doesn't quite cut it, check out some of the smaller islands nearby. The secluded **Ko Man Klang** and **Ko Man Nok** offer upmarket accommodation packages that include boat transport and meals. These holidays should be arranged by phone in advance through the Bangkok reservation numbers.

Public transport to the pier departure points for Ko Man Klang and Ko Man Nok can be arranged in Ban Phe. On weekends and holidays there may be sŏrng·tăa·ou out to the piers; otherwise charter a vehicle from the market for around 100B one-way, and arrange a pick up for your return.

Raya Island Resort (☎ in Bangkok 0 2316 6717; 1-night, 2-day packages per person 1800-3000B;) This comfortable getaway has 15 bungalows and plenty of hush. It is 8km off Laem Mae Phim (27km east of Ban Phe), on Ko Man Klang.

Ko Nok Island Resort (☎ in Bangkok 0 2860 3025; www.munnorkislandresort.com; packages per person 3800-4400B;) On Ko Man Nok, this classy resort has one-night, two-day packages in a variety of villas. The island is 15km off Pak Nam Prasae (53km east of Ban Phe).

weekends). It's also common to find rising prices as different places start to fill up – one bungalow could go from 500B on Friday morning to 800B by the end of the day. Most bungalow operations have an attached restaurant and/or bar. They can also help you arrange boats to the mainland or many of the activities that are available on the island.

HAT SAI KAEW

Known as 'Diamond Sand', the sand here is white and relatively clean, though the seafront is lined with hotels, restaurants and umbrellas packed so tight they nearly form a roof. It's a favourite for Thais from Bangkok, and at the weekends expect a cacophony of jet skis and karaoke.

Saikaew Villa (☎ 0 3864 4144; r 500-1550B; 🗲) Big rooms or small rooms, fan or air-con, Saikaew Villa conjures up a wide range of accommodation options amid a manicured space that (almost) goes too far with the holiday-camp atmosphere. Don't expect much privacy, but do expect food, drinks and activities all on tap.

Sinsamut (☎ 0 3864 4207; www.sinsamut-kohsamed .com; r 900-1500B; 🗲) Bright, light and colourful (but slightly shabby), rooms come with brick walls and the bathrooms have gravel floors with stepping stones. Fan rooms have cold-water showers, while air-con rooms come with TVs, hot water and refrigerators.

AO HIN KHOK

It's wall-to-wall faràng on Ao Hin Khok, a pretty stretch of sand lined with trees and boulders. This is the island's traditional backpacker hub, and while the ambience is slowly moving upmarket, there's still loads of energy from independent travellers to make it a fun spot – especially after dark.

Naga Bungalows (☎ 0 3864 4035; r 300-600B; 🖵) At Naga, Ko Samet's backpacker spirit lives on. Simple fan bungalows are set into a forested hillside, and movies are shown nightly in the outstanding restaurant. Ex-pat Sue runs the post office, library, and charity (ask how you can be involved), and is an excellent source of island information.

Tok's (☎ 0 3864 4072; r 300-1500B; 🗲) Same, same, but different (there are some air-con rooms at Tok's). You'll need a torch after dark to negotiate the steep hillside to the simple bungalows – especially if you've been taking part in Tok's regular drinking games. Some snazzy updated bungalows are also available

on the beach but don't expect much from the reception.

Jep's Bungalows (☎ 0 3864 4112; www.jepbungalow .com; r 600-2600B; 🗲 🖵) Spearheading the evolution of Ao Hin Khok, the long-established Jep's offers rooms ranging from dingy fan bungalows to air-con rooms with satellite TV. There's not much of a welcome but it's an OK place to lay your head.

AO PHAI

More upmarket than at Ao Hin Khok and still quite busy, this lovely white-sand bay with great swimming is just over the headland.

Silver Sand (☎ 08 6530 2417; bungalows 800-4200B; 🗲 🖵) Silver Sand's verdant property is perfectly manicured, while the evening bar action throws a little chaos into the mix. The massive tiled bungalows with terraces are very comfortable

Samed Villa (☎ 0 3864 4094; www.samedvilla.com; r incl breakfast 1800-2800B; 🗲 🖵) This place was getting upgraded when we passed by but it was already the nicest in the area. The bungalows are spotless and comfortable and stretch along the white beach out to a shady rocky point lapped by waves. Inviting wooden deck chairs sit under trees all along the shore.

AO PHUTSA & AO NUAN

At Ao Phutsa, you start to feel the seclusion of the island since there are actual stretches of empty sand. Tubtim Resort has a little floating dock that you can swim out to.

Tubtim Resort (☎ 0 3864 4025; www.tubtimresort .com; Ao Phutsa; r 600-2500B; 🗲) Tubtim has a whole range of stylish, modern bungalows climbing a rugged hill from the beach up into the jungle. Spend the extra 200B and go for an upgraded fan bungalow – they have sparkling bathrooms and varnished fixtures, and are noticeably better than the rickety cheapies. The restaurant serves up some fantastic dishes within 3m of the crashing tide.

Ao Nuan (bungalows 700-1200B) Hidden among thick foliage, the simple wooden bungalows have a tiny beach to themselves. The funky, intimate restaurant is packed with colourful books and board games, while dishing out delicious home-cooked faves. There's no phone and it doesn't take reservations.

AO CHO (AO LUNGWANG)

A five-minute walk across the next headland from Ao Nuan, this bay can also be reached by road from Hat Sai Kaew, or you can take a boat directly from Ban Phe to Ao Wong Deuan and walk. It's a lovely white beach.

Lungwang Wonderland Resort (☎ 0 3864 4162; r 500-3000B; 🔀) The grounds could use some TLC and the air-con rooms are overpriced, but the simple bungalows are good – they're decked out in cheerful colours and bright, mismatched tiles. Kayak rentals are 200B per hour and the whole place feels like a low-key Thai holiday camp.

AO WONG DEUAN

This crescent-shaped bay has good nightlife with a chilled after-dark vibe, but your daytime soundtrack may be jet skis and speedboats. Ferries (80B each way) run to and from Ban Phe, with increased services at the weekend.

PJ House (☎ 0 3864 4182; r 500B; 🔀) Next to Baywatch Bar, this small place is pretty basic but 500B scores you an air-con room. There's a pool table downstairs dominated by the local 10-year-old sharks.

Blue Sky (☎ 08 1509 0547; r 600-850B; 🔀) One of the last budget spots on Ao Wong Deuan, Blue Sky has simple bungalows set on a rocky headland. The restaurant does tasty things with seafood.

Vongduern Villa (☎ 0 3864 4260; www.vongduernvilla.com; r 1200-3500B; 🔀) Sprawling along the bay's southern edge are bungalows, either near the beach or higher on the cliff top for better views. The Beach Front Bar is a sociable spot for sundowner cocktails, but romantic couples may prefer the subdued ambience of the Rock Front Restaurant.

AO THIAN (CANDLELIGHT BEACH)

Better known by its English name, Candlelight Beach, Ao Thian has stretches of sand with rocky outcrops. To get here, catch a ferry to Ao Wong Deuan and walk south over the headland. It's also a quick walk to the west side of the island – look for the marked trail near Tonhard Bungalows.

Candlelight Beach (☎ 08 1762 9387; bungalows 700-1300B; 🔀) On the beach, these fan and air-con bungalows have a natural, woody ambience.

Tonhard Bungalow (☎ 08 1435 8900; r 700-1500B; 🔀) On a wooded and sandy part of the beach, this place is quiet, friendly, and somewhat private. Most bungalows differ from each other. At the southern end of Candlelight Beach.

Lung Dam Apache (☎ 08 1659 8056; bungalows 850-1200B; 🔀) These quirky bungalows look like they've been thrown together from marine debris. Some have enclosed verandahs and wraparound windows.

Viking Holiday Resort (☎ 0 3864 4353; r from 2000B; 🔀) Rooms are large and luxurious, and there's only nine of them so book ahead.

AO WAI

The southern reaches of the island are still practically untouched, with only a couple of hotels spread over as many kilometres of coastline. Lovely Ao Wai is about 1km from Ao Thian, but can be reached from Ban Phe by chartered speedboat (1500B for two people).

Samet Ville Resort (☎ 0 3865 1682; www.sametville resort.com; r incl breakfast 2000-6000B; 🔀) Under a forest canopy, it's a case of 'spot the sky' at the very secluded Samet Ville. It's a romantic spot, but if you do have a fight with your loved one, take advantage of the water sports on offer and cool off in separate kayaks for the day. At dusk, patch things up over cocktails and subdued beats in the beachfront bar. There is a huge range of different fan and air-con rooms for all budgets.

WEST COAST (HAT AO PHRAO)

West-facing Ao Prao gets fabulous sunsets, and offers a smattering of chic hotels for the posh set. Speedboat transfers from the mainland are included (of course).

Lima Coco Resort (☎ 0 2938 1811; www.limacoco.com; r 2600-7000B; 🔀) White-washed rooms could go either way: Mediterranean or bland. No matter what, they're bright and a little different than the norm.

Ao Prao Resort (☎ 0 2437 7849; www.samedresorts.com; r from 6300B; 🔀 🖳) This resort opened in the 1990s as the island's first luxury accommodation. It's holding its age well, with private bungalows cascading down a hill to the gorgeous beach. High ceilings create a spacious ambience and there is an excellent restaurant.

AO NOI NA

Northwest of Na Dan, the beach at Ao Noi Na is only average, but there is a refreshing solitude with a couple of good places to stay.

Baan Puu Paan (☎ 0 3864 4095; r 700-1200B; 🔀) This English-run spot has a couple of standalone huts above the ocean at the end of a pier. Bring a big book – it's a good place to get away.

Eating & Drinking

Most places to stay have restaurants that moonlight as bars at sunset. The food won't blow you away, but it's OK value, with Thai and Western favourites for around 80B to 130B. Most choice is on Hat Sai Kaew, Ao Hin Khok, Ao Phai and Ao Wong Deuan, but hotels on the remote stretches won't make you go to bed hungry. Look for nightly beach barbecues, particularly along Ao Hin Khok and Ao Phai.

Drinking-wise, many places offer nightly 'toss-a-coin' promotions. Basically heads or tails decides if you end up paying for your drink or not. Ao Wong Deuan is slightly more upmarket, but not much.

For seriously cheap eats, check out the food stalls which set up in the late afternoon on the road between Na Dan and Hat Sai Kaew.

Rabeang Bar (Na Dan; dishes 30-100B; ☺ breakfast, lunch & dinner) Right by the ferry terminal, this over-the-water spot has decent waiting-for-the-next-boat kind of food.

Miss You Café (coffee 40-90B; ☺ breakfast, lunch & dinner; ☎) Located beside the National Parks main office, this spot has 13 different kinds of coffee, and almost as many variations on cake and ice cream. Have a latté as you hitch your laptop to its wi-fi network.

Jep's (☎ 0 3864 4112; Ao Hin Khok; dishes 40-150B; ☺ breakfast, lunch & dinner) With Thai, Indian, Mexican, Japanese and European food, you should find something you like at this sand-between-the-toes spot that also does regular beach barbecues.

Naga Bar (☎ 0 3864 4035; Ao Hin Khok; dishes 60-150B) Has a huge menu with Thai set meals (so you can taste everything), meat pies, real coffee and fresh-baked goods. There's a bar across the road next to the *moo·ay tai* (Thai boxing) ring where you can duke out to see who pays for the next round.

Tok's Little Bar (☎ 0 3864 4072; Ao Hin Khok; dishes 60-150B) With sticks-n-straw decor, a few locals who fancy themselves as lady-killers, and nightly drinking games, you won't mistake this place for a sophisticated cocktail bar.

Silver Sand Bar (☎ 0 6530 2417; Ao Phai; dishes 60-180B; ☺ breakfast, lunch & dinner) As well as a regular menu, Silver Sand offers fresh crêpes (sweet and savoury), a juice bar and nightly movies. Once the movies end, the action progresses (regresses?) to cocktail buckets and fire shows on the beach. There is even a burger bar to appease the midnight munchies.

Baywatch Bar (☎ 08 1826 7834; Ao Wong Deuan; kebabs 190-290B; ☺ breakfast, lunch & dinner) There's chill-out platforms and Asian umbrellas, and bean-bag chairs on the sand after dark. The cocktails are strong and it's a fun evening crowd.

Getting There & Away

Ferries (one-way/return 50/100B, 40 minutes, hourly) depart from 7am to 5pm from Ban Phe's Saphan Nuan Tip pier – opposite the 7-Eleven, where the buses and sŏrng·tǎa·ou stop. Tickets can be bought from a small **tourist information centre** (☎ 0 3889 6155; ☺ 7am-5pm) on the pier itself. Ferries return to Ban Phe from the pier in Na Dan hourly from 7am to 5pm – buy your ticket at the pier. Despite what you may be told, you don't need to buy a round-trip ticket.

From Ban Phe, two scheduled ferries (9am and noon) also make the run to Ao Wong Deuan (one-way/return 70/110B, one hour). They make the trip in reverse at 8.30am and noon. In the high season boats run to other bays if enough people show an interest. Alternatively, you can charter a speedboat to any of the island's beaches. They are quite expensive (1200B to Na Dan or 1600B to Ao Wai), but they take up to 10 passengers for this price, so it's worthwhile if you're travelling in a group.

Ignore the touts that congregate around the ferry terminal, as they charge inflated prices for boat tickets and will hassle you into pre-booking expensive accommodation – just go straight to the ticket office.

To get off Ko Samet in a hurry, charter a speedboat. Ask at your hotel, or call **Jimmy's Tours** (☎ 08 9832 1627). Prices start at 1200B from Na Dan.

Getting Around

Ko Samet's small size makes it a great place to explore on foot. It's only a 15-minute walk from Na Dan to Hat Sai Kaew, but if you are carting luggage or want to go further, sŏrng·tǎa·ou meet arriving boats at the pier and provide drop-offs all along the length of the island. Set fares for transport around the island from Na Dan are posted at the main stop by the 7-Eleven; you shouldn't have to pay much more than 20B to get to Hat Sai Kaew, 30B to go halfway down the island, or 40B to reach the southern beaches. If drivers don't have enough people to fill the vehicle, they either won't go, or they will charge passengers 200B to 500B to charter the whole vehicle.

Motorcycles and mountain bikes can be rented from almost every bungalow operation on the island. Expect to pay about 300B per day or an hourly rate of 100B. The dirt roads are *very* rough – you may want to walk or rent a mountain bike (100B per hour) instead.

CHANTHABURI & AROUND
จันทบุรี
pop 488,397

Chanthaburi town has earned a global reputation as the centre for gem trading in Southeast Asia. All day Friday and Saturday, and on Sunday mornings, shops along Th Si Chan and Th Thetsaban 4 are overflowing with the banter and intrigue of the hard sell. You'll be offered the 'deal of a lifetime', but walk away unless you really know what you're doing. You're better off just filling up at the food stalls (try the famous Chanthaburi rice noodles, *gŏo·ay·dĕe·o sên jan*) surrounding the commercial bustle.

If you grab a taxi or local bus from Chanthaburi town, you can reach the quiet provincial villages along the water. Tourists often overlook these hushed coral sands and sleepy fishing villages as they beeline for livelier beach holidays. The **Tha Mai** district has the area's nicest beaches, the most charming being **Hat Chao Lao**, which is stocked with delicious seafood restaurants. Our readers have also enjoyed the laid-back ambience in the lagoonside town of **Khlung**. The jagged peninsula of Laem Singh is a picturesque beach option and home to the region's most popular tourist destination, **Oasis Sea World** (☎ 0 3936 3238; Laem Singh; admission 400B). Dolphins are the main attraction and the price of admission includes the opportunity to get in the water with the lovable creatures and assist the trainers with tricks and feeding. Visits can be arranged by most tour operators between Pattaya and Ko Chang.

Sleeping
Accommodation in Chanthaburi can get busy. Try and book ahead, especially from Friday to Sunday when the gem traders are in town.

River Guest House (☎ 0 3932 8211; Th Si Chan 3/5-8; r incl breakfast 150-350B; ✸ 🖳) Painted in shades of soft taupe and beige, Chanthaburi's real gems are the clean rooms and relaxed sitting area by the river at this friendly place. There's a fair bit of highway noise, but air-con should drown it out. The cheapest rooms share baths.

Le Village de Napoleon (☎ 0 3944 4575; www .napoleonvillage.net; Laem Singh; r from 1500B; ✸ 🖳 🖳) Situated on the quiet cape of Laem Singh, about 30km from Chanthaburi town, this is a five-room hotel with all the conveniences of a luxury resort. Spend the day poolside with a delicious cocktail, savour delicious international cuisine for dinner, and relax in the evening while watching cult classics in the cinema room.

Getting There & Away
Buses operate between Chanthaburi town (200B, 4½ hours) and Bangkok's Eastern bus terminal every half-hour throughout the day and less frequently at night. Buses also travel to Rayong (90B, 2½ hours, five daily) and Trat (67B, 1½ hours, hourly).

TRAT & AROUND
อ.เมืองตราด
pop 21,590

Trat, a charming provincial capital of old alleyways, markets, coffee shops and book stores, is the perfect antidote to too many days on the beach. The town's main road, Th Sukhumvit, is a roaring drag-way of honking sŏrng·tǎa·ou, but you just have to step into a side street to appreciate the gentle pace of everyday life along the slithering canal. The city's architecture is a striking cornucopia of styles: hidden pedestrian lanes are lined with century-old teak houses, while loud colours are splashed across the boxy department stores nearby. If you decide stay the night, you'll find some of the cheapest lodging in this part of Thailand.

The day market beneath the municipal shopping centre off Th Sukhumvit, the old day market off Th Tat Mai, and another nearby day market are all worth a look. The latter becomes an excellent night market in the evening. Don't leave town without buying some of Trat's famous *nám·man lěu·ang* (yellow oil), a herb-infused liquid touted as a remedy for everything from arthritis to stomach upsets.

Information
Bangkok Trat Hospital (☎ 0 3953 2735; Th Sukhumvit; ⏲ 24hr) Best health care in the region.

EASTERN GULF COAST

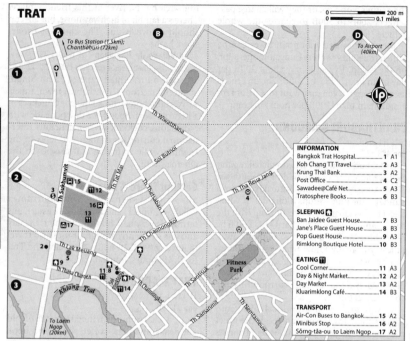

TRAT

0 — 200 m
0 — 0.1 miles

INFORMATION
Bangkok Trat Hospital.................... 1 A1
Koh Chang TT Travel...................... 2 A3
Krung Thai Bank............................. 3 A2
Post Office....................................... 4 C2
Sawadee@Café Net........................ 5 A3
Tratosphere Books......................... 6 B3

SLEEPING
Ban Jaidee Guest House................ 7 B3
Jane's Place Guest House.............. 8 B3
Pop Guest House............................ 9 A3
Rimklong Boutique Hotel............ 10 B3

EATING
Cool Corner................................... 11 A3
Day & Night Market..................... 12 A2
Day Market.................................... 13 A2
Kluarimklong Café........................ 14 B3

TRANSPORT
Air-Con Buses to Bangkok........... 15 A2
Minibus Stop................................. 16 A2
Sŏrng-tǎa-ou to Laem Ngop 17 A2

Koh Chang TT Travel (☎ 0 3953 1420; 109 Th Ratanuson; ☻ 8.30am-7pm) Excellent agent for transport by land, air or sea.

Krung Thai Bank (Th Sukhumvit) Has an ATM and currency-exchange facilities.

Post office (Th Tha Reua Jang)

Sawadee@Café Net (☎ 0 3952 0075; Th Lak Meuang; per min 1B; ☻ 10am-10pm) Internet and Skype are both available.

Tratosphere Books (Soi Rimklong 23; ☻ 8am-10pm) Has secondhand titles in English and pretty much every other language. Owner Serge is a good source of information and sells *nám·man lěuang*.

Sleeping & Eating

Trat has a small and charming super-budget guesthouse scene; just take a stroll through the quiet lanes lining Lak Meuang and pick one that tickles your fancy. For the best cheap eats head to the town's many markets.

There are also bungalows at the piers in Laem Ngop and Laem Sok but Trat is only 20km away, transport is omni-present and town is a much nicer option.

Ban Jaidee Guest House (☎ 0 3952 0678; 6 Th Chaimongkol; r 150-200B) Meaning 'good heart',

this lovely Thai-style home is Trat's long-running favourite. The simple rooms share a bathroom and the whole place abounds with leafy greens.

Rimklong Boutique Hotel (☎ 08 1861 7181; 194 Th Rakmuang; rimklong2008@hotmail.com; r 800B; ☒ ☁) The only real midranger in the area, the three ground-level rooms here are huge, clean and have hot water. There's an espresso bar attached and it's a short walk to the excellent, lounge-style Kluarimklong Café on Soi Rimklong that's owned by the same friendly people.

ourpick Cool Corner (☎ 08 4159 2030; 49-51 Th Thana Charoen; dishes 50-150; ☻ breakfast, lunch & dinner) Though it's no longer on the corner since the original building burned down in 2008, hip artist/owner Morn still serves up great vibes, good beats, and some of the best breakfasts in Thailand.

Also recommended:

Pop Guest House (☎ 0 3951 2392; popson1958@hotmail.com; 1/1 Th Thana Charoen; r 150-600B; ☒ ☐) Over 40 comfy rooms are spread around four tidy properties. The owner will wheel and deal you with one hand and pamper you with the other.

Jane's Place Guest House (☎ 0 3951 1827; 140-142 Th Lak Meuang; r 200B) A new place with three spacious wooden rooms with balconies overlooking a garden. The bathroom is shared.

Getting There & Around

To reach the islands in the Ko Chang Archipelago, travellers will have to transfer to one of the piers along the coast. Most tourists will end up around Laem Ngop. Motorbike taxis around Trat cost around 20B.

TRAT

Bangkok Airways (☎ in Bangkok 0 2265 5555, Trat Airport 0 3952 5767; www.bangkokair.com) flies three times a day to/from Trat and Bangkok. The airport is 40km from town; minibuses and taxis meet all flights and a taxi is 400B.

Air-conditioned buses from Bangkok to Trat (223B to 300B, five to six hours) leave hourly from the Ekamai and Mo Chit bus terminals between 8.30am and 10.30pm and from the Suvarnabhumi Airport bus terminal (248B, five hours) six times per day between 6.30am and 6.30pm. The price and frequency for the return trip to Bangkok are the same. All buses leave from and arrive at Trat's bus station 1.5km north of town centre. A sŏrng·tǎa·ou or motorbike taxi to the guesthouse area will cost around 25B to 40B.

Direct minibuses from Trat to Hat Lek (120B, one hour) leave every 45 minutes from the bus station. Sŏrng·tǎa·ou (around 50B) also trundle from the bus station to Hat Lek, but you will have to wait for enough people to show up. Agents around town also sell minibus tickets to Bangkok (300B) and far flung destinations such as Siem Reap (800B) in Cambodia.

LAEM NGOP

Sŏrng·tǎa·ou for Laem Ngop and Centrepoint Pier (50B) leave Trat from a stand on Th Sukhumvit next to the municipal shopping centre market and from the bus station. They depart regularly throughout the day, but after dark you will have to charter your own (250B to 300B). There are travel agents in Laem Ngop that can book you on direct bus links to other major destinations on the eastern coast (for a reasonable price).

TRAT TO CAMBODIA

A thin necklace of sandy beaches lines the skinny scrap of land between Trat town and the Cambodian border. **Hat Sai Si Ngoen** (Silver Sand Beach) lies just north of the 41km marker

---

GETTING TO ANGKOR IN CAMBODIA

For travel to Sihanoukville or a more scenic route to Phnom Penh, cross the Thai-Cambodian border at Hat Lek (see p148) if you're coming from the eastern gulf coast. To get to Siem Reap and the Temples of Angkor, however, it's far easier to travel by bus from Chanthaburi via Sa Kaew (137B, three hours) to Aranya Prathet (35B, 40 minutes). From here catch a túk-túk (60B, 10 minutes) to the border where you can cross over to the Cambodian border town of Poipet. This border is open between 7am and 8pm but Poipet after dark is not a pleasant place to be so plan on getting there well before dusk.

Scams abound. Túk-túk drivers will take you to a fake 'Cambodian Consulate' where you'll be told to fill out forms for a visa and pay 1200B. Pick up your pack and walk away. Cambodian visas are given in Cambodia, not in Thailand. Some people have reported being told they have to exchange US$100 into riel – this is also a scam. Go straight to Thai immigration to get stamped out then walk to the Cambodian visa office where you'll be issued a visa for 1000B or US$20. If you don't have an ID photo you'll be charged an extra 100B. Another option is to get a one-month e-visa (US$25) online from www.mfaic.gov.kh – this takes three business days to issue but can help you avoid the scam zone.

Once you're through the sleazy armpit casino strip of Poipet, and beyond the border gates, your best option is to move on – this is Cambodia's ickiest town. Try not to get roped into the 'free' tourist shuttle to the 'International Tourist Terminal,' which arranges transport to major cities, but at inflated prices: Phnom Penh (US$15, seven hours); Siem Reap (US$10, two hours); Battambang (US$9, two hours). Instead, walk to the bus company offices for cheaper fares. The vast majority of buses depart very early (before 8am). It is also possible to negotiate taxis. Aim to pay no more than US$30 to Siem Reap (153km), which should take less than two hours in a good vehicle.

For more information on Thai visas see p411.

GETTING TO CAMBODIA'S ISLANDS, BEACHES & PHNOM PENH

Hat Lek is much easier to reach and depart from nowadays thanks to direct boats to/from the Ko Chang Archipelago (see p162). This is the border to cross if you're heading to Sihanoukville or Phnom Penh, but for Siem Reap it's better to cross at Aranya Prathet (see the boxed text, p147). The border at Hat Lek is open between 7am and 8pm daily but note that it gets very busy – and slow – on Fridays when lots of Cambodians cross into Thailand for a weekly market. Motorcycles and minivans are available from Hat Lek to the border for 50B to 60B.

Once on the Cambodian side of the border you can take a *moto* (motorcycle with driver; 100B plus 11B toll) or taxi (200B plus 44B toll) to Krong Koh Kong. It is now quick and easy to travel by road from Krong Koh Kong to Phnom Penh or Sihanoukville. Buses to Sihanoukville (US$7 to US$13, four hours) and Phnom Penh (US$5 to US$8, five hours) usually depart before 9.30am; morning share taxis to both destinations (US$10) leave from the bus and taxi station. The fast boat services that used to connect Krong Koh Kong with Sihanoukville have been suspended for some time, although they could resume during the lifetime of this book.

A visa is usually available at the border for 1200B (US dollars are no longer preferred) – and yes, that's 200B more expensive than Cambodian visas at other border crossings; haggle politely for hours and you might get it for 1000B. It's cheaper to get a Cambodian visa in Bangkok or you can get a one-month e-visa (US$25) online from www.mfaic.gov.kh, which takes three business days to issue. There are plenty of travel agencies in Trat and Ko Chang that can arrange the trip for a few hundred baht extra, but there's no guarantee your trip will be scam-free. See p411 for information on Thai visas.

Getting stuck in Krong Koh Kong isn't so bad – it has some seedy border-town attributes but can be a fun place to explore, especially the surrounding mountains, estuaries and islands. If you need or want to stay try **Dugout Hotel** (☎ 016-650325; thedugouthotel@yahoo.com; St 3; r with fan/air-con 300/400B; 🛏), a clean, quiet establishment smack in the centre of town.

---

off Hwy 3. Nearby, at the 42km marker, is **Hat Sai Kaew** (Crystal Sand Beach), while at the 48km marker you'll find **Hat Thap Thim** (Sapphire Beach); neither one quite lives up to its whimsical name. The most promising beach is **Hat Ban Cheun**, a long stretch of clean sand near the 63km marker.

In the little town of Khlong Yai, travellers can stop by the **immigration office** (☎ 0 3958 8108) to have their passport stamped upon re-entry from Cambodia. The small border outpost of **Hat Lek** is the departure point for boats to Krong Koh Kong in Cambodia. For information on crossing to Cambodia, see above.

KO CHANG ARCHIPELAGO

อุทยานแห่งชาติเกาะช้าง

Named after the largest island in the area, this stunning archipelago comprises nearly 50 islands and is made up of several marine parks and governmental subdistricts. Only about 2500 inhabitants call these furry specks of jungle home.

Ko Chang is the darling of southeast Thailand and has beach and forest that will enchant most visitors. Other islands have recently begun throwing their hats into the tourist ring and are quickly becoming idyllic tropical destinations themselves. Ko Mak and Ko Kood have dozens of places to stay but feel particularly remote since each resort usually sits alone on one of the myriad bays. Smaller islands such as Ko Whai, Ko Rayang, Ko Kham and Ko Kradat also have a sprinkling of resorts along their flaxen sands.

Diving & Snorkelling

The seamounts off the southern tip of Ko Chang stretch over 32km to Ko Kood, offering a new frontier of diving opportunities in Thailand. **Hin Luk Bat** and **Hin Lap** are rocky, coral-encrusted seamounts with depths of around 18m to 20m that act as a haven for schooling fish. Both **Hin Phrai Nam** and **Hin Gadeng** (between Ko Whai and Ko Rang) are formed by spectacular rock pinnacles and have coral visible to around 28m. Southwest of Ko Chang's Ao Salak Phet, reef-fringed **Ko Whai** features a good variety of colourful hard and soft corals at depths of 6m to 15m.

EASTERN GULF COAST

KO CHANG MARINE NATIONAL PARK

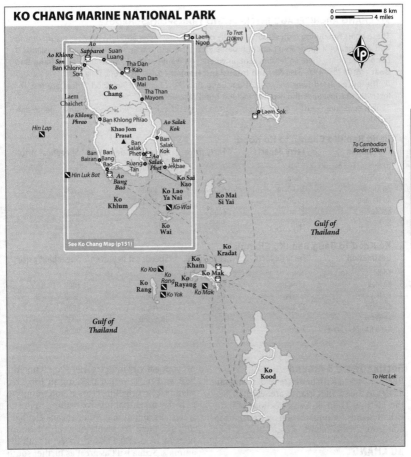

EASTERN GULF COAST

The region's most renowned diving is to be found around **Ko Rang**. Visibility here is much better than near Ko Chang and averages between 10m and 20m but some locals complain that this area gets too crowded with snorkellers and some of the coral has been damaged by boat anchors and people's feet. In the same area, **Ko Yak** and **Ko Laun** are shallow dives perfect for beginners. These two small rocky islands can be circumnavigated and have lots of coral, schooling fish, puffer fish, morays, barracuda, rays and the occasional turtle. **Hin Kuak Maa** (also known as Three Finger Reef) is probably the top dive and is home to a coral-encrusted wall sloping from 2m to 14m and attracting swarms of marine life.

Most dive operators are based on Ko Chang, the largest island in the archipelago (see p153).

Tours

The best way to explore this quiet realm is by joining a live-aboard tour. The **JYSK Sea Safari** (☎ 0 2630 9371; www.jysktravel.com; 3-day trip 8900B) takes passengers on an authentic fishing vessel for a three- to four-day adventure around the archipelago with sea kayaks and snorkelling equipment. This isn't a holiday cruise – there's one bathroom and everyone sleeps on deck, but it's a fantastic way to experience life at sea. You can decide where you prefer to end your voyage; JSYK also runs New Road Guesthouse in Bangkok (p96).

KO CHANG ARCHIPELAGO INTER-ISLAND TRANSPORT SCHEDULE

These boats run during high season – usually between November and July. Services dry up during bad weather or if there aren't enough passengers. The ferries only stop at the smaller islands if people are going there so tell the captain where you want to get off. Boats are run by **Bang Bao Boat** (☎ 08 7054 4300; Bang Bao) and **Interisland Hopper** (☎ 08 1865 0610; Bang Bao).

The prices listed here are to go from Bang Bao (Ko Chang) or Ko Kood. Prices are less for inter-island trips. Speedboat prices include hotel pick up.

This schedule is just a guide and is apt to change: check times with local tourist agents and hotels.

Bang Bao (Ko Chang) to Ko Kood:

Destination	Ferry departs	Ferry price	Speedboat departs	Speedboat price
Bang Bao (Ko Chang)	8.50am	–	11.50am	–
Ko Whai	10am	300B	12.15pm	400B
Ko Kham	10.40am	400B	12.30pm	600B
Ko Rayang	10.50am	400B	12.40pm	600B
Ko Mak	11am	400B	1pm	600B
Ko Kood	2pm	700B	2pm	900B

Ko Kood to Bang Bao (Ko Chang):

Destination	Ferry departs	Ferry price	Speedboat departs	Speedboat price
Ko Kood	9am	–	9am	–
Ko Mak	11.50am	300B	10am	600B
Ko Rayang	midday	400B	10.20am	600B
Ko Kham	12.10pm	400B	10.30am	600B
Ko Whai	1pm	400B	10.45am	600B
Bang Bao (Ko Chang)	2pm	700B	11am	900B

Getting There & Around

Boat services to Ko Chang are year-round but ferries to the smaller islands are seasonal. See the 'Getting There & Away' sections of individual islands for information on transport to and from the mainland.

KO CHANG

เกาะช้าง

Despite how built up the west coast of the island is getting, Ko Chang still feels like an adventurous getaway. High mountains mean that you'll have to chug up and down vertiginous, often slippery paved roads to get anywhere. Nearly the whole island is covered in vast swathes of flourishing rainforests that hide waterfalls, exotic reptiles and endless potential for rugged exploration. Emerge from the jungle and you'll reach isolated lookouts that gaze down on beaches ranging from secret sandy spits to sweeping stretches crammed with sun-worshippers.

If your time on other Thai islands has included a few too many days laying on the beach, Ko Chang can help brush the cobwebs off your activity muscles. Here you'll find the best and most varied trekking in the Thai islands from gruelling cross-island tramps to easy day hikes that involve bathing in lots of waterfalls. Being that *chang* means elephant in Thai, there are plenty of elephant camps offering treks and a chance to swim with the animals. Scuba isn't as great as further south down the peninsula but is still very worthwhile; there are plenty of twee islands to kayak to and rivers to explore. Try your hand deep sea or squid fishing, take a cooking class, motorbike around the island – the options are limitless.

Each holiday season brings new development, but rest assured, many years remain before this mega-island will no longer be synonymous with 'paradise.'

Orientation

Most of Ko Chang's development straddles the western coastline, while the majority of the rest of the island remains a dripping rainforest. Boats from the mainland arrive at the northern pier at Ao Sapparot while

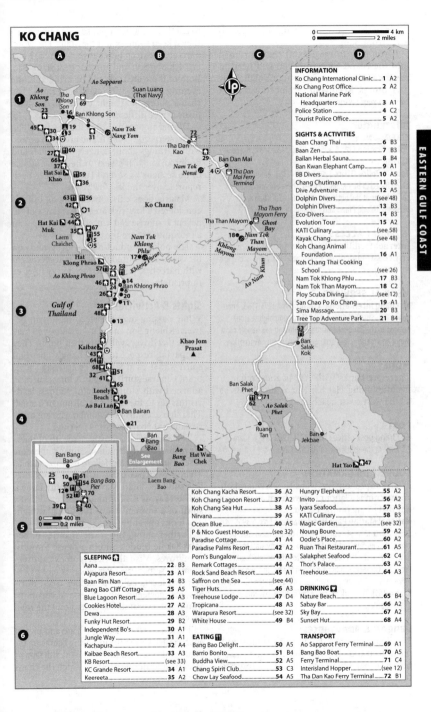

KO CHANG

0 |————————| 4 km
0 |————————| 2 miles

INFORMATION

Ko Chang International Clinic	**1** A2
Ko Chang Post Office	**2** A2
National Marine Park Headquarters	**3** A1
Police Station	**4** C2
Tourist Police Office	**5** A2

SIGHTS & ACTIVITIES

Baan Chang Thai	**6** B3
Baan Zen	**7** B3
Bailan Herbal Sauna	**8** B4
Ban Kwan Elephant Camp	**9** A1
BB Divers	**10** A5
Chang Chutiman	**11** B3
Dive Adventure	**12** A5
Dolphin Divers	(see 48)
Dolphin Divers	**13** B3
Eco-Divers	**14** B3
Evolution Tour	**15** A2
KATI Culinary	(see 58)
Kayak Chang	(see 48)
Koh Chang Animal Foundation	**16** A1
Koh Chang Thai Cooking School	(see 26)
Nam Tok Khlong Phlu	**17** B3
Nam Tok Than Mayom	**18** C2
Ploy Scuba Diving	(see 12)
San Chao Po Ko Chang	**19** A1
Sima Massage	**20** B3
Tree Top Adventure Park	**21** B4

SLEEPING

Aana	**22** B3
Aiyapura Resort	**23** A1
Baan Rim Nan	**24** B3
Bang Bao Cliff Cottage	**25** A5
Blue Lagoon Resort	**26** A3
Cookies Hotel	**27** A2
Dewa	**28** A3
Funky Hut Resort	**29** B2
Independent Bo's	**30** A1
Jungle Way	**31** A1
Kachapura	**32** A4
Kaibae Beach Resort	**33** A3
KB Resort	(see 33)
KC Grande Resort	**34** A1
Keereeta	**35** A2

EATING

Bang Bao Delight	**50** A5
Barrio Bonito	**51** B4
Buddha View	**52** A5
Chang Spirit Club	**53** C3
Chow Lay Seafood	**54** A5

Koh Chang Kacha Resort	**36** A2
Koh Chang Lagoon Resort	**37** A2
Koh Chang Sea Hut	**38** A5
Nirvana	**39** A5
Ocean Blue	**40** A5
P & Nico Guest House	(see 32)
Paradise Cottage	**41** A4
Paradise Palms Resort	**42** A2
Porn's Bungalow	**43** A3
Remark Cottages	**44** A2
Rock Sand Beach Resort	**45** A1
Saffron on the Sea	(see 44)
Tiger Huts	**46** A3
Treehouse Lodge	**47** D4
Tropicana	**48** A3
Warapura Resort	(see 32)
White House	**49** B4

Hungry Elephant	**55** A2
Invito	**56** A2
Iyara Seafood	**57** A3
KATI Culinary	**58** B3
Magic Garden	(see 32)
Noung Boure	**59** A2
Oodie's Place	**60** A2
Ruan Thai Restaurant	**61** A5
Salakphet Seafood	**62** C4
Thor's Palace	**63** A2
Treehouse	**64** A3

DRINKING

Nature Beach	**65** B4
Sabay Bar	**66** A2
Sky Bay	**67** A2
Sunset Hut	**68** A4

TRANSPORT

Ao Sapparot Ferry Terminal	**69** A1
Bang Bao Boat	**70** A5
Ferry Terminal	**71** C4
Interisland Hopper	(see 12)
Tha Dan Kao Ferry Terminal	**72** B1

Ban Bang Bao

See Enlargement

0 |————| 400 m
0 |————| 0.2 miles

boats to the rest of the Chang Archipelago leave from Bang Bao.

If you plan to venture off the main road into the island's interior, you will need to pay the 400B park entry fee at one of the four park offices. Keep your receipt so you don't have to pay twice.

Information

EMERGENCY
Police Station (☎ 0 3958 6191, 0 3952 1657) Based at Ban Dan Mai.
Tourist Police Office (☎ 0 3965 1351, emergency 1155) Based in Ban Khlong Phrao. There are also smaller police boxes at the northern end of Hat Sai Khao and between Khlong Phrao and Hat Kaibae.

INTERNET ACCESS
Internet facilities run the length of the western coast, charging between 1B and 2B per minute.

MEDICAL SERVICES
Ko Chang International Clinic (☎ 0 3955 1555, emergency 1719; Hat Sai Khao; ✆ 24hr during high season) Related to the Bangkok Hospital Group and can handle most minor emergencies and arrange for emergency evacuations.

MONEY
There are banks with ATMs and exchange facilities along Hat Sai Khao, and ATMs at all the west coast beaches.

POST
Ko Chang post office (☎ 0 3955 1240; ✆ 8.30am-3.30pm) At the south end of Hat Sai Khao.

TOURIST INFORMATION
The comprehensive website www.iamkoh chang.com is a labour of love from an irreverent Brit living on the island.
National Marine Park Headquarters (☎ 0 3955 5080; ✆ 8.30am-4.30pm Mon-Fri) On the main road between Khlong Son and Hat Sai Khao. Friendly staff try their best, despite the language barrier, to offer as much info as they can. Campers can book a site in the brush beyond the office at Nam Tok Than Mayom or on the isolated isle of Ko Rang (p165). The park entrance fee is 400B, payable at one of these offices.

Dangers & Annoyances
Ko Chang's biggest danger is its skinny and often steep and slick 'ring road.' As one guesthouse owner bluntly put it, 'Many tourists rent motorbikes and then they die. You want to tell them to at least put some clothes on so they'll keep some skin if they fall.' The worst parts are the steep hills between Hat Sai Khao and Khlong Son and another near Bang Bao. Both of these areas should be avoided in the evening or after rain (even light rain). The road is poorly lit at night and the many sharp turns can be difficult to navigate.

During monsoon season, the beaches along the western side of the island are often posted with warnings about dangerous riptides and undercurrents. It's best to heed the advice of these signs as several fatalities have been reported over the last few years.

Malaria does exist on Ko Chang but it's considered a low-risk area. Liberal use of repellent at sunrise and sunset and sleeping with a mosquito net are the best protections.

The police conduct regular drug raids on the island's accommodation. If you get caught with narcotics, you could face heavy fines or imprisonment.

Sights & Activities
While passing over the steep mountain between Khlong Son and Hat Sai Khao, you may notice that drivers will honk their horns. They are paying respect to Ko Chang's guardian spirit who lives at **San Chao Po Ko Chang** – a vibrant Chinese spirit temple. A long staircase, adorned with stone elephant statues, leads visitors up to the entrance, although a small Thai sign explains that women who are menstruating are barred from entering.

The east coast is mostly made up of mangrove forests and plantations. Inland, there are several stunning **waterfalls** to explore, such as Than Mayom (see p154). The stretch of shoreline south of Than Mayom is locally known as **Ghost Bay**, as it's commonly believed that a spirit of a woman roams the beach at night and looks out at the sea.

Further along, the rustic shanties of **Ban Salak Kok** lie hidden within a dense forest of mangroves. Visit the rickety docks and explore the serpentine river by kayak (see p155). Nearby, locals cultivate rubber trees, durians, mangosteens, pineapples and coconuts. You'll see several **shrimp farms** along the road as well.

There's another fishing village and pier at **Ao Salak Phet**. Climb the imposing **lighthouse** for panoramic views, and stop by the **fish farm** at Salakphet Seafood (p160) to watch the chaos during feeding time.

WHERE TO BEACH YOURSELF ON KO CHANG

Ko Chang is the second biggest island in Thailand – meaning it's huge – and the beach where you choose to stay will define your experience. Many visitors arrive by boat and hope that the sŏrng·tăa·ou will just drop them off at the main beach. Well, there isn't really a main beach – decide where you want to go before you arrive. The following beaches are listed from north to south:

- **Ao Khlong Son** has the island's largest village, a lovely bay and is near good trekking, elephant camps and the ferry. For beach-side fun you're better off elsewhere unless you're staying at the plush Aiyapura Resort.
- **Hat Sai Khao (White Sands Beach)**, the longest beach strip on the island, packs in a concentration of bungalows, bars and restaurants. Great shopping lines the concrete-dominated main drag and there are tons of very comfortable midrange options plus a mellow backpacker area, reached only on foot at the golden northern section of the beach. While most of Hat Sai Khao is swathed in lovely white sand, the southern part, Ko Muk, hardly has a beach at all.
- **Hat Khlong Phrao** is small, quiet and romantic with sunset vistas over a scattering of karst islands. Luxury resorts are moving in fast but there's still a budget option or two and some good midrangers. This is a great location for kayaking up the Khlong Phrao or to the fringing islands.
- **Hat Kaibae** is similar to Hat Khlong Phrao in terms of stunning looks but is more popular with families. The main road area is clogged with a colourful collection of simple shops and stalls.
- **Lonely Beach**, the laid-back backpacker hold out with thumping music as late as you want, is anything but lonely. Most sleeping options are off the beach but it's a short walk to lush sands where party-goers sleep it off between water buffalo bathing in murky streams.
- **Bang Bao** has a rickety pier that's very touristy with tons of shops, some of the island's best seafood and some interesting places to stay. The cape, walking distance from the pier, offers lots of sea views, rocky cliffs and small quiet beaches.
- **Hat Yao** is where you go for a lost beach experience. The beach is one of the island's best but once you're here you're stuck.

DIVING & SNORKELLING

While the best sites in Thailand are undoubtedly along the Andaman and southern Gulf coasts, divers around Ko Chang will have the benefit of exploring reefs that are still quite pristine. Some local enthusiasts claim that there's diving throughout the year, but most operations function with a skeleton crew during monsoon season as the visibility is lousy and the seas can be incredibly rough and often impassable. The best time to strap on your gear is between December and March. See p148 for detailed information about diving around the Ko Chang Archipelago.

Diving prices are somewhat standardised across Ko Chang so there's no need to spend your time hunting around for the best deal. You can, however, ask your operator of choice about discounted accommodation – several companies often hook their clients up with great lodging rates as an added incentive. Additional price cuts are given if you bring your own equipment. A typical fun-dive excursion usually includes two guided dives, transport, equipment and food, and will set you back about 2500B to 3000B. PADI Open Water certification costs 13,500B to 15,000B per person, and is available in several different languages. Be wary of dive centres that offer too many price cuts – safety is paramount, and a shop giving out unusually good deals is probably cutting too many corners.

The following dive operations plus many travel agencies also offer snorkelling tours around Ko Chang (500B to 550B) and Ko Rang (650B to 700B). Prices include snorkel gear and lunch. Evolution Tour (p154) also offers full-day snorkelling trips.

BB Divers (☎ 0 3955 8040, 08 6129 2305; www.bbdivers .com) Based in Bang Bao, with a swimming pool at the south end of Lonely Beach.

Dive Adventure (☎ 08 1762 6482; www.thedive kochang.com) Also based in Bang Bao. Offers captained boat rentals from 8000B per day.

Dolphin Divers (☎ 08 7028 1627; www.scubadiving kohchang.com) Based in Khlong Phrao and also has a small booking office at the Amari Resort. Offers a variety of other water sports including surfing, kayaking and wake-boarding.

Eco-Divers (☎ 0 3955 7296; www.ecodivers.fr) Main office also located at Khlong Phrao, with additional locations on most of the other west coast beaches.

Ploy Scuba Diving (☎ 0 3955 8033; www.ployscuba .com) Has a shop on nearly every beach in Ko Chang; the main office is in Bang Bao.

ELEPHANT TREKKING

Chang means elephant, so it's not surprising that there are three operations on the island offering travellers the opportunity to play with these gentle giants.

Ban Kwan Elephant Camp (☎ 08 9815 9566, 08 1919 3995; changtone@yahoo.com; 40-/90min adventure 500/900B; ☽ 8.30am-4.30pm), about 2km inland from Ban Khlong Son, takes in older pachyderms that were once used for labour and helps them live out their days close to nature. The informative 1½-hour 'experience' involves feeding, bathing, an elephant ride and the chance to learn about the creatures' lives in a wild setting.

Chang Chutiman (☎ 08 9939 6676, 08 7135 7424; 1-/2hr ride 500/900B; ☽ 8am-5pm) and **Baan Chang Thai** (☎ 0 3955 1474; 1-/2hr ride 500/900B) are both based in Khlong Phrao and offer similar programs to Ban Kwan in a less dramatic setting.

Transfers are included in these prices, but make sure you book in advance. Most accommodation can arrange these adventures within a day's notice.

HIKING

If your muscles are starting to shrivel after too many days of beach bumming, try stretching your legs in Ko Chang's breathtaking inland jungle of soaring mountain vistas, lush vegetation and gushing waterfalls.

Many consider **Nam Tok Khlong Phlu** (park admission 400B; ☽ 8am-5pm) to be Ko Chang's most impressive waterfall. It's easily accessible from the resorts at Khlong Phrao on the western coast. Set amid striking jungle scenery, the chute is

---

KEEPING YOU ABREAST

Topless sunbathing is not just considered to be offensive to Thais – it is forbidden by law in all of Thailand's national parks. This includes Ko Chang Marine National Park and all beaches on Ko Chang, Ko Kood, Ko Mak, Ko Whai etc.

---

quickly reached by walking 600m along a well-marked jungle path. Khlong Phlu dumps out into a cool pool; it's the perfect place to dunk your body after a sweaty day's adventure.

Another stunning cascade, **Nam Tok Than Mayom** (park admission 400B; ☽ 8am-5pm) can be reached via Tha Than Mayom or Ban Dan Mai on the east coast. The view from the top is marvellous and there are inscribed stones bearing the initials of Rama V, Rama VI and Rama VII nearby.

There are many freelance guides on the island who charge from around 500B for day hikes (the price depends on how much car travel and equipment is involved). Should you decide to set off on your own adventure (which is not particularly advisable), steer clear of the mountainous area between Bang Bao and Ao Salak Phet, unless you are an experienced tropical hiker with moderate orienteering skills. If you don't get lost, this rewarding hike will take four to six hours and you may find the isolated **Hat Wai Chek**. If you do get lost, try to find a stream and follow the current – it will usually take you either to the sea or a village, then you can either follow the coast or ask for directions.

If you plan to do several hikes, make sure you hold on to your park fee receipt, as you only have to pay once to access the park. The following operations offer all-inclusive tour packages. Your hotel can probably book you on similar trips as well.

Evolution Tour (☎ 0 3955 1058; www.evolutiontour .com; Khlong Phrao) Offers a huge assortment of hiking and boating trips. Snorkelling tours are also available.

Jungle Way (☎ 08 9223 4795; www.jungleway .com) Runs one- and two-day excursions (800B to 1000B) through the island's interior, including an intense hike through the Chang Noi peninsula; book through your hotel.

Trekkers of Koh Chang (☎ 08 1578 7513) Offers ornithological day trips (1200B to 1400B); book through your hotel.

KAYAKING

The most professional sea-kayaking outfit is the new British-run **Kayak Chang** (☎ 08 7673 1753; www.kayakchang.com; Amari Resort). Courses range from two-hour introductory jaunts (900B) to eight-day expeditions (25,000B) and everything in between. Groups have a maximum of six people so this is a wonderfully intimate way to discover secret beaches, snorkelling spots and uninhabited islands of the archipelago.

PRESERVING THE SPIRIT OF KO CHANG

Pittaya Homkrailas is the founder of the **Chang Spirit Project** (www.changspirit.net; for the project's activities see below), a pioneer community-based tourism project at Salak Kok on the eastern side of Ko Chang. He's also involved with the eco-conscious **Ban Kwan Elephant Camp** (opposite).

Here Pittaya explains his vision:

'All I want to do on Ko Chang is to try and take good care of people and nature. Living here is so beautiful and peaceful – I don't want to lose it.

'Years ago Ko Chang's goal was ecotourism and everyone agreed because we have very good nature and beautiful villages. But this was mixed by the different people who came to Ko Chang as tourists, officers, investors, etc. Different people look at Ko Chang and think differently. Yes, we should make a balance and I agree. But can Ko Chang be different from other Thai islands? Yes, Ko Chang can.

'Four years ago I set up the Chang Spirit Project at Salak Kok as a pilot project. My goal is to save this peaceful fishing village as well as the largest mangrove forest on Ko Chang. Here tourists, the villagers, the government and nature can all work together. The villagers can love each other because they own the same business and work together towards the same goal. This project uses only human energy, less pollution and good exercise plus 5% of the profit is used to protect the mangrove forest. The villagers still keep their old ways as fishers and fruit gardeners but welcome the tourists. The tourists help save the community and the mangrove forest; Salak Kok and the mangrove forest remain beautiful and peaceful. The government can help by offering funds for support and know that when the villagers become as one they are easier to reach.

'Let's live happily together!'

For a more low-key local experience organised by the **Chang Spirit Project** (see boxed text, above), **Salak Kok Kayak Station** (☎ 08 1919 3995; Ban Salak Kok; 1hr rental 100B, 90min tour 900B), in a traditional stilt village in the island's southeast, hires kayaks for viewing the mangrove-forested bay. It also runs a three-hour 'dinner cruise' (see p160).

Many guesthouses rent out kayaks; prices generally run from 100B per hour and 300B to 500B per day.

OTHER SPORTS

Some guesthouses rent out inflatable beach rafts, sailboards, masks and snorkels, and boogie boards. Mountain bikes can be hired for 150B per day at several places on the island, most of which are located at Hat Sai Khao and Hat Kaibae.

The **Tree Top Adventure Park** (☎ 08 4310 7600; www .treetopadventurepark.com; admission 900B; 9am-5pm), near Ao Bai Lan, is an exciting obstacle course suspended high in the trees. The price includes a couple of hours of jungle fun and complementary hotel transfers. Last entry at 3pm.

Deep sea fishing trips (5-7hr trip 1200B) can be organised through virtually any tour office, hotel or on the pier at Bang Bao. Trips during the day or at night from sunset include a buffet lunch or dinner. You can also organise more basic night-time **squid fishing trips** (6pm-12am; 450B) through the agents on the dock at Bang Bao.

SPA & YOGA

The proliferation of top-end resorts has meant a similar increase in the number of spas. Today there are places to get pampered on every beach on the west coast.

If you're into yoga, reiki, bamboo massage and/or meditation, look no further than **Baan Zen** (☎ 08 6530 9354; www.baanzen.com) in Khlong Phrao. Run by a friendly French couple, this serene teak retreat sits on a quiet lagoon near the ocean. Reserve in advance for private workshops (two to four people only), led by an experienced Sivananda yoga instructor.

When the natural humidity isn't enough to cleanse your pores, try a sauna treatment at **Bailan Herbal Sauna** (☎ 0 6252 4744; www.bailan-koh chang.com; Ao Bai Lan; admission 200B; 3-9pm). Sweat to a variety of herbs including kaffir lime and lemon grass. Mud masks and salt scrubs are also on offer in a lush garden setting.

Sima Massage (☎ 08 1489 5171; Ao Khlong Phrao; massage per hr 250B; 8am-10pm) is regarded by some as the best massage on the island; locals head here for sports injuries or to work out stress. Try the After Sun Body Treatment (600B). It's on the road next to KATI cooking school (p156).

Courses

Thai cooking classes are available at **KATI Culinary** (☎ 0 3955 7252, 08 9028 9969; kati_culinary@ hotmail.com; lunch courses 1000B; ☺ 10.30am-3pm) and **Koh Chang Thai Cooking School** (☎ 08 1940 0649; info cookingschool@yahoo.com; Blue Lagoon Resort; afternoon courses 1000B). Both are fun and friendly options that include transportation, a cookbook and, of course, your meal.

VOLUNTEERING

You'll notice fewer stray animals on Ko Chang compared to other places in Thailand thanks to the efforts of the **Koh Chang Animal Foundation** (☎ 08 9042 2347; www.kohchanganimalfoundation.org; Ban Khlong Son). Funded entirely by donations, the foundation offers free-of-charge vet services and provides refuge and treatment for stray animals around the island. Volunteer visits by travelling vets and veterinarian nurses are particularly appreciated, but the foundation also welcomes day visits from anyone who loves animals and can help bathe and socialise with abused animals.

Sleeping

Accommodation on Ko Chang continues to multiply with every season. Prices have been climbing as well, and even though several cheapies remain, the island's prices are more inflated than similar island destinations such as Ko Tao and Ko Pha-Ngan.

During the low season, the ferries usually stop servicing all of the piers on Ko Chang except Ao Sapparot and Tha Dan Kao, and several remote resorts close their doors. Places that do stay open often lower their prices around 25%.

For more detailed descriptions of each beach see p153.

BAN KHLONG SON

This is the island's largest village, with a network of piers, a wát, a school, several noodle shops and an ATM.

Jungle Way (☎ 08 9223 4795; www.jungleway .com; bungalows 200-400B) Stilted bungalows and a funky restaurant with a wildlife-viewing platform are tucked into the jungle near the Ban Kwan Elephant Camp. You're nowhere near the beach, but there's trekking on offer, mountain bikes for rent (80B per day) and the staff are fun and friendly.

Aiyapura Resort (☎ 0 3955 5111; www.aiyapura.com; bungalows 4000-14,000B; ⚡ ☐ ⚡ ⚡) If you want to be treated like a king or queen, then Aiyapura is the perfect place to drop your luggage. This rambling resort sits alone on a hilly promontory and fashionable bungalows are nestled in between shivering coconut palms and fruit-bearing trees. Amenities include a long jogging track, state-of-the-art spa, gargantuan pool, beachside restaurant and unbelievably friendly staff.

HAT SAI KHAO (WHITE SANDS BEACH)

If you're arriving on Ko Chang from Trat, busy White Sands will be your first stop after coming over the headland. The less attractive southern end of the beach is known as Hat Kai Muk (Pearl Beach).

There's a mellow backpacker enclave at the north of the beach reached only on foot. To get there turn towards the beach at the 7-Eleven in front of the KC Grande. When you reach the beach, turn right and walk for a few hundred metres.

our pick **Independent Bo's** (☎ 0 3955 1165; r 300-750B) A colourful place that clambers up the jungled hillside, Bo's is what the Swiss Family Robinson would've built if the family were on acid. All bungalows are funky and unique, and very clean. The cheapest rooms are 'way, way' up in the jungle. No phone bookings are accepted so you just have to show up.

Rock Sand Beach Resort (☎ 08 4781 0550; www .rocksand-resort.com; r from 500B; ⚡) Just past Bo's, Rock Sand lacks character but is more comfy and solidly built than the other backpacker beach cheapies. Simple fan bungalows share bathrooms, while the highest-priced air-con rooms look out over the sea. The restaurant hovers over the clear blue water.

Koh Chang Lagoon Resort (☎ 0 3955 1201; www .kohchanglagoonresort.com; r 1200-1600B; ⚡) Spread out over three buildings, every room at this place is spotless, has wood floors, a good bathroom and offers excellent value. The only rooms of character are found at the beachside location, which is built with polished rocks in cement and has gnarled vine-lined walkways. Rooms here have floor-to-ceiling hardwoods and feel almost like cabins. The beach in front is backed by a shady, grassy area and a few massage huts.

Koh Chang Kacha Resort (☎ 0 3955 1224; www .kohchangkacha.com; r 1400-1600B; ⚡ ⚡) The name makes you want to say 'gazuntite' and hand someone a tissue, but this place is one of the more stylish midrangers on this beach.

There are two areas here: nestled in a jungly garden along the skinny white beach you'll find Balinese-style bungalows and villas while crisp rooms are in a brand-new block building across the road. Each section has a good pool and the whole place is popular with families.

Remark Cottages (☎ 0 3955 1261; www.remark cottage.com; bungalows 2000-3300B; ✸) A wonderfully overgrown garden conceals 15 Balinese-style bungalows in a supremely relaxing location off a quiet rocky beach. Relax in the wooden spa dipping pool or treat yourself with a course of shower spray therapy.

Other notable options:

Saffron on the Sea (☎ 0 3955 1253; r from 1200B; ✸) Nestled in a pebbled cove with sitting areas over the water, tiny Saffron strives for boutique beauty.

Paradise Palms Resort (☎ 08 9094 6023; www .paradisepalmsresort.net; d/f 1400/2500B; ✸) A lovely, clean family-run place that was the first built in the area – Hat Muk is named after the owners' daughter. Updated bungalows sit on one of the nicest parts of this beach and the price includes free motorbike usage.

Cookies Hotel (☎ 0 3955 1107; www.kohchangcookies hotel.com; r 1500-4000B; ✸ ▢ ▣) Occupies two horseshoe-shaped buildings: one along the beach, and one bordering the jungle across the road. It's got a bit of a package tour vibe but is a great bargain.

Keereeta (☎ 0 3955 1304; www.keereeta.com; r 2500B; ✸ ▣) Nowhere near the beach but lovely rooms with beautiful Balinese decoration; a soothing pool graces the Zen-like central courtyard.

KC Grande Resort (☎ 0 3955 1199; www.kckohchang .com; r & bungalows from 7000B; ✸) KC is 'grande' with over 60 rooms. It's on the best part of the beach but it's overpriced unless you find a good deal on the web.

AO KHLONG PHRAO

About 4km south of Hat Sai Khao, Ao Khlong Phrao is developing as the island's luxury hub, but a few affordable places remain.

Blue Lagoon Resort (☎ 08 1940 0649; www.koh changcookery.com; r 600-1200B; ✸) White-washed bungalows with private decks and softly striped curtains sit right above a calm lagoon, and further back two-storey air-con bungalows stand in a shady grove. A wooden walkway leads to the beach and there's a Thai cooking class (opposite).

Baan Rim Nam (☎ 08 7005 8575; www.iamkohchang .com; r from 1100B; ✸ ▢ ☎) Run by some of the most helpful people on Ko Chang, this converted fisherman's-house-turned-guesthouse teeters over a river in the mangroves. Free kayaks help you explore upriver or down to the beach (under five minutes) and offshore islands. Rooms are spotless and comfortable and the estuary keeps the whole place relatively cool.

Dewa (☎ 0 3955 7339; www.thedewakohchang.com; r & bungalows 4400-12,600B; ✸ ▢ ▣) The Dewa takes polished grey cement structures and tops them with thatch creating a stunning and contemporary eco-chic. This unique dual style permeates the interiors as well – rooms are adorned with velvet day beds and dark teak panelling. At night the restaurant spreads over the beach and you can dine in tiki-torchlight with views over the calm sea.

ourpick Tropicana (☎ 0 2642 4420; www.kohchang tropicana.com; r 4900-8800B; ✸ ▢ ▣) Live out your jungle fantasies in the utmost comfort at this beachside gem swimming in lush yet impeccably maintained gardens. All the structures are built with a mix of cement, bamboo and thatch, and have some quirky features such as spiral teak staircases and lovely Thai wooden furniture. There's an infinity pool overlooking a blissful stretch of beach, a little river running through the property, charming wooden walkways everywhere and lovely service.

Also recommended:

Tiger Huts (☎ 08 1762 3710; bungalows 300-600B) Forty unadorned thatch huts line a strip of sandy beach and come in two models: shared bathrooms or private bathrooms. They're simple, but well located.

Aana (☎ 0 3955 1539; www.aanarsort.com; r from 7000B; ✸ ▢ ▣) Round walls, crisp whitewashed rooms and a riverside location makes Aana fresh and unique. The rooms are effortlessly romantic and a few come with personal spas.

KAIBAE

Porn's Bungalow (☎ 08 9251 9233; www.pornsbunga lows-kohchang.com; huts 300-800B) Aah it's a remaining slice of backpacker heaven at Porn's where rustic huts are cheap and an eclectic clientele of every age and nationality play pool, eat, drink and just hang out. There's a multilevel chill space where idlers watch the sun bleed red as it dips behind four jagged islands. The restaurant here is also excellent.

Kaibae Beach Resort (☎ 0 3955 7132; www.kaibae beach.com; r 900-1500B; ✸) Clean and sturdy wooden fan-cooled bungalows sit plumb on a lovely, slender stretch of white sand; newer concrete air-con bungalows are tucked back on a murky river but are very comfortable. A large open-air restaurant fires up nightly barbecues.

EASTERN GULF COAST

KB Resort (☎ 0 3955 7125, 08 1862 8103; www.kbresort
.com; bungalows 1150-5000B; ❄) Right on a stretch
of palm-lined beach and soft grass overlooking
some off-shore islands, this family-oriented
place is a little overpriced but the location
is so good few people complain. Bungalows
are very spacious and comfortable but basic.
There's also a mediocre cement pool.

LONELY BEACH (HAT THA NAM) & AO BAI LAN

A backpacker fave, Lonely Beach is moving
upscale with flashier resorts moving in. The
better accommodation (what we have listed)
is mainly inland but there are a scattering
of basic, poorly maintained bamboo beach
huts on the sand in the heart of never-ending
thumping music from 350B per night.

Little Ao Bai Lan is just south of Lonely
Beach and is *very* quiet.

P & Nico Guest House (☎ 08 4362 6673; Hat Tha Nam;
bungalows 200-400B) Tidy, small huts decorated in
summertime blue and yellow are good for a
quiet sleep but still well placed for bars and
restaurants. Bathrooms are attached and have
hot water.

our pick Paradise Cottage (☎ 0 3955 8122, 08 1773
9337; fan bungalows 300-500B; air-con bungalows 1000B;
❄ 🖳) While Paradise just went through a
major upgrade, the thoughtful management
decided to keep some of their old rickety backpacker cheapies 'to not disappoint returning customers'. The rest of the place is now
relatively luxurious with clean, good-value,
modern polished-concrete bungalows with
hot-water bathrooms. Laze the day away in a
private gazebo and listen to relaxing, smooth
jazz as gushing water overflows from over-
turned urns. The beach is rocky but you can
swim here.

Kachapura (☎ 0 3955 8020; www.kachapura.com; fan/
air-con bungalows 500/1000B; ❄) The wood bungalows here with their massive windows, Zen-
style beds and big semi-outdoor hot-water
bathrooms pack a lot of style and comfort
for relatively few baht. The units are linked
by wooden walkways and run down a shady,
flower-filled slope.

White House (☎ 08 1409 8307; www.whitehousekoh
chang.com; r 1600-2000B; ❄ 🖳) Bright white bungalows surround a small pool at this midsized
beachfront resort in Ao Bai Lan. The beds
are size XL but the best feature is the sunken
bathrooms, decked out with clean white tiles.
Less-expensive hotel-type rooms are set back

from the beach and pool, but have less restaurant noise.

our pick Warapura Resort (☎ 08 9122 9888; wara
pura@gmail.com; r incl breakfast 1700-3300B; ❄ 🖳 🖳) If
you're digging the Lonely Beach mojo but can't
live without a little luxe, then Warapura's a
dream come true. Flat-roofed, near-Mexican-
feeling, white-washed buildings house bright
rooms with floor-to-ceiling windows and
more modern style than anything else on Ko
Chang in this price range. It's all about white
and minimalism without losing a cosy appeal
or being ostentatious. The staff are lovely, the
pool is relaxing and the candle-lit restaurant
romantic. Plus there's always a great Lonely
Beach party scene just steps away.

BANG BAO

our pick Bang Bao Cliff Cottage (☎ 08 5904 6706;
www.cliff-cottage.com; bungalows 300B; 🖳) Rustic
wooden huts with mosquito nets, hard beds
and shared bathrooms sit atop a hill with spectacular views either out to sea for sunset or
over Bang Bao for sunrise. There's an excellent
chill space and restaurant down by the water
and it's a seven-minute walk to Bang Bao pier.
Easy-access swimming can be had along the
rocky shore or you can walk to some small,
secluded beaches. For backpacker calm and
simplicity, this place is bliss.

Ocean Blue (☎ 08 1889 2348; www.oceanbluethailand
.com; r fan/air-con 600/1200B; ❄) Simple fan rooms
line a long, polished-wood hallway at this
traditional pier house. Toilets are the bucket
variety, and showers are cold, but the rooms
are clean and you can hear the ocean slosh
beneath you. The young crew running the
place is quirky and funny.

Koh Chang Sea Hut (☎ 08 1285 0570; www.kohchang
-seahut.com; r incl breakfast 2500B; ❄) These 'shanty-
chic' bungalows look like bobbing octagonal
buoys connected by an intricate network of
thin planks. The ebbing ocean curls under
your cabin floor and fresh ocean breezes float
through wooden shutters. Free boat shuttles
or kayaks are available to get to the beach.

Nirvana (☎ 0 3955 8061; www.nirvanakohchang.com;
r 3500-9950B; ❄) Ko Chang's premium resort is
hidden away on a quiet peninsula, and almost
impossible to spot among rambling vegetation. 'Balinese' was the initial design idea, but
each bungalow is furnished slightly differently
in muted earth tones with subtle Asian accents. Tantra, the resort's restaurant, offers a
superb dining experience over the water.

EAST COAST

This part of the island is less developed than the west coast, mostly due to the lack of beaches.

Treehouse Lodge (☎ 08 1847 8215; www.tree-house .org; Hat Yao; huts 300B) This rustic bohemian booby trap for backpackers has recently changed management and everyone is hoping this groovy, peaceful lost paradise will remain the same. Reports are good so far and no matter what there will always be that fantastic, quiet beach to lounge on.

Funky Hut Resort (☎ 0 3958 6177; www.funkyhut -thailand.com; Ao Dan Kao; r 1600-1850B; 🍽 🖳 🕿) Under new ownership, these bungalows are decidedly less funky and certainly more comfortable than their predecessors. Sporting a full face-lift and some pleasant landscaping, the invitingly roomy bungalows still smell of fresh paint and are a good value. Warm hosts Cheryl and Julian can pick you up from the ferry if you contact them in advance.

Eating & Drinking

Virtually every place to stay has a place to eat. Independent restaurants are quickly becoming popular, and there are several special options throughout the island.

WHITE SANDS BEACH (HAT SAI KHAO)

Noung Boure (mains from 40B; 🍽 breakfast, lunch & dinner) Those looking for un-watered down Thai fare should head straight to this simple semi-open air restaurant. A delicious whole steamed fish with lemon (for two people) costs 300B, pad thai starts at 40B and the menu is a tome of seafood and noodle choices.

Thor's Palace (mains 70-170B; 🍽 breakfast, lunch & dinner) Only on Ko Chang is Thor the name of a camp *gà·teu·i* (also spelt *kàthoey*; ladyboy) instead of a burly Scandinavian lumberjack. Savour excellent dishes in an upbeat atmosphere of pumping tunes and colourful knick-knacks.

Hungry Elephant (mains 120-300B; 🍽 10am-10pm) Some of the best French food on the island can be found at this humble roadside place in Hat Kai Muk. Try the mussels with garlic butter (120B) or a filet steak with shallots and red wine (280B) then wash it down with the Italian house red.

Oodie's Place (☎ 0 3955 1193; pizzas 170-260B; 🍽 dinner) After the nightly movie, Mr Oodie straps on the guitar and plays to the crowd as they sling back French and Thai dishes, or Mongolian barbecue with a couple of beers.

our pick **Invito** (☎ 0 3955 1326; mains 320-490B; 🍽 lunch & dinner) Set in a charming teak house, Invito offers wood-fired pizzas, handmade pasta, braised-beef dishes and mouthwatering desserts. It's everyone's favourite *ristorante* on the island, and it'll even deliver to your bungalow.

Bustling Sai Khao has a lively night scene relative to the rest of the island. **Sabay Bar** (☎ 0 3955 1098) has a great night-time vibe and a daily onslaught of talented Filipino bands. **Sky Bay** (☎ 0 3955 1319), towards Khlong Phrao, is a popular pub choice with a plastic cartoon elephant that greets patrons out the front.

KHLONG PHRAO

KATI Culinary (☎ 0 3955 7252, 08 9028 9969; mains 40-120B; 🍽 dinner) This charming twig hut is swathed in warm lighting as the serenades of Serge Gainsbourg drift through the air. Dishes burst with fresh ingredients, and essential side orders of rice are served in an adorable variety of shapes – we got a heart. If you enjoy your meal (and we're pretty sure you will), enrol in KATI's Thai cooking course.

Iyara Seafood (☎ 0 3955 1353, 08 1751 0058; mains from 100B; 🍽 10am-10pm) Iyara isn't your standard island seafood warehouse: after dining in the lovely bamboo *săh·lah* (often spelt *sala*; opensided room), guests are invited to kayak along the adjacent lagoon to watch the flickers of wild fireflies.

LONELY BEACH (HAT THA NAM)

Treehouse (☎ 08 1847 8215; mains 30-80B; 🍽 breakfast, lunch & dinner) Once you hunker down on a bed-sized cushion here, you'll never want to leave. After negotiating the sea of colourful flip-flops left at the entrance, make sure you watch your step while finding a place to relax: the planks of wood are uneven after years of wear and tear.

Magic Garden (☎ 0 3955 8027; mains 60-120B; 🍽 dinner) Magic Garden's pagoda is the Lonely Beach place to chill out and watch a movie. You have to get up to grab some grub – most people get seduced by the squishy pillows and fall asleep.

Barrio Bonito (🍽 breakfast, lunch, dinner) Surprisingly good Mexican fare is served up in this stylish place under ceiling fans by a French/Mexican couple. Try the chicken fajitas (180B), tequila-flambéed prawn with cream, parsley and cilantro (250B) or stop by for a hearty Mexican-style breakfast (150B).

There's also a bar, a small swimming pool and free internet.

For some post-dinner partying, check out the DJ-ed beats at Om Bar, Sunset Hut or the funky discotheque at Nature Beach, all down by the beach.

BANG BAO

Bang Bao Delight (☺ 7am-10pm) Fresh pastries, espresso, fantastic breakfasts, light lunches, free wi-fi and cheap internet (1B per minute), hooray!

Buddha View (☎ 08 9936 1848; www.thebuddhaview .com; mains 80-250B; ☺ breakfast, lunch & dinner) For something chic and international as well as less seafood-oriented, Buddha View is a great place to relax with a cocktail, eat pasta or steak and watch the waves roll in at sunset. Potted jungle flowers abound and the furniture is made from various incarnations of tubular bamboo.

The Bang Bao pier is seafood paradise and the best way to choose where to wield your spoon is to cruise the restaurants' live tanks till you see what you fancy eating swimming around in one of them. The restaurants with the best reputations are **Ruan Thai Restaurant** (☎ 08 9833 5117; mains 100-300B; ☺ breakfast, lunch & dinner) and **Chow Lay Seafood** (☎ 0 3955 5081, 08 1917 9084; www.chowlayseafood.com; mains 100-300B; ☺ breakfast, lunch & dinner).

EAST COAST

Salakphet Seafood (☎ 08 1429 9983; www.kohchang salakphet.com; Ao Salak Phet; mains 40-300B; ☺ breakfast, lunch & dinner) This lonely restaurant hit it big when Thailand's prime minister rolled up, strapped on a bib and declared the food 'delicious'. Since then, other celebrities have stopped by and posed for a photograph for the 'wall of fame'. Salakphet also has a large fish farm with submerged nets full of humongous critters – feeding time is a memorable frenzy.

our pick **Chang Spirit Club** (☎ 08 1919 3995; set menu 1200B; ☺ dinner) Based at the rustic fishing village of Salak Kok, this unique dining experience is a romantic sunset adventure aboard a wooden catamaran. Fresh seafood is served as the quiet craft meanders through gnarled mangroves. For more info on the Chang Spirit Club see p155.

Getting There & Away

There is year-round service between the mainland and Ko Chang. From Tha Ko Chang Centrepoint, 4km from Laem Ngop, there are ferries approximately every hour to and from Ko Chang's Tha Dan Kao (100B, 45 minutes) from 7am until 7pm daily. This is also a vehicle ferry – cars and motorbikes can ride this ferry free with every paying passenger. A sŏrng·tăa·ou from Trat to Tha Ko Chang Centrepoint costs around 60B per person.

Another way to get to Ko Chang is via the more on-schedule hourly vehicle ferry from Tha Thammachat. This ferry arrives at Ao Sapparot pier (per person/car 80/100B, 30 minutes) and may be the only boat running during rough seas.

A new bus links Suvarnabhumi Airport in Bangkok to Ko Chang (around six hours) including boat ticket for 308B. At the time of research there was only one service per day leaving at 7.30am but more are planned. The bus departs back to the airport from Ko Chang at 1.30pm

For transport information to the smaller islands in the archipelago, consult the section of your desired destination.

Getting Around

There are loads of places along the west coast that rent out motorbikes for around 250B per day. Jeeps can be hired for around 2000B per day in the high season. See p152 for important safety protocols.

The sŏrng·tăa·ou meeting the boats at Tha Dan Kao and Ao Sapparot charge from 50B to 120B per person, depending on how far down the west coast you want to go. Expect to pay between 60B and 150B for east coast deliveries.

KO KOOD

เกาะกูด

There's nowhere else in Thailand quite like Ko Kood. It's vast, it's studded with spectacular strips of white sand as well as a few rickety fishing villages, and it has a slightly hilly lush-rainforest interior. While the locals are exceptionally nice and the island is easy to get to, Ko Kood is still scarcely developed and only the wiliest tourists have caught on that this is such a refreshingly mellow place to visit. The people who do make it here are spread out between the 20 or so resorts, nearly each one with its own private beach, so it feels like you have the island to yourself. Think romance; think ultimate peace and quiet; think not going to stay this way for long.

Orientation

Almost all of the resorts are located along Ko Kood's western beaches. A dirt road runs through the west side, connecting the villages of Ban Khlong Hin Dam and Ban Khlong Chao, and then turns northeast before ending in Ao Salat on the other side of the island.

Information

There are no banks or ATMs on the island, and credit cards are rarely accepted. Some bungalow operators can exchange small amounts of foreign currency, but it's best to bring along all the cash you'll need.

Most resorts have a computer terminal or two for guests' use but the internet connection is slow and unreliable. Mobile phones work surprisingly well throughout the island.

Sights

If you have your sights set on finding a secluded strip of sand, you can pretty much choose from any beach on the island.

Two waterfalls on the island are short hiking destinations. The larger and more popular **Nam Tok Khlong Chao** is wide and pretty with a massive plunge pool. Expect to share it with dozens of other visitors, especially on weekends. It's a quick jungle walk to the base, or you can kayak up Khlong Chao. Further north is **Nam Tok Khlong Yai Ki**, which is smaller but also has a large pool to cool off in.

Ao Salat and **Ao Yai**, two east coast bays, both have very ambient and authentic shanty-filled fishing villages. In the early evening visitors can purchase freshly caught seafood as it's coming off the boat.

Ngamkho Resort (right) rents mountain bikes (per day 150B), and **bicycling** is a pleasant, if dusty, way to tour the hilly island.

Activities

With its gin-clear waters and quiet coves, Ko Kood's surrounds are great for **snorkelling** and **kayaking**. Most resorts offer equipment.

Ploy Scuba Diving, next to Away Resort, and Paradise Divers at Ko Kood Beach Resort run programs from Ao Salat and Ban Khlong Chao. For detailed information about **diving** around Ko Kood and the other islands of the Ko Chang Archipelago, see p148. Most bungalow operations have rentable **snorkelling** equipment for around 100B to 200B and run **snorkelling tours** including a 'pearl farm visit,' which is actually just a visit to the farm's shop.

For island tours you can rent out a sŏrng·tăa·ou with a Thai-speaking driver for 1200B per day. He'll know where to take you.

Sleeping & Eating

Prepaid all-inclusive holidays dominate Ko Kood's tourism, although an independent visit is definitely doable. If you're a backpacker arriving spontaneously, get off the boat at the Ban Khlong Chao pier. From here you can walk into the village where there are a handful of small, simple guesthouses and homestays with rooms from 400B. Beaches are everywhere and they're all good so no matter where you stay, you can't go wrong.

For resorts, book in advance since everything is very spread apart and the island is vast. Speedboat operators will usually drop you off at your accommodation. Prices drop by around 30% in the low season at the places that remain open.

Besides a few scattered local-style places, dining on Ko Kood is limited to resorts but the food is generally very tasty.

our pick Ngamkho Resort (☎ 08 1825 7076, 08 4653 4644; www.kohkood-ngamkho.com; Ao Ngam Kho; bungalows 650B) A great budget option with stylish, well-maintained but miniscule bamboo huts with hammocked terraces and brick attached bathrooms. There's a snoozy, cruisy vibe, 'Uncle Joe' is a superb host and the beach is perfect.

Away Resort (Bai Kood Shambala; ☎ 08 1835 4517, 08 7147 7055, in Bangkok 0 2696 8239; www.awayresorts.com; Ban Klong Chao; safari tents 1800B; bungalows from 3000B; 🈺 💻) Overlooking the sweeping sands at the mouth of the Khlong Chao river, Away is one of the more elegant choices on the island with modern cottages along a manicured coconut palm grove. Up the hill are more rustic safari tents in a shady glade of trees. The metropolitan-designed outdoor restaurant is excellent and there are more activities available here than anywhere else on the island.

Beach Natural Resort (☎ 08 6009 9420, in Bangkok 0 2222 9969; www.thebeachkohkood.com; Ao Bang Bao; bungalows incl breakfast 2200-3400B; 🈺 💻) Balinese-style bungalows here have loads of rustic-chic details such as antique-looking glass doorknobs on the wooden double doors and halved-barrel sinks in the bathrooms. The setting is a shady garden of hibiscus, orchids and bromeliads that cascades down a hillside to a rocky beach – a stretch of stunning white sand is only a short walk away.

ourpick Koh Kood Beach Resort (☎ in Bangkok 0 2630 9371; www.kohkoodbeachresort.com; Ao Bang Bao; r 3200-3700B, f 9600B; 🍴 🖳 🏊) This resort has perfectly maintained grounds that rest beneath a canopy of skyscraping palms. There are two types of bungalows: the Balinese cottages are the most private and have slanted roofs with plenty of thatch; the Thai-style units are duplexes with outdoor whirlpools. It's one of the only resorts on the island with a swimming pool and a dive centre. Free snorkelling gear and delicious food are extra bonuses but it's the stellar service that really sets this place apart.

Shantaa (☎ 08 1817 9648; www.shantaakohkood.com; Ao Yai Kee; bungalows incl breakfast 4500-5900B; 🍴) Stylish bungalows top a sunny cliff at one of the classiest spots on the island. The whole place is luxurious but the best feature is the bathrooms. Stepping stones lead into a private garden, complete with two, leafy outdoor showers or a soaking tub, and herbal toiletries complete the experience. Other amenities include stereos, king-sized beds, a private beach, and a welcome lack of TVs.

The huge Six Senses **Soneva Kiri Resort** (www .sixsenses.com/soneva-kiri) was still under construction and fenced-off like a high-security prison when we passed. When it opens its doors it will be the biggest and flashiest place on the island.

Other quality options available include the following:

Mangrove Bungalows (☎ 08 5279 0278; www.koh koodmangrove.com; Baan Khlong Chao; bungalows incl breakfast 800-1500B; 🍴) Situated along mangrove-smothered Khlong Chao, clean concrete bungalows sport polished wood floors and hot-water showers. Kayaks are on offer for heading upriver.

Siam Beach (☎ 08 1945 5789, 08 1899 6200; sb_koh kood@yahoo.com; Ao Bang Bao; d 800-1500B, f 1200-2000B; 🍴 🖳) One of the more social spots on the island with cute white cottages and less-charming family-sized concrete bungalows. The sand and garden is a little sparse but there's great swimming and lots of activities.

Dusita (☎ 0 3951 2902; fan bungalows d/tr/q 900/1400/1800B, air-con bungalows d/tr/q 1400/1900/2400B; 🍴) Sweet service and a peaceful beach. A huge variety of rooms sit in a coconut grove on soft Japanese grass.

Getting There & Around

For inter-island ferries between the islands in the Ko Chang Archipelago including Ko Chang and Ko Mak see p150. For the mainland, speedboats depart from Tha Laem Sok, 22km (45 minutes) southeast of Trat, daily at 1pm for Ko Kood (600B, 1¼ hours). In the reverse direction, boats leave Ko Kood at 9.30am and 1pm. A ferry runs from the same pier, departing at noon and returning from Ko Kood at 10am (350B, 2¼ hours). Share taxis to and from Laem Sok to Trat are included in ticket prices.

From Tha Dan Kao, 5km east of Trat (not to be confused with Ko Chang's Tha Dan Kao), a speedboat departs at 9am daily during the high season (550B, 1¼ hours). It departs Ko Kood for the mainland at 1pm.

Ao Thai Marine Express (☎ Ko Kood 08 1863 3525, Hat Lek 08 0092 3408; one-way 1250B; 🕐 Wed, Fri & Sun) runs speedboats to/from Hat Lek at the Cambodian border to Ko Kood via Ko Mak. Departures from Ko Kood are at 1pm arriving at Hat Lek at 2pm. From Hat Lek, boats depart at 4pm and arrive on Ko Kood at 5pm. For information about the border crossing at Hat Lek see p148.

On-island transport is thin on the ground, and you're better off renting a motorbike or mountain bike. Motorbikes are widely available with prices ranging from 300B to 500B for 24 hours.

KO MAK
เกาะหมาก

Flat and palm-fringed Ko Mak is nearly entirely dedicated to tourism these days but it still feels like a beach-bum's secret. Most of the island remains covered with rainforest or coconut and rubber plantations, leaving many beaches untouched yet easily discovered by bike, motorbike or even on foot. Lounge and wander all day and make merry at chummy beach bars at night – this is the kind of island that can melt your brain into never, ever wanting to leave.

Orientation & Information

Ko Mak is cross-shaped and most of the tourist development has evolved along the western arm at Hat Khao beach to the south and much quieter Ao Suan Yai to the north. The eastern part of the island has a small town with around 50 families, but remains rather quiet despite the main passenger pier at Ao Nid.

There are no banks or ATMs on the island, so stock up on cash before visiting. Most places to stay have an internet terminal or two.

Ball's Café (☎ 08 1925 6591; Ao Nid Pier; per min 1B; 🕐 9am-6pm) Has internet access and can help arrange accommodation and tours.

Ko Mak Health Centre (☎ 08 9403 5986; on cross-island road near Ao Nid Pier; ☽ 8.30am-4.30pm) Can handle basic first-aid emergencies and illnesses.
Police (☎ 0 3952 5741) Near the Health Centre.

Activities

With an array of dirt roads curving across the island as well as mellow terrain, Ko Mak has good opportunities for **cycling**. Near the health clinic, **Chan Chao** (☎ 08 9728 0703) rents sturdy bikes (per hour/day 50/150B) and has routes mapped out. Many guesthouses also rent bikes, as does Ko Mak Cococape resort (right), which has similar prices.

Snorkelling and **diving trips** can be arranged through most guesthouses, though **Kok Mak Divers** (☎ 08 3297 7724; on road behind Island Huts) has a good reputation and is actively involved in coral development projects. Snorkelling with lunch and transport included costs 650B, while a dive trip is 2300B. For more information about diving around Ko Mak and the other islands of the Ko Chang Archipelago, see p148. Most resorts have rentable **snorkelling** equipment (100B to 200B) for an impromptu afternoon of blowing bubbles.

Sleeping & Eating

Ko Mak has a whole range of places to stay but all of them offer the same kick-back, beach cool. We have listed high-season prices – expect discounts of up to 50% in the low season at the places that remain open.

The whole island, including accommodation operators, shows up to meet the daily boat from the mainland although inter-island speedboats sometimes drop everyone off at Monkey Island. Don't worry, your hotel or guesthouse will find you.

Restaurants on Ko Mak are often affiliated with bungalows but the stand-alone options are slightly cheaper. A few chow shacks gather near Tha Maka Thanee, where a mixed bag of locals and tourists feasts on an assortment of cheap noodles and barbecued seafood.

our pick **Island Hut** (☎ 08 7139 5537; Hat Khao; huts 100-400B) Wood-and-thatch huts (all with attached bathrooms), over-water swings and lazy hammocks give this simple, lovingly maintained spot a funky feel. Palms, papaya trees and potted orchids wind their way around adorable turtle-shaped stepping-stone paths to the shady beach. The friendly owners have been on the island for many generations and they'll make you feel like part of the family.

Monkey Island (☎ 08 9501 6030; www.monkey islandkohmak.com; Hat Khao; bungalows 300-3000B; ⚋ 🖵) Somewhat of a backpacker hub, very sociable Monkey's funky bungalows range from simple bamboo affairs with shared bathrooms to deluxe wooden villas with bay windows and outdoor lounge settings. Live-music shows at night are animated by friendly Mr Tee, the dreadlocked glee-captain of the resort, although it's a mellow scene that's more Rasta than techno.

Baan Koh Maak (☎ 0 3952 4028; www.baan-koh-mak .com; Hat Khao; bungalows 700-1400B; ⚋) Competing for most stylish flashpacker digs on the island, Baan Koh Maak's bungalows are bright and funky. The white picket fences give it a fairy-tale Thai suburbia feel, but the neon-green and fuchsia paint add a rebellious bit of psychedelia. The mattresses are softer than the usual mid- to low-range variety. It also operates Koh Mak Cottages with simple fan bungalows (550B), next door.

Ko Mak Cococape (☎ 08 1937 9024; www.kohmak cococape.com; Ao Suan Yai; r 1000-10,000; ⚋ 🖵 🕾) Owned by a couple of Bangkok architects (and it shows), this sprawling place has a collection of naturalistic-chic bungalows blending hard woods, thatch, whitewashed cement and bamboo. The cheapest options are bamboo huts that totter over tide pools with a shared bathroom and a fan; the priciest options have huge lounging spaces, Thai cushions and hammocks everywhere and bathrooms as monster sized as the rooms. There are long stretches of empty beach on either side of the resort and the view over the aqua bay is dotted with corduroy-green islets.

Lazy Day the Resort (☎ 08 9433 0970; www.lazy daytheresort.com; Hat Khao; bungalows 2200-2700B; ⚋ 🖵) Right at the quiet, clean end of Hat Khao, super-spacious immaculate white bungalows here have floor-to-ceiling windows, a comfy modern design, big terraces and tons of light. All sit in a green grassy coconut grove and look out over the sunset. The restaurant sits way back from the beach surrounded by trees and ponds and the service is extremely friendly and helpful. This place is a steal.

Cinnamon Art Resort & Spa (☎ 08 5906 5042; www.cinnamonartresort.com; Laem Son; r 3500-5000B; ⚋ 🖵 🕾) Tucked away on a lonely stretch of magnificent beach on the northeast of Ko Mak, this new resort was built with ecofriendly materials and without cutting down the area's trees. Although the design, based on rounded thatch roofs, isn't very trendy, the whole place is very comfortable and unpretentious and the service is outstanding. An infinity pool sits at the edge of the shallow bay.

Other worthy options to check out include the following:

Buri Huts (☎ 08 9752 5285; www.kohmakburihut.com; Baan Lang; bungalows 500-1300B; ⊠ ⊡) On the eastern side of the island, Buri has cylindrical, African-style huts that perch cheerfully on a tiered bluff above the water. An earthen-coloured pool is surrounded by lounge chairs.

Koh Mak Resort (☎ 0 3950 1013; www.kohmaak.com; Ao Suan Yai; bungalows 1400-6600B; ⊠ ⊡) This place is like several resorts melded into one along a never-ending strip of gorgeous beach. Flashy new near-Japanese-style bungalows with lots of glass are the priciest while the old concrete mainstays are on the best part of the beach. There are also three restaurants and a dive centre.

Makathanee (☎ 08 7600 0374; www.makathaneekoh mak.com; Hat Khao; bungalows 3000B, r 3000-4800B; ⊠ ⊡ ⊡) The gorgeous, comfy, sort of colonial-style bungalows on the beach are fantastic but the big cement hotel block behind is a bit of a buzz-kill.

Getting There & Around

Several speedboat companies run frequent trips between Ko Mak and the mainland; the best way to book them is through your guesthouse. Panan Speedboat leaves from the Ko Mak Resort pier on the northwest side of the island at 8am and 1pm, and departs Tha Laem Ngop at 10am and 4pm (450B, one hour). Leelawadee Speedboat has departures outside Makathanee Resort (see above) at 8am, 9am, 10.30am and 1.30pm, and Laem Ngop at 10.30am, 12pm, 2pm and 4pm (450B, 1¼ hours). A slow ferry (via Ko Whai) leaves Ko Mak's Ao Nid Pier at 8am for Tha Laem Ngop, leaving the mainland to go back at 3pm (300B, three hours). Also, all of the boats from Laem Sok to Ko Kood as well as services to Hat Lek at the Cambodian border stop at Ko Mak (see p162).

See p150 for the boat schedules for inter-island travel around the archipelago including Ko Chang and Ko Kood.

Once on the island, you can pedal your way around (see p163), or it's small enough to explore by foot if you're so inclined. Motorbikes go for 60B to 80B per hour or 300B to 450B per day.

OTHER ISLANDS

A few other small islands offer seclusion, azure waters and overnight accommodation.

Most speedboats make stops here upon request but between June and October boats stop running and most bungalow operations close down. See p150 for inter-island boat schedules.

In addition to the following islands, there is also accommodation on the wee islets of **Ko Kradat** (☎ 08 9099 7917, in Bangkok 0 2368 2675), **Ko Lao Ya Nai** (☎ 0 3951 2818), **Ko Mai Si Yai** (☎ 08 7077 2018) and **Ko Sai Kao** (☎ 08 1929 8669).

Ko Whai
เกาะหวาย

Ko Whai is teensy and somewhat primitive, but endowed with excellent coral reefs. BB Divers (p153) has an on-site outpost and can hook you up with scuba equipment. For the mainland, there's a daily ferry (300B, 2½ hours) between Ko Whai and Laem Ngop departing Ko Whai at 8am and returning from Laem Ngop at 3pm.

There are now several places to lay your head, all along the northern side of the island. Expect to share the bulk of your afternoons with day-trippers, and the remainder of your time in peace.

Koh Wai Paradise (☎ 08 1762 2548; bungalows from 250B) is a reliable, popular place with rustic wooden bungalows on the beach and run by a friendly family that speaks English. You'll probably have to share the coral out front with snorkelling day-trippers but it's an easy walk to other nearby beaches.

Good Feeling (☎ 08 8503 3410; bungalows 300B) offers up basic thatch huts with shared bathrooms, and is run by a lovely family. **Grand Mer** (bungalows 400B) has six huts positioned along a quiet smile of beach, with a small restaurant. It's on the northeastern side of the island.

Koh Wai Pakarang (☎ 08 4113 8946; www.kohwaipa karang.com; bungalows 800-2500B; ⊠ ⊡) has clean, concrete air-con bungalows on a lovely strip of sand near the boat dock. There's also a half-hearted coral information centre and turtle hatchery, as well as a good restaurant-bar.

Koh Wai Beach Resort (☎ 08 1306 4053; www .kohwaibeachresort.com; r incl breakfast 2500-3500B; ⊠ ⊡), the newest and flashiest place on Ko Whai, is tucked away on the southeastern part of the island. Beachfront rooms are in a cement block divided by pebble walls right on the beach while Thai teak houses are darker but have terraces. All are equipped with everything from hot water to cable TV.

Ko Kham & Ko Rayang
เกาะขาม/เกาะรายาง

Little Ko Kham and Ko Rayang bob like brilliant green apples just 1km off the coast of Ko Mak. Braids of hardened lava suggest the presence of ancient volcanic activity, but today these islands boast shimmering turquoise vistas, swimmable beaches and vibrant coral reefs. These quiet spots are easily accessible by speedboat from Ko Mak, and during the high season there are daily passenger ferries that stop here.

Ko Kham Resort (☎ 08 1303 1229; bungalows 400-2000B) is so close to Ko Mak, you could kayak across from Ao Suan Yai. Enjoy quiet starlit evenings, although there tends to be a lot of day-tripping snorkellers in the afternoon. **Rayang Island Resort** (☎ 08 3118 0011, 0 3955 5082; www.rayang-island.com; bungalows from 1700B) is a serene place with 15 refurbished one- and two-bedroom bungalows. There are no day-trippers, so it's wonderfully quiet.

Ko Rang
เกาะรัง

Dazzling Ko Rang is the largest landmass of an island chain called Mu Ko Rang (Ko Rang Archipelago). This area boasts one of the best strings of coral in the region and a long stretch of sand called **Hat San Chao**. Although there are no resorts on the island, campers are allowed to pitch a tent as long as they register with the **national park office** (☎ 0 3955 5080; ⊗ 8.30am-4.30pm Mon-Fri) on Ko Chang. There is a 400B fee per person to access the marine park. Crude washrooms and running water have been set up; however, visitors must bring their own consumables.

Northwestern Gulf Coast

Thai vacationers have been flocking to Thailand's northwestern gulf coast for decades, yet somehow foreign tourists never got the memo. This thin isthmus connecting the Asian continent to the Malay Peninsula offers sleepy seaside towns, rugged shell-strewn sand dunes and plenty of intriguing detours, making it a great place to slough off Bangkok's urban smog.

Most tourists will only experience the region through the window of a speeding bus or train destined for the kingdom's southern treasures. Those who decide to stop will enjoy a unique vacationing experience steeped in local tradition.

Quiet Phetchaburi makes for a pleasant afternoon of temple gazing. Stop in Cha-am to master the lyrics of your favourite Thai pop-rock song as it blares along the beach during the usual weekend bustle. Countless guesthouses and resorts are crammed along the beachfront thoroughfare, much like in Hua Hin, further south, which is the favoured resort destination of the royal family.

The dramatic crags of Khao Sam Roi Yot National Park are definitely worth a visit, especially for wildlife enthusiasts. And at the southernmost point of the region, Chumphon earns its spot on the map as the official gateway to southern Thailand and the obligatory transfer point for the diving-centric Ko Tao.

While transport between major destinations is a cinch, navigating the quieter regions requires a little ingenuity and may put your independent travel spirit to the test.

NORTHWESTERN GULF COAST

HIGHLIGHTS

- Searching for hidden street stalls and secret seaside shanties in charming **Hua Hin** (p176)
- Listening for rustling leaves while trying to spot a furry monkey at **Khao Sam Roi Yot National Park** (p183)
- Eavesdropping on Thai gossip from under your beachside umbrella in **Cha-am** (p172)
- Ogling crumbling temples scattered around **Phetchaburi** (opposite)
- Pressing binoculars against your face while anticipating the arrival of a rare bird in **Kaeng Krachan National Park** (p172)

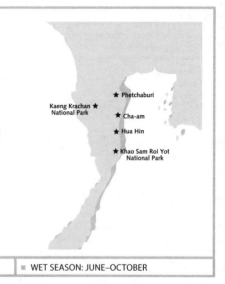

★ Phetchaburi

Kaeng Krachan ★
National Park

★ Cha-am

★ Hua Hin

★ Khao Sam Roi Yot
National Park

■ DRY SEASON: NOVEMBER–MAY	■ WET SEASON: JUNE–OCTOBER

Climate

The northwestern gulf coast shares its weather patterns with the rest of central Thailand. Temperatures peak in the March to May hot season, followed by monsoon rains falling in the June to October wet season. November through February is known as the 'cool' season and is the best time to visit. The afternoon temperatures seem to hover around 32°C throughout the year, but evenings tend to be cooler and there is little rain.

National Parks

Kaeng Krachan (p172) is the largest national park in Thailand, covering nearly half of Phetchaburi Province. This unending expanse of jungle is known for the Pala-U waterfall and excellent birdwatching. The undulating hills of Khao Sam Roi Yot (p183) offer breathtaking views of the gulf amid limestone cliffs. This is another spot bird fanatics can check off their lists.

PHETCHABURI (PHETBURI)

อ.เมือง เพชรบุรี

pop 47,200

Unlike many other centres of worship around the world, quiet Phetchaburi (also called Phetburi) feels surprisingly devoid of tourist traffic. Dozens of temples lie frozen within the city's slowly paced quotidian life, each one a relic reflecting the achievements of empires that flourished long ago. The Khmer first settled here in the 11th century, and since then the town has seen a steady stream of inhabitants that have used the convenient riverside location as a central trading post. Today the town has barely changed, and a stroll through the city centre reveals a place teeming with crumbling wát mixed with old teak houses and misplaced concrete indicators of a modern future.

If you're light on time, the sleepy religious town can be tackled in an afternoon visit – glimpse the diverse array of wát along the eastern riverbank during a half-day walking tour (see the boxed text, p170). The underground Buddhist shrine at the Khao Luang caves is also worth a visit.

Orientation & Information

If you've come by bus, you'll be getting off close to Khao Wang and will have to take a motorcycle taxi into the centre of town. Train users should follow the road southeast of the tracks until you come to Th Ratchadamnoen,

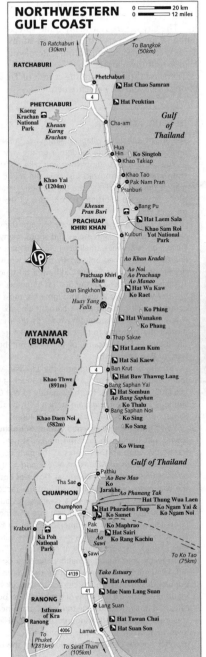

NORTHWESTERN GULF COAST

then turn right and follow the main boulevard to the second major intersection (Th Chisa-In). The city centre is actually quite spread out, and there is very little shade on sunny days. Wear sunscreen and bring water if you plan to tour the temples.

There are three banks at the corner of Th Phongsuriya and Th Panichjaroen.

Police station (☎ 0 3242 5500; Th Ratwithi) Near the intersection of Th Ratchadamnoen.

Post office (cnr Th Ratwithi & Th Damnoen Kasem) There's a telephone centre upstairs.

TAT office (☎ 0 3240 2220; Th Ratwithi; ☯ 8.30am-4.30pm) Set in a wátlike structure, this tourist office doesn't have loads of brochures, but the staff can point you in the direction of temples, cheap food and lodging.

DETOUR: AMPHAWA

The quaint, canalside village of Amphawa in Samut Songkhram is less than 100km from Bangkok and makes for a wonderful detour on the way down to the northwestern gulf coast.

Your adventure begins when you take a stab into Thonburi looking for the **Wong Wian Yai train station** in Bangkok. Just past the traffic circle (Wong Wian Yai) is a fairly ordinary food market that camouflages the unceremonious terminal of this commuter line, known in English as the Mahachai Shortline. Hop on one of the hourly trains (10B) to Samut Sakhon and you're on your way.

Only 15 minutes out of the station and the city density yields to squatty villages where you can peek into homes, temples and shops, many of which are only arm's length from the tracks. Further on palm trees, small rice fields and marshes filled with giant elephant ears and canna lilies line the route, tamed only briefly by little whistle-stop stations. The backwater farms evaporate quickly as you enter **Samut Sakhon**, a bustling port town several kilometres from the Gulf of Thailand and the end of the first rail segment.

After working your way through what must be one of the most hectic fresh markets in the country, you'll come to a vast harbour clogged with water hyacinth and wooden fishing boats. A few rusty cannons pointing towards the river testify to the town's crumbling fort, built to protect the kingdom from sea invaders. Before the 17th century, the town was known as Tha Jiin (Chinese Pier) because of the large number of Chinese junks that called here. Board the ferry to **Ban Laem** (3B).

Arriving on the opposite side, the Jao Mae Kuan Im Shrine at **Wat Chong Lom** is a 9m-high fountain in the shape of the Mahayana Buddhist Goddess of Mercy. To get here, take a motorcycle taxi (10B) from the pier for the 2km ride to Wat Chong Lom. Conveniently located just beside the shrine is Tha Chalong, a train station with two afternoon departures for your next destination, Samut Songkhram (10B, 1.30pm and 4.40pm).

You'll know you've reached **Samut Songkhram** when it looks like you've crashed into the town's wet market. In fact, the market is held directly on the train tracks, and vendors must frantically scoop up their wares as the daily comes through.

At the mouth of Mae Nam Mae Klong is the province's most famous tourist attraction: a bank of fossilised shells known as **Don Hoi Lot**. The shell bank can really only be seen during the dry season when the river surface has receded to its lowest level (typically April and May), but most visit for the perennial seafood restaurants that have been built at the edge of Don Hoi Lot. To get there you can hop into a sŏrng·tăa·ou (pick-up truck) in front of Somdet Phra Phuttalertla Hospital at the intersection of Th Prasitwatthana and Th Thamnimit; the trip takes about 15 minutes (10B). Or you can charter a boat from the Mae Klong Market pier (tâh dà·làht mâa glorng), a scenic journey of around 45 minutes (1000B).

To reach your final destination, charter a boat (1000B, 45 minutes) or hop in a sŏrng·tăa·ou (8B, 15 minutes) near the market for the ride to **Amphawa**. This canalside village has become a popular destination among city folk who seek out its quintessentially 'Thai' setting. This urban influx has sparked a few signs of gentrification, but the canals, old wooden buildings, atmospheric cafes and quaint waterborne traffic still retain heaps of charm. On weekends Amphawa puts on a reasonably authentic floating market. Alternatively, visit on a weekday and you'll have the whole town to yourself. Steps from Amphawa's central footbridge is **Wat Amphawan Chetiyaram**, a graceful temple believed to be located at the place of the family home of Rama II, and which

Sights & Activities

Looming west of the city, **Khao Wang** is studded with wát and topped by various components of King Mongkut's 1860 palace, **Phra Nakhon Khiri** (Holy City Hill; ☎ 0 3240 1006; admission 40B; ☉ 9am-4pm). You can make the strenuous upward climb along the cobblestone paths or head to the west side of the hill and take a funicular straight to the peak (adult one way 40B). The views here are great, especially at sunset, and the entire hill teems with meandering monkeys looking for attention. The ticket office will sell you an information pamphlet (5B) that includes a map of the palace grounds.

The cave sanctuary of **Khao Luang** (donation encouraged; ☉ 8am-6pm) is 5km north of Phetchaburi.

---

features accomplished murals. A short walk from the temple is **King Buddhalertla (Phuttha Loet La) Naphalai Memorial Park** (☎ 0 3475 1376; Km 63, Route 35, Samut Songkhram; adult/child 20/5B; ☉ park 8.30am-5.30pm daily, museum 9am-6pm Wed-Sun), a museum housed in a collection of traditional central Thai houses set on 1.5 landscaped hectares. Dedicated to Rama II, the museum contains a library of rare Thai books and antiques from early-19th-century Siam.

At night long-tail boats zip through Amphawa's sleeping waters to watch the star-like dance of the *hìng hôy* (fireflies). Several operators lead tours, including **Niphaa** (☎ 08 1422 0726), an experienced and well-equipped outfit located at the mouth of the canal, near the footbridge.

Sleeping & Eating

Amphawa is popular with Bangkok's weekend warriors, and it seems like virtually every other house has opened its doors to tourists in the form of homestays. These can range from little more than a mattress on the floor and a mosquito net to upscale guesthouse-style accommodation.

Baan Song Thai Plai Pong Pang (☎ 0 3476 7333; Amphawa; r 850B) organises basic homestays and has been recognised for ecotourism excellence. Two new midrange options are **Baan Torsang Ampawa** (☎ 0 3475 1390; www.bantorsang.com; 23 Moo 8 Th Suanluang; r 1000-1500B) and **Thanicha Boutique Resort** (☎ 0 3472 5511; www.thanicha.com; 261 Amphawa Samut Songkhram; r 800-1200B). For something a bit more upscale there's **Baan Ku Pu** (☎ 0 3472 5920; Th Rim Khlong, Amphawa; r 1600-4000B; 🗙), a self-styled 'resort' featuring wooden bungalows, and **Baan Tai Had Resort** (☎ 0 3476 7220; www.baantaihad.com; 1 Moo 2, Th Tai Had, Samut Songkhram; r 1600-5600B; 🗙 🗩), a sleek new riverside resort boasting heaps of activities.

In the imposing ferry building, the seafood **Tarua Restaurant** (☎ 0 3441 1084; Ferry Terminal Bldg, 859 Th Sethakit, Samut Sakhon; dishes 60-200B) offers views over the harbour and an English-language menu.

The open-air seafood restaurant **Khrua Chom Ao** (☎ 0 85190 5677; Samut Sakhon; dishes 60-200B) looks over the gulf and has a loyal local following. It is a brief walk from Wat Chong Lom, down the road running along the side of the temple opposite the statue of the Chinese goddess Kuan Im.

If you're in town on a weekend, get your eats on at the fun **Amphawa Floating Market** (*dà·làht nám am·pá·wah*; ☎ 0 3475 2847; dishes 20-40B; ☉ noon-9pm Fri-Sun), where *pàt tai* and other noodle dishes are served directly from boats.

Getting There & Away

Trains leave Thonburi's Wong Wian Yai station (Map pp70–1) for Samut Sakhon roughly every hour from 5.30am. You'll need to leave before 8.30am in order to reach Samut Songkhram by train.

Samut Songkhram is the southernmost terminus of the Mahachai Shortline. There are four departures from Ban Laem to Samut Songkhram (10B, one hour, approximately 7.30am, 10.10am, 1.30pm and 4.40pm) and four return trips (6.20am, 9am, 11.30am and 3.30pm).

Between Bangkok and Amphawa, buses (70B) run every 40 minutes from Thonburi's Southern bus terminal (Map pp70–1). There are also regular buses from Samut Sakhon (60B) and Samut Songkhram (65B). Alternatively, you can catch one of several buses to/from Damnoen Saduak (80B) that ply the highway near Amphawa.

For a more leisurely approach to visiting Amphawa's floating market, consider joining a four-day Suburban Lifestyle Tour run by **Visit Beyond** (☎ 0 2630 9371; www.visitbeyond.com). The tour explores the lesser-known tourist attractions around Bangkok, including Amphawa.

NORTHWESTERN GULF COAST

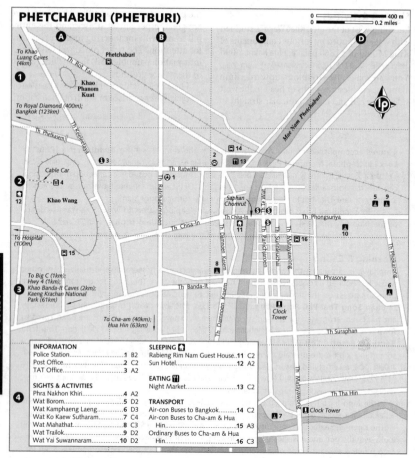

PHETCHABURI (PHETBURI)

INFORMATION	
Police Station..................1 B2	
Post Office.....................2 C2	
TAT Office.....................3 A2	

SIGHTS & ACTIVITIES	
Phra Nakhon Khiri.............4 A2	
Wat Borom....................5 D2	
Wat Kamphaeng Laeng........6 D3	
Wat Ko Kaew Sutharam........7 C4	
Wat Mahathat.................8 C3	
Wat Trailok....................9 D2	
Wat Yai Suwannaram..........10 D2	

SLEEPING 🏠	
Rabieng Rim Nam Guest House..11 C2	
Sun Hotel.....................12 A2	

EATING 🍴	
Night Market..................13 C2	

TRANSPORT	
Air-con Buses to Bangkok.........14 C2	
Air-con Buses to Cha-am & Hua	
Hin........................15 A3	
Ordinary Buses to Cha-am & Hua	
Hin........................16 C3	

The caverns here are filled with ageing Buddha images in various stances, many of them originally placed by King Mongkut (Rama IV). The best time to visit is around 5pm, when evening light pierces the ceiling, surrounding artefacts below with an ethereal glow. There are multiple chambers to wander through, which feature easily anthropomorphised rock formations, and showers of stalactites.

Another cave sanctuary – perhaps even more magical than Khao Luang – is at **Khao Banda-It** (donation encouraged; ⏰ 9am-4pm), 2km west of town. English-speaking guides will lead you through the caves and answer your questions. A săhm·lór (three-wheeled pedicab) from the city centre to either site costs about 55B; a motorcycle taxi is 40B.

Walking Tour

Sleepy Phetchaburi is known throughout Thailand for its collection of varied wát. The following tour ambles through some of the town's most striking relics from previous empires.

After crossing Mae Nam Phetchaburi (Phetchaburi River), walk about 300m along Th Phongsuriya until you come to a big temple on the right. This is **Wat Yai Suwannaram (1)**, originally built during the 17th century and renovated during the reign of King Rama V (r 1868–1910). Legend has it that the gash in the ornately carved wooden doors dates to the Burmese attack of Ayuthaya. The main bòht (central sanctuary) is surrounded by a cloister filled with sombre Buddha images. The murals inside the *bòht* date back to the 1730s and are in good condition. Next to the *bòht*, set on a murky pond, is a beautifully designed old *hŏr drai* (Tripitaka library).

Wat Borom (2) and **Wat Trailok (3)** are next to each other opposite Wat Yai Suwannaram on Th Phongsuriya, a little to the east. They aren't especially attractive, but they do have distinctive monastic halls and long, graceful wooden 'dormitories' on stilts.

South of the two wàt, on Th Phokarong, is the pleasant, 13th-century Khmer site **Wat Kamphaeng Laeng (4)**. It has five *bràhng* (Khmer-style towers) and part of the original *gampaang laang* (laterite wall) is still standing. The front *bràhng* contains a Buddha footprint. Two others contain images dedicated to famous *lŏo·ang pôr* (venerated monks), and two have been restored. If you're feeling peckish, there's a decent on-site restaurant that serves up the usual assortment of Thai treats.

Follow Th Phrasong back towards the town centre, turning left onto Th Matayawong. After about 800m turn right at the clock tower and look for signs to the Ayuthaya-period **Wat Ko Kaew Sutharam (Wat Ko; 5)**. The *bòht* features

---

WALK FACTS

Start Wat Yai Suwannaram
Finish Wat Mahathat
Distance 2.7km
Duration 1½ hours

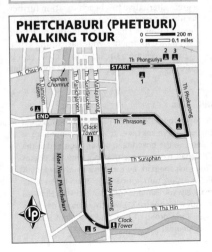

PHETCHABURI (PHETBURI) WALKING TOUR

---

early-18th-century murals that are among the best in Thailand. One panel depicts what appears to be a Jesuit priest wearing the robes of a Buddhist monk, while another shows other foreigners undergoing Buddhist conversion. There is also a large wooden monastic hall on stilts – similar to the ones at Wat Borom and Wat Trailok but in much better condition.

Follow Th Panichjaroen in front of Wat Ko towards central Phetchaburi and turn left onto Th Phrasong; soon you'll reach **Wat Mahathat (6)**. Its large white *bràhng* can be seen from a distance – a typical late Ayuthaya–early Ratanakosin adaptation of the *bràhng* of Lopburi and Phimai.

If you have extra time, continue along Th Phrasong, turn left on Th Ratchadamnoen, a quick right on Th Banda-It, and make a right at Th Keeleetaya. You'll find the cobbled staircase up to the top of Khao Wang (Map p170), which provides stunning views of all the temples you've just visited.

Festivals & Events

In early February the **Phra Nakhon Khiri Fair** centres on Khao Wang and the city's historic temples. Festivities include a sound-and-light show held at the Phra Nakhon Khiri palace, temples festooned with lights, and performances of *lá·kon chah·dree* (classical Thai dance-drama), *lí·gair bàh* (folk dance-drama) and modern-style historical dramas. A twist on the usual beauty contest provides a showcase for Phetchaburi widows.

Sleeping & Eating

Phetchaburi is a popular stop for temple oglers, so it's surprising that such a small collection of lodging and dining options exists. Western tourists have yet to make their mark, so most chow houses are hidden in the urban fray. Try the night market on Monday evenings for cheap, tasty treats.

The town is famous for its local cuisine, which includes *kôw châa pét·bù·ree* (moist, chilled rice served with sweetmeats – a hot-season speciality) and the widely known *môr gaang* (egg custard).

Rabieng Rim Nam Guest House (☎ 0 3242 5707; 1 Th Chisa-In; s/d 120/240B) Set in a large, creaky teak structure sitting along the lazy river, this popular backpacker choice has simple rooms that are nothing fancier than a wooden closet with a mattress. If you aren't impressed with the rooms, the owner will point across the bridge to the Jomklow Hotel, which is the same price. Don't bother walking over there; the place feels like a prison. Rabieng's riverside restaurant is open for all three meals, serving an enormous selection of Thai staples. Go for a *yam* (spicy salad) – it's yum. The wafting '70s music matches the record jackets glued to the walls (think ABBA and Elvis). Extras include laundry service (5B per piece) and motorcycle rental (250B per day). Trips to Kaeng Krachan National Park (below) can be organised from here.

Sun Hotel (☎ 0 3240 0000; 43/33 Soi Phetkasem 1; r 800-1500B, ste 1700B; ✴) Located opposite the cable car to Phra Nakhon Khiri, Sun Hotel is backcountry Thailand's attempt at boutique sophistication. The enormous rooms are mostly painted in cool greys and browns, with one brightly coloured accent wall. There's a restaurant in the open-air lobby that's quite popular with the Thai guests. The professional staff will turn your food order into room service for an extra 5B. Discounted room rates are usually given.

Royal Diamond (☎ 0 3241 1061; www.royaldiamondhotel.com; 555 Moo 1, Th Phetkasem; r 1200-2000B; ✴) It's a bit of a hike to get there, but Royal Diamond has a good selection of comfortable lodging. The rates are pretty good value, especially for the roomy cheaper (standard) rooms, which come with wall-to-wall carpeting. The attached karaoke bar is a good place to make some noise during your visit to quiet Phetchaburi.

Getting There & Away

Buses pulling into town make several stops depending on travellers' requests. Most buses stop at the Big C (a multistorey shopping centre) and a large lime-coloured hospital. It is best to get off near the hospital (just west of Khao Wang), as it is closer to the town's sites. There are frequent air-con bus services to/from Bangkok's Southern bus station (120B, 2½ hours). The bus terminal for air-con buses to/from Bangkok is across from the night market. Figure on around 1B per kilometre to reach nearby destinations such as Cha-am (35B, 40 minutes) and Hua Hin (50B, 70 minutes).

Trains are less convenient than buses, unless you factor in the time taken to get to or from Bangkok's bus terminals. There are frequent services to/from Bangkok's Hualamphong train station. Fares vary depending on the train and class (2nd class around 200B, 3rd class around 100B, three hours).

Getting Around

Sǎhm·lór and motorcycle taxis go anywhere in the town centre for 30B; you can also charter them for the whole day (from 300B). Sǒrng·tǎa·ou (pick-up trucks) cost 10B to 20B around town. Rabieng Rim Nam Guest House rents out motorcycles (250B per day).

CHA-AM

อำเภอชะอำ

pop 65,500

After Hua Hin struck it big when King Rama IV moved in, the quiet fishing town was transformed into a cosmopolitan beach destination. Little Cha-am, just 25km up the coast, has managed to escape a similar fate – this sandy stretch of casuarinas and umbrellas caters mostly to weekending Thais. It can be a great alternative to a beach vacation further south: the prices are cheaper, the cuisine is geared towards Thai tastebuds and you'll have the chance to practise your bargaining skills.

Each weekend a stream of tour buses expels giddy revellers who grab a shaded spot under

---

DETOUR: KAENG KRACHAN NATIONAL PARK

The largest national park in Thailand and home to the gorgeous Nam Tok Pala-U, **Kaeng Krachan** (adult/child 200/100B) is easily reached from Phetchaburi. There are caves to explore, mountains, a huge lake and excellent birdwatching opportunities (see the boxed text, p186) to be had in the evergreen forest that blankets the park. Kaeng Krachan has fantastic trekking, and it is one of the few places to see elephants roaming wild. To reach the park by car, drive south on Hwy 4 about 20km from Phetchaburi, and at the Kern Pet Junction, turn right and go 38km to Pet Dam, then 3km more to the park headquarters. Alternatively you can arrange a tour in Hua Hin (see p178). In Phetchaburi, contact Rabieng Rim Nam Guest House (p171), which arranges day trips (2000B per person, minimum four people, or 6000B for a group of two) and overnight visits in rustic bungalows (2400B per person, minimum four people).

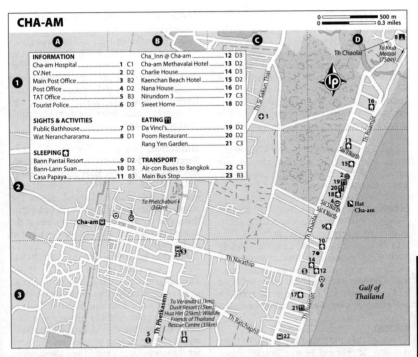

CHA-AM

INFORMATION	
Cha-am Hospital	1 C1
CV.Net	2 D2
Main Post Office	3 B2
Post Office	4 D2
TAT Office	5 B3
Tourist Police	6 D3

SIGHTS & ACTIVITIES	
Public Bathhouse	7 D3
Wat Neranchararama	8 D1

SLEEPING	
Bann Pantai Resort	9 D2
Bann-Lann Suan	10 D3
Casa Papaya	11 B3

Cha_Inn @ Cha-am	12 D3
Cha-am Methavalai Hotel	13 D2
Charlie House	14 D3
Kaenchan Beach Hotel	15 D2
Nana House	16 D1
Nirundorn 3	17 C3
Sweet Home	18 D2

EATING	
Da Vinci's	19 D2
Poom Restaurant	20 D2
Rang Yen Garden	21 C3

TRANSPORT	
Air-con Buses to Bangkok	22 C3
Main Bus Stop	23 B3

the millions of beachside parasols for days filled with picnics and frenzied chatter. On weekdays, Cha-am is virtually deserted, making it a great time to cash in on the lowered room rates and quiet sands.

Lately Cha-am has become a popular stop for touring Scandinavians – you'll find countless restaurants and guesthouses proudly waving Nordic flags at the entrance.

Orientation

On the west side of Th Phetkasem (Phetkasem Hwy, or just the 'highway') you'll find all of the civic facilities: the main post office, the train station, the police station and government offices. The road that fronts the beach, Th Ruamjit, about 2km from the train station, is a long string crammed with hotels, restaurants, souvenir stalls and public bathhouses.

Information

There are large clusters of banks and ATMs at the intersections of Th Phetkasem and Th Narathip, and Th Narathip and Th Ruamjit.

Cha-am Hospital (☎ 0 3247 1808; Th Leapkhlong) Northwest of the beach.

CV.Net (Th Ruamjit; per hr 40B; ☾ 9am-10pm) An internet cafe on the main drag.

Post office (Th Ruamjit) This small branch is on the main beach strip; the main office is near the train station.

TAT office (☎ 0 3247 1005; tatphet@tat.or.th; 500/51 Th Phetkasem; ☾ 8.30am-4.30pm) Has English-speaking staff and information on Cha-am, Phetchaburi, Hua Hin and Prachuap Khiri Khan.

Tourist police (☎ 0 3251 5995, emergency 1155; cnr Th Ruamjit & Th Narathip)

Sights & Activities

The beautiful **Wat Neranchararama** (Th Chaolai) features an unusual six-armed Buddha statue. Each hand covers a sensory organ in a symbolic gesture denying the senses – kinda like 'see no evil, hear no evil, speak no evil'.

Colourful Cha-am is largely the domain of Thai tourists who spend their holidays under giant parasols along the beach. If you abide by the 'when in Rome...' philosophy, you can hire a beach chair anywhere along the sand. At the end of the day, follow your fellow travellers to one of the many **public bathhouses** (admission 5-10B) along the main strip.

Volunteering

If you love animals and aren't afraid of a bit of hard work, then consider a stint at the **Wildlife Friends of Thailand Rescue Centre** (☎ 0 3245 8135; rescue centre www.wfft.org, volunteering www .wildlifevolunteer.org). Based 35km northwest of Cha-am,the centre cares for a menagerie of creatures rescued from animal shows and exploitative owners. An average day could involve feeding sun bears, building enclosures for macaques and establishing island refuges for gibbons. Volunteering costs US$140 per week, including all accommodation and meals. Volunteers are expected to stay for two to three months.

Sleeping

Sleeping options run from hovel-like guest-houses to futuristic boutique hotels. The seaside lodging in central Cha-am is tightly packed and generally in need of renovation (some exceptions to this rule are listed following). Consider booking ahead on the weekend and expect prices to increase or decrease for any number of seemingly illogical reasons.

BUDGET

Nirundorn 3 (☎ 0 3247 1038, 0 3243 3450; 247/7 Th Ruamjit; r 600-1000B; ❄) Nirundorn is an endearing spot with clean cottages, friendly managers and cute decor details that play with positive and negative space. Fan accommodation is rather lacklustre – go for an upper-floor room for the best views.

Charlie House (☎ 0 3243 3799; Soi 1 North, 241/60-61 Th Ruamjit; r from 650B; ❄) With pastel leather stools and accent lighting (even in the superbly designed bathrooms), this friendly place gets points for colour and flare. Don't confuse it with Charlie Place or Charlie TV (both on the same soi).

Nana House (☎ 0 3243 3632, 0 3247 1357; www.nana house.net; 203/3-4 Th Ruamjit; r 700-800B; ❄) Seems like pink and purple paint was on sale when this place was under construction. But don't let the cutesy pastels put you off; inside you'll find the best budget rooms in town. Nana House has spread across several buildings at the northern end of the strip, but all of the accommodation is comfy and sparkling clean.

Bann-Lann Suan (☎ 0 3243 3171, 0 3247 1893; 261/2 Th Ruamjit; r 800-1500B; ❄) This trendy address is easily the most stylish option squished along Cha-am's beachside road. Remember to keep your curtains shut in the evening as the rooms face one another along a narrow scrap of synthetic jungle.

Cha_Inn @ Cha-am (☎ 0 3247 1879; www.cha-inn. com; 274/34 Th Ruamjit; r from 900B; ❄ ☎) Modern and minimalist, this is one of Cha-am's newest and sleekest sleeping spots. Rooms have bamboo mats over polished cement floors, honest-to-goodness art on the walls, and tantalising verandahs. After one night here you'll feel tranquil.calm.

MIDRANGE

Sweet Home (☎ 0 3241 1039; 279/1 Th Ruamjit; bungalows 1500B; ❄) It must have taken an entire forest to build Sweet Home – everything's constructed of beautiful burnished teak. The bathrooms are surprisingly basic, but everything else oozes rustic charm, including the shaded picnic table contraptions in front of each bungalow.

Kaenchan Beach Hotel (☎ 0 3247 0777; 241/4 Th Ruamjit; bungalows 1500B, r 2150-3300B, ste 5700B; ❄ ⊕) This tangerine tower is a popular midrange choice for vacationing Thais and expats. Kaenchan's spacious rooms boast loads of lacquered cherry-wood furnishings and windows that face the sea. Additional bungalow-style accommodation sits behind the hotel for those who aren't too fussed about ocean views. The complimentary breakfast feels a bit like an anthropological study – it's a Thai interpretation of a Western buffet. Walk-ins can usually score 50% discounts even on the busiest weekends of the year.

TOP END

There are numerous top-end options around Cha-am, but the most lavish resorts are located several kilometres south. Most of the pricey places in the area offer taxi shuttles to and from nearby Hua Hin.

Casa Papaya (☎ 0 3247 0678; www.casapapayathai .com; 810/4 Th Phetkasem; r from 3000B; ❄ ⊒ ☎ ⊕) Designer Mexican chic runs riot at this terrific spot right on the beach 6km south towards Hua Hin. The beachfront and sea-view bungalows have rooftop decks to enjoy the sunlight, and inside there are king-size beds, and bathrooms in wonderfully brave colours.

Cha-am Methavalai Hotel (☎ 0 3243 3250-3; www .methavalai.com; 220 Th Ruamjit; r 3200-4200B, ste 6500-10,400B; ❄ ⊒ ⊕) Methavalai doesn't compete with the armada of sleek boutique resorts popping up along the king's coast, but there's something very charming about this older stalwart. Flowers spill from the white, terraced balconies like green pom-poms, and Thai-style cottages hide throughout the grounds of manicured foliage.

Bann Pantai Resort (☎ 0 3243 3111; www.bannpan tai.com; Th Ruamjit; r 4000-8000B; ❄ ▯ ▣) The sexiest option in the heart of Cha-am, Bann Pantai is a chic village oozing trendy decor details yanked straight out of a magazine. Sleek hotel pods sit on the edge of the amoeba-shaped overflow pool, which drips a refreshing turquoise tint.

Dusit Resort (☎ 0 3252 0009; http://huahin.dusit .com; 1349 Th Phetkasem; r 7000-8000B, ste 14,000-58,000B; ❄ ▯ ▣) This stunning, colonial-style resort pretends to be in Hua Hin, however, it's technically within Cha-am's city limit, despite being several kilometres south of town. Dusit is one of the most respected names in Thai vacation luxury, and this beachside avatar is probably the flagship. Amenities include a fitness centre, minigolf course, horse-riding facilities, a pool, tennis and squash courts and polo grounds.

Veranda (☎ 0 3270 9000-99; www.verandaresort andspa.com; 737/12 Th Mung Talay; r 8400-9800B, ste 19,800B, villa 35,000-45,000B; ❄ ▯ ▣) If the Starship *Enterprise* were disassembled and turned into a beachside resort, it would probably look a bit like sleek Veranda. Muted tones and trendsetting details permeate the plush oasis, while Speedo-clad jetsetters lounge around the pool absorbing sunrays and the chic ambiance in equal measure.

Eating

There are loads of options along the main coastal drag – some are affiliated with hotels, while others are stand-alone venues and beachside food stalls.

Rang Yen Garden (☎ 0 3247 1267; 259/40 Th Ruamjit; dishes 50-180B; ❄ lunch & dinner Nov-Apr) This lovely patio-style restaurant serves up Thai favourites under the stars. It's only open in the high season.

ourpick Krua Medsai (☎ 08 1763 6070, 0 3243 0196; dishes 60-280B; ❄ dinner) This fantastic local haunt rarely registers on Cha-am's tourism radar because it sits just north of the beachside town. Try succulent *'boo nim* (soft-shell crab) and order a bowl of spicy *dôm yam gûng* (prawn and lemon grass soup) with coconut. To find Krua Medsai, go north along the main ocean road until the rows of accommodation end; you'll pass over a small bridge and a few hun-

dred metres later there's a large blue billboard pointing to the restaurant on the right-hand side of the road.

Poom Restaurant (☎ 0 3247 1036; 274/1 Th Ruamjit; dishes 100-200B; ❄ lunch & dinner) Poom is the restaurant of choice for weekending Thais – there's copious indoor and outdoor seating, and the long tables are conducive to a sociable evening with a large group of friends. It's slightly pricier than similar establishments, but the portions are massive, and, according to the lengthy menu, everything's 'cooked the way you lick it'. We 'licked' everything we ate.

Da Vinci's (☎ 0 3247 1871; 274/5 Th Ruamjit; mains 120-400B; ❄ lunch & dinner) Trimmed with a Euro-Asian mix of old-style lamps and shady palms, Da Vinci's chic patio is easily the classiest spot to dine in Cha-am. The setting largely reflects the menu; a variety of international eats are up for grabs.

Getting There & Away

All of the top-end hotels, as well as some of the midrange hotels, have shuttles to Hua Hin. Expect to pay about 300B to 450B one way.

Ordinary and air-conditioned buses stop in the town centre, on Th Phetkasem. Some air-conditioned buses to/from Bangkok go to the beach, stopping on Th Chaolai a few hundred metres south of the Th Narathip intersection.

Frequent bus services operating to/from Cha-am include Bangkok (around 150B, three hours), Phetchaburi (35B, 40 minutes) and Hua Hin (25B, 30 minutes).

The train station is inland on Th Narathip, west of Th Phetkasem, and a 30B motorcycle ride to/from the beach. From Bangkok, three train stations have daily services to Cha-am: Hualamphong (3.50pm), Sam Sen (9.27am) and Thonburi (7.15am, 1.30pm and 7.05pm). Tickets cost from 60B to 180B and the journey is around four hours. Cha-am isn't listed on the English-language train schedule – ask at the ticket counter in Bangkok to be sure the train is stopping at Cha-am.

Getting Around

From the city centre to the beach it's a quick motorcycle taxi (30B) or share taxi (10B) ride. Motorcycle taxis around town cost 30B.

Bicycles and motorbikes are available for rent all along Th Ruamjit. Motorcycles generally go for 300B per day, while the hot-pink bicycles are 20B per hour or 100B per day. They're a great way to get about town.

HUA HIN
อำเภอหัวหิน

pop 49,800

The humble fishing village of Hua Hin became the poster child for a traditional Thai beach holiday back in 1922 when King Rama IV chose the quiet site for his rambling summer palace. Today his teak fortress is still used by his progeny when they need to unwind from the daily chore of ruling a nation. Western developers have followed suit, creating high-rise skyscrapers and rambling resorts offering visitors the chance to live like royalty.

Growing development has encroached on government land, completely obstructing the ocean view from the beach road of Th Naresdamri. Girlie bars are starting to make an appearance, and although they are relegated to a few small side streets, it may be a sign of things to come. Many beachseekers are heading to nearby towns such as Cha-am (p172) or Pranburi (p182) for a quieter vacation closer to the sand. Adventure types might want to try Khao Sam Roi Yot National Park (p183).

Although the city is light on for sights, there are plenty of activities to keep you busy throughout the day. Play a round of golf at one of the nearby private courses, or go horse riding on the nearby polo grounds. Make mealtime an event and try a leisurely lunch at one of the seafood restaurants jutting out over the bay along the pier. Dinners can be easily arranged at one of the charming colonial hotels around town. Evening drinks can last through the night until the sun rises for another day of casting rays over this urban jungle by the sea.

Orientation

Th Naresdamri is the tourist backbone and home to a cacophony of restaurants, souvenir stalls and persistent tailors, some of whom try to get passers by into an 'original' Armani suit. Guesthouses and busy outdoor restaurants line the waterfront area, and it's here that the catches of the day flounder, awaiting a tasty fate. Small soi veer off this thoroughfare and hide more guesthouses, old teak houses, jumping bars (of the girlie and nongirlie variety) and travel agencies. It's a lively place to visit, but if you want some quiet time it may be best to stay elsewhere.

The beachfront is completely obscured by tourism enterprises – the best stretch of sand can be found by the Sofitel resort, where the peach-coloured beach is broken up by round, smooth boulders (Hua Hin means 'stone head') and is ideal for year-round swimming. The train station lies at the western end of town, and its beautifully restored royal waiting room is a great spot to get snap-happy.

Information

BOOKSHOPS
Bookazine (☎ 0 3253 2071; 166 Th Naresdamri; ⊙ 9am-10pm) Has loads of maps, books in English and travel books, including Lonely Planet guides.

EMERGENCY
Tourist police (☎ 0 3251 5995, emergency 1155; Th Damnoen Kasem)

INTERNET ACCESS
Internet access is available all over Hua Hin.
World News Coffee (Th Naresdamri; per hr 40B; ⊙ 8am-11pm; 🔀) This cafe has fast internet connection in air-con comfort.

INTERNET RESOURCES
Hua Hin After Dark (www.huahinafterdark.com) A good resource for night-time shenanigans.

MEDIA
Hua Hin Observer (www.observergroup.net) A free, home-grown magazine with short features in English (and a few in German). Available at most hotels around town, it contains snippets on eating out, culture and entertainment.

MEDICAL SERVICES
Hospital San Paolo (☎ 0 3253 2576; 222 Th Phetkasem) For basic and emergency care.

MONEY
There are currency exchange booths and ATMs up and down Th Naresdamri, as well as on several side streets. Nearer to the bus stations are a couple of banks on the northern part of Th Phetkasem.
Bank of Ayudhya (Th Naresdamri; ⊙ 10am-8pm) Exchange window conveniently located close to the beach.

POST
Post office (☎ 0 3251 1350; Th Damnoen Kasem)

TOURIST INFORMATION
Free maps, pamphlets and brochures – almost everything you'll need – can be found in most restaurants and hotels.
Tourist information office (☎ 0 3253 2433; cnr Th Phetkasem & Th Damnoen Kasem; ⊙ 8.30am-8pm Mon-Fri, to 5pm Sat) Has lots of info on Hua Hin and the

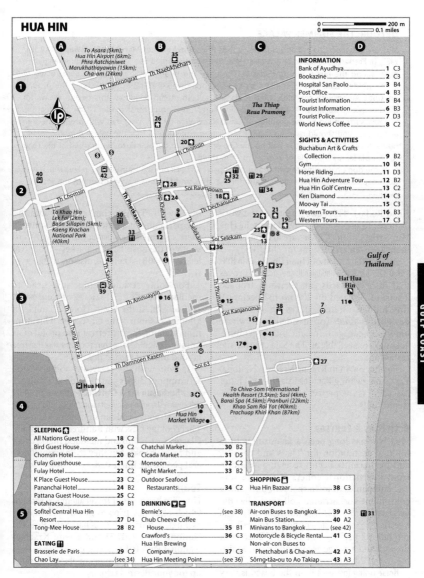

HUA HIN

0 |======| 200 m
0 |======| 0.1 miles

INFORMATION
Bank of Ayudhya	1 C3
Bookazine	2 C3
Hospital San Paolo	3 B4
Post Office	4 B3
Tourist Information	5 B4
Tourist Information	6 B3
Tourist Police	7 D3
World News Coffee	8 C2

SIGHTS & ACTIVITIES
Buchabun Art & Crafts Collection	9 B2
Gym	10 B4
Horse Riding	11 D3
Hua Hin Adventure Tour	12 B2
Hua Hin Golf Centre	13 C2
Ken Diamond	14 C3
Moo•ay Tai	15 C3
Western Tours	16 B3
Western Tours	17 C3

Tha Thiap
Reua Pramong

Gulf of
Thailand

Hat Hua
Hin

To Asara (5km);
Hua Hin Airport (6km);
Phra Ratchaniwet
Marukhathayawan (15km);
Cha-am (24km)

To Khao Hin
Lek Fai (2km);
Baan Sillapin (5km);
Kaeng Krachan
National Park
(40km)

To Chiva-Som International
Health Resort (3.5km); Sasi (4km);
Barai (4.5km); Pranburi (22km);
Khao Sam Roi Yot (40km);
Prachuap Khiri Khan (87km)

Hua Hin
Market Village

SLEEPING
All Nations Guest House	18 C2
Bird Guest House	19 C2
Chomsin Hotel	20 B2
Fulay Guesthouse	21 C2
Fulay Hotel	22 C2
K Place Guest House	23 C2
Pananchai Hotel	24 B2
Pattana Guest House	25 C2
Putahracsa	26 B1
Sofitel Central Hua Hin Resort	27 D4
Tong-Mee House	28 B2

EATING
Brasserie de Paris	29 C2
Chao Lay	(see 34)
Chatchai Market	30 B2
Cicada Market	31 D5
Monsoon	32 C2
Night Market	33 B2
Outdoor Seafood Restaurants	34 C2

DRINKING
Bernie's	(see 38)
Chub Cheeva Coffee House	35 B1
Crawford's	36 C3
Hua Hin Brewing Company	37 C3
Hua Hin Meeting Point	(see 36)

SHOPPING
Hua Hin Bazaar	38 C3

TRANSPORT
Air-con Buses to Bangkok	39 A3
Main Bus Station	40 A2
Minivans to Bangkok	(see 42)
Motorcycle & Bicycle Rental	41 C3
Non-air-con Buses to Phetchaburi & Cha-am	42 A2
Sŏrng•tăa•ou to Ao Takiap	43 A3

surrounding areas, and gives out loads of brochures. There is a handy, second location right beside the Starbucks near the central clock tower.

Sights

Although the sights are a bit thin on the ground in Hua Hin, there are several spots orbiting the urban core that are worth a quick look. For views of city and sea make the 2km trek to **Khao Hin Lek Fai**, also known as Khao Radar. The scenery is best appreciated at dusk.

For insight into Hua Hin's thriving artistic community, hit up **Baan Sillapin** (☎ 0 3253 4830; 81 Moo 14; ☻ 10am-5pm, Tue-Sun) located around 5km west of town (around 3km beyond

---

DETOUR: THE SUMMER PALACE

Midway between Cha-am and Hua Hin stands **Phra Ratchaniwet Marukhathayawan** (☎ 0 3247 2482; Th Phetkasem; admission by donation; ⏰ 8.30am-4pm Mon-Fri, to 5pm Sat & Sun), a summer palace built during the reign of King Rama VI. The one- and two-storey buildings are constructed of prime golden teak and interlinked by covered boardwalks, all raised high above the ground on stilts. Along with the high, tiled roofs and tall, shuttered windows, this design allows for maximum air circulation – a building design sorely missing in most modern Thai architecture. It's now surrounded by the grounds of Camp Rama VI, a military post, but with proper check-in at the gate you should have no trouble receiving permission to tour the palace during opening hours. If you take one of the half-hourly Cha-am–Hua Hin buses, ask to be dropped at the road to this place; it's a couple of kilometres from there.

If you don't have time to visit the summer palace, check out the train station in Hua Hin. It was designed to be the royal waiting room for the king, and features a similar flamboyant design.

Khao Radar). This retreat features the work of Tawee Kesa-Ngam, the president of the Hua Hin Artist Group. Classes are also on offer – there are even art sessions for children.

About 30km west of Hua Hin, **Hua Hin Hills** (☎ 0 3252 6351; www.huahinhillsvineyard.com) proves that lush vineyards can thrive in tropical Thailand. Situated on 200 *râi* (32 hectares), this hidden estate features an intricately designed *săh·lah* (open-sided hall) where onlookers can gain insight into viticulture. Tastings are available at 'The Sala', the on-site restaurant.

Further on, in in Kraeng Krachan National Park, the gushing **Nam Tok Pala-U** – an 11-tier cascade – is the perfect reward for more intrepid souls.

Activities & Courses

Hua Hin has long been a favourite golfing holiday destination for Thais and royalty, and has recently begun receiving attention from international golfers. There are several companies in town that rent out golfing equipment and arrange golf tours. **Hua Hin Golf Centre** (☎ 0 3253 1096; www.huahingolf.com; Th Naresdamri; ⏰ noon-10pm), opposite the Hilton, can tailor a package to any of the courses in the area and arrange accommodation, equipment, a caddy and transfers.

Horse riding (per hr 450B) on the beach is very common around these parts. Horses and their owners can usually be found at the beach at the end of Th Damnoen Kasem.

Moo·ay tai (Thai boxing; ☎ 0 3251 5269; 8/1 Th Phunsuk; admission 300B) matches take place every Tuesday and Friday at 9pm. The fighters aren't pros by any stretch of the imagination, but they put on a good show. If you're inspired by the

moo·ay tai (Thai boxing) matches and feel like partaking in a little kickboxing yourself, there's a **gym** (Th Phetkasem) south of town – just south of the hospital and market – that gives lessons (300B). Daily admission to the gym is 180B.

For some serious pampering, head to the **Barai Spa** (☎ 0 3251 1234; www.thebarai.com; 91 Th Khao Takiap) at the Hyatt Hotel, a couple of kilometres south of the city centre. This stunning, state-of-the-art retreat is so proud of its unique design details that it offers regular free guided tours of the facility.

If you wish to re-create some of the scrumptious dishes you've eaten in Thailand, visit **Buchabun Art & Crafts Collection** (☎ 0 1572 3805; www.siambeing.com/restaurant/cookingcourse; 22 Th Dechanuchit) where you can sign up for a half-day Thai cooking class with Ratthreeya Buchabun. Classes cost 1000B and include a market visit and recipe book – but they're only run if several people are interested.

Tours

Hua Hin has loads of travel agencies, most of which offer day trips to nearby places such as Phetchaburi (p167), Khao Sam Roi Yot National Park (p183) and Kaeng Krachan National Park (p172). You may have to wait a day or two before a quorum of tourists signs up for your desired trip.

Hua Hin Adventure Tour (☎ 0 3253 0314; www.hua hinadventuretour.com; Th Naep Khehat; ⏰ 8.30am-7pm) Runs kayaking trips in the Khao Sam Roi Yot National Park (1900B), among several other options. Tours include pick-up from your hotel.

Ken Diamond (☎ 0 3251 3863; www.travel-huahin.com; 4/34 Th Naresdamri) A German-run outfit that has dozens of trips to destinations in the vicinity, including waterfalls, national parks, and diving and snorkelling locations. It also arranges car rentals.

Western Tours (☎ 0 3253 3303; www.westerntours huahin.com; 11 Th Damnoen Kasem) Has tours to surrounding attractions, golf packages (including equipment rentals), hotel bookings, bus tickets and help with local transportation. It's an authorised agent for Thai Airways. There's another branch on Th Amnuaysin.

Festivals & Events

The annual **Hua Hin Jazz Festival** (http://jazzfestival huahin.com; ☼ mid-Jun) is held near the beachfront and showcases Thailand's best jazz talent.

Sleeping

Lodging in Hua Hin generally falls at the extremes of the pricing spectrum. There are some great deals around town for the budget traveller, and some of Thailand's best boutique hotels for those who can drop the big bucks. Cha-am (25km north) and Pranburi (23km south) offer some fantastic sleeping options as well.

Hua Hin's proximity to Bangkok means that rates sometimes skyrocket on weekends (especially holiday weekends), while weekdays are noticeably less expensive.

Although the 'girlie bar' scene may not be as raucous in Hua Hin as, say, Pattaya or Patong, travellers should watch out for the burgeoning prostitution scene, especially when choosing accommodation. The budget and midrange categories (especially in the Th Chomsin area) are rife with unsavoury characters that hide behind the boutique facades. We've experienced solicitation firsthand and recommend caution if steering away from our list of reviewed accommodation.

BUDGET

All Nations Guest House (☎ 0 3251 2747; www.geocities .com/allnationsguesthouse; 10-10/1 Th Dechanuchit; d with shared bathroom 350-500B) All Nations' backpacker lodging is simple, but it gets the job done. The lobby bar is decorated with foreign flags and currencies, and the televisions are conveniently stuck on the sports channel. Single travellers get a 50% discount.

Pattana Guest House (☎ 0 3251 3393; huahinpat tana@hotmail.com; 52 Th Naresdamri; r 350-600B) Blink and you'll miss the narrow soi that leads to little Pattana. This charming teak habitat is adorned with a variety of colourful collectibles, including a giant wooden rooster, toy ships and endless stacks of tattered paperbacks.

Rooms are small and far less memorable, but they'll do the trick for any bargain-basement backpacker.

Bird Guest House (☎ 0 3251 1630; birdguesthousehua hin@hotmail.com; 31/2 Th Naresdamri; r 400-600B; 🖳) Bird doesn't sing like it used to, but it's a decent budget choice if you're seeking out a charming, pier-shanty ambiance. It's a bit smaller than some of the other guesthouses nearby, so there's a homely, relaxed atmosphere.

Tong-Mee House (☎ 0 3253 0725; 1 Soi Raumpown; r 550B; 🖳) This hidden gem is tucked away along a quiet residential soi. Fresh potted plants cheer the stairwell, and although the rooms are cosy (ie small), they have polished wooden floors and immaculate bathrooms. There's a neat little cafe, a small library and plenty of genuine smiles.

Pananchai Hotel (☎ 0 3251 1707, 0 3251 1633; 71 Th Naep Khehat; d incl breakfast 650B; 🖳) Pananchai feels like a small European hotel with its teeny check-in desk and thin, rickety elevator. The rooms have small windows and are decked out in faded floral patterns.

K Place Guest House (☎ 0 3251 1396; kplaceus@yahoo .com; 116 Th Naresdamri; r 800-1000B; 🖳) Smack in the heart of things on Th Naresdamri, but tucked away behind the associated minimart, K Place's spacious rooms are good value, but not all have natural light.

MIDRANGE

Fulay Guesthouse (☎ 0 3251 3145; www.fulay-huahin .com; 110/1 Th Naresdamri; r 750-1500B; 🖳) One of the best pier guesthouses jutting out over the sea, Fulay has charming marine-themed rooms with fresh coats of white and blue paint, and the odd framed portrait of a wooden frigate. Guests fall asleep to the soft crashing of the waves below.

Fulay Hotel (☎ 0 3251 3670, 0 3251 3145; fishshop@ hotmail.com; 110/1 Th Naresdamri; r 850-1500B; 🖳 🛜) Across from Fulay Guesthouse is this narrow, teak-facade hotel right in the thick of things. The hotel is good value, and there's also a romantic, fancy-looking restaurant downstairs.

Chomsin Hotel (☎ 0 3251 5348; www.chomsinhuahin .com; 130/4 Th Chomsin; r 900-1500B; 🖳 🛜) Friendly Chomsin is a great addition to the spread of low-priced accommodation in Hua Hin. The rooms are immaculate, and feature polished hardwood floors, modern bathrooms and sun-filled picture windows.

All Seasons Guesthouse (☎ 0 3251 5151; Soi 63, 77/18-19 Th Phetkasem; r 1000-1300B; 🖳) All Seasons has spacious, sun-soaked rooms with enormous bathrooms befitting a top-end resort. The friendly, UK-born owner rents out DVD players, so you can finally watch any purchases you've made. The seven rooms can fill up quickly so it's best to call ahead.

TOP END

our pick **Putahracsa** (☎ 0 3253 1470; www.putahracsa .com; 22/65 Th Naep Khehat; r 4500-11,000B; 🅿 🖳 🛜 🐾) How do you say 'swanky' in Thai? It's 'Putahracsa'. This stunning complex features a variety of structures shaped like cubic Tetris pieces, which sit along a beachfront lawn with blades of bright green grass. The design is elegant yet simple, with teak veneers covering smooth white walls. This terrific resort is hard to spell, but definitely easy to love.

Sofitel Central Hua Hin Resort (Hua Hin Railway Hotel; ☎ 0 3251 2021-38; www.accorhotels.com/asia; 1 Th Damnoen Kasem; r from 4943B, ste from 12,578B; 🅿 🖳 🛜 🐾) In 1922 the State Railway of Thailand (then the Royal Thai Railway) extended the national rail network to Hua Hin to allow easier access to the Hua Hin summer palace. The area proved to be a popular vacation spot with the general population too, so in the following year the Hua Hin Railway Hotel was built – a graceful colonial-style inn by the sea. Today the property is under the management of Accor's Sofitel branch, and it remains a beautiful complex with plenty of beach views, three pools, rolling grounds and first-class spa services. Discounts of up to 40% may be possible during the week and in the low season.

Dune (☎ 0 3251 5051; www.dunehuahin.com; 5/5 Th Naep Kaehat; r incl breakfast 5900-15,800B; 🅿 🖳 🛜 🐾) Little Dune has five luxurious suites stocked with a cache of boutique design details. Cool club beats gently waft through the air as guests recline on imported furniture made from handcrafted textiles. It's located just beyond the city centre near Soi 45, between the town and the airport.

Asara (☎ 0 3254 7555; www.asaravillaandsuite.com; 35 Hua Hin Soi 5; r from 9500B; 🅿 🖳 🛜 🐾) Beautiful Asara is a veritable village of modern villas. Located 5km north of the city centre, this lagoon-filled property boasts ocean vistas, private plunge pools, two restaurants and a vast spa offering world-class spa packages. The friendly staff tend to guests with ear-to-ear smiles.

Chiva-Som International Health Resort (☎ 0 3253 6536; www.chivasom.com; 73/4 Th Phetkasem; r US$460-

---

LIVE LIKE A KING

King Rama IV made Hua Hin his royal summer residence back in 1922, and today, you too can find your very own palace in the form of a stunning, world-class resort. While the following options may break the bank, they sure are worth the splurge.

- **Chiva-Som International Health Resort** (left; Hua Hin)
- **Evasons** (p183; Pranburi)
- **Veranda** (p175; Cha-am)
- **Putahracsa** (left; Hua Hin)
- **Asara** (left; Hua Hin)

1600; 🅿 🖳 🛜 🐾) Set along seven acres of beach, Chiva-Som is the ultimate vacation playground for the overworked, overstressed and overpaid. The name means 'haven of life' in Thai-Sanskrit, and the staff of 200 fuse Eastern and Western approaches to wellness with planned nutrition, step and aqua aerobics, and Thai, Swedish or underwater massage. Rates include three meals per day along with health and fitness consultations, spa treatments and recreational activities. Lengthier packages are also available (up to one month), as are specialised detox and fitness regimes.

Eating

Seafood rules the culinary roost in Hua Hin and fresh delights from the sea are available all over town. You can get seafood snacks on the beach throughout the day; cracked crab and cold Singha beer can be ordered without leaving your deckchair. The best seafood to eat in Hua Hin is *ƀlah săm·lee* (cotton fish or kingfish), *ƀlah grà·pong* (perch), *ƀlah mèuk* (squid), *hŏy má·laang pôo* (mussels) and *ƀoo* (crab). The concentration of outdoor wharfside seafood restaurants on Th Naresdamri, at the intersection of Th Dechanuchit, offers the widest choice in ocean fare.

Night Market (🕑 around 5pm-midnight) After sampling the sea's offerings, it's well worth heading here for a heady assortment of steamed eats. The pedestrian street comes alive every evening, although weekends tend to be livelier when holidaying Thais pop into town as an escape from the Bangkokian buzz. There are plenty of spots to grab a bite – it's best to stick to the street-side fare; we found that most of the adjacent restaurants cater to tourists and offer up less-than-stellar eats.

Cicada Market (3pm-midnight Sat) This newer market sits near the Hyatt Regency, and although the focus leans more towards performance arts and homemade crafts, there are several food stalls that offer authentic local cuisine. An expansion of opening hours is in the works.

Chatchai Market (Th Dechanuchit) This colourful and inexpensive market is one of Hua Hin's major attractions. Vendors gather nightly in the centre of town (off Th Phetkasem) to fry, steam, grill, parboil or bake fresh gulf seafood for hordes of hungry Thais. Don't leave town without trying the famous *roti Hua Hin* (10B) served at this market, a delicious snack made with special dough and filled with sweets such as strawberries, custard or raisins.

Chao Lay (☎ 0 3251 3436; 15 Th Naresdamri; dishes 60-400B; lunch & dinner) Probably the best of the wharf restaurants, this place certainly manages to fill its two levels of pier seating. There's a veritable fish market out front where you can choose your catch of the day, and a small army of waiters to deliver the end product.

Baan Itsara (☎ 0 3253 0574; 7 Th Naebkhehars; dishes 90-400B; lunch & dinner) Baan Itsara is a destination for aficionados of the ocean's produce. Considered by some to be one of the best seafood places in town, this restaurant, located a short walk north of the town centre, has tables right on the ocean and a small imported wine list. The tiger prawns in sweet basil sauce are a perennial favourite.

Monsoon (☎ 0 3253 1062; 62 Th Naresdamri; dishes 100-250B; set menu 390B; lunch & dinner) Beautiful Monsoon feels like a far-flung railway station deep within Indo-China. There are large leather chairs plucked directly from a posh lodge and the menu offers imported teas and a mix of regional and foreign cuisine. The 50B water surcharge was the only thing that marred the experience.

Brasserie de Paris (☎ 0 3253 0637; 3 Th Naresdamri; dishes 180-500B; breakfast, lunch & dinner) An actual French chef serves up real French food (crab Hua Hin is a speciality) in this lovely, light and airy restaurant. There's a good view of *la mer* from upstairs.

Sasi (☎ 0 3253 6606; 83/159 Nhongkae; set menu 350-450B; dinner) Set in the round in an open air show space, Sasi offers an elaborate Thai dance and theatrical show at dinner.

Drinking

Countless faràng bars can be found at the Hua Hin Bazaar and on the little soi off Th Naresdamri and Th Damnoen Kasem. Some of these offer a Thai-hostess atmosphere, but a few bill themselves as sports bars and have a widescreen TV tuned to events around the world.

Hua Hin Brewing Company (Th Naresdamri) This maze of barges, decks and masts is one of the most popular entertainment venues around. There's often live music and it attracts a mix of hotel guests, expats, tourists and some local 'ladies of the night'. It's not at all sleazy, however – it's attached to one of the classiest hotels in town.

Bernie's (Hua Hin Bazaar, Th Damnoen Kasem) A British-run sports bar – the owner is a big golf nut with loads of info on swinging a club in the area.

Hua Hin Meeting Point (☎ 0 3253 1132; 3 Th Phunsuk) The corner location ensures this place sees plenty of action. It serves meals but is also a popular place for a few drinks. There's indoor seating around a slick, modern white bar (in the comfort of air-con) or sit on the outside patio, which has a giant projection screen.

Crawford's (☎ 0 3251 1517; 5 Th Phunsuk) Hua Hin's favourite Irish bar has imported everything directly from the motherland (minus the cold weather). There are two wood-finished levels of air-conditioned, Guinness-drinking comfort. It's not too rowdy and there's a friendly expat 'drink with your mates' mood here, as well as the occasional sports match on one of its many TVs.

Chub Cheeva Coffee House (☎ 0 3251 33380; 2/8 Th Nahb Kahat) Wonderfully offbeat, Chub Cheeva sits on a grassy space that feels like an orphanage for unwanted patio furniture. Fruit shakes, coffee and delicious ice cream are on offer throughout the day, though our favourite time to visit is in the late afternoon for sundowner drinks.

Getting There & Away

SGA (☎ in Hua Hin 0 3252 2300; in Bangkok 0 2134 3233; www.sga.aero) flies a 12-seat shuttle two times a day (one-way around 3000B, 40 minutes, noon and 5.30pm) from Bangkok's Suvarnabhumi airport to Hua Hin.

There are air-con buses to/from Bangkok's Southern bus station (171B, 3½ hours, every half hour). These leave on Th Sasong (outside the Siripetchkasem Hotel). Air-con minivans to Bangkok (180B) leave every half hour from the Yamaha Sign near the junction of Th Chomsin and Th Phetkasen.

The main government bus station, on Th Liap Thang Rot Fai, has air-con buses to many destinations throughout the country. Be sure to ignore the touts here and go to the window for assistance and ticket purchase. There is at least one air-con bus per day to each destination: Phetchaburi (80B, 1½ hours), Cha-am (40B, 30 minutes), Prachuap Khiri Khan (80B, 1½ hours), Chumphon (160B, four hours), Phuket (378B, eight hours), Krabi (389B, eight hours), Koh Samui (320B, nine hours) and Songkhla (457B, 11 hours). Frequent non-air-con buses to Phetchaburi (50B, 1½ hours) and Cha-am (25B, 30 minutes) leave from near the intersection of Th Chomsin and Th Phetkasem.

There are frequent trains running to/from Bangkok's Hualamphong train station (2nd class 292B to 382B, 3rd class 234B to 294B, four hours) and other stations on the southern railway line.

The Lomprayah ferry service runs bus/boat combos down to Ko Pha-Ngan at 9am and midnight daily. See p232 for more details. If you arriving in Hua Hin from the islands, you will mostly be dropped off on the side of the highway near the Hua Hin Market Village, south of the town centre on Th Phetkasem.

Getting Around

The airport is 6km north of town – about a 150B taxi ride away.

Local buses (10B) and sŏrng·tăa·ou (10B) to Ao Takiap (for resorts south of Hua Hin) leave from the corner of Th Sasong and Th Dechanuchit.

Even though săhm·lór fares in Hua Hin have been set by the municipal authorities, haggling is still often required. Some sample fares: from the train station to the beach, 20B; from the air-con bus terminal to Th Naresdamri, 30B to 40B (depending on the size of your bags); and from Chatchai Market to Tha Thiap Reua Pramong, 20B. Most drivers will ask for at least twice as much.

Motorcycles and bicycles can be rented from a couple of places on Th Damnoen Kasem near the Sofitel Central Hua Hin Resort. Motorcycle rates are reasonable: 200B to 250B per day for 100cc to 125cc bikes. Occasionally, larger bikes (400cc to 750cc) are available for 600B to 700B a day. Car and 4WD rental can

also be arranged at most travel agencies, including Ken Diamond and Western Tours (see p178). Expect to pay around 1300B to 1500B for a small Suzuki 4WD. Bicycle rental costs 50B to 100B per day.

PRANBURI
ปราณบุรี
pop 75,000

Pranburi, about 35km south of Hua Hin, is quickly becoming the choice destination for high-end travellers heading along the king's coast. Flanked by verdant pineapple orchards and creamy brown sands, this little hamlet has caught the eye of cinematographers capitalising on the area's natural beauty and seclusion.

The region of Pranburi sits slightly inland from the ocean, while the beach area is commonly known as Pak Nam Pran. A long, sandy road snakes directly along the coast cutting a path between the seaside resorts and the cool, crashing tides. For an interesting perspective on the local fishing culture, try a serene **boat tour** (☎ 08 3849 7061; 6-person boat 1000B), which takes in views of the vibrant trollers docked near hidden temples. Boat depart from Ban Pranburi.

Information
Pranburi Hospital (☎ 0 3262 1757, 0 3262 1767)
Tourist Police (☎ 0 3251 5995, emergency 1155)

Sleeping & Eating
As the region continues to increase in popularity, heaps of new hotels are popping up, including a tantalising array of boutique options. There are a few independent restaurants and bars along the main beach street, but most guests tend to dine at the fantastic resort restaurants.

Palm Beach Pranburi (☎ 0 3263 1966; www.palmbeachpranburi.com; 494 Moo 2; r from 1500B; ❀) A new 'boutique' operation along the sand, Palm Beach is a solid holiday option with prim rooms sporting subtle Thai touches and an inviting poolside patio.

Lawana Beach Resort (☎ 0 3263 2222; www.lawanapranburi.com; 5/1 Moo 1; bungalows 2800-12,000B; ❀ ▣) Just 200m from the local village, this sprawling complex of palm fronds and thatched cottages (some with awesome personal plunge pools!) sits along a sandy ribbon on the Pranburi river.

Huaplee Lazy Beach (☎ 0 3263 0555; www.huapleelazybeach.com; 163 Moo 4; r 3300-7000B; ❀) Charming, sun-drenched rooms line a miniature pasture by the sea. The interiors are white-on-white, with an occasional blue accent that feels distinctly Mediterranean. Handcrafted furniture and little knick-knacks such as seashell mobiles and colourful teapots give the Lazy Beach an extra pinch of *je ne sais quoi*.

Evasons (☎ 0 3262 2111; www.sixsenses.com/evason -hua-hin; 9 Moo 5, Pak Nam Pran; r & bungalows 5750-16,000B; ❑ ❑ ❑ ❑) This stunning resort is actually made up of two different properties: one offers charming hotel-style lodging and the other features ultraprivate villas, some with exquisite plunge pools. The super-smiley staff don pastel uniforms while catering to guests' every whim and shuttling them around the complex and beyond. Several fantastic adventure activities can be arranged, including biking, hiking, diving and other water sports. There are two on-site spas offering an eclectic assortment of treatments in a garden setting that blends with the naturally occurring foliage. The resort has an entire department dedicated to environmental management and conversation; the primary focus is limiting the impact of tourism and fishing on the surrounding nature.

Aleenta (☎ 0 2508 5333; www.aleenta.com; 183 Moo 4; r 8000-20,000B; ❑ ❑ ❑ ❑) Delicate Aleenta offers villas and suites set within an adobe-and-thatch fortress. Rambling staircases cross the sandy grounds like an Escher print, and the quiet rooms fuse modern amenities and natural textiles. This place prides itself on providing a secluded getaway – almost to the point of snootiness.

Getting There & Away

There are two **minivan services** (☎ 08 6007 4742, 08 5242 5268) that transport passengers between Bangkok and Pranburi (220B). The communication might be a little tricky over the phone as the operators speak very little English. The pick-up and drop-off site is Pranburi's sole 7-Eleven, and in Bangkok, plan to get out at the Victory Monument. It is best to book ahead as these shuttles can fill up rather quickly. If you are trying to connect to a city between Pranburi and Bangkok, simply inform the driver of your intended destination. Taxis from Hua Hin cost 400B, or 500B from Hua Hin airport.

KHAO SAM ROI YOT NATIONAL PARK

อุทยานแห่งชาติเขาสามร้อยยอด

Long ago, a wooden merchant ship was trolling the coast, and when it reached this region

it sprang a leak and rapidly began to sink. Miraculously, all 300 individuals aboard swam to shore escaping a watery grave. From then on, the area became known as Khao Sam Roi Rot, which roughly means 'land of the 300 saved'. After many retellings, this nickname started to change – the memory of the ancient ship became overshadowed by the region's natural virtues, which include myriad skyscraping mountains. The 'rot' ('saved') changed to 'yot' and today this jagged jungle is known as the land of the 300 peaks.

More recently, in 1996 this tropical realm was given national park status, preserving the stunning mounds, caves and trails from developers' hands. The area is home to a vibrant ecosystem that includes friendly dusky langur monkeys, barking deer, Javan mongooses, otters and palm civets. Birdwatchers also hold the park in high esteem, since over 300 species of migratory birds descend on the region's ponds and mangroves each year (see the boxed text, p186).

Other wildlife you may be able to spot around Khao Sam Roi Yot includes crab-eating macaques, slow loris, Malayan pangolins, fishing cats, serows and monitor lizards. Unfortunately, as is the case with many of Thailand's natural resources, the encroachment of industry (in this case shrimp farms) is taking its toll on the natural habitat of the park's varied fauna.

Information

There are three park headquarters (Hat Laem Sala, Ban Rong Jai and Ban Khao Daeng) and three visitors centres (Hat Laem Sala, Hat Sam Phraya and Ban Khao Daeng) where you can obtain information on the area. A nature study centre lies at the end of a 1.5km road leading north from Ban Rong Jai. There are a couple of checkpoints – one on the road south from Pranburi and the other on the road east of Hwy 4. You'll have to pay admission (adult/child under 14 years 400/200B) at these checkpoints or, if you've left the park and are returning, show proof that you've already paid.

Sights & Activities

HIKING

Well worth the steep 45-minute climb, the **Khao Daeng viewpoint** is reached by a well-marked trail beginning 500m from Ban Khao Daeng. The views from the top are breathtaking and the vista spans the length of the

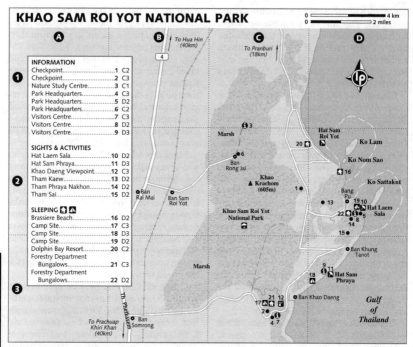

KHAO SAM ROI YOT NATIONAL PARK

	0	4 km
0		2 miles

To Hua Hin (40km)

To Pranburi (18km)

INFORMATION
Checkpoint	1	C2
Checkpoint	2	C3
Nature Study Centre	3	C1
Park Headquarters	4	C3
Park Headquarters	5	D2
Park Headquarters	6	C2
Visitors Centre	7	C3
Visitors Centre	8	D2
Visitors Centre	9	D3

SIGHTS & ACTIVITIES
Hat Laem Sala	10	D2
Hat Sam Phraya	11	D3
Khao Daeng Viewpoint	12	C3
Tham Kaew	13	D2
Tham Phraya Nakhon	14	D2
Tham Sai	15	D2

SLEEPING
Brassiere Beach	16	D2
Camp Site	17	C3
Camp Site	18	D3
Camp Site	19	D2
Dolphin Bay Resort	20	C2
Forestry Department Bungalows	21	C3
Forestry Department Bungalows	22	D2

Marsh

Ban Rong Jai

Khao Krachom (605m)

Ban Rai Mai

Ban Sam Roi Yot

Khao Sam Roi Yot National Park

Marsh

Th. Phetkasem

To Prachuap Khiri Khan (40km)

Ban Somrong

Hat Sam Roi Yot

Ko Lam

Ko Nom Sao

Ko Sattakut

Bang Pu

Hat Laem Sala

Ban Khung Tanot

Hat Sam Phraya

Ban Khao Daeng

Gulf of Thailand

---

park, from the limestone cliffs to the wiggling coastline below. If you have the time, or are visiting the park on your own steam, try the hike to **Khao Krachom** (605m) for a whole different perspective.

BEACHES

Both of the park's beaches have plenty of facilities, including food stalls, picnic areas and washrooms.

Hat Laem Sala, a sandy beach flanked on three sides by dry limestone hills and casuarinas, has a small visitors centre, a restaurant, bungalows and a camping area. The trail to Tham Phraya Nakhon starts here. Boats to the beach (250B return), which take up to 10 people, can be hired from Bang Pu. You can also reach the beach from Bang Pu via a steep trail (20 minutes' walk).

Hat Sam Phraya, 5km south of Hat Laem Sala, is about 1km in length and has a restaurant and washrooms.

CAVES

The three main caves in this park are all worth a detour.

Tham Phraya Nakhon is probably the most photographed cave in Thailand and can be reached by boat or foot. The boat trip takes about 30 minutes there and back, while it's 30 minutes each way by foot along a steep, rocky 430m-long trail from Hat Laem Sala. The cave is made up of two large sinkholes, and when the sun shines through in the early morning the effect is truly mystical. In one cave there's a royal *săh·lah*. It was built for King Chulalongkorn (Rama V), who would stop off here when travelling back and forth between Bangkok and Nakhon Si Thammarat. Check out 'Pagoda Rock', covered with colourful talismans, and 'Crocodile Rock', which actually looks more like an alligator.

Tham Kaew, 2km from the Bang Pu turn-off, features a series of chambers connected by narrow passageways; you enter the first cavern by a ladder. The stalactites and limestone formations glitter with calcite crystals as though they were encrusted with diamonds (hence the cave's name, 'Jewel Cave'). Tham Kaew is best visited in the company of a park guide because of the dangerous footing. Guides can be arranged at Bang Pu.

Tham Sai is a hill cave near Ban Khung Tanot, about 2.3km from the main road between Laem Sala and Sam Phraya beaches. You can rent lamps for a small fee from a shelter near the cave's mouth. A 280m-long trail leads up the hillside to the cave, which features a large single cavern. Be mindful of steep drop-offs in the cave.

Sleeping & Eating

Just outside the northerly checkpoint, roads turn off towards a long sandy bay and Hat Sam Roi Yot. Here, several private resorts offer midrange to top-end accommodation along the uninterrupted and spotless beach. This bay is supposedly a breeding ground for a school of dolphins.

You can pitch your own tent at camp sites near the Khao Daeng Viewpoint, at Hat Laem Sala or at Hat Sam Phraya. There are basic restaurants at all these locations, serving decent food priced for between 30B and 120B.

Forestry Department (☎ in Bangkok 0 2562 0760; campsites per person 30B, bungalows per 5-6 people 1200-1400B, per 6-9 people 1600-2200B) The forestry department hires out yellow and green bungalows with metal roofing at Hat Laem Sala and at the visitors centre near the Khao Daeng viewpoint. Two-person tents are available for rent at these spots for 150B per night.

Dolphin Bay Resort (☎ 0 3255 9333; www.dolphin bayresort.com; 227 Moo 4, Phu Noi; r & bungalows 1490-6800B; 🍴 🏊) This well-priced option is a great place to take the family. There's plenty of space to frolic around and the large swimming pool has a slippery slide. A wide range of trips is on offer to nearby islands and peaks around the national park.

our pick **Brassiere Beach** (Brassiere Cozy Hotel; ☎ 0 3263 0555, 0 2511 1397; brassierebeach@hotmail.com; 210 Moo 5, Tambol Samroiyod; villas from 4275B; 🍴 🛜 🏊) When you check into Brassiere Beach, the first thing you'll notice are two breastlike islands bobbing just off the coast (hence the name). The second thing you'll notice is the key to your room – it's attached to a colourful miniature bra. Each of the stunning Mediterranean-style villas has loads of personalised charm. When we visited, a Thai pop star was getting ready to shoot a music video on the premises.

Getting There & Away

The park is approximately 40km south of Hua Hin and is best seen by car or motorcycle. From Hua Hin take Hwy 4 (Th Phetkasem) to Pranburi. In Pranburi turn left at the main intersection and 4km later, at the police substation, turn right. From there, it's 19km to the park's entrance. If you're trying to reach the park from the south, there's an entrance off Hwy 4 – make a right at Km286.5 marker.

If you don't have your own wheels, catch a bus or train to Pranburi (possible from both Bangkok and Hua Hin, as well as other regional places). From Pranburi, take a sŏrng·tǎa·ou (50B, every half-hour during daylight hours) to Bang Pu, a small village inside the park. Bang Pu is virtually on Hat Laem Sala.

You can also hire a taxi for 350B, or a motorcycle taxi for 300B, from Pranburi all the way to the park. Be sure to mention you want to go to the ù·tá·yahn hàang châht (national park) rather than Ban Sam Roi Yot.

PRACHUAP KHIRI KHAN & AROUND

อ.เมืองประจวบคีรีขันธ์

Prachuap Khiri Khan is the administrative centre for the province with the same name. The little town is light on attractions, but it's an OK place to stretch your legs and grab a bite to eat. If you really need some exercise, hike the 418 steps to the golden-spired **Wat Thammikaram**, established by King Rama IV. Hordes of monkeys provide endless entertainment along the way. The view from the top stretches west to the Myanmar border, only 11km away.

Located in the Muang district, the **King Mongkut Memorial Park of Science and Technology** (☎ 0 3266 1104; www.nfe.go.th/waghor; 🕘 9am-4pm) is a sprawling science complex that features a giant aquarium with a walk-through tunnel, a soothing butterfly garden and a planetarium for astronomy enthusiasts.

Fishing still provides the main source of income for the town's inhabitants and you're likely to see brightly painted vessels bobbing up and down the coastline like rainbow-coloured sea birds. Not surprisingly, the seafood here is excellent and considerably cheaper than at the more popular tourist hang-outs along the coast.

Uncrowded beaches and broad bays sweep north and south around town, and locals are always happy to see the few faràng that make the effort to get off the well-trodden tourist trail. **Ao Manao** and **Hat Wa Kaw**, both south of Prachuap town, and **Ao Noi**, to the north, all have calm casuarina-lined dunes along quiet rolling waters. Beautiful Ao Manao is under the supervision of the local Thai Air Force.

Orientation & Information

The city of Prachuap Khiri Khan stretches along the 8km-long Ao Prachuap. While the bay isn't the best for swimming, a well-lit esplanade runs the length of the town, and is ideal for morning or twilight ambling.

Bangkok Bank (cnr Th Maitri Ngam & Th Sarachip)

Internet cafes (Th Sarachip; per hr 30B; ⏰ 8am-10pm) These two unsigned internet options are right next to each other.

Kasikorn Bank (Th Phitak Chat)

Police station (☎ 0 3261 1148; Th Kong Kiat) Just west of Th Sarachip.

Post office (cnr Th Maitri Ngam & Th Suseuk) Right by a telephone office with internet access.

Tourist office (☎ 0 3261 1491; Th Chai Thaleh) At the northern end of town. The staff speak good English and offer detailed information about the town.

Sleeping

The accommodation options in Prachuap Khiri Khan leave a lot to be desired, but there are a few passable establishments here and some better ones a few kilometres north and south of town, in particular at Ao Manao.

Yuttichai Hotel (☎ 0 3261 1055; 115 Th Kong Kiat; r from 150B) Yuttichai offers large, old decent rooms with fan, and has friendly and informative staff. The squeaky-clean units are fine for a kip, but the mattresses are on the stiff side.

Happy Inn (☎ 0 3260 2082; 149-151 Th Suanson; bungalows from 400B) One kilometre north of town, Happy Inn offers simple bungalows (no hot showers) that face each other along a brick path. The highlight here – besides the coy, geishalike staff – is the sitting area over the mangrove-lined water.

Hadthong Hotel (☎ 0 3260 1050-6; www.hadthong .com; 21 Th Suseuk; r 700-1600B; 🛎) Right on the beach, this place has a light and airy lobby and is hands down the best option in town. Some rooms have views of Khao Chong Krajok and others have windows facing the sea.

Baan Forty (☎ 0 3266 1437; www.baanfortyresort .com; 555 Th Prachuap-Khlong Wan; bungalows from 800B; 🛎 🛜) Located along Ao Khlong Wan, south of town, is this complex of concrete along a private slice of sand. The friendly owner arranges tours and rents out bicycles and motorcycles.

Prachuap Beach Hotel (☎ 0 3260 1288; 123 Th Suseuk; r from 900B; 🛎 🖳 🛜) The newest addition to sleeping options in PKK, this fine option has crisp white linen and splashy accent walls. Go for a room with the sea views, as the mountain views aren't particularly stellar.

Eating & Drinking

Prachuap Khiri Khan has a well-deserved reputation for fine seafood. One of the must-try specialities is *ʰblah săm·lee dàat dee·o* – whole cotton fish that's sliced lengthwise, left to dry in the sun and then fried in a wok. It's often

---

FOR THE BIRDS

Kaeng Krachan and Khao Sam Roi Yot National Parks vie for the title of Thailand's top birdwatching spot. We'll leave the battle for that honour to the ornithologists, but there's no denying that these world-renowned birding sites are a feast for their avid eyes.

Kaeng Krachan National Park is so huge it is still largely unexplored. So far, over 250 bird species have been recorded in the tropical, broad-leaved evergreen forests of this national treasure. The best places for birdwatching are in the northern parts of the park, particularly around Huai Nam Yen. With a bit of patience, birds you're likely to see here include the rufous-bellied eagle, oriental hobby, wreath hornbill, silver-breasted broadbill, banded broadbill, yellow-vented pigeon, chestnut-breasted malkoha, great barbet, white-throated laughing thrush, white-hooded babbler, black-thighed falconet, brown fish owl, grey peacock-pheasant, bay woodpecker, grey treepie, large scimitar-babbler, blue pitta, yellow-bellied warbler and narcissus fly-catcher.

In **Khao Sam Roi Yot National Park** the best locales to look are around marshland areas near the nature study centre and the mangrove areas along the coast. The park lies at the intersection of the East Asian and Australian fly ways, and as many as 300 migratory and resident bird species have been recorded here. Spotters can see the yellow bittern, cinnamon bittern, purple swamp hen, water rail, ruddy-breasted crake, bronze-winged jacana, grey heron, painted stork, whistling duck, spotted eagle and black-headed ibis. The park has Thailand's largest freshwater marsh, along with mangroves and mudflats, and is one of only three places in the country where the purple heron breeds.

served with mango salad on the side, and it tastes way better than it sounds. An all-day market lines the street on Th Maitri Ngam daily, starting at around 6am.

Phloen Samut Restaurant (☎ 0 3261 1115; 44 Th Chai Thaleh; dishes 50–120B; ⏰ 10am-10pm) One of a few seafood restaurants along the promenade, Phloen Samut offers sea views and loads of seafood, albeit with slow service.

4K (☎ 0 3260 1412; mains from 180B; ⏰ dinner) North of PKK in the township of Kuiburi, 4K (that's 'fork' for the uninitiated) is spicing things up along the shores at the swank X2 resort. Minimalist decor and a sparkling red bar gives this place a distinctly jetsetter feel, and there's a menu to match: sample a bevy of international dishes prepared with locally sourced ingredients.

MC Club Thailand (Th Chai Thaleh; ⏰ noon-late) Half-heartedly decorated with motorcycle memorabilia (notice the dangling tyre), this bar is a good place to jump-start a big night out on the town in PKK. During high season, the club sets up on the promenade beside the beach.

Getting There & Away
There are frequent air-con buses to/from Bangkok (around 200B to 250B, five hours), Hua Hin (around 80B to 100B, 1½ hours), Cha-am (around 90B, 2½ hours) and Phetchaburi (around 100B, three hours) leaving from Th Phitak Chat near the town centre. For southern destinations such as Phuket or Krabi, hike 2km northwest out to the police station on the highway to catch passing buses (motorcycle taxis will take you for 40B). Ordinary (read: slow) buses to Hua Hin (60B), Bang Krut (50B), Bang Saphan (50B) and Chumphon (155B, 3½ hours) leave from the southeast corner of Th Thetsaban Bamrung and Th Phitak Chat.

There are frequent train services to/from Bangkok (2nd class 317B to 357B, 3rd class 250B, six hours). Trains also run to Ban Krut (one hour) and Bang Saphan Yai (1½ hours).

Getting Around
Prachuap is small enough to get around on foot, but you can hop on a motorcycle taxi around town for 30B. Other destinations include Ao Noi (50B) and Ao Manao (40B). At Ao Manao motorcycles aren't permitted past the gate unless both driver and passenger are wearing helmets.

You can rent motorbikes in front of the Hadthong Hotel for 200B per day. The roads in the area are very good and it's a great way to see the surrounding beaches. Opposite the post office, bicycles can be rented for 100B per day.

BAN KRUT & BANG SAPHAN YAI
หาดบ้านกรูด/บางสะพานใหญ่

Things start to get quiet between the administrative centres of Prachuap Khiri Khan and Chumphon. This wooded realm is dotted with plantations, a gold mine and rice fields that spread between the flaxen shoreline and the Myanmar border. The long strings of sand are popular holiday spots for weekending Thai tourists. During the week, the beaches are virtually deserted, save for a few colourful long-tail vessels.

The main beach of Hat Ban Krut is right beside a road, making the 10km beach handy to cars and services, but detracting from a 100% peaceful beach experience. Sitting atop a headland to the north, **Wat Tan Sai** has multiple golden spires that reach to the sky like a fantasy Disneyland castle. You can clamber up to the top for sensational views of the area. Just beyond, there's **Hat Sai Kaew**, which is quieter but slightly out of the way, making it a better beach experience.

Bang Saphan Yai, 20km south of the town, is starting to experience development. Accommodation is also strung along the sand between Bang Saphan Yai and Bang Saphan Noi, 15km further south. Islands off the coast to the south, including **Ko Thalu** and **Ko Sing**, offer good **snorkelling** and **diving** from the end of January to mid-May. Coral Hotel in Bang Saphan Yai can arrange half-day diving excursions to these islands, as well as outings to virtually every site in the region.

Sleeping & Eating
There are plenty of places to spend the night in Ban Krut and Bang Saphan Yai. Big-spenders won't find five-star palaces, and penny-pinchers will be hard-pressed to track down dirt-cheap shacks, but there are a couple of unique options within this zone of decidedly midrange places. If you know where you want to stay, it's best to book ahead – public transport is a bit rough around these parts, and the resort of your choice can probably arrange some of your transport. Virtually all beachside accommodation options offer a place to eat.

DAN SINGKHON BORDER

Southwest of Prachuap Khiri Khan, near the narrowest slice of Thailand's trim waist (12km from the coast to the border) lies the town of Dan Singkhon. Once a military point, the village now makes for an interesting half-day jaunt from the sand. Saturday mornings are the best time to visit. Merchants cross the border from Myanmar to hawk their wares: jewellery, handicrafts and, most interesting of all, orchids. The area truly comes alive, however, during Songkran (13–15 April) when the people from both countries perform elaborate festival dances.

Don't forget: if you plan to cross the border into Myanmar, you'll need your passport.

BAN KRUT

Banito Beach Resort (☎ 0 2964 2175; www.banitobeach .com; bungalows 1300-9000B; ✕ ⚛) Colourful Banito feels like it was plucked from a Caribbean island and set down in sleepy Ban Krut. Accommodation is arranged in houses along a long street that connects the ocean to a large swimming pool bizarrely placed at the back of the resort. Have a look at a couple of rooms before plopping down your bags – some options have been renovated more recently than others.

Rachavadee Resort (☎ 0 3269 5155; www.racha vadee.com; bungalows 1800-4800B; ✕) Rachavadee offers a rugged serenity within its faux-brick walls and skyscraping cantilevered roofs. Free bus transfers are also on offer.

Baan Klang Aow Beach Resort (☎ 0 3269 5123; www.baanklangaowresort.com; bungalows 1800-5200B; ✕ ▢ ⚛) Further south on the same beach as Suan Bankrut, the one- and two-bedroom bungalows here have large verandahs and are hidden in leafy thickets. Bicycles, kayaks and two swimming pools will get you hungry for your next meal at the resort's scenic restaurant.

Suan Bankrut Beach Resort (☎ 0 3269 5217; www .suanbankrut.com; bungalows 2200-6400B; ✕) Suan Bankrut offers charming bungalows with plenty of thatch that squat beneath furry palms.

BANG SAPHAN YAI

Vanveena Hotel (☎ 0 3269 1251; www.vanveena.com; r 270-1500B; ✕) Vanveena's rooms are noticeably spartan, with a few stencil drawings to liven up the walls, but this cookie-cutter hotel is beach-adjacent and there's a charming bamboo restaurant on the sand.

Western Hotel (☎ 0 3269 1015; r 600-1500B; ✕) If the bungalows along Bang Saphan Yai are full, try the Western Hotel. The drab decor feels a bit like 'Soviet Gulag takes a tropical holiday', but the rooms are clean enough if you're on a tight budget.

Coral Hotel (☎ 0 3269 1667; www.coral-hotel.com; 171 Moo 9; r 1525B, bungalows 1210-4410B; ✕ ⚛) Set amid a coconut grove, this upmarket French-managed hotel is right on the beach. There's a huge pool, a very good restaurant and all rooms are equipped with TV, fridge and hot water. Fill your days with water sports or exploring the area on an organised tour. Four-person bungalows are also available for families.

Sailom Resort (☎ 0 3269 1003; www.sailomresort bangsaphan.com; r 2900-5900B; ✕ ⚛) Manicured grounds, a huge swimming pool, Asian chic decor – this new spot has certainly shaken things up in sleepy Bang Saphan Yai.

Getting There & Around

From Chumphon there are many connections to Ban Krut and Bang Saphan Yai, departing Chumphon every day at 8am, 9.30am, 11.45am, 1pm, 4pm, 6pm, 7pm and 8pm (70B). To leave either town you'll have to wait on the side of the highway (Th Phetkasem) for a passing bus. Buses from every direction usually stop in front of the Rama Inn, a white hotel in the heart of Bang Saphan Yai. Otherwise you can organise transport with your accommodation. The towns are positioned along the main train artery between Bangkok and the south; however, you will need to hire a motorcycle taxi to get you to the beach.

There is one **motorcycle shop** (☎ 0 3269 1059) in Bang Saphan Yai that rents out automatic and manual motorcycles (250B and 300B respectively). Its rows of scooters out the front are hard to miss. Other than that, transport can be a bit of a problem. Once you get to the beaches, however, most resorts can hook you up with motorcycle rental for a similar price to the shop.

When booking transport, don't confuse Bang Saphan Yai with Bang Saphan Noi, which is 15km further south.

CHUMPHON
อ.เมืองชุมพร
pop 81,700

Chumphon doesn't pretend to be a destination in itself. The air is thick with anticipation: tourists are eager to arrive in Ko Tao, or they're wrapping up an island getaway and want to get back to Bangkok. Either way, Chumphon feels like a border town. There's even a big, vanilla archway near the train station welcoming passengers to Thailand's south. The sleepy town has embraced its status as a link in the transport chain – it's one of the few cities in Thailand with more travel agencies than 7-Elevens.

Information

There are dozens of travel agencies around town that can organise all of your booking needs, such as transport, lodging, even scuba lessons on Ko Tao. Most agencies offer internet access for 40B per hour, and complimentary wi-fi for those with laptops. There are numerous banks and ATMs scattered around town.

Chumphon Hospital (☎ 0 7750 3672; Th Phisit Phayaban) The main hospital in town.

Chumphon Tourist Services Centre (Th Sala Daeng; ☯ 8.30-4.30 Mon-Sat) The travel agencies usually offer better tourism details.

Kiat Travel (☎ 0 7750 2127; www.chumphonguide .com; 115 Th Tha Taphao) One of the better full-service agencies. Friendly and knowledgeable staff are more than happy to answer questions.

New Infinity Travel (☎ 0 7750 0176; new_infinity@ hotmail.com; 68/2 Th Tha Taphao) Extremely helpful and friendly agency with loads of information on the area. Purchase a second-hand book for some entertainment on the journey to your next destination.

Post office (☎ 0 7751 1012; Th Poramin Mankha) In the eastern part of town.

Festivals & Events

The city hosts the **Chumphon Marine Festival** some time in March – it features cultural and folk-art exhibits, a sailboarding competition at Hat Thung Wua Laen and a marathon. **Lang Suan Buddha Image Parade & Boat Race Festival** is a five-day festival that includes a procession of temple boats and a boat race on Mae Nam Lang Suan. It's held in October.

Sleeping

The accommodation options in Chumphon are quite utilitarian, as the city is mostly used as a transfer centre. There are a few resort-style places a few kilometres away along the coast.

CITY CENTRE

Farang Bar (☎ 0 7750 1003; farangbar@yahoo.com; 69/36 Th Tha Taphao; r 150B) The cheap rooms at Farang Bar could definitely use a fix-up, but the hip Thai staff foster a good backpacker vibe, and they can answer virtually every travel query. Showers cost 20B.

Suda Guest House (☎ 0 7750 4366; 8 Soi Bangkok Bank; r 200-500B; ⊠) A fantastic find hidden within the urban chaos, this little guesthouse has a homey vibe and a low price tag. The owner, Suda, speaks perfect English and keeps her rooms spick and span. It's best to book ahead – if it's fully booked she'll send you down the street to another guesthouse that ain't half bad.

Chumphon Palace Hotel (☎ 0 7757 1715-22; 328/15 Th Pracha Uthit; r 440-2250B; ⊠) Keep an eye out for

NORTHWESTERN GULF COAST

STAR LIGHT, STAR BRIGHT, FIRST SQUID I SEE TONIGHT...

After the fiery equatorial sun plunges deep into the ocean, stars begin to emerge overhead and a strange concentration of greenish lights materialises on the horizon. The brilliant lights look like a flotilla of UFOs as they illuminate the night sky with their powerful beams – these are the squid fishermen of Thailand, and you are likely to see them ply their trade along the length of the country.

Squid are best fished after dark. The powerful lights mimic sunlight and are used to attract plankton and small fish that usually feed in the daytime near the surface. Squid, which feed on these organisms, follow their mobile meals into waiting nets. The lights are so powerful that they can be seen in satellite photos taken 800km from earth – that's a lot of candle power.

As fishing techniques improve collection rates, overfishing is becoming a growing problem in Thailand and the government has attempted to impose limits, much to the chagrin of fishermen. Regardless, squid fishing is a huge industry and you are likely to see these galaxies of bobbing beams for a while yet.

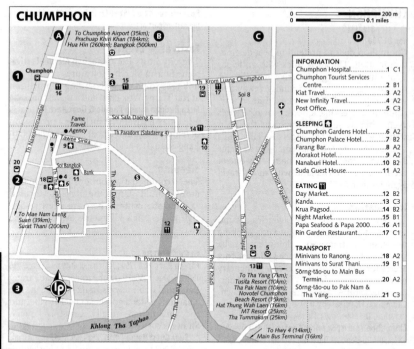

a purple sign saying 'Hotel', and you'll find the pink, frilly Chumphon Palace Hotel hiding just off the main drag. Upstairs, the rooms are clean and crisp, and the beds have rose-coloured ruffles like at granny's house.

Morakot Hotel (☎ 0 7750 3628-32; fax 0 7757 0196; Th Tawee Sinka; r 450-1300B; ☒) The staff here don't speak much English, but the rooms are spotless and some have great views. It's in a large green structure and the reception is located behind a motorcycle showroom that rents out motorcycles for 150B per day.

Chumphon Gardens Hotel (☎ 0 7750 6888; 66/1 Th Tha Taphao; r 540-700B, ste 2000B; ☒) Chumphon Gardens is the go-to spot for businesspeople passing through town. The lobby is a bit drab, but the rooms are sparkling clean.

Nanaburi Hotel (☎ 0 7750 3888; 355/9 Th Paradorn; r incl breakfast 700-2200B; ☒) A newer addition to uninspired Chumphon, Nanaburi is a darn good deal. Sleek rooms employ a black-and-white theme.

SEASIDE

MT Resort (☎ 0 7755 8153; www.mtresort-chumphon .com; Hat Tummakam Noi; bungalows incl breakfast 1500B;

☒) This low-key hang-out, right beside the Lomprayah ferry pier, is a scenic option if you'd rather stay outside of Chumphon's grimy downtown core while waiting for the boat to Ko Tao. There are free kayaks for wandering around the nearby islands and mangroves. Call ahead to organise transport, or grab a cab for around 300B.

Chumphon Samet Island Resort (☎ 08 9795 8680; http://chumphonsamedisland.inspiredyou.net; Ko Samet; r & bungalow from 1000B; ☒) Not to be confused with the Ko Samet near Bangkok, this quiet spot is the only place to crash on the lonely island near the gulf island ferry piers. Bungalows and motel-style rooms are simple, but offer views of the sea through the thickets of palms. To reach the island, head to Hat Paradon Pharb and hop on a long-tail boat for the 15-minute ride.

Novotel Chumphon Beach Resort (☎ 0 7752 9529; info@novotel-chumphon.com; 110 Moo 4, Hat Paradonpab; r from 4500B; ☒ ▯ ☲ ☒) The sparkling Novotel is breathing new life into Chumphon's quiet coast nearby. Despite its chain status, this plush getaway is a great place to hang your hat if you want to turn a layover into a mini vacation.

Tusita Resort (☎ 0 7757 9073; www.tusitaresort.com; 259/9 Moo 1, Paktako, Tungtako; bungalows 7600-23,000B; ❄ 🖳 🛜 📺) A worthy option if you're not yet ready to hit the islands, this Indian-style resort features large teak *sǎh·lah* dotting the windswept sand, and private bungalows hidden among a patchwork of coconut palms and jungle vines. Tusita is 10km from the city centre – take a taxi to Kaao Pii junction (30B to 45B) and then call the resort for a free pick-up. There are no public phones, so you'll need a mobile phone or ask to use someone else's.

Eating

Krua Pagsod (☎ 0 7757 1731; 110/32 Th Paradorn; dishes 50-200B; ✷ lunch & dinner) Delicious vegetarian options are available at this prim, modern establishment that blows cool gusts of air-conditioned air over weary travellers.

Papa Seafood & Papa 2000 (☎ 0 1569 6161, 0 7751 1972; 188/181 Th Krom Luang Chumphon; dishes 80-200B; ✷ lunch & dinner) This large patio restaurant right in the heart of town dishes out tasty barbecued seafood and steak under flickering fairy lights. As the evening turns to night, Papa fills up with locals who toss back a few beers before heading to the adjacent Papa 2000 discotheque.

Rin Garden Restaurant (☎ 0 7751 1531; Th Krom Luang Chumphon; ✷ lunch & dinner) and **Kanda** (☎ 0 7751 1707; Th Poramin Mankha; ✷ lunch & dinner) both have good local reputations if you want to chow down off the tourist trail.

Chumphon's **night market** (Th Krom Luang Chumphon) can be a little hit-or-miss depending on the day of the week (and the weather), but when things start to get moving, it can be a good distraction while waiting for the next link in your chain of transport. The food isn't fantastic, but it's dirt cheap. A bustling day market runs north–south between Th Pracha Uthit and Th Poramin Mankha.

Getting There & Away

Travel agencies in Bangkok and all over southern Thailand sell Lomprayah and Seatran Discovery bus/boat packages from Bangkok to Ko Tao, Ko Samui and Ko Pha-Ngan via Chumphon. Taking a train/boat combination is another way of getting to these islands. If you're arriving in Chumphon from Ko Tao, the Lomprayah shuttle from the ferry drops passengers off at either Fame Travel Agency or New Infinity, depending on the day.

BOAT

The small island of Ko Tao (p233), north of Ko Samui and Ko Pha-Ngan, can be reached by boat from one of three piers south of town. Services continue to Ko Samui and Ko Pha-Ngan.

The *Lomprayah Express* catamaran (350B, 1½ hours) leaves from Tha Tummakam (25km from town) at 7am and 1pm, and return services depart Ko Tao at 10.15am and 2.45pm. Transfers between Chumphon and Tha Tummakam are included in the ticket price. The *Songsrem Express* (300B, three hours) leaves Tha Yang (7km from town) at 7am; the return service departs Ko Tao at 2.30pm. Most travel agencies will provide free transfers to this pier as well.

There is also a midnight boat (300B) that leaves from Tha Pak Nam (10km from town) and arrives at Ko Tao at 6am. The return service from Ko Tao departs at 11pm and arrives at Tha Pak Nam early in the morning. Consider nixing this option if there's a chance of rain, as some boats leak and you might end up wet and cold. A shared taxi to Tha Pak Nam costs 50B. Sǒrng·tǎa·ou to Tha Pak Nam or Tha Yang are 15B.

BUS

The main bus terminal is inconveniently located on the main highway, 16km from Chumphon – it's better to take the train if you are arriving from Bangkok. To get here you can catch a local bus or sǒrng·tǎa·ou from a stop on Th Nawaminruamjai for 20B. There are several buses travelling daily from Bangkok to Chumphon: one VIP bus (500B, seven hours, departs 9.30pm), three regular air-conditioned buses (around 350B, seven hours) and three 2nd-class buses (250B). From Bangkok, all buses leave from the Southern bus terminal. There are several private bus companies running buses to Bangkok for around 400B; tickets can be bought at any travel agency and include a free pick-up from your hotel.

Figure on around 1B per kilometre when paying for your ticket on government buses. Destinations include Hua Hin (230B, five hours), Bang Saphan (100B, two hours), Prachuap Khiri Khan (160B, 3½ hours), Ranong (130B, three hours), Surat Thani (170B, 3½ hours), Krabi (270B, eight hours), Phuket (320B, eight hours) and Hat Yai (310B, 10 hours). Tickets can be bought at travel agencies.

MINIVAN

Air-conditioned minivans run hourly to/ from Ranong (100B to 200B, three hours) and leave from a stop on Th Tha Taphao. Half-hourly minivans to/from Surat Thani (150B to 200B, 3½ hours) run all day and leave from a stop just off Th Krom Luang Chumphon.

TRAIN

The southern line has several trains a day to/from Bangkok. If you catch the train in mid-afternoon, you will arrive in Chumphon in time to find a room and crash for the night. Early evening trains arrive in the wee hours of the morning; however, you may miss your connection to Ko Tao and be forced to lounge around Chumphon until the afternoon ferry. If this is the case, scout out a travel agency that has comfy chairs and plenty of space for your luggage.

Trains to and from towns all along the southern line leave and arrive several times a day. Third-class trains head out to Prachuap Khiri Khan (40B, three hours), Surat Thani (45B, three hours) and Hat Yai (90B, 12 hours). Southbound rapid and express trains – the only trains with 1st and 2nd class – are much less frequent and can be difficult to book out of Chumphon in the high season (November to April).

Getting Around

Motorcycle taxis around town cost a flat 20B per trip. Most travel agencies can arrange motorbike rentals, as can the Morakot Hotel (p190), which has dozens of motorbikes sitting around the lobby.

Southwestern Gulf Coast

This stunning coast features a Thailand holiday trifecta: Ko Samui, Ko Pha-Ngan and Ko Tao. This family of spectacular islands lure millions of tourists every year with their powder-soft sands and emerald waters. Ko Samui is the oldest brother, with a business-minded attitude towards vacation. High-class resorts operate with Swiss efficiency as uniformed butlers cater to every whim. Ko Pha-Ngan is the slacker middle child with tangled dreadlocks and a penchant for hammock-lazing and all-night parties. Baby Ko Tao has plenty of spirit and spunk – offering high-adrenaline activities including world-class diving and snorkelling.

A thin archipelago of pin-sized islets creates a small barrier between these three busy destinations and the quieter beachside towns along the coast. Known as Ang Thong Marine National Park, this ethereal realm of greens and blues offers some of the most picture-perfect moments in the entire kingdom. As the rugged coastline swerves south, travellers will uncover quiet Songkhla, whose urban soundtrack mixes the rhythmic lapping of the tides with the muezzin's call to prayer.

For the last few years, the political situation in the southernmost provinces (Yala, Pattani and Narathiwat) has been unstable, and travelling here can be a risky venture. Sect violence and bouts of terror-inducing attacks are the norm, and although tourists aren't the targets of these aggressive outbursts, it's better not to risk it. It's a shame though – these sleepy towns silently simmer in 2000 years' worth of mystical kingdoms, aromatic spice markets, and imperialist mercantilism. If, by the time you read this, the heated situation has cooled, consider editing your itinerary to include a little looksee. If not, thumb through the end of this chapter – you might learn a bit more about the many faces in the 'land of smiles'.

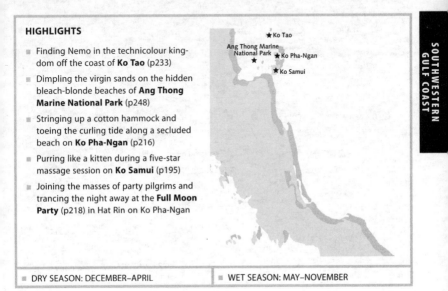

HIGHLIGHTS

- Finding Nemo in the technicolour kingdom off the coast of **Ko Tao** (p233)
- Dimpling the virgin sands on the hidden bleach-blonde beaches of **Ang Thong Marine National Park** (p248)
- Stringing up a cotton hammock and toeing the curling tide along a secluded beach on **Ko Pha-Ngan** (p216)
- Purring like a kitten during a five-star massage session on **Ko Samui** (p195)
- Joining the masses of party pilgrims and trancing the night away at the **Full Moon Party** (p218) in Hat Rin on Ko Pha-Ngan

★ Ko Tao
Ang Thong Marine National Park ★ ★ Ko Pha-Ngan
★ Ko Samui

- DRY SEASON: DECEMBER–APRIL
- WET SEASON: MAY–NOVEMBER

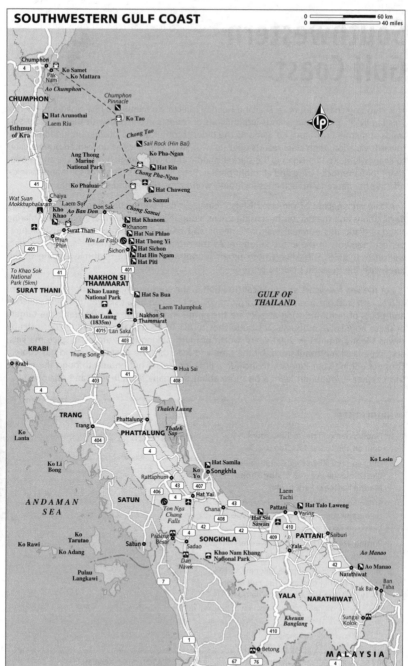

SOUTHWESTERN GULF COAST

0 — 60 km
0 — 40 miles

Climate
The best time to visit gulf islands is during the hot and dry season, from February to late June. From July to October (southwest monsoon) it can rain on and off, and from October to January (northeast monsoon) there are sometimes strong winds. However, many travellers have reported fine weather (and fewer crowds) in October. November tends to receive some of the rain that affects the east coast of Malaysia.

National Parks
There are a couple notable parks in this region. Ang Thong Marine National Park (p248), the setting for the perfect beach in the movie *The Beach* (although much of the movie was actually filmed on Ko Phi-Phi Leh; p358), is a stunning archipelago of 40 small jagged limestone islands. Khao Luang National Park (p256) is known for its beautiful mountain and forest walks, waterfalls and fruit orchards. It is also home to a variety of elusive animals, from clouded leopards to tigers.

Getting There & Away
Travelling to the lower southern gulf is fairly straightforward. It's extremely easy to hop on a bus or train in Bangkok and then catch a ferry to the Gulf islands. Several daily flights connect Bangkok, Phuket and Pattaya to Ko Samui. Bus and train travel from Bangkok is generally cheap, relatively efficient and mostly takes place overnight.

Getting Around
Numerous boats shuttle back and forth between Ko Samui, Ko Pha-Ngan, Ko Tao and Surat Thani, while buses and trains link Surat Thani with destinations further south. Consider using the port in Chumphon (p189) to access the Gulf islands from the mainland.

GULF ISLANDS

KO SAMUI
เกาะสมุย
pop 39,681
At first glance, Ko Samui could be mistaken for a giant golf course floating in the Gulf of Thailand. The greens are perfectly manicured, sand traps are plentiful, and there's a water hazard or two thrown in for good measure.

Middle-aged men strut about donning white polo shirts that contrast with their cherry-red faces, while hired lackeys carry around their stuff. But Samui is far from being an adults-only country club – a closer look reveals steaming street-side food stalls, 2am jetsetter parties, secreted Buddhist temples, and backpacker shanties plunked down on a quiet stretch of sand.

Ko Samui is a choose-your-own-adventure kinda place that strives, like a genie, to grant every tourist their ultimate holiday wish. You want ocean views, daily massages and personal butlers? Poof – here are the keys to your private poolside villa. It's holistic aura-cleansing vacation you're after? Shazam – take a seat on your yoga mat before your afternoon colonic. Wanna party like a rockstar? Pow – trance your way down the beach with the throngs of whisky-bucket-toting tourists.

Beyond the merry-making machine, the island will also offer interested visitors a glimpse into local life. Chinese merchants from Hainan Island initially settled Samui and today these unique roots have blossomed into a small community that remains hidden beneath the glossy holiday veneer.

Orientation
Ko Samui is quite large – the ring road around the island is almost 100km total. The island has been blessed with picturesque beaches on all four sides. The most crowded are Hat Chaweng (Map p199) and Hat Lamai (Map p201), both on the eastern side of the island.

The beaches on the island's northern coast, which include Choeng Mon, Mae Nam, Bo Phut (Map p207), Bang Po, and Big Buddha Beach (Bang Rak), are starting to become quite busy as well, but the prices are still decent and secluded nooks can still be found. For a quieter experience, try the secluded beaches along the southern coast, and western shore south of Na Thon.

Information
BOOKSHOPS
There are several places around the island where you can snag a paperback to read in your hammock. Many hotels also have libraries or book trades. The **Bookazine** (Map p199; ☎ 0 7741 3616; Hat Chaweng; ⓨ 10am-11pm) chain sells a smattering of popular reads including several Lonely Planet guides for southeast Asia.

EMERGENCY
Tourist police (Map p197; ☎ 0 7742 1281, emergency 1155) Based at the south of Na Thon.

IMMIGRATION OFFICES
If you are planning to obtain a visa extension, it is imperative that you know the ins and outs of the extension process. If you entered Thailand by plane but without preregistering for a 60-day visa, then you will only be granted seven additional days at 1900B. If you entered Thailand overland, only seven days can be added to your original 14. Tourists with a '60+30' stamp in their passport can earn their extra 30 days for 1900B, but if you are late to apply for the extension you will not be granted clemency. Late fines are 500B per day. Located about 2km south of Na Thon is Ko Samui's **Immigration Office** (Map p197; ☎ 0 7742 1069; ☒ 8.30am-noon & 1-4.30pm Mon-Fri). During our visits here we've watched dozens of tourists wait through exhausting lines only to get curtly denied an extension for no particular reason (it even happened to us). On a particularly bad day expect extensions to take the entire afternoon.

INTERNET ACCESS
There are countless places all over the island for internet access, even at the less popular beaches. Prices range from 1B to 2B per minute. Keep an eye out for restaurants that offer complimentary wi-fi service.

INTERNET RESOURCES
The following websites cover dive centres, accommodation and tours. They also have transportation timetables.
Sawadee.com (www.samui.sawadee.com)
Tourism Association of Koh Samui (www.samuitourism.com)

MEDIA & MAPS
The Siam Map Company puts out quarterly booklets including a *Spa Guide, Dining Guide,* and an annual directory, which lists thousands of companies and hotels on the island. Their *Siam Map Company Samui Guide Map* is fantastic, free, and easily found throughout the island. Also worth a look is the *Samui Navigator* pamphlet. **Essential** (www.essential-samui) is a pocket-size pamphlet focused on promoting Samui's diverse activities. *Samui Guide* looks more like a magazine and features mostly restaurants and attractions.

MEDICAL SERVICES
Ko Samui has four private hospitals, all near Chaweng's Tesco-Lotus supermarket on the east coast (where most of the tourists tend to gather). The government hospital in Na Thon has seen significant improvements in the last couple years but the service is still a bit grim since funding is based on the number of Samui's legal residents (which doesn't take into account the heap of illegal Burmese workers).

GULF ISLANDS IN...

One Week
First, shed a single tear that you have but one week to explore these idyllic islands. Then start on one of Ko Pha-Ngan's secluded beaches in the north or east to live out your ultimate castaway fantasies. For the second half of the week choose between partying in Hat Rin, pampering over on Ko Samui, or diving on li'l Ko Tao.

Two Weeks
Start on Ko Tao with a 3½-day Open Water certification course (or, if you already have your diving licence, sign up for a few fun dives). Slide over to Ko Pha-Ngan and soak up the sociable vibe in party-prone Hat Rin. Then, grab a longtail and your luggage and make your way to one of the island's hidden coves for a few days of detoxing and quiet contemplation. Ko Samui is next on the agenda. Try Bo Phut for boutique sleeps, or live it up like a rockstar on Chaweng or Choeng Mon beach. And, if you have time, do a daytrip to Ang Thong Marine Park.

One Month
Follow the two-week itinerary at a more relaxed pace, infusing many extra beach-book-and-blanket days on all three islands. Be sure to plan your schedule around the Full Moon Party, which takes place at Hat Rin's Sunrise Beach on Ko Pha-Ngan.

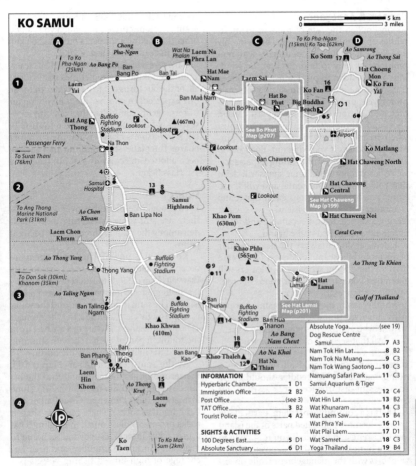

KO SAMUI

INFORMATION	
Hyperbaric Chamber......................... 1 D1	
Immigration Office............................ 2 B2	
Post Office.................................(see 3)	
TAT Office.. 3 B2	
Tourist Police.................................. 4 A2	
SIGHTS & ACTIVITIES	
100 Degrees East............................ 5 D1	
Absolute Sanctuary......................... 6 D1	

Absolute Yoga...........................(see 19)	
Dog Rescue Centre	
Samui.. 7 A3	
Nam Tok Hin Lat............................. 8 B2	
Nam Tok Na Muang........................ 9 C3	
Nam Tok Wang Saotong............... 10 C3	
Namuang Safari Park...................... 11 C3	
Samui Aquarium & Tiger	
Zoo.. 12 C4	
Wat Hin Lat.................................... 13 B2	
Wat Khunaram................................ 14 C3	
Wat Laem Saw................................ 15 B4	
Wat Phra Yai.................................. 16 D1	
Wat Plai Laem................................ 17 D1	
Wat Samret..................................... 18 C3	
Yoga Thailand................................ 19 B4	

Bandon International Hospital (Map p207; ☎ 0 7742 5840, emergency 0 7742 5748)

Bangkok Samui Hospital (Map p199; ☎ 0 7742 9500, emergency 0 7742 9555) Your best bet for just about any medical problem.

Hyperbaric Chamber (Map p197; ☎ 0 7742 7427; Big Buddha Beach) The island's dive medicine specialists.

Samui International Hospital (Map p199; ☎ 0 7742 2272; www.sih.co.th; Hat Chaweng) Emergency ambulance service is available 24 hours and credit cards are accepted. Near the Amari Resort in Chaweng.

MONEY

Changing money isn't a problem on the east and north coasts, and in Na Thon. Multiple banks and foreign exchange booths offer daily services and there's an ATM every couple hundred metres. You should not have to pay credit card fees like on neighbouring Ko Tao.

POST

In several parts of the island there are privately run post office branches charging a small commission. You can almost always leave your stamped mail with your accommodation. **Main post office** (Map p197; Na Thon) Near the TAT office; not always reliable.

TOURIST INFORMATION

TAT office (Map p197; ☎ 0 7742 0504; Na Thon; ⏰ 8.30am-4.30pm) At the northern end of Na Thon; this office is friendly, helpful and has handy brochures and maps – although travel agents throughout the island can provide similar information.

Dangers & Annoyances

As on Phuket, the rate of road accident fatalities on Samui is quite high. This is mainly due to the large number of tourists who rent motorcycles only to find out that the winding roads, sudden tropical rains, and frenzied traffic can be lethal. If you decide to rent a motorcycle, protect yourself by wearing a helmet, and ask for one that has a plastic visor. Shoes and appropriate clothing are also a must when driving – jeans will save you from skinning your knees if you wipe out. Even if you escape unscathed from a riding experience, we've heard reports that some shops will claim that you damaged your rental and will try to extort you for some serious cash. Car rental is another option on the island – we suggest leasing a vehicle from a reputable and internationally recognised name brand.

Lately, jet ski rentals are the newest avatar of the motorbike scam. Incidents of injury are high on these water scooters, and leasers will claim that you damaged their goods in order to collect some extra money.

Another scam, that's rapidly gaining popularity, involves timeshares. It's best to avoid anyone who approaches you offering a vacation deal that seems too good to be true.

Beach vendors are registered with the government and should all be wearing a numbered jacket. No peddler should cause an incessant disturbance – seek assistance if this occurs.

Theft is a continuing problem, particularly around the more populated parts of the island like Chaweng and Lamai. If you're staying in a beach bungalow, consider depositing your valuables with the management while on excursions around the island or while you're swimming at the beach. Consider asking for a receipt listing the items stored with the staff.

Lastly, never give your passport to anyone as collateral. If a company demands identification, give them your drivers licence or any other form of ID. A fraudulent operation can try to extort money from you, or track you down when filing for a new passport.

TRANSPORT

There are over 400 registered taxis on Samui, which means that the competition for passengers is fierce. Unlike Bangkok, cabs will refuse to use their meters so you must *always* negotiate your price before stepping into a cab. A 35B taxi ride in Bangkok will probably set you back about 350B on Samui. It's a flagrant crime, but there's not much you can do other than taking a sŏrng·tǎa·ou (small pickup truck) instead. Fares start at 200B.

Take care when making train and bus reservations: bookings are sometimes not made at all, or the bus turns out to be far inferior to the one expected. In another scam involving air tickets, agents claim that the economy-class seating is fully booked and force tourists to book in business class – when the customer boards the plane, they find out that they've been allotted an economy seat but paid for a 1st-class ticket.

Sights

Even though the island has over 500 resorts, there are still some interesting things hidden among the island's three million coconut palms.

Ko Samui is one of Thailand's premiere beach destinations and there's a reason why **Chaweng** (Map p199) is the most popular spot – it's the longest and most beautiful beach on the island. The sand is powder soft, and the water is surprisingly clear, considering the number of boats and bathers. Picture ops are best from the southern part of the beach, with stunning views of the hilly headland to the north.

At the south end of **Lamai** (Map p201), the second-largest beach, you'll find the infamous **Hin-Ta** and **Hin-Yai** (Map p201) stone formations (also known as Grandfather and Grandmother rocks). These genitalia-shaped rocks provide endless mirth to giggling Thai tourists. **Hua Thanon**, just beyond, is home to a vibrant Muslim community, and their anchorage of high-bowed fishing vessels is a veritable gallery of intricate designs.

Although the **northern beaches** have coarser sand and aren't as striking as the beaches in the east, they have a laid-back vibe and stellar views of Ko Pha-Ngan. **Bo Phut** (Map p207) stands out with its charming Fisherman's Village; a collection of narrow Chinese shophouses that have been transformed into trendy resorts and boutique hotels.

Many visitors spend the day on the wild, rugged beaches of **Ang Thong Marine Park** (p248). This stunning archipelago might just have the most beautiful islands in all of Thailand.

WATERFALLS

At 30m, **Nam Tok Na Muang** (Map p197) is the tallest waterfall on Samui and lies in the centre

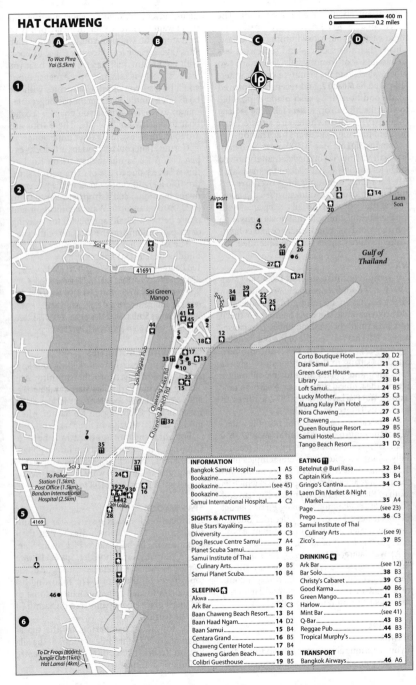

HAT CHAWENG

400 m
0.2 miles

To Wat Phra
Yai (5.5km)

To Police
Station (1.5km);
Post Office (1.5km);
Bandon International
Hospital (2.5km)

To Dr Frogs (800m);
Jungle Club (1km);
Hat Lamai (4km)

Airport

Soi 4

41691

Soi Green
Mango

Soi Solo

Soi Reggae Pub

Chaweng Lake Rd

Chaweng Beach Rd

Soi 3

Soi Colibri

4169

Laem
Son

Gulf of
Thailand

INFORMATION
Bangkok Samui Hospital **1** A5
Bookazine.......................................**2** B3
Bookazine.................................(see 45)
Bookazine.......................................**3** B4
Samui International Hospital.......**4** C2

SIGHTS & ACTIVITIES
Blue Stars Kayaking **5** B3
Diveversity **6** C3
Dog Rescue Centre Samui...........**7** A4
Planet Scuba Samui......................**8** B4
Samui Institute of Thai
    Culinary Arts............................**9** B5
Samui Planet Scuba....................**10** B4

SLEEPING
Akwa **11** B5
Ark Bar **12** C3
Baan Chaweng Beach Resort.....**13** B4
Baan Haad Ngam **14** D2
Baan Samui..................................**15** B4
Centara Grand **16** B5
Chaweng Center Hotel **17** B4
Chaweng Garden Beach **18** B3
Colibri Guesthouse **19** B5

Corto Boutique Hotel...................**20** D2
Dara Samui **21** C3
Green Guest House.......................**22** C3
Library **23** B4
Loft Samui.....................................**24** B5
Lucky Mother **25** C3
Muang Kulay Pan Hotel..............**26** C3
Nora Chaweng **27** C3
P Chaweng **28** A5
Queen Boutique Resort **29** B5
Samui Hostel................................**30** B5
Tango Beach Resort **31** D2

EATING
Betelnut @ Buri Rasa **32** B4
Captain Kirk **33** B4
Gringo's Cantina..........................**34** C3
Laem Din Market & Night
    Market.....................................**35** A4
Page ....(see 23)
Prego **36** C3
Samui Institute of Thai
    Culinary Arts .... (see 9)
Zico's...**37** B5

DRINKING
Ark Bar ....(see 12)
Bar Solo **38** B3
Christy's Cabaret **39** C3
Good Karma **40** B6
Green Mango **41** B3
Harlow...**42** B5
Mint Bar ....(see 41)
Q-Bar..**43** B3
Reggae Pub **44** B3
Tropical Murphy's **45** B3

TRANSPORT
Bangkok Airways.........................**46** A6

of the island about 12km from Na Thon. The water cascades over ethereal purple rocks, and there's a great pool for swimming at the base. This is the most scenic – and somewhat less frequented – of Samui's falls. There are two other waterfalls in the vicinity; a smaller waterfall called **Na Muang 2**, and recently, improved road conditions have also made it possible to visit the high drop at **Nam Tok Wang Saotong** (Map p197). These chutes are situated just north of the ring road near Hua Thanon.

Nam Tok Hin Lat (Map p197), near Na Thon, is worth visiting if you have an afternoon to kill before taking a boat back to the mainland. After a mildly strenuous hike over streams and boulders, reward yourself with a dip in the pool at the bottom of the falls. Keep an eye out for the Buddhist temple that posts signs with spiritual words of moral guidance and enlightenment. Sturdy shoes are recommended.

WÁT

For temple enthusiasts, **Wat Laem Sor** (Map p197), at the southern end of Samui near Ban Phang Ka, has an interesting, highly venerated old Srivijaya-style stupa. At Samui's northern end, on a small rocky island linked by a causeway, is **Wat Phra Yai** (Temple of the Big Buddha; Map p197). Erected in 1972, the modern Buddha (sitting in the Mara posture) stands 15m high and makes an alluring silhouette against the tropical sky and sea. Nearby, a new temple, **Wat Plai Laem** (Map p197), features an enormous 18-armed Buddha.

On the eastern part of Samui, near the waterfalls of the same name, **Wat Hin Lat** (Map p197; ☎ 0 7742 3146) is a meditation temple that teaches daily *vipassana* courses. Several temples have the mummified remains of pious monks including **Wat Khunaram** (Map p197), which is south of Rte 4169 between Th Ban Thurian and Th Ban Hua. The monk, Luang Phaw Daeng, has been dead for over two decades but his corpse is preserved sitting in a meditative pose and sporting a pair of sunglasses.

At **Wat Samret** (Map p197), near Th Ban Hua, you can see a typical Mandalay sitting Buddha carved from solid marble – a common sight in India and northern Thailand, but not so common in the south.

Activities

DIVING

If you're serious about diving, head to Ko Tao and base yourself there for the duration of your diving adventure. If you're short on time and don't want to leave Samui, there are plenty of operators who will take you to the same dive sites (at a greater fee, of course). Try to book with a company that has its own boat (or leases a boat) – it's slightly more expensive, but you'll be glad you did it. Companies without boats often shuttle divers on the passenger catamaran to Ko Tao, where you board a second boat to reach your dive site. These trips are arduous, meal-less, and rather impersonal.

Certification courses tend to be twice as expensive on Ko Samui as they are on Ko Tao, this is largely due to use of extra petrol, since tiny Tao is significantly closer to the preferred diving locations. You'll drop between 16,000B to 22,000B on an Open Water certification, and figure between 3200B and 6200B for a diving daytrip depending on the location of the site.

The island's hyperbaric chamber is at Big Buddha Beach (Hat Bang Rak).

100 Degrees East (Map p197; ☎ 0 7742 5936; www .100degreeseast.com; Bang Rak) Highly recommended.

Diveversity (Map p199; ☎ 0 7741 3196; www.dive versity.nl; Hat Chaweng) Based at the Amari Hotel.

Samui Planet Scuba (SIDS; Map p199; ☎ 0 7723 1606; samuiplanetscuba@planetscuba.net; Hat Chaweng)

OTHER WATER ACTIVITIES

For those interested in snorkelling and kayaking, book a daytrip to the stunning Ang Thong Marine Park. **Blue Stars Kayaking** (Map p199; ☎ 0 7741 3231; www.bluestars.info; trips 2000B), based in Hat Chaweng on Ko Samui, offers guided sea-kayak trips in the park.

For some instant gratification, head to Chaweng – from there you can hire sailboats, catamarans, snorkelling gear, boats for waterskiing, and so forth. Be wary of scams involving jet ski rentals, see p198 for details.

SPAS & YOGA

Competition for Samui's five-star accommodation is fierce, which means that their spas are of the highest calibre. Pick up the Siam Map Company's free booklet, **Spa Guide** (www .siamspaguide.com), for a detailed catalogue of the top centres on the island. The following list of resort-affiliated retreats includes some of the finest places to be pampered on Samui (if not the world).

For top-notch pampering, try the spa at Anantara (p207), the Hideaway Spa at the Sila Evason Resort (p206), or the wellness centre at Tamarind Retreat (p205).

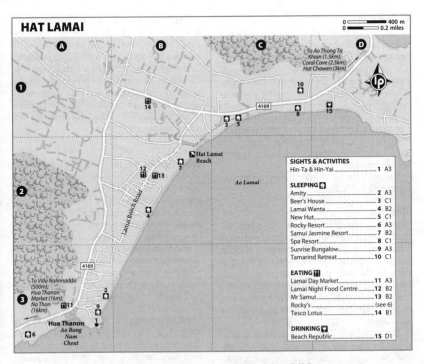

HAT LAMAI

SIGHTS & ACTIVITIES	
Hin-Ta & Hin-Yai	1 A3
SLEEPING	
Amity	2 A3
Beer's House	3 C1
Lamai Wanta	4 B2
New Hut	5 C1
Rocky Resort	6 A3
Samui Jasmine Resort	7 B2
Spa Resort	8 C1
Sunrise Bungalow	9 A3
Tamarind Retreat	10 C1
EATING	
Lamai Day Market	11 A3
Lamai Night Food Centre	12 B2
Mr Samui	13 B2
Rocky's	(see 6)
Tesco Lotus	14 B1
DRINKING	
Beach Republic	15 D1

Absolute Sanctuary (Map p197; ☎ 0 7760 1190; www
.absoluteyogasamui.com) is a wellness resort offering
detox programs and every type of yoga under
the sun. Try Yoga Thailand (p209) for the
latest in wellness and fitness.

The Spa Resort (p204), in Lamai, is the island's original health destination, and is still
known for its effective 'clean me out' fasting
regime.

Courses

If you're contemplating a Thai cooking course,
Samui Institute of Thai Culinary Arts (SITCA; Map p199;
☎ 0 7741 3434; www.sitca.net; Hat Chaweng) is the place
to do it. It has daily Thai-cooking classes and
courses in the aristocratic Thai art of carving
fruits and vegetables into intricate floral designs. Lunchtime classes begin at 11am, while
dinner starts at 4pm (both cost 1950B for a
three-hour course with three or more dishes).
Included is an excellent tutorial about pro-
curing ingredients in your home country. Of
course you get to eat your projects, and even invite a friend along for the meal. Complimentary
DVDs with Thai cooking instruction are also
available so you can practise at home.

Ko Samui for Children

If seawater and sandcastles just aren't enough
to keep the tykes entertained, there are plenty
of family-friendly activities around the
island.

At Choeng Mon, there's a new creation
called **football golf** (☎ 08 9771 7498; ☺ 9am-6.30pm)
where you 'putt' your football into a rubbish-
bin-sized hole. It's great for the kids and each
game (300B) comes with a complimentary soft
drink. It's a par 66.

Namuang Safari Park (Map p197; ☎ 0 7742 4098),
near Na Muang Falls, has safari options and
packages galore. Adventure tours (from 900B)
vary in length and can include elephant trekking, monkey shows, 4WD rides, and even a
visit to a rubber plantation to drain the trees
(now that's excitement). Prices include hotel
transfer.

In the same vein, **Samui Aquarium & Tiger Zoo**
(Map p197; ☎ 0 7742 4017; orchid@sawadee.com; admission
350B; ☺ 9am-6pm) has picture-worthy aquariums
and tigers, as well as a large aviary. Nancy
and Woody, two 'crazy' otters, hang out and
frolic in a swimming pool. You can call for
transport.

Volunteering

Donations of time and/or money are hugely appreciated at the aptly named **Dog Rescue Centre Samui** (☎ 0 7741 3490; www.samuidog.org). The organisation has played an integral role in keeping the island's dog population under control through an active spaying and neutering program. The centre also vaccinates dogs against rabies. Volunteers are always needed to take care of the pooches at the kennel/clinics located in Chaweng (Map p199) and Taling Ngam (Map p197). Call the centre for volunteering details.

See p413 for more information about volunteering in Thailand.

Sleeping

'Superior', 'standard', 'deluxe', 'standard deluxe', 'deluxe superior', 'superior standard' – what does it all mean? Trying to decode Samui's obnoxious hotel lingo is like trying to decipher the ancient Mayan language. The island's array of sleeping options is overwhelming – we've compiled a list of our favourites, but the following inventory is by no means exhaustive.

If you're looking to splurge, there is definitely no shortage of top-end resorts sporting extravagant bungalows, charming spas, private infinity pools, and 1st-class dining. Bo Phut, on the island's northern coast, has a charming collection of boutique lodging – the perfect choice for midrange travellers. Backpack-toting tourists will have to look a little harder, but budget digs do pop up once in a while along all of the island's beaches.

Private villa services have become quite popular in recent years. Rental companies often advertise in the various tourist booklets that circulate on the island.

This large section is organised as follows: we start on the popular east coast with Chaweng and Lamai, then move anticlockwise around the island covering the smaller beaches. These tinier areas are grouped according to location – Bo Phut and Choeng Mon, for example, are subcategories under 'Northern Beaches', and so forth.

CHAWENG

Packed end-to-end with hotels and bungalows, this beach is the eye of the tourist storm. The main street in central Chaweng feels like a non-descript soi in the heart of Bangkok. Despite the chaos, there's a striking stretch of beach, and most resorts are well protected from street noise. In the last couple years, the beach has experienced a bit of a renaissance – new budget spots are opening their doors (although prices are still a bit high relative to the rest of the island), and previously derelict areas are getting facelifts. At the south end of the beach, a small headland separates a sliver of sand (called Chaweng Noi) from the rest of the hustle.

Budget

Samui Hostel (Map p199; ☎ 08 9874 3737; dm 180B; ✖ 🖳) It doesn't look like much from the front, but the dorm rooms here are surprisingly spic and span. It's a great place for solo travellers on a tight budget, although couples should know that a private double room can be scouted in Chaweng for around 400B.

Green Guest House (Map p199; ☎ 0 7742 2611; www.greenguestsamui.com; r 400-1000B; ✖ 🖳) If penny-pinching is your game, you won't find anything cheaper than Green, although there isn't much in the way of atmosphere at this old-school relic.

P Chaweng (Map p199; ☎ 0 7723 0684; r 400-600B, ste 1000B; ✖ 🖳) This vine-covered cheapie doesn't even pretend to be close to the beach, but the pink-tiled rooms are spacious and squeaky clean (minus a couple of bumps and bruises on the wooden furniture). Pick a room facing away from the street – it seems a tad too easy for someone to slip through an open window and pilfer your stuff.

Lucky Mother (Map p199; ☎ 0 7723 0931; r & bungalows 500-1500B; ✖) First, let's take a moment to giggle at the resort's name. OK, now we can appreciate the old utilitarian huts – a dying breed in Chaweng. For those wanting hot showers and air-con, modern hotel rooms are also available, but most of them look out onto a parking lot.

Loft Samui (Map p199; ☎ 0 7741 3420; www.theloftsmaui.com; r from 590B; ✖ 🖳 📶) A new budget operation in Chaweng, The Loft is giving has-beens like The Wave a run for their money with cheap digs furnished by a couple of quirky details like adobe styling and savvy built-ins. It seems to be quite popular with travelling Israelis.

our pick **Jungle Club** (Map p199; ☎ 0 1894 2327; bungalows 600-2900B; ✖ 🖳 📶 🐾) The perilous drive up the slithering dirt road is totally worthwhile once you get a load of the incredible views from the top. This isolated mountain getaway is a huge hit among locals and tourists alike. There's a relaxed back-to-nature vibe – guests chill around the stunning horizon pool or tuck themselves away for a catnap under the canopied roofs of an open-air *săh·lah*. Jungle Club is Ko Samui's best bang for your baht by far. Call ahead for a pick up – you don't want to spend your precious jungle vacation in a body cast. Taxis from the main road cost 50B. It's 100B from central Chaweng and 400B if you need an airport pick up.

Akwa (Map p199; ☎ 08 4660 0551; www.akwa guesthouse.com; r from 700B; 🔀 🖳 🛜) A charming B&B-style sleeping spot, Akwa has a few funky rooms decorated with bright colours. Expect teddy bears adorning each bed, quirky bookshelves stocked with DVDs and cartoon paintings all over.

Colibri Guesthouse (Map p199; ☎ 0 7723 0574; colibri@samart.co.th; r from 700B; 🔀 🛜) A step up from P Chaweng next door, Colibri offers comfy tiled digs with freshly renovated bathrooms. It's not worth getting a room with a balcony since the views aren't particularly memorable.

Queen Boutique Resort (Map p199; ☎ 0 7741 3148; queensamui@yahoo.com; r from 800-1200B; 🔀 🖳 🛜) Despite the less-than-friendly staff, Queen offers up boutique sleeps for backpacker prices. Make sure, however, that you get a room with tiled floors; the ones with scuffed linoleum are far less appealing.

Midrange

Chaweng Center Hotel (Map p199; ☎ 0 7741 3747; cha wengcenter@hotmail.com; r 1200B; 🔀 🛒) Although the views of McDonald's across the street are far from charming, this central cheapie has fresh-faced rooms that are well-priced and pull off 'minimal-chic' instead of feeling spartan.

Corto Boutique Hotel (Map p199; ☎ 0 7723 0041; www.corto-samui.com; r 1500-4000B, tr 3000B; 🔀 🛒) As adorable as it is memorable, Corto looks like it just fell out of a comic book – maybe 'Tintin and the Mystery of Surprisingly Cheap Accommodation in Chaweng'? Rooms are outfitted with cheerful pastels, wooden moulding, and the occasional stone feature.

Chaweng Garden Beach (Map p199; ☎ 0 7796 0394; www.chawenggardnessamui.com; r from 1600B; 🔀 🖳 🛜 🛒) A popular 'flashpacker' choice, this campus of accommodation has a large variety of room types serviced by an extra-smiley staff.

SAMUI SLEEPING SUPERLATIVES

There are hundreds upon hundreds of places to stay in Samui – the choices are endless and dizzying. The following list includes our favourite sleeping spots:

Swanky Splurges

- **Library** (p204)
- **Sala Samui Resort & Spa** (p205)
- **Sila Evason Hideaway** (p206)

Small Budgets

- **Jungle Club** (opposite)
- **L'Hacienda** (p206)
- **Lodge** (p206)

Families

- **Centara Grand** (p204)
- **Ibis Bo Phut** (p206)

Romantic Retreats

- **Anantara** (p207)
- **Zazen** (p207)

Baan Samui (Map p199; ☎ 0 7723 0965; www.see2sea .com; r from 2400B; 🔀 🖳 🛜 🛒) In sharp contrast to the austere Library next door, Baan Samui is a campus of colourful beachside units. If the Flintstones had a holiday ranch house, it would probably look something like this.

Nora Chaweng (Map p199; ☎ 0 7791 3666; www .norachawenghotel.com; r from 2600B; 🔀 🖳 🛜 🛒) Nora Chaweng is not on the beach, but this newer addition to the Chaweng bustle has swankily designed rooms, an inviting on-site pool and a relaxing spa studio.

Tango Beach Resort (Map p199; ☎ 0 7742 2470; www.tangobeachsamui.com; r incl breakfast 2650-6250B; 🔀 🖳 🛜 🛒) A midrange all-star, the newly-completed Tango features a string of bungalows arranged along a teak boardwalk that meanders away from the beach.

Ark Bar (Map p199; ☎ 0 7742 2047; www.ark-bar.com; bungalows 3000B; 🔀 🛜 🛒) You'll find two of every creature at Ark Bar – hardcore partiers, chilled out hippies, teenagers, forty-somethings, even Canadians. Lately, the perennially popular resort has started to shift gears – higher-end digs is now the name of the game.

Top End

Baan Chaweng Beach Resort (Map p199; ☎ 0 7742 2403; www.baanchawengbeachresort.com; bungalows 4000-7000B; ❄ ▭ ▨) A pleasant option for those who want top-end luxury without the hefty bill, Baan Chaweng is one of the new kids on the block and is keeping the prices relatively low. The immaculate rooms are painted in various shades of peach and pear, with teak furnishings that feel both modern and traditional.

Muang Kulay Pan Hotel (Map p199; ☎ 0 7723 0849-51; www.kulaypan.com; r incl breakfast 4725-13,540B; ❄ ▭ ▨) No, that's not a rip in the wallpaper – it's all part of the design concept. The architect cites a fusion between Zen and Thai concepts, but we think the decor is completely random. The seaside grounds have been purposefully neglected to lend an additional sense of chaos to this unique resort.

Baan Haad Ngam (Map p199; ☎ 0 7723 1500, 0 7723 1520; www.baanhaadngam.com; bungalows 6400-14,000B; ❄ ▭ ▨) Vibrant Baan Haad Ngam shuns the usual teak and tan – every exterior is painted in an interesting shade of green – like radioactive celery. It's sassy, classy and a great choice if you've got the dime.

Dara Samui (Map p199; ☎ 0 7723 1323; www .darasamui.com; r & bungalows from 8160B; ❄ ▭ ▨) Inserted in the middle of Chaweng's seamless chain of accommodation, Dara can feel a tad cramped but the rooms are elegant and the pool area looks like a scene from a Rudyard Kipling novel.

Centara Grand (Map p199; ☎ 0 7723 0500; www .centralhotelsresorts.com; r 8900-19,500B; ❄ ▭ ▨) Centara is a massive, manicured compound in the heart of Chaweng, but the palm-filled property is so large that you can safely escape the streetside bustle. Rooms are found in a hotel-like building that is conspicuously Western in theme and decor. Grown-ups can escape to the spa, or one of the four restaurants, and leave the children at the labyrinth of swimming pools under the watchful eye of an in-house babysitter.

ourpick Library (Map p199; ☎ 0 7742 2407; www.the library.name; bungalows 9000-12,000B; ❄ ▭ ▨) This place is too cool for school, which is ironic since it's called 'The Library'. The entire resort is a sparkling white mirage accented with black trimming and slatted curtains. Besides the futuristic iMac computer in each page (rooms are called 'pages' here), our favourite feature is the large monochromatic wall art – it glows brightly in the evening and you can adjust the colour depending on your mood. Lifesize statues are engaged in the act of reading, and if you too feel inclined to pick up a book, the on-site library houses an impressive assortment of colourful art and design books. The large rectangular pool is not to be missed – it's tiled in piercing shades of red, making the term 'bloodbath' suddenly seem appealing.

LAMAI

Once upon a time, people in the know used to say 'skip Chaweng and head to Lamai', but these days Lamai has become the island's has-been and the unofficial HQ of Samui's wretched girly bar scene. South of Lamai, Hua Thanon is a small, quieter area with a couple memorable options.

Budget & Midrange

New Hut (Map p201; ☎ 0 7723 0437; newhut@hotmail .com; Lamai North; huts 200-500B) New Hut is a rare beachfront cheapie with tiny-but-charming A-frame huts. The wooden structures, including the welcoming restaurant, are covered with layers of thick black paint.

Beer's House (Map p201; ☎ 0 7723 0467; Lamai North; bungalows 200-550B) These tiny shade-covered bungalows are lined up right along the sand. Some huts have a communal toilet, but all have plenty of room to sling a hammock and laze the day away. Those with their own bathroom will be pleased to find freshly retiled surfaces. The lights take a little while to turn on after you flick the switch, so don't be too hasty when summoning the management.

Amity (Map p201; ☎ 0 7742 4084; Lamai South; bungalows 350-1500B; ❄) Amity offers alluring modern bungalows and a few ramshackle cheapies with shared bathroom – there's no theme, just a mishmash of accommodation that changes style depending on the price range (we liked the 700B huts). The air-con cottages are a welcome addition to the repertoire.

Sunrise Bungalow (Map p201; ☎ 0 7742 4433; www .sunrisebungalow.com; Lamai South; bungalows 400-1300B; ❄) Steps away from the awkward giggles at Hin Ta Hin Yai (the island's infamous genital-shaped rocks), Sunrise offers budget travellers a relaxing place to hang their backpack. The owner is a sixth-generation Samui native.

Spa Resort (Map p201; ☎ 0 7723 0855; www.spasamui .com; Lamai North; bungalows 900-3500B; ❄) This health spa has a bevy of therapeutic programs on offer, and no one seems to mind that the lodging is cheap by Lamai's standards. Programs include colonics, massage, aqua detox, hypnotherapy and yoga, just to name a few. The bathrooms leave a bit to be desired, but who needs a toilet when you're doing a weeklong fast? Accommodation tends to book up quickly, so it's best to reserve in advance (via email). Nonguests are welcome to partake in the programs.

Lamai Wanta (Map p201; ☎ 0 7742 4550, 0 7742 4218; www.lamaiwanta.com; Central Lamai; r & bungalows 1600-3400B; ✗ ☲ ⌨) The pool area feels a bit retro, with its swatchbook of beige- and blue-toned tiles, but there are modern motel rooms and bungalows out the back with fresh coats of white paint. On the inside, rooms feel sparse and threadbare rather than 'minimal'.

Top End

Tamarind Retreat (Map p201; ☎ 0 7723 0571; www.tamarindretreat.com; Lamai North; villas 3500-11,600B; ✗ ⌨) Tucked far away from the beach within a silent coconut-palm plantation, Tamarind's small collection of villas are each elaborately decorated with a different design schema. Some have granite boulders built into walls and floors; others offer private ponds or creative outdoor baths. There's a seven-night minimum stay (three nights in low season) and free pick up at the airport is included. Advance reservations are a must.

Samui Jasmine Resort (Map p201; ☎ 0 7723 2446; www.samuijasmineresort.com; Central Lamai; r & bungalows 3800-5000B; ✗ ⌨) Pleasant Samui Jasmine is a great deal along Lamai's sun-bleached sands. Go for the lower-priced rooms – most have excellent views of the ocean and the crystal-coloured lap pool. The design scheme features plenty of varnished teak and frilly accessories such as lavender pillows.

ourpick Rocky Resort (Map p201; ☎ 0 7741 8367; www.rockyresort.com; Hua Thanon; r 4200-14,000B; ✗ ⌨) Our favourite spot in Lamai (well, actually just south of Lamai) Rocky finds the right balance between an upmarket ambience and an unpretentious, sociable atmosphere. During the quieter months the prices are a steal, since ocean views abound, and each room has been furnished with beautiful Thai-inspired furniture that seamlessly incorporates a modern twist. The pool has been carved in between a collection of boulders mimicking the rocky beach nearby (hence the name).

Villa Nalinnadda (Map p201; ☎ 0 7723 3131; www.nalinnadda.com; Hua Thanon; bungalows 6000-6500B; ✗ ⌨) Villa Nalinnadda's exterior walls are swathed in undulating waves of white adobe that mimic the bubbling water in the rectangular plunge pool. Seven suites of various shapes and sizes face out towards the swaying ocean offering a blend of romantic solitude while also fostering a convivial atmosphere among guests.

NORTHERN BEACHES

Ko Samui's northern beaches have the largest range of accommodation. Choeng Mon has some of the most opulent resorts in the world, while Mae Nam and Bang Po cling to their backpacker roots. Bo Phut, in the middle, is the shining star in Samui's constellation of beaches.

Choeng Mon & Around

While technically known as Plai Lam, this rugged outcropping is often called Choeng Mon after the largest beach in the area. If you happen to be the CEO of a Fortune 500 company, Choeng Mon is where you'll stay. These resorts are locked in an unwavering battle to out-posh one another.

Ô Soleil (☎ 0 7742 5232; r & bungalows from 400B; ✗) One of the cheaper beachfront properties on the island, old Ô Soleil offers a scatter of bungalows and semi-detached rooms extending inland from the sand. It's a very casual affair, so be sure to safely store your valuables.

White House (☎ 0 7724 7921, 0 7724 5318; www.hotelthewhitehouse.com; r 5000-6600B; ✗ ⌨) You can check Angkor Wat off your 'to do' list – The White House feels like the seat of an ancient empire hidden deep within the thickest jungle. Sandstone temples bleed luscious tropical ferns from every crevice, and praying deity statues hide among the twisting jungle foliage.

ourpick Sala Samui (☎ 0 7724 5888; www.salasamui.com; bungalows US$360-1100; ✗ ☲ ⌨) Look out folks, these guys mean business – they quote their room rates in US dollars instead of baht. Is the hefty price tag worth it? Definitely. The design scheme is undeniably exquisite – regal whites and lacquered teaks are generously lavished throughout, while subtle turquoise accents draw on the colour of each villa's private plunge pool.

Tongsai Bay (☎ 0 7724 5480-5500; www.tongsaibay.co.th; ste 11,000-30,000B; ✗ ⌨) For serious pampering, head to this secluded luxury gem. Expansive and impeccably maintained, the hilly grounds make the cluster of bungalows look more like a small village. Golf carts whiz around the vast landscape transporting guests to various activities like massages or dinner. All the extra-swanky split-level suites have day-bed rest areas, gorgeous romantic decor, stunning views, large terraces and creatively placed bathtubs (you'll see). Facilities include salt- and fresh-water pools, a tennis court, the requisite spa, a dessert shop, and several restaurants.

ourpick Sila Evason Hideaway (☎ 0 7724 5678; www.sixsenses.com/hideaway-samui/index.php; bungalows from 18,000B; ✗ ☐ ⚑) We're not saying that you should sell all your earthly possessions (because then you'll have nothing to pack), but this hidden bamboo paradise is worth the once-in-a-lifetime splurge. Set along a rugged promontory, Sila Evason strikes the perfect balance between opulence and rustic charm, and defines the term 'barefoot elegance'. Most of the villas have stunning concrete plunge pools and offer magnificent views of the silent bay below. The regal, semi-outdoor bathrooms give the phrase 'royal flush' a whole new meaning. Beige golf buggies move guests between their hidden cottages and the stunning amenities are strewn throughout the property – including a world-class spa and two excellent restaurants.

Big Buddha Beach (Bang Rak)

This area gets its moniker from the huge golden Buddha that acts as overlord from the small nearby quasi-island of Ko Fan. Its proximity to the airport means lower prices at the resorts.

Samui Mermaid (☎ 0 7742 7547; www.samui-mermaid.info; r 400-2500B; ✗ ☐ ⚑) Samui Mermaid is a great choice in the budget category because it feels like a full-fledged resort. There are two large swimming pools, copious beach chairs, two lively restaurants and every room has cable TV. The landing strip at Samui's airport is only a couple kilometres away, so sometimes there's noise, but free airport transfers sweeten the deal.

Shambala (☎ 0 7742 5330; www.samui-shambala.com; bungalows 600-1000B; ✗) While surrounding establishments answer the call of upmarket travellers, this laid-back, English-run place is a backpacking stalwart with a subtle hippy feel. There's plenty of communal cushion seating, a great wooden sundeck, and the bungalows are bright and roomy. Staff doles out travel tips and smiles in equal measure.

Ocean 11 (☎ 0 7741 7118; www.o11s.com; bungalows 1900-3200B; ✗ ⚑) A little slice of luxury at a very reasonable price, Ocean 11's 'residences' are a steal (get it?!) Silly film references aside, this mellow spot with cottagey, Med-style decor is a great midrange getaway along a relatively quiet patch of sand.

Prana (☎ 0 7724 6362; www.pranaresorts.com; r 5600-8000B; ✗ ☐ ⚑) Vegetarians unite! This trendy crash-pad is the ultimate retreat for those who shun the carnivore lifestyle. Beautiful oceanfront bedrooms extend along the beach beyond the infinity-edge lap pool.

Bo Phut

The beach isn't breathtaking, but Bo Phut has the most dynamic lodging in all of Samui. A string of vibrant boutique cottages starts deep within the clutter of Fisherman's Village and radiates outward along the sand.

Khuntai (Map p207; ☎ 0 7724 5118, 08 6686 2960; r 400-850B; ✗) This clunky orange guesthouse is as cheap as decent rooms get on Samui. A block away from the beach, on the outskirts of Fisherman's Village, Khuntai's 2nd-floor rooms are drenched in afternoon sunshine and feature outdoor lounging spots.

ourpick L'Hacienda (Map p207; ☎ 0 7724 5943; www.samui-hacienda.com; r 1000-3000B; ✗ ⚑) Polished terracotta and rounded archways give the entrance a Spanish mission motif. Similar decor permeates the eight adorable rooms, which sport loads of personal touches such as pebbled bathroom walls and translucent bamboo lamps. There's a charming surprise waiting for you on the roof, and we're pretty sure you'll love it as much as we did.

Lodge (Map p207; ☎ 0 7742 5337; www.apartmentsamui.com; r 1350-1900B; ✗ ⚑) Another great choice in Bo Phut, The Lodge feels like a colonial hunting chalet with pale walls and dark wooden beams jutting across the ceiling. Every room has scores of wall hangings and a private balcony overlooking the beach. The 'pent-huts' on the top floor are very spacious. Reservations are a must – this place always seems to be full.

Ibis Bo Phut (Map p207; ☎ 0 7791 4800; www.ibishotel.com/thailand; r from 1600B; ✗ ☐ ⚑ ⚑) The biggest resort on the island, the brand new Ibis still has that new car smell in its shiny, efficient rooms. Families will love the children's bunk beds and the grassy grounds perfect for a game of tag. If you're looking for a resort with traces of Thai character, this is not the place for you.

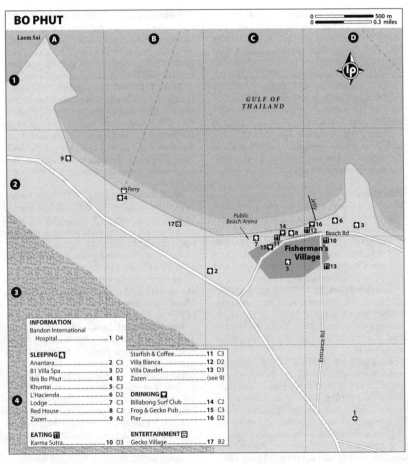

BO PHUT

GULF OF
THAILAND

Laem Sai

Ferry

Public
Beach Arena

Fisherman's
Village

Beach Rd

Entrance Rd

SOUTHWESTERN
GULF COAST

Red House (Map p207; ☎ 0 7742 5686; www.design
-visio.com; r 2000B; ✷) To reach the small reception
area at the back, guests must pass through a
sleek shoe shop that looks like a swish Chinese
bordello. The four rooms are decorated with
a similar spiciness. Intricate oriental patterns
liven the walls and canopied beds are swathed
in streamers of ruby and chartreuse. A cache
of reclining beach chairs and potted plants is
the perfect rooftop escape.

B1 Villa Spa (Map p207; ☎ 0 7742 7268; www.b1villa
.com; ste 3500-5000B; ✷ ☒) There's a refreshing
burst of character at this inn-style option
along the beach in Fisherman's Village. Each
room displays a unique collection of wall art,
and has been given a special moniker – the
2nd-storey spaces are named after the stars

in Orion's belt. Oh, and it's B1 as in 'B1 with
yourself', get it?

our pick **Zazen** (Map p207; ☎ 0 7742 5085; www
.samuizazen.com; r 5300-12,800B; ✷ ☒ ☒) What was
once a simple place has now transformed into
the boutique-iest boutique resort on Samui –
every inch of this charming getaway has been
thoughtfully and creatively designed. It's
'Asian minimalism meets modern Rococo'
with a scarlet accent wall, terracotta goddesses, a dash of feng shui and generous smattering of good taste. Guests relax poolside on
comfy beach chairs gently shaded by canvas
parasols. The walk-in prices are scary, so it's
best to book in advance.

our pick **Anantara** (Map p207; ☎ 0 7742 8300; www
.anantara.com; r 7000-15,000B; ✷ ☒ ☒) Anantara's

stunning palanquin entrance satisfies every fantasy of a far-flung oriental kingdom. Low-slung torches spurt plumes of unwavering fire, and the residual smoke creates a light fog around the fanned palm fronds higher up. Clay and copper statues of grimacing jungle creatures abound on the property's wild acreage, while guests savour wild teas in an open-air pagoda, swim in the lagoon-like infinity-edged swimming pool, or indulge in a relaxing spa treatment. The 'deluxe' hotel-style rooms have moveable window-walls in the bathroom, but feel a tad small when considering the steep price tag.

Mae Nam

Mae Nam doesn't have the most beautiful tract of sand, but it offers cheap accommodation relative to the other beaches.

Shangrilah (☎ 0 7742 5189; bungalows 300-2000B; 🐾) A backpacker's Shangri La indeed – these are some of the cheapest huts around and they're in decent condition.

Coco Palm Resort (☎ 0 7742 5095; bungalows 1200B; 🐾) The bungalows at Coco Palm have been crafted with tonnes of rattan. A rectangular pool is the centrepiece along the beach – and the price is right for a resort-like atmosphere.

Maenam Resort (☎ 0 7742 5116; www.maenamresort.com; bungalows 1200-2700B; 🐾 🖳) Palm-bark cottages are set in several rows amid a private, jungle-like garden. They're decked out in a mix of wicker and wooden furnishings, and vary in price according to their distance from the beach. Suites are a steal for families.

Harry's (☎ 0 7742 5447; www.harrys-samui.com; bungalows 1200-3000B; 🐾 🖳) Arriving at Harry's feels like entering sacred temple grounds. Polished teak wood abounds in the lobby and the classic pitched roofing reaches skyward. The concrete bungalows, stashed in a verdant garden, do not retain the flamboyant architectural theme out front, but they're cute and comfortable nonetheless.

Sea Fan (☎ 0 7742 5204; www.seafanresort.com; r 2200-2700B; 🐾 🖳) Offering huge thatch and wood bungalows connected by wooden walkways, with colourful flora abounding, this is a fine place to stay. The beautiful beachside pool has a small kid's area.

Bang Po

This small enclave has a cache of budget bungalows.

Sunbeam (☎ 0 7742 0600; bungalows 500-1000B) Quiet Sunbeam has just over a dozen rustic cottages by the sea. They're spacious, comfy, and offer beach views from the porch. Brick paths wind through a lush garden, and cool breezes pass through the shanty-like bar.

Moon (☎ 0 7724 7740; bungalows 600-1800B) Moon is a throwback to an earlier time when Samui was rife with seaside shacks. Several modern concrete cottages have recently sprung up on the property – they're comfortable and clean, and they don't detract from the general laid-back jungle-on-the-beach atmosphere. The large wood-beamed restaurant is the heart of the action.

Health Oasis Resort (☎ 0 7742 0124; www.healthoasisresort.com; bungalows 800-4500B; 🐾) If you're lookin' to get 'cleansed' – whether it's your aura or your colon, then you've happened upon the right place. New Age is all the rage at the Health Oasis. Guests can choose from a variety of healing packages involving everything from meditation to fasting. Bungalows are modern and receive plenty of sunshine. There's also a vegetarian restaurant on site, of course.

Four Seasons Koh Samui (☎ 0 7724 3000; www.fourseasons.com/kohsamui; villas 30,000B; 🖳 🐾 🛜 🖳) Four Seasons Koh Samui feels more like a private village than a resort. The international luxury brand has purchased an entire peninsula at the far western corner of Bang Po, and transformed it into a hilly enclave. A ridiculous amount of on-site amenities means that you'll probably never leave the grounds. Each villa has a large private plunge-pool and spacious sitting areas. Should you decide to be more social, there's a beautiful stretch of flaxen sand offering beach chairs and water sports.

WEST COAST

Largely the domain of Thai tourists, Samui's west coast doesn't have the most picturesque beaches, but it's a welcome escape from the east-side bustle.

Na Thon

The island's main settlement is dominated by the ferry pier and is not much to look at. There's really no reason to stay here, but if for some reason you feel compelled, try the following.

Jinta Hotel (☎ 0 7742 0630, 0 7723 6369; www.jintasamui.com; r 500-650B; 🐾 🖳) Jinta's white walls and linoleum floors feel a bit institutional, but it gets the job done. All rooms have satellite TV.

Grand Sea View Hotel (☎ 0 7742 0441; www .grandseaviewbeachhotel.com; r 1000-2000B; 🍴 💻) Na Thon's pick of the litter, this five-floor hotel is popular with visiting businessmen. Spacious rooms have sparkling tile floors, light wooden framing, air-conditioning and cable TV. The higher levels have great views over the town and sea.

Taling Ngam

A quiet stop south of Na Thon, Taling Ngam is a charming hideaway with a quaint local village nearby.

Wiesenthal (☎ 0 7723 5165; fax 0 7741 5480; bungalows incl breakfast 1500-2500B; 🍴 🛜 💻) The name sorta sounds like a smoky German beer hall made from thick trunks of cedar, but this Thai-owned operation is a breezy beachside paradise. Cast modesty aside, spread your curtains wide, and welcome sunshine and sea views in through your floor-to-ceiling windows. Lounge-worthy porch furniture further contributes to the comfy, casual vibe established at the open-air restaurant and pool.

Ban Sabai (☎ 0 7742 8200; www.bansabaisunset.com; bungalows 6800-25,000B; 🍴 💻 🛜 💻) Beautiful Ban Sabai has 20 rooms on a secluded stretch of sand and palms. Villas along the beach have multi-room lavatories under a charming patchwork of thatching and starlight. Rooms have a private waterfall – the bathtubs receive water from a lovely cascade-like faucet. The intimate common spaces and semi-detached cottages make this resort a great place to relax with friends.

Baan Taling Ngam Resort (☎ 0 7742 9100; www.baan-taling-ngam.com; bungalows 8500-16,000B; 🍴 💻 🛜 💻) Unlike most of Samui's five-star digs, Baan Taling Ngam has been designed in a 'classic Thai' theme. Luxuriously appointed guest accommodation contains custom-made Thai-style furnishings and the service here is impeccable. As it's not right on the beach, a shuttle service transports guests back and forth; airport and ferry transfers are also provided.

SOUTH COAST

The southern end of Ko Samui is spotted with rocky headlands and smaller sandy coves. The following options are all well worth the baht, in fact, these resorts represent some of our favourite places to stay on the island.

Easy Time (☎ 0 7792 0110; www.easytimesamui.com; Phang Ka; r from 1300B; 🍴 💻 🛜 💻) Safely tucked away from the throngs of tourists, this little haven – nestled inland around a serene swimming pool – is a great place to unwind. Duplex villa units and a chic dining space create an elegant mood that is refreshingly unpretentious.

Elements (☎ 0 7791 4678; www.elements-koh-samui .com; Phang Ka; r from 4400B; 🍴 💻 🛜 💻) A refreshing twist on the modern boutique sleep, Elements occupies a lonely strand of palm-studded sand. Rooms are arranged in condo-like blocks, each one featuring an eye-pleasing blend of Thai and West styling. Hidden villas dot the path down to the fire-coloured restaurant and ocean-side lounge area.

Yoga Thailand (☎ 0 7792 0090; www.yoga-thai land.com; Phang Ka; retreats from €650; 🍴 💻 🛜) Secreted away along the southern shores, Yoga Thailand is ushering in a new era of therapeutic holidaying with its state-of-the-art facilities and dedicated team of trainers. Accommodation is located in a comfy apartment block up the street while yoga studios, wellness centres and a breezy cafe sit calmly along the shore.

Eating

If you thought it was hard to pick a place to sleep, the island has even more options when it comes to dining. From roasted crickets to beluga caviar – Samui's got it and is not afraid to flaunt it.

Influenced by the mainland, Samui is peppered with *kôw gaang* (rice and curry) shops, usually just a wooden shack displaying large metal pots of southern Thai–style curries. Folks pull up on their motorcycles, lift up the lids to survey the vibrantly coloured contents, and pick one for lunch. *Kôw gaang* shops are easily found along the Ring Rd (Rd 4169) and sell out of the good stuff by 1pm. Any build up of local motorcycles is usually a sign of a good meal in progress.

The upmarket choices are even more numerous and although Samui's swanky dining scene is laden with Italian options, visitors will have no problem finding flavours from around the globe. Lured by high salaries and spectacular weather, world-class chefs regularly make an appearance on the island.

CHAWENG

Dozens of the restaurants on the 'strip' serve a mixed bag of local bites, international cuisine, and greasy fast food. For the best ambience, get off the road and head to the beach, where many bungalow operators set up tables on the sand and have glittery fairy lights at night.

Laem Din Market & Night Market (Map p199; dishes from 30B; ⏱ 4am-6pm, night market 6pm-2am) A busy day market, Laem Din is packed with stalls selling fresh fruits, vegetables and meats that stock local Thai kitchens. Pick up a kilo of sweet green oranges or wander the stalls trying to spot the ingredients in last night's curry. For dinner, come to the adjacent night market and sample the tasty southern-style fried chicken and curries.

our pick Gringo's Cantina (Map p199; ☎ 0 7741 3267; dishes 140-280B; ⏱ 2pm-midnight) Wash down a Tex-Mex classic with a jug of sangria or a frozen margarita. We liked the *chimichangas* (mostly because we like saying '*chimichanga*'). There are burgers, pizzas and vegie options too, for those who don't want to go 'south of the border'.

Captain Kirk (Map p199; ☎ 08 1270 5376; dishes 140-480B; ⏱ dinner) Beam yourself up to this beautiful rooftop garden for a vast selection of international eats. Patrons often lounge on the cushioned bamboo furniture and indulge in post-repast cocktails.

Page (Map p199; ☎ 0 7742 2767; dishes 180-850B; ⏱ breakfast, lunch & dinner) If you can't afford to stay at the ultra-swanky Library (p204), have a meal at their beachside restaurant. The food is expensive (of course) but you'll receive glances from the beach bums on the beach as they try to figure out if you're a jetsetter or movie star. Lunch is a bit more casual and affordable, but you'll miss the designer lighting effects in the evening.

Prego (Map p199; ☎ 0 7742 2015; www.prego-samui.com; mains 200-700B; ⏱ dinner) This smart ministry of culinary style serves up fine Italian cuisine in a barely-there dining room of cool marble and modern geometry. Reservations are accepted for seatings at 7pm and 9pm.

Dr Frogs (Map p199; ☎ 0 7741 3797; mains 380-790B; ⏱ lunch & dinner) Perched atop a rocky overlook, Dr Frogs combines incredible ocean vistas with delicious international flavours (namely Italian and Thai favourites). Delectable steaks and crab cakes, and friendly owners puts this spot near the top of our dining list.

Betelnut @ Buri Rasa (Map p199; ☎ 0 7741 3370; mains 600-800B; ⏱ dinner) Fusion can be confusing, and often disappointing, but Betelnut will set you straight. Chef Jeffrey Lords claims an American upbringing and European culinary training, but most importantly he spent time in San Francisco, where all good food is born. The menu is a pan-Pacific mix of curries and chowder, papaya and pancetta.

Zico's (Map p199; ☎ 0 7723 1560; menu 790B; ⏱ 6pm-late) This palatial *churrascaria* puts the '*carne*' in Carnival. Vegetarians beware – Zico's is an all-you-can-eat Brazilian meat-fest complete with saucy dancers sporting peacock-like outfits.

our pick Samui Institute of Thai Culinary Arts (SITCA; Map p199; ☎ 0 7741 3434; course 1950B; ⏱ lunch & dinner Mon-Sat) Go one better than savouring a traditional Thai meal: cook it yourself! See p201 for details.

LAMAI

As Samui's second-most populated beach, Lamai has a surprisingly limited assortment of decent eateries when compared to Chaweng next door. The newly opened **Tesco Lotus** is a great place to pick up snacks for a beachside picnic. Most visitors, however, dine wherever they're staying.

Lamai Day Market (Map p201; dishes from 30B; ⏱ 6am-8pm) The Thai equivalent of a grocery store, Lamai's market is a hive of activity, selling food necessities and takeaway food. Visit the covered area to pick up fresh fruit or to see vendors shredding coconuts to make coconut milk. Or hunt down the ice-cream seller for homemade coconut ice cream. It's next door to a petrol station.

Hua Thanon Market (Map p201; ☎ 0 7742 4630; dishes from 30B; ⏱ 6am-6pm) Slip into the rhythm of this village market slightly south of Lamai; a window into the food ways of southern Thailand. Vendors shoo away the flies from the freshly butchered meat and housewives load bundles of vegetables into their baby-filled motorcycle baskets. Follow the market road to the row of food shops delivering edible Muslim culture: chicken biryani, fiery curries, or toasted rice with coconut, bean sprouts, lemongrass and dried shrimp.

Lamai Night Food Centre (Map p201; ☎ 0 7742 4630; dishes from 30B; ⏱ dinner) Eating becomes a circus sideshow at Lamai's outdoor food centre, next door to a 7-Eleven. The vendor stalls whip up all the Thai standards – a spectacle in itself. And then the hostesses at the nearby girly bars crank up the music for pole dancing or a few rounds of *moo·ay tai* (also spelled *muay thai;* Thai boxing).

Mr Samui (Map p201; ☎ 0 7742 4630; dishes 100-180B; ⏱ lunch & dinner) Enter Baan Soi Gemstones (look for the 'illy' sign out front) and pass the veritable garage sale of oriental knick-knacks to find a tiny cluster of tables and cushions. Savour your nutty massaman curry amid flamboyant Chinese wall art, dripping chandeliers and gaudy geometric pillows (everything's for sale).

Rocky's (Map p201; ☎ 0 7741 8367; dishes 300-800B; 🕙 lunch & dinner) Easily the top dining spot on Lamai, Rocky's gourmet dishes are actually a bargain when you convert the baht into your native currency. Try the signature beef tenderloin with blue cheese – it's like sending your tastebuds on a Parisian vacation. On Tuesday evenings, diners enjoy a special Thai-themed evening with a prepared menu of local delicacies.

NORTHERN BEACHES
Some of Samui's finest establishments are located on the northern coast. Boho Bo Phut has several trendy eateries to match the string of yuppie boutique hotels.

Choeng Mon & Big Buddha Beach (Bang Rak)
BBC (☎ 0 7742 5264; dishes 60-200B; Big Buddha Beach; 🕙 breakfast, lunch & dinner) No, this place has nothing to do with *Dr Who* – BBC stands for Big Buddha Café. It's popular with the local expats, and there's a large international menu and exquisite ocean views from the patio.

Elephant & Castle (☎ 0 7743 0394; Big Buddha Beach; dishes 80-250B; 🕙 lunch & dinner) The ultimate hangout for homesick Brits, Elephant & Castle is the perfect replica of a London pub. There's beer by the pint and the steak-and-kidney pies will give you meat sweats for days.

ourpick Dining On The Rocks (☎ 0 7724 5678; reservations-samui@sixsenses.com; Choeng Mon; menus from 2200B; 🕙 dinner) Samui's ultimate dining experience takes place on nine cantilevered verandahs of weathered teak and bamboo that yawn over the gulf. After sunset (and a glass of wine), guests feel like they're dining on a wooden barge set adrift on a starlit sea. Each dish on the six-course prix-fixe menu is the brainchild of the experimental cooks who regularly dabble with taste, texture and temperature. If you're celebrating a special occasion, you'll have to book well in advance if you want to sit at 'table 99' – the honeymooners' table – positioned on a private terrace. Dining On The Rocks is located at the isolated Sila Evason Hideaway (p206).

Bo Phut
Starfish & Coffee (Map p207; ☎ 0 7742 7201; mains 130-180B; 🕙 breakfast, lunch & dinner) This streamer-clad eatery was probably named after the Prince song, since we couldn't find any starfish on the menu (there's loads of coffee though). Evenings feature standard Thai fare and sunset views of rugged Ko Pha-Ngan.

Karma Sutra (Map p207; mains 130-260B; 🕙 breakfast, lunch & dinner) A haze of purples and pillows, this charming chow spot in the heart of Bo Phut's Fisherman's Village serves up international and Thai eats listed on colourful chalkboards. Karma Sutra doubles as a clothing boutique.

Villa Daudet (Map p207; dishes from 130-380B; 🕙 lunch & dinner Mon-Sat) Villa Daudet is French-owned (so you know the food's gonna be good) and sits in a quaint garden decorated with a flower trellis and elephant-themed paintings.

Villa Bianca (Map p207; ☎ 0 7724 5041, 08 9873 5867; dishes from 200B; 🕙 lunch & dinner) Another fantastic Italian spot on Samui, Villa Bianca is a sea of crisp white tablecloths and woven lounge chairs. Who knew wicker could be so sexy?

Zazen (Map p207; ☎ 0 7742 5085; dishes 550-850B; set menu from 1300B; 🕙 lunch & dinner) The chef describes the food as 'organic and orgasmic', and the ambient 'yums' from elated diners definitely confirm the latter. This romantic dining experience comes complete with ocean views, dim candle lighting and soft music. Reservations recommended.

Mae Nam & Bang Po
Angela's Bakery (☎ 0 7742 7396; Mae Nam; dishes 80-200B; 🕙 breakfast & lunch) Duck through the screen of hanging plants into this beloved bakery, smelling of fresh bread and hospitality. Angela's sandwiches and cakes have kept many Western expats from wasting away in the land of rice.

Ko-Seng (☎ 0 7742 5365; Mae Nam; dishes 100-300B; 🕙 dinner) Hidden down a narrow side street near Mae Nam's Chinese temple, Ko Samui's best kept secret is a welcome escape from the island's restaurants that fuss over the decor instead of their food. It's a local haunt that dishes out top-notch soft-shell crab and plump, flash-fried prawns in a peppery sauce.

Bang Po Seafood (☎ 0 7742 0010; Bang Po; dishes from 100B; 🕙 dinner) A meal at Bang Po Seafood is a test for the tastebuds. It's one of the only restaurants that serves traditional Ko Samui fare (think of it as island roadkill, well, actually its more like local sea-kill): recipes call for ingredients like raw sea urchin roe, baby octopus, sea water, coconut, and local turmeric.

WEST COAST
The quiet west coast features some of the best seafood on Samui. Na Thon has a giant **day market** on Th Thawi Ratchaphakdi – it's worth stopping by to grab some snacks before your ferry ride.

Big John Seafood (☎ 0 7742 3025; www.bigjohn samui.com; Thong Yang; dishes 60-300B; ⏰ breakfast, lunch & dinner) Big John's menu looks like an encyclopaedia of marine life. The seafood is freshly caught every day from various fishing hotspots off the coast of Samui. Dinnertime is particularly special – live entertainment kicks in around 6pm just as the sun plunges below the watery horizon.

ourpick About Art & Craft Café (☎ 08 9724 9673; Na Thon; dishes 80-180B; ⏰ breakfast & lunch) An artistic oasis in the midst of hurried Na Thon, this cafe serves an eclectic assortment of healthy and wholesome food, gourmet coffee, and, as the name states, art and craft, made by the owner and her friends. Relaxed and friendly, this is also a gathering place for Samui's dwindling population of bohemians and artists.

ourpick Five Islands (☎ 0 7741 5359, 08 1447 5371; www.thefiveislands.com; Taling Ngam; dishes 150-500B, tours 2000-6500B; ⏰ lunch & dinner) Five Islands defines the term 'destination dining' and offers the most unique eating experience on the island. Before your meal, a traditional longtail boat will take you out into the turquoise sea to visit the haunting Five Sister Islands where you'll learn about the ancient and little-known art of harvesting bird nests to make bird's nest soup, a Chinese delicacy. This perilous task is rewarded with large sums of cash – a kilo of bird's nests is usually sold for 100,000B to restaurants in Hong Kong (yup, that's five zeros). The lunch tour departs at 10am, and the dinner program leaves at 3pm. Customers are also welcome to dine without going on the tour and vice versa.

Drinking & Entertainment
Samui's biggest party spot is, without a doubt, noisy Chaweng. Lamai and Bo Phut come in second and third respectively, while the rest of the island is generally quiet, as the drinking is usually focused on self-contained resort bars.

CHAWENG & LAMAI
Making merry in Chaweng is a piece of cake. Most places are open until 2am and there are a few places that go strong all night long. **Soi Green Mango** has loads of girly bars. **Soi Colibri** and **Soi Reggae Pub** are raucous as well.

Ark Bar (Map p199; ☎ 0 7742 2047; www.ark-bar .com; Hat Chaweng) The 'it' destination for a Wednesday-night romp on Samui. Drinks are dispensed from the multicoloured bar draped in paper lanterns, and guests lounge on pyramidal pillows strewn down the beach. The party usually starts around 4pm.

Good Karma (Map p199; ☎ 08 7741 3857; Hat Chaweng) Open all day, this snazzy lounge lures the hip 'hi-so' (Thai high society) crowd with canopied daybeds and a hidden pond.

Harlow (Map p199; ☎ 08 3692 7911, 08 4744 9207; Hat Chaweng) This hole-in-the-wall hotspot feels like a hidden metropolitan lounge whose address is known only by the poshest of jet-setters.

Bar Solo (Map p199; ☎ 0 7741 4012; Hat Chaweng) A sign of things to come, Bar Solo has future-fitted Chaweng's outdoor beer halls into an urban setting with sleek cubist decor and a cocktail list that doesn't scream holiday hayseed. The evening drink specials lure in the front-loaders preparing for a late, late night at the dance clubs on Soi Solo and Soi Green Mango.

Q-Bar (Map p199; ☎ 08 1956 2742; www.qbarsamui .com; Hat Chaweng) Overlooking Chaweng Lake, Q Bar is a little piece of Bangkok nightlife planted among the coconut trees. The upstairs lounge opens just before sunset treating cocktail connoisseurs to various highbrow tipples and a drinkable view of southern Chaweng – mountains, sea and sky. After 10pm, the night-crawlers descend upon the downstairs club where DJs spin the crowd into a techno amoeba. A taxi there will cost between 200B and 300B.

Tropical Murphy's (Map p199; ☎ 0 7741 3614; Hat Chaweng; dishes 50-300B) A popular faràng joint, Tropical Murphy's dishes out steak-and-kidney pie, fish and chips, lamb chops and Irish stew. Come night-time, the live music kicks on and this place turns into the most popular Irish bar on Samui (yes, there are a few).

Green Mango (Map p199; ☎ 0 7742 2661; Hat Chaweng) This place is so popular it has an entire soi named after it. Samui's favourite power drinking house is very big, very loud and very faràng. Green Mango has blazing lights, expensive drinks and masses of sweaty bodies swaying to dance music.

Reggae Pub (Map p199; ☎ 0 7742 2331; Hat Chaweng) This fortress of fun sports an open-air dance floor with music spun by foreign DJs. It's a towering two-storey affair with long bars, pool tables, and a live-music stage. The whole place doubles as a shrine to Bob Marley.

Mint Bar (Map p199; ☎ 08 7089 8726; Hat Chaweng) The street scene on this party street is too entertaining to keep the crowds corralled in this stylish club on ordinary nights. But the Mint is able to lure a few DJ heavyweights for a Samui spin on extraordinary nights. Watch the entertainment listings for special events.

Christy's Cabaret (Map p199; ☎ 08 1894 0356; Hat Chaweng) This flashy joint offers free *kàthoey* (transgender males) cabaret every night at 11pm and attracts a mixed clientele of both sexes. Other lady-boys loiter out front and try to drag customers in, so to speak.

Beach Republic (Map p201; ☎ 0 7745 8100; Hat Lamai) Recognised by its yawning thatch-patched awnings, Beach Republic would be the perfect spot to shoot one of those MTV Spring Break episodes. There's an inviting wading pool, comfy lounge chairs and an endless cocktail list.

NORTHERN & WEST COAST BEACHES

Billabong Surf Club (Map p207; ☎ 0 7743 0144; Bo Phut) Billabong's all about Aussie rules football – it's playing on the TV and the walls are smothered with memorabilia from Down Undah. There are great views of Ko Pha-Ngan and hearty portions of ribs and chops to go with your draught beer.

Frog & Gecko Pub (Map p207; ☎ 0 7742 5248; Bo Phut) This tropical British watering hole and food stop is famous for its noodle-bending 'Wednesday Night Pub Quiz' competitions and its wide selection of music. Live sporting events are shown on the big screen.

Pier (Map p207; ☎ 0 7743 0681; Bo Phut; dishes 200-390B; ☏ lunch & dinner) This sleek black box sticks out among Bo Phut's narrow Chinese tenements. It's the hippest address in Fisherman's Village, sporting multilevel terraces, a lively bar, and plenty of wide furniture to lounge around and watch the rickety fishing vessels pull into the harbour.

Gecko Village (Map p207; ☎ 0 7724 5554; Bo Phut) For electronica fans, Gecko Village is the original maven of beats. It's a beachfront bar and resort that has used its London connections to lure international DJs to Samui paradise. The New Year's Eve parties and Sunday sessions are now legends thanks to the big names that grace the turntables.

Nikki Beach (☎ 0 7791 4500; Lipa Noi) The acclaimed luxury brand has brought their international *savoir faire* to the secluded west coast of Ko Samui. Expect everything you would from a chic address in St Barts or St Tropez: haute cuisine, chic decor and gaggles of jetsetters.

Getting There & Away
AIR
Samui's airport is located in the northeast of the island near Big Buddha Beach. **Bangkok Airways** (www.bangkokair.com) operates flights roughly every 30 minutes between Samui and Bangkok (from 3000B, one to 1½ hours). **Thai Airways International** (THAI; ☎ in Bangkok 0 2134 5403; www.thaiair.com) operates between Samui and Bangkok (from 5000B, twice a day). Both airlines usually land at Bangkok's Suvarnabhumi Airport.

There is a **Bangkok Airways Office** (Map p199; ☎ 0 7742 0512-9) in Chaweng and another at the **airport** (☎ 0 7742 5011). The first (at 6am) and last (10pm) flights of the day are always the cheapest.

Bangkok Air also flies from Samui to Phuket (2000B to 3000B, one hour, three daily) and Pattaya (3000B, one hour, three daily). International flights go directly from Samui to Singapore (4200B to 5400B, three hours, daily) and Hong Kong (12,000B to 16,000B, four hours, five days a week).

During the high season, make your flight reservations far in advance as seats do sell out. If Samui flights are full, try flying into Surat Thani from Bangkok and taking a short ferry ride from Samui. Flights to Surat Thani are generally cheaper than a direct flight to the island, although they are much more of a hassle (see p250).

BOAT
The ferry situation is rather convoluted: schedules and prices are always in flux, and there are heaps of entry and exit points on Samui and the mainland. Your exit and entry point will probably depend on what's available when you arrive in Surat Thani (after all, you probably don't want to hang around town). The four main piers on the mainland are Ao Ban Don, Tha Thong, Don

Sak and Khanom – Tha Thong (in central Surat) and Don Sak being the most common. On Samui, the three oft-used ports are Na Thon, Mae Nam and Big Buddha. Service quality can also vary greatly within the same ferry company – some boats are rusty and rundown, others are much more modern and are even outfitted with TVs. Expect complimentary taxi transfers with high-speed ferry services.

There are frequent daily boat departures between Samui and Surat Thani. The hourly

---

POP'S CULTURE: LIFE AS A LADYBOY

Pop, age 45, is what Thais call a *ga·teu·i*, usually referred to as a 'ladyboy' in English. Thailand's transgender population is the subject of many debates and conversations, especially among tourists. Although tolerance is widespread in Buddhist Thailand, concealed homophobia prevails – for *ga·teu·i*, this can be a challenging life, with the entertainment and sex industries the only lucrative career avenues open. We spent the day with Pop and got the skinny on what life was really like as a member of Thailand's oft-talked-about 'third sex'.

Let's start with a question that many tourists in Thailand would like to ask: why does there seem to be so many *ga·teu·i* in Thailand? Well, that's like asking me why I am a ladyboy! I have no idea. I didn't ask to have these feelings. I think the more important thing to notice is why there are so many ladyboys in the cabaret or sex industry. First, however, let me start by staying that the word *ga·teu·i* is the informal way of saying 'person with two sexes'; the term *phuying kham pet* is generally more polite. Also, *ga·teu·i* is strictly reserved for people who still have male body parts but dress as female, so I am not technically *ga·teu·i* anymore.

Most tourists think that there are tonnes of ladyboys in Thailand because they are in places that many tourists visit. Yes, some ladyboys want to be cabaret dancers, just like some women want to be cabaret dancers, but most of them don't. These types of jobs are the only ones available to ladyboys, and the pay is lousy. Life is not as 'Hollywood' for a ladyboy as it may seem on stage. Most ladyboys don't have the chance to have a job that is respected by the community. We are not allowed to become doctors or psychologists and most corporations do not allow ladyboy employees because they don't want *ga·teu·i* to be associated with their company's image. Since many of us cannot have proper jobs, many ladyboys don't even bother going to school, and lately this educational gap in the culture has become huge. You see many *gàteui* dropping out of school at a young age because they know they don't have a future in a respectable job. Ladyboys work in the sex industry because they aren't given the opportunity to make a lot of money doing something else. I feel like a second-class citizen; we are not allowed to use male *or* female bathrooms! I used to have to climb 14 flights of stairs to use the special ladyboys' bathroom at my old job! Also, Thai law states that my ID cards and passport must always have an 'M' for male because the definition of a female in Thailand is someone who can bear children. It's hard for me to leave the country because my passport says 'male' but I look like a female. They will never let me through security because it looks like a fraudulent passport.

When did you first realise that you might be a transgender person? I realised that I was different when I was about six years old. I always wanted to dress up like my sister and would get upset when my parents dressed me in boy's clothing. It felt wrong being in boy's clothes. I felt good in my sister's outfits.

How does one tell the difference between a ladyboy and a woman on the street? Sometimes it's really hard to tell…sometimes a ladyboy can be more beautiful than a woman! There is no set way to figure it out, unless you ask them for their ID card. These days, doctors are really starting to perfect the operations, and the operations are expensive – mine was 150,000B! I had the 'snip', then I had breast implants, my Adam's apple was shaved off, and I also had a nose job (I didn't like my old nose anyways). Other operations available include silicone implants in the hips, jaw narrowing, cheekbone shaving and chin sculpting – to make it rounder. But before anyone can have an operation, you have to have a psych evaluation. The operation was extremely painful.

Seatran ferry is a common option. Ferries cost around 230B and take one to five hours, depending on the boat. A couple of these departures can connect with the train station in Phun Phin (for an extra 100B to 140B). The slow night boat to Samui (250B) leaves from central Surat Thani each night at 11pm, reaching Na Thon around 5am. It returns from Na Thon at 9pm, arriving at around 3am. Watch your bags on this boat.

There are almost a dozen daily departures between Samui and Ko Pha-Ngan. These

---

I spent seven days in the hospital and it took me about two months to fully recover. Younger patients tend to heal faster – I was about 40 years old when I had the operation.

Why didn't you have the operation earlier? I didn't 'change' earlier because I didn't want to give up my job, and I knew that after the operation I would be forced to quit. I was working as a software instructor at a university, and university teachers are not allowed to be transgender. I also waited until my father passed away so that it would be easier on my family when I made the transition.

How has your family handled the transition? Well, contrary to what some tourists believe, no family particularly *wants* a transgender child, even a family with only boys. Some of my close friends no longer speak to their families. My mother was always very comforting. A month before my operation she told me 'you will always be my child, but never lie to anyone about who you are – accept who you are'. I have two adopted sons who are now quite grown-up, and after I made the change, they bought me presents on Mother's Day instead of Father's Day – I thought that was very sweet. My father on the other hand was never very supportive. When he found I was sleeping with men, he…well…let's put it this way, he practised his *moo·ay thai* boxing on me.

What was the first thing that passed through your mind when you woke up after the operation? How has life been since the operation? I woke up with a big smile. Life is great. I am happy that I can be on the outside what I am on the inside – I can stop feeling sad every time I look down! Finding a job after my surgery was hard. I wrote on my CV 'transgender post-op' so that there would be no surprises in the interview, but I never heard back from any companies. Oh, actually one company asked me to come for an interview, but they spent the meeting asking me inappropriate questions about my personal life. It was very disheartening. I finally found a queer-friendly company, where I am employed as a hospitality software implementer, meaning that I go around to hotels around Thailand and teach front-desk staff how to use the hotel's computer system. I adore my job.

Now that my surgery is far behind me, I have to take female hormones regularly until I die. I take a pill twice per week, but some male-to-females take one injection per month (I hate needles). Some people have a bad reaction to the medication at first. I have had friends that got a lot of pimples and got really fat. Sometimes it takes a while before you find the right amount of hormones. Besides the hormones, there is a certain amount of…maintenance…that needs to take place in order to keep my new parts working. Put it this way, when you get your ears pierced, if you don't regularly wear earrings…well… Anyways, my aunt, who moved to the United States, asked me if I wanted to move too, but I am happy in Thailand. Even though transgender individuals don't have a lot of rights, I'm not convinced that it is that much better anywhere else.

And finally, what do you feel is the biggest misconception about gàteui in Thailand? This is an easy question. The biggest misconception is that we are all promiscuous whores and liars. Like any human being, we are just looking for love. It is true that many ladyboys do try to trick the people around them, but this is because they are afraid of being rejected for who they really are. Also, many of them lie because they desperately want to be real women, but they will never be real women. I know that – that's why I always show the real me – I am comfortable with who I am. I wish everyone else would be too.

For more information about ladyboys in Thailand, visit www.thailadyboyz.net (although the site is currently in Thai only). As told to Brandon Presser.

leave either from the Na Thon, Mae Nam or Big Buddha piers and take from 20 minutes to one hour (220B to 450B). On Ko Pha-Ngan there are two piers (Hat Rin and Thong Sala). The boats departing from Big Buddha service Hat Rin, and the other boats alight at Thong Sala. Ferries from Mae Nam slide up Ko Pha-Ngan's remote eastern coast. From the same piers, there are also around six daily departures between Samui and Ko Tao. These take 1¼ to 2½ hours and cost 350B to 600B.

Car ferries from Don Sak and Khanom land at Thong Yang, about 10km south of Na Thon. There are no car ferries from Samui to Ko Pha-Ngan or Ko Tao.

BUS & TRAIN

A bus/ferry combo is more convenient than a train/ferry package for getting to Ko Samui because you don't have to switch transportation in Phun Phin (a tiny town near Surat Thani). However, the trains are much more comfortable and spacious – especially at night. If you prefer the train, you can get off at Chumphon and catch the Lomprayah catamaran service the rest of the way. See p252 for more details.

Getting Around

See p198 for the dangers and annoyances concerning transportation around the island. You can rent motorcycles (and bicycles) from almost every resort on the island. The going rate is 200B per day, but for longer periods try to negotiate a better rate.

Sŏrng·tăa·ou drivers love to try to overcharge you, so it's always best to ask a third party for current rates, as they can change with the season. These vehicles run regularly during daylight hours only. It's about 30B to travel along one coast, and no more than 75B to travel halfway across the island. Figure about 20B for a five-minute ride on a motorcycle taxi.

TO/FROM THE AIRPORT

Taxi service on Samui is quite chaotic and prices can vary greatly depending on your driver's mood. Ask your resort about complimentary airport transfers or try the **Samui Shuttle** (www.samuishuttle.com). Taxis typically charge 300B to 500B for airport transfer. Some Chaweng travel agencies arrange minibus taxis for less.

KO PHA-NGAN
เกาะพะงัน
pop 12,100

In the family of southern gulf islands, Ko Pha-Ngan sits in the crystal sea between Ko Samui, it's business-savvy older brother, and little Ko Tao, the spunky younger brother full of dive-centric energy. Ko Pha-Ngan is the slacker middle child; a chilled-out beach bum with tattered dreadlocks, a tattoo of a Chinese serenity symbol, and a penchant for white nights and bikini-clad pool parties.

But like any textbook teenager, this angst-ridden island can't decide what it wants to be when it grows up. Should the party personality persist or will the stunning and secluded northern beaches finally come out from under Hat Rin's shadow?

While Pha-Ngan's slacker vibe and reputation will no doubt dominate for years to come, the island is secretly starting to creep upmarket. Each year, tired old shacks are replaced by crisp modern abodes. In Hat Rin, you'll be hard-pressed to find a room on Sunrise Beach – home to the world-famous Full Moon Party (p218) – for less than 1000B. Soon, the phrase 'private infinity pool' and 'personal butler' will find a permanent place in the island's lexicon, replacing 'pass the dutch' and 'another whiskey bucket please'. But don't fret yet – the vast inland jungle continues to feel undiscovered, and there are still plenty of secluded bays to string up a hammock and watch the tide roll in.

Orientation

Ko Pha-Ngan is the fifth-largest island in Thailand, measuring 193 sq km. The town of Thong Sala is its administrative capital, Hat Rin is party central, and the fishing village in Chalok Lam, on the northern part of the island, is starting to come into its own as another commercial centre.

Most of the island's visitors stay on the thin peninsula known as Hat Rin. This mountainous cape is flanked by beaches on either side, and is home to the infamous Full Moon Parties held every month (p218). For a detailed layout of the area, see p222. The rest of the island is noticeably quieter, although gradual development has meant an increase in population on the west and south coasts. The northern coast has a few good beaches that have modern amenities but feel relaxed and remote. The quiet eastern shore is more deserted, but still offers a few great places to stay.

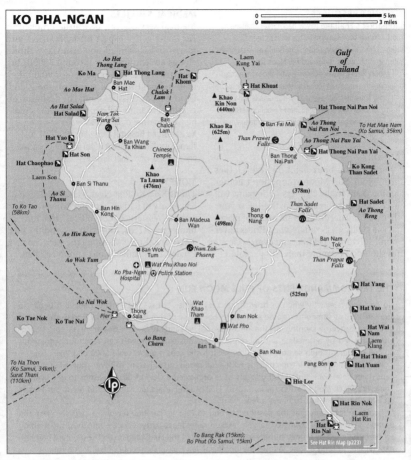

KO PHA-NGAN

About half of Ko Pha-Ngan's population lives in and around the small port of Thong Sala, where the ferries to and from Ko Tao, Surat Thani and Ko Samui dock. Samui-bound ferries also depart from Hat Rin.

Information

BOOKSHOPS

D's Books & Café (Map p223; ☎ 08 4667 7730) Tucked away just off the main drag, D's is almost a carbon-copy of the successful bookshop-cum-cafe on Ko Phi-Phi. Sit in the chill courtyard with an iced coffee while catching up on your holiday reading.

EMERGENCY

Main police station (Map p217; ☎ 0 7737 7114, 191) Located about 2km north of Thong Sala. The police station in Hat Rin (near Hat Rin school) will not let you file a report; to do so you must go to Thong Sala. Local police have been known to charge 200B to file a report. Do not pay this – it should be free. Note that if you are arrested you do have the right to an embassy phone call; you do not have to agree to accept the 'interpreter' you are offered.

INTERNET ACCESS

Hat Rin and Thong Sala are the main centres of internet activity, but every beach with development now offers access. Rates are generally 2B per minute, with a 10B to 20B minimum and discounts if you stay on for more than an hour. Places offering a rate of 1B per minute usually have turtle-speed connections.

INTERNET RESOURCES

Backpacker's Thailand (www.backpackersthailand .com) A handy site managed by the island's friendly Backpacker's Information Centre. Offers info on local news, transportation, water sports and Full Moon fun.

Full Moon Party (www.fullmoonpartykohphangan.com) An informative site about the ubiquitous Full Moon Party, with party schedules, hotel listings, venue details and videos.

Phangan Info (www.phangan.info) An online version of the helpful island pamphlet available at most bungalows and the Thong Sala pier.

LAUNDRY

If you got neon body paint on your clothes during your Full Moon romp, don't bother sending them to the cleaners – the paint will never come out. Trust us, we tried. For your other washing needs, there are heaps of places that will gladly wash your clothes. Prices hover around 30B to 40B per kilo, and express cleanings shouldn't be more than 60B per kilo.

MEDICAL SERVICES

Medical services can be a little crooked in Ko Pha-Ngan – expect unstable prices and many underqualified doctors. Many clinics charge an 'entrance fee' (around 3000B) before treatment – see opposite for vital information about medical scams on the island. Serious medical issues should be dealt with on nearby Ko Samui. All dental problems should be treated on Ko Samui as well.

Ko Pha-Ngan Hospital (Map p217; ☎ 0 7737 7034; Thong Sala; ⏱ 24hr) About 2.5km north of Thong Sala, offers 24-hour emergency services.

MONEY

Thong Sala, Ko Pha-Ngan's financial 'capital', has plenty of banks, currency converters and several Western Union offices. Hat Rin has numerous ATMs, especially around the pier. There are also ATMs along the west coast, in Chalok Lam, and around Thong Nai Pan.

THE TEN COMMANDMENTS OF FULL MOON FUN

No one knows exactly when or how these crazy parties got started – many believe it began in 1987 or 1988 as someone's 'going away party', but none of that is relevant now. Today, thousands of bodies converge monthly on the kerosene-soaked sands of Sunrise Beach for an epic trance-a-thon fuelled by adrenaline and a couple other substances. Crowds can reach an outrageous 40,000 partiers in high season, while low season still sees a respectable 5000 pilgrims.

If you can't make your trip coincide with a full moon but still want to cover yourself in fluorescent paint, fear not – enterprising locals have organised a slew of other reasons to get sloshed. There are Black Moon Parties (at Ban Khai), Half Moon Parties (at Ban Tai) and Moon-set Parties (at Hat Chaophao) just to name a few.

Some critics claim that the party is starting to lose its carefree flavour, especially since the island's government is trying to charge a 100B entrance fee to partygoers. Despite the disheartening schemes hatched by money-hungry locals, the night of the Full Moon is still the ultimate partying experience, so long as one follows the unofficial Ten Commandments of Full Moon fun:

- Thou shalt arrive in Hat Rin at least three days early to nail down accommodation during the pre–Full Moon rush of backpackers. See p222 for information about sleeping in Hat Rin.
- Thou shalt double-check the party dates as sometimes they coincide with Buddhist holidays and are rescheduled.
- Thou shalt secure all valuables, especially when staying in budget bungalows.
- Thou shalt savour some delicious fried fare in Chicken Corner before the revelry begins.
- Thou shalt wear protective shoes during the sandy celebration, unless ye want a tetanus shot.
- Thou shalt cover thyself with swirling patterns of neon body paint.
- Thou shalt visit Magic Mountain or The Rock for killer views of the heathens below.
- Thou shalt not sample the drug buffet, nor shalt thou swim in the ocean under the influence of alcohol.
- Thou shalt stay in a group of two or more people, especially women, and especially when returning home at the end of the evening.
- Thou shalt party until the sun comes up and have a great time.

POST

The **main office** (Thong Sala; ⌚ 8.30am-4.30pm Mon-Fri, 9am-noon Sat) offers reliable service. There's a smaller satellite office right at the pier in Hat Rin with similar hours of operation.

TOURIST INFORMATION

There are no government-run TAT offices on Ko Pha-Ngan, instead tourists get their information from local travel agencies and brochures. Most agencies are clumped around Hat Rin and Thong Sala. Agents take a small commission on each sale, but collusion keeps prices relatively stable and standardised. Choose an agent you trust if you are spending a lot of money – faulty bookings do happen on Ko Pha-Ngan, especially since the island does not have a unit of tourist police.

Several mini-magazines also offer comprehensive information about the island's accommodation, restaurants, activities and Full Moon Parties. Our favourite option is the pocket-sized **Phangan Info** (www.phangan .info).

The friendly **Backpacker's Information Centre** (Map p223; ☎ 0 7737 5535; www.backpackersthailand.com; Hat Rin) is the perfect resource for travellers looking to book transportation and tours (water sports, diving, live-aboards, jungle safaris etc). Not just for backpackers, it's an expat-run travel agency that offers piece of mind with every purchase. They also run the Crystal Dive shop next door.

Dangers & Annoyances

Some of your fondest vacation memories may be forged on Ko Pha-Ngan; just be mindful of the following situations that can seriously tarnish your experience on this hot-blooded jungle island. For information directly related to the Full Moon Party, see opposite, but don't forget to read-up on the following points as well.

MOTORCYCLES & JET SKIS

Fatal crashes, scarring injuries and broken bones – these days it seems like everyone has a horror story to tell regarding motorbikes. In fact, Ko Pha-Ngan has more motorcycle accidents than injuries incurred from Full Moon tomfoolery. Nowadays there's a system of paved roads, but much of it is still a labyrinth of rutty dirt-and-mud paths. The island is also very hilly, and even if the road is paved, it can be too difficult for most to

take on. The *very* steep road to Hat Rin is a perfect case in point. Too many injuries (and outrageous motorcycle damage fees) result from drivers being too proud to turn around and hail a taxi instead.

Hospitals and clinics around the island actually offer a commission to the locals that bring injured travellers in for treatment! Once you're inside, nurses (some lowly trained) tend to your injuries with astronomically priced equipment and procedures. Injuries have become so widespread on the island that locals are closing down their travel agencies to reopen as chemists!

The threat of bodily harm isn't as great with jet skis; the main danger here is a scam where local outfitters try to fleece tourists for 'damage fees' (sometimes as high as 50,000B!) This practice is now very common and widespread on the island; we know of several reputable operators who now refuse to deal with jet skis altogether. We strongly suggest you do not rent one.

DRUGS & ALCOHOL

You're relaxing on the beach when suddenly a local walks up and offers you some local herb at a ridiculously low price. 'No thanks', you say, knowing that the penalties for drug-use in Thailand are fierce. But the vender drops his price even more and practically offers you the weed for free. Too good to be true? Obviously. As soon as you take a toke, the seller rats you out to the cops and you're whisked away to the local prison. By paying a wallet-busting fine you might avoid a lengthy trial. This type of scenario happens all the time on Ko Pha-Ngan so it's best to avoid the call of the ganja.

Here's another important thing to remember: your travel insurance does not cover any drug-related injury or treatment. Drug-related freak-outs *do* happen – we've heard firsthand accounts of partiers slipping into extended periods of delirium.

Although the consumption of alcohol isn't a one-way ticket to the slammer, excess drinking is easily the biggest problem on the island (especially in Hat Rin). There's a reason why the 'buckets' of booze are so cheap: as a general rule, if your server doesn't explicitly show you that they're cracking open a new bottle of spirits, then you should assume that you are drinking bathtub gin or moonshine. Most travellers complain about stunning hangovers (which is partially due to the sweaty tropical climate), but we've received reports that more potent mixtures have caused blackouts and memory loss similar to the effects of rohypnol (commonly known as the 'date rape' drug). Excess drinking is responsible for dozens of avoidable accidents – even death (drowning or motorbike collisions) – each month, and these situations are by no means limited to Full Moon shenanigans.

FIRE SHOWS

The clichéd fire shows that light up oh-so many beaches around Thailand are taken to the next level in Hat Rin. Over the last few years a couple of the beach bars have started to include tourists in the nightly fire routines. A popular game is 'fire jump rope' where travellers get to skip over a blazing string as it zips by. Severe burns are not uncommon, and they take *forever* to heal in a sweltering tropical environment. Although the lure of a free bucket might almost be too tempting to pass up, we highly recommend against playing any of these risky games.

WOMEN'S SAFETY

Female travellers should be extra careful when partying on the island. We've received many reports about drug- and alcohol-related sexual assault (once again, these situations are not limited to Full Moon Parties). Another disturbing problem is the unscrupulous behaviour of some of the local motorcycle-taxi drivers. Several complaints have been filed about drivers groping female passengers.

Sights

For those who tire of beach-bumming, this large jungle island has many natural features to explore including mountains, waterfalls and, most importantly, some of the most spectacular beaches in all of Thailand.

BEACHES & WATERFALLS

There are many **waterfalls** throughout the island's interior, four of which gush throughout the year. **Than Sadet** features boulders carved with the royal insignia of Rama V, Rama VII and Rama IX. King Rama V enjoyed this hidden spot so much that he returned over a dozen times between 1888 and 1909. The river waters of Khlong Than Sadet are now considered sacred and used in royal ceremonies. Also near the eastern coast, **Than Prawet**

is a series of chutes that snake inland for approximately 2km.

In the centre of the island, **Nam Tok Phaeng** is protected by a national park; this waterfall is a pleasant reward after a short-but-rough hike. Continue the adventure and head up to **Khao Ra**, the highest mountain on the island at 625m. Those with eagle-eyes will spot wild crocodiles, monkeys, snakes, deer and boar along the way, and the **viewpoint** from the top is spectacular – on a clear day you can see Ko Tao. Although the trek isn't arduous, it is very easy to lose one's way, and we *highly* recommend hiring an escort in Ban Madeua Wan (near the falls). The local guides have crude signs posted in front of their homes, and, if they're around, they'll take you up to the top for 500B. Most of them only speak Thai.

Pha-Ngan's stunning **beaches** are definitely worth visiting, however caution should also be exercised for those travelling on foot. The 'Green Dot' trail from Hat Rin to Hat Yuan is overgrown, as is most of the route between Chalok Lam and Hat Khuat (Bottle Beach). Save yourself the strife and charter a water taxi.

Hat Khuat, also called Bottle Beach, is a classic fave. Visitors flock to this shore for a relaxing day of swimming and snorkelling – some opt to stay the night at one of the several bungalow operations along the beach. For additional seclusion, try the isolated beaches on the east coast, which include **Hat Sadet**, **Hat Yuan**, **Hat Thian**, and the teeny **Ao Thong Reng**. For additional enchanting beaches, consider doing a day trip to the stunning **Ang Thong Marine Park** (p248).

WÁT

Remember to change out of your beach clothes when visiting one of the 20 wát on Ko Pha-Ngan. Most temples are open during daylight hours.

The oldest temple on the island is **Wat Phu Khao Noi**, near the hospital in Thong Sala. While the site is open to visitors throughout the day, the monks are only around in the morning. **Wat Pho**, near Ban Tai, has an **herbal sauna** (admission 50B; ☎ 3-6pm) accented with natural lemon grass. The **Chinese Temple** is known to give visitors good luck. It was constructed about 20 years ago after a visiting woman had a vision of the Chinese Buddha who instructed her to build a fire-light for the island. **Wat Khao Tham**, also near Ban Tai, sits high on a hill and has resident female monks. At the temple there is a bulletin board detailing a meditation retreat taught by an American-Australian couple. For additional information, write in advance to Wat Khao Tham, PO Box 8, Ko Pha-Ngan, Surat Thani 84280.

Activities
DIVING & SNORKELLING
With Ko Tao, the high-energy diving behemoth, just a few kilometres away, Ko Pha-Ngan enjoys a much quieter, more laidback diving scene focused on fun diving rather than certifications. A recent drop in Open Water certification prices has made local prices competitive with Ko Tao next door. Group sizes tend to be smaller on Ko Pha-Ngan since the island has less divers in general. Like the other islands in the Samui Archipelago, Pha-Ngan has several small reefs dispersed around the island. The clear favourite snorkelling spot is **Ko Ma**, a small island in the northwest connected to Ko Pha-Ngan by a charming sandbar. There are also some rock reefs of interest on the eastern side of the island.

A major perk of diving from Ko Pha-Ngan is the proximity to **Sail Rock** (Hin Bai), the best dive site in the Gulf of Thailand and a veritable beacon for whale sharks. This large pinnacle lies about 14km north of the island. An abundance of corals and large tropical fish can be seen at depths of 10m to 30m, and there's a rocky vertical swim-through called 'The Chimney'.

Dive shops on Ko Tao sometimes visit Sail Rock, however the focus tends to be more on swallow reefs (for newbie divers) and the shark-infested waters at Chumphon Pinnacle. The most popular trips departing from Ko Pha-Ngan are three-site day trips which stop at Chumphon Pinnacle, Sail Rock and one of the other premiere sites in the area (see p238). These three-stop trips cost around 3650B to 3800B and include a full lunch. Two-dive trips to Sail Rock will set you back around 2350B to 2500B.

The following list features the top dive operators on the island:

Haad Yao Divers (☎ 08 6279 3085; www.haadyao divers.com) Established in 1997, this dive operator has garnered a strong reputation by maintaining European standards of safety and customer service.

Lotus Diving (☎ 0 7737 4142; www.lotusdiving.net) This well-reputed dive centre has top-notch instructors, and owns not one, but two beautiful boats (that's two more vessels than most of the other operations on Ko Pha-Ngan). Trips can be booked at their office in Chalok Lam, or at the Backpacker's Information Centre (p217). Recommended.

Reefers (☎ 08 6471 4045, 08 7894 0637; www.reefers diving.com) Based at Shiralea (p227), Reefers is a new dive school on the island. Vic and Kim, the owners, are wonderfully chill, not to mention top-notch and professional instructors. Recommended.

Sail Rock Divers (☎ 0 7737 4321; www.sailrockdivers resort.com) The responsible and friendly staff at Sail Rock satisfies customers at their purpose-built facility, featuring air-con classrooms and a small wading pool.

OTHER WATER SPORTS
The staff at Backpacker's Information Centre (p219) has their finger on the pulse when it comes to water sports.

Jamie passes along his infinite wakeboarding wisdom to eager wannabes at **Wake Up** (☎ 08 7283 6755, 08 0039 6353; www.wakeupwakeboarding .com; ⊙ Jan-Oct), his small water-sports school in Chalok Lam. Fifteen minutes of 'air-time' will set you back 1500B (or 500B for 'two rounds of the bay'), which is excellent value considering you get one-on-one instruction. Kite-boarding, wake-skating and water-skiing sessions are also available, as are 'round-the-island' daytrips (2000B per person; six-person quorum needed).

Located at Holiday Beach Resort in Ao Bang Charu, **Cuttlebone Kiteboarding Centre** (☎ 08 1940 1902; www.cuttlebone.net; ⊙ Nov-Apr) offers top-notch private lessons for those interested in taking on the arduous sport of kiteboarding. Pascal, the all-star owner and main instructor, does his darnedest to make sure that all of his students 'catch the wind'.

Avoid renting jet skis – see p219 for details.

YOGA & WELLNESS
Serious yogaholics should head to Ko Samui, but if you're keen on sticking around, try the Sanctuary (p229) on the island's east coast.

Inexpensive massage stalls are set up in various spots along the west coast and around Hat Rin. You needn't look too hard as you'll undoubtedly hear the nasal 'massaaaaaaaaaaaage' catcalls from work-hungry locals. Figure around 300B for one hour of pummelling. Beware of indoor 'spas' around Hat Rin that offer shady 'happy endings'.

Tours

The exceedingly popular **Eco Nature Tour** (☎ 08 4850 6273) offers a 'best of' island trip, which includes elephant trekking, snorkelling, and a visit to the Chinese temple, a stunning viewpoint and Nam Tok Phaeng. The daytrip, which costs 1400B, departs at 9am and returns around 3pm. Eco Nature Tour also offers half-day boat trips for a similar price. Bookings can be made at their office in Thong Sala or at the Backpacker's Information Centre (p219). **Pha-Ngan Safari** (☎ 0 7737 4159, 08 1895 3783) offers a similar trip for 1900B.

Hiking and snorkelling daytrips to Ang Thong Marine Park (p248) generally depart from Ko Samui, but recently tour operators are starting to shuttle tourists from Ko Pha-Ngan as well. **Grand Sea Discovery** (☎ 0 7742 7001; www.grandseatours.com; daytrip 2100B) offers day-long trips to the marine park, which includes snorkelling, kayaking and a buffet lunch. Ask at your accommodation for details about additional boat trips as companies often come and go due to unstable petrol prices. Note that the marine park is closed from October until Christmas.

For all other around-island boat tour bookings – like 'Snoop Dogg' or 'Munchies' (figure around 700B for a half-day trip) – stop by Backpacker's Information Centre in Hat Rin.

Sleeping

Ko Pha-Ngan's legendary history of laid-back revelry has solidified its reputation as *the* stomping ground for the gritty backpacker lifestyle. Recently, however, the island is starting to see a shift towards a more upmarket clientele. Many local mainstays have collapsed their bamboo huts and constructed newer, sleeker accommodation aimed at the ever-growing legion of 'flashpackers'.

On other parts of the island, new tracts of land are being cleared for Samui-esque five-star resorts. But backpackers fear not; it'll still be many years before the castaway lifestyle goes the way of the dodo. For now, Ko Pha-Ngan can revel in its three distinct classes of lodging: pinch-a-penny shacks, trendy midrange hangouts, and blow-the-bank luxury.

Hat Rin sees an exorbitant amount of visitors relative to the rest of the island. Party pilgrims flock to this picturesque peninsula for the legendary festivities, and although most of them sleep through the daylight hours, the setting remains quite picturesque despite the errant beer bottle in the sand. The southern part of Sunrise Beach is starting to reek of kerosene due to the nightly fire-related shenanigans at Drop-In Bar – needless to say it's best to sunbathe at the quieter northern part of the sand.

Pha-Ngan also caters to a subculture of seclusion-seekers who crave a deserted slice of sand. The northern and eastern coasts offer just that – a place to escape.

The following sleeping options are organised into five sections: we start in Hat Rin, move along the southern coast, head up the west side, across the northern beaches and down the quiet eastern shore.

HAT RIN

The thin peninsula of Hat Rin features three separate beaches. Hat Rin Nok (Sunrise Beach) is the epicentre of Full Moon tomfoolery, Hat Rin Nai (Sunset Beach) is the less impressive stretch of sand on the far side of the tiny promontory, and Hat Seekantang (also known as Hat Leela), just south of Hat Rin Nai, is a smaller, more private beach. The three beaches are linked by Ban Hat Rin (Hat Rin Town) – a small inland collection of restaurants and bars.

Needless to say, the prices listed below are meaningless during periods of maximum lunar orbicularity. Also, during Full Moon events, bungalow operations expect you to stay for a minimum number of days. If you plan to arrive the day of the party (or even the day before), we strongly suggest booking a room in advance, or else you'll probably have to sleep on the beach (which you might end up doing anyway). Full Mooners can also stay on Samui and take one of the hourly speedboat shuttles (from 550B) to access the festivities.

Budget

Sea Garden (Map p223; ☎ 0 7737 5281; www.seagarden _resort.com; Ban Hat Rin; r 200-1500B; 🞲) A campus of bungalows and motel-style accommodation, Sea Garden has a variety of rooms for every budget (although have a look at a few different room types before hanging your hat). Go for the dingy, closet-sized digs if you're just looking for a place to drop your bags during the Full Moon fun – make sure you secure your values.

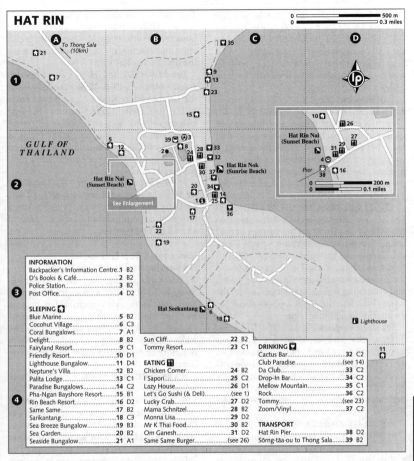

HAT RIN

INFORMATION
Backpacker's Information Centre..1	B2
D's Books & Café.................................2	B2
Police Station...................................3	B2
Post Office..4	D2

SLEEPING
Blue Marine......................................5	B2
Cocohut Village................................6	C3
Coral Bungalows.............................7	A1
Delight..8	B2
Fairyland Resort..............................9	C1
Friendly Resort..............................10	D1
Lighthouse Bungalow...................11	D4
Neptune's Villa..............................12	B2
Palita Lodge...................................13	C1
Paradise Bungalows......................14	C2
Pha-Ngan Bayshore Resort..........15	B1
Rin Beach Resort...........................16	D2
Same Same......................................17	B2
Sarikantang....................................18	C3
Sea Breeze Bungalow....................19	B3
Sea Garden.....................................20	B2
Seaside Bungalow.........................21	A1
Sun Cliff...22	B2
Tommy Resort................................23	C1

EATING
Chicken Corner..............................24	B2
I Sapori..25	C2
Lazy House.....................................26	D1
Let's Go Sushi (& Deli)............(see 1)	
Lucky Crab.....................................27	D2
Mama Schnitzel.............................28	B2
Monna Lisa....................................29	D2
Mr K Thai Food..............................30	D2
Om Ganesh....................................31	D2
Same Same Burger...................(see 26)	

DRINKING
Cactus Bar......................................32	C2
Club Paradise...........................(see 14)	
Da Club...33	C2
Drop-In Bar....................................34	C2
Mellow Mountain..........................35	C1
Rock..36	C2
Tommy.......................................(see 23)	
Zoom/Vinyl.....................................37	C2

TRANSPORT
Hat Rin Pier....................................38	D2
Sŏrng·tǎa·ou to Thong Sala.......39	B2

Paradise Bungalows (Map p223; ☎ 0 7737 5244; Hat Rin Nok; bungalows 250-1200B; ⚡) The world-famous Full Moon Party was hatched at this scruffy batch of bungalows, and the place has been living on its name fame ever since. The backpackers keep on coming to wax nostalgic, although the grounds are starting to look more like a junkyard than a resort and new construction (including a bizarre roof-slide) is making it even more frenetic. Paradise lost.

Sun Cliff (Map p223; ☎ 0 7737 5134; Hat Rin Nai; bungalows 250-2000B; ⚡) Perched on a palm-studded knoll, Sun Cliff overlooks the sea and basks in the tropical sun amid huge boulders and rolling vegetation. Each bungalow is a completely different species; some are dipped in pastels, others embody the quintessential island hut.

Seaside Bungalow (Map p223; ☎ 08 6940 3410, 08 7266 7567; Hat Rin Nai; bungalows 300-600B; ⚡) Seaside sees loads of loyal customers who return for the mellow atmosphere, cheap drinks, free pool table, and comfy wooden bungalows staggered along Sunset Beach. At 500B, we're pretty sure that these huts are the cheapest air-con rooms on the island.

Lighthouse Bungalow (Map p223; ☎ 0 7737 5075; Hat Seekantang; bungalows 350-800B) Hidden at the far end of Hat Rin, this low-key collection of humble huts gathers along a sloping terrain punctuated by towering palms. To access this secluded resort, walk through Leela Beach Bungalows (don't bother stopping) and follow the wooden boardwalk as it curves to the left (southeast) around the sea-swept boulders.

Same Same (Map p223; ☎ 0 7737 5200; www.same -same.com; Ban Hat Rin; r 500-800B; 🖸) Although still a sociable spot for Scandinavians during the Full Moon madness, Same Same is but a faint flicker of what it used to be. The no-frills motel rooms upstairs continuously get bad reviews from our readers.

Coral Bungalows (Map p223; ☎ 0 7737 5023; www.coral haadrin.com; Hat Rin Nai; bungalows 500-800B; 🖸 🖵 🖭) This party-centric paradise has firmly planted its flag in 'Backpackerland' as the go-to spot for a booze-addled rompfest. By day, sun-worshippers straddle beachside chaises. Then, by night, like a vampire, Coral transforms into a sinister pool party machine fuelled by one too many vodka Red Bulls.

our pick **Sarikantang** (Map p223; ☎ 0 7737 5055, 08 1444 1322; www.sarikantang.com; Hat Seekantang; bungalows 500-3500B; 🖸 🖭) Don't get too strung out over trying to pronounce the resort's name – you can simply call this place 'heaven'. Cream-coloured cabins, framed with teak posts and lintels, are sprinkled among swaying palms and crumbling winged statuettes. Inside, the rooms look like the set of a photo shoot for an interior design magazine.

Sea Breeze Bungalow (Map p223; ☎ 0 7737 5162; Ban Hat Rin; bungalows 500-8000B; 🖸 🖭) Sea Breeze gets a good report card from our readers, and we agree; the labyrinth of secluded hillside cottages is an ideal hammocked retreat for any type of traveller. Several bungalows, poised high on stilts, deliver stunning views of Hat Rin and the sea.

Neptune's Villa (Map p223; ☎ 0 7737 5251; Hat Rin Nai; r from 600B; 🖸) An old favourite among travellers, Neptune's is an ever-expanding spot with a mixed bag of accommodation spread across several motel-style units.

Blue Marine (Map p223; ☎ 0 7737 5079; Hat Rin Nai; bungalows 600-1200B; 🖸) The shimmering blue-tiled roofs act like a beacon luring in curious backpackers in search of a good deal, and most of them stay since the cheery interiors are usually well kept. Try to nab a concrete cottage closer to the beach as a few affiliated bungalows have sprung up on the far side of the rutty road.

Cocohut Village (Map p223; ☎ 0 7737 5368; www .cocohut.com; Hat Seekantang; r 600B, bungalows 1900-10,000B; 🖸 🖵 📶 🖭) This super-social place is the unofficial gathering spot for vacationing Israelis. In fact, Cocohut is so happenin' that guests might forget that they are just up the street from the brouhaha on Sunrise Beach.

The backpacker digs, with shared locker-room-styled toilets, are slightly sub-par, however the pricier options, such as the cliff villas and beachfront bungalows, are some of the best bets in Hat Rin.

Delight (Map p223; ☎ 0 7737 5527; www.delightresort .com; Ban Hat Rin; r 700-2000B; 🖸 🖭) Tucked behind the bright yellow Kodak sign in the centre of Hat Rin, Delight offers some of the best lodging around. Spic-and-span hotel rooms come with subtle designer details (such as peacock murals) and are sandwiched between an inviting swimming pool and a lazy lagoon peppered with lily pads.

Friendly Resort (Map p223; ☎ 0 7737 5167; Hat Rin Nai; friendly_resort@hotmail.com; r from 800B; 🖸 🖭) Looking out over the pier, Friendly has a tangle of accommodation wrapped around a small central pool.

Midrange & Top End

Pha-Ngan Bayshore Resort (Map p223; ☎ 0 7737 5227, 0 7737 5224; www.phanganbayshore.com; Hat Rin Nok; r 800-5000B; 🖸 🖵 🖭) After a much-needed overhaul, this hotel-style operation has primed itself for the ever-increasing influx of flash-packers in Hat Rin. Sweeping beach views and a giant swimming pool make Pha-Ngan Bayshore one of the top addresses on Sunrise Beach.

Rin Beach Resort (Map p223; ☎ 0 7737 5112; www .kohphanganrinbeach.com; Hat Rin Nai; bungalows 1000-3000B; 🖸 🖭) Giant amphorae, spewing forth gushes of water, welcome weary travellers as they tumble off the wooden ferry. Cottages are bright and airy with dark cherry wood accents and colourful sutra paintings. The enormous flower-shaped pool is a booby trap for sun-seekers.

Fairyland Resort (Map p223; ☎ 0 7737 5076, 08 5057 1709; www.haadrinfairyland.com; Hat Rin Nok; bungalows from 1400B; 🖸) Although the name sounds like a board game for six-year-old girls, these prim bungalows are serious competition for the older resorts on Sunrise Beach. Walk-ins might be lucky enough to score a 60% discount depending on the time of the month and year – be sure to ask the other vacationers how much they're paying before you decide to check in.

Palita Lodge (Map p223; ☎ 0 7737 5172; www.pali talodge.com; Hat Rin Nok; bungalows 1500-4500B; 🖸 🖭) Smack in the heart of the action, Palita is a tribute to the never-ending party that is Hat Rin's Sunrise Beach. Spacious concrete bungalows, with wooden accents and modern design elements, are neatly pressed together on this beachy wedge of sand and shrubs. Week-long bookings are a must during Full Moon revelry.

Tommy Resort (Map p223; ☎ 0 7737 5215; www .phangantommyresort.com; Hat Rin Nok; r 1800-2200B; 🗶 🖳 🖳) Tommy is a trendy address in the heart of Hat Rin, striking a good balance between chic boutique and carefree backpacker hangout. The rectangular swimming pool changes things up, since every other artificial body of water on the island looks like it was manufactured at the kidney-shaped pool factory.

SOUTHERN BEACHES

The accommodation along the southern coast is the best bang for your baht on Ko Pha-Ngan. There are fleeting views of the islands in the Ang Thong Marine Park; however, the southern beaches don't have the postcard-worthy crystal waters you might be longing for. This section starts at the port in Thong Sala and follows the coast east towards Hat Rin.

Thong Sala

There's really no reason to stay in Thong Sala, unless you're paranoid about missing a morning ferry, or feeling ill and seeking medical attention nearby.

Bua Kao Inn (☎ 0 7723 7226; buakao@samart.co.th; s & d from 450-850B; 🗶) If you're looking for a town vibe rather than a strip of sand, Bua Kao is your best bet. The beds are comfy and the rooms are well kept (although some have the faint smell of cigarette smoke) and the restaurant downstairs teems with chatty expats.

Pha-Ngan Chai Hotel (☎ 0 7737 7068, 0 7737 7286; r 700-1200B; 🗶 🖳) Think 'Soviet tenement meets tropical holiday' and you'll immediately spot this dowdy behemoth while landing at the Thong Sala pier. The convenient location is the hotel's best feature, although you'll need some cab fare to find a swimmable beach.

Ban Tai

The waters at Ban Tai tend to be shallow and opaque, especially during low season, but lodging options are well-priced compared to other parts of the island, and you're not too far from Hat Rin.

Chokana (☎ 0 7723 8085; bungalows 400-1200B; 🗶) Chokana is the Jabba the Hut of huts; these

wooden beachside bungalows are enormous. The bubbly owner genuinely cares about her clientele – the cabins have loads of personal touches such as wooden carvings and mosaics, and it feels as though all of the guests are repeat customers.

Coco Garden (☎ 0 7737 7721, 08 6073 1147; www .cocogardens.com; bungalows 500-1000B; 🗶 🛜) The best budget spot along the southern coast, Coco Garden one-ups the nearby resorts with well-manicured grounds and sparkling bungalows that are almost pathologically clean.

Holiday Resort (☎ 0 7737 7468; www.holiday beachresort.net; bungalows 800-1700B; 🗶) The owners aren't too fussed about landscaping, but the bungalows are kept very tidy – the best deals are the 900B bungalows (loaded with air-con and a TV) right along the water. There's a funky bar doused in fluorescent blues and greens, a couple of volleyball nets strung up, and a well-worn pool table hilariously positioned a mere 5m from the rolling tide.

Phangan Great Bay Resort (☎ 0 7723 8659; fax 0 7723 8697; bungalows 1250-2000B; 🗶 🖳 🖳) Take your pick from motel rooms housed in a mauve structure, or comfy bungalows further a field that also make use of ostentatious colours such as radioactive carrot and lime. Idle away the day trying to anthropomorphise the curious shape of the pool, or catch a movie on the TV in the restaurant.

Milky Bay Resort (☎ 0 7723 8566; www.milkybay .com; bungalows 1400-5000B; 🗶 🖳 🖳) Milky white walls, which permeate the grounds, are peppered with large black stones resembling the spots on a cow. These bovine bulwarks snake through the resort linking the airy, thatched bungalows to the sea.

B52 (www.b52-beach-resort-phangan.info; bungalows from 1800B; 🗶) Find your very own love shack at B52's campus of Thai-styled bungalows sporting plenty of thatch, polished concrete floors and rustic tropical tree trunks.

Ban Khai

Like Ban Tai, the beaches aren't the most stunning, but the accommodation is cheap and there are beautiful views of Ang Thong Marine Park in the distance.

Lee's Garden (☎ 08 5916 3852; bungalows 250-600B) If Lee's Garden had a soundtrack it would probably be Bob Marley's greatest hits. The clump of comfy wooden huts is a wonderful throwback to a time when Pha-Ngan attracted a grittier backpacker who wasn't fussed about hot showers or air-con.

Boom's Cafe Bungalows (☎ 0 7723 8318; www .boomscafe.com; bungalows 300-1000B; ⌘) Staying at Boom's is like visiting the Thai family you never knew you had. The friendly owners lovingly tend their sandy acreage and dote on the contented clientele. No one seems to mind that there's no swimming pool, since the curling tide rolls right up to your doorstep. Boom's is located at the far eastern corner of Ban Khai, near Hat Rin.

Mac Bay (☎ 0 7723 8443; bungalows 500-1500B; ⌘ ⌘) Home to the Black Moon Party (another lunar excuse for Ko Pha-Ngan to go wild), Mac Bay is a sandy slice of Ban Khai where even the cheaper bungalows are spic and span. At beer o'clock, grab a shaded spot on the sand and watch the sun dance amorphous shadows over the distant islands of Ang Thong Marine Park.

Morning Star (☎ 0 7737 7756; morningstarkpn@yahoo .com; bungalows 1190-2490B; ⌘ ⌘) This collection of wooden and concrete jungle cottages has spotless interiors; some rooms are furnished with noticeably ornate dressers and vanities, others have subtle dark-wood trimming. A dozen white wooden beach chairs orbit the adorable kidney-bean-shaped swimming pool.

WEST COAST BEACHES

The west coast has seen a lot of development in recent years, now that there's a smooth road between Thong Sala and Chalok Lam. The atmosphere is a pleasant mix between the east coast's quiet seclusion and Hat Rin's sociable vibe.

Ao Nai Wok to Si Thanu

Close to Thong Sala, the resorts peppered along this breezy strip mingle with patches of gnarled mangroves. Despite the lack of appealing beaches, the prices are cheap and the sunsets are memorable.

Loy Fa (☎ 0 7737 7319; loyfabungalow@yahoo.com; Ao Srithanu; bungalows 300-800B) Loy Fa scores high marks for its friendly, French-speaking Thai staff, charming gardens, and sturdy huts guarding sweeping ocean views. Modern bungalows tumble down the promontory onto an uber-private sliver of ash-coloured sand.

Cookies Bungalows (☎ 0 7737 7499; cookies_bunga low@hotmail.com; Ao Plaay Laem; bungalows 300-1000B; ⌘) A time warp back to the days of old Pha-Ngan,

Cookie's offers a standard-issue assemblage of bamboo, thatch and wooden slats.

Pimmada (☎ 0 7737 7325; Ao Plaay Laem; bungalows 400-800B; ⌘ ⌘) Next to Cookie's, Pimmada is a noticeable step up with newer digs and a welcoming pool tiled in deep green hues.

Beck's Resort (☎ 0 7737 7140; Ao Plaay Laem; bungalows 500-800B; ⌘) Just a 10-minute hop from Thong Sala, Beck's offers a gathering of prim white bungalows – it's a solid option for penny pinchers trying to avoid cab fare.

Sea Scene (☎ 0 7737 7516; www.seascene.com; Ao Plaay Laem; bungalows 500-1700B; ⌘) Sea Scene's family-sized bungalows are sprawled along a tangle of old mangroves and offer front-row seats to the blazing sunsets over Ang Thong Marine Park in the distance.

Chills Resort (☎ 08 9875 2100; www.chillsresort .com; Ao Srithanu; r from 1000B; ⌘ 🛜 ⌘) Set along a stunning secluded beach, Chills' cluster of delightfully simple-but-modern rooms all have peaceful ocean views letting in plenty of sunlight and sea breezes. The natural rock-pool perched along the breakers is the perfect place to swig an afternoon cocktail while watching the sunset.

Grand Sea Resort (☎ 0 7737 7777; www.grandsea resort.com; Ao Nai Wok; bungalows 1200-3000B; ⌘ ⌘) A good choice for those wanting a bit of sand close to Thong Sala, Grand Sea feels like a collection of wooden Thai spirit houses.

Hat Chaophao

Like Hat Yao up the coast, this rounded beach is lined with a variety of bungalow operations. There's an inland lake further south, and a 7-Eleven to cure your midnight munchies.

Sunset Cove (☎ 0 7734 9211; www.thaisunsetcove.com; bungalows 1500-3350B; ⌘ 🖵 ⌘) There's a feeling of Zen symmetry among the forested assortment of boutique bungalows; the towering bamboo shoots are evenly spaced along the cobbled paths weaving through brush and boulders. The beachside abodes are particularly elegant sporting slatted rectangular windows and barrel-basined bathtubs.

Pha-Ngan Paragon (☎ 08 4728 6064; www.phangan paragon.com; bungalows 2500-13,000B; ⌘ 🖵 🛜 ⌘) A tiny hideaway with seven rooms, Paragon's decor incorporates stylistic elements from the ancient Khmer, India and Thailand, without forfeiting any modern amenities. The 'royal bedroom' deserves a special mention – apparently the canopied bed has been imported from Kashmir.

Hat Yao & Hat Son

One of the busier beaches along the west coast, Hat Yao sports a swimmable beach, numerous resorts and a few extra services such as ATMs and convenience stores.

Ibiza (☎ 0 7734 9121; www.ibizabungalows.com; Hat Yao; bungalows 150-1300B; 🔀) Ibiza brings Hat Rin's youthful backpacker vibe up the west coast to Hat Yao. The no-frills bungalows are run of the mill, but the friendly staff members, appealing central garden, and cheap rates keep budget travellers coming back for more.

Tantawan Bungalows (☎ 0 7734 9108; www.tantawanbungalow.com; Hat Son; bungalows 450-550B; 🛋) Little Tantawan sits high up in the jungle like a tree house, boasting soaring sea views from the sprinkle of rugged bungalows. Guests can take a dip in the trapezoidal swimming pool or enjoy the sunrise on their small bamboo porches. Don't forget to try the tasty French and Thai dishes at the on-site restaurant.

our pick Shiralea (☎ 08 0719 9256; www.shiralea.com; Hat Yao; bungalows 500B; 🔀 🛜 🛋) Although this batch of fresh-faced poolside bungalows is not right on the beach (about 100m away), you'll be hard-pressed to find a better deal on the island. Reefers (p221) the on-site dive outfit offers world-class diving at your doorstep, and don't forget to ask the friendly owner where the name Shiralea comes from – we're pretty sure you'll quite surprised.

High Life (☎ 0 7734 9114; www.highlifebungalow.com; Hat Yao; bungalows 500-2000B; 🔀 🛜 🛋) We can't decide what's more conspicuous: the dramatic ocean views from the infinity-edged swimming pool, or the blatant double entendre in the resort's name. True to its moniker, the 25 bungalows, of various shapes and sizes, sit on a palmed outcropping of granite soaring high above the cerulean sea. Advance bookings will set you back an extra 200B.

Haad Son Resort (☎ 0 7734 9104; www.haadson.info; Hat Son; bungalows 1000-8000B; 🔀 🖳 🛜 🛋) The word 'complex' has a double meaning at this vast resort; we suggest leaving a trail of breadcrumbs along the serpentine paths if you ever want to find the way back to your room. The poshest rooms aren't worth the baht, so go for the budget digs; they're simple, but you'll have access to all of the on-site amenities.

Haad Yao Bay View Resort (☎ 0 7734 9193, 0 7734 9141; www.haadyao-bayviewresort.com; Hat Yao; r & bungalows 1500-5000B; 🔀 🖳 🛜 🛋) Sparkling after a facelift in 2008, this conglomeration of bungalows and hotel-style accommodation looks like a tropical mirage on Hat Yao's northern headland. Vacationers, in various states of undress, linger around the large turquoise swimming pool catching rays and Zs. Others nest in their private suites amid polished hardwood floors and wicker daybeds.

Haad Yao See Through Boutique Resort (☎ 0 7734 9315; www.haadyao.net; Hat Yao; r from 1750B; 🔀) After a slice of Hat Yao beach was cut up among brothers, 'See Through' came into existence along a thin tract of land. Rooms are decorated with a vibrant swatchbook of yellows, greens and reds, however the exterior – an imposing block of polished concrete – looks more like a construction site instead of boutique chic.

Hat Salad

One of the better beaches on the west coast, Hat Salad has a string of quality accommodation along the sand.

our pick Cookies Salad (☎ 0 7734 9125, 08 3181 7125; www.cookies-phangan.com; bungalows 1500-3000B; 🛋) The resort with a tasty name has delicious Balinese-styled bungalows orbiting a two-tiered lap pool tiled in various shades of blue. Shaggy thatching and dense tropical foliage gives the realm a certain rustic quality, although you won't want for creature comforts.

Green Papaya (☎ 0 7737 4182; www.greenpapayaresort.com; bungalows 4000-7500B; 🔀 🖳 🛋) The polished wooden bungalows at Green Papaya are a clear standout along the lovely beach at Hat Salad, however they come at quite a hefty price.

Ao Mae Hat

The northwest tip of the island has excellent ocean vistas, and little Ko Ma is connected to Pha-Ngan by a stunning sandbar.

Royal Orchid (☎ 0 7737 4182; royal_orchid_maehaad@hotmail.com; bungalows 300-800B; 🔀 🖳) Handsome backpacker bungalows are arranged like a zipper along a slender garden path – most have fleeting views of the serene beach and idyllic sandbar that extends to scenic Ko Ma offshore.

Pha-Ngan Utopia Resort (☎ 0 7737 4093; www.phanganutopia.com; bungalows 1500-3000B; 🔀 🖳 🛋) It's pretty audacious to name one's resort 'Utopia', but the owners have done an excellent job of creating an idyllic jungle retreat perched high above the sea. Our favourite rooms – the two-storey villas – slope down the mountainside and have an entire level dedicated to an extra-large spa bath.

NORTHERN BEACHES

Stretching from Chalok Lam to Thong Nai Pan, the dramatic northern coast is a wild jungle with several stunning and secluded beaches – it's the most scenic coast on the island.

Chalok Lam (Chaloklum) & Hat Khom

The cramped fishing village at Chalok Lam is like no other place on Ko Pha-Ngan. The conglomeration of teak shanties and huts is a palpable reminder that the wide-reaching hand of globalisation has yet to touch some parts of the world. Sŏrng·tăa·ou ply the route from here to Thong Sala for around 100B per person. There's a dirt road leading from Chalok Lam to Hat Khom, and water taxis are available as well (50B to 100B).

Coral Bay (☎ 0 7737 4245; Hat Khom; bungalows 150-600B) Perched on a small promontory separating Chalok Lam from Hat Khom, Coral Bay's seemingly secluded selection of classic backpacker digs can be easily accessed by road or water taxi from the heart of Chalok Lam.

Fanta (☎ 0 7737 4132; fantaphangan@yahoo.com; Chalok Lam; bungalows 300-700B) Not to be confused with Fantasea next-door, Fanta sits at the far eastern side of Chalok Lam and boasts rows of old-school Pha-Ngan bungalows (think lots of worn wood and thatch) on a sizeable chunk of sand.

Malibu (☎ 0 7737 4013; Chalok Lam; bungalows 300-1300B; 🐾) The casual vibe around the large backyard beach (over the lagoon bridge) sets Malibu apart from the other budget bungalows around Chalok Lam. A drink-wielding hut, stationed on the private sandbar, lures guests of every ilk. The cheapest huts are a bit rough around the edges, although the new round bungalow-like concoctions are overpriced.

Mandalai (☎ 0 7737 4316; www.mymandalai.com; Chalok Lam; r 2750-5600B; 🐾 🖥 🏊) Like an ash-white Riyadh from a distant Arabian land, this small boutique hotel quietly towers over the surrounding shantytown of fishermen's huts. Floor-to-ceiling windows command views of tangerine-coloured fishing boats in the bay, and there's an intimate wading pool hidden in the inner cloister.

Bottle Beach (Hat Khuat)

This isolated dune has garnered a reputation as a low-key getaway, and has thus become quite popular. During high season, places can fill up fast so it's best to try to arrive early. Grab a long-tail taxi boat from Chalok Lam for 50B to 120B (depending on the boat's occupancy).

Bottle Beach II (☎ 0 7744 5156; bungalows 350-400B) At the far eastern corner of the beach, this is the spot where penny pinchers can live out their castaway fantasies.

Smile (☎ 08 1956 3133; smilebeach@hotmail.com; bungalows 400-700B) At the far west corner of the beach, Smile features an assortment of wooden huts that climb up a forested hill. The two-storey bungalows (700B) are our favourite.

Haad Khuad Resort (☎ 0 7744 5153; r 1800-2200B; 🐾) Although significantly more expensive than the other sleeping spots on Bottle Beach, this small hotel is worth the splurge. The rooms are fastidiously clean and they all feature floor-to-ceiling windows that face the cerulean bay.

Thong Nai Pan

The pair of rounded bays at Thong Nai Pan looks a bit like buttocks; Ao Thong Nai Pan Yai (*yai* means 'big') is the southern half, and Ao Thong Nai Pan Noi (*noi* means 'little') curves just above. These beaches have been increasing in popularity over the last few years as a pleasant alternative to the raucous Hat Rin. See p233 for information on getting to Thong Nai Pan.

Dolphin (bungalows 500-1400B; 🐾) This hidden retreat gives yuppie travellers a chance to rough it in style, while granola-types will soak up every inch of the laidback charm. Quiet afternoons are spent lounging on the comfy cushions in one of the small pagodas hidden throughout the jungle. Lodging is only available on a first-come basis.

Starlight (☎ 0 7744 5026; bungalows from 500B; 🐾) A solid second choice if Dolphin is full, this streamer of cookie-cutter concrete accommodation swerves from the shoreline into the canopy of jungle ferns. Reception is in the supermarket next door.

Havana (☎ 0 7744 5162; www.phanganhavana.com; r 3000-4500B, ste 7000-8000; 🐾 🏊) One of the newer spots in Thong Nai Pan, Havana features psychedelic ocean-inspired murals in the rooms, which are arranged in apartment-style complexes around an inviting swimming pool.

Ra Sa Nan Da (☎ 0 7723 9555; www.rasananda.com; villas from 10,000B; 🐾 🖥 📶 🏊) Ra Sa Nan Da represents the future of Ko Pha-Ngan. This attempt at five-star luxury is a sweeping sandside property with a smattering of semi-detached villas – many bedecked with private plunge pools. A savvy mix of modern and traditional *săh·lah* styling prevails, although the staff are still working out the kinks of running a high-end operation on an undoubtedly laidback island.

EAST COAST BEACHES

Robinson Crusoe; eat your heart out. The east coast is the ultimate hermit hangout. For the most part, you'll have to hire a boat to get to these beaches, but water taxis are available in Thong Sala and Hat Rin. Some of these secluded beaches can even be reached by taking the ferry connecting Thong Nai Pan and Mae Nam on Ko Samui (see p232).

Than Sadet & Thong Reng

Accessible by 4WD vehicles and colourful taxi boats, quiet Than Sadet and Thong Reng are the island's best-kept secrets for seclusion seekers.

Treehouse (treehouse.kp@googlemail.com; Thong Reng; bungalows from 200B) Ko Chang's (the big Ko Chang) legendary backpacker hangout has recently set up shop along the secluded waters of Thong Reng. Follow the cheery plastic flowers over the hill from Than Sadet to find uber-basic digs drenched in bright shades of paint.

Plaa's (☎ 0 7744 5191; Than Sadet; bungalows 600B; 🖳) Plaa's colourful village of bungalows sits on the northern headland of Than Sadet overlooking the bay below. Grab a Corona, 'cause this is the perfect place to shoot one of those idyllic beach beer commercials.

Mai Pen Rai (☎ 0 7744 5090; www.thansadet.com; Than Sadet; bungalows 600B; 🖳) 'Mai pen rai' is the Thai equivalent of 'don't worry, be happy', which isn't too surprising since this bay elicits nothing but sedate smiles. Bungalows mingle with Plaa's on the hilly headland, and sport panels of straw weaving with gabled roofs.

Hat Thian

Geographically, Hat Thian is quite close to Hat Rin; however, there are no roads and the crude hiking trail is lengthy and confusing. Ferry taxis are available from Hat Rin for around 150B.

our pick **Sanctuary** (☎ 08 1271 3614; www.thesanctuarythailand.com; dm 120B, bungalows 400-2900B) If you're looking for Alex Garland's mythical beach, this is about as close as it gets. A friendly enclave promoting relaxation, The Sanctuary is an inviting haven offering splendid lodging while also functioning as a holistic retreat (think yoga classes to detox sessions). Accommodation, in various manifestations of twigs, is scattered around the resort, married to the natural surroundings. You'll want to Nama-stay forever.

Beam Bungalows (☎ 0 7927 2854, 08 6947 3205; bungalows 300-500B) Beam is set back from the beach and tucked behind a coconut palm grove. Charming wooden huts have dangling hammocks out front, and big bay windows face the ocean through the swaying palms.

Hat Yuan

Hat Yuan has a few bungalow operations, and is quite secluded as there are no roads connecting this little beach to Hat Rin down the coast.

Barcelona (☎ 0 7737 5113; bungalows 200-600B) Solid wood huts come in two shades: natural wood or creamy white. They climb up the hill on stilts behind a palm garden and have good vistas and jovial staff.

Eating

Ko Pha-Ngan is no culinary capital, especially since most visitors quickly absorb the lazy lifestyle and wind up eating at their accommodation. Those with an adventurous appetite should check out Thong Sala and the island's southern coast.

HAT RIN

This bustling 'burb has the largest conglomeration of restaurants and bars on the island, yet most of them are pretty lousy. The infamous **Chicken Corner** is a popular intersection stocked with several faves such as **Mr K Thai Food** (Map p223; Ban Hat Rin; dishes 30-80B) and **Mama Schnitzel** (Map p223; Ban Hat Rin; dishes 40-100B) who promise to cure any case of the munchies, be it noon or midnight.

Let's Go Sushi (& Deli) (Map p223; ☎ 0 7773 5535; Ban Hat Rin; snacks from 40B, sandwiches from 80B, sushi sets from 120B; 🕙 noon-10pm; 🛜) Finally! A place in Hat Rin that isn't overcharging the tourists. This brand new establishment offers fresh-from-the-sea sushi and sashimi, homemade sandwiches, fresh fruit smoothies and a heaping portion of free wi-fi. Everything's available for take away, so grab it to go and enjoy your healthy nibbles on the sand down the street.

Om Ganesh (Map p223; ☎ 0 7737 5123; Hat Rin Nai; dishes 70-190B; ❤ breakfast, lunch & dinner) Customers meditate over curries, biryani rice, roti and lassis though the local expats joke that every dish tastes the same. Platters start at 350B.

Lazy House (Map p223; ☎ 0 7737 5432; Hat Rin Nai; dishes 90-270B; ❤ lunch & dinner) Back in the day, this joint was the owner's apartment – everyone liked his cooking so much that he decided to turn the place into a restaurant and hangout spot. Today, Lazy House is easily one of Hat Rin's best places to veg out in front of a movie with a scrumptious shepherd's pie.

Lucky Crab (Map p223; Hat Rin Nai; dishes 100-400B; ❤ lunch & dinner) Lucky Crab is your best bet for seafood in Hat Rin. Rows of freshly caught creatures are presented nightly atop miniature longtail boats loaded with ice. Once you've picked your prey, grab a table inside amid dangling plants and charming stone furnishings.

Same Same Burger (Map p223; ☎ 0 7737 5200; www.same-same.com; Hat Rin Nai; burgers 180-230B; ❤ lunch & dinner) Owned by the folks who run the backpacker digs with the *same same* name, this bright-red burger joint is the *same same* as McDonald's (except pricier).

Monna Lisa (Map p223; ☎ 08 0696 7378; Hat Rin Nai; pizza & pasta from 200B; ❤ breakfast, lunch & dinner) The best spot in Hat Rin for a pizza, Monna Lisa is a relatively new operation run by a team of friendly Italians. The mushroom and ham pizza practically knocked our socks off – as did the homemade truffle pasta.

I Sapori (Map p223; ☎ 08 2800 5951; Hat Rin Nok; pizza & pasta from 200B; ❤ breakfast, lunch & dinner) Behind Drop In Bar onSoi Sea Garden, this new joint offers tasty individual pizzas as well.

SOUTHERN BEACHES

ourpick Night Market (Thong Sala; dishes 25-180B; ❤ 6.30-10.30pm) A heady mix of steam and snacking locals, Thong Sala's night market is a must for those looking for a dose of culture while nibbling on a low-priced snack. The best place to grab some cheap grub is the stall in the far right corner with a large white banner. Hit up the vendor next door for tasty seafood platters, such as red snapper served over a bed of thick noodles. Banana pancakes and fruit smoothies abound for dessert.

Boom's Cafe (☎ 0 7723 8318; www.boomscafe.com; Hin Lor; dishes 30-100B; ❤ breakfast, lunch & dinner) A family-run operation nestled between impassable boulders, this secluded option promises scrumptious local meals, scraped together at a moment's notice as the super-smiley owner cheerfully clangs her weathered pots and pans.

Ando Loco (☎ 08 6780 7200; Ban Tai; mains from 59B; ❤ dinner) This outdoor Mexican hangout looks like an animation cell from a vintage Hanna-Barbera cartoon, with assorted kitschy accoutrements such as papier-mâché cacti. Down a super-sized margarita and show your skills on the beach volleyball court. Ando Loco closes during low season (around September to December).

A's Coffee Shop & Restaurant (☎ 0 7737 7226; Thong Sala; dishes 80-260B; ❤ breakfast, lunch & dinner Mon-Sat) Located on Soi Krung Thai Bank, A's is the perfect place to nab some heart-clogging British pub grub if you're stuck in town waiting for the ferry.

Vantana Restaurant (☎ 0 7723 8813; dishes 80-150B; Thong Sala; ❤ breakfast, lunch & dinner) Spilling out onto Soi Krung Thai Bank, Vantana offers a hearty selection of English eats. The gut-busting Sunday Brunch (260B) is the perfect cure for homesick Brits.

Maew Hot Pan BBQ (☎ 08 1970 4077; Ban Tai; buffet 110B; ❤ dinner) The island's best do-it-yourself dinner joint, Maew is an all-you-can-eat affair where diners cook their meats, vegies and quail eggs (a local fave) over a gurgling hot pot. Maew can be easy to miss; it is located on the ocean side of Ban Tai's main road near the 7-Eleven.

Kaito (☎ 0 7737 7738; Thong Sala; dishes from 130B; ❤ 3-9pm Thu-Mon) Authentic Japanese imports are the specialty here – slurp an Asahi while savouring your tangy seaweed salad and *tonkatsu* (pork cutlet). The upstairs level has cosy cushion sitting while the main sitting area is flanked with *manga* and pocket-sized Japanese novels.

ourpick Mason's Arms (☎ 08 5884 7271; Thong Sala; mains from 160B; ❤ 10.30am-11.30pm) Suddenly, a clunky structure emerges from the swaying palms; it's a Tudor-style manse, plucked directly from Stratford-upon-Avon and plunked down in the steamy jungle. This lodge-like lair is one blood pudding away from being an official British colony. The fish 'n' chips is a local favourite.

Pizza Chiara (☎ 0 7737 7626; Thong Sala; pizzas 180-320B; ❤ lunch & dinner) The quintessential chequered tablecloths confirm it (in case you didn't guess from the name): Pizza Chiara is all about tasty Italian fare. Go for the Pizza

Cecco smothered with prosciutto, salami, mushrooms and *cotto* cheese.

OTHER BEACHES

Tantawan (☎ 0 7734 9108; www.tantawanbungalow.com; Hat Son; dishes 60-200B; ☒ lunch & dinner) This charming teak nest, tucked among jungle fronds, is dripping with clinking chandeliers made from peach coral and khaki-coloured seashells. Diners sit in a sea of geometric cushions while gobbling up some of the tastiest Thai and French-inspired dishes on the island.

Cookies Salad (☎ 0 7734 9125, 08 3181 7125; Hat Salad; mains from 100B; ☒ breakfast, lunch & dinner) Worth tracking down if you're staying on the west coast, this casual restaurant, perched atop a cliff on the south side of Hat Salad, offers a stunning assortment of Thai treats (don't miss the Penang curry) and unique smoothies (including a rich nutella swirl). Sadly cookie salads are not on offer.

ourpick **Sanctuary** (☎ 08 1271 3614; Hat Thian; mains from 130B) Forget what you know about health food, The Sanctuary's restaurant proves that wholesome eats can also be delicious. Enjoy a tasty parade of plates – from Indian pakoras to crunchy Vietnamese spring rolls – as an endless playlist of music (undoubtedly the island's best) wafts overhead. Don't forget to wash it all down with a shot of neon-green wheatgrass. Yum!

Cucina Italiana (Jenny's; ☎ 08 3640 1797; Chalok Lam; pizza 180B; ☒ dinner) Cucina Italiana is starting to have a cult following on Ko Pha-Ngan. The friendly Italian chef is passionate about his food, and creates all of his dishes from scratch. On Thursday and Sunday, you can order unlimited toppings on your oven-roasted pizza for only 180B.

Ra Sa Nan Da The Bistro @ The Beach (☎ 0 7723 9555; Thong Nai Pan; mains 120-400B; ☎) The swirling, spaceship-like wine cellar is reason enough to dine at Ra Sa Nan Da's sexy beachside restaurant. Pha-Ngan's most swanked-out dining spot offers a broad range of international eats while providing respite from the rice-wielding bamboo shacks further down the sand.

Drinking

Every month, on the night of the full moon, pilgrims pay tribute to the party gods with trance-like dancing, wild screaming, and glow-in-the-dark body paint. The throngs of bucket-sippers and fire twirlers gather on the infamous Sunrise Beach (Hat Rin Nok)

and party til the sun replaces the moon in the sky.

Recently, a few other noteworthy party spots have opened up around the island – they're definitely worth a look if you want something a bit mellower.

HAT RIN

Hat Rin is the beating heart of the legendary Full Moon fun, and the area can get pretty wound up even without the influence of lunar phases. When the moon isn't lighting up the night sky, partygoers flock to other spots on the island's south side. See p218 for details. The following party venues flank Hat Rin's infamous Sunrise Beach from south to north:

Rock (Map p223; ☎ 0 7737 5244) Great views of the party.

Club Paradise (Map p223; ☎ 0 7737 5244) Paradise basks in its celebrity status as the genesis of the lunar *loco*-motion.

Drop-In Bar (Map p223; ☎ 0 7737 5374) This dance shack blasts the chart toppers that we all secretly love. The other nights of the year are equally as boisterous.

Zoom/Vinyl (Map p223) An ear-popping trance venue.

Cactus Bar (Map p223; ☎ 0 7737 5308) Smack in the centre of Hat Rin Nok, Cactus pumps out a healthy mix of old school tunes, hip hop and R&B.

Da Club (Map p223) A newer spot on the sand where trance beats shake the graffiti-ed walls.

Tommy (Map p223; ☎ 0 7737 5215) One of Hat Rin's largest venues lures the masses with black lights and trance music blaring on the sound system. Drinks are dispensed from a large ark-like bar.

Mellow Mountain (Map p223; ☎ 0 7737 5347) Also called 'Mushy Mountain' (you'll know why when you get there), this trippy hangout sits at the northern edge of Hat Rin Nok delivering stellar views of the shenanigans below.

OTHER BEACHES

Eagle Pub (☎ 08 4839 7143; Hat Yao) At the southern end of Hat Yao, this drink-dealing shack, built right into the rock face, is tattooed with the neon graffiti of virtually every person that's passed out on the lime green patio furniture after too many *caipirinhas*.

Flip Flop Pharmacy (Thong Nai Pan) This open-air bar on the sands of Thong Nai Pan is the area's preferred hangout spot.

Amsterdam (☎ 0 7723 8447; Ao Plaay Laem) Near Hat Chaophao on the west coast, Amsterdam attracts tourists and locals from all over the island who are looking for a chill spot to watch the sunset.

Pirates Bar (☎ 08 4728 6064; Hat Chaophao) This popular and wacky drinkery is a replica of a pirate ship built into the cliffs. When you're sitting on the deck and the tide is high (and you've had a couple drinks), you can almost believe you're out at sea. These guys host the well-attended Moon Set parties, three days before Hat Rin gets pumpin' for the Full Moon fun.

Sheesha Bar (☎ 0 7737 4161; Chalok Lam) The antithesis of grungy Hat Rin, Sheesha Bar swaps buckets of Samsung for designer drinks. The enticing patchwork of beige sandstone and horizontal slats of mahogany fit right in with the arabesque Mandalai Hotel across the street (owned by the same family).

Getting There & Away

As always, the cost and departure times are in flux. Rough waves are known to cancel ferries between the months of October and December. Beware of travel agencies in Bangkok selling fake 1st-class boat/train or boat/bus combinations. Passengers needing to do a visa run (or those planning to travel on to Malaysia) can book boat/bus combos at the Backpacker's Information Centre (p219). It costs 1150B to reach Penang (Butterworth), 1850B to reach KL and 1850B to reach Singapore.

BANGKOK, HUA HIN & CHUMPHON

The Lomprayah and Seatran Discovery service has bus/boat combination packages that depart from Bangkok and pass through Chumphon. It is also quite hassle-free to take the train from Bangkok to Chumphon and switch to a ferry service (it works out to be about the same price and the train is comfier if you get a couchette). Lomprayah and Seatran charge 1300B from Ko Pha-Ngan to both Bangkok and Hua Hin. Passengers that disembark in Chumphon pay 850B. Songserm offers a slightly slower and less comfortable service to Bangkok for 850B. Travellers can also opt for the government bus to Bangkok (1100B, or 1400B for the VIP bus). For additional information about travelling through Chumphon see p189. Bangkok-bound passengers can choose to disembark in Hua Hin.

KO SAMUI

There are around a dozen daily departures between Ko Pha-Ngan and Ko Samui (220B to 450B). These boats leave throughout the day from 7am to 6pm and take from 30 minutes

to an hour. All leave from either Thong Sala or Hat Rin on Ko Pha-Ngan and arrive either in Na Thon, Mae Nam or the Bang Rak pier on Ko Samui. If the final location matters, state your preferences while buying your ticket.

The *Haad Rin Queen* (220B) goes back and forth between Hat Rin and Big Buddha Beach. Ferry service from Samui's Mae Nam pier leaves at noon and wanders up the eastern coast of Ko Pha-Ngan, stopping in Hat Thian, Than Sadet and Thong Nai Pan. Boats running in the other direction leave Thong Nai Pan at 9am.

There are no car ferries between Ko Pha-Ngan and Ko Samui, you must return to the mainland and take a separate boat.

At the time of research there were rumours of a high-speed boat service to Ko Samui starting up that would run frequently and cut travel time down to 15 minutes between the islands.

KO TAO

Ko Tao–bound Lomprayah ferries (450B) depart from Thong Sala on Ko Pha-Ngan at 8.30am and 1pm and arrive at 9.45am and 2.15pm. The Seatran service (450B) departs from Thong Sala at 8.30am and 2pm daily. Taxis depart Hat Rin for Thong Sala one hour before the boat departure. Songserm (350B) leaves Ko Pha-Ngan at 12.30pm and alights at 2.30pm.

SURAT THANI & THE ANDAMAN COAST

Combination boat/bus tickets are available at any travel agency, simply tell them your desired destination and they will sell you the necessary links in the transport chain. Most travellers will pass through Surat Thani as they swap coasts. There are approximately six daily departures between Ko Pha-Ngan and Krabi (650B) on the Raja Car Ferry, Songserm or Seatran. These boats leave from Thong Sala throughout the day from 7am to 8pm. Every night, depending on the weather, a night boat runs from Surat, departing at 11pm. Boats in the opposite direction leave Ko Pha-Ngan at 10pm. Figure around 850B for a taxi/boat/bus connection from Hat Rin to Ko Lanta, 780B to Khao Lak, 1050B to Ko Phi-Phi, 1000B to Satun province, and 2050B to reach little Ko Lipe. See the webiste of the **Backpacker's Information Centre** (www.backpackersthailand.com) for detailed departure times to additional Andaman destinations.

Getting Around

See p219 for important information about the dangers of riding motorbikes around the island. You can rent motorcycles all over the island for 150B to 250B per day. Always wear a helmet – it's the law on Ko Pha-Ngan, and local policemen are starting to enforce it. If you plan on riding over dirt tracks it is imperative that you rent a bike comparable to a Honda MTX125 – gearless scooters cannot make the journey. Bicycle rentals are discouraged unless you're fit enough to take on Lance Armstrong. Car rentals are around 1200B a day.

Some places can only be reached by boat, such as Bottle Beach and some sections of the eastern coast. If you do find trails, keep in mind that they are often overgrown and not suitable for solo navigation.

Pick-up trucks and sŏrng·tǎa·ou chug along the island's major roads and the riding rates double after sunset. Ask your accommodation about free or discount transfers when you leave the island. The trip from Thong Sala to Hat Rin is 100B, further beaches will set you back around 150B.

Long-tail boats depart from Thong Sala, Chalok Lam and Hat Rin, heading to a variety of far-flung destinations such as Hat Khuat (Bottle Beach) and Ao Thong Nai Pan. Expect to pay anywhere from 50B for a short trip, to 300B for a lengthier journey. You can charter a private boat ride from beach to beach for about 150B per 15 minutes of travel.

KO TAO
เกาะเต่า
pop 1,382

First there was Ko Samui, then Ko Pha-Ngan; now, the cult of Ko Tao ('Ko Taoism' perhaps?) has emerged along Thailand's crystalline gulf coast. Today, thousands of visitors come to worship the turquoise waters offshore, and quite often they stay. The secret to Ko Tao's undeniable appeal? Simple: although the island is only 21 sq km, tiny Tao sure knows how to pack it in – there's something for everyone, and nothing is in moderation. Diving enthusiasts cavort with sharks and rays in a playground of tangled neon coral. Hikers and hermits can re-enact an episode from *Lost* in the dripping coastal jungles. And when you're Robinson Crusoe-ed out, hit the pumpin' bar scene that rages on until dawn.

Many years have passed since the first backpacker came to the scrubby island and planted a flag in the name of self-respecting shoestring travellers everywhere, but fret not, there's still plenty of time to join the tribe. Ko Tao has several years to go before corporate resort owners bulldoze the remaining rustic cottages, and visitors start discussing stockholdings rather than sea creatures spotted on their latest dive.

Orientation

'The Rock', as it's known, is significantly smaller than neighbouring Ko Pha-Ngan and Ko Samui, but is quite similar in topography: rolling, jungle-clad hills and thick, sandy beaches. Ferries pull into Mae Hat, on the western side of the island. This seaside town has all the tourist amenities one would need: travel agencies, accommodation, dive shops, restaurants, internet cafes and motorcycle rentals.

The biggest village on the island is Sairee Beach (sometimes called Hat Sai Ri), about 2km up the coast. Here, travellers will find similar amenities but in greater quantity. Chalok Ban Kao, on the muddy southern coast, is the island's third largest settlement.

The island's eastern and northern coasts are fairly undeveloped compared to the bustling west coast, with only a few bungalow enterprises on each little bay. A paved road connects the west coast to Tanote Bay (Ao Tanot), the busiest bay in the east. A 4WD vehicle should be used when navigating any of the other rugged roads in the area.

About the only thing of historic interest on the island is a large boulder, which has the initials of King Rama V, commemorating his royal visit in 1899.

Information

EMERGENCY
Police station (Map p236; ☎ 0 7745 6631) Between Mae Hat and Sairee Beach along the rutty portion of the beachside road.

INTERNET ACCESS
Rates are generally 2B per minute, with a 20B minimum and discounts if you log on for one hour or longer. You may find, however, that certain useful tourism websites have been firewalled at internet cafes affiliated with travel agencies. The larger dive schools on the island usually have a wireless connection available for laptop-toting tourists.

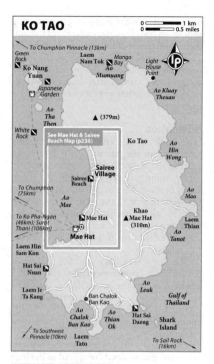

KO TAO

Sabai Jai is a newer publication on the island dedicated to eco efforts.

MEDICAL SERVICES

All divers are required to sign a medical waiver before exploring the sea. If you have any medical condition that might hinder your ability to dive (including mild asthma), you will be asked to get medical clearance from a doctor on Ko Tao. If you're unsure about whether or not you are fit to dive consider seeing a doctor before your trip as there are no official hospitals on the island, and the number of qualified medical professionals is limited. Also, make sure your traveller's insurance covers scuba diving. On-island medical 'consultations' (and we use that term very lightly) cost 300B. There are several walk-in clinics and mini-hospitals scattered around Mae Hat and Sairee. All serious medical needs should be dealt with on Ko Samui. If you are diving ask your outfitter to point you in the proper direction of medical advice.

Diver Safety Support (Map p236; ☎ 08 1083 0533; kohtao@sssnetwork.com; Mae Hat; ☻ on call 24hr) Has a temporary hyperbaric chamber and offers emergency evacuation services.

MONEY

There are 24-hour ATMs at the island's 7-Elevens. There's also a cluster of ATMs orbiting the ferry docks at Mae Hat. There is a money exchange window at Mae Hat's pier and a second location near Choppers in Sairee. There are several banks near the post office in Mae Hat, at the far end of town along the island's main inland road. They are usually open from 9am to 4pm on weekdays. Almost all dive schools accept credit cards, however there is usually a 3% or 4% handling fee.

POST

Post Office (Map p236; ☎ 0 7745 6170; ☻ 9am-5pm Mon-Fri, 9am-noon Sat) A 10- to 15-minute walk from the pier; at the corner of Ko Tao's main inner-island road and Mae Hat's 'down road'.

TOURIST INFORMATION

There's no government-run TAT office on Ko Tao. Transportation and accommodation bookings can be made at most dive shops or at any of the numerous travel agencies, all of which take a small commission on services rendered.

INTERNET RESOURCES

Koh Tao.com (www.kohtao.com) Handy site with loads of practical information including ferry schedules.

Koh Tao Community (www.kohtao-community.com) A forum offering general info about the various goings-on around the island.

Koh Tao Online (www.kohtaoonline.com) An online version of the handy *Koh Tao Info* booklet.

LAUNDRY

After a few dives, you'll probably want to wash your swim trunks (especially if you saw a shark and 'accidentally' peed your wetsuit). Almost every bungalow operation (and even some restaurants) offers laundry service. One kilo of laundry should be around 40B. You may want to ask your diving instructor where he or she gets their washing done, as sometimes items get conveniently lost. Express service is usually available for 60B per kilo.

MEDIA

The ubiquitous *Koh Tao Info* booklet lists loads of businesses on the island and goes into some detail about the island's history, culture and social issues. The pocket-sized

Dangers & Annoyances

There's nothing more annoying than enrolling in a diving course with your friends and then having to drop out because you scraped your knee in a motorcycle accident. The roads on Ko Tao are horrendous, save the main drag connecting Sairee Beach to Chalok Ban Kao. While hiring a moped is extremely convenient, this is not the place to learn how to drive. The island is rife with abrupt hills and sudden sand pits along gravel trails. Even if you escape unscathed from a riding experience, scamming bike shops may claim that you damaged your rental and will try to extort you for some serious cash.

Like several other Thai islands experiencing rapid tourist growth, Ko Tao now has a gaggle of transvestite prostitutes that hawk their wares along the main drag in Sairee Beach. The influx of cheesy cabarets and seedy skin trade has – much to the chagrin of the local expat community – encouraged a culture of thieving and drugs. This is best avoided, and hopefully the lack of business will encourage these shady characters to seek business elsewhere. Always keep your valuables in a safe place, especially when you're out on the dive boat.

Travellers should also be aware that mosquito-borne dengue fever (and a similar but less-severe cousin) is a real and serious threat – your author caught it on his most recent research trip. The virus can spread quickly due to tightly packed tourist areas and small size of the island. See p432 for more information.

Sights

Sightseeing on Ko Tao revolves around its scenic **beaches**. While the beautiful Sairee Beach offers spectacular sunset vistas, it's by no means the stunning, secluded beach you were dreaming about. To find a hidden cove, venture through the jungle to the less-developed east and northern coasts. Follow the weaving dirt road east from Sairee until you roll down the steep hill at **Hin Wong** – a stunning, rounded bay. There's no beach here, but the water is impossibly clear and the giant schools of black sardines look like an oozing oil spill as they swish through the sea. Hundreds of thick coconut palms bend over the cove as though they were vying for a sip of seawater. The boulder-strewn inlet at **Ao Tanot** (Tanote Bay) has a similarly magical juxtaposition of jungle and sea, though it is a bit more developed. **Ao Leuk**, further south, is the choice retreat for many, and **Ao Thian Ok** (Shark Bay) is another stunning option, although despite the nickname, there are no sharks in the bay.

In the far north, **Ao Mamuang** (Mango Bay) has become a choice spot for scuba rookies – the bay is shallow and swimmable, with a picture-perfect backdrop featuring a rolling forest dotted with the occasional pitched roof of a hidden bungalow. In good weather you can get there by sŏrng·tăa·ou; otherwise take a water taxi.

Just off the island's northwest coast, the rugged **Ko Nang Yuan** is a lonely island featuring three dramatic cone-shaped peaks connected by a remarkable sandbar. This idyllic beige strip is a stunning natural phenomenon that finds its way onto virtually every local postcard. Ferries from Mae Hat and water taxis from northern Sairee stop regularly at Ko Nang Yuan. There is a 100B levy to access the island.

Activities

DIVING

Never been diving before? Ko Tao is *the* place to lose your scuba virginity. The island issues more scuba certifications than in any other place around the world. The shallow bays scalloping the island are the perfect spot for newbie divers to take their first stab at scuba. On shore, over 40 dive centres are ready to saddle you up with some gear and teach you the ropes in a 3½-day Open Water certification course. We know, we know, homework on a holiday sucks, but the intense competition among scuba schools means that certification prices are unbeatably low, and the standards of service are top notch, as dozens of dive shops vie for your baht.

It's no surprise that this underwater playground has become exceptionally popular with beginners; the waters are crystal clear, there are loads of neon reefs, and temperatures feel like bathwater. The best dive sites are found at offshore pinnacles within a 20km radius of the island (see p238), but seasoned scubaholics almost always prefer the top-notch sites along the Andaman coast. The local marine wildlife includes groupers, moray eels, batfish, bannerfish, barracudas, titan triggerfish, angelfish, clownfish (Nemos), stingrays, reef sharks, and frequent visits by almighty whale sharks.

MAE HAT & SAIREE BEACH

0 — 300 m
0 — 0.1 miles

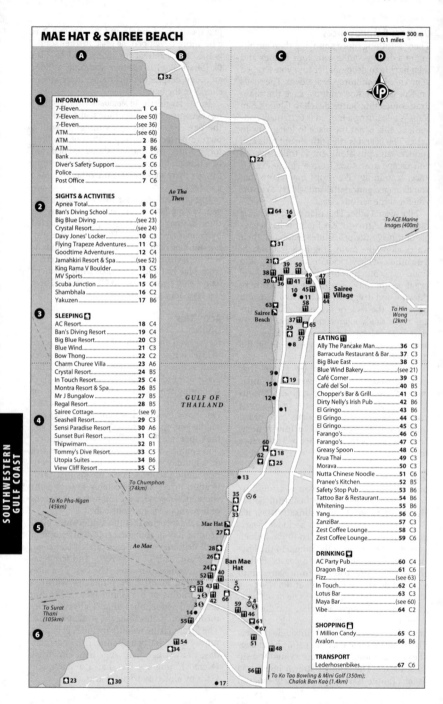

INFORMATION
7-Eleven.............................. **1** C4
7-Eleven.............................(see 50)
7-Eleven.............................(see 36)
ATM....................................(see 60)
ATM..................................... **2** B6
ATM..................................... **3** B6
Bank.................................... **4** C6
Diver's Safety Support......... **5** C6
Police................................... **6** C5
Post Office........................... **7** C6

SIGHTS & ACTIVITIES
Apnea Total.......................... **8** C3
Ban's Diving School.............. **9** C4
Big Blue Diving...................(see 23)
Crystal Resort.....................(see 24)
Davy Jones' Locker.............. **10** C3
Flying Trapeze Adventures... **11** C3
Goodtime Adventures......... **12** C4
Jamahkiri Resort & Spa......(see 52)
King Rama V Boulder........... **13** C5
MV Sports............................ **14** B6
Scuba Junction..................... **15** C4
Shambhala........................... **16** C2
Yakuzen............................... **17** B6

SLEEPING
AC Resort............................. **18** C4
Ban's Diving Resort............. **19** C4
Big Blue Resort.................... **20** C3
Blue Wind............................ **21** C3
Bow Thong........................... **22** C2
Charm Churee Villa.............. **23** A6
Crystal Resort...................... **24** B5
In Touch Resort................... **25** C4
Montra Resort & Spa........... **26** B5
Mr J Bungalow..................... **27** B5
Regal Resort........................ **28** B5
Sairee Cottage....................(see 9)
Seashell Resort.................... **29** C3
Sensi Paradise Resort.......... **30** A6
Sunset Buri Resort............... **31** C2
Thipwimarn......................... **32** B1
Tommy's Dive Resort.......... **33** C5
Utopia Suites....................... **34** B6
View Cliff Resort.................. **35** C5

EATING
Ally The Pancake Man.......... **36** C3
Barracuda Restaurant & Bar...... **37** C3
Big Blue East........................ **38** C3
Blue Wind Bakery...............(see 21)
Café Corner.......................... **39** C3
Café del Sol......................... **40** B5
Chopper's Bar & Grill........... **41** C3
Dirty Nelly's Irish Pub......... **42** B6
El Gringo.............................. **43** B6
El Gringo.............................. **44** C3
El Gringo.............................. **45** C3
Farango's.............................. **46** C6
Farango's.............................. **47** C3
Greasy Spoon....................... **48** C3
Krua Thai.............................. **49** C3
Morava................................. **50** C3
Nutta Chinese Noodle.......... **51** C6
Pranee's Kitchen.................. **52** B5
Safety Stop Pub................... **53** B6
Tattoo Bar & Restaurant...... **54** B6
Whitening............................ **55** B6
Yang..................................... **56** C6
ZanziBar................................ **57** C3
Zest Coffee Lounge............. **58** C3
Zest Coffee Lounge............. **59** C6

DRINKING
AC Party Pub....................... **60** C4
Dragon Bar........................... **61** C6
Fizz.....................................(see 63)
In Touch............................... **62** C4
Lotus Bar............................. **63** C3
Maya Bar.............................(see 60)
Vibe..................................... **64** C2

SHOPPING
1 Million Candy.................... **65** C3
Avalon.................................. **66** B6

TRANSPORT
Lederhosenbikes.................. **67** C6

Ao Tha Then

To ACE Marine Images (400m)

Sairee Village

To Hin Wong (2km)

Sairee Beach

GULF OF THAILAND

To Chumphon (74km)

To Ko Pha-Ngan (45km)

Ao Mae

Mae Hat

To Surat Thani (105km)

Ban Mae Hat

To Ko Tao Bowling & Mini Golf (350m);
Chalok Ban Kao (1.4km)

When you alight at the pier in Mae Hat, swarms of touts will try to coax you into staying at their dive resort with promises of a 'special price for you' – some touts even start accosting tourists on the boat ride over to the island. There are dozens of dive centres on Ko Tao, so it's best to arrive armed with the names of a few reputable dive schools. If you aren't rushed for time, consider relaxing on the island for a couple of days before making any diving decisions – you will undoubtedly bump into swarms of scubaphiles and instructors who will gladly offer their advice and opinions. Remember: the success of your diving experience (especially if you are learning how to dive) will largely depend on how much you like your instructor. There are other factors to consider as well, like the size of your diving group, the condition of your equipment, and the condition of the dive sites, to name a few.

For the most part, diving prices are standardised across the island, so there's no need to spend your time hunting around for the best deal. A **PADI** (www.padi.com) Open Water certification course costs 9800B; an **SSI** (www.ssithailand.com) Open Water Certification is slightly less (9000B, because you do not have to pay for instructional materials). An Advanced Open Water certification will set you back 8500B, a rescue course is 9500B and the Divemaster program costs a cool 25,000B. Fun divers should expect to pay roughly 1000B per dive, or around 7000B for a 10-dive package. These rates include all dive gear, boat, instructors/guides and snacks. Discounts are usually given if you bring your own equipment. Be wary of dive centres that offer too many price cuts – safety is paramount, and a shop giving out unusually good deals is probably cutting too many corners.

Most dive schools can hook you up with cheap (or even free) accommodation. Expect large crowds and booked-out beds during December, January, June, July and August, and a monthly glut of wannabe divers after the Full Moon Party on Ko Pha-Ngan next door. If you are planning to do 'diving detox' after a Full Moon romp, make sure you purchase your ferry tickets before the eve of the lunar lunacy – boats sell out quickly.

The following dive schools are among the best operators on the island, and most actively support the Save Koh Tao initiative (p240):

Ban's Diving School (Map p236; ☎ 0 7745 6466; www.amazingkohtao.com; Sairee Beach) A well-oiled diving machine and relentlessly expanding conglomerate, Ban's certifies more divers per year than any other scuba school in the world and recent refurbishments have given it a five-star feel. Classroom sessions tend to be conducted in large groups, but there's a reasonable amount of individual attention in the water. A breadth of international instructors means that students can learn to dive in their native tongue. The affiliated resort (p241) is quite popular with party-seekers.

Big Blue Diving (Map p236; ☎ 0 7745 6415, 0 7745 6772; www.bigbluediving.com; Sairee Beach) If Goldilocks were picking a dive school, she'd probably pick Big Blue – this midsize operation (not too big, not too small) gets props for fostering a sociable vibe while maintaining a high standard of service. Divers of every ilk can score dirt-cheap accommodation at their resort (p240).

Buddha View (☎ 0 7745 6074; www.buddhaview -diving.com; Chalok Ban Kao) Another big dive operation on Ko Tao, Buddha View offers the standard fare of certification and special programs for technical diving (venturing beyond the usual parameters of recreational underwater exploration). Discounted accommodation is available at their friendly resort (p242).

Crystal (Map p236; ☎ 0 7745 6107; www.crystaldive .com; Mae Hat) Crystal is the Meryl Streep of diving operators, winning all the awards for best performance year after year. It's one of the largest schools on the island (and around the world), although high-quality instructors and intimate classes keep the school feeling quite personal. Multilingual staff members, air-conditioned classes and two on-site swimming pools sweeten the deal. Highly recommended; your author did his Divemaster training here. Crystal offers accommodation in both Mae Hat and Sairee (see p241).

Davy Jones' Locker (DJL; Map p236; www.davyjones locker.asia; Sairee Beach) Gaining momentum in the last year, this popular dive outfitter (with a strangely ominous name) has become a favourite in northern Sairee. Friday night pool parties are a big draw.

New Heaven (☎ 0 7745 6587; www.newheavendive school.com; Chalok Ban Kao) The owners of this small diving operation dedicate a lot of their time to preserving the natural beauty of Ko Tao's underwater sites by conducting regular reef checks and contributing to reef restoration efforts. A special CPAD research diver certification program is available in addition to the regular order of programs and fun dives.

Scuba Junction (Scuba J; Map p236; ☎ 0 7745 6164; www.scuba-junction.com; Sairee Beach) A groovy new storefront and team of outgoing instructors lure travellers looking for a more intimate dive experience. Scuba Junction guarantees a maximum of four people per diving group.

SOUTHWESTERN GULF COAST

DIVE SITES AT A GLANCE

In general, divers don't have a choice as to which sites they explore. Each dive school chooses a smattering of sites for the day depending on weather and ocean conditions. Deeper dive sites such as Chumphon Pinnacle are always visited in the morning. Afternoon boats tour the shallower sites such as Japanese Gardens. Divers hoping to spend some quality time searching for whale sharks at Sail Rock should join one of the dive trips departing daily from Ko Pha-Ngan.

- **Chumphon Pinnacle** (36m max depth), 13km west of Ko Tao, has a colourful assortment of sea anemones along the four interconnected pinnacles. The site plays host to schools of giant trevally, tuna, and large grey reef sharks. Whale sharks are known to pop up once in a while.

- **Green Rock** (25m max depth) is an underwater jungle gym featuring caverns, caves and small swim-throughs. Rays, grouper and triggerfish are known to hang around. It's great place for a night dive.

- **Japanese Gardens** (12m max depth), between Ko Tao and Ko Nang Yuan, is a low-stress dive site perfect for beginners. There's plenty of colourful coral, and turtles, stingray and pufferfish often pass by.

- **Mango Bay** (16m max depth) might be your first dive site if you putting on a tank for the first time. Lazy reef fish swim around as newbies practice their skills on the sandy bottom.

- **Sail Rock** (34m max depth), best accessed by Ko Pha-Ngan, features a massive rock chimney with a vertical swim-through, and large pelagics like barracuda and kingfish. This is one of the top spots in southeast Asia to see whale sharks.

- **Southwest Pinnacle** (33m max depth) offers divers a small collection of pinnacles that are home to giant groupers and barracudas. Whale sharks and leopard sharks are sometimes spotted (pun partially intended).

- **White Rock** (29m max depth) is home to colourful corals, angelfish, clown fish and territorial triggerfish. Another popular spot for night divers.

SNORKELLING

Snorkelling is a popular alternative to diving, although scuba snobs will tell you that strapping on a snorkel instead of an air tank is like eating spray cheese when there's camembert on the table. Orchestrating your own snorkelling adventure is simple, since the bays on the east coast have small bungalow operations offering equipment rental for 100B to 200B per day.

Most snorkel enthusiasts opt for the do-it-yourself approach on Ko Tao, which involves swimming out into the offshore bays or hiring a longtail boat to putter around further out. Guided tours are also available and can be booked at any local travel agency. Tours range from 500B to 700B (usually including gear, lunch and a guide/boat captain) and stop at various snorkelling hotspots around the island. **Laem Thian** is popular for its small sharks, **Shark Island** has loads of fish (and ironically no sharks), **Hin Wong** is known for its crystalline waters, and **Light House Point**, in the north, offers a dazzling array of colourful sea anemones. Dive schools will usually allow snorkellers on their vessels for a comparable price – but it's only worth snorkelling at the shallower sites such as Japanese Gardens. Note that dive boats visit the shallower sites in the afternoons.

FREEDIVING

For those interested in tackling freediving – exploring the sea using breath-holding techniques rather than scuba gear – we highly recommend the capable staff at **Apnea Total** (Map p236; ☎ 08 7183 2321; www.apnea-total.com; Sairee Beach) who have earned several awards in the freediving world and possess a special knack for easing newbies into this heart-pounding sport.

TECHNICAL DIVING & CAVE DIVING

Well-seasoned divers and hardcore Jacques Cousteaus should contact **Trident** (www.techthailand.com), a branch of **Master Divers** (☎ 0 7745 6314; www.master-divers.com), if they want to take their underwater exploration to the next level and try a technical dive. According to PADI, tec diving, as it's often known, is 'diving other than conventional commercial or recreational diving that takes divers beyond recreational diving limits'. Technical diving exceeds depths of 40m, requires stage decompressions and a variety of gas mixtures are often used in a single dive.

In the last few years, Trident has made a name for itself in the diving community after successfully locating dozens of previously undiscovered wrecks in the Gulf of Thailand. Their most famous discovery was the USS *Lagarto* an American naval vessel that sunk during WWII. The gulf has long been an important trading route and new wrecks are being discovered all the time, from old Chinese pottery wrecks to Japanese *marus* (merchant ships).

Recently, cave diving has taken Ko Tao by storm, and the most intrepid scuba buffs are lining up to make the half-day trek over to Khao Sok National Park (p290). Beneath the park's main lake lurks an astonishing submarine world filled with hidden grottos, limestone crags and skulking catfish. In certain areas divers can swim near submerged villages that were flooded in order to create a reservoir and dam. Most cave-diving trips depart from Ko Tao on the afternoon boat service and return to the island on the afternoon boat service of the following day. Overnight stays are arranged in or near the park.

Stop by Buddha View (p242) on Saturdays for a free introduction into the world of tec diving, or hit the waters with the Trident team on 'wreck Wednesdays'. If you aren't diving with Buddha View or Master Divers, your dive school of choice can easily help you get sorted.

UNDERWATER PHOTOGRAPHY & VIDEOGRAPHY

If your wallet is already full of PADI certification cards, consider renting an underwater camera or enrolling in a marine videography course. Many scuba schools hire professional videographers to film Open Water certifications, and if this piques your interests, you could potentially earn a few bucks after completing a video internship. Your dive operator can put you in touch with any of the half-dozen videography crews on the island. We recommend **ACE Marine Images** (☎ 0 7745 7054; www.acemarineimages.com; Sairee Beach), one of Thailand's leading underwater videography studios. Their interactive eight-dive course

(30,000B) includes an independent diver certification and one-on-one instruction in the editing room. **Deep Down Productions** (☎ 08 7133 4102; www.deepdown-productions.com) and **Oceans Below** (☎ 08 6060 1863; www.oceansbelow.net) offer videography courses and internships that are a bit easier on the pocketbook.

OTHER WATERSPORTS

If diving isn't your bag, there are plenty of activities to keep the blood flowing on top of the waves. Many dive operators, including Buddha View (p237) and **Black Tip Divers** (☎ 0 7745 6204; www.black-tip.com; Chalok Ban Kao) offer a variety of watersports including kiteboarding and sailing. Alternatively, the friendly folks at **MV Sports** (☎ 0 7745 6065) in Mae Hat can pull you behind a speedboat while you ride a variety of items like water skis, wakeboards or even an inflatable sumo suit.

SPAS

All of that shark ogling might leave you with a serious backache, so why not indulge in a post-scuba session? (Though be warned that a massage treatment directly after diving can be dangerous as it pushes residual nitrogen throughout the body.)

Jamahkiri Resort & Spa (Map p236; ☎ 0 7745 6400/1; www.jamahkiri.com) Offers aloe vera wraps (great for sunburn), massages, and facials atop a huge island peak on the east coast. Call for free transport, or swing by their wooden storefront near the Mae Hat pier.

Yakuzen (☎ 0 7745 6229, 08 4837 3385; Mae Hat; ☺ 5pm-10pm Thu-Tue) Japanese-style bathhouse in Mae Hat changes things up by offering this unique form of relaxation. Sixty-minute soaks cost 700B.

YOGA

Ko Tao's only full-time yoga centre is **Shambhala** (Map p236; ☎ 08 4440 6755), housed in beautiful wooden *săh·lah* located on the forested grounds of Blue Wind in Sairee Beach. The two-hour classes, led by Kester, the energetic yogi, are 300B.

OTHER ACTIVITIES

Although most activities on Ko Tao revolve around the sea, the friendly crew at **Goodtime Adventures** (Map p236; ☎ 08 7275 3604; www.gt adventures.com; Sairee Beach, ☺ noon-late) offer a wide variety of land-based activities to get the adrenaline pumping. Hike through the island's jungly interior, score a do-it-yourself bouldering kit (1000B), swing from rock to rock during a climbing and abseiling session (from 2000B), or unleash your inner daredevil during an afternoon of cliff jumping.

The newest craze to hit Ko Tao is the uber-popular **Flying Trapeze Adventures** (FTA; Map p236; ☎ 08 0696 9269; www.flyingtrapezeadventure .com; Sairee Beach; ⏲ 2-10pm). Find out if you're a great catch while donning a pair of hot pink tights during a one-hour group trapeze lesson (950B; discounts if you enrol in a series of classes). All courses are recorded and a DVD is available for 550B. Large groups should book via email, and individual bookings are best done over the phone. Participants must be at least six years old. Search 'trapezee at ko tao' on YouTube to get a preview.

Ko Tao Bowling & Mini Golf (☎ 0 7745 6316; ⏲ noon-midnight), on the main road between Mae Hat and Chalok Ban Kao, has several homemade bowling lanes where the employees reset the pins after every frame (300B per hour). The 18-hole mini golf course has a landmark theme – putt your ball through Stonehenge or across the Golden Gate Bridge.

Volunteering

The **Save Koh Tao** (0 7745 7045; www.marineconser vationkohtao.com) group, spearheaded by New Heaven diving school, is an initiative focused on keeping the island as pristine as possible by promoting sustainable tourism. They don't have a structured volunteer program, although there are always projects that need a helping hand, both on land and in the sea. Save Koh Tao has several large-scale projects including Biorock, an artificial reef built beyond the headland at the northern end of Sairee Beach.

The **Secret Garden** (www.secretgarden-kohtao.com) offers opportunities for work for travellers who are interested in conservation and educational programs. Conservation projects include beach clean-ups, erosion prevention initiatives and marine protection. Native English speakers can help out in the classroom offering English lessons to the local Thai children, or lending a hand during the yearly summer camp. Contact the Secret Garden directly on their website to learn more about volunteering.

Regular **beach clean-ups** attract a large number of volunteers as well. Contact Crystal (opposite) in Mae Hat, Big Blue (right) in Sairee Beach, New Heaven (p243) in Chalok Ban Kao, and Black Tip (p243) in Tanote Bay.

See p413 for more information about volunteering in Thailand.

Sleeping

If you are planning to dive while visiting Ko Tao, your scuba operator will probably offer you discounted accommodation to sweeten the deal. Some schools have on-site lodging, while others have deals with nearby bungalows. It's important to note that you only receive your scuba-related discount on the days you dive. So, for example, if you buy a 10-dive package, and decide to take a day off in the middle, your room rate will not be discounted on that evening. Also, a restful sleep is important before diving, so scope out these 'great room deals' before saying yes – some of them are one roach away from being condemned.

There are also many sleeping options that have absolutely nothing to do with the island's diving culture. Ko Tao's secluded eastern coves are dotted with stunning retreats that still offer a true getaway experience, but these can be difficult to reach due to the island's dismal network of roads. You can often call ahead of time and arrange to be picked up from the pier in Mae Hat.

Note that Ko Tao is not Ko Samui – if you are looking for impeccable service and perfect five-star standards you will not find it here…yet.

SAIREE BEACH

Giant Sairee is the longest and most developed strip on the island, with a string of dive operations, bungalows, travel agencies, minimarkets and internet cafes. The narrow 'yellow brick road' stretches the entire length of the beach (watch out for motorcycles).

Blue Wind (Map p236; ☎ 0 7745 6116, 0 7745 6015; bluewind_wa@yahoo.com; bungalows 300-900B; 🐱) Hidden within a clump of bodacious lodging options, Blue Wind offers a breath of fresh air from the high-intensity dive resorts strung along Sairee Beach. Sturdy bamboo huts are peppered along a dirt trail behind the beachside bakery. Large, tiled air-conditioned cabins are also available, boasting hot showers and TVs.

Big Blue Resort (Map p236; ☎ 0 7745 6050; www .bigbluediving.com; r 400-1000B; 🐱 🖳) This scuba-centric resort has a summer camp vibe – diving classes dominate the daytime, while evenings are spent en masse, grabbing dinner or watching fire twirling. Both the basic fan bungalows and motel-style air-con rooms offer little when it comes to views, but who has the time to relax when there's an ocean out there to explore?

Sairee Cottage (Map p236; ☎ 0 7745 6126, 0 7745 6374; saireecottage@hotmail.com; bungalows 400-1500B; ✕) The air-con bungalows are hard to miss since they've been painted in various hues of fuchsia. Low prices means low vacancy – so arrive early to score one of the brick huts facing out onto a grassy knoll.

AC Resort (Map p236; ☎ 0 7745 6197; www.phoenix -divers.com; bungalows from 400B; ✕ ▢ ⬚ ▣) A large sign, half-covered by an artificial waterfall, welcomes vacationers to the party at AC Resort. Backpackers will find a standard issue of well-worn huts. The air-conditioned cottages have gargantuan beds, but the bathrooms are microscopic. Divers get a 30% to 40% discount, which increases depending on how long you stay.

Ban's Diving Resort (Map p236; ☎ 0 7745 6466, 0 7745 6061; www.amazingkohtao.com; r from 400; ✕ ▢ ▣) This dive-centric party palace offers a wide range of quality accommodation from basic backpacker digs to sleek hillside villas. Post-scuba chill sessions happen on Ban's prime slice of beach, or at one of the two swimming pools tucked within the strip of jungle between the two motel-like structures. Evenings are spent at the Fish Bowl bar downing international cuisine and 'buckets' in equal measure.

Seashell Resort (Map p236; ☎ 0 7745 6299; www .seashell-resort.com; bungalows 450-3800B; ✕) Several bungalows have ocean views from their porches (a rarity in Sairee), while others sit in a well-maintained garden of colourful vegetation and thin palm trunks. Seashell welcomes divers and non-divers alike.

In Touch Resort (Map p236; ☎ 0 7745 6514; bungalows 500-1200B; ✕) Older bungalows are a mishmash of bamboo and dark wood, while several rounded air-con rooms have a cave theme – it's all very 'Flintstones', except the shower nozzle hasn't been replaced with the trunk of an elephant.

Bow Thong (Map p236; ☎ 0 7745 6266; bungalows from 600B; ✕ ▣) A member of the quieter northern section of silky Sairee Beach, Bow Thong has a cluster of reasonably priced bungalows if you're looking to be near the waves and aren't affiliated with a dive school.

Sunset Buri Resort (Map p236; 0 7745 6266; bungalows 700-2500B; ✕ ▢ ▣) A long beach-bound path

is studded with beautiful white bungalows featuring enormous windows and flamboyant temple-like roofing. The kidney-shaped pool is a big hit, as are the large beach recliners sprinkled around the resort.

Thipwimarn (Map p236; ☎ 0 7745 6409; www.thip wimarnresort.com; bungalows from 3000B; ✕ ⬚ ▣) North of the Sairee action, Thipwimarn occupies a secluded strip of land overlooking the quiet crystal sea. A circular restaurant with an outstanding view offers intimate, floor-level tables. Attractive bungalows spill down the hillside among boulders and greenery, with myriad stairs to keep you fit.

MAE HAT

All ferry arrivals pull into the pier at the busy village of Mae Hat. Busy village accommodation is spread throughout, but the more charming options extend in both directions along the sandy beach.

North of the Pier

Mr J Bungalow (Map p236; ☎ 0 7745 6066, 0 7745 6349; bungalows 250-1000B) Even though Mr J tried to charge us 50B for his business card, we still think he's well worth the visit. The eccentric owner entangles guests in a philosophical web while tending to his flock of decent bungalows. Ask him about reincarnation if you want to hear some particularly twisted conjectures.

View Cliff Resort (Map p236; ☎ 0 7745 6353; www .viewcliff.com; bungalows from 400B, r 1500B; ✕) A photogenic strip of Italianate double-decker bungalows links the narrow street with the rocky shoreline. The perfectly manicured lawns feel almost like the green of a golf course, and large rounded balconies overhead offer glimpses of the turquoise sea.

Tommy's Dive Resort (Map p236; ☎ 0 7745 6039; bungalows 700-2500B) Follow the undulating curve of the motel's porches as they slope down a hill, and check out the seaside views from the 700B rooms – these are the best bang for your baht at Tommy's. The convenient location between the bustle of Mae Hat and Sairee is a big plus.

Crystal Resort (Map p236; ☎ 0 7745 6107; www .crystaldive.com; bungalows 800-1500B; ✕ ▣) The bungalow and motel-style accommodation at Crystal is reserved for its divers, and prices drop significantly for those taking courses. Guests can take a dip in the refreshing pool when it isn't overflowing with bubble-blowing newbie divers.

Regal Resort (Map p236; ☎ 0 7745 6007; www .kohtaoregal.com; r from 2000B; 🏊 🖳 🛜 🖭) Home to the most beautiful swimming pool on the island, Regal is a new behemoth along the sands of Mae Hat. Set slightly away from the pier, this is a solid option for travellers seeking a sprinkle of air-con and ocean views from their balcony.

Montra Resort & Spa (Map p236; ☎ 0 7745 7057; www.kohtaocoral.com; r from 3500B; 🏊 🖳 🛜 🖭) A newer address virtually at the Mae Hat pier, Montra is an upmarket affair with all the modern bells and whistles. The hotel structure is rather imposing when compared to the scatter of humble bungalows next door.

South of the Pier

Utopia Suites (Map p236; ☎ 0 7745 6729, 0 7745 6672; r/ste from 600/2000B, monthly from 20,000B) Utopia is located in the charming fishing village, just a stone's throw from the pier. The beachside apartment-style accommodation is perfect for families and small groups. Ask about discounts for extended stays.

Sensi Paradise Resort (Map p236; ☎ 0 7745 6244; www.sensiparadise.com; bungalows 2500-9000B; 🏊) There are one too many geckos in the bathroom to call this place 'natural chic', but if you like to be at one with nature then you'll appreciate that these rustic cottages are somehow simultaneously upscale. Friendly caretakers and several airy teak *săh·lahs* add an extra element of charm.

Charm Churee Villa (Map p236; ☎ 0 7745 6393; www .charmchureevilla.com; bungalows 3200-12,200B; 🏊 🖳 🖭) Tucked gently under sky-scraping palms, the luxuriant villas of Charm Churee are dedicated to the flamboyant spoils of the Far East. Gold-foiled oriental demigods pose in arabesque positions, with bejewelled eyes frozen in a Zen-like trance. Staircases, chiselled into the rock face, dribble down a palmed slope revealing teak huts strewn across smoky boulders. The villas' unobstructed views of the swishing indigo waters are nothing short of charming.

The following sleeping spots are located further south and can be accessed by a quick ride in a boat taxi.

Sai Thong Resort (☎ 0 7745 6868; www.sai thong-resort.com; Hat Sai Nuan; bungalows 300-2500B; 🏊 🖳 🖭) As the rush of Mae Hat dwindles away along the island's southwest shore, Sai Thong emerges along sandy Hat Sai Nuan. Bungalows, in various incarnations of weav-

ing and wood, have colourful porch hammocks and palm-filled vistas. Guests frequent the restaurant's relaxing sun deck – a favourite spot for locals too.

Tao Thong Villa (☎ 0 7745 6078; Ao Sai Nuan; bungalows from 500B) Very popular with long-termers seeking peace and quiet, these funky, no-frills bungalows have killer views. Tao Thong actually straddles two tiny beaches on a craggy cape about halfway between Mae Hat and Chalok Ban Kao. The pair of neighbouring swim spots is the perfect place for a hermitic afternoon.

CHALOK BAN KAO

Ao Chalok, about 1.7km south of Mae Hat by road, is the third-largest concentration of accommodation on Ko Tao, but can feel a lot more crowded because the beach is significantly smaller than Sairee and Mae Hat. The beach itself isn't tops as low tides are often muddy.

Budget

Buddha View Dive Resort (☎ 0 7745 6074; www.buddha view-diving.com; r 300-1500B; 🏊) Like the other large diving operations on the island, Buddha View offers its divers discounted on-site digs in a super-social atmosphere. If you plan on staying a while, ask about the 'Divers Village' across the street, which offers basic accommodation from around 4,000B per month.

Tropicana (☎ 0 7745 6167; www.koh-tao-tropicana -resort.com; r from 400) Tropicana ups the ante when it comes to quality budget digs. Low-rise hotel units are peppered across a garden campus providing fleeting glimpses of the ocean between fanned fronds and spiky palms.

JP Resort (☎ 0 7745 6099; bungalows from 400B) This little cheapie promises a colourful menagerie of prim motel-style rooms stacked on a small scrap of jungle across the street from the sea. Sun-soaked rooms have polished pastel-coloured linoleum floor, and many of the tiled bathrooms have been recently refurbished.

Freedom Beach (☎ 0 7745 6596; bungalows 400-1500B; 🏊) On its own secluded beach at the eastern end of Ao Chalok, Freedom feels like a classic backpacker haunt, although there's a variety of accommodation to suit various humble budgets. The string of bungalows (from wooden shacks to sturdier huts with air-con) links the breezy seaside bar to the resort's restaurant high on the cliff.

Viewpoint Resort (☎ 0 7745 6666; www.kohtaoview point.com; bungalows 800-1300B) A hot-shot architect from Bangkok allegedly designed this friendly, family-run retreat at the end of civilisation. Cottages are spartan but airy and well maintained. Some have partial sea views; others quietly sit in a gorgeous hillside garden that thrums with cicadas at night.

Midrange & Top End

New Heaven Resort (☎ 0 7745 6422; newheavenresort@ yahoo.co.th; r & bungalows 1200-3900B) Just beyond the clutter of Chalok Ban Kao, New Heaven delivers colourful huts perched over impossibly clear waters. A steep path of chiselled stone tumbles down the shrubby rock face revealing views ripped straight from the pages of *National Geographic*.

Ko Tao Resort (☎ 0 7745 6133; www.kotaoresort.com; r & bungalows 1600-3900B; 🅿 🖳 🛋) The entrance is a throwback to the days when taste and architecture weren't particularly synonymous (the '70s perhaps?), but the facilities themselves fit the true definition of a resort. The rooms are well stocked, water sports equipment is on offer, and there are several bars primed to serve an assortment of fruity cocktails.

Chintakiri Resort (☎ 0 7745 6133; www.chintakiri .com; r & bungalows 2900-4000B; 🅿 🖳 🛋) Perched high over the gulf waters overlooking Chalok Ban Kao, Chintakiri (which sounds a bit too much like the top-end fave Jamahkiri) is one of Ko Tao's newest luxury additions as the island furtively creeps upmarket. Rooms are spread around the inland jungle, and sport crisp white walls with lacquered finishing.

EAST COAST BEACHES

The serene eastern coast is, without a doubt, one of the best places in the region to live out your island paradise fantasies. The views are stunning, beaches are silent, yet all of your creature comforts are 10 minutes away. Accommodation along this coast is organised from north to south.

Hin Wong

A sandy beach has been swapped for a boulder-strewn coast, but the water is crystal clear. The road to Hin Wong is paved in parts, but sudden sand pits and steep hills can toss you off your motorbike.

Hin Wong Bungalows (☎ 0 7745 6006, 08 1229 4810; bungalows from 300B) Pleasant wooden huts are scattered across vast expanses of untamed

tropical terrain – it all feels a bit like *Gilligan's Island* (minus the millionaire castaways). A rickety dock, jutting out just beyond the breezy restaurant, is the perfect place to dangle your legs and watch schools of black sardines slide through the cerulean water.

View Rock (☎ 0 7745 6548/9; viewrock@hotmail .com; bungalows 300-400B) When coming down the dirt road into Hin Wong, follow the signs as they lead you north (left) of Hin Wong Bungalows. View Rock is precisely that: views and rocks; the hodgepodge of wooden huts, which looks like a secluded fishing village, is built into the steep crags offering stunning views of the bay.

Laem Thian

Laem Thian is a scenic cape with a small patch of sand.

Laem Thian (☎ 0 7745 6477; r & bungalows 400-1500B; 🅿) Nestled far from civilisation on a lush stretch of jungle, this small boulder-filled resort is the only operation on Laem Thian. The modern rooms tend to be better than the bungalows, so long as you don't mind the ugly facades. The road here is very rough; call for a pick up.

Tanote Bay (Ao Tanot)

Tanote Bay is more populated than some of the other eastern coves, but it's still rather quiet and picturesque. It is the only bay on the east coast that is accessible by a decent road. Discounted taxis (around 100B) bounce back and forth between Tanote Bay and Mae Hat, ask at your resort for a timetable and price details.

Poseidon (☎ 0 7745 6735; poseidonkohtao@hotmail .com; bungalows from 300B) Poseidon keeps the tradition of the budget bamboo bungalow alive with a dozen basic-but-sleep-able huts scattered near the sand.

Bamboo Huts (☎ 0 7745 6531; bungalows 300-500B) Sitting on scraggly boulders in the centre of Tanote Bay, Bamboo Huts caters to pennypinchers with the usual crew of cheap bungalows. The sociable restaurant, serving Thai and Western fare, is an added bonus.

Diamond Beach (☎ 0 7745 6591; bungalows 300-1100B; 🅿) Diamond's beachy batch of huts sits directly on Tanote's sand. There's a mix of bungalow types, including A-frames for tinier wallets.

Black Tip Dive Resort (☎ 0 7745 6488; www.blacktip -kohtao.com; bungalows 600-2800B; 🅿 🖳 🛜) Part dive shop and water-sports centre, Black Tip also has a handful of lovely wooden bungalows with thatched roofing. The scuba centre is housed in a wacky structure made of rippling white adobe and strange geometric protrusions. Guests get a 50% discount when enrolled in a diving course and 'fun divers' get 25% off room rates.

Ao Leuk & Ao Thian Ok

The dirt roads to Ao Leuk and Ao Thian Ok are steep, rough and rutty, especially towards the end; don't attempt it on a motorcycle unless you're an expert. Both bays are stunning and serene.

Ao Leuk Bungalows (☎ 0 7745 6692; bungalows 400-1500B) Lodging at Ao Leuk comes in several shapes and sizes ranging from backpacker shacks to modern family-friendly options. Flickering torches and ambient cackles of curious cicadas accent the jet-black evenings.

Jamahkiri Resort & Spa (☎ 0 7745 6400; www .jamahkiri.com; bungalows 6900-13,900B) The flamboyant decor at this whitewashed estate is decidedly focused around tribal imagery. Wooden gargoyle masks and stone fertility goddesses abound amid swirling mosaics and multi-armed statues. Feral hoots of distant monkeys confirm the overarching jungle theme, as do the thatched roofs and tiki-torched soirees. The resort's seemingly infinite number of stone stairways can be a pain, so it's a good thing Ko Tao's most luxurious spa is located on the premises.

NORTH COAST

Mango Bay, an isolated rocky bay, has one sleeping option set in a dramatic backdrop of tangled jungle vines and rocky hills.

Mango Bay Grand Resort (☎ 0 7745 6097; www .mangobaygrandresortkohtaothailand.com; bungalows 1400-3000B; ⊠) Spacious mahogany bungalows are perched high on stilts above the ashen boulders lining the bay. A thin necklace of mosaic-lined paths winds through the tropical shrubbery, connecting the secluded villas.

KO NANG YUAN

Photogenic Ko Nang Yuan, just off the coast of Ko Tao, is easily accessible by the Lomprayah catamaran, and by water taxis that depart from Mae Hat and Sairee.

Ko Nangyuan Dive Resort (☎ 0 7745 6088, 0 7745 6093; www.nangyuan.com; bungalows 1500-7000B; ⊠) Although the obligatory 100B tax to access the island is a bit off-putting (as is the 100B water taxi ride each way), Nangyuan Dive Resort is nonetheless a charming place to stay. The rugged collection of wood and aluminium bungalows winds its way across three coolie-hat-like conical islands connected by an idyllic beige sandbar. The resort also boasts the best restaurant on the island, but then again, it's the only place to eat…

Eating

With super-sized Samui lurking in the horizon, it's hard to believe that quaint little Ko Tao is a worthy opponent in the gastronomy category. Most resorts and dive operators offer on-site dining, and stand-alone establishments are multiplying at lightning speed in Sairee Beach and Mae Hat. The diverse population of divers has spawned a broad range of international cuisine, including Mexican, French, Italian, Indian and Japanese. On our quest to find the tastiest Thai fare on the island, we discovered, not surprisingly, that our favourite local meals were being dished out at small, unnamed restaurants on the side of the road.

SAIREE BEACH

Ally the Pancake Man (Map p236; pancakes from 20-40B; ☺ lunch & dinner) Stop by the 7-Eleven beside Big Blue Resort to check out Ally The Pancake Man as he dances around – like an Italian chef making pizza – while cooking your tasty snack. The 'banana nutella' is a fave.

Café Corner (Map p236; snacks & mains 30-120B; ☺ breakfast & lunch) The flaky *pain au chocolat* can easily be mistaken for a Parisian patisserie. Customers enjoy their desserts at swirling stainless steel countertops while watching movies on a swanky plasma TV. Swing by at 5pm to stock up for tomorrow morning's breakfast; the scrumptious baked breads are buy-one-get-one-free before being tossed at sunset.

Blue Wind Bakery (Map p236; ☎ 0 7745 6116; mains 50-120B; ☺ breakfast, lunch & dinner) This beachside shanty dishes out Thai favourites, Western confections and freshly blended fruit juices. Enjoy your thick fruit smoothie and flaky pastry while reclining on tattered triangular pillows.

Krua Thai (Map p236; ☎ 08 7892 9970; dishes 50-120B; ☺ lunch & dinner) Popular with the tourists who want their food 'faráng spicy' rather than 'Thai spicy', Krua Thai offers a large assortment of classic faves served in a well-maintained storefront.

Chopper's Bar & Grill (Map p236; ☎ 0 7745 6641; dishes 60-200B; ☺ breakfast, lunch & dinner) So popular that it's become a local landmark, Chopper's is a two-storey hangout where divers and tourists can widen their beer belly. There's live music, sports on the big-screen TVs, billiards, and a cinema room. Friday nights are particularly popular; the drinks are 'two for one', and dishes are half-priced as well. Cheers for scored goals are interspersed with the exaggerated chatter about creatures seen on the day's dive.

Big Blue East (Map p236; ☎ 0 7745 6416; dishes 70-250B; ☺ 6am-11pm) Big Blue Resort's busy chow house, located about 2m from the crashing tide, dispatches an assortment of Thai and international eats, including tasty individual pizzas. The joint fills up around sunset with divers chuckling at the daily dive bloopers shown on the big-screen TV.

El Gringo (Map p236; ☎ 0 7745 6323; dishes 80-150B; ☺ 9am-11pm) As if there aren't already enough nicknames for white people in Thailand. The self-proclaimed 'funky Mexican joint' slings burritos of questionable authenticity in both Sairee Beach and Mae Hat. Delivery available.

ZanziBar (Map p236; ☎ 0 7745 6452; sandwiches 90-140B; ☺ breakfast, lunch & dinner) The island's outpost of sandwich yuppie-dom slathers a mix of unpronounceable condiments betwixt two slices of wholegrain bread.

Barracuda Restaurant & Bar (Map p236; ☎ 08 0146 3267; mains 180-400B; ☺ lunch & dinner) Brand new to Ko Tao's ever expanding dining scene, Barracuda offers a refined selection of seafood and gourmet bites. The owner, a masterful chef with many years in the biz, makes an earnest attempt to use only locally sourced ingredients.

Morava (Map p236; ☎ 0 7745 6270; dishes 200-350B; ☺ breakfast, lunch & dinner) This Sairee splurge has out-swanked the competition with smooth decor and equally stylish dishes. The carefully refined menu features delicious options such as tender lamb steaks and fresh-from-the-sea sashimi.

MAE HAT

Yang (Map p236; ☎ 0 7745 6226; dishes 30-70B; ☺ breakfast, lunch & dinner) Simply put, Yang's offers mounds of cheap Thai chow for pennies.

Nutta Chinese Noodle (Map p236; dishes 30-90B; ☺ dinner) Green-tinged neon lights and a lone, surly fish in the aquarium – that's how far the

decor goes at this scruffy hole-in-the-wall. But it's well worth stopping by for some grub – try the 'number three', a mix of three types of pork on a bed of rice with a side of savoury soup. Pour the soup over the pork and voila; a cheap and tasty meal.

Pranee's Kitchen (Map p236; dishes 50-120B; ☺ 7am-10pm; ☎) An old Mae Hat fave, Pranee's serves scrumptious curries and other Thai treats in an open-air pavilion sprinkled with lounging pillows, wooden tables and TVs. English movies (with hilariously incorrect subtitles) are shown nightly at 6pm.

Safety Stop Pub (Map p236; ☎ 0 7745 6209; mains 60-250B; ☺ 7am-late; ☎) A haven for homesick Brits, this pier-side restaurant and bar feels like a tropical beer garden. Stop by on Sundays to stuff your face with an endless supply of barbecued goodness.

Farango's (Map p236; ☎ 0 7745 6205; dishes 80-230B; ☺ 11am-10pm) Ko Tao's first faràng restaurant spins tasty pizzas and other signature Italian fare. Free delivery. There's a second location on the outskirts of Sairee Village.

Tattoo Bar & Restaurant (Map p236; ☎ 08 9291 9416; hamburger 150B) Just 30m south of Whitening (at the edge of the fishing village), Tattoo is a casual affair with a cosy area for TV watching. If you're hungry, try the massive Aussie burger, homemade meat pies and sausage rolls.

Dirty Nelly's Irish Pub (Map p236; ☎ 0 7745 6569; mains 180-250B) True to its name, Dirty Nelly's is unapologetically Irish; the draught beers, the managers – everything's been imported straight from the motherland (except the weather). There's billiards, sports on the big-screen TV, a menu of hearty eats, and regular weekend BBQs.

Zest Coffee Lounge (Map p236; ☎ 0 7745 6178; dishes 70-190B; ☺ 6am-6pm; ☎) Indulge in the street-cafe lifestyle at Zest – home to the best cup of joe on the island. Idlers can nibble on *ciabatta* sandwiches or sticky confections while nursing their creamy caffe latte. There's a second branch in Sairee, although we prefer this location.

our pick Café del Sol (Map p236; ☎ 0 7745 6578; dishes 70-250B; ☺ 8am-11pm; ☐ ☎) Even the pickiest eater will be satisfied with the menu's expansive selection of 'world cuisine'. Located just steps away from the pier, this is our favourite breakfast spot on the island – go for the 'Del Sol breakfast' (delicious fruit salad, yoghurt and coffee) with a scrumptious spinach omelette on the side. Lunch and dinner dishes range from hearty pepper hamburgers to homemade pasta.

Greasy Spoon (Map p236; ☎ 08 6272 1499; English breakfast 120B; ⏱ 7am-6pm) Although completely devoid of character, Greasy Spoon stays true to its name offering a variety of heart-clogging breakfast treats: eggs, sausage, stewed vegies and chips (their speciality) that'll bring a tear to any Brit's eye.

our pick **Whitening** (Map p236; ☎ 0 7745 6199; dishes 160-300B; ⏱ dinner) This beachy spot falls somewhere between being a restaurant and chic seaside bar – foodies will appreciate the tasty twists on indigenous and international dishes while beertotalers will love the beachy, breached-white atmosphere which hums with gentle lounge music. Dine amid dangling white Christmas lights while keeping your bare feet tucked into the sand. This is the top spot on the island for a celebratory dinner. And the best part? It's comparatively easy on the wallet.

CHALOK BAN KAO

Tukta Thai Food (☎ 0 7745 6109; dishes 40-180B; ⏱ breakfast, lunch & dinner) On the main road coming into Chalok Ban Kao, Tukta is solid option for Thai staples.

New Heaven Restaurant (☎ 0 7745 6462; lunch dishes 60-180B, dinner dishes 60-350B; ⏱ lunch & dinner) The best part about New Heaven Restaurant is the awe-inducing view of Shark Bay (Ao Thian Ok) under the lazy afternoon moon. The turquoise waters below are so translucent that the curving reef is easily visible from your seat. The menu is largely international, and there are nap-worthy cushions tucked under each low-rise table.

Drinking & Entertainment

After diving, Ko Tao's favourite pastime is drinking, and there's definitely no shortage of places to get tanked. In fact, the island's three biggest dive centres each have bumpin' bars – **Fish Bowl** (Map p236), **Crystal Bar** (Map p236) and **Buddha On The Beach** – that attract swarms of travellers and expats alike. It's well worth stopping by even if you aren't a diver. Fliers detailing upcoming parties are posted on various trees and walls along the island's west coast (check the two 7-Elevens in Sairee). Also keep an eye out for posters touting 'jungle parties' held on nondescript patches of scrubby jungle in the centre of the island. Two large-scale party venues, **Club H2O** and **Castle**, are tak-

ing things to a new level with internationally acclaimed DJs and dedicated clubbing spaces for hundreds of partiers. The tides also play an integral part of the island's night scene. On evenings when the tides are high, there tends to be less of the raucous along Sairee Beach since there's not a lot of room to get wild.

In addition to the following options, several places in our 'eating' section (p244) – like Dirty Nelly's, Choppers and Safety Stop Pub – double as great hangout joints for a well-deserved post-dive beer.

Just remember; don't drink and dive.

Fizz (Map p236; ☎ 08 7887 9495; Sairee Beach) Recline on mattress-sized pillows and enjoy designer cocktails while listening to Moby, or Enya, mixed with hypnotic gushes of the rolling tide. Stick around for dinner – the tuna steaks (200B) earn top marks.

Lotus Bar (Map p236; ☎ 0 7745 6358; Sairee Beach) This bar, next door to Fizz, is the de facto late-night hangout spot along the northern end of Sairee. Muscular fire twirlers toss around flaming batons, and the drinks are so large there should be a lifeguard on duty.

Dragon Bar (Map p236; ☎ 0 7745 6423; Mae Hat) This bar caters to those seeking snazzy, cutting-edge surroundings. There is a happening 'Communist chic' retro styling throughout, and everything's dimly lit, moody and relaxing. Dragon Bar is rumoured to have the best cocktails on the island.

Vibe (Map p236; Sairee Beach) Sairee's top spot for sundowner drinks, Vibe has the largest (and best) playlist of any drinking spot on the island.

Clumped at the southern end of Sairee Beach, the following nightspots take turns reeling in the partiers throughout the week:

AC Party Pub (Map p236; ☎ 0 7745 6197)
In Touch (Map p236; ☎ 0 7745 6514)
Maya Bar (Map p236; ☎ 0 7745 6195)

Shopping

Although most items are cheap when compared to prices back home, diving equipment is a big exception to the rule. On Ko Tao you'll be paying Western prices plus shipping plus commission on each item (even with 'discounts') so it's better to do your scuba shopping at home or on your computer.

If you're having trouble scrubbing the sea salt out of your hair, then stop by **Avalon** (Mae Hat; 10am-7pm Mon-Sat) for some locally made (and eco-friendly) body and hair care products.

Sweet tooths should swing by **1 Million Candy** (Map p236; ☎ 08 7272 9758; candy from 20B; 4-8pm Mon-Sat) in Sairee plaza for a sugary reminder of home.

Getting There & Away

As always, the cost and departure times are in flux. Rough waves are known to cancel ferries between the months of October and December. Beware of travel agencies in Bangkok selling fake 1st-class boat/train combinations. When the waters are choppy we recommend taking the Seatran rather than the Lomprayah catamaran if you are prone to seasickness. The catamarans ride the swell, whereas the Seatran cuts through the currents as it crosses the sea. Note that we highly advise purchasing your boat tickets *several* days in advance if you are accessing Ko Tao from Ko Pha-Ngan in January, February, March, July or August – especially after Full Moon.

BANGKOK, HUA HIN & CHUMPHON

Bus/boat package tickets from Bangkok – such as the Lomprayah service – cost 900B and are available from travel agencies all over Bangkok and the south. Watch out for scams – many agencies will book you on a shabby bus while tricking you into paying '1st class' prices. Also, bring all of your valuables onto the bus with you as thieves are known to rifle through luggage stored in the under-bus compartments. Buses switch to boats in Chumphon and BKK-bound passengers can choose to disembark in Hua Hin (for the same price as the Ko Tao–Bangkok ticket).

If you are planning to travel through the night, the train's couchettes are a much more comfortable option than the bus. Travellers can plan their own journey by taking a boat to Chumphon, then making their way to Chumphon's town centre to catch a train up to Bangkok (or any town along the upper southern gulf); likewise in the opposite direction.

From Ko Tao, the high-speed catamaran departs for Chumphon at 10.15am and 2.45pm (350B, 1½ hours), the Seatran leaves the island at 4pm (350B, two hours), and a Songserm fast boat makes the same journey at 2.30pm (300B, three hours). There may be fewer departures if the swells are high.

There's also a midnight boat from Chumphon (300B) arriving early in the morning. It returns from Ko Tao at 11pm. Don't take this boat if there's a good chance of rain; some boats leak and you'll be wet, cold and miserable.

Boat/couchette connections can be arranged for 950B to 1350B (depending on whether or not you want fan or air-con).

See p166 for more information.

KO PHA-NGAN

The Lomprayah Catamaran offers twice daily service (350B), leaving Ko Tao at 9.30am and 3pm and arriving on Ko Pha-Ngan around 10.50am and 4.10pm. The Seatran Discovery Ferry offers an identical service. The Songserm Express Boat departs daily at 10am and arrives on Ko Pan-Ngan at 11.30am. Hotel pick ups are included in the price. See p232 for departure times if you coming from Ko Pha-Ngan.

KO SAMUI

The Lomprayah Catamaran offers twice daily service (500B), leaving Ko Tao at 9.30am and 3pm and arriving on Samui around 11.30am and 4.40pm. The Seatran Discovery Ferry offers an identical service. The Songserm Express Boat departs daily at 10am and arrives on Samui at 12.45pm. Hotel pick ups are included in the price.

SURAT THANI & THE ANDAMAN COAST

If you are heading to the Andaman Coast and do not want to stop on Ko Pha-Ngan

SOUTHWESTERN GULF COAST

or Ko Samui along the way, then there are two routes which you can take. The first, and more common approach is through Surat Thani. First, board a Surat-bound boat (the Songserm or the night ferry, unless you want to change ships) then transfer to a bus upon arrival. The night boat (550B; nine hours) leaves Ko Tao at 8.30pm. Daily buses to the Songserm Express Boat depart from Surat Thani at 8am and arrive at 2.30pm. Return passengers leave Ko Tao at 10am and arrive in Surat Thani at 4.30pm.

The second option is to take a ferry to Chumphon on the mainland and then switch to a bus or train bound for the provinces further south.

All boat/bus combination tickets are available at any travel agency, simply tell them your desired destination and they will sell you the necessary links in the transport chain.

Getting Around

Sŏrng·tăa·ou, pick-up trucks and motorbikes crowd around the pier in Mae Hat as passengers alight. If you're a solo traveller, you will pay 100B to get to Sairee Beach or Chalok Ban Kao. Groups of two or more will pay 50B each. Rides from Sairee to Chalok Ban Kao cost 80B per person, or 150B for solo tourists. These prices are rarely negotiable, and passengers will be expected to wait until their taxi is full unless they want to pay an additional 200B to 300B. Prices double for trips to the east coast, and the drivers will raise the prices when rain makes the roads harder to negotiate. If you know where you intend to stay, we highly recommend calling ahead to arrange a pick up. Many dive schools offer free pick ups and transfers as well.

Renting a motorcycle is a dangerous endeavour (see p235) if you're not sticking to the main, well-paved roads. Daily rental rates begin at 150B for a scooter. Larger bikes start at 350B. Discounts are available for weekly and monthly rentals. Try **Lederhosenbikes** (Map p236; ☎ 08 1752 8994; www.lederhosenbikes.com; Mae Hat; ☺ 8.30am-6pm Mon-Sat). Do not rent all-terrrain-vehicles (ATVs) or jet skis – they are unsafe.

Boat taxis depart from Mae Hat, Chalok Ban Kao and the northern part of Sairee Beach (near Vibe Bar). Boat rides to Ko Nang Yuan will set you back at least 100B. Long-tail boats can be chartered for around 1500B per day, depending on the number of passengers carried.

ANG THONG MARINE NATIONAL PARK

อุทยานแห่งชาติหมู่เกาะอ่างทอง

The 40-some jagged jungle islands of Ang Thong Marine Park stretch across the cerulean sea like a shattered emerald necklace – each piece a virgin realm featuring sheer limestone cliffs, hidden lagoons and perfect peach-coloured sands. These dream-inducing islets inspired Alex Garland's cult classic The Beach about dope-dabbling backpackers.

February, March and April are the best months to visit this ethereal realm of greens and blues; crashing monsoon waves means that the park is almost always closed from October to Christmas.

Sights

Every tour stops at the park's head office on **Ko Wua Talap**, the largest island in the archipelago. The island's **viewpoint** might just be the most stunning vista in all of Thailand. From the top, visitors will have sweeping views of the jagged islands nearby as they burst through the placid turquoise water in easily anthropomorphised formations. The trek to the lookout is an arduous 450m trail that takes roughly an hour to complete. Hikers should wear sturdy shoes and walk slowly on the sharp outcrops of limestone. A second trail leads to **Tham Bua Bok**, a cavern with lotus-shaped stalagmites and stalactites.

The **Emerald Sea** (also called the Inner Sea) on **Ko Mae Ko** is another popular destination. This large lake in the middle of the island spans an impressive 250m by 350m and has an ethereal minty tint. You can look but you can't touch; the lagoon is strictly off-limits to the unclean human body. A second dramatic **viewpoint** can be found at the top of a series of staircases nearby.

The naturally occurring stone arches on **Ko Samsao** and **Ko Tai Plao** are visible during seasonal tides and weather conditions. Because the sea is quite shallow around the island chain, reaching a maximum depth of 10m, extensive coral reefs have not developed, except in a few protected pockets on the southwest and northeast sides. There's a shallow coral reef near Ko Tai Plao and Ko Samsao that has decent but not excellent snorkelling. There are also several novice dives for exploring shallow caves and colourful coral gardens and spotting banded sea snakes and turtles. Soft powder beaches line **Ko Tai Plao**, **Ko Wuakantang** and **Ko Hintap**.

Tours

The best way to experience Ang Thong is through one of several guided tours departing from Ko Samui and Ko Pha-Ngan. The tours usually include lunch, snorkelling equipment, hotel transfers, kayaking, and (with fingers crossed) a knowledgable guide. If you're staying in luxury accommodation, there's a chance that your resort has a private boat for group tours. Some midrange and budget places also have their own boats, and if not, they can easily set you up with a general tour operator. Dive centres on Ko Samui and Ko Pha-Ngan offer scuba trips to the park, although Ang Thong doesn't offer the same calibre of diving that can be found around Ko Tao.

Due to the tumultuous petrol prices, tour companies come and go like the wind. Check out p200 and p222 for additional details.

Sleeping

Ang Thong does not have any resorts; however, the national park has set up five bungalows on Ko Wua Talap, which each house between two and eight guests. The marine park also allows campers to pitch a tent in certain designated zones. Advance reservations can be made with the **National Parks Services** (☎ 0 7728 6025, 0 7728 0222; www.dnp.go.th; bungalows 500-1400B). Online bookings are possible, although customers must forward a bank deposit within two days of making the reservation. Check out their website for detailed information.

Getting There & Around

The best way to reach the park is to catch a private day-tour from Ko Samui or Ko Pha-Ngan (located 28km and 32km away, respectively). The islands sit between Samui and the main pier at Don Sak; however, no ferries stop along the way. There is a dedicated tourist booth at the pier in Na Thon on Ko Samui for those interested in planning a trip, although virtually any travel agency on Samui or Ko Pha-Ngan can sort you out. Private boat charters are another possibility, although high gas prices will make the trip quite expensive.

MAINLAND

Noticeably devoid of awe-inducing attractions, the southwestern gulf's mainland is usually encountered as travellers make their way between the Andaman and gulf coasts.

SURAT THANI & AROUND

อ.เมืองสุราษฎร์ธานี

pop 126,900

Known in Thai as 'City of Good People', Surat Thani was once the seat of the ancient Srivijaya empire. Today, this busy junction has become a transport hub that indiscriminately moves cargo and people around the country. Travellers rarely linger here as they make their way to the deservedly popular islands of Ko Samui, Ko Pha-Ngan and Ko Tao.

Information

Scores of tourists pass through town every day sparking many unscrupulous travel agencies to develop innovative scams involving substandard buses, phantom bookings and surprise 'extra' fees. Also, a common annoyance is having valuables stolen from large luggage stored under the bus. Locks do not help – take all items of importance with you to your seat. Not everyone's a crook, of course; just make sure to ask a lot of questions and trust your instincts. Traffic in Surat Thani flows both ways, so when you happen upon tourists travelling in the opposite direction, ask them about their experiences.

Th Na Meuang has a bank on virtually every corner in the heart of downtown. If you're staying near the 'suburbs', the Tesco-Lotus has ATMs as well.

Boss Computer (per hr 20B; ☽ 9am-midnight) The cheapest internet connection around. Located near the post office.

Post Office (☎ 0 7727 2013, 0 7728 1966; Th Talat Mai; ☽ 8.30am-4.30pm Mon-Fri, 8.30am-12.30pm Sat) Across from Wat Thammabucha. The local One Tambon One People (OTOP) craft house is located inside.

Siam City Bank (Th Chonkasem) Has a Western Union office.

Taksin Hospital (☎ 0 7727 3239; Th Talat Mai) The most professional of Surat's three hospitals. Just beyond the Talat Mai Market in the northeast part of downtown.

TAT office (☎ 0 7728 8817; tatsurat@samart.co.th; 5 Th Talat Mai; ☽ 8.30am-4.30pm) Friendly office southwest of town. Distributes plenty of useful brochures and maps, and staff speak English very well.

Sleeping

For a comfy night in Surat, escape the grimy city centre and hop on a sŏrng·tăa·ou heading towards the Phangna district. When you climb aboard, tell the driver 'Tesco-Lotus', and you'll be taken 4km out of the town centre to a large, boxlike shopping centre. When looking away from the mall, head right, and as you start walking you'll spot the billboards of at least four hotel options that have low prices and refreshingly modern amenities.

Sleeping options in the downtown area are cheaper, but many tend to offer 'by the hour' service, so things can get a bit noisy as clients come and go. If you're on a very tight schedule or budget, consider zipping straight through town and take the night ferry (see opposite). When the weather is nice, you may even sleep better on the boat than in a noisy hotel. But if there's a chance of rain, beware – you're likely to be wet and weary in the morning.

Home Stay (☎ 08 6475 7747; Khlong Roi Sai; r 100B) Situated behind the TAT office, this rather informal homestay is the cheapest place to crash in the entire region and gives travellers a cultural counterpoint to the unmemorable box-motels further afield. English may be a little thin on the ground so consider asking the TAT office to hook you up, or, if you call, ask for Ms Bow or Mr Panook. Mini boat tours are available along the canal at around 7pm when the fireflies sparkle.

Queen Hotel (☎ 0 7731 1003; 916/10-13 Th Sri Sawat, Phun Phin; r 500B; 🛱) If you are stuck in the cruddy transport junction of Phun Phin, or want to catch a very early train, don't despair; there is one tolerable option. The Queen Hotel is just a block away from the train station. It's no luxury vacation, but at least you won't have to sleep on the streets. Have a look at a couple rooms before putting down your bags – some choices are larger and less dingy than others.

100 Islands Resort & Spa (☎ 0 7720 1150; www .roikoh.com; 19/6 Moo 3, Bypass Rd; r from 590B; 🛱 🖳 🛱) Across the street from the suburban Tesco-Lotus, 100 Islands is as good as it gets in Thailand for under 600B. This teak palace looks out of place along the suburban highway, but inside, the immaculate rooms surround an overgrown garden and lagoon-like swimming pool.

Wangtai Hotel (☎ 0 7728 3020; www.wangtaisurat .com; 1 Th Talat Mai; r 790-2000B; 🛱 🖳 🛱) Across the river from the TAT office, Wangtai tries its best to provide a corporate hotel atmosphere. Polite receptionists and tux-clad bellboys bounce around the vast lobby, and upstairs, rooms have unmemorable furnishings, but there are good views of the city from the upper floors.

Eating & Drinking

Surat Thani isn't exactly bursting with dining options. Head to the **night market** (commonly called Sarn Chao Ma; Th Ton Pho) for fried, steamed, grilled or sautéed delicacies – don't forget to try the crunchy insects, we hear they're a great source of protein. There are additional evening food stalls near the departure docks for the daily night boats to the islands, a seafood market at **Pak Nam Tapi**, and an afternoon **Sunday market** (🕑 4-9pm) near the TAT office. During the day many food stalls near the downtown bus terminal sell *kôw gài òp* (marinated baked chicken on rice), which is very tasty. If you're looking for something a bit more familiar (KFC and the like), try the Colosseum mall, two blocks from the Talat Kaset 1 terminal, or the Tesco-Lotus megamart 4km out of town. There's also a Big C supermarket 800m north-west of the hospital.

Crossroads Restaurant (☎ 0 7722 1525; Bypass Rd; dishes 50-200B; 🕑 11am-1am) Located 2km south-west of Surat across from the Tesco-Lotus mall, Crossroads has a quaint bluesy vibe enhanced by dim lighting and live music. Try the oysters – Surat Thani is famous for its giant molluscs, and the prices are unbeatable. There's a second location on the far side of the river near the centre of town.

GM Pub (30/16 Th Karunarat; dishes 40-140B; 🕑 lunch & dinner) GM has a good mix of locals and faràng English teachers who return time and time again for the mellow atmosphere, tasty international menu, and wide selection of beer and cocktails.

Getting There & Away

In general, if you are departing Bangkok or Hua Hin for Ko Pha-Ngan or Ko Tao, consider taking the train or a bus/boat package that goes through Chumphon rather than Surat. You'll save time, and the journey will be more comfortable. Travellers heading to/from Ko Samui will most likely pass through. If you require any travel services, try **Holiday Travel** (Th Na Meuang) or **Pranthip Co** (Th Talat Mai) – both are reliable and English is spoken.

AIR

Although flights from Bangkok to Surat Thani are cheaper than the flights to Samui, it takes quite a bit of time to reach the gulf islands from the airport. In fact, if you are attempting to fly back to Bangkok from the gulf islands, you'll probably have to leave your beachside

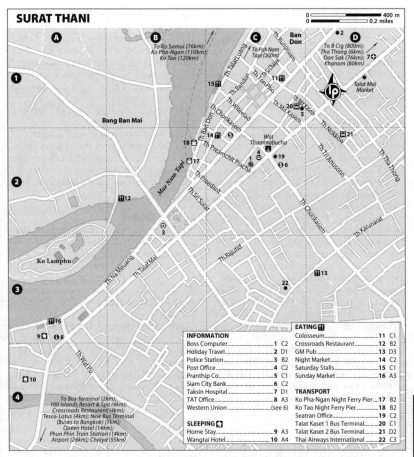

SURAT THANI

0 ——— 400 m
0 ——— 0.2 miles

INFORMATION		
Boss Computer	1	C2
Holiday Travel	2	D1
Police Station	3	B2
Post Office	4	C2
Pranthip Co	5	C1
Siam City Bank	6	C2
Taksin Hospital	7	D1
TAT Office	8	A3
Western Union	(see 6)	

SLEEPING		
Home Stay	9	A3
Wangtai Hotel	10	A4

EATING		
Colosseum	11	C1
Crossroads Restaurant	12	B2
GM Pub	13	D3
Night Market	14	C2
Saturday Stalls	15	C1
Sunday Market	16	A3

TRANSPORT		
Ko Pha-Ngan Night Ferry Pier	17	B2
Ko Tao Night Ferry Pier	18	B2
Seatran Office	19	C2
Talat Kaset 1 Bus Terminal	20	C1
Talat Kaset 2 Bus Terminal	21	D2
Thai Airways International	22	C3

bungalow the evening before your flight and spend the night in Surat. Not ideal. If you want to fly through Surat, there are daily shuttles to Bangkok on **Thai Airways International** (THAI; ☎ 0 7727 2610; 3/27-28 Th Karunarat) for around 3000B (70 minutes). See p213 for flights directly to Samui.

BOAT

In the high season travellers can usually find bus/boat services to Ko Samui and Ko Pha-Ngan directly from the Phun Phin train station. These services don't cost any more than those booked in Surat Thani and can save you some serious waiting time. There are also several ferry and speedboat operators that connect Surat Thani to Ko Tao, Ko Pha-Ngan

and Ko Samui. Most boats – such as the Raja and Seatran services – leave from Don Sak (about one hour from Surat; bus transfers are included in the ferry ticket) although the Songserm leaves from the heart of Surat town. Be warned that the Raja service can be a very frustrating experience, especially for travellers who are tight on time. The boat trip usually takes around 90 minutes to Ko Samui and 2½ hours to Ko Pha-Ngan, although oftentimes the captain will cut the engines to half propulsion, which means that the journey can take up to five hours. See the Getting There & Away section of your desired destination for more details.

From the centre of Surat there are nightly ferries to Ko Tao (550B, eight hours, departs at 10pm), Ko Pha-Ngan (350B, seven hours, departs at 10pm) and Ko Samui (200B, six hours, departs at 11pm). These are cargo ships, not luxury boats, so bring food and water and watch your bags. If Thai passengers are occupying your assigned berth, it's best to grab a different one nearby rather than asking them to move.

BUS & MINIVAN

The most convenient way to travel around the south, frequent buses and minivans depart from two main locations in town known as Talat Kaset 1 and Talat Kaset 2. Talat Kaset 1, on the north side of Th Talat Mai (the city's main drag) offers speedy service to Nakhon. This is also the location of Pranthip Co; one of the more trustworthy agencies in town. Buses to Phun Phin also leave from Talat Kaset 1. At Talat Kaset 2, on the south side of Th Talat Mai, you'll find frequent transportation to Hat Yai (220B) and minibuses to Nakhon, Trang, Khanom (120B) and Krabi (180B). Andaman-bound buses (usually destined for Phuket; 250B) depart every hour from 7am to 3.30pm, stopping at Takua Pa (150B) for those who want to access Khao Sok National Park. The 'new' bus terminal (which is actually a few years old now, but still referred to as new by the locals) is located 7km south of town on the way to Phun Phin. This hub services traffic to and from Bangkok. Buses to Bangkok start at 500B.

TRAIN

When arriving by train you'll actually pull into Phun Phin, a cruddy town 14km west of Surat. From Phun Phin, there are buses to Phuket, Phang-Nga and Krabi – some via Takua Pa, a junction city further west and the stopping point for Khao Sok National Park. Transport from Surat moves with greater frequency, but it's worth checking the schedule in Phun Phin first – you might luck out and save yourself a slow ride between towns. See right for more info.

If you plan on travelling during the day, go for the express railcars. Night travellers should opt for the air-con couchettes. Odd-numbered trains are travelling from Bangkok south – even-numbered trains are travelling in the opposite direction. Trains passing through Surat stop in Chumphon and Hua Hin on their way up to the capital, and in the other direction you'll call at Trang, Hat Yai and Sungai

Kolok before hopping the border. Figure 578B for a 2nd-class seat on a 'special express' train, 1179/758B for a an upper berth couchette in 1st/2nd class, or 1379/848B for a lower berth couchette in 1st/2nd class. If you take an early evening train from Bangkok you'll arrive here in the morning. Tickets can be purchased online (don't forget to click the 'EN' in the top right corner of the site), at a travel agency or at the train station itself.

The train station at Phun Phin has a 24-hour left-luggage room that charges around 20B a day. The advance ticket office is open from 6am to 6pm daily (with a nebulous one-hour lunch break somewhere between 11am and 1.30pm).

Getting Around

Air-conditioned vans to/from the Surat Thani airport cost around 70B per person and they'll drop you off at your hotel.

To travel around town, sŏrng·tǎa·ou cost 10B to 30B (it's 15B to reach Tesco-Lotus from the city centre), while sǎhm·lór (also spelt as sǎamláw; three-wheeled vehicles) charge from 20B to 40B.

Fan-cooled Orange buses run from Phun Phin train station to Surat Thani every 10 minutes (15B, 25 minutes). For this ride, taxis charge a cool 200B for a maximum of four people, while share-taxis charge 100B per person. Other taxi rates are posted just north of the train station (at the metal pedestrian bridge).

CHAIYA
ไชยา

pop 12,500

It's hard to believe that Chaiya, a sleepy town 60km north of Surat Thani, was once an important seat of the Srivijayan Empire. These days, most foreigners who visit are on their way to the outstanding meditation retreats held at the progressive Suan Mokkhaphalaram monastery.

Surrounded by lush forest, **Wat Suan Mokkhaphalaram** (Wat Suanmokkh; www.suanmokkh .org), which means 'the Garden of Liberation', charges 1500B for a 10-day program that includes food, lodging, and instruction (although technically the 'teaching' is free). English retreats begin on the first day of every month and registration takes place the night before. Founded by Ajahn Buddhadasa Bhikkhu, arguably Thailand's most famous monk, the temple's philosophical teachings are ecumenical in nature, comprising Zen, Taoist and Christian elements, as well as the traditional Theravada schemata.

To reach the temple, located 7km outside of Chaiya, you can catch a 3rd-class local train from Phun Phin (10B to 20B, one hour) or catch a sŏrng·tăa·ou (40B to 50B, 45 minutes) from Surat's Talat Kaset 2 bus terminal. If you're heading to Surat Thani by train from Bangkok, you can get off before Surat Thani at the small Chaiya train station. Take a motorcycle taxi from the station for an additional 40B.

AO KHANOM
อ่าวขนอม

Little Khanom, halfway between Surat Thani and Nakhon Si Thammarat, quietly sits along the blue gulf waters. Overlooked by tourists who flock to the jungle-islands nearby, this pristine region, simply called Khanom, is a worthy choice for those seeking a silent beach setting unmarred by enterprising corporations.

Information
The police station and hospital are located just south of Ban Khanom at the junction leading to Kho Khao Beach. There's a 7-Eleven (with an ATM) in the heart of Ban Khanom.

Sights
The most unique feature in Khanom, are the **pink dolphins** – a rare breed of albino dolphins that have a stunning pink hue. They are regularly seen from the old ferry pier and the electric plant pier around dawn and dust.

The area is also home to a variety of pristine geological features including **waterfalls** and **caves**. The largest of the falls, known as **Samet Chun**, has tepid pools for cooling off, and great views of the coast. To reach the falls, head south from Ban Khanom and turn left at the blue Samet Chun sign. Follow the road for about 2km and after crossing a small stream, take the next right and hike up into the mountain following the dirt road. After about a 15-minute walk, listen for the waterfall and look for a small trail on the right. The scenic **Hin Lat Falls** is the smallest cascade, but it's also the easiest to reach. There are pools for swimming and several huts providing shade. It's located south of Nai Phlao.

There are also two beautiful caves along the main road (Hwy 4014) between Khanom

and Don Sak. **Khao Wang Thong** has a string of lights guiding visitors through the network of caverns and narrow passages. A metal gate covers the entrance; stop at the house at the base of the hill to retrieve the key (and leave a small donation). Turn right off the main highway at Rd 4142 to find **Khao Krot Cave**, which has two large caverns, but you'll have to bring a torch (flashlight).

For a postcard-worthy vista of the undulating coastline, head to **Dat Fa Mountain**, located about 5km west of the coast along Hwy 4014. The hillside is usually deserted, making it easy to stop along the way to snap some photos.

Sleeping & Eating
In the last few years, there has been talk of further developing Khanom's beaches into a more laidback alterative to the islands nearby. The area is still far from booming, but large-scale development is on the cards. A recent surge in gulf oil rigging has meant that developers are eyeing Khanom as a potential holiday destination for nearby workers. There are enough options here that prebooking isn't a must – in fact we advise checking out a few places before picking a spot to crash. Many of the resorts see very few customers and the constant disuse (not regularly flushing the toilets etc) means that some rooms are dank as the relentless jungle reclaims them. It's best to stay away from the large hotels and stick to beachside bungalow operations.

For some cheap eats, head to **Kho Khao Beach** at the end of Rd 4232. You'll find a steamy jumble of BBQ stands offering some tasty favourites such as mŏo nám dòk (spicy pork salad) and sôm đam (spicy green papaya salad). On Wednesdays and Sundays, there are markets further inland near the police station.

Suchada Villa (☎ 0 7552 8459; bungalows 800B; ❄) Right along the main road – Suchada is recognisable by its cache of brightly coloured bungalows. Rooms are cute and clean with quirky designer details such as strings of shells dangling in front of the bathroom doors.

Talkoo Beach Resort (☎ 0 7552 8397, 08 3692 2711; bungalows 1470B; ❄ 🐾) This charming operation has dozens of snazzy white cottages featuring quirky fixtures such as sinks made from hollowed-out tree trunks. This is best lodging option in the vicinity.

Racha Kiri (☎ 0 7552 7847; www.rachakiri.com; bungalows 3500-12,500B; ❄ 🛜 🐾) Khanom's upscale retreat is a beautiful campus of rambling villas. The big price tag means no crowds, which can be nice, although the resort feels like a white elephant when the property isn't being used as a corporate retreat.

One More Beer (☎ 08 1396 4447; www.1morebeer. net; ✂ ▢ ☞) One More Beer is a popular expat-owned hangout spot serving a variety of tasty dishes from all over the globe. Ask for a spicy salad with *yordt ma plao* (heart of palm) instead of green papaya.

Getting There & Away
From Surat Thani, you can catch any Nakhon-bound bus and ask to be let off at the junction for Ban Khanom. Catch a motorcycle taxi (60B) the rest of the way. You can get a share taxi from Nakhon Si Thammarat's share taxi terminal to Khanom town for 85B. From Khanom town you can hire motorcycle taxis out to the beaches for about 60B. There are three separate bus stops in the vicinity. Ask your driver to stop near the fruit market or the hospital, as these are closer to the beach. Motorbikes can be rented at One More Beer for 300B per day.

NAKHON SI THAMMARAT
อ.เมืองนครศรีธรรมราช
pop 118,100
The bustling city of Nakhon Si Thammarat (usually shortened to 'Nakhon') won't win any beauty pageants. However, travellers who stop in this historic town will enjoy a decidedly cultural experience amid some of the most important wát in the kingdom. Hundreds of years ago, an overland route between the western port of Trang and eastern port of Nakhon Si Thammarat functioned as a major trade link between Thailand and the rest of the world. This ancient influx of cosmopolitan conceits is still palpable today, and can be found in the recipes of local cuisine, or housed in the city's temples and museums.

Orientation
Most of Nahkon's commercial activity (hotels, banks and restaurants) takes place in the northern part of downtown. South of the clock tower, visitors will find the city's historic quarter with the oft-visited Wat Mahathat. Th Ratchadamnoen is the main thoroughfare and is loaded with cheap sŏrng·tăa·ou heading in both directions.

Information
Several banks and ATMs hug Th Ratchadamnoen in the northern end of downtown. There is an English-language bookstore on the 3rd floor of Robinson Ocean shopping mall.

Bovorn Bazaar (Th Ratchadamnoen) A mall housing a few internet cafes.

Police station (☎ 1155; Th Ratchadamnoen) Opposite the post office.

Post office (Th Ratchadamnoen; ✇ 8.30am-4.30pm)

TAT office (☎ 0 7534 6515) Housed in a 1926-vintage building in the northern end of the Sanam Na Meuang (City Park). Has some useful brochures in English. The local OTOP craft house is just a block away on the west side of Sanam Na Meuang Park.

Sights
The most important wát in southern Thailand, **Wat Phra Mahathat Woramahawihaan** (simply known as 'Mahathat') is a stunning campus boasting 77 *chedi* and an imposing 77m *chedi* crowned by a gold spire. According to legend, Queen Hem Chala and Prince Thanakuman brought relics to Nakhon over a thousand years ago, and built a small pagoda to house the precious icons. The temple has since grown into a rambling site, and today, crowds gather daily to purchase the popular Jatukham amulets (see opposite). Mahathat's resident monks live across the street at **Wat Na Phra Boromathat**.

When the Tampaling (or Tambralinga) kingdom traded with merchants from Indian, Arabic, Dvaravati and Champa states, the region around Nakhon became a melting pot of crafts and art. Today, many of these relics are on display behind the rundown facade of the **national museum** (Th Ratchadamnoen; admission 30B; ✇ 9am-4pm Wed-Sun).

Nakhon's noteworthy shadow puppets are also worthy of exploration. Traditionally, there are two styles of puppet: *năng đà·lung* and *năng yài*. At just under 1m tall, the former are similar in size to the Malay-Indonesian-style puppets and feature moveable appendages and parts (including genitalia); the latter are unique to Thailand, nearly life-sized, and lack moving parts. Both are intricately carved from buffalo-hide. Nowadays performances are rare and usually limited to festivals.

Festivals & Events
Every year during mid-October there is a southern-Thai festival called **Chak Phra Pak Tai**

JATUKHAM RAMMATHEP

If you've spent more than 24 hours in Thailand then you've probably seen a Jatukham Rammathep dangling around someone's neck – these round amulets are everywhere.

The bearers of the Jatukham Rammathep are supposed to have good fortune and protection from any harm. The origin of the amulet's name remains a mystery, although a popular theory suggests that Jatukham and Rammathep were the aliases of two Srivajayan princes that buried relics under Nakhon's Wat Mahathat some 1000 years ago.

A notorious Thai police detective first wore the precious icon, and firmly believed that the guardian spirits helped him solve a particularly difficult murder case. He tried to popularise the amulet, but it wasn't a market success until his death in 2006. Thousands of people attended his funeral including the crown prince, and the Jatukham Rammathep took off.

The talismans are commissioned at the Mahathat temple, and in the last several years, southern Thailand has seen an incredible economic boom. The first amulet was sold in 1987 for 39B, and today, over 100 million baht are spent on the town's amulets every *week*. The desire for these round icons has become so frenzied that a woman was crushed to death on the temple grounds during a widely publicised discount sale (she was not wearing her talisman).

Everyday, trucks drive along Nakhon's main roads blaring loud music to promote new shipments. These thumping beats have started to shake the ground beneath the temple, and the repeated hammering has, in an ironic metaphor, bent the main spire of Wat Mahathat.

---

held in Nakhon Si Thammarat (as well as Songkhla and Surat Thani). In Nakhon Si the festival is focused on Wat Phra Mahathat and includes performances of *năng dà·lung* and *lá·kon*, as well as the parading of Buddha images around the city to collect donations for local temples.

In the third lunar month (February to March) the city holds the colourful **Hae Phaa Khun That**, in which a lengthy cloth *jataka* (stories of the Buddha's previous lives) painting is wrapped around the main *chedi* at Wat Phra Mahathat.

Sleeping

Lodging options are limited to a few respectable places.

Thai Hotel (☎ 0 7534 1509; fax 0 7534 4858; 1375 Th Ratchadamnoen; fan r 220-270B; air-con r 340-450B, ste 750B; 🕱) Thai Hotel is the most central sleeping spot in town – look for a small sign (which actually says 'Thai Hotet' in Thai) pointing down a busy sidestreet. The walls are thin, but the air-con options are a good deal for the price. Each room has a TV and the higher floors have good views of the urban bustle.

Nakorn Garden Inn (☎ 0 7532 3777; 1/4 Th Pak Nakhon; r 445B; 🕱) The motel-style Nakorn Garden Inn offers a pleasant alternative to the usual cement cube. Rooms are encased in exposed crimson brick and set around a sandy garden. Each unit is identical, sporting a TV and fridge; try to score a room that gets plenty of sunlight.

Grand Park Hotel (☎ 0 7531 7666-73; fax 0 7531 7674; 1204/79 Th Pak Nakhon; r 700-1700B; 🕱) Grand Park offers fine, modern rooms with TV and fridge – nothing too fancy or luxurious. The rooms are on seven floors, some with sweeping vistas of the city. Guests can loiter in the spacious lobby and restaurant.

Twin Lotus Hotel (☎ 0 7532 3777; www.twinlotushotel .net; 97/8 Th Phattanakan Khukhwang; r 1100-3000B; 🕱 🕱) Its age is starting to show, but Twin Lotus is still a nice spot for a little pampering while visiting Nakhon. The well-equipped hotel gym is very popular with the local English teachers. This 16-storey behemoth sits several kilometres southeast of the city centre.

Eating & Drinking

Nakhon is a great place to sample cuisine with a distinctive southern twist. In the evening, Muslim food stands sell delicious *khâo mòk* (chicken biryani), *má·dà·bà* (*murdabag*, a stuffed Indian pancake) and roti. Several tasty options cluster around Bovorn Bazaar on Th Ratchadamnoen.

For an all-night dance fest, head south towards the Twin Lotus Hotel and you'll find the popular **Venice Pub**. For a tamer evening of beers and pub grub, check out **Bar 60** (known as 'Bar Hok Sip'), near the corner of Th Ratchadamnoen and Th Phra Ngoen.

Hao Coffee (☎ 0 7534 6563; Bovorn Bazaar; dishes 30-60B; 🕑 breakfast & lunch) Dishes out quick and convenient breakfasts, and the coffee is pretty darn good.

Rock 99 (☎ 0 7531 7999; 1180/807 Bavorn Bazaar; dishes 40-100B; 🕑 dinner) The choice faràngout (faràng-hangout) in Nakhon, Rock 99 has a good selection of international fare – from taco salads and steak sandwiches, to pizzas and fried potatoes. There's live music on Wednesday, Friday and Saturday nights, but expect to bump into friendly expats almost all the time.

Khrua Nakhon (☎ 0 7531 7197; Bovorn Bazaar; dishes 60-200B 🕑 breakfast & lunch) This joint, next to Hao Coffee, has a great selection of traditional Nakhon cuisine. Order one of the sharing platters which comes with five types of curry (including an unpalatable spicy fish sauce), or try the *khâo yam* (southern-style rice salad). There's a second location in Robinson Ocean Mall.

Krua Talay (Th Pak Nakhon; dishes 40-300B; 🕑 lunch & dinner) Located Near the Kukwang Market, Krua Talay is the top spot in town for succulent seafood. It can be a little pricey compared to the other non-touristy chow spots around town, but the locals agree that it's definitely worth it.

Country Home (☎ 08 1968 0762; 119/7 Th Ratchadamnoen) This large, open-air bar invokes the Wild West with saloon-style seating and an odd smattering of straw hats. There's live music every night and the joint gets packed with beer-toting locals.

Getting There & Away

Several small carriers (plus Thai Airways) fly from Bangkok to Nakhon everyday. There are about six daily one-hour flights priced around 3500B.

There are two daily train departures from Bangkok to Nakhon (stopping through Hua Hin, Chumphon and Surat Thani along the way). They are both 12-hour night trains leaving at 5.35pm and 7.15pm. Second-class fares cost upwards of 600B. These trains continue on to Hat Yai and Sungai Kolok.

Buses from Bangkok depart either between 6am and 8am, or between 5.30pm and 10pm. There are about seven daily departures (1st class/2nd class around 700/600B, 12 to 13 hours). Ordinary buses to Bangkok leave from the bus terminal, but a couple of private buses leave from booking offices on Th Jamroenwithi, where you can also buy tickets.

When looking for minivan stops to leave Nakhon, keep an eye out for small desks along the side of the downtown roads (minivans and waiting passengers may or may not be present nearby). It's best to ask around as each destination has a different departure point. Krabi and Don Sak minivans are grouped together – just make sure you don't get on the wrong one. Stops are scattered around Th Jamroenwithi, Th Wakhit and Th Yommarat. There are frequent minivans (that leave when they're full) to Krabi (180B to 240B, 2½ hours) and Phuket (175B to 275B, five hours), Surat Thani (100B, one hour), Khanom (85B, one hour) and Hat Yai (around 120B, three hours).

Getting Around

Sŏrng·tăa·ou run north-south along Th Ratchadamnoen and Th Si Thammasok for 10B (a bit more at night). Motorcycle-taxi rides start at 20B and cost up to 50B for longer distances.

KHAO LUANG NATIONAL PARK

อุทยานแห่งชาติเขาหลวง

Known for its beautiful mountain and forest walks, cool streams, waterfalls and orchards, **Khao Luang National Park** (☎ 0 7530 9644-7; adult/child 400/200B) surrounds the 1835m peak of Khao Luang and is covered in virgin forest. An ideal source for streams and rivers, the mountains show off impressive waterfalls and provide a habitat for a plethora of bird species – this place is a good spot for any budding ornithologist. Fans of flora will also get their kicks here; there are over 300 species of orchid in the park, some of which are found nowhere else on earth.

Park bungalows can be rented for 600B to 1000B per night and sleep six to 12 people. Camping is permitted along the trail to the summit. To reach the park, take a sŏrng·tăa·ou (25B) from Nakhon Si Thammarat to the village of Khiriwong, at the base of Khao Luang. The entrance to the park and the offices of the Royal Forest Department are 33km from the centre of Nakhon on Rte 4015, an asphalt road that climbs almost 400m in 2.5km to the office and a further 450m to the car park.

DEEP SOUTH

Culturally speaking, the provinces of Thailand's deep south have much more in common with neighbouring Malaysia, and the language, religion and even foods of Pattani, Narathiwat and much of Songkhla provide a fascinating contrast with the largely Thai-speaking, Buddhist areas to the north. Unfortunately, due to a long running violent conflict (see p28), experiencing this fascinating culture, not to mention exploring many of the region's largely unspoiled beaches is, at the time of writing, generally not a safe proposition. Thankfully, the region's gem, Songkhla, has been largely spared from the violence, but we encourage those considering a visit anywhere in Thailand's deep south to do their homework and be aware of the situation on the ground (see p258).

SONGKHLA & AROUND
สงขลา
pop 87,822

Unlike many of the urban centres in Thailand's deep south, Songkhla has enough going for itself to entertain visitors for a couple of days. The city is surrounded by pleasant beaches, has several green parks and has a pretty historical centre. Due to the generous sea breezes, Songkhla manages to feel gracefully cool just about year-round, and also boasts some great food, including copious seafood and two vibrant night markets.

Information

Banks can be found all over town.

Click Me! (cnr Th Phetchakhiri & Th Saiburi; per hr 15B; 8am-10pm) Internet service.

Corner Bookshop (☎ 0 7431 2577; cnr Th Saiburi & Th Phetchakhiri; 7am-7.30pm) Stocks a small selection of English-language novels, maps, newspapers, magazines and Lonely Planet guides.

Indonesian Consulate (☎ 0 7431 1544; Th Sadao)

Malaysian Consulate (☎ 0 7431 1062; 4 Th Sukhum)

Police station (☎ 0 7432 1868; Th Laeng Phra Ram) North of the town centre.

Post office (Th Wichianchom) Opposite the market; international calls can be made upstairs.

Sights & Activities

KO YO
เกาะยอ

A popular day trip from Songkhla, this island in the middle of Thale Sap is actually connected to the mainland by bridges and is famous for its cotton-weaving industry. There's a roadside market selling cloth and ready-made clothes at excellent prices.

If you visit Ko Yo, the **Thaksin Folklore Museum** (☎ 0 7459 1618; admission 100B; 8.30am-

4.30pm) actively aims to promote and preserve the culture of the region, and is a must-see. The pavilions here are reproductions of southern Thai-style houses and contain folk art, handicrafts and traditional household implements.

Frequent sŏrng·tăa·ou to Ko Yo depart from Th Ramwithi in Songkhla (15B, 20 minutes). To stop at the small market ask for *nâh dà·làht* (in front of the market). To get off at the museum ask for *pí·pí·tá·pan*.

NATIONAL MUSEUM
พิพิธพัณฑสถานแห่งชาติ

The 1878 building that now houses the **national museum** (☎ 0 7431 1728; Th Wichianchom; admission 150B; 9am-4pm Wed-Sun, closed public holidays) was originally built in a Chinese architectural style as the residence of a luminary. This museum is easily the most picturesque national museum in Thailand and contains exhibits from all Thai art-style periods, particularly the Srivijaya. Also on display are Thai and Chinese ceramics and sumptuous Chinese furniture owned by the local Chinese aristocracy.

BEACHES

The residents are taking better care of the windy strip of white sand along **Hat Samila**, and it is now quite a pleasant beach for strolling. A **bronze mermaid**, depicted squeezing water from her long hair in tribute to Mae Thorani (the Hindu-Buddhist earth goddess), sits atop some rocks at the northern end of the beach. Nearby are the **cat and rat sculptures**, named for the Cat and Rat Islands (Ko Yo and Ko Losin). At the northern tip of Laem Songkhla a **Naga statue** rather unceremoniously shoots water into the ocean.

A few kilometres south of Hat Samila is **Kao Seng**, a quaint beachfront Muslim fishing village – this is where the tourist photos of gaily painted fishing vessels are taken. Sŏrng·tăa·ou run regularly between Songkhla (from near the stand to Ko Yo) and Kao Seng for 10B.

WAT MATCHIMAWAT (WAT KLANG)

This large temple compound typifies the Sino-Thai temple architecture in Songkhla around the 18th century. The walls of the adjacent *bòht* (central sanctuary or chapel) are decorated with some of the most beautiful temple murals in southern Thailand, some of which depict life in 19th-century Songkhla. The doors of the *bòht* are often locked; contact

SOUTHWESTERN GULF COAST

one of the resident monks if you'd like to take a look inside.

OTHER ATTRACTIONS

The area around Th Nang Ngam has a long-standing Chinese community and is lined with quaint, rickety old Thai houses and a few multicoloured Chinese temples.

North of the centre are two forested hills, **Khao Tang Kuan** and **Khao Noi** (also known as Monkey Mountain, since hordes of monkeys live here). There's a **cable car** (round-trip 30B; 8.30am-6.30pm) on the eastern side of Khao Tang Kuan and vendors selling food you can give to the hairy little guys.

Kids will enjoy cuddling with baby tigers at the **Songkhla Zoo** (☎ 0 7433 6038; Khao Rup Chang; adult/child 50/15B; 7.30am-5pm) or pointing at clown fish at the brand-new **Songkhla Aquarium** (☎ 0 7432 2787; Laem Songkhla; www.songkhlaaquarium.com; adult/child 150/80B; 9am-5pm Wed-Mon).

Sleeping

Suk Somboon 2 (☎ 0 7431 3809-10; fax 0 7432 1406; 14 Th Saiburi; r 200-450B;) This is actually two buildings, a very old and a more modern, right next

to each other. The newer half has pleasant but smallish rooms that are among the nicest in this price range in town, while the rooms in the old half are very basic indeed.

Romantic Guest House (☎ 08 1599 2914; 10/1-3 Th Platha; r 250-380B;) The abodes here are massive and airy and all come with a TV and sturdy-looking bamboo bed frames. All fan-cooled rooms have shared bathrooms. Motorcycles are available for rent here (250B per day).

Green World Palace Hotel (☎ 0 7443 7900-8; fax 0 7443 7899; 99 Th Samakisuk 2; r 900-1050B;) Judging by the chandeliers, spiralling staircase in the lobby and 5th-floor swimming pool with views, you'd think this place would charge an arm and a leg. It doesn't – and the immaculate rooms here, with a whole stack of mod-cons in the more expensive ones, are deservedly popular. It's south of the town.

BP Samila Beach Hotel (☎ 0 7444 0222; www.bphotel sgroup.com; 8 Th Ratchadamnoen; r 1440-1500B;) This beachfront hotel provides Songkhla's swankiest accommodation and has all the amenities, including an IDD phone, fridge, satellite TV and sea or mountain views.

TRAVELLING IN THE DEEP SOUTH   *Austin Bush*

When I told Thai friends I was going to Thailand's deep south to do research for this guide-book, the typical reaction was a blank stare followed by a bewildered, 'Why?'. Since 2004, the provinces of Pattani, Narathiwat and parts of Songkhla have been the setting of a violent insurgency that has claimed the lives of nearly 4000 people (for the historical background to the insurgency, see the boxed text, p28). To date, tourists have not been specifically targeted in the unrest, but during the week I spent in the region there were several violent incidents, some resulting in deaths, in the same provinces that I was visiting. I wasn't witness to any of these incidents, and emerged from the trip entirely unscathed, yet a backdrop of roadblocks, security checks and heavily armed soldiers was a constant reminder that I was in potentially dangerous territory.

Although there's no sure-fire way of avoiding danger, while in Pattani and Narathiwat I did my best to avoid early-morning and late-evening travel, as these are generally when most violent incidents have taken place. This wasn't a problem, as most restaurants in the deep south tend to close early, and there's not a lot of nightlife to speak of anyway, so most nights I found myself in bed quite early. And at the region's morning markets, which still continue to draw shoppers despite being the site of several fatal bombings since 2004, I simply did my best to stay away from parked motorcycles, as they have been used as vehicles for remote-controlled bombs.

My overall impression of the region was that of an area experiencing extraordinarily turbulent times, but populated by people who have continued, more or less, to conduct their lives as normal. From a traveller's point of view, the biggest downside of the conflict was the inability to explore the region's numerous remote and untouched beaches. Travel via rented motorcycle is a risky venture, and many rural towns are under the influence of violent militias, leaving me and most travellers more or less restricted to the region's urban centres. And although visiting these cities can provide a rare insight into Thai Muslim culture and, in this case, life in a conflict zone, they offer little in the way of bona-fide 'sights'.

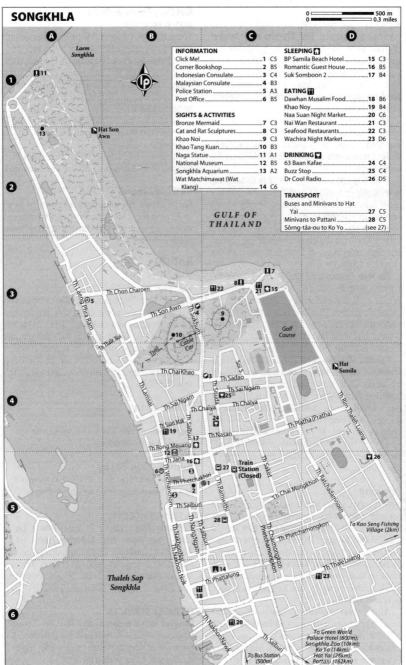

SONGKHLA

| | | | 0 | 500 m |
| | | | 0 | 0.3 miles |

INFORMATION
Click Me!..**1** C5
Corner Bookshop.........................**2** B5
Indonesian Consulate................**3** C4
Malaysian Consulate..................**4** B3
Police Station................................**5** A3
Post Office.....................................**6** B5

SIGHTS & ACTIVITIES
Bronze Mermaid...........................**7** C3
Cat and Rat Sculptures..............**8** C3
Khao Noi...**9** C3
Khao Tang Kuan..........................**10** B3
Naga Statue..................................**11** A1
National Museum.......................**12** B5
Songkhla Aquarium...................**13** A2
Wat Matchimawat (Wat
  Klang).......................................**14** C6

SLEEPING
BP Samila Beach Hotel..............**15** C3
Romantic Guest House...............**16** B5
Suk Somboon 2............................**17** B4

EATING
Dawhan Musalim Food..............**18** B6
Khao Noy.......................................**19** B4
Naa Suan Night Market.............**20** C6
Nai Wan Restaurant...................**21** C3
Seafood Restaurants..................**22** C3
Wachira Night Market................**23** D6

DRINKING
63 Baan Kafae..............................**24** C4
Buzz Stop......................................**25** C4
Dr Cool Radio...............................**26** D5

TRANSPORT
Buses and Minivans to Hat
  Yai...**27** C5
Minivans to Pattani...................**28** C5
Sŏrng·tăa·ou to Ko Yo..........(see 27)

SOUTHWESTERN GULF COAST

Eating

Songkhla has two excellent night markets for you to sample. The **Wachira night market** (Th Thale Luang), so called for the school it sets up in front of, features a solid kilometre of vendors hocking everything from noodles to curries. Another, known by locals as the **Naa Suan night market** (Th Saiburi), has a palpable Muslim influence.

The seafood in Ko Yo has a reputation for being some of the best in the area. On the mainland, there are several cheap, excellent **seafood restaurants** around the beach along Th Som Awm.

Khao Noy (☎ 0 7431 1805; 14/22 Th Wichianchom; dishes 30-50B; ☺ breakfast & lunch, Thu-Tue) Songkhla's most lauded *ráhn kôw gaang* (curry shop) serves up an amazing variety of authentic southern-style curries, soups, stir-fries and salads. Look for the glass case holding several stainless steel trays of food just south of the sky-blue Chokdee Inn.

Nai Wan Restaurant (☎ 0 7431 1295; Th Ratchadamnoen; dishes 35-200B; ☺ lunch & dinner) Popular for its crab dishes (bring moist wipes!), the menu also offers Thai salads, soups and other seafood offerings, as well as a few vegie entries. Note, there's no Roman-script sign, but it's located near the BP Samila Beach Hotel.

Dawhan Musalim Food (☎ 0 7431 5637; 140 Th Phattalung; dishes 40-60B; ☺ lunch & dinner) Praised by locals, Dawhan is located in the tall pink building (there's no Roman-script sign). It has a small selection of Thai-Muslim soups, stir-fries and rich curries, as well as a popular chicken biryani. If you don't see anything you fancy here, there are several other similar Muslim restaurants along this strip of Th Phattalung.

Drinking

Several casual bars and restaurants are found on and around happening Th Sisuda. **Buzz Stop** (☎ 0 7444 0231; 24 Th Sisuda; ☺ 9am-1am), a quasi-Irish boozer, offers a variety of imported draught beers and an expansive menu of pub grub. **63 Baan Kafae** (☎ 08 6956 8066; Th Sisuda; ☺ 10am-1am) is an open-air garden where locals nibble on spicy snacks and drink beer over low tables.

Along Hat Samila is strip of quasi-beachfront restaurant-bars. **Dr Cool Radio** (☎ 0 7431 2758; Th Rim Thaleh Luang) has great sea views and is filled most nights with Thai students listening to local DJs spinning pop hits.

Getting There & Away
BUS & MINIVAN

Songkhla's bus station is located a 500m south of the town centre. Between two and four 2nd-class buses go daily to Bangkok (563B), stopping in Nakhon Si Thammarat (125B), Surat Thani (197B) and Chumphon (312B), among other places. One VIP bus to Bangkok leaves at 5pm (1126B).

To Hat Yai, buses (19B) and minivans (30B) take around 40 minutes and leave from Th Ramwithi.

Minivans to Pattani (90B) leave from 6am to 5pm from further south on Th Ramwithi.

Getting Around

Sŏrng·tăa·ou circulate around town or head to Ko Yo for 15B. Motorcycle taxis around town cost around 30B during the day; rates double at night.

HAT YAI
หาดใหญ่
pop 193,732

Hat Yai literally means 'Big Beach', but you won't find a drop of sea in this landlocked urban monstrosity. Instead, the city functions as a significant transit hub to virtually every other destination in the region. If you're heading to an island or beach in the deep south, you'll undoubtedly be passing through at some point.

Information
EMERGENCY
Tourist police (☎ 0 7424 6733; Th Niphat Uthit 3; ☺ 24hr) Near the TAT office.

IMMIGRATION OFFICE
Immigration Office (☎ 0 7425 7019; Th Phetkasem) Near the railway bridge, it handles visa extensions.

INTERNET ACCESS
Patcharin Tour (106/1-2 Th Niphat Uthit 2; per hr 20B; ☺ 9am-10pm) and **Sahachai Travel** (49 Th Thamnoonvithi; per hr 20B; ☺ 8am-9pm) offer internet and other computer-related services. There's also an **internet cafe** (per hr 20B; ☺ 8am-9pm) on the 2nd floor of the OH (Oriental Hotel).

MEDICAL SERVICES
Bangkok Hatyai Hospital (☎ 0 7436 5780-9; bhhimc @bgh.co.th; 75 Soi 15 Th Pechkasam) One of the best health-care providers in southern Thailand, it has English-speaking staff. It's northeast of the centre.

MONEY

Hat Yai is loaded with banks. Several after-hours exchange windows are located along Th Niphat Uthit 2 and 3 near the Th Thamnoonvithi intersection. If you have Malaysian ringgit the banks won't take them, but many midrange and top-end hotels have exchange windows that will.

POST

Main post office (1 Th Niphat Songkhrao) At the very north of town. A more convenient branch lies two blocks northeast of the train station on Th Rattakan.

TELEPHONE

Telephone office (Th Niphat Songkhrao; ⏰ 7am-11pm) Adjacent to the main post office.

TOURIST INFORMATION

Tourist maps and pamphlets are available at hotels throughout town.

TAT Office (☎ 0 7424 3747; tatsgkhla@tat.or.th; 1/1 Soi 2, Th Niphat Uthit 3) Very helpful staff here speak excellent English and have loads of info on the entire region.

TRAVEL AGENCIES

Hat Yai is full of travel agencies, but **Cathay Tour** (☎ 08 9466 2491, 0 7423 2202; cathay_ontours@hotmail .com; 93/1 Th Niphat Uthit 2; ⏰ 7.30am-7pm) stands out for its super-friendly staff and full range of services, from tickets to tours to visa runs.

Sights

BULLFIGHTING

A more innocuous version than its Spanish equivalent, **bullfighting** (☎ 0 7438 8753; tickets 300-600B; ⏰ 10am-3pm) revolves around two bulls butting heads in opposition, but the real sport here is gambling. Fights occur on the first Saturday of the month, or the second Saturday if the first Saturday is a *wan prá* (Buddhist worship day; full or new moon). Fights are held at **Noen Khum Thong Stadium**, west of the city on the way to the airport (20/80B by sŏrng·tăa·ou/túk-túk).

WAT HAT YAI NAI
วัดหาดใหญ่ใน

About 1.5km west of town, on Th Phetkasem, this wát features a 35m reclining Buddha (Phra Phut Mahatamongkon). Inside the image's gigantic base is a curious little museum and mausoleum with a souvenir shop. To get here, get a motorcycle taxi (50B) or hop on a sŏrng·tăa·ou near the intersection of Th Niphat Uthit l and Th Phetkasem and get off after crossing the river – it costs about 12B.

Sleeping

Hat Yai has dozens of hotels within walking distance of the train station.

Cathay Guest House (☎ 0 7424 3815; fax 0 7435 4104; 93/1 Th Niphat Uthit 2; r 160-250B) Ludicrously helpful staff and plentiful information about onward travel make up for the rundown rooms at this popular cheapie.

Ladda Guest House (☎ 0 7422 0233; 13-15 Th Thamnoonvithi; r 250-450B; 🞩) Virtually next door to Louise Guest House, Ladda offers equally tidy rooms at a similar price.

Louise Guest House (☎ 0 7422 0966; 21-23 Th Thamnoonvithi; r 300-500B; 🞩) This place has more appealing rooms than the Cathay – though not its buzz. The numerous portraits of the Thai royal family on the walls and the apartment-style layout give the place a homey feel.

SOUTHWESTERN
GULF COAST

MAKING A (VISA) RUN FOR THE BORDER FROM HAT YAI

The Malaysian border is about 60km south of Hat Yai, and many travellers come through town just to extend their Thai visas.

To get an in-and-out stamp, head to Padang Besar, the nearest Malaysian border town. Buses cost 39B (two hours, every 25 minutes, 5.30am to 7pm) and minivans are 50B (1½ hours, hourly, 6am to 7pm). It's also possible to get a train, but this option is not very fast or frequent. The **immigration office** (☎ 0 7452 1020) on the Thai side is open from 5am to 9pm daily.

There's another border at Dan Nawk, south of Sadao, which can be reached by minivan (55B, 1½ hours, 6am to 6pm), but this route sees more through traffic than day trippers. The **immigration office** (☎ 0 7430 1107) on the Thai side is open from 5am to 11pm daily.

If you need a longer Thai visa, you'll have to see the Thai consulate in Georgetown, on Penang Island (accessible through the mainland town of Butterworth). Buses from Hat Yai to Butterworth are run by private tour companies and start from 250B (four hours). Again, trains from Hat Yai to Butterworth are slower and less frequent.

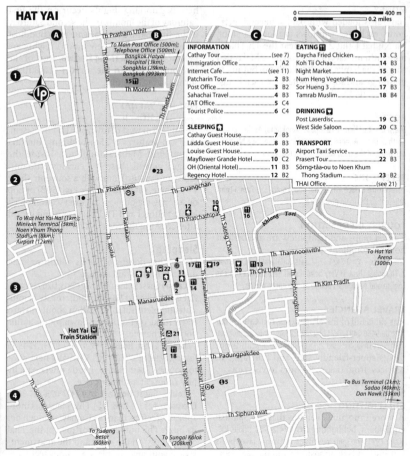

HAT YAI

INFORMATION		EATING	
Cathay Tour	(see 7)	Daycha Fried Chicken	13 C3
Immigration Office	1 A2	Koh Tii Ochaa	14 B3
Internet Cafe	(see 11)	Night Market	15 B1
Patcharin Tour	2 B3	Num Heng Vegetarian	16 C2
Post Office	3 B2	Sor Hueng 3	17 B3
Sahachai Travel	4 B3	Tamrab Muslim	18 B4
TAT Office	5 C4		
Tourist Police	6 C4	DRINKING	
		Post Laserdisc	19 C3
SLEEPING		West Side Saloon	20 C3
Cathay Guest House	7 B3		
Ladda Guest House	8 B3	TRANSPORT	
Louise Guest House	9 B3	Airport Taxi Service	21 B3
Mayflower Grande Hotel	10 C2	Prasert Tour	22 B3
OH (Oriental Hotel)	11 B3	Sŏrng·tǎa·ou to Noen Khum	
Regency Hotel	12 B2	Thong Stadium	23 B2
		THAI Office	(see 21)

OH (Oriental Hotel; ☎ 0 7423 0142; fax 0 7435 4826; 135 Th Niphat Uthit 3; r 500-550B; ❄ ▯) OH offers rooms with TV (no cable), hot water, a fridge and some truly psychedelic carpets. Lack of a desk is a downside if you plan to do any writing, but an internet cafe and a central location make it a convenient place to stay.

Mayflower Grande Hotel (☎ 0 7423 4888; may flowergrande@hotmail.com; 150 Th Saeng Chan; r 890-1190; ❄ ▯ ☎) Blonde wood floors, full-length windows and minimalist design give the rooms here a real Scandinavian feel. Free wi-fi and a chic coffee shop seal the deal.

Regency Hotel (☎ 0 7435 3333-47; www.regency -hatyai.com; 23 Th Prachathipat; r 898-1398B; ❄ ▯) This hotel has that grand old-world charm that's so very rare nowadays. The rooms in the old

wing are smaller (and cheaper) and feature attractive wood furnishings, while rooms on the upper floors of the new wing boast amazing views.

Eating

Hat Yai is southern Thailand's gourmet mecca, offering Muslim roti and curries, Chinese noodles and dim sum, and fresh seafood.

The **night market** (Th Montri 1) boasts heaps of local eats including several stalls selling the famous Hat Yai–style deep-fried chicken and kà·nŏm jeen (fresh rice noodles served with curry), as well as a couple of stalls peddling grilled seafood.

On Th Niyomrat, between Niphat Uthit 1 and 2, starting at **Tamrab Muslim**, is a string of casual and inexpensive Muslim restaurants open from about 7am to 9pm daily. Meals at these places cost between 20B to 60B.

Num Heng Vegetarian (☎ 0 7435 1032; 99/3-4 Th Prachathipatai; dishes 20-30B; ☯ breakfast, lunch & dinner) Those who eschew flesh will appreciate this clean and yummy-looking vegie corner.

Daycha Fried Chicken (☎ 08 1098 3751; Th Chi Uthit; dishes 30-50B; ☯ lunch & dinner) Locals claim that Daycha does the best Hat Yai–style fried chicken. Enjoy your spicy bird over fragrant yellow rice, or with a plate of *sôm·dam*.

Koh Tii Ochaa (☎ 0 7423 4243; 134-136 Th Niphat Uthit 3; dishes 30-80B; ☯ breakfast & lunch) This classic eatery sells all your Sino favourites, including some you didn't even know about such as the delicious *bà·gùt·děh*, pork ribs in a fragrant dark broth.

Sor Hueng 3 (☎ 08 1896 3455; 79/16 Th Thamnoonvithi; dishes 30-120B; ☯ 4pm-3am) This popular local legend with branches all over town prepares heaps of delicious Thai-Chinese and southern Thai faves. Simply point to whatever looks good or order something freshly wok-fried from the extensive menu.

Drinking & Entertainment

Th Thamnoonvithi boasts a string of lively bars and pubs.

Post Laserdisc (☎ 0 7423 2027; 82/83 Th Thamnoonvithi; ☯ 1pm-1.30am) Unlike most other places in town, this longstanding pub has no 'theme', but this makes it all the more authentic. The live music here is relatively good, and the happy hour is among the most generous in Thailand.

West Side Saloon (☎ 0 7435 4833; 135/5 Th Thamnoonvithi; ☯ 6pm-midnight) This 'saloon' attracts Thais, Malays and faràng to its dim, rustic, publike space. Tables are set in front of a stage, where live music rocks from 8.30pm nightly.

Getting There & Away
AIR
Thai Airways International (THAI; ☎ 0 7423 0445; 182 Th Niphat Uthit 1) operates eight flights daily between Hat Yai and Bangkok (1915B to 4290B, 90 minutes).

Nearly all of the low-cost airlines now operate flights to and from Bangkok:

Air Asia (☎ 0 2515 9999; www.airasia.com) Eight daily flights between Hat Yai and Bangkok (1410B to 1910B).

Nok Air (☎ 0 2900 9955; www.nokair.com) Eight daily flights between Hat Yai and Bangkok's Don Meuang Airport (1655B to 3265B).

One-Two-Go (☎ in Bangkok 1126, elsewhere 1141 ext 1126; www.fly12go.com; New World Hotel, Th 152-156 Niphat Uthit 2) Two daily flights to/from Bangkok's Don Meuang Airport (1600B).

BUSES FROM HAT YAI

Destination	Transport	Fare	Duration
Bangkok	air-con bus	535-688B	14hr
	VIP bus	1070B	14hr
Ko Samui	air-con bus	420B	8hr
Krabi	air-con bus	169-218B	5hr
	VIP bus	535B	5hr
Nakhon Si Thammarat	ordinary bus	90B	3hr
	air-con bus	140B	3hr
Narathiwat	minibus	150B	3hr
Padang Besar	ordinary bus	39B	2hr
	minibus	50B	1½hr
Pattani	minibus	100B	2½hr
Phuket	air-con bus	267-344B	8hr
Sadao	minibus	45B	1hr
Satun	air-con bus	65B	2hr
	minibus	70B	1½hr
Songkhla	ordinary bus	19B	1hr
	minibus	30B	1hr
Sungai Kolok	minibus	180B	4hr
Surat Thani	air-con bus	200-240B	5hr
Trang	ordinary bus	80B	3hr
	air-con bus	100B	2½hr
	minibus	150B	2½hr

BUS & MINIVAN

Most inter-provincial buses and south-bound minivans leave from the bus terminal 2km southeast of the town centre, while most north-bound minivans now leave from a minivan terminal 5km west of town at Talat Kaset, a 60B túk-túk ride from the centre of town. Destinations from Hat Yai are shown in the boxed text, p263.

Prasert Tour (☎ 0 7435 4050; Th Niphat Uthit 1) conducts minibuses to Surat Thani (240B, 4½ hours, 8am to 5pm), and **Cathay Tour** (☎ 0 7423 2202; 93/1 Th Niphat Uthit 2) can also arrange minivans to many destinations in the south.

TRAIN

There are four overnight trains to/from Bangkok each day, and the trip takes at least 16 hours. Sample fares include 339B for a 3rd-class seat, 455/675B (fan/air-con) for a 2nd-class seat, 605/945B for a 2nd-class sleeper (in the lower berth) and 1394B to 1594B for a 1st-class sleeper. There are also seven trains daily that run along the east coast to Sungai Kolok (43B to 286B) and two daily trains running west to Butterworth (180B to

332B) and Padang Besar (57B to 272B), both in Malaysia.

There is an advance booking office and left-luggage office at the train station; both are open 7am to 5pm daily.

Getting Around

An **Airport Taxi Service** (☎ 0 7423 8452; 182 Th Niphat Uthit 1) makes the run to the airport four times daily (80B per person, 6.45am, 9.30am, 1.45pm and 6pm). A private taxi for this run costs 280B.

Sŏrng·tǎa·ou run along Th Phetkasem (10B per person). Túk·túk and motorcycle taxis around town cost 20B to 40B per person.

PATTANI
อ.เมืองปัตตานี
pop 44,800

Despite the city's interesting past, there's little of interest in Pattani except its access to some excellent nearby beaches. Unfortunately, the ongoing insurgency (see the boxed text, p258) has made all but a few of these sandy destinations unsafe for the independent traveller.

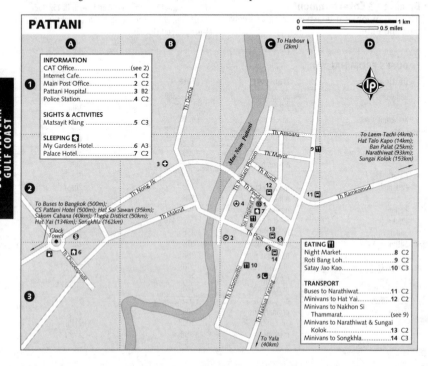

PATTANI

INFORMATION	
CAT Office	(see 2)
Internet Cafe	1 C2
Main Post Office	2 C2
Pattani Hospital	3 B2
Police Station	4 C2

SIGHTS & ACTIVITIES	
Matsayit Klang	5 C3

SLEEPING	
My Gardens Hotel	6 A3
Palace Hotel	7 C2

To Harbour (2km)

To Laem Tachi (4km); Hat Talo Kapo (14km); Ban Palat (25km); Narathiwat (93km); Sungai Kolok (153km)

To Buses to Bangkok (500m); CS Pattani Hotel (500m); Hat Soi Sawan (35km); Sakom Cabana (40km); Thepa District (50km); Hat Yai (134km); Songkhla (162km)

Clock Tower

EATING	
Night Market	8 C2
Roti Bang Loh	9 C2
Satay Jao Kao	10 C3

TRANSPORT	
Buses to Narathiwat	11 C2
Minivans to Hat Yai	12 C2
Minivans to Nakhon Si Thammarat	(see 9)
Minivans to Narathiwat & Sungai Kolok	13 C2
Minivans to Songkhla	14 C3

To Yala (40km)

ISLAM IN SOUTHERN THAILAND

At approximately 4% of the population, Muslims make up Thailand's largest religious minority, living side by side with the majority Theravadan Buddhists. There are some 3000 mosques in Thailand – over 200 in Bangkok alone. Of these mosques, 99% are associated with the Sunni branch of Islam (in which Islamic leadership is vested in the consensus of the Ummah, or Muslim community), and 1% with the Shi'ite branch (in which religious and political authority is given to certain descendants of the Prophet Mohammed).

Islam was introduced to Thailand's southern region between AD 1200 and 1500 through the influence of Indian and Arab traders and scholars. To this day, most of Thailand's Muslims reside in the south, concentrated in the regions of Pattani, Narathiwat, Satun and Yala. These southerners trace their heritage to the former Kingdom of Pattani, an Islamic kingdom whose territory straddled the present-day border between Thailand and Malaysia. Accordingly, the south shares both a border and a cultural heritage with its predominantly Muslim neighbour. Indeed, most of Thailand's southern Muslims are ethnically Malay and speak Malay or Yawi (a dialect of Malay written in the Arabic script) in addition to Thai.

These cultural differences, inflamed by a history of perceived religious and linguistic discrimination, have led to a feeling of disconnection with the Buddhist mainstream among a radical few of the southern Muslims (see the boxed text, p40). Some have called for secession, and fewer still have, in the past, taken up armed insurgency (see the boxed text, p28).

Proper etiquette in Thai Muslim communities is simple and predictable. Islam forbids the consumption of pork and alcohol. In very conservative communities, multigender groups will be split off into separate rooms upon arrival. Men and women will be reunited as they depart.

Just as is the case when visiting wát, mosques will not permit entry to those in shorts or shoes. Women should not wear short skirts, sleeveless tops or any particularly revealing clothing; simply think conservative. Unless invited to do so, avoid entering the mosque's main prayer hall, as this is a sacred space intended for Muslims. Do not bring cameras, and remember to turn off mobile (cell) phones.

Friday is the day of the Sabbath, with religious activities culminating between 11am and 2pm. Locals may be too busy on Friday for visitors and most restaurants close down during this time.

Information

There are several banks along the southeastern end of Th Pipit, near the Th Naklua Yarang intersection.

Internet cafe (cnr Th Peeda & Soi Thepiweat 2; per hr 20B)

Main post office (Th Pipit) The attached CAT office provides an overseas phone service from 7am to 10pm daily.

Pattani Hospital (☎ 0 7333 5134-6; Th Nong Jik)

Police station (☎ 0 7334 8555; Th Pattani Phirom) In a central location.

Sights

Along Th Ruedi you can see what is left of old Pattani architecture – the Sino-Portuguese style that was once so prevalent in this part of southern Thailand.

BEACHES

Despite the ongoing conflict in the south, there are a few beaches in the area that the locals still frequent. **Laem Tachi**, a sandy cape that juts out over the northern end of Ao Pattani, can be reached by boat taxi from Pattani harbour. **Hat Talo Kapo**, 14km east of Pattani near Yaring Amphoe, is a pretty beach that's also a harbour for *gowlŏw*, the traditional fishing boats of southern Thailand. And although it's technically in Songkhla Province, **Thepa District**, located 35km northwest of Pattani, is the most developed beach destination in the area. There you'll find a few slightly aged resorts that cater mostly to middle-class Thais. At **Hat Soi Sawan**, near the Songkhla-Pattani provinces border, several families have set up informal beachfront restaurants that are popular with locals on the weekends.

Dress modestly on or near the beaches.

MOSQUES

Thailand's second-largest mosque is the **Matsayit Klang** (Th Naklua Yarang), a traditional structure with a green hue that is probably still the south's most important mosque. It was built in the 1960s.

Sleeping & Eating

My Gardens Hotel (☎ 0 7333 1055-8; fax 0 7333 6217; 8/28 Th Charoenpradit; r 200-800B; ✖) A favourite with travelling businesspeople, My Gardens is good value. Rooms are well maintained and comfortable with satellite TV, bath, good hot-water showers and fridge.

Palace Hotel (☎ 0 7334 9171; 10-12 Soi Thepiwat 2; r 250-500B; ✖) Despite its location in a grubby market soi, the rooms here, in particular those with air-con on the lower floors, are neat and comfortable.

Sakom Cabana (☎ 0 7431 8065; 136 Moo 4, Tambon Sakom; r 600-800B; ✖) Located in Thepa District, 40km from Pattani, this basic resort features a clean compound with several attractive wooden duplex bungalows a short walk from the beach.

CS Pattani Hotel (☎ 0 7333 5093/4; cspatani@cscoms.com; 299 Muu 4 Th Nong Jik; r 1500-5500B; ✖ 🖳 🖳) Pattani's poshest digs has a gorgeous colonial lobby, two pools, an excellent restaurant, a sauna and steam room…the list goes on. Breakfast is included. Ask about discounts. It's 3km southwest of town.

Roti Bang Loh (☎ 0 81096 9555; Th Naklua Yarang; dishes 15-20B; ✆ 6-9am & noon-8pm) This delicious roti vendor is known around town for the several prizes he's won – if you speak Thai or Yawi ask him about them and he'll go on for ages!

Satay Jao Kao (☎ 0 89737 5417; 37/20 Th Udomwithi; dishes 20-30B; ✆ 10am-6pm) This well respected open-air restaurant serves beef satay local style with cubes of rice and a sweet dipping sauce. Several other restaurants along this stretch of Th Udomwithi come highly recommended by Pattani's Muslim foodies.

A variety of food vendors convenes at the **night market** (Soi Thepiwat 2).

Getting There & Around

Minivans are the most common way to get around this part of Thailand, and just to make things more difficult for visitors, there's no single minivan or bus terminal in Pattani. See Map p264 for pick-up and drop-off locations. All minivans and buses run from approximately 6am to 5pm.

Buses to Bangkok depart from the small lot beside a petrol station near the CS Pattani Hotel – call ☎ 0 7334 8816 for ticket purchase and reservations. The trip takes 15 to 16 hours

BUSES FROM PATTANI			
Destination	Transport	Price	Duration
Hat Yai	minivan	100B	1½hr
Narathiwat	ordinary bus	60B	2½hr
	minivan	100B	2hr
Songkhla	minivan	90B	1½hr
Sungai Kolok	minivan	130B	2½hr

and costs 1187B (VIP), 890B (1st class) and 594B (2nd class).

Sŏrng·tăa·ou go anywhere in town for 10B per person.

NARATHIWAT
อ.เมืองนราธิวาส
pop 44,200

Sitting on the banks of the Bang Nara River, Narathiwat is probably the most Muslim large city in Thailand. Some of the Sino-Portuguese buildings lining the riverfront are over a century old, and some pleasant beaches are just outside town. Unfortunately the security situation in this part of the country (see the boxed text, p258) has suffocated the little tourism that this region used to see. Be sure to check the latest situation before travelling in this region.

Information

There's a bunch of banks in the town centre.
CAT office (Th Pichitbamrung; ✆ 8.30am-10pm Mon-Fri, 9am-5pm Sat & Sun) Same location as the post office.
Internet cafes (✆ 9am-10pm) Can be found near the clock tower, on Th Puphapugdee and Th Worakhamphiphit. Most charge 15B per hour.
Phanwiphaa (☎ 0 7351 1161; Th Puphapugdee; ✆ 8am-5pm) This ticket office, located across from the large Krung Thai Bank, arranges airline tickets as well as transport to the airport.
Post office (Th Pichitbamrung)
TAT (☎ 0 7352 2411; tatnara@cscoms.com) Inconveniently located a few kilometres southeast of town, just across the bridge, on the road to Tak Bai.

Sights
BEACHES

Just north of town is **Hat Narathat**, a 5km-long sandy beach, which serves as a kind of public park for locals. The beach is only 2km from the town centre – you can easily walk there or take a săhm·lór.

Five kilometres south of town, **Ao Manao** used to be a popular sun and sand destination, but today is mostly frequented by locals catching fish. Nonetheless, there's accommodation, and on weekends, basic food and drinks.

MATSAYIT KLANG
มัสยิดกลาง

Towards the southern end of Th Pichitbamrung stands this interesting old, wooden mosque built in the Sumatran style. It was reputedly built by a prince of the former kingdom of Pattani over a hundred years ago.

Sleeping & Eating

Most of the town's accommodation is located on and around Th Phupha Phakdi (signposted as 'Puphapugdee') along the Bang Nara River.

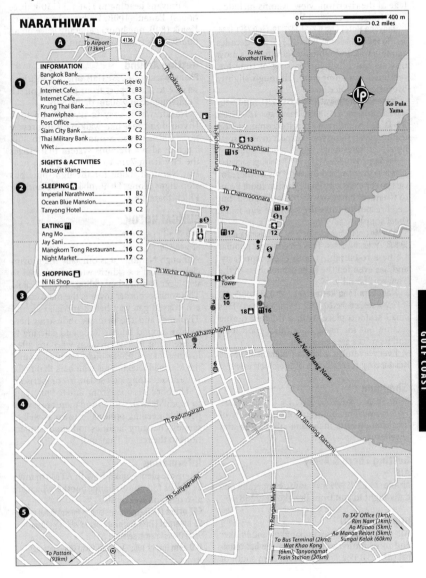

NARATHIWAT

0 — 400 m
0 — 0.2 miles

INFORMATION
Bangkok Bank.............................1 C2
CAT Office..............................(see 6)
Internet Cafe...........................2 B3
Internet Cafe...........................3 C3
Krung Thai Bank........................4 C3
Phanwiphaa.............................5 C3
Post Office..............................6 C4
Siam City Bank.........................7 C2
Thai Military Bank......................8 B2
VNet....................................9 C3

SIGHTS & ACTIVITIES
Matsayit Klang.........................10 C3

SLEEPING
Imperial Narathiwat...................11 B2
Ocean Blue Mansion...................12 C2
Tanyong Hotel.........................13 C2

EATING
Ang Mo................................14 C2
Jay Sani...............................15 C2
Mangkorn Tong Restaurant..........16 C3
Night Market..........................17 C2

SHOPPING
Ni Ni Shop.............................18 C3

To Airport (13km)
4136
To Hat Narathat (1km)

Ko Pula Yama

Th Kokkean
Th Pichitbamrung
Th Puphapugdee
Th Sophaphisai
Th Jitpatima
Th Chamroonnara
Th Wichit Chaibun
Clock Tower
Th Worakhamphiphit
Th Padungaram
Mae Nam Bang Nara
Th Jaturong Rattami
Th Suriyapradit
Th Rangae Munka

To Pattani (93km)

To Bus Terminal (2km); Wat Khao Kong (6km); Tanyongmat Train Station (20km)

To TAT Office (1km); Rim Nam (1km); Ao Manao (5km); Ao Manao Resort (5km); Sungai Kolok (60km)

SOUTHWESTERN GULF COAST

Ao Manao Resort (☎ 0 7354 2193; bungalows 300B; ✗) This accommodation, 5km southeast of town at Ao Manao, features large, clean cement cottages in a small compound. A motorcycle taxi here costs 40B.

Ocean Blue Mansion (☎ 0 7351 1109; 297 Th Puphapugdee; r 350-1500B; ✗) This hotel/apartment is the only one in town to really take advantage of the riverfront view. Rooms include a huge fridge and cable TV.

Tanyong Hotel (☎ 0 7351 1477-79; fax 0 7351 1834; 16/1 Th Sophaphisai; r 650-750B; ✗) A few decades ago this was undoubtedly Narathiwat's most upscale hotel, but the passing of time has rendered it a competent, although slightly overpriced, choice.

Imperial Narathiwat (☎ 0 7351 5041; narathiwat@ imperialhotels.com; 228 Th Pichitbamrung; r 1200-2200B; ✗ 🖳 🖴) Narathiwat's nicest accommodation features everything you'd expect in an upscale hotel. Cut rates make this excellent value.

Jay Sani (☎ 0 89657 1546; 50/1 Th Sophaphisai; dishes 30-60B; ☼ breakfast, lunch & dinner) This is where locals go for excellent Thai-Muslim food. Point to whatever curry or stir-fry looks good, but be sure not to miss the sublime *súp néu·a* (beef soup).

Ang Mo (cnr Th Puphapugdee & Th Chamroonnara; dishes 30-80B; ☼ lunch & dinner) This exceedingly popular Chinese restaurant is both cheap and tasty, and has even fed the likes of members of the Thai royal family.

Mangkorn Tong Restaurant (☎ 0 7351 1835; 433 Th Puphapugdee; dishes 60-160B; ☼ lunch & dinner) This small seafood place, with a floating dining section out the back, does quite good food and its prices are reasonable.

Every evening a ragtag **night market** (Th Pichitbamrung) forms north of the clock tower.

Shopping

Ni Ni Shop (☎ 0 89736 3346; 436 Th Puphapugdee; ☼ 9am-8pm) This boutique offers a variety of local handicrafts including silks, batik and jewellery.

Getting There & Away

AIR

Air Asia (☎ 0 2515 9999; www.airasia.com) operates one daily flight to and from Bangkok (1226B).

BUS & MINIVAN

Air-conditioned buses to Bangkok and Phuket and most minivans leave from the **bus terminal** (☎ 0 7351 1552; Th Rangae Munka) 2km south of

town. The buses to Phuket (530B, 12 hours) originate in Sungai Kolok, pass Narathiwat three times daily (7am, 9am and 6.30pm) and continue via Pattani, Hat Yai, Songkhla, Trang, Krabi and Phang-Nga. Buses to Bangkok (VIP/1st/2nd class 1296/833/669B) take at least 15 hours and depart several times during the day.

Minivans heading to Hat Yai (150B, three hours), Pattani (100B, 1½ hours) and Sungai Kolok (80B, one hour) generally leave on an hourly basis from 5am to 5pm.

Getting Around

Phanwiphaa (☎ 0 7351 1161) offers a minivan service to the airport from its office on Th Puphapugdee at 9.30am daily (80B).

Narathiwat is easy to navigate on foot. If you don't feel like walking, motorcycle taxis will take you around for 20B to 40B. There is also a free bus system that circles the city from 7am to 6pm, stopping near Hat Narathat. Look for the light-blue bus stop signs along Th Puphapugdee and Th Phichitbamrung.

SUNGAI KOLOK
สุไหงโกลก
pop 40,500

Although Narathiwat is officially the provincial capital, it's a skinny wimp compared to its bigger and brasher sibling, Sungai Kolok. This soulless border town is the main southern coastal gateway between Malaysia and Thailand, and the primary industries here revolve around border trade and catering to weekending Malaysian men who are often looking for sex. Every night the area around the Marina Hotel booms with bars that make Pattaya or Patong look sedate in comparison.

The border is open from 5am to 9pm (6am to 10pm Malaysian time) and there are several passable sleeping options in town as well as money-changing facilities and good connections to the rest of Thailand.

Information

There are plenty of banks with ATMs in town as well as foreign-exchange booths, which are also open on weekends.

CAT office (Th Thetpathom) Handles international calls.

CS Internet (Th Charoenkhet; per hr 20B; ☼ 10am-9pm) Offers internet service.

D.D.com (per hr 10B; ☼ 10am-9pm) Offers internet service.

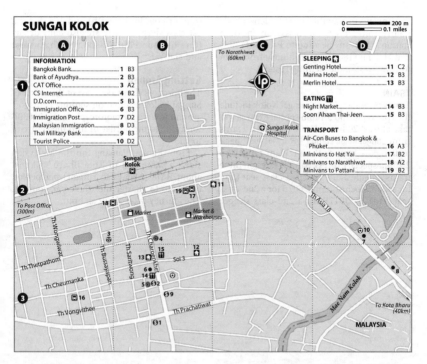

SUNGAI KOLOK

INFORMATION
Bangkok Bank................................**1** B3
Bank of Ayudhya...........................**2** B3
CAT Office.....................................**3** A2
CS Internet....................................**4** B2
D.D.com...**5** B3
Immigration Office........................**6** B3
Immigration Post...........................**7** D2
Malaysian Immigration...................**8** D3
Thai Military Bank..........................**9** B3
Tourist Police...............................**10** D2

SLEEPING
Genting Hotel..............................**11** C2
Marina Hotel...............................**12** B3
Merlin Hotel................................**13** B3

EATING
Night Market...............................**14** B3
Soon Ahaan Thai-Jeen..................**15** B3

TRANSPORT
Air-Con Buses to Bangkok &
   Phuket......................................**16** A3
Minivans to Hat Yai......................**17** B2
Minivans to Narathiwat................**18** A2
Minivans to Pattani......................**19** B2

Immigration offices Border (☎ 0 7361 4114; ☻ 5am-9pm); Sungai Kolok (☎ 0 7361 1231; Th Charoenkhet; ☻ 8.30am-4.30pm Mon-Fri) The in-town branch is a larger office across from the Merlin Hotel.

Post office (Th Asia 18) A hike to the western edge of town.

Tourist Police (Th Asia 18) At the border, it has a small selection of free maps and brochures.

Sleeping & Eating

There's heaps of accommodation options here, but most hotels are pretty grubby and cater to the 'by the hour' market.

Merlin Hotel (☎ 0 7361 8111; 68 Th Charoenkhet; r 390-580B; ☒) Don't let the lobby fool you – the rooms here are very plain indeed, but a good choice if you need a cheap room with a view.

Genting Hotel (☎ 0 7361 3231-40; fax 0 7361 1259; 250 Th Asia 18; r 570-1520B; ☒ ☒) Geared towards the conference trade, this place comes equipped with a barber, a snooker room, entertainment venues, a pub and a karaoke lounge. There are some good, only slightly scuffed, midrange rooms and it's away from the seedier areas.

Marina Hotel (☎ 0 7361 3881-5; fax 0 7361 3385; 173 Soi 3, Th Charoenkhet; r 980-2400B; ☒ ☒) Don't be alarmed by the chirping in the lift; this hotel's elevator shaft doubles as a home to swifts whose nests are a Chinese delicacy. Located right in the epicentre of the entertainment district, the Marina also has multiple bars, clubs and a restaurant all on site.

Despite the mix of cultures and emphasis on tourism, Sungai Kolok is definitely not a culinary destination. A small **night market** unfolds next to the immigration office – exceptionally good and cheap eats can be got at the stall in the centre that only has Chinese writing.

Soon Ahaan Thai-Jeen (Thai-Chinese Food Centre; ☎ 0 7341 8207; cnr Th Charoenkhet & Soi 3; dishes 20-60B; ☻ breakfast & lunch) This small food court serves a variety of mostly Chinese-style dishes.

Getting There & Away
BUS & MINIVAN

The **long-distance bus station** (☎ 0 7361 2045) is located west of downtown, and there are three daily air-conditioned buses for the 18-hour trip to Bangkok; one VIP (1369B, noon), one 1st class (880B, 1pm) and one 2nd class (706B, 8.30am). Buses head off to Phuket (556B) at 6am, 8am and 5.30pm via Krabi (428B).

SOUTHWESTERN
GULF COAST

Minivans to Narathiwat (80B) depart half-hourly from Th Asia 18, across from the train station. Minivans heading to Pattani (130B) and Hat Yai (180B) depart hourly from 5am to 7pm, west of the Genting Hotel.

TRAIN
Trains from Bangkok to Sungai Kolok include the 1pm rapid and 3.10pm special express and take at least 20 hours (180B to 893B). Trains from **Sungai Kolok station** (☎ 0 7461 4060) back to Bangkok include the 11.30am rapid and 2.20pm special express. Sample fares on these trains include 370B for a 3rd-class seat (fan, for sadomasochists only), 607B for a 2nd-class seat (fan), 677/917B for a 2nd-class sleeper (fan/air-con, lower berth) and 1753B for a 1st-class sleeper. There are also daily departures to Phun Phin, Nakhon Si Thammarat and Hat Yai.

Getting Around
The border is about 1km east of the centre of Sungai Kolok or the train station. Transport around town is by motorcycle taxi – it's 30B for a ride to the border or into the centre of town.

From Rantau Panjang (on the Malaysian side), a share taxi to Kota Bharu will cost about RM8 (Malaysian ringgit) per person or RM40 to charter the whole car yourself. The journey takes about an hour.

Northern Andaman Coast

Whether you've got designer-villa wishes, bamboo-hut desires or anything in between, the northern Andaman coast serves it up with a warm shot of turquoise ocean to wash it down. Phuket, on the southern extremity, is the audacious starlet of the region, flaunting glitzy five-star hotels that grace ultrawhite beaches, and where sleep is an afterthought to parties, water sports and spa pampering. Ranong, to the far north, is a mix of Burmese and Thais who eke out a living in a dusty frontier removed from the tourist industry. Travel the 300km between Ranong and Phuket and you'll see it all: Muslim and Moken stilt villages and vertical limestone karsts; resorts out of the pages of *Architectural Digest* and bays abuzz with jet skis; tangled mangrove swamps and skittish clouds of nesting swallows.

Phuket is the second-most visited location in Thailand (Pattaya is first) and its fame for fine dining, cabarets, general hedonism and outstanding beaches makes it easy to overlook the rest of this coast. But head north and you'll find the jaw-dropping underwater coral gardens of the Surin and Similan Islands, and the islands of Ko Chang and Ko Phayam, both blessed with sweet beach bungalows and a back-to-nature spirit. In the wet season, much of the far north shuts down and Phuket's beaches empty out, leaving fabulous deals on accommodation and the best surf in Thailand.

HIGHLIGHTS

- Searching for elusive whale sharks on a live-aboard cruise of the **Similan Islands Marine National Park** (p295) and **Surin Islands Marine National Park** (p289)
- Experiencing the beautiful beaches, sublime vistas and Thai-Muslim culture on **Ko Yao** (p300)
- Cruising the art galleries and hole-in-the-wall restaurants and bars of Old Phuket in **Phuket Town** (p308)
- Kayaking around the beautiful bay of **Ao Phang-Nga** (p297)
- Finding gluttonous hedonism in the hair-raising clubs and on the packed beaches of **Hat Patong** (p322) – love it or hate it
- Exploring the emerging jungled isles of **Ko Chang** (p275) and **Ko Phayam** (p277)

- DRY SEASON: NOVEMBER–APRIL
- WET SEASON: MAY–OCTOBER

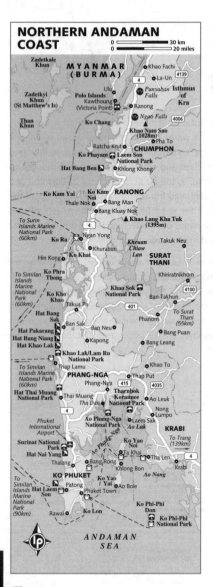

Climate

The Andaman coast is wetter than the southern gulf provinces, with the low season months between May and October logging the highest rainfall. During this time, seas are rough and passenger boats to some islands, such as the Surin and Similan archipelagos, are suspended. On the upside, peninsular

Thailand is narrow, so if the weather turns sour on the Andaman coast, you can always pack your bags and chase the sun to the eastern seaboard.

National Parks

Some of the northern Andaman coast's most visited areas are national parks. Ao Phang-Nga National Park (p299) swarms with day-trippers drawn by the expanse of turquoise water and pristine islands – it's no wonder Scaramanga (of *The Man with the Golden Gun* fame) chose to build his lair here. Divers and snorkellers are now flocking to Surin Islands Marine National Park (p289) and Similan Islands Marine National Park (p295), mostly on two-day to week-long liveaboard cruises.

Even built up Phuket Province has its share of parks: Khao Phra Taew Royal Wildlife & Forest Reserve (p332) is a remnant rainforest in the heart of Phuket's concrete jungle and Sirinat National Park (p330) is one of the wildest coastal stretches on the island.

Further off the beaten track in the far north is Laem Son National Park (p277), where you'll find mangrove forests, stunning, empty beaches and turtle nesting sites.

RANONG & AROUND

อ.เมืองระนอง

pop 27,772

Some consider this rough and ready border town and provincial capital rather charmless. Others dig the frontier atmosphere that comes with the setting – Ranong lies on the tea-brown Pak Chan estuary, a short boat ride from Myanmar – and the local blend of Burmese and Thais working the underground angles of international commerce. For years, the town has been known as a visa-run gateway, but now tourists only get 15 days when crossing overland or by sea, so unless you're an expat looking for a long-stay extension, it makes (much) less sense to go this route. But with its natural hot springs, tremendous local food, and easy access to luscious Ko Chang and Ko Phayam, Ranong is still worth a night or two.

Information

IMMIGRATION OFFICES

The main Thai immigration office is on the road to Saphan Plaa, about halfway between town and the main piers, across from a branch of the Thai Farmer's Bank. If entering Thailand from Myanmar via Kawthoung, you'll have to visit this office to get your passport stamped with a visa on arrival, but you'll still only get 15 days.

There is also a smaller immigration post in the vicinity of Tha Saphan Plaa. If you're just going in and out of Myanmar's Kawthoung for the day, a visit to the small post will suffice.

For details on getting a new Thai visa or making a day trip to Victoria Point (Myanmar), see the boxed text, p276.

INTERNET ACCESS
No Name Internet Shop (225 Th Ruangrat; per hr 20B; ⏰ 10am-midnight)

MONEY
Most of Ranong's banks and ATMs are near the intersection of Th Tha Meuang and Th Ruangrat.

POST
Main post office (Th Chonrau; ⏰ 9am-4pm Mon-Fri, to noon Sat)

TELEPHONE
Communications Authority of Thailand (CAT; Th Tha Meuang; ⏰ 24hr)

TRAVEL AGENCIES
Plenty of agencies along Th Ruangrat offer visa-run services, bus and boat tickets, accommodation arrangements for the nearby islands

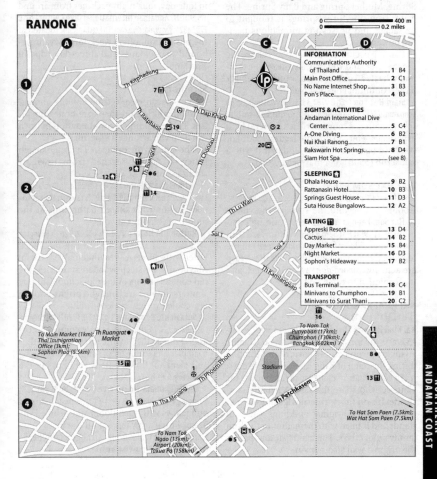

RANONG

INFORMATION
Communications Authority	
of Thailand	**1** B4
Main Post Office	**2** C1
No Name Internet Shop	**3** B3
Pon's Place	**4** B3

SIGHTS & ACTIVITIES
Andaman International Dive	
Center	**5** C4
A-One Diving	**6** B2
Nai Khai Ranong	**7** B1
Rakswarin Hot Springs	**8** D4
Siam Hot Spa	(see 8)

SLEEPING
Dhala House	**9** B2
Rattanasin Hotel	**10** B3
Springs Guest House	**11** D3
Suta House Bungalows	**12** A2

EATING
Appreski Resort	**13** D4
Cactus	**14** B2
Day Market	**15** B4
Night Market	**16** D3
Sophon's Hideaway	**17** B2

TRANSPORT
Bus Terminal	**18** C4
Minivans to Chumphon	**19** B1
Minivans to Surat Thani	**20** C2

To Main Market (1km); Thai Immigration Office (3km); Saphan Plaa (5.5km)

To Nam Tok Punyaban (17km); Chumphon (130km); Bangkok (602km)

To Hat Som Paen (7.5km); Wat Hat Som Paen (7.5km)

To Nam Tok Ngao (13km); Airport (20km); Takua Pa (158km)

of Ko Chang and Ko Phayam, and day trips to Kawthoung (in Myanmar).

Pon's Place (☎ 0 7782 3344; www.ponplace-ranong.com; Th Ruangrat; ☯ 7.30am-midnight) Also rents out motorcycles and cars.

Sights & Activities
HOT SPRINGS
บ่อน้ำร้อน

Ranong may lack the sophistication of your standard spa town, but it is well known for its hot springs. You can sample them near Wat Tapotaram, where **Rakswarin Hot Springs** (Th Petchkasem; admission free; ☯ 8am-5pm) offers pools hot enough to boil eggs in (65°C). Like the three bears of *Goldilocks* fame, the Thai names of the springs translate as Father Spring, Mother Spring and Baby Spring. The water from the three springs is thought to be sacred and possessing miraculous healing powers.

Bathing occurs in outdoor pools above the mocha river, and you may also lie on the thermally heated concrete slab – one incredibly large, communal heating pad.

Siam Hot Spa (☎ 0 7781 3551; www.siamhotsparanong.com; 73/3 Th Petchkasem), opposite the public springs, offers a more sterilised mineral bath experience. You can dip into Jacuzzi (600B) or standard bath tubs (300B), and pair it with a salt scrub (550B) or a massage (200B).

WAT HAT SOM PAEN
วัดหาดส้มแป้น

About 7km beyond the springs, the village of **Hat Som Paen** is a former tin-mining community. At **Wat Hat Som Paen**, visitors feed fruit to the huge *blah ploo ang* (black carp) in the temple stream. The faithful believe these carp are actually *tair·wá·dah*, a type of angel, and it's forbidden to catch and eat them.

NAI KHAI RANONG
ในค่ายระนอง

Nai Khai Ranong (Th Ruangrat; admission free; ☯ 9am-4.30pm) is the former home of Koh Su Chiang, a Hokkien who became governor of Ranong during the reign of King Rama V. These days, it is a combination clan house (clubhouse for Chinese who share the same surname) and shrine. It's on the northern edge of town.

Of the three original buildings, one still stands and is filled with mementos of the Koh family's glory days. The main gate and part of the original wall also remain.

WATERFALLS
Of the several well-known waterfalls in Ranong Province, **Nam Tok Ngao** and **Nam Tok Punyaban** are within walking distance of Hwy 4. Ngao is 13km south of Ranong, while Punyaban is 15km north of town. Take a sŏrng·tăa·ou (small pickup truck with two benches in the back, used as bus/taxi) in either direction and ask to be let off at the *nám dòk* (waterfall).

DIVING
Live-aboard diving trips run from Ranong to world-class bubble-blowing destinations, including the Burma Banks and the Surin and Similan Islands. Try **A-One-Diving** (☎ 0 7783 2984; www.a-one-diving.com; 256 Th Ruangrat). It specialises in four-day, four-night packages from around 15,900B. **Andaman International Dive Center** (☎ 0 7783 4824; www.aidcdive.com; Th Petchkasem), located at the bus station, offers week-long Myanmar-bound live-aboards and three-day trips in Thailand.

Sleeping
Don't expect fireworks from Ranong's hotels; most offer little more than bare-bones amenities. Those running accommodation in town can help you arrange a visa run.

The places on or near Th Petchkasem (Hwy 4) can be reached from town by sŏrng·tăa·ou 2.

Springs Guest House (☎ 0 7781 2818; Th Kamlangsap; r with shared bathroom 250B) This has quirky retro-cool rooms with shared bathrooms at the mouth of Ranong canyon.

Rattanasin Hotel (☎ 0 7781 1242; 226 Th Ruangrat; r 250-350B; 🕮) The Rattanasin is a big, block hotel with an eerie, yet undeniable, charm. Maybe it's the steep wooden staircases, the red concrete floors or the old-school Chinese shutters. Rooms are large and bright, and the fan-cooled variety is a good value.

Suta House Bungalows (☎ 0 7783 2707; Th Ruangrat; r 390-420B; 🕮) One of the more comfy choices and right in the town centre, this off-the-road place has a cluster of simple bungalows – and plenty of flowers. Beds are hard but the showers are hot.

our pick Dhala House (☎ 0 7781 2959; 323/5 Th Ruangrat; r 400-500B; 🕮 🛜) Cute, peach-tinted bungalows with tiled floors and pebbled tile baths, lining a garden; set off the main drag. Management will happily arrange a late checkout if you're on a visa run.

Eating & Drinking

Appreski Resort (☎ 08 7817 7033; 129/6 Moo 1, Th Petchkasem; sandwiches 45B; ☻ breakfast, lunch & dinner) Built into Ranong canyon across the river from the hot springs, it has cultivated a reputation for Danish-style open sandwiches piled with imported cheese, pork liver pâté, or gravlax cured in-house.

our pick **Cactus** (Th Ruangrat; dishes from 69B; ☻ dinner) OK, it looks cheesy. What, with its bevy of long-legged ladies in short shorts and stilettos tending tables of somewhat shady blokes, who seem fine with wearing sunglasses at night. And, yes, there is a karaoke machine, but there also happens to be something exceptional – and exceptionally spicy – happening in that kitchen. Its *dôm yam gûng* (prawn and lemon grass soup with mushrooms) was the best we had in Thailand, so was the cashew chicken, and its tender squid could not be fresher. Service is swift and impeccable.

Sophon's Hideaway (☎ 0 7783 2730; Th Ruangrat; mains 80-250B; ☻ 10am-midnight; ☎) This expat favourite has everything, including internet access, a free pool table, a pizza oven, full bar, water features and rattan furnishings aplenty.

On Th Kamlangsap, not far from Hwy 4, there is a night market that sells great Thai dishes at low prices. The day market on Th Ruangrat offers inexpensive Thai and Burmese meals.

Getting There & Away

The bus terminal is on Th Petchkasem 1km from town, though some Bangkok-bound buses stop at the main market. Sŏrng·tăa·ou 2 (blue) passes the terminal.

Destination	Bus type	Price	Duration
Bangkok	VIP	665B	10hr
	1st class	428B	10hr
	2nd class	357B	10hr
	ordinary	220B	10hr
Chumphon	2nd class	100B	3hr
Hat Yai	2nd class	410B	5hr
Khuraburi	air-con	100B	1½hr
Takuapa	air-con	140B	3hr
Khao Lak	air-con	170B	3½hr
Krabi	air-con	300B	6hr
Phang-Nga	ordinary	250B	5hr
Phuket	air-con	240B	5-6hr
Surat Thani	1st class	180B	4-5hr
	2nd class	100B	4-5hr

Minivans head to Surat Thani (250B, 3½ hours, four times daily) and Chumphon (120B, three hours, hourly from 6am to 5pm); see the map for departure locations.

Getting Around

Motorcycle taxis will take you almost anywhere in town for 20B, to the hotels along Th Petchkasem for 25B and to the pier (for 50B) for boats to Ko Chang, Ko Phayam and Myanmar. Pon's Place (opposite) can assist with motorcycle and car rentals.

KO CHANG

เกาะช้าง

This little-visited rustic isle is a long way – in every respect – from its much more popular Trat Province namesake. Pass the time exploring the island's tiny village capital (where the boats dock during the dry season) or wend your way around the island on one of the dirt trails. Sea eagles, Andaman kites and hornbills all nest here and, if you're lucky, you'll catch sight of them floating above the mangroves and the jungled east coast. The wide, westcoast beach of **Ao Yai** has gorgeous marbled white and black sand in the south, which obscures the otherwise clear water. A short trail leads over the bluff to **Ao Tadeng**, another marbled beach strewn with boulders and the island's best sunset spot. White sand snobs will be happiest at Ao Yai's north end.

There are no banks or cars on Ko Chang, but internet has arrived at **Cashew Resort** (Ao Yai; per min 2B).

Bungalow operations on the island can arrange **boat trips** to Ko Phayam and other nearby islands for around 200B per person (including lunch) in a group of six or more. Dive trips are also possible. **Aladdin Dive Safari** (☎ 0 7782 0472; www.aladdindivecruise.de) runs PADI courses and offers a range of live-aboard dive safaris. A five-day live-aboard trip to Myanmar costs 28,500B; a four-day trip visiting both the Surin and Similan islands costs 20,400B.

Trails lead south from the village in the island's interior to the national park station on the east coast. That's where you'll find the island's best stretch of intact jungle. Elsewhere it's all been tamed into cashew orchards and rubber plantations.

Sleeping & Eating

Basic bamboo huts reign supreme on Ko Chang and, for the most part, they're only open from November to April. Electricity is limited and a few places have solar and wind power.

Ao Yai is the main beach where you'll find most lodging options and a few more places are tucked away on Ao Tadaeng to the south, which is linked to Ao Yai via a short walking track. More isolated options can be found on the beaches to the north and far south of the island.

Crocodile Bungalow (☎ 08 0533 4138; Ao Yai; bungalows 200-350B) Outstanding bamboo bungalows perched on Ao Yai's southern headland. Although it's not 'on' the beach, it gets huge points for its superb bay views. Its kitchen turns out homemade yoghurt, breads, cookies, good espresso and a variety of vegie and seafood dishes.

Hornbill Bungalow (☎ 0 7787 0240; Ao Hornbill; bungalows 200-250B) A slice of paradise is yours when you book one of these sizeable, attractive wooden bungalows right on a secluded golden beach and jade cove.

Koh Chang Resort (☎ 08 1896 1839, 08 3969 4022; kohchangandaman.com; Ao Yai; bungalows 200-900B) Once the cream of the crop, the bungalows here are looking a little weathered, but the best ones still share an incredible perch with wraparound balconies extending over the bay.

Mama's (☎ 0 7782 0180, 08 0530 7066; mamasbun galows@yahoo.com; Ao Tadaeng; huts 250-300B) Tucked into a pretty corner on a rocky, hibiscus-laden hillside above Ao Tadaeng. The good-sized wooden huts here all have private bathrooms. Mama serves some of the best Thai food around.

Full Moon Bungalows (☎ 08 7623 6728, 08 4745 4670; familymoon99@hotmail.com; Ao Yai; bungalows 250-600B) Next door to Sawasdee, both the older, smaller wood bungalows and large, new pastel-tinted variety are awash in good vibrations. The new digs have stencilled motifs on the bathroom walls. The owner has lived on this island for 30 years.

Sunset Bungalows (☎ 08 5655 5002; Ao Yai; bungalows 300-400B) Sweet wooden bungalows with bamboo decks right on Ao Yai's best stretch of beach. The restaurant is charming and offers a tasty menu, and there's a stocked lender library.

our pick Sawasdee (☎ 08 6906 0900, 08 1803 0946; sawadeekohchang@hotmail.com; Ao Yai; bungalows 400-600B)

RENEWING YOUR VISA AT VICTORIA POINT

The dusty, tumbledown port at the southernmost tip of mainland Myanmar was named Victoria Point by the British, but is known as Ko Song (Second Island) by the Thais. The Burmese appellation, Kawthoung, is most likely a corruption of the Thai name. Most travellers come here to renew their visas, but the place also makes an interesting day trip.

Fishing and trade with Thailand keep things ticking over, but Kawthoung also churns out some of Myanmar's best kickboxers. Nearby islands are inhabited by bands of nomadic *chow lair* (sea gypsies).

The easiest way to renew your visa is to opt for one of the 'visa trips' (from 800B per person including visa fees) offered by travel agencies in Ranong (p273), but you can do the legwork yourself.

When the Thailand–Myanmar border is open, boats to Kawthoung leave from the pier at Saphan Plaa (Pla Bridge; off Map p273) about 5km from the centre of Ranong. Take sŏrng·tăa·ou (small pickup truck) 2 from Ranong (20B) to the pier, where long-tail captains will lead you to the immigration window then to their boat (per person one way/return 100/200B). When negotiating your price, confirm whether it is per person or per ride, and one way or return. At the checkpoint, you must inform the authorities that you're a day visitor – in which case you will pay a fee of US\$10 (it must be a crisp bill, you can get one from harbour touts for 500B). It's also possible to stay overnight in one of Victoria Point's dingy hotels. If you have a valid Myanmar visa in your passport, you'll be permitted to stay for up to 28 days.

If you're just coming to renew your Thai visa, the whole process will take a minimum of two hours. Bear in mind when you are returning to Thailand that Myanmar's time is 30 minutes behind Thailand's. This has caused problems in the past for returning visitors who got through Burmese immigration before its closing time only to find the **Thai Immigration office** (🕒 8.30am-4.30pm) closed. It's a good idea to double-check Thai immigration closing hours when leaving the country – if you don't get stamped in you'll have to return to Myanmar again the next day.

The best all-around property on the island. The new A-frame wooden bungalows have vented walls to keep things cool. Its alfresco restaurant (think: driftwood furniture spread beneath a massive tree dangling with lanterns) is as classy as it is delicious, and ownership and its staff practically glow with good energy.

Little Italy (☎ 08 4851 2760; Ao Yai; mains 120-200B) The owner's Sicilian grandma dreamed up these plates, which are served in the woods about 80m inland from Wat Pah Ko Chang on Ao Yai. It also has two bungalows (300B to 400B) stilted high in the trees, with private bathrooms down below.

Tsunami Bar (Ao Yai; ☼ 9am-late) Because every Thai isle needs a groovy reggae bar. Its solar-powered sound system pumps as long as customers are swilling. It also has two stilted bamboo tree houses for rent (250B).

Isolated from the rest of Ko Chang, but stunningly beautiful, Ao Lek is all about turquoise sea solitude. There are five bungalow properties in the area, and if you call ahead staff will buzz out to fetch you off the Ko Phayam–bound boat from Ranong. Ko Chang's taxi boats don't come this far south. The best accommodation option is **Tommy's Garden** (☎ 08 4993 8545; Ao Lek; bungalows 150-450B). Bungalows range from rickety wooden ones with shared bathroom to large, tiled and concrete cottages with private bathrooms and sunrise views.

Getting There & Away

From Ranong take a sŏrng·tăa·ou (25B) from the day market on Th Ruangrat to Tha Ko Phayam near Saphan Plaa. Alternatively most Ranong guesthouses will arrange for a taxi to shuttle you to the pier for 100B.

Two speedboats to Ao Yai (per person 350B, 10am and 2.30pm, 45 minutes) leave daily from late October to April. They return to Ranong at 9am and 1pm. It's cheaper and just as convenient to travel on one of three daily long-tail taxi boats (per person 150B, 9.30am, noon, 2pm). They stop at all the west-coast beaches. Taxi boats return at 7.30am and 1.30pm. During the monsoon months boats make the crossing three days a week, and dock at the main pier on the northeast coast.

A new taxi boat service connecting Ko Chang and Ko Phayam is operated on week-days only by Koh Chang Resort (opposite). Taxi boats (per person 300B, one hour) leave Ko Chang at 10am weekdays and return at

3pm. You can also charter a long-tail boat to Ko Phayam through Koh Chang Resort (1200B) or Mama's (800B; see opposite).

LAEM SON NATIONAL PARK
อุทยานแห่งชาติแหลมสน

This **national Park** (☎ 0 7786 1431; www.dnp.go.th; adult/child 200/100B) covers 315 sq km, includes about 100km of Andaman Sea coastline – the longest protected shore in the country – and over 20 islands. Much of the coast here is edged with mangroves and laced with tidal channels, home to various species of birds, fish, deer and monkeys (including crab-eating macaques). Sea turtles nest on Hat Praphat.

The most accessible beach is **Hat Bang Ben**, where the park headquarters are located. This wide, 3km-long sweep of white sand – backed by towering casuarinas – is drop-dead gorgeous. Look south and peninsulas jut out into the ocean like so many fingers. In between are isolated coves accessible only by long-tail boat. All of the beaches are said to be safe for swimming year-round. From here you can also see several islands, including the nearby Ko Kam Yai, Ko Kam Noi, Mu Ko Yipun, Ko Khang Khao and, to the north, Ko Phayam. Park staff arrange boat trips to any of these islands for 1500B to 1800B depending upon the destination. If there is a prettier sunset picnic spot on the north Andaman coast, we missed it.

Ko Phayam is a beautiful, vibrant up-and-coming island destination that's about to go mainstream. With spectacular beaches on the northwest and southwest coasts dotted with beach bungalows, breezy restaurants and bars, a wooded interior laced with concrete streets, and one of the Andaman coast's best ecolodges, you can certainly understand the appeal. Fauna in the area includes wild pigs, monkeys and snakes, and there is tremendous bird life. Look for sea eagles, toucans and hornbills. There's one 'village' on the island, where you will also find the main pier and a majestic golden Buddha at **Wat Phayam**. The motorcycle 'highway', running down the middle of the island, feeds smaller concrete roadways and dirt trails, some of which can be rutted to the point of hazardous. Take it slow and easy if you rent your own bike. You can also access the Surin Islands from here via live-aboard dive expeditions or regular speedboat transfer. For dive trips and PADI courses contact **Phayam Divers** (☎ 08 6995 2598; www.phayamlodge.com; Ao Yai).

Ao Yai is long, wide and chilled out, attracting everyone from gap-year backpackers to glam-packing couples to young families to retirees. Ao Khao Kwai is a rugged yet luscious cove with golden sand, jungled bluffs and a rock reef offshore that is preferred by hippies, stoners and the occasional German package tourist. It's a terrific swimming beach, too, except at low tide, when the sea recedes leaving mud flats on the southern end where the beach is at its softest and whitest. Swimming is always possible at Ao Yai. The island's best snorkelling is found off **Leam Rung**, Ao Yai's northernmost point.

Ko Khang Khao is known for a beach on its northern end, which is covered with colourful pebbles. Although underwater visibility isn't great around the island, it's a little better than on Ko Chang as it's further from the mouth of the Mae Nam Chan. The beach on **Ko Kam Noi** has relatively clear water for swimming and snorkelling (April is the best month), plus the added bonus of fresh water year-round and plenty of grassy areas for camping. **Ko Kam Yai** is 14km southwest of Hat Bang Ben. It's a large island with a pretty beach and great snorkelling. One island on the other side of Ko Kam Yai is **Ko Kam Tok** (also called Ko Ao Khao Khwai). It's only about 200m from Ko Kam Yai, and, like Ko Kam Noi, has a good beach, soft coral, fresh water and a camping ground.

About 3km north of Hat Bang Ben, across the canal, is another beach, **Hat Laem Son**, which is almost always deserted. The only way to get here is to hike from Hat Bang Ben. In the opposite direction, about 50km south of Hat Bang Ben, is **Hat Praphat**, very similar to Bang Ben with casuarinas and a long beach.

From Ao Khao Kwai, you could opt for the increasingly popular two-day/one-night snorkelling trips to **Surin Islands Marine National Park** (per person all-inclusive 5000B), run by Mr Gao (right).

Sleeping & Eating

HAT BANG BEN

Small family-owned bungalow outfits tend to come and go in these parts. Camping is allowed anywhere among the casuarinas for 80B per person (pay at the park office just inside the park entrance) or you can rent a tent from 150B per night.

National Park Bungalows (☎ 0 2562 0760; reserve@ dnp.go.th; bungalows with fan 1200B, houses with air-con 1600B; 🔀) Choose from basic fan-cooled bungalows and bigger, air-conditioned houses. The on-site restaurant serves three meals per day. Park staff speak decent English.

KO PHAYAM

The following places are either on Ao Yai, a pleasant 3km-long sweep of sandy beach, Ao Khao Kwai further north, or Ao Hin-Khow on the wind-swept eastern shore – an increasingly popular kite-boarding spot.

Electricity is often only available from sunset to 10pm or 11pm. Most resorts are open year-round and have attached eateries serving Thai fare with grilled seafood available in the evenings. Some properties have internet connections for the standard 2B per minute. If yours doesn't, look for Phayam Guesthouse in the village.

Mr Gao (☎ 0 7787 0222; www.mr-gao-phayam.com; Ao Khao Kwai; bungalows from 250B) The varnished wood bungalows are a step up in style and comfort from the classic bamboo crash pad and are very popular with couples. It has 24-hour electricity, an internet cafe (2B per minute), kayak rental, and arranges transport and multiday trips to the Surin Islands (see left).

Aow Yai Bungalows (☎ 0 7787 0216, 08 9819 8782; Ao Yai; bungalows 300-600B) The thatched bamboo bungalow pioneer that started it all 24 years ago. This French-Thai operation was Phayam's first and remains one of the island's best. Choose between small wooden and bamboo bungalows in the palm grove and a larger beachfront model on the southern end of Ao Yai. It rents snorkel gear, kayaks and body boards, too.

Vijit (☎ 0 7783 4082; www.kohpayam-vijit.com; Ao Khao Kwai; bungalows 300-800B; 🖳) Its tree-shaded bungalows are immaculate, huge, have indoor/outdoor bathrooms and little artistic touches.

Bamboo Bungalows (☎ 0 7782 0012; www.bamboo-bungalows.com; Ao Yai; bungalows 350-1500B; 🔀 🛜) A sweet beachfront property. There's a lush garden and an attractive lounge-restaurant with hammocks and cool log swings out the-front. Bungalows range from older bamboo jobs to fairly luxurious peaked-roof cottages that have tiled floors, ceiling fans and outdoor rain showers. There's 24-hour electricity and free kayaks. No wonder upwardly mobile backpackers flock here.

Archanpan Bungalows (☎ 08 0719 9060; Ao Khao Kwai; bungalows 400B) These are rustic, wooden bungalows set in a palm grove bordering a jungle rustling with hornbills, toucans and monkeys.

Jansom Bungalows (☎ 08 9587 8252; Ao Khao Kwai; bungalows 400B) These huge thatched wooden bungalows are above a rocky beach (but just a short stroll from a sandy one). All have new tiles in the bathrooms, 24-hour electricity, and wide terraces out front and there's a restaurant with outstanding views and one of the best and most authentic kitchens on the island.

Frog Beach House (☎ 08 3542 7559; frogbeach@gmail .com; Ao Yai; bungalows 500-800B) You'll see the gorgeous wooden restaurant-lounge as you stroll along the calmer northern stretch of Ao Yai. But you'll have to venture behind it to reach this classy, affordable row of Thai-style cottages with wood floors, outdoor bathrooms, glass-bowl sinks and mosquito nets.

ourpick PP Land (☎ 08 1678 4310; payamppland beach.com; Ao Hin-Khow; bungalows 600B) A stunning ecolodge, north of the pier on the windward side. The stylish concrete bungalows are powered by the wind and sun and have terraces that overlook the sea. The Belgian-Thai owners also preserved a vast tract of jungle south of the resort, and good birdwatching is available from the top floor of their tasty restaurant. They have an organic garden, make their own all-natural laundry detergent and treat the sewage with a cutting-edge grey-water system. Some people talk green; these folks live it. So we'll forgive the soft rock early '80s soundtrack.

JJ's Seafood (Ao Yai; dishes 80-150B; ☺ lunch & dinner) One of a few beach bars and cafes scattered on the beach. Choose a bamboo table sunk into the sand and enjoy exquisite Thai food and market-priced fresh catch.

Drinking

Hippy Bar (Ao Khao Kwai; ☺ 11am-2am Nov-Apr) An amazing beach bar cobbled out of found driftwood, bottles, seashells and anything else that has happened to wash up on shore. The lounge resembles the bow of a pirate ship. There are orchids, waterfall fountains and dub tunes on the sound system.

River Bar (Ao Yai; ☺ 11am-2am) A highly recommended watering hole that sits by the river mouth on Ao Yai. If it has a party going on, be there.

Getting There & Away

The turn-off for Laem Son National Park is about 58km from Ranong down Hwy 4 (Petchkasem Hwy), between the Km 657 and Km 658 markers. Buses heading south from Ranong can drop you off here (ask for Hat Bang Ben). Once you're off the highway, however, you'll have to flag down a pickup truck going towards the park. If you can't get a ride all the way, it's a 10km walk from Hwy 4 to the park entrance. The road is paved, so if you're driving it's a breeze.

From Ranong, take a sŏrng·tăa·ou from Th Ruangrat Market (25B) or one of the many shuttles that service most guesthouses (50B) to the Phayam Pier near Saphan Plaa. If you have three or more people in your group it makes better sense to hire a driver (100B).

There are daily ferries from here to Ko Phayam's main pier (150B, 1½ to two hours) at 9am and 2pm, and speedboats (350B, 45 minutes) at 10am and 2.30pm. A motorcycle taxi from the pier to the main beaches costs 70B per person each way. From Ko Phayam back to Ranong the boats run at 9am and 1pm. Long-tail boat charters to Ko Chang are 1200B, or you can take the taxi boat (300B, one hour) that departs from the main pier on weekdays only at 3pm.

Boats out to other various islands can be chartered from the park's visitors centre; the general cost is 1200B to 1500B per day.

Getting Around

Motorcycle taxis provide transport around Ko Phayam; there are no cars or trucks, and roads are pleasantly motorcycle sized. A ride to your bungalow will cost 80B. Walking is possible but distances are long – it's about 45 minutes from the pier to Ao Khao Kwai, the nearest bay. The outlying dirt roads get bumpy, rutted and worse. Make sure to take your bike for a test drive and check the brakes before venturing off. Motorbike rentals are available at **Phayam Guesthouse** (☎ 08 7071 3695; www.phayam-guesthouse.com; per day approx 150B), in the village, and from most of the larger resorts.

KHURABURI
คุระบุรี/ตะกั่วป่า

Blink and you'll miss it. But if you keep your eyes wide you'll enjoy this soulful, dusty gateway to the Surin islands (p289). For locals it's a market town relied upon by hundreds of squid fishermen that live in ramshackle stilted bamboo villages or new princess-sponsored subdivisions tucked away in the rolling jade hills. Many fishermen have Moken roots

---

COMMUNITY-BASED TOURISM IN PHANG-NGA PROVINCE

Post tsunami, Phang-Nga looks pretty much back to normal if you stay in tourist areas. What the majority of visitors don't know is that many fishing communities have had their way of life changed forever, either by the loss of life of key family members, destruction of fishing equipment or relocation inland out of necessity or fear. Recovery nowadays is taking the form of community development and visitors can help out by enjoying a glimpse of 'real life' on the Andaman coast via community tourism.

Andaman Discoveries (☎ 08 7917 7165; www.andamandiscoveries.com; Khuraburi), formerly Northern Andaman Tsunami Relief, runs highly recommended community-based tours of one to seven days, including to Ban Talae Nok, a historic nearby fishing village, surrounded by tropical forest and mangroves, just down the road from 6km of uninhabited beach. There's an award-winning homestay here featuring cultural and handicraft activities, and fishing and snorkelling trips to uninhabited islands. Pair it with a visit to Muang Kluang, where you can explore Kapoe Bay with warm-hearted residents, who also offer handicraft and sustainable agriculture demonstrations.

Andaman Discoveries also manages three community-service projects: a learning centre for children of Burmese migrant workers; an orphanage outside of Khao Lak; and a school for disabled children in Phuket. Volunteer placement is available, and whatever you decide to do, it will be an unforgettable experience.

---

and moved inland after the 2004 Boxing Day Tsunami destroyed their seaside villages. If you'd like to explore the real Khuraburi, there are some excellent community-based tourism opportunities through Andaman Discoveries (see the boxed text, above).

For internet access, stop into **Good Net** (385-386 Th Pekasem; per hr 40B; ⏰ 10am-11pm) next to the bus stop on the northbound traffic side of the road. For tourist information try **Tom & Am Tour** (☎ 08 6272 0588) right next door. There's an ATM at the 7-Eleven adjacent to the petrol station at the north end of Khuarburi's commercial strip, and another at Krung Thai Bank (Th Pekasem).

Sleeping & Eating

Tararain River Hut Resort (☎ 0 7649 1789; bungalows 300-500B; ❄) Tumbledown but charming, the fan rooms have more character, but its new air-conditioned concrete bungalows on the river are more comfy.

ourpick **Boon Piya Resort** (☎ 0 7649 1969, 08 1752 5457; 175/1 Th Pekasem; bungalows 650B; ❄) These spacious, sparkling modern concrete bungalows with blue roofs and granite floors, set in a garden compound off the main road, are always the first to sell out. Amenities include hot water, cable TV, free bottled water and air-con. It also does laundry and offers free overnight parking if you book your Surin transport with the resort.

Kurarean Thai Hotel (☎ 08 4502 8475; www.kurareanthai.com; r 650B; ❄) Brand-new concrete

bungalows with tiled floors, queen-sized beds, hot water, cable TV and high ceilings. Management doesn't speak much English but is beyond warm and welcoming. It's off the main highway, so it works best if you have your own wheels.

ourpick **Kan-Eng Restaurant** (☎ 08 9727 0254; dishes 30-80B) This cinderblock, tin-roof, street-side shack is the best restaurant in town. It has the hard to find *pla tod kamin* (fried fish with turmeric), a tremendous selection of soups and arguably the best prawns on the north coast.

Morning Market (Th Pekasem; meals 25B; ⏰ 6am-10am) Before you blow town for the Surin Islands, hit Khuarburi's phenomenal market, across the street from Boon Piya Resort, and eat with the locals who descend from all Khuraburi corners for pork and rice porridge, coconut waffles and Thai donuts, which you'll dunk into muddy local coffee.

Getting There & Away

Any Ranong- or Phuket-bound bus will stop in Khuraburi. Take a Phuket-bound bus to Takua Pa, about 50km south of Khuraburi, to transfer to destinations such as Surat Thani (ordinary/air-con 80/100B, three hours), Krabi (ordinary 120B, four hours) and Khao Sok National Park (60B to 80B, one hour).

The pier for the Surin islands is about 9km north of town. Whoever books your boat to the islands will arrange free transfer.

(Continued on page 289)

Diving & Other Activities

Scuba diving over a coral reef in Similan Islands Marine National Park (p295)

Clownfish and anemone
ERNEST MANEWAL

A trip to Thailand's islands and beaches: days lounging in the shade of a coconut palm, evenings spent watching the fiery sunset – the true definition of paradise. But after several extended sessions of muscle-shrivelling relaxation, it becomes increasingly difficult to avoid that little voice in your head encouraging you to get back on your feet and explore. Good thing Thailand has some of the best scuba diving in the entire world, not to mention excellent hiking, rock climbing and sea kayaking. At the end of your trip, you might be surprised to find that you'll need a vacation from your vacation!

DIVING

Those who have explored the deep can undoubtedly agree with Jacques Cousteau: 'the sea, once it casts its spell, holds one in its

top five
DIVE HUBS

Ko Tao (p233) Fantastic frenetic dive energy and scores of shallow dive sites that are often visited by plankton-guzzling whale sharks. This is the best (and cheapest) place in Thailand to lose your scuba virginity. Sail Rock (more readily accessible from Ko Pha-Ngan) and Chumphon Pinnacle are the star sites.

Khao Lak (p292) The gateway to the hushed tropical archipelagos of the Surin and Similan Islands chains. Explore myriad dive sites on a live-aboard trip and check out Richelieu Rock – a stunning diving spot discovered by Jacques Cousteau.

Ko Lanta (p358) Another top spot for crystal-clear waters and loads of marine life including recurrent visits by manta rays and the odd whale shark. Try the submerged pinnacles at Hin Daeng and Hin Muang.

Ko Phi-Phi Don (p351) A triumphant comeback after the tsunami: loads of shimmering reefs swaying under perfectly clear waters. Hin Bida or Ko Bida Nok are the local faves, as is the *King Cruiser* wreck.

Ko Lipe (p386) Not as impressive as most of the other hubs around the kingdom, but the noticeable lack of divers and wonderfully laid-back vibe set the region apart.

net of wonder forever'. In fact, when Mr Cousteau sang that sea's praises, he was probably talking about the land of smiles, since he himself discovered several of the frequented sites explored by many today. Those who are willing to strap on some scuba gear can easily access this stunning realm, which rivals the beauty of the kingdom's idyllic on-land scenery captured in photographs and postcards, then flaunted to jealous friends back home.

For detailed information about the ins and outs of diving in Thailand, see p393.

Andaman Coast vs Gulf Coast

Thailand's unique coastal topography sits at the junction of two distinct oceanic zones – the Andaman Sea waters wash in from the west, while the Gulf of Thailand draws its waters from the islands of Indonesia and the South China Sea. Although marine life is somewhat similar on both sides of the peninsula, each region has telltale differences that easily distinguish one from the other. An ideal diving vacation in Thailand would involve stops along both bodies of water.

The most popular dive sites throughout the kingdom are reef-encrusted limestone outcrops and submerged limestone pinnacles. These sights are often surrounded by deep water and are feeding stations for large pelagic fish including manta rays, reef sharks and whale sharks. Underwater caverns, walls and seamounts are quickly gaining popularity as the 'older' sites become overrun with divers. The seas off both coasts benefit from their equatorial positioning and offer bathwater-like temperatures that hover around 29°C throughout the year.

When the weather is right, the Andaman Sea has some of the finest diving in Southeast Asia. Many would argue that the Andaman has better diving than the gulf, but this is mostly attributed to excellent visibility during the few months of favourable sea conditions. After several post-tsunami evaluations of the coral reefs in the Andaman, most divers agree that the damage was surprisingly small. In fact, some say that the sea has been shining a more brilliant blue in recent years. At least 210 hard corals and 108 species of reef fish have been recorded here, and encounters with large pelagic creatures are quite frequent along the southern provinces. Live-aboard dive trips regularly depart Khao Lak and Phuket for the quiet archipelagos further west known as the Surin and Similan Islands. To the south, Ko Phi-Phi, Ko Lanta and even little Ko Lipe are great places to hang your rucksack and put on some fins.

Many-host goby and sea plants MICHAEL AW

The best part about diving the Gulf of Thailand is that sea conditions are generally favourable throughout the year. This C-shaped coastline is about twice as long as the Andaman side and changes drastically as it links the Malaysian border to Thailand's eastern neighbour, Cambodia. The southwestern gulf coast has the finest diving spots, located near the islands of Ko Tao and Ko Pha-Ngan. Ko Tao currently certifies more divers than any other place in world. Pattaya, just a quick two-hour hop from the Bangkok bustle, offers a few memorable dives as well including a couple wrecks. On the far eastern side of the coast, the Ko Chang Archipelago provides for some pleasant scuba possibilities, although choppy seas limit the season to November to May.

Thailand's Marine Life

If speaking were possible underwater, almost every dive site in Thailand would be a noisy jumble of 'oohs' and 'aahs' as divers gleefully point to passing creatures. Thailand's aquatic food chain is as colourful as it is complicated. Hard and soft corals provide the foundation for schooling fish ranging in size from teeny 'Nemos' (clownfish), to large visitors such as giant trevallies, tunas, groupers, barracudas, kingfish, manta rays and reef sharks. The gigantic whale shark is the big kahuna. For more information on whale sharks, see the boxed text above.

HITTING THE UNDERWATER JACKPOT

Most divers come to Thailand with the hope of hitting the underwater jackpot: spotting an elusive whale shark – the largest fish in the sea – with a giant mouth that can measure about 2m wide (so just imagine how big their bodies are). Don't worry; they are filter feeders, which means that they mostly feed on plankton, krill and other tiny organisms. In fact, divers often report that adult whale sharks are quite friendly and enjoy swimming through the streamers of bubbles emitted by divers. Usually these gentle creatures gravitate towards submerged pinnacles and often hang out at a site for several days before continuing on. So, if rumours are flying around about a recent sighting, then strap on your scuba gear and hit the high seas.

In the past there were 'spotting seasons', but recent shifts in weather patterns mean that they can be spotted at any time of the year. Recently the number of whale sharks has greatly increased – in 2007 most diving instructors averaged around four sightings per year, but these days the scuba pros we encountered said they are personally averaging between 20 and 40 gentle giants annually!

Diving with a whale shark near Ko Tao (p233)

Snorkelling near Ko Chang (p275)

DAVID GREEDY

SNORKELLING

Snorkelling is a popular choice for those who cringe at the thought of breathing air out of a tank; it's also a great option for those who are simply on a tighter budget. Orchestrating your own snorkelling adventure is a cinch – along all of the coasts there are loads of resorts and dive shops that rent out gear for 100B to 200B per day. Many islands, including the Trang island chain (p371), Ko Tao (p238), Ko Pha-Ngan (p247), Ko Phi-Phi (p351) and the islands in the Ko Chang Archipelago (p148), have phenomenal snorkelling spots right off shore.

Snorkelling tours are becoming just as popular as diving day trips; in fact, many dive operators are now starting to offer snorkelling outings as well. Expect to pay between 500B and 1000B for a day trip, depending on how far you travel to find favourable conditions. High-end excursions usually use fancy speedboats and expensive equipment, while cheaper deals tend to focus more on the social aspect of the trip, taking customers to so-so reefs. Consider chartering your own speedboat or long-tail boat if you are serious about snorkelling. With a little research, it's not too difficult to scout out undisturbed reefs nearby.

In general you can see plenty of marine life while snorkelling, though at busy tourist destinations such as Ko Phi-Phi the number of travellers is starting to harm the marine environment. The general rule is that the further you get from human inhabitation, the better the condition of the reefs. However, some developed islands have hidden corners where healthy coral still persists, usually coinciding with areas of rocky shoreline.

SEA KAYAKING

Although Thailand's coastal regions are famous for the action occurring below sea level, sea kayaking is a great way to check out some remote islands and hidden coves that are inaccessible to larger watercraft.

The thin chain of islands between Ko Samui and the mainland, known as Ang Thong Marine Park (p248), is a must for any kayaking fanatic. This stunning collection of easily anthropomorphised islands stretches along the cerulean waters like an emerald necklace. All of the islands are uninhabited (save five bungalows operated by the marine parks system) and feature pristine terrain that can only be accessed by long-tail boat or kayak. Tours depart from Ko Samui (p200) and Ko Pha-Ngan (p222), both located about an hour's ride away by speedboat.

Sea-kayaking tours of remote islands and mangroves around the Andaman Sea are hugely popular at tourist centres such as Phuket (p305), Ao Nang (p342) and elsewhere along the coast.

In some cases equipment can be rented for solo expeditions, but more typically outings are organised tours, which include transfers, guides, gear, lunch and usually snorkelling equipment as a bonus.

CAVING

Spelunking is just as much fun as it sounds. Bounding through angled crevices and dangling stalactites is a popular activity among visitors. Millions of years worth of monsoon rains have etched elaborate systems of tunnels throughout Thailand. Join a cave tour in Ko Lanta (p361), Ko Muk (p373) or Khao Sok National Park (p291), or visit the undulating coastline in Trang Province (p367), which offers a fascinating mix of intense crawl spaces and hidden shrines.

The newest fad in cavern exploration is underwater caving – a popular option for scuba-philes with a significant amount of diving experience. Several operators on Ko Tao (p238) offer one-day/one-night trips out to the submerged grottos in Khao Sok National Park.

Kayaking at Ao Phang-Nga (p297)

AUSTIN

Many caves throughout Thailand have been transformed into unusual religious sanctuaries – although these caverns are by no means a heart-pumping expedition, their context is important in understanding the kingdom's history and customs. The dramatic caves at Khao Sam Roi Yot (p184) are a cherished royal stomping ground, and feature a dazzling golden pavilion that shimmers as the afternoon sunlight pours in from above. The popular temple town of Phetchaburi (p169) has a couple of interesting cave shines as well.

HIKING

Despite the region's focus on water sports, Thailand's coasts and islands have numerous hiking opportunities featuring unique biodiversity and photo opportunities befitting the pages of *National Geographic*.

If you're travelling between the Andaman and gulf coasts, consider breaking up the trip with a stopover in the centre of the isthmus of Kra – the long strip of land that separates the two coasts. This network of inland jungles stretches in a ribbon from Phetchaburi, near Bangkok, all the way down into Malaysia. Along the way, visitors will find the oldest rainforest in the world with over 500 species of birds. Two virgin archipelagos are bookends to coastal Thailand – Ko Chang Archipelago hugs the Cambodian border and features dozens of tiny islands primed for exploration, while the Ko Tarutao Marine Park near the Malaysian border benefits from strict governmental laws prohibiting development on all but one island.

For information on responsible hiking see p393.

ROCK CLIMBING

Thailand's numerous jagged outcrops of sky-reaching limestone make most tourists drool, but for rock-climbing enthusiasts it's

top five
TREKS

Khao Sok National Park (p290) This majestic park protects the world's oldest rainforest, which features shimmering limestone outcrops, gushing waterfalls, giant flowers, curious creatures and thickets of dripping jungle ferns.

Khao Sam Roi Yot National Park (p183) A network of easily navigable paths criss-crosses a steep jungle of overgrown flora and leaping dusky langur monkeys.

Ko Chang (p150) Endless acres of untouched terrain lie hidden deep within this gargantuan floating jungle. Try exploring the island's nether-regions on the back of a gentle elephant.

Ko Tarutao Marine National Park (p383) One of the original marine parks in Thailand, this pristine archipelago is home to 51 jungle islands with loads of opportunities for nature enthusiasts to tread quietly among tumbling vegetation and scampering wildlife. Ko Adang and Ko Rawi are our faves.

Kam Ru National Park (p292) The quiet national park at Khao Lak is a stunning expanse of dramatic hills, sea cliffs, estuaries and forested valleys. Scurrying fauna includes tapirs, monkeys and black bears.

Ban Kwan Elephant Camp (p154), Ko Chang

DAVID GREEDY

a whole other story. These swirling stone masses are a world-class playground of crags and crevices that lures scores of adventurers from around the globe.

The Andaman coast delivers the goods, with several iterations of rocky crags along the sharp, twisting coast. With nearly 500 bolted routes and top-notch views from the summits, Railay (p346) can safely claim to be one of the best places in the world to climb. Try your hand at One, Two, Three Wall, which boasts over 40 climbs ranging from 4b to 8b on the French grading system. Advanced climbers should test their muscles at Thaiwand Wall, a slippery, sky-scraping limestone mass at the southern end of Hat Rai Leh West. 'Deep water soloing' is a recent craze – adventurers are free-climbing steep, limestone ledges and using the deep seas below as their safety net when they fall in. The Trang Islands (p371) are another popular spot for some monkey action, as are Ko Phi-Phi (p354) and Ko Tao (p239).

Tuition costs generally hover around 5000B to 6000B for a three-day course, while half-day courses will set you back around 800B to 1000B. If you are an experienced climber, equipment can be rented for around 1000B per day. For those who intend to bring their own gear, include a 60m rope, plenty of slings and quickdraws, chalk (sweaty palms are inevitable in the tropics) and a small selection of nuts and cams as backup for thinly protected routes. Final anchors are usually fixed at two or three points and have opposing karabiners or double rings for lowering off. A woven rattan mat (available locally for 100B to 150B) will help keep the sand out of your gear. Bolts are replaced every few years and are generally solid, though some of the more-remote routes are re-bolted less frequently and may be off-limits for safety reasons.

Rock climbing at Railay (p346)

CHRISTOPHER GROEN

(Continued from page 280)

SURIN ISLANDS MARINE NATIONAL PARK (MU KO SURIN NATIONAL PARK)
อุทยานแห่งชาติหมู่เกาะสุรินทร์

The five gorgeous islands that make up the **Surin Islands Marine National Park** (www.dnp.go.th; admission 400B; mid-Nov–mid-May) sit 60km offshore, just 5km from the Thailand–Myanmar marine border. Here you can explore healthy rainforest and comb postcard-perfect white-sand beaches on glassy turquoise bays with rocky headlands that jut into the ocean. Look up and you'll see a range of jungled mountains knife into the sky, look down and you'll notice that the clearest of water nurtures abundant marine life and offers visibility up to 20m. The islands' sheltered bays also attract *chow lair* (sea gypsies), which live in a village onshore during the May to October monsoon season. This group is known as the Moken people, from the local word *ôr gaang*, meaning 'salt water'.

Ko Surin Neua (north) and Ko Surin Tai (south) are the two largest islands. Park headquarters and all visitor facilities are at Ao Chong Khad and Ao Mai Ngam on Ko Surin Neua, near the jetty. The setting of flaxen sand and sparkling blue-green bays is spectacular.

Khuraburi is the jumping-off point for the park. The pier is about 9km north of town, as is the mainland **national park office** (0 7649 1378; 8am-5pm), with good information, maps and helpful staff.

Sights & Activities
DIVING & SNORKELLING
Dive sites in the park include **Ko Surin Tai** and **HQ Channel** between the two main islands. **Richelieu Rock** (a seamount 14km southeast) is also technically in the park, but is relatively far off. It also happens to be one of the best, if not the best, dive sites on the Andaman coast. Whale sharks are sometimes spotted here during March and April. Sixty kilometres northwest of the Surins – but often combined with dive trips to the park – are the famed **Burma Banks**, a system of submerged seamounts. The three major banks, **Silvertip**, **Roe** and **Rainbow**, provide five-star diving experiences, with coral gardens laid over flat plateaus, and large oceanic and smaller reef marine species. There's presently no dive facility in the park itself, so dive trips (four-day live-aboards around 20,000B) must be booked

from the mainland; see Getting There & Away (p290), and the Khao Lak (p293) and Ranong (p274) sections, for more information.

Snorkelling is excellent due to relatively shallow reef depths of 5m to 6m. Two-hour snorkelling trips (per person 80B, gear per day 150B) leave the park headquarters at 9am and 2pm daily. Expect to be in the company of mostly Thais who swim fully clothed. If you'd like a more serene snorkelling experience, charter your own long-tail from the national park (half day 1000B), or better yet, directly from the Moken themselves in **Ban Moken**. The most beautiful, vibrant soft corals we saw were at **Ao Mae Yai**, an enormous North Island bay around the corner from Chong Khod. The best section of reef is between the white buoys along the northern peninsula. There are more fish off tiny **Ko Pajumba**, but the coral isn't in great shape. **Ao Suthep**, off the South Island, has vast schools of iridescent fish and shallow blue holes with milky bottoms.

WILDLIFE & HIKING
Around park headquarters you can explore the forest fringes, looking out for crab-eating macaques and some of the 57 resident bird species, which include the fabulous Nicobar pigeon, endemic to the Andaman islands. Along the coast you're likely to see the Brahminy kite soaring and reef herons on the rocks. Twelve species of bat live here, most noticeably the tree-dwelling fruit bats (also known as flying foxes).

A rough-and-ready **walking trail** winds 2km along the coast and through forest, up and over the jagged mountains and back down to the beach at **Ao Mai Ngam**, where there's good snorkelling, as well as camping facilities and its own canteen. At low tide it's easy to walk along the coast between the two campsites.

OTHER ACTIVITIES
Ban Moken (Moken Village) at Ao Bon on the South Island welcomes visitors. Post-tsunami, Moken have settled in this one sheltered bay where a major ancestral worship ceremony (Loi Reua) takes place in April. The national park offers a **Moken Village Tour** (per person 300B). You'll stroll through the village, hike the 800m **Chok Madah trail** over the jungled hills to an empty beach, visit its interpretative centre and, if your luck is exceptional, maybe even row a traditional *kabang* (houseboat carved and lashed with all-natural materials). Tours

depart at 9.15am and must be reserved the day before. You can also organise a ride over from the park's HQ (per person 100B). If you do visit the village, bring cash to buy handicrafts to help support its economy. There's also a clothing donation box at park headquarters for the Moken, so this is a good, responsible place to lighten your load.

Sleeping & Eating

Park accommodation is decent, but because of the island's short, narrow beaches it can feel seriously crowded when full (around 300 people). Book online at www.dnp.go.th or with the mainland **national park office** (☎ 0 7649 1378; ⌚ 8am-5pm) in Khuraburi. The clientele is mostly Thai, giving the place a lively holiday-camp feel. You can camp on both Ao Chong Klod and Ao Mae Ngam. The former has the more spectacular beach, the latter fills up last, is more secluded and with its narrow white sand sliver tucked into mangroves, it feels a bit wilder. There are no bungalows on Ao Mae Ngam.

Bungalows (2000B) have wood floors and private terraces, as well as private terracotta bathrooms and fans that run all night. **Tents** (2-/4-person 300/450B, bedding per person 60B) are available for rent or you can pitch your own **tent** (per night 80B). There's generator power until 10pm.

A park **restaurant** (dishes from 80B, set menus 170-200B) serves decent Thai food.

Getting There & Away

A 'big boat', which was docked when we passed through, theoretically leaves the Khuraburi pier at 9am daily when the park is open, returning at 1pm (return 1300B, 2½ hours one way). But most tour operators now use speedboats (return 1600B, one hour one way) exclusively. They leave around 9am and honour open tickets. Return whenever you please.

Several tour operators also run day tours (2700B including food and park lodging) to the park. The best in safety, service and value is **Barracuda Diving** (☎ 0 7649 1900; www .barracudadiving.com; 179-180 Th Pekasem), which is co-managed by Boon Piya Resort (p280). Agencies in Hat Khao Lak (p293), Phuket (p304) and Ranong (p273) are the most convenient booking options for live-aboard dive trips. Transfers from the place of purchase are always included.

KO PHRA THONG

เกาะพระทอง

Legend has it that many centuries ago, pirates docked here and buried a golden Buddha beneath the sands. Translated as 'Golden Buddha Island', it is now unlikely that Ko Phra Thong will give up its secret, but tourists can still make good use of its pleasant sandy beaches.

The island is as quiet as a church mouse, and fishing (squid, prawns and jellyfish) remains its key industry. The local delicacy is pungent gà·bì (fermented prawn paste).

our pick **Golden Buddha Beach Resort** (☎ 08 1892 2208; www.goldenbuddharesort.com; bungalows 3300-16,800B) is the island's top resort, attracting a stream of yoga aficionados keen for a spiritual getaway. Accommodation is in naturalistic-chic wooden houses. All have open-air bathrooms with views of the sea and the surrounding forest.

There are no regular boats to Ko Phra Thong, but if you're set on going to the island independently you can hop on a Surin-bound diving boat at the Khuraburi pier (see p280) and ask the boat driver to drop you off for a small fee. It's better to contact Golden Buddha Beach Resort in advance to arrange transport.

Locals of Tung Dap village on the southern tip of the island have requested that tourists not visit their area, so please be respectful and avoid this corner.

KHAO SOK NATIONAL PARK

อุทยานแห่งชาติเขาสก

If your leg muscles have atrophied after one too many days of beach-bumming, consider venturing inland to the wondrous Khao Sok National Park. Many believe this lowland jungle – the wettest spot in Thailand – to be over 160 million years old, making it one of the oldest rainforests on the globe. It features dramatic limestone formations and waterfalls that cascade through juicy thickets drenched with rains and morning dew. A network of dirt trails snakes through the quiet park, allowing visitors to spy on the exciting array of indigenous creatures.

Information

The **park headquarters** (☎ 0 7739 5025; www.khao sok.com; park admission 400B) and visitors centre are 1.8km off Rte 401, close to the Km 109 marker.

The best time of year to visit is between December and April – the dry season. During the June to October wet season, trails can be extremely slippery, and flash flooding is a common and sometimes fatal occurrence. On the other hand, animals leave their hidden reservoirs throughout the wet months, so you're more likely to stumble across big fauna.

Sights & Activities

Khao Sok's vast terrain makes it one of the last viable habitats for **large mammals**. During the wetter months you may happen upon bear, boar, gaur, tapirs, gibbons, deer, wild elephants and perhaps even a tiger. There are more than 300 bird species, 38 bat varieties and one of the world's largest flowers, the rare *Rafflesia kerrii*, which is found only in Khao Sok (within Thailand). These **giant flowers** can reach 80cm in diameter. They have no roots or leaves of their own; instead they live as parasites inside the roots of the liana, a jungle vine.

The stunning **Kheuan Chiaw Lan** sits about an hour's drive east of the visitors centre. The lake was created in 1982 by an enormous shale-clay dam called Ratchaprapha (Kheuan Ratchaprapha or Kheuan Chiaw Lan). The limestone outcrops protruding from the lake reach a height of 960m, over three times higher than the formations in the Phang-Nga area. Technical divers can drop into the emerald waters and glimpse ghostly stalagmites with the tech-diving team from **Big Blue** (☎ 0 7745 6415; www.bigbluekhaosok.com), which is based on the gulf island of Ko Tao.

A cave known as **Tham Nam Thalu** contains striking limestone formations and subterranean streams, while **Tham Si Ru** features four converging passageways used as a hideout by communist insurgents between 1975 and 1982. The caves can be reached on foot from the southwestern shore of the lake. You can rent boats from local fishermen to explore the coves, canals, caves and cul-de-sacs along the lakeshore.

Elephant trekking, kayaking and rafting are popular park activities. The hiking is also excellent, and you can arrange park tours from any guesthouse – just be sure you get a certified guide (they wear an official badge). Various hiking trails from the visitors centre lead to the waterfalls of **Sip-Et Chan** (4km), **Than Sawan** (9km) and **Than Kloy** (9km), among other destinations.

Sleeping

The road leading into the park is lined with charming fan bungalows offering comfortable digs in natural surroundings. Try to arrive in the daytime, so you can walk along the short road leading up to the park and pick where you want to stay. All the resorts offer tours and transport throughout the park.

Jungle Huts (☎ 0 7739 5160; huts 300-1200B) A solid choice for backpackers. Free monkey and waterfalls tours are on offer.

Khao Sok Rainforest Resort (☎ 0 7739 135; www.krabidir.com/khaosokrainforest; bungalows 400-600B) This resort has budget huts stilted along the snaking river. In-house conservation programs target low-impact hiking and forest restoration.

Tree Tops River Huts (☎ 08 1958 0629; www.treetopsriverhuts.com; bungalows 500-1400B) More cosy tree houses with limestone cliff views.

Our Jungle House (☎ 08 1417 0546; huts 800-2400B) This offers tree houses and loads of tours and activities (think: river tubing, elephant trekking, guided hikes and moonlight safaris).

Cliff & River Jungle Resort (☎ 08 7271 8787; www.thecliffandriver.com; bungalows 1800B) This beautiful property with stilted bamboo bungalows is set below the jagged cliffs and is removed from Khao Sok's budget huddle. The food is terrific, too.

Getting There & Around

Minivans to Khao Sok from Surat Thani (150B to 200B, one hour, 100km) leave at least twice daily. Tickets can be arranged through most travel agents in Surat. Otherwise, catch a bus going towards Takua Pa. On the Andaman coast, you can take a Surat Thani–bound bus from Phuket (220B, three hours), Khao Lak (150B, 1½ hours) or Takua Pa (60B to 80B, one hour). Buses drop you off along the highway (Rte 401), 1.8km from the visitors centre. If guesthouse touts don't meet you, you'll have to walk to your chosen nest (from 50m to 2km).

To explore Chiaw Lan Lake, charter a longtail (2000B per day) at the dam's entrance.

HAT PAKARANG & HAT BANG SAK

หาดปะการัง/หาดบางสัก

Essentially one long, sleepy stretch of sand, the beaches at Pakarang and Bang Sak had been attracting an ever-growing number of tourists until the 2004 tsunami washed away scores of businesses and hotels in an instant. The biggest casualties were in the nearby squid fishing village of **Baan Nam Kem**, where you'll find a moving **Tsunami Memorial Park** – a black-granite and terracotta, wave-shaped monument steps from the beach. More than five years later, the creamy white sand remains virtually empty. With thick mangroves, ample rolling pasture and rubber tree plantations forming a wide buffer between the coast and highway, you really feel like you've gotten away from it all when you land here.

If you've spent your life looking for a consistent, long wave on an empty beach with almost no surfers in the water, **Hat Pakarang** is your dream break. **Pakarang Surf Shop** (☎ 0 7648 5350; pakarangsurfshop.com; Th Petchkasem) in Khao Lak offers board rental (per hour 200B), lessons (1000B, 1½ hours) and local surf secrets.

Sleeping & Eating

There are just a few hotels along this pretty beach, making it an ideal romantic hideaway.

White Sand Beach Bungalow (☎ 0 7648 7580; Hat Pakarang; cottages 1500B; ❄) Next door to the Sarojin are eight, simple, clean, air-conditioned cottages with queen-sized beds, hot water and a five-star slice of sand. Day-trippers descend from Khao Lak to the attractive beachside restaurant. At night it will be all yours.

Le Meridian (☎ 0 7642 7500; www.lemeridian.com; Hat Bang Sak; r from 6320B, villas from 11,200B; ❄ 🖳 🛜 🏊) A four-star megaresort, its 243 rooms and 20 villas are the only nests on Hat Bang Sak. It lacks the boutique touch and five-star service of the Sarojin, but it is slightly cheaper and is certainly majestic, sprawling nearly all the way from the highway to the sea.

Sarojin (☎ 0 7642 7900-4; www.sarojin.com; Hat Pakarang; r 12,500-23,250B; ❄ 🖳 🛜 🏊) A quiet retreat with a Japanese-meets-modern-Thai style, service here is stellar and the whole setting (there are only 56 rooms) is elegant and intimate. The very private spa (treatments from 2300B), which takes in views of coconut groves and is nestled at the edge of the mangroves, is one of the best on the Andaman coast. We especially love the pool with its stylish lounging huts that hover above the crystal-blue water. Its cooking class takes place on the banks of the muddy Takuapa river, where you can watch water buffalo stroll by, and it arranges private diving and snorkelling trips to the Similan and Surin islands. No kids allowed.

Getting There & Away

From Khao Lak catch a frequent public sŏrng·tǎa·ou (60B) between 8.30am and 5pm. Buses running between Takua Pa and Phuket will also get you here, but the highway is a bit of a stroll from most resorts. Your best bet is to take public transport to Khao Lak and charter a sŏrng·tǎa·ou (500B to 700B) from there.

HAT KHAO LAK
หาดเขาหลัก

Just before you arrive you'll round a bend and suddenly Khao Lak's vast horseshoe bay, backed by rolling granite hills thick with tropical rainforest, will reveal itself. You'll notice resort rooftops peeking above the swaying coconut palms, tourists lounging and strolling on the golden sand, as the turquoise sea gently licks the shore in overlapping ovals.

Keep driving through the main drag, however, and you'll soon confront Khao Lak's shadow, in the form of an armoured police boat (Boat 813) stranded in an empty field, surrounded by tourists snapping photos. Consider it proof that while there has been significant tourism resurgence since the tsunami, Khao Lak's wounds run deep. Nowhere outside of Aceh was hit harder on 26 December 2004. But it's that combination of beauty and experience that makes Khao Lak such an amazing place to visit.

It also happens to be the most practical base for exploring the Similan islands as well as the mainland wonders of Khao Sok and Khao Lak/Lam Ru National Parks; which explains why there are shops, restaurants, bars and tour offices crowding the highway.

Internet is widely available and banks and ATMs are everywhere.

Sights & Activities

The area immediately south of Hat Khao Lak has been incorporated into the vast 125 sq km **Khao Lak/Lam Ru National Park** (☎ 0 7642 0243; www .dnp.go.th; adult/child 100/50B; ❦ 8am-4.30pm), a collage of sea cliffs, 1000m-high hills, beaches, estuaries, forested valleys and mangroves. Wildlife includes hornbills, drongos, tapirs, gibbons, monkeys and Asiatic black bears. The visitors centre, just off Hwy 4 between the Km 56 and Km 57 markers, has little in the way of maps or printed information, but there's a very nice open-air restaurant perched on a shady slope overlooking the sea. From the restaurant you can take a fairly easy 3km round-trip nature trail that heads along the cape and ends at often-deserted Hat Lek beach.

Guided hikes along the coast or inland can be arranged through many tour agencies in town, as can long-tail boat trips up the scenic **Khlong Thap Liang** estuary. The latter affords opportunities to view mangrove communities of crab-eating macaques. Between Khao Lak and Bang Sak is a network of sandy **beach trails** – some of which lead to deserted beaches – which are fun to explore on foot or by rented motorcycle. Most of the hotels in town rent motorbikes for 250B per day.

The Nanthong beach road runs parallel, just down hill from the main drag, and offers public access to the best beach in Khao Lak proper.

About 2.5km north of Hat Khao Lak, **Hat Bang Niang** is well worth a trip if you are looking for a little more peace and quiet. You won't miss **Boat 813** perched in an open field nearly 1km from shore. More than five years later, it remains the region's most prominent reminder of nature's power. There's an information booth nearby with a tsunami timeline in both Thai and English, as well as some compelling photo books for sale. It's just a 50B sŏrng·tăa·ou between here and Khao Lak.

DIVING & SNORKELLING
Diving or snorkelling day excursions to the Similan and Surin islands are immensely popular, but if you can, opt for a live-aboard. Since the islands are around 60km from the mainland (about three hours by boat), you'll have a more relaxing trip and experience the islands sans day-trippers. All dive shops offer live-aboard trips from around 10,000/19,000B for two- /three-day packages and day trips for 4900B to 6500B.

Although geared towards divers, all dive shops welcome snorkellers who can hop on selected dive excursions or live-aboards for a discount of around 40%; otherwise, tour agencies all around town offer even cheaper snorkelling trips to the Similan islands for around 2700B. PADI Open Water certification courses cost anywhere from 10,000B to 18,000B depending upon where you dive. You can go on a 'discover scuba' day trip to the Similans for around 6000B to 6500B.

Recommended dive shops:

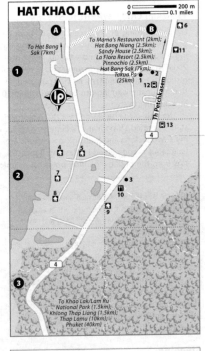

HAT KHAO LAK

SIGHTS & ACTIVITIES	
Big Blue...1 B1
IQ Dive.......................................(see 3)
Liquid..2 B1
Wicked Diving................................3 B2

SLEEPING	
Greenbeach....................................4 A2
Khao Lak Bhandari.........................5 A2
Khao Lak Youth Club......................6 B1
Nangthong Bay Resort....................7 A2
Nangthong Beach Resort.................8 A2
Walker's Inn...................................9 B2

EATING	
Phu Khao Lak................................10 B2

DRINKING	
Happy Snapper..............................11 B1

TRANSPORT	
Bus Stop (Northbound)..................12 B1
Bus Stop (Southbound)..................13 B2

Big Blue (☎ 0 7648 5544; www.bigbluekhaolak.com) Japanese and Swedish owned; its speedboat, live-aboard and dive instructors are among the best in Khao Lak.
IQ Dive (☎ 0 7648 5614; www.iq-dive.com) Another highly recommended and responsible outfitter with a variety of day-trip and live-aboard options.

TSUNAMI EARLY WARNING SYSTEM

On the morning of 26 December 2004, an earthquake off the coast of the Indonesian island of Sumatra sent enormous waves crashing against much of Thailand's Andaman coast, claiming around 8000 lives and causing millions of dollars of damage to homes and businesses. In 2005 Thailand officially inaugurated a national disaster warning system, which was created in response to the country's lack of preparedness in 2004. The Bangkok-based centre anticipates that a tsunami warning can be issued within 30 minutes of the event being detected by existing international systems.

The public will be warned via the nationwide radio network, Channel 5 army TV network, the state-operated TV pool and SMS messages. For non-Thai speakers, the centre has installed warning towers along the high-risk beachfront areas that will broadcast announcements in various languages accompanied by flashing lights. The **call centre** (☎ 1860) also handles questions and tips from the public regarding potential or unfolding disasters.

Liquid (☎ 0 7648 5068; www.liquid-adventure.com) It runs day trips on its own speedboat and acts as an agent for Khao Lak–based live-aboards, with boats and itineraries to suit all budgets.

our pick Wicked Diving (☎ 0 7648 5868; www.wicked diving.com) An exceptionally well-run and environmentally conscious outfit that runs diving and snorkelling overnight trips, where you can sleep in national park bungalows, as well as a range of live-aboards; including Whale Sharks & Mantas, Turtle & Reefs and Sharks & Rays conservation trips, run in conjunction with Ecocean (www.whaleshark.org). It does all the PADI courses, too.

Sleeping

Backpacker accommodation predominates in the congested centre of town, while three- and four-star resorts dominate the coast.

BUDGET

our pick Khaolak Youth Club (☎ 0 7648 5900; www .khaolakyouthclub.com; dm 250B, bungalows 1200B; ✖ ☎) Budgeteers will dig the large, bright, fan-cooled, unisex dorm. Of course, for some others high ceilings, brick feature walls and an MTV's *Real World* vibe cannot compete with private bathrooms. Which is why they'll opt for a very cute, shabby chic, wooden bungalow with air-con and a flat screen TV.

Walker's Inn (☎ 0 7648 5668; Th Petchkasem; r 400-750B; ✖ ☎) The Walker's comprises large, basic, tiled rooms with air-con and hot showers, above a pub. Some rooms have private balconies.

Sandy House (☎ 0 7648 6224; www.infothesandyhouse .com; r 800B; ✖ ☎) Just inland from La Flora in Bang Niang and just a short walk from a beautiful beach is this coral-coloured three-floor walk-up with queen-sized beds, tiled floors, minifridge and cable TV.

MIDRANGE

Khao Lak/Lam Ru National Park Bungalows (☎ 0 2562 0760; reserve@dnp.go.th; bungalows 800-2000B) There is a handful of four- and six-bed bungalows in the national park. Standards are basic, but the setting will suit those after an eco-experience.

Greenbeach (☎ 0 7648 5845; greenbeach_th@yahoo .com; bungalows 1300-2300B; ✖) On an excellent stretch of beach and extending back into a garden, this place has a warm family-style soul. The wooden bungalows have glass doors, air-con and fan, shady terraces and views of a towering, ancient banyan tree. Even the cheapest rooms have sea views.

Nangthong Bay Resort (☎ 0 7648 5088; www .nangthong.com; r 1500-3000B; ✖ ☐ ☎ ☎) Until its sister property opened, this was the best midranger on the beach. Rooms are designed with a sparse black-and-white chic decor. The cheapest rooms are set back from the beach, but are fantastic value. Grounds are lush and service is excellent.

our pick Nangthong Beach Resort (☎ 0 7648 5911; www.nangthong.com; r 2000-2200B, bungalows 2500-3000B; ✖ ☐ ☎ ☎) The best choice in Khao Lak proper has large, well-appointed rooms, and even larger bungalows, with ceramic-tile floors, dark-wood furnishings, a bourgeoning garden, impeccable service and the best stretch of sand in town.

TOP END

Khao Lak Bhandari (☎ 0 7648 5751; www.khaolak bhandari.com; chalets 4900B, bungalows 6900B; ✖ ☐ ☎ ☎) Ageing but still classy, these Thai-style bungalows and chalets are large, with soaring ceilings, peaked roofs, showers and baths, across the street from the beach.

Its high-quality spa (massages from 600B, skin scrubs from 800B) is the best value in the area.

La Flora Resort (☎ 0 7642 8000; www.lafloraresort .com; Hat Bang Niang; r 5700-7700B, villas 9000-10,500B; 🅿 🖳 🛜 🆒) This classy four-star resort was utterly destroyed by the tsunami, but you'd never know from looking at it. Villas are large and modern with sexy beachfront infinity pools. Rooms have marble floors, ceramic sinks, striking modern art, iPod docks and aromatherapy diffusers.

Eating & Drinking

Venture out of the hotel dining rooms and you'll find some terrific restaurants hidden in plain sight.

our pick **Mama's Restaurant** (☎ 08 4850 7417; Th Petchkasem; dishes 60-300B) Nobody, and we do mean nobody, does seafood better than Mama, who is still holding it down across from Boat 813. Her fish cakes are insane, so is the barracuda sautéed in yellow curry. And, lest you forget, you are in squid country.

Phu Khao Lak (☎ 0 7648 5141; Th Petchkasem; dishes 80-240B; ⏰ breakfast, lunch & dinner) With it's dangling lanterns and clothed tables spilling onto a lawn at the south end of the Khao Lak strip, it's hard to miss. And you shouldn't because the dishes are impeccably prepared.

Pinocchio (☎ 0 7644 3079; 67/61 Th Hat Bang Niang, Hat Bang Niang; mains 240-480B) This beautiful candle-lit garden restaurant features a huge stone pizza oven, imported wine and cheese, tremendous sourdough bread, even better pizza, homemade pasta, and gelato, and the bizarre assumption that all faràng speak German.

Happy Snapper (☎ 0 7648 5500; Th Petchkasem) Here's a bar stocked with good liquor, with a map of the world on the ceiling, the tree of life on the wall and a rockin' house band on stage six nights a week in the high season, led by the owner, a Bangkok-born bass legend.

Getting There & Away

Any bus running along Hwy 4 between Takua Pa (50B, 45 minutes) and Phuket (80B, two hours) will stop at Hat Khao Lak if you ask the driver. Buses will also stop near the Merlin resort and the Khao Lak/Lam Ru National Park headquarters. By taxi it's only one hour to Phuket International Airport (1200B to 500B).

SIMILAN ISLANDS MARINE NATIONAL PARK (MU KO SIMILAN NATIONAL PARK)

อุทยานแห่งชาติหมู่เกาะสิมิลัน

Known to divers the world over, beautiful **Similan Islands Marine National Park** (www.dnp.go.th; admission 400B; ⏰ Nov-May) is 60km offshore. Its smooth granite islands are as impressive above water as below, topped with rainforest, edged with white-sand beaches and fringed with coral reefs.

Two of the nine islands, Island 4 (Ko Miang) and Island 8 (Ko Similan), have ranger stations and accommodation; park headquarters and most visitor activity centres are on Island 4. 'Similan' comes from the Malay word *sembilan*, meaning 'nine', and while each island is named, they're more commonly known by their numbers.

Hat Khao Lak is the jumping-off point for the park. The pier is at Thap Lamu, about 10km south of town, where you'll find a cluster of tour operators. The **mainland park office** (☎ 0 7659 5045; ⏰ 8am-4pm) is about 500m before the pier, but there's no information in English available.

Sights & Activities
DIVING & SNORKELLING

The Similans offer exceptional diving for all levels of experience, at depths from 2m to 30m. There are seamounts at **Fantasy Rocks**, rock reefs at **Ko Payu** (Island 7) and dive-throughs at **Hin Pousar** (Elephant Head), with marine life ranging from tiny plume worms and soft corals to schooling fish and whale sharks. There are dive sites at each of the six islands north of Ko Miang; the southern part of the park (Islands 1, 2 and 3) is off-limits to divers and is a turtle nesting ground. No facilities for divers exist in the national park itself, so you'll need to take a dive tour. Agencies in Hat Khao Lak (p293) and Phuket (p304) book dive trips (three-day live-aboards from around 13,500B). The best Similan islands for diving are Island 9 (which has excellent coral slopes) and Islands 5 and 6.

If you're a snorkeller trying to decide between the Surin or Similan islands, opt for the Surin islands (see p289) where the majority of corals are relatively close to the surface. That said, snorkelling is good at several points around Island 4, especially in the main channel, and on Islands 7 and 8; you can hire snorkelling gear (per day 100B) from the park headquarters. Day-tour operators usually visit three or four different snorkelling sites. Plenty of tour agencies in Hat Khao Lak offer snorkelling-only day/overnight trips (from around 2700/4900B).

WILDLIFE & HIKING

The forest around the park headquarters on Ko Miang (Island 4) has a couple of walking trails and some great wildlife. The fabulous Nicobar pigeon, with its wild mane of grey-green feathers, is common here. Endemic to the islands of the Andaman Sea, it's one of some 39 bird species in the park. Hairy-legged land crabs and fruit bats (flying foxes) are relatively easily seen in the forest, as are flying squirrels.

A small **beach track**, with information panels, leads 400m to a tiny, pretty snorkelling bay. Detouring from it, the **Viewpoint Trail** – 500m or so of steep scrambling – has panoramic vistas from the top. A 500m walk to **Sunset Point** takes you through forest to a smooth granite platform facing – obviously – west.

On Ko Similan (Island 8) there's a 2.5km forest hike to a **viewpoint**, and a shorter, steep scramble off the main beach to the top of **Sail Rock** (aka Balance Rock).

Sleeping & Eating

Accommodation in the park is available for all budgets. Book online at www.dnp.go.th or with the mainland **national park office** (☎ 0 7645 3272) at Hat Khao Lak. Tour agents in Hat

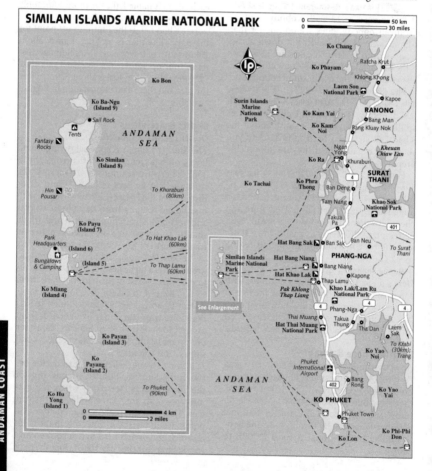

SIMILAN ISLANDS MARINE NATIONAL PARK

Khao Lak also arrange overnight to multiday trips that include transport, food and lodging at the park – these cost little more than it would to go solo.

On Ko Miang there are sea-view **bungalows** (r 2000B; ❄️) with balconies; two dark five-room wood-and-bamboo **longhouses** (r 1000B; ❄️) with fans, and **tents** (2-/4-person 300/450B). There's electricity from 6pm to 6am.

Tents are also available on Ko Similan. You can pitch your own **tent** (per night 80B) on either island.

A **restaurant** (dishes 100-150B) near the park headquarters serves simple Thai food.

Getting There & Away

There's no official public transport to the park, but theoretically independent travellers can book a speedboat transfer (return 1700B, 1½ hours one way) with a Hat Khao Lak snorkelling operator, though they much prefer that you join the snorkelling tour and generally discourage independent travel to the Similans. Most will collect you from Phuket or Hat Khao Lak, but if you book through national parks (which uses the same tour operators' boats anyway), be aware that you'll have to find your own way to their office and then wait for a transfer to the pier.

Agencies in Hat Khao Lak and Phuket book day/overnight tours (from around 2700/4900B) and dive trips (three-day liveaboards from around 13,500B). Generally these cost little more than what you'd pay trying to get to the islands independently when you factor in meals, bus tickets etc.

AO PHANG-NGA & PHANG-NGA

อ่าวพังงา/อ.เมืองพังงา

pop 11,000

With turquoise bays peppered with craggy limestone rock towers, brilliant-white beaches and tumbledown fishing villages, Ao Phang-Nga is one of the region's most spectacular escapes. Little wonder then that it was here, among the towering cliffs and swifts' nests that James Bond's nemesis, Scaramanga (*The Man with the Golden Gun*), chose to build his lair. Wanted assassins with goals of world domination would not be recommended to hide out here nowadays, since the area is swarming with tourists in motorboats and sea kayaks nearly year-round. Much of the bay, and some of the coastline, has now been incorporated into the Ao Phang-Nga National Park (p299).

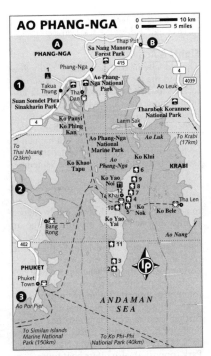

Information

Phang-Nga town doesn't have a tourist office, but the one in Phuket Town (TAT; p309) provides maps and good information on the region.

Immigration office (☎ 0 7641 2011; ⏱️ 8.30am-4.30pm Mon-Fri) A few kilometres south of town, you'll probably never find it on your own. Take a motorbike taxi.

Siam Commercial Bank (Hwy 4; ⏰ 9am-4pm Mon-Fri) On the main road; has an ATM and exchange facilities.

Sights & Activities

The old 'city of contrasts' cliché really does apply to the town of Phang-Nga. A scruffy, luckless town, it backs up against some beautiful limestone cliffs and, while the main street looks rather downtrodden, there are a couple of decent places to bed down. There isn't a whole lot to see or do unless you happen to be here during the annual **Vegetarian Festival** (see the boxed text, p312) in late September or October.

About 8.5km south of the town centre is Tha Dan. From here, you can charter boats to see half-submerged **caves**, oddly shaped islands and **Ko Panyi**, a Muslim village on stilts. There are tours to the well-trod **Ko Phing Kan** ('James Bond Island'; the island rock in *The Man with the Golden Gun*; see also opposite) and **Ao Phang-Nga National Park** (500B per person for a two- to three-hour tour); see opposite for more information. Takua Thung, another pier area about 10km further west of Tha Dan, also has private boats for hire at similar prices to tours. The park office, inside Ao Phang-Nga National Park (opposite), also offers boat tours.

Although it can be a pain to haggle with boatmen, it is nice to create your own itinerary. Of course, it's much easier (and cheaper) to go with an organised tour through an agency in town. **Sayan Tours** (☎ 0 7643 0348; www.sayantour.com) has been doing tours of Ao Phang-Nga for many years now, and continues to receive good reviews from travellers. Half- /full-day tours cost from 700/1000B per person and include **Tham Lawt** (a large water cave), Ko Phing Kan and Ko Panyi, among other destinations. For an extra 300B you can add a bit of kayaking. It also offers a **river rafting trip** (per person 1600B) to the Son Pat Waterfall 25km south of Phang-Nga, and tours to nearby destinations, including **Sa Nang Manora Forest Park**.

Sleeping

Old Lukmuang Hotel (☎ 0 7641 2125; 1/2 Moo 1, Th Petchkasem, Phang-Nga; r from 200B) This place is awfully dingy, but Bond fanatics will be interested to know that it housed some of the crew from *The Man with the Golden Gun* when they based themselves here during filming.

Phang-Nga Guest House (☎ 0 7641 1358; Th Petchkasem, Phang-Nga; r 250-380B; ❄) Nothing fancy. Just a clean block of cheap and cherry-tiled rooms in the otherwise drab centre of town.

ourpick Phang-Nga Inn (☎ 0 7641 1963; 2/2 Soi Lohakit, Phang-Nga; r 400-1500B; ❄) This converted residential villa is an absolute gem and features heavy wood staircases, louvered cabinets and peaceful gardens. It's well furnished, there's a little eatery and the staff are gracious.

Eating

Several food stalls on the main street of Phang-Nga sell delicious *kà·nŏm jeen* (thin wheat noodles) with chicken curry, *nám yah* (spicy ground-fish curry) or *nám prík* (spicy sauce). *Roti gaang* (fried flatbread dipped in mild curry sauce, served with jam or fruit fillings) is available from the morning market, which is open from 5am to 10am daily. There's also a small night market on Tuesday, Wednesday and Thursday evenings, located just south of Soi Lohakit.

Duang's (Th Petchkasem, Phang-Nga; dishes 60-200B; ⏰ lunch & dinner) A kosher Thai's worst nightmare, this street side diner stir-fries prawns and pork every which way.

ourpick Kror Son Thong (☎ 08 4182 4684; 29/1 Th Rongua, Phang-Nga; mains 70-200B; ⏰ lunch & dinner) Overlooking the river, south of the commercial strip, is this kitchen, which verges on gourmet. Try the *pla tod kamin*, crab omelette or roast duck with kale. It's all excellent.

Getting There & Away

If you're arriving in the Ao Phang-Nga area from Krabi on Hwy 4, you can go two ways. South of Thap Put, you can either continue straight on Hwy 4 or head west onto Hwy 415. Turning onto Hwy 415 will keep you on the shorter, straighter path, while staying on Hwy 4 will take you onto a narrow, very curvy and pretty stretch of highway, which is 5km longer than the direct route.

Phang-Nga's bus terminal is located just off the main street on Soi Bamrung Rat. Bangkok buses to/from Phang-Nga include VIP (889B, 12 hours, one daily), 1st class (546B, 12 to 13 hours, two daily) and 2nd class (449B, 12 hours, three to four daily).

There are several other bus services available:

Destination	Price	Frequency	Duration
Hat Yai	300B	2 daily	6hr
Ko Pha-Ngan	480B	3 daily	6hr
Ko Samui	390B	3 daily	5hr
Krabi	85B	frequent	1½hr
Phuket	85B	frequent	1½hr
Ranong	270B	4 daily	5hr
Surat Thani	150B	frequent	3hr
Trang	260B	frequent	3½hr

Getting Around

Most places in town are accessible on foot. Motorcycle taxis around town cost 20B.

Sayan Tours (opposite), located at the bus terminal, can assist with motorbike rental (200B per day). Sörng·tǎa·ou/motorcycle taxis to Tha Dan cost 30B.

AROUND PHANG-NGA
Ao Phang-Nga National Park
อุทยานแห่งชาติอ่าวพังงา

Established in 1981 and covering an area of 400 sq km, Ao Phang-Nga National Park (☎ 0 7641 1136; www.dnp.go.th; admission 200B; ☀ 8am-4pm) is noted for its classic karst scenery created by fault movements on the mainland that pushed massive limestone blocks into geometric patterns. As these blocks extend southwards into Ao Phang-Nga, they form over 40 islands with huge vertical cliffs, some with caves that are accessible at low tide and lead into hidden hôrngs (lagoons surrounded by solid rock walls). The bay itself is composed of large and small tidal channels that originally connected with the mainland fluvial system. The main tidal channels – Khlong Ko Phanyi, Khlong Phang-Nga, Khlong Bang Toi and Khlong Bo Saen – run through vast mangroves in a north–south direction and today are used by fisher folk and island inhabitants as aquatic highways. These are the largest remaining primary mangrove forests in Thailand.

Unfortunately dramatic beauty and precious ecosystems don't necessarily garner the kind of protection one might expect from a national park system. And in a way, it's our own fault. After all, we are the ones buzzing the bay in droves of long-tails and speedboats, especially in the peak season when the bay can become a package-tourist superhighway. But if you explore in the early morning (best done from Ko Yao Noi or Ko Yao Yai) or stay out a bit late, you'll find a slice of beach, sea and a limestone karst to call your own. The best way to experience

the park is by kayak. John Gray of John Gray's Seacanoe (☎ 0 7622 6077; www.johngray-seacanoe .com) – see also p305 – was the first kayak outfitter in the bay and remains the most ecologically minded. He's constantly clamouring for more protection for his beloved hôrngs among local national park rangers and their supervisors in Bangkok. His Hong By Starlight daytrip (per person 3950B) dodges the crowds, involves plenty of sunset paddling and will introduce you to Ao Phang-Nga's famed bio-luminescence once night falls.

The biggest tourist drawcard in the park is the so-called 'James Bond Island', known to Thais as Ko Phing Kan (literally 'Leaning on Itself Island'). Once used as a location setting for The Man with the Golden Gun, the island is now full of vendors hawking coral and shells that should have stayed in the sea, along with butterflies, scorpions and spiders encased in plastic. It's much wiser to venture further afield. Ko Nok, set halfway between Phuket and Krabi, is far enough from tour epicentres that you'll usually have it to yourself. Ko Klui, the big island north of Ko Yao Noi, has tidal access to a huge hôrng, which some call the Blue Room, and a pristine white-sand beach with plenty of hornbills and monkeys.

PLANTS & ANIMALS

Two types of forest predominate in the park: limestone scrub forest and true evergreen forest. The marine limestone environment favours a long list of reptiles, including Bengal monitor lizards, flying lizards, banded sea snakes, dogface water snakes, shore pit vipers and Malayan pit vipers. Keep an eye out for a two-banded monitor (Varanus salvator), which looks like a crocodile when seen swimming in the mangrove swamp and can measure up to 2.2m in length.

Amphibians in the Ao Phang-Nga region include marsh frogs, common bush frogs and crab-eating frogs. Avian residents of note are helmeted hornbills (the largest of Thailand's 12 hornbill species, with a body length of up to 127cm), the edible-nest swiftlets (Aerodramus fuciphagus), white-bellied sea eagles, ospreys and Pacific reef egrets.

In the mangrove forests and on some of the larger islands reside over 200 species of mammals, including white-handed gibbons, serows, dusky langurs and crab-eating macaques.

ROCK ART

Many of the limestone islands in Ao Phang-Nga feature prehistoric rock art painted or carved onto the walls and ceilings of caves, rock shelters, cliffs and rock massifs. In particular you can see rock art on Khao Khian, Ko Panyi, Ko Raya, Tham Nak and Ko Phra At Thao. Khao Khian (Inscription Mountain) is probably the most visited of the sites. The images contain scenes of human figures, fish, crabs, prawns, bats, birds and elephants, as well as boats and fishing equipment, and seem to reference some sort of communal effort tied to the all-important sea harvest. The rock paintings don't fall on any one plane of reference; they may be placed right-side up, upside-down or sideways. Most of the paintings are monochrome, while some have been traced in orange-yellow, blue, grey and black.

GETTING THERE & AROUND

From the centre of Phang-Nga, drive about 6km south on Hwy 4, turn left onto Rte 4144 (the road to Tha Dan) and travel 2.6km to the park headquarters. Without your own transport you'll need to take a sŏrng·tăa·ou to Tha Dan (30B).

From the park office, you can hire a boat (1500B, maximum four passengers) for a three-hour tour of the surrounding islands.

Ko Yao
เกาะยาว

The captivating islands of **Ko Yao Yai** (Big Long Island) and **Ko Yao Noi** (Little Long Island) are part of the Ao Phang-Nga National Park (p299) and are not to be missed. Their mountainous backbones and unspoilt shorelines, populated by Muslim fishermen and their families, offer both a great vantage point for kicking back and soaking up the bay's beautiful scenery, as well as the best base to access the islands before and after the hordes descend from Phuket, Railay, Krabi, Ko Phi-Phi and all points in between.

Despite being the relative pipsqueak, Ko Yao Noi is the main population centre of the two, with fishing, coconut farming and tourism sustaining its small, year-round population. Bays on the east coast recede to mud flats at low tides, and don't expect postcard-perfect white-sand beaches and turquoise lagoons even when the tide is high. That said, **Hat Pa Sai** and **Hat Paradise** are both gorgeous. Bring along a mountain bike (pick one up from your resort in Phuket) if you want to explore the island's numerous dirt trails, or join up with Phuket's **Amazing Bike Tours** (☎ 08 7263 2031; www .amazingbiketoursthailand.com; Ko Yao Noi; day trip 2900B). **Ta Khai**, the largest settlement on Ko Yao Noi, is a subdistrict government seat where you'll also find a strip of market stalls, a 7-Eleven with an attached ATM, and another ATM around the corner at Government Savings Bank. Half-day three-island snorkelling tours (1700B, maximum six passengers) through Ao Phang-Nga are easily organised from any guesthouse or with long-tail captains on the beach.

Ko Yao Yai is far less developed than Ko Yao Noi; it offers an even more remote and wild getaway. It's twice the size of Yao Noi with a fraction of the development (the only ATM is out of the way in the far north near the Klong Hia Pier, so you'd be wise to carry plenty of cash), which is why villagers are still pleasantly surprised to see tourists pedalling their bicycles or buzzing the concrete streets on rented motorbikes. Amazing, considering how close the island is to Phuket. If you explore some of the island's dirt trails that wind into the hills you may glimpse wild boar, monkeys, flying squirrels or the confounding yet intriguing small barking deer.

Hat Lo Pa Red and **Hat Tiikut** are two of the island's best beaches – the former lined with coconut palms, the latter with casuarina trees. But **Hat Chonglard**, best accessed from Twison Beach Resort, trumps them both. The powder-white sand extends into a jutting palm-shaded peninsula to the north, and it's perfectly oriented to the limestone islands that layer the eastern horizon. On Ko Yao Yai's west coast, **Elixir Divers** (☎ 08 7897 0076; www.elixirdivers.com) leads two-tank trips around Ao Phang-Nga and beyond. **Koh Yao Diver** (☎ 08789 575 517; kohyao-diver.com) does the same on Ko Yao Noi.

Ko Bele, a small island east of the twin Ko Yao islands, features a large tidal lagoon, three white-sand beaches, and easily accessible caves and coral reefs.

Please remember to respect the beliefs of the local Muslim population and wear modest clothing when away from the beaches.

SLEEPING & EATING
Ko Yao Noi

Sabai Corner Bungalows (☎ 0 7659 7497; www.sabai cornerbungalows.com; bungalows 500-2000B) Tucked into a rocky headland, the wooden and bamboo bungalows here are full of character and blessed with gorgeous views. The restaurant is also quite good.

Tha Khao Bungalow (☎ 08 1676 7726; www .kohyaobungalow.com; bungalows 500B) Thatch-and-wood bungalows are the staple at these Hat Tha Khao digs. Well set up for tourists, it rents bikes (250B) and kayaks, and serves tasty food.

Suntisook Resort (☎ 08 9868 8639; www.suntisook kohyao.com; Hat Tha Khao; bungalows 700-1500B; 🔀) Cute wooden bungalows with kitschy interiors are across the street from a long stretch of beach with life-altering views. Cheaper fan-cooled bungalows are actually the nicest and most spacious options.

Ko Yao Beach Bungalows (☎ 08 7896 3815; Hat Tha Khao; bungalows 1500B; 🔀) Attractive, spacious, tiled bungalows with hot water and air-con across the road from a fantastic swimming beach. This is the best value on the island.

Lom Lea (☎ 0 7659 7486; www.lomlae.com; bungalows 2100-5000B) Stylish, naturalist wooden bungalows are fronted by a stunning and secluded beach with views of Phang-Nga's signature karst islands. There's a dive centre, a good restaurant and plenty of activities on offer. We found the bungalows a bit rustic for the price, but the setting and service do merit extra baht.

Paradise Hotel (☎ 08 1892 4878; www.theparadise .biz; Hat Paradise; r from 7500B) Tucked into a private cove on the far north, and accessible only by long-tail or by a rutted earthen road that winds through the rubber trees, rooms and bungalows are built into a hillside and sprinkled throughout a blooming garden. The restaurant and pool are nestled just behind an arc of golden sand that disappears into a turquoise lagoon.

Six Senses Hideaway (☎ 0 7641 8500; www.sixsenses .com/hideaway-yaonoi; r 32,000-400,000B; 🔀 💻 🐾) Known for creating and managing some of the worlds best spa resorts, this swanky five-star property – where 56 hillside pool villas (and their tremendous spa) have been built to resemble an old *chow lair* village – doesn't disappoint. Views of distant limestone are jaw-dropping; its Thai kitchen is tantalising; its loungy bar and white-sand beach are both worthy of the fashionistas that frequently fly in for photo shoots; and its commitment to sustainability is unparalleled among global five-star chains. Even broken dishes are saved and used as filtration for its on-site wastewater treatment plant.

Pradu Seafood (☎ 0 7659 7015; meals 150-250B; 🍴 lunch & dinner) No matter where you stay, make sure to dine here. The local chef still fetches fresh ingredients daily on her motorbike and makes some of the best seafood in southern Thailand. You'll dine among mango trees and coconut palms while watching the sunset in the mangroves.

Ko Yao Yai

Fa Sai Beach Bungalows (☎ 08 1691 3616; bungalows 500B) Basic but clean cold-water bungalows are stilted in the mangroves south of Tha Lo Jak, and just back from a gorgeous strip of white sand.

OUR PICK Twison Beach Resort (☎ 08 1737 4420; www.twisonbeach.com; bungalows with fan 700B, bungalows with air-con 1500B; 🔀) Easily the cleanest, and sweetest, of the island's bungalow properties. Here are proper wooden bungalows with polished floors, outdoor baths, and wide patios facing the best beach on the island. Beachfront bungalows are the largest, but fan rooms are tremendous value.

Yao Yai Beach Resort (☎ 08 1968 4641; www.yaoyai resort.com; bungalows 1500-2400B; 🔀) Located on the gem of a beach at Loh Pared on the western side of the island, the funky bungalows here are hand painted and comfy. There's an on-site restaurant and a great laid-back vibe.

Elixir (☎ 08 7808 3838; www.elixirresort.com; bungalows 8000-25,500B; 🔀 🐾 💻) The first of Yao Yai's two four-star resorts (Ko Yao Yai Village was still under construction when we visited) offers tasteful beachfront and hillside peaked-roof villas steeped in classic Thai style. There are dark-wood floors and high ceilings, indoor and outdoor showers, and ceramic-bowl sinks. It's set on a private beach, where you'll also find a common pool, dive centre, massage pagodas and spectacular sunsets over Phuket.

GETTING THERE & AROUND

Although both islands fall within Phang-Nga Province, the easiest access points are Phuket and Krabi. To get to Ko Yao Noi from Phuket, take a taxi (600B to 800B) from one of the resort areas to Tha Bang Rong. From here, there are hourly boats (long-tail/speedboat 40/20 minutes, 120/180B) between 7.30am and 5.40pm. Speedboats leave at 9.40am, 3pm and 5.40pm. They all dock at Tha Klong Hia on Ko Yao Yai upon request before crossing to Ko Yao Noi. Boats begin returning to Phuket at 6.30am. There are also six boats per day from Krabi's Tha Len pier to Ko Yao Noi piers at Tha Manok and Tha Khao. Once you arrive on Ko Yao Noi, it's 70B to 100B for túk-túk (pronounced đúk đúk; motorised vehicle) transport to the resorts.

The best way to reach Ko Yao Yai from Phuket is to catch a speedboat or ferry from Tha Rasada near Phuket Town. Ferries depart at 8.30am, 10.30am and 2pm (one hour, 100B). Speedboats (30 minutes, 150B) make the run at 4pm and 5pm. On Fridays the schedule shifts to accommodate prayer times.

To get from Ko Yao Noi to Ko Yao Yai, catch a shuttle boat from Tha Manok (100B to 150B, 15 minutes) to Tha Klong Hia. On the islands, you can travel by túk-túk for about 150B per ride or rent a motorbike from most guesthouses for 200B to 250B per day. Before leaving Ko Yao Noi you'd be wise to arrange transport to meet you at Tha Klong Hia. Drivers do not gather and wait for arriving boats. Any guesthouse or resort can help you out, or contact **Yao Yai Taxi Service** (☎ 08 6267 5931, 08 9909 9057).

Suan Somdet Phra Sinakharin Park
สวนสมเด็จพระศรีนครินทร์

This public **park** (admission free; ۞ dawn-dusk) has two entrances. The most dramatic is through a huge hole in a limestone cliff near the Phang-Nga Bay Resort Hotel in Tha Dan. The main – less scenic – entrance is at the southern end of Phang-Nga. Surrounded by limestone cliffs and bluffs, the park is cut through with caves and tunnels. Wooden walkways link the water-filled caverns so visitors can admire the ponds and amazing limestone formations. One of the larger caves, **Tham Reusi Sawan**, is marked by a gilded statue of a *reu-sĕe* (Hindu sage). The other main cavern is known locally as **Tham Luk Seua** (Tiger Cub Cave).

Sa Nang Manora Forest Park
สวนป่าสระนางมโนราห์

This beautiful and little-visited **park** (admission free; ۞ dawn-dusk) features an impressive fairy-land setting, with lots of dense rainforest, rat-tan vines, moss-encrusted roots and rocks, and multilevel waterfalls with several pools suitable for swimming. Primitive trails run along (and at times through) the falls, level after level and beyond – you could easily get a full day's hiking in without walking along the same path twice. Bring plenty of drinking water – although the shade and the falls

moderate the temperature, the humidity in the park is quite high.

The park's name comes from a local folk belief that the mythical Princess Manora bathes in the pools of the park when no one else is around. Facilities include some picnic tables and a small restaurant.

To get here, head north out of Phang-Nga on Hwy 4. Go 3.2km past the Shell petrol station, then turn left and go down a curvy road for another 4km. Motorcycle taxis from Phang-Nga cost 75B.

Wat Tham Suwankhuha
วัดถ้ำสุวรรณคูหา

A cave *wát* (temple), **Wat Tham Suwankhuha** (Heaven Grotto Temple; admission 20B; ۞ dawn-dusk) is full of Buddha images. The shrine consists of two main caverns, the larger one containing a 15m-high reclining Buddha and tiled with *lai-krahm* and *benjarong* (two coloured patterns more common in pottery), and the smaller cavern displaying spirit flags and a *reu-sĕe* statue. Royal seals of several kings, including Rama V, Rama VII and Rama IX – as well as those of lesser royalty – have been inscribed on one wall of the latter cave. Many monkeys hang around the area: if you don't lock your car doors they're likely to break in to get at your travel snacks.

The *wát* is 10km southwest of Phang-Nga. To get here without your own transport, hop on any *sŏrng·tăa·ou* running between Phang-Nga and Takua Thung (90B). The *wát* is down a side road.

PHUKET PROVINCE

Waking up with Phuket is glorious. Especially if you head to an out-of-the-way beach early enough to see the fishing boats return home. When the sun is just high enough to dance on the glassy Andaman Sea.

It's a scene that repeats itself up and down both coasts of this rather large tourist magnet. But it's the 17 west-coast beaches that lure 5.3 million tourists here annually. From the earthy, rocky coves of Rawai and Hat Nai Han, to that wide web of lust that is pulsing Patong, to chic Hat Surin, and on to the gorgeous yet discreet north of Ao Nai Thon, Hat Nai Yang and Hat Mai Khao, Phuket's coastline contorts and twists into various shapes and sizes, giving each stretch of sand its own rhythm.

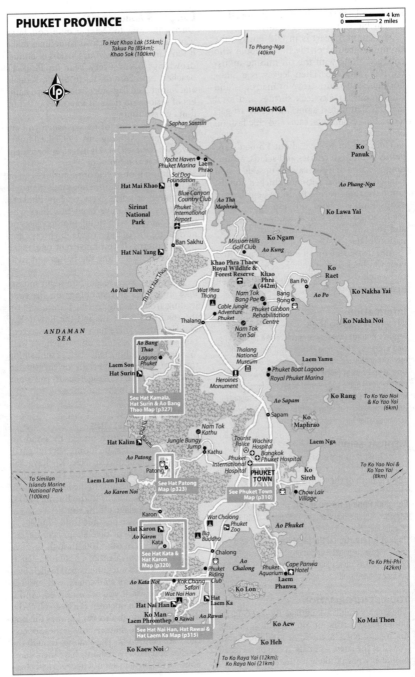

PHUKET PROVINCE

0 ————— 4 km
0 ————— 2 miles

To Hat Khao Lak (55km);
Takua Pa (85km);
Khao Sok (100km)

To Phang-Nga
(40km)

PHANG-NGA

Saphan Sarasin

Ko
Panuk

Yacht Haven
Phuket Marina
Laem
Phrao

Soi Dog
Foundation

Ao Phang-Nga

Hat Mai Khao

Blue Canyon
Country Club

Ao Tha
Maphrao

Sirinat
National
Park

Phuket
International
Airport

Ko Lawa Yai

Ban Sakhu

Mission Hills
Golf Club

Ko Ngam

Hat Nai Yang

Ao Kung

Ko
Raet

Khao Phra Thaew
Royal Wildlife &
Forest Reserve

Khao
Phra
(442m)

Ban Po

Ko
Nakha Yai

Ao Nai Thon

Wat Phra
Thong

Nam Tok
Bang Pae

Bang
Bong

Ao Po

Cable Jungle
Adventure
Phuket

Phuket Gibbon
Rehabilitation
Centre

Ko Nakha Noi

*ANDAMAN
SEA*

Thalang

Nam Tok
Ton Sai

Thalang
National
Museum

Ao Bang
Thao
Laguna
Phuket

Laem Yamu

Laem Son
Hat Surin

Phuket Boat Lagoon
Royal Phuket Marina

See Hat Kamala,
Hat Surin & Ao Bang
Thao Map (p327)

Heroines
Monument

Ao Sapam

Ko Rang

To Ko Yao Noi
& Ko Yao Yai
(6km)

Sapam

Ko
Maphrao

Nam Tok
Kathu

Hat Kalim

Jungle Bungy
Jump

Tourist
Police

Wachira
Hospital

Laem Nga

Kathu

Bangkok
Phuket Hospital

Ao Patong

Phuket
International
Hospital

To Similan
Marine
National Park
(100km)

Patong

**PHUKET
TOWN**

Ko
Sireh

To Ko Yao Noi &
Ko Yao Yai
(8km)

Laem Lam Jiak

See Hat Patong
Map (p323)

Ao Karon Noi

See Phuket Town
Map (p310)

Chow Lair
Village

Karon

Hat Karon

Wat Chalong

Ao Karon

Phuket
Zoo

Ao Phuket

Kata

Big
Buddha

To Ko Phi-Phi
(42km)

See Hat Kata &
Hat Karon
Map (p320)

Chalong

Ao
Chalong

Cape Panwa
Hotel

Ao Kata Noi

Phuket
Riding
Club

Phuket
Aquarium

Laem
Phanwa

Kok Chang
Safari

Wat Nai Han

Hat Nai Han

Hat
Laem Ka

Ko Lon

Ko Man

Rawai

Ao Rawai

Laem Phromthep

See Hat Nai Han, Hat Rawai &
Hat Laem Ka Map (p315)

Ko Aew

Ko Mai Thon

Ko Heh

Ko Kaew Noi

To Ko Raya Yai (12km);
Ko Raya Noi (21km)

But they all have one thing in common: their undeniable, soul-soothing beauty.

The cultural heart is in Old Phuket, the stomping ground of the Baba people who emerged along with the tin-mining industry 100 years ago. Their legacy is a Sino-Portuguese treasure trove of mansions and shophouses, creaky teak shrines and local markets that unfurl alongside funky art galleries, hip restaurants, cafes and chic fashion boutiques.

There's a lot to love about Phuket's appetite. With Thai curries and salads, a stunning selection of fresh seafood, upscale fusion kitchens and local roti and chicken stands, you have some eating to do. When the sun drops Phuket's wild side emerges. Think seedy go-go bars, stylish lounges, live rock and roll and slick nightclubs hosting international DJs.

And if you stay up all night, you may find your way back to that quiet beach, where you can watch the sunrise until it's high enough to dance once more.

Information
INTERNET RESOURCES
Jamie's Phuket (www.jamie-monk.com) A fun insider's blog written by a long-time Phuket expat resident with excellent photos and travel tips.

One Stop Phuket (www.1stopphuket.com) A user-friendly travel guide and internet booking referral service.

Phuket Dot Com (www.phuket.com) Offers a sophisticated compendium of many kinds of information, including accommodation on the island.

MEDICAL SERVICES
Local hospitals are equipped with modern facilities, emergency rooms and outpatient-care clinics. Both of the following have hyperbaric chambers:

Bangkok Phuket Hospital (Map p303; ☎ 0 7625 4425; www.phukethospital.com; Th Yongyok Uthit) Reputedly the favourite with locals.

Phuket International Hospital (Map p303; ☎ 0 7624 9400; www.phuketinternationalhospital.com; Th Chalermprakiat) International doctors rate this hospital as the best on the island.

TOURIST INFORMATION
The weekly English-language *Phuket Gazette* publishes information on activities, events, dining and entertainment around the island, as well as the latest scandals. It can be accessed online at www.phuketgazette.net.

Dangers & Annoyances
During the May to October monsoon, large waves and fierce undertows sometimes make it too dangerous to swim. Dozens of annual drownings occur every year on Phuket's beaches, especially on Laem Singh, Kamala and Karon. Red flags are posted to warn bathers of serious rip tides. If a red flag is flying, don't go swimming.

Keep an eye out for jet skis when you are in the water. Although in 1997 the Phuket governor declared jet skis illegal, enforcement of the ban is another issue.

Renting a motorcycle or motorbike can be a high-risk proposition. Thousands of people are injured or killed every year on Phuket's highways. Some have been travellers who weren't familiar with riding motorcycles and navigating the island's roads, highways and traffic patterns. If you must rent one, make sure you at least know the basics and wear a helmet.

There have been recent late-night motorbike muggings and stabbings on the road leading from Patong to Hat Karon, and on the road between Kata and the Rawai–Hat Nai Han area. There have been a few recent random sexual assaults on women, as well. Women should think twice before sunbathing topless and alone, especially on an isloated beach, and it can be dangerous to run alone at night or early in the morning.

Activities
DIVING & SNORKELLING
Phuket island is surrounded by good-to-excellent dive sites, including several small islands to the south (Ko Hae, Ko Raya Yai, Ko Raya Noi, Hin Daeng and Hin Muang). Live-aboard excursions to the fantastic Surin and Similan islands, or to the Burma Banks/Mergui Archipelago off the southern coast of Myanmar, are also possible from Phuket.

There are heaps of 'dive' shops here – at last count there were over 100, though most of them are the equivalent of a booking agency. The more serious ones often operate their own boat(s) while others send you off with another operator, so ask if you're concerned. And it doesn't hurt if an operator is a five-star PADI dive centre, though this isn't always the best criterion for dive shops. Many of these operations are centred on Hat Patong, though the smaller beach towns certainly have their share. Some of the bigger (but not necessarily better) places have multiple branch offices all over Phuket. See also the boxed text, below.

Typical one-day dive trips to nearby sites cost around 3500B, including two dives and equipment. Nondivers (and snorkellers) are permitted to join such dive trips for a significant discount. PADI Open Water certification courses cost around 15,000B for three days of instruction and equipment.

It's wise to obtain your own private diving insurance before travelling. PADI or DAN are best. Regular insurance doesn't often cover diving accidents or decompression costs, but you could check with your insurance representative. Your dive shop will also have some insurance, but some have better policies than others; ask.

Phuket International Hospital (Map p303; ☎ 0 7624 9400) and **Bangkok Phuket Hospital** (Map p303; ☎ 0 7625 4425) both have hyperbaric chambers.

Snorkelling is best along Phuket's western coast, particularly at the rocky headlands between beaches. Mask, snorkel and fins can be rented for around 250B a day. As with scuba diving, you'll find better snorkelling, with greater visibility and variety of marine life, along the shores of small outlying islands such as Ko Raya Yai and Ko Raya Noi.

As elsewhere in the Andaman Sea, the best diving months are December to May, when the weather is good and the sea is smooth and clear.

The best dive supply shops on Phuket:

All 4 Diving (Map p323; ☎ 0 7634 4611; 5/4 Th Sawatdirak, Hat Patong)

Dive Supply (☎ 0 7638 3414; www.divesupply.com; 88/5 Th Patak, Chalong) In new digs, this is Phuket's scuba superstore.

HORSE RIDING
Phuket Riding Club (☎ 0 7628 8213; www.phuketridingclub.com; 95 Th Viset, Rawai) offers one-hour (per person 800B) and two-hour (1500B) rides in the jungle around Rawai and along nearby beaches.

SEA KAYAKING
Several companies based on Phuket offer canoe tours of scenic Ao Phang-Nga. Kayaks can enter semisubmerged caves (which Thai fishermen have called *hôrng* or 'room' for centuries) inaccessible to long-tail boats. A day paddle costs from 3950B per person including meals, equipment and transfer; many outfits also run all-inclusive, three-day (from 13,700B) or six-day (from 27,100B) kayak/camping trips.

John Gray's Seacanoe (off Map p310; ☎ 0 7625 4505-7; www.johngray-seacanoe.com; 124 Soi 1, Th Yaowarat) The original, still the most reputable and by far the most ecologically sensitive company on the island. Like any good brand in Thailand, his 'Seacanoe' name and itineraries have been frequently copied. He's north of Phuket Town.

Paddle Asia (☎ 0 7621 6145; www.paddleasia.com; 9/71 Moo 3, Th Rasdanusorn, Ban Kuku) Another popular company that caters to small groups, and offers several day and multiday trips to Ao Phang-Nga and Khao Sok National Park on classic kayaks rather than sit-on-tops or inflatables.

WHICH DIVE SHOP?
Choosing the right dive shop can be an intimidating business. After all, there are so many flashy shops advertising the wonders of the diving world – over 100 in Phuket alone. How on earth can you be sure you're making the right choice?

When choosing a dive company on Phuket (or anywhere in Thailand, for that matter) there are a few key questions you should ask. For example, how long has the dive shop existed? How many divers will be on the boat? What is the dive instructor-to-client ratio? What kind of insurance does it have and what does it cover? Is it a licensed Tourism Authority of Thailand (TAT) operator? If it's a live-aboard trip, is there oxygen on board? Talk to the staff (if they're not out diving): how experienced are they and how much of this experience is local? Do they make you feel comfortable and confident? If you're taking a class, what kind of certification do the instructors have? And do they speak your language well enough that you understand each other? One last thing: look at the equipment – is it in good shape and well maintained?

Perhaps the best way to choose an excellent dive operation, however, is to get a glowing recommendation from other divers who've already done the underwater deed. Word of mouth is often the best indicator of the quality of a company – and in the competitive diving world, a good reputation can really make or break a business.

SURFING

Phuket is an undercover surf paradise. Once the monsoons bring their midyear swell, glassy seas fold into barrels. The best waves arrive between June and September, when annual competitions are held in Kata and Kalim. **Phuket Surf** (www.phuketsurf.com) is based in Kata, at the south end of the bay near the best break, which typically tops out at 2m. Hat Nai Han can get huge (up to 3m) near the yacht club. Be warned, both Kata and Nai Han have vicious undertows that can claim lives.

Hat Kalim, just north of Patong, is sheltered and has a consistent break that also gets up to 3m. This is a hollow wave, and is considered the best break on the island. The **Phuket Boardriders Club** (www.phuket boardriders.com) sponsors an August contest here. Kamala's northernmost beach has a nice 3m beach break, and Laem Singh, just up the coast in front of the Amanpuri, gets very big and fast, plus it's sheltered from wind by the massive headland.

Hat Nai Yang has a consistent if soft wave that is perfect for veteran boardriders who'd rather not take a pounding. It breaks more than 200m offshore, swells get up to 3m high and there is no undertow.

There are a few surf shops with boards for rent:

Phuket Surf (Map p320; ☎ 08 7889 7308, 08 1684 8902; www.phuketsurf.com) On Hat Kata Yai's southern cove; offers surf lessons starting at 1500B for a half-day, as well as board rentals for 100/300B per hour/day. Check its website for more info about local surf breaks.

Phuket Surfing (Map p320; ☎ 0 7628 4183; www .phuketsurfing.com) Just in front of Phuket Surf and sharing a roof with Nautilus dive, it rents boards by the hour for 100B to 150B.

KITE BOARDING

One of the world's fastest growing sports is also one of Phuket's coming fads. The three best spots are Hat Nai Yang, Karon (in the low season) and Rawai (ideal conditions for beginners in the high season). Phuket's two kiteboarding outfitters are both affiliated with the International Kiteboarding Organization (think: PADI for kites)

Kite Boarding Asia (Map p320; ☎ 08 1591 4594; www.kiteboardingasia.com; lessons from 4000B) Its main office is on Hat Nai Yang, but it has a kiosk on the south end of Hat Karon that's open in the low season. It also offers lessons off Rawai's Friendship Beach.

Kite Zone (Map p315; ☎ 0833 952 005; www.kite surfingphuket.com; beginner lessons from 1100B) With locations in Nai Yang and Rawai, it is the younger, hipper of the two schools, with a tremendous perch on Friendship Beach. Courses range in length from an hour to five days.

YACHTING

Phuket is one of Southeast Asia's main yachting destinations, and you'll find all manner of craft anchored along its shores – from 80-year-old wooden sloops to the latest in hi-tech motor cruisers.

Marina-style facilities with year-round anchorage are presently available at a few locations:

Phuket Boat Lagoon (☎ 0 7623 9055; fax 0 7623 9056) This is located at Ao Sapam, about 10km north of Phuket Town on the eastern shore. It offers an enclosed marina with tidal channel access, serviced pontoon berths, 60- and 120-tonne travel lifts, a hard-stand area, plus a resort hotel, laundry, coffee shop, fuel, water, repairs and maintenance services.

Royal Phuket Marina (☎ 0 7637 9397; www.royal phuketmarina.com) The US$25 million Royal Phuket Marina is located just south of Phuket Boat Lagoon. It's more luxurious with shiny new townhouses, upscale restaurants and a convention centre overlooking 190 berths.

Yacht Haven Phuket Marina (☎ 0 7620 6704; www .yacht-haven-phuket.com) This marina is at Laem Phrao on the northeastern tip. The Yacht Haven boasts 130 berths with deep-water access, and a scenic restaurant. It also does yacht maintenance.

Port clearance is rather complicated; the marinas will take care of the paperwork (for a fee, of course) if notified of your arrival in advance. Expect to pay from 17,000B per day for a high-season, bareboat charter.

For information on yacht charters (both bareboat and crewed), contact the following:

Asia Marine (www.asia-marine.net; Yacht Haven Phuket Marina)

Tawan Cruises (☎ 08 8194 3234; www.tawancruises .com)

If you're interested in a more affordable sailing trip, seek out **Phuket Sail Tours** (☎ 08 7897 0492; www.phuketsailtours.com; Ao Por). Its day trips through Ao Phang-Nga (3000B all-inclusive) come highly recommended.

Tours

It's not hard to find elephant rides and 4WD tours of the island's interior, though none of those will win their way into the hearts of

PHUKET'S MOO•AY TAI EXPLOSION

Over the past few years, spurred in no small part by the increasing global presence and popularity of Mixed Martial Arts, several *moo•ay tai* (also spelled *muay thai;* Thai boxing) gyms catering to international male and female athletes have sprouted off the beach in Phuket. Based on the original *moo•ay tai* camp concept, fighters live and train on site with seasoned *moo•ay tai* professionals.

The whole thing started with Pricha 'Tuk' Chokkuea and his gym, **Rawai Muay Thai** (Map p315; ☎ 08 1476 9377; www.rawaimuaythai.com; 43/42 Moo 7, Th Sai Yuan). He and former business partner, Danny Avison, a Phuket-based triathlete, decided to train tourists as a fundraising mechanism so Tuk could also train impoverished, up-and-coming Thai fighters, without dipping deeply into their fight purse (the traditional *moo•ay tai* business model, and something Tuk always resented). For years his was the only gym around, but in Rawai alone there are now more than half-a-dozen gyms. The best new gym is Avison's **Promthep Muay Thai Camp** (☎ 08 5786 2414; www .promthepmuaythai.com; 91 Moo 6, Soi Yanui). In addition to training fighters, Avison has a tremendous multisport cross-training weight-loss program. Wherever you enter the ring, be warned: this is no wussie watered-down-for-Westerners theme-park ride. Prepare to sweat, cringe, grapple and bleed. If you're the truth, maybe you'll even win a fight under the Bang-la Stadium lights?

animal rights activists or environmentalists, so why not take a bike ride? **Amazing Bike Tours** (☎ 0 7628 3436; www.amazingbiketoursthailand.asia; 32/4 Moo 9, Th Chaofa, Chalong; day trips from 1600B), Phuket's best new adventure outfitter, leads small groups on half-day bicycle tours through the Khao Phra Thaew Royal Wildlife & Forest Reserve, and it offers terrific day trips around Ko Yao Noi and the gorgeous beaches and waterfalls of Thai Muang in nearby Phang-Nga province.

Courses

Mom Tri's Boathouse (☎ 0 7633 0015; www.boat housephuket.com; 2/2 Th Kata (Patak West), Hat Kata) Offers a thrilling Thai cooking class (per person one day/weekend 2000/3000B) each weekend with its renowned executive chef, Tamanoon. See also p318.

Phuket Thai Cookery School (☎ 0 7634 6269; www .phuketthaicookeryschool.com; Ko Sireh; ⏱ 8.30am-5pm) Get intimate with aromatic Thai spices at this popular cooking school set on a quiet seafront plot on Ko Sireh's east coast. Courses (per day 2500B to 2900B) can last up to six hours. It provides hotel pick-ups, market tours and a cookbook.

Pum Thai Cooking School (Map p323; ☎ 0 7634 6269; www.pumthaifoodchain.com; 204/32 Tha Rat Uthit, Hat Patong) This restaurant chain (three locations in Thailand and two in France) holds several daily one- to six-hour classes (per person 4650B). Longer classes begin with a market tour and end with a meal.

Phuket for Children

There's plenty for kids to do on Phuket. And while the seedier face of the sex industry is on full show in Patong (we wouldn't bring our kids there, although many people do), the rest of the island is fairly G-rated.

In terms of activities, the usual array of water sports is offered at the bigger resorts up and down the coast. Many of the activities already mentioned will also appeal to children of all ages. Elephant treks are always a big hit with kids, with the best options available on the Kata–Hat Nai Han road. The **Phuket Aquarium** (p314) and a visit to the tremendous **Phuket Gibbon Rehabilitation Centre** (p332) are also terrific animal-themed activities that are sure to please.

The main family-flogged feature of Phuket, however, is **Phuket Fantasea** (p327), which is a pricey extravaganza of wild animals, costumes, song, dance, special effects, pyrotechnics, a lousy dinner and magic (marvel at the disappearing elephants) – but it's all very cheesy.

Volunteering

Soi Dog Foundation (☎ 08 7050 8688; www.soidog.org) is a well-organised unit aimed at sterilising, providing medical care for and feeding stray dogs. Volunteers are needed for feeding the dogs but it's just as helpful to donate funds towards the projects. Check the website for updates and details.

Getting There & Away

AIR

Thirty kilometres northwest of Phuket Town, **Phuket International Airport** (☎ 0 7632 7230) has a post office, bookshop, restaurants and cafes; **internet connection** (per 15min 100B) in the domestic departure area, and a **left luggage** (per bag per day 80B) facility on the 1st floor. There are plenty of foreign-exchange booths, ATMs and a tourist office in the arrivals area. It takes around 45 minutes to an hour to reach the southern beaches from here.

Some domestic airline carriers:

Air Asia (www.airasia.com) Serves Phuket beautifully. In addition to several daily Bangkok flights (from 790B), it also flies direct to Hong Kong (4295B), Chiang Mai (1524B), Ho Chi Minh City (790B), Kuala Lumpur (from 990B), Singapore (1796B) and Jakarta (1270B).

Bangkok Airways (Map p310; ☎ 0 7622 5033; www .bangkokair.com; 58/2-3 Th Yaowarat) Has daily flights to Ko Samui (1905B) and Bangkok (2290B).

Nok Air (www.nokair.com) Links Phuket with Bangkok.

One-Two-Go (www.fly12go.com) Also links Phuket with Bangkok.

THAI (Map p310; ☎ 0 7621 1195; www.thaiairways.com; 78/1 Th Ranong, Phuket Town) Operates up to 10 daily flights to Bangkok (from 3035B) with connections to/from several other cities in Thailand, as well as international destinations.

Several international airlines have offices in Phuket Town:

Dragonair (Map p310; ☎ 0 7621 5734; Th Phang-Nga, Phuket Town)

Malaysia Airlines (Map p310; ☎ 0 7621 6675; 1/8-9 Th Thungkha, Phuket Town)

Silk Air (Map p310; ☎ 0 7621 3891; www.silkair.com; 183/103 Th Phang-Nga, Phuket Town)

FERRY

During the high season, several boats ply the waters between Ao Ton Sai on Ko Phi-Phi and ports on Phuket. **Chao Koh Group** (☎ 0 7624 6513) boats depart from Tha Rasada, near Phuket Town, for Ko Phi-Phi at 8.30am and 2.30pm and return at 9am and 2.30pm (400B one way).

MINIVAN

Some Phuket travel agencies sell tickets (including ferry fare) for air-con minivans down to Ko Samui and Ko Pha-Ngan. Air-con minivan services to Krabi, Ranong, Trang, Surat Thani and several other locations are also available. Departure locations vary: for details, visit the TAT office (opposite) in Phuket Town. Prices are slightly more than the buses, which all stop in Phuket Town (see p313).

PHUKET TOWN
อ.เมืองภูเก็ต
pop 94,325

One of the least-visited and most-authentic corners of the island, Phuket Town (officially called Phuket City, but that name is seldom used) was the island's first settlement and is a magical place to wander. Here you'll find eclectic art galleries, fantastic shopping, crumbling Sino-Portuguese relics, Chinese Taoist shrines and some damn good food.

The southern Chinese immigrants who first arrived in Phuket in the 19th century to work the tin mines lived among these narrow alleys and canals that were already steeped in the spice-island experience of local Arabian, Indian and Portuguese entrepreneurs. Within a generation Phuket had its own subculture. Lifelong Phuket Town residents celebrate their Chinese heritage through both ritual and cuisine, yet the town – especially the architecture – has a distinctly European vibe.

But it's not just some lost-in-time cultural archive. Bubbling up throughout the emerging Old Town is an infusion of relevant art and music, and an abundance of hip restaurants and cafes. It's no wonder that people who live and work in Phuket spend their evenings here.

If you're on a budget, Phuket Town has some of the best lodging bargains on the island and is a good option if you have a night to burn before or after your ferry leaves for Ko Phi-Phi or Lanta from nearby Tha Rasada. From here you can hop on regular sŏrng·tǎa·ou to any of Phuket's beaches (which will take between 30 minutes and 1½ hours; see p314) for more details.

Information

There are numerous internet cafes and ATMs around Th Phuket, Th Ranong, Th Montri and Th Phang-Nga.

DHL World Wide Express (☎ 0 7625 8500; 61/4 Th Thepkasatri) Offers a swift and reliable courier service.

Main post office (Th Montri; ☉ 8.30am-4pm Mon-Fri, 9am-noon Sat)

Phuket CAT office (Th Phang-Nga; ☉ 8am-midnight) Offers Home Country Direct telephone service.

Police (☎ 191, 0 7622 3555; cnr Th Phang-Nga & Th Phuket)

Southwind Books (☎ 08 9724 2136; 1/2/5 Th Phang-Nga; ☉ 9am-7pm Mon-Sat, 10am-3pm Sun) Peruse these dusty secondhand stacks. There are titles in 18 languages, including Polish.

TOP FIVE PHUKET SPAS

There seems to be a massage shop on every corner on Phuket. Most are low-key family affairs where traditional Thai massage goes for about 250B per hour, and a basic mani-pedi costs around 100B – a real steal. The quality of service at these places varies, and changes rapidly as staff turnover is high. Go with your gut instinct or ask fellow travellers or your hotel staff for recommendations. No matter where you choose, it's hard to go wrong. Especially if it's sporting a wood-fired herbal sauna on the premises.

If you're looking for a more Westernised spa experience, head to one of Phuket's plentiful spa resorts. These places are often affiliated with a ritzy hotel (but nearly all are open to nonguests). They are *haute couture* affairs with sumptuous Zen designs and huge treatment menus. Prices vary depending on location, but treatments generally start at around 1000B and go up and up from there.

Our top five Phuket spa picks:

- The **Bua Luang Spa** (p332) at the Anantara Phuket combines the best of Thai and Ayurvedic healing traditions. Why not follow that Turmeric Body Scrub with a Thai Herbal Compress Massage?
- The **Six Senses Spa** (p315) at the Evason Phuket Resort is sublimely back-to-nature in setting, yet cutting edge as far as treatments are concerned. Try the Energising Journey (three hours, 7600B), which includes a body toner, an Energiser massage, followed by foot acupressure.
- Get wrapped in Asian White Clay (2000B) or detoxifying seaweed (2500B) and follow it with a Tri Phase Stone Therapy Massage (2900B) at the **Sala Resort & Spa** (p331).
- One of Phuket's first spas, **Hideaway Day Spa** (p329) still enjoys an excellent reputation. More reasonably priced than many hotel counterparts, the Hideaway offers treatments in a tranquil setting by a lagoon.
- Another reasonable, refreshing choice is the **Raintree Spa** at Sino House (p311) in Phuket Town. When locals crave spa therapy (massages 500B to 1000B) they come here.

TAT office (☎ 0 7621 2213; www.tat.or.th; 73-75 Th Phuket; ☺ 8.30am-4.30pm) Has maps, information brochures, a list of standard sŏrng·tǎa·ou fares out to the various beaches, and the recommended charter costs for a vehicle.

Sights & Activities

Phuket's historic **Sino-Portuguese architecture**, found along along thanets Thalang, Dibuk, Yaowarat, Ranong, Phang-Nga, Rasada and Krabi and sweet Soi Romanee, is the town's most evocative sight. The most magnificent examples in town are the **Standard Chartered Bank** (Th Phang-Nga), Thailand's oldest foreign bank; the **THAI office** (78/1 Th Ranong); and the **old post office building**, which now houses the **Phuket Philatelic Museum** (Th Montri; admission free; ☺ 9.30am-5.30pm). The best-restored residential properties are found along Th Dibuk and Th Thalang. The fabulous **Phra Phitak Chyn Pracha Mansion** (9 Th Krabi) was being restored and turned into a branch of the upscale Blue Elephant restaurant chain at research time.

A handful of Chinese temples inject some added colour. Most are standard issue, but

the **Shrine of the Serene Light** (Saan Jao Sang Tham; ☺ 8.30am-noon & 1.30-5.30pm), tucked behind Wilai restaurant and accessible via a narrow walk marked by a red arch off Th Phang-Nga, is a cut above the rest. Built by a local family in 1889, you'll see Taoist etchings on the walls and vaulted ceilings stained from incense plumes. The altar is always alive with fresh flowers and burning candles.

For a bird's-eye view of the city, climb **Khao Rang** (Phuket Hill), northwest of the town centre. It's best during the week, when the summit is relatively peaceful, but keep an eye out for mobs of snarling dogs. If, as many people say, Phuket is a corruption of the Malay word *bukit* (hill), then this is probably its namesake.

Festivals & Events

The **Vegetarian Festival** (see p312) is Phuket's most important event and usually takes place during late September or October. The TAT office in Phuket prints a helpful schedule of events for the Vegetarian Festival. If you plan to attend the street processions, consider

NORTHERN
ANDAMAN COAST

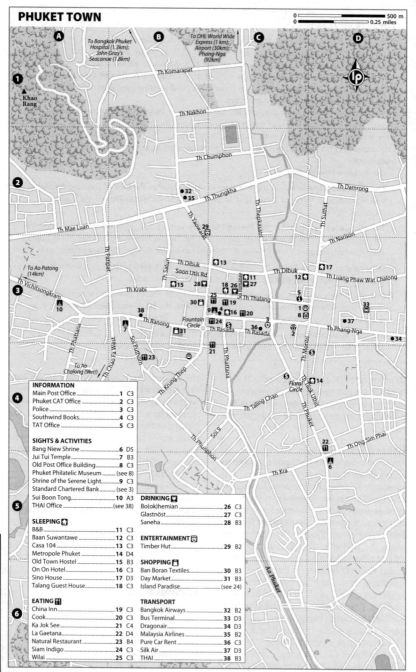

PHUKET TOWN

bringing earplugs to blunt the firecrackers' never-ending blast.

Sleeping

Phuket Town is the cheapest place on the island to get some 'z's and is a treasure trove of budget lodging. Head out to the beaches for more midrange and top-end options.

BUDGET

On On Hotel (☎ 07621 1154; 19 Th Phang-Nga; r 180-400B; ✹) This bare-bones classic scooped a bit part in *The Beach* (2000), and despite its musty rooms and peeling paint, retains a whiff of Old Phuket. Expect sagging beds, squeaking fans, squat toilets and padlocked doors. New, charmless but cleaner air-con rooms are downstairs off the dingy old-school cafe.

Talang Guest House (☎ 0 7621 4225; talanggh@ phuket.ksc.co.th; 37 Th Thalang; r 280-370B; ✹) This decrepit shophouse is something of an architectural classic. Rooms are huge with high ceilings and sparkling-clean tile floors. If you really want to soak up the atmosphere, check in to the 3rd-floor room overlooking the street.

Old Town Hostel (☎ 0 7625 8272; phuketoldtownhostel .com; 42 Th Krabi; r 400-550B; ✹) Spacious newly tiled rooms with lavender walls, sparkling bathrooms and friendly management. Upstairs air-con rooms have wood floors, hot water and indoor-outdoor bathrooms.

B&B (☎ 08 4991 7029, 08 1538 1233; 22 Soi Romanee; r 500-650B; ✹) A shophouse turned B&B on charming Soi Romanee. The remodelling didn't completely restore the building's grace (a bit too much tile downstairs), but you'll enjoy the pastel walls, high ceilings and gushing fountains.

MIDRANGE & TOP END

Baan Suwantawe (☎ 0 7621 2879; www.baansuwantawe .co.th; 1/10 Th Dibuk; r from 1200B; ✹ ▢ ▣) With Zen art, hardwood floors, good-sized bathrooms and comfy lounge areas, these studio-style rooms are a steal. Higher-priced rooms have terraces overlooking the blue-tiled pool and lily pond and the whole place smells like lemongrass.

our pick **Casa 104** (☎ 0 7622 1268; 104 Th Yaowarat; r 1200B; ✹ ⌆) An instant classic, here's an absolutely stunning renovation of a 100-year-old shophouse. Old Shanghai aficionados will love it here, what with its burgundy walls, dangling chandeliers, bouquets of bamboo and pea-

cock feathers, and early days' swing on the sound system. And that's just the lobby bar. Guestrooms are more spare, but still elegant with white concrete floors, rain showers and original art nouveau fixtures. By far the best deal in town.

Sino House (☎ 0 7623 2494; www.sinohousephuket .com; 1 Th Montri; r 2000-2500B; ✹ ▢) Shanghai style meets *Mad Men* chic at this impressive Old Town offering. Rooms are massive with mod furnishings, fantastic handmade ceramic basins and quarter-moon shower tubs in their bathrooms. There's an on-site Raintree Spa (see p309) and long-term rates (18,000B per month) are available.

Metropole Phuket (☎ 0 7621 5050; www.metro polephuket.com; 1 Soi Surin, Th Montri; r from 2300B; ✹ ▣) The best of Phuket Town's tower hotels, the Metropole fancies itself as a big hitter. The seahorse fountain is a little kitsch, but the 1960s furnishings give the rooms unintentionally dated grace. There are tremendous views of Ao Chalong from the upper reaches.

Eating

There's good food in Phuket Town, and meals here cost a lot less than those at the beach.

Cook (☎ 0 7625 8375; 101 Th Phang-Nga; dishes 60-120B) The Thai owner-chef used to cook Italian at a megaresort, so when he opened this ludicrously inexpensive Old Town cafe he fused the two cultures. So, you'll order the sensational green curry pizza with chicken, or the pork curry coconut milk pizza, and love it.

our pick **Wilai** (☎ 0 7622 2875; 14 Th Thalang; dishes from 65B; ☙ breakfast & lunch) Phuket soul food is fried and steamed at this local lunch counter. It does Phuketian *pàt tai* (thin rice noodles fried with tofu, vegetables, egg and peanuts) with some kick to it, and a fantastic *mee sua*, think: noodles sautéed with egg, greens, prawns, chunks of sea bass, and incredibly tender squid. Wash it down with fresh chrysanthemum juice.

China Inn (☎ 0 7635 6239; Th Thalang; dishes 80-250B) The organics movement meets Phuket cuisine at this turn-of-the-century shophouse. There's red curry with crab, a host of vegie options, tremendous homemade yoghurt and fruit smoothies flavoured with organic honey. There's also a terrific gallery here with handmade lacquer, textiles, carvings and clothes from Myanmar and Laos.

Siam Indigo (☎ 0 7625 6697; www.siamindigo .com; 8 Th Phang-Nga; dishes 130-290B; ☙ lunch & dinner

VEGETARIAN FESTIVAL *Celeste Brash*

Loud popping sounds like machine-gun fire fill the streets, the air is nearly opaque with grey-brown smoke and men and women traipse along blocked-off city roads, their cheeks pierced with skewers and knives or, more surprisingly, lamps and tree branches; some of the flock have blood streaming down their fronts or open lashes across their backs. No this isn't a war zone, this is the **Vegetarian Festival**, one of Phuket's most important festivals.

The festival, which takes place during the first nine days of the ninth lunar month of the Chinese calendar – usually late September or October, celebrates the beginning of 'Taoist Lent', when devout Chinese abstain from eating meat. But more obvious to the outsider are the daily processions winding their way through town with floats of ornately dressed children and ladyboys, near armies of flag-bearing colour-coordinated young people and, most noticeably, men and women engaged in outrageous acts of self-mortification. Shop owners along Phuket's central streets set up altars in front of their shopfronts offering nine tiny cups of tea, incense, fruit, firecrackers, candles and flowers to the nine emperor gods invoked by the festival.

Those participating as mediums bring the nine deities to earth by entering into a trance state, piercing their cheeks with an impressive variety of objects. On the day we ventured into the crowds these ranged from model ships and skewers to flag poles, sledge hammers and a machine gun. Every time we thought the piercing object couldn't get more outrageous, we'd walk around a corner and there would be a guy casually wandering along with, say, an iron bed head hanging out of his cheek. All this made the guys sawing their tongues with giant knives, whipping their backs with spiky metal balls and so on seem somewhat less interesting. Whatever form the self-flagellation takes, the mediums (primarily men) walk in procession, stopping at shopfront altars, where they picked up the offered fruit. They also drink one of the nine cups of tea, grab some flowers to stick in their waistbands or set strings of firecrackers alight. The shop owners and their families stand by with their palms together in a *wâi* gesture, out of respect for these mediums who are temporarily possessed by deities. As the day wears on the main procession thins out, there's an even more intense feeling of fervour in the remaining participants and firecrackers pop nonstop, filling the scene with smoke. Surreal and overwhelming hardly describes it. In Phuket Town, the festival activities are centred around five Chinese temples, with the Jui Tui temple on Th Ranong the most important, followed by Bang Niew and Sui Boon Tong temples. There are also events at temples in the nearby towns of Kathu (where the festival originated) and Ban Tha Reua. If you stop by the procession's starting point early enough in the morning, you may see a surprisingly professional, latex-glove-clad crew piercing the devotee's cheeks – not for the faint-hearted. Other ceremonies occur throughout the festival at the temples and can include firewalking and knife-ladder climbing. Beyond the headlining gore, fabulous vegetarian food stalls line the side streets offering a perfect opportunity to sample cheap local treats and strike up interesting conversations with the locals.

The TAT office (p309) in Phuket prints a helpful schedule of events for the Vegetarian Festival each year. The festival also takes place in Trang, Krabi and other southern Thai towns.

Oddly enough, there is no record of these sorts of acts of devotion associated with Taoist Lent in China. The local Chinese claim the festival was started by a theatre troupe from China that stopped off in nearby Kathu around 150 years ago. The story goes that the troupe was struck seriously ill because the members had failed to propitiate the nine emperor gods of Taoism. The nine-day penance they performed included self-piercing, meditation and a strict vegetarian diet.

For more info, visit www.phuketvegetarian.com.

Wed-Mon) A stylish gem set in an 80-year-old Sino-Portuguese relic that specialises in Thai cuisine with a twist. There's a fiery seared tuna *lâhp* (spicy salad), minced, spiced pork satay, and grilled duck breast sliced and stewed in massaman curry.

Ka Jok See (☎ 0 7621 7903; kajoksee@hotmail.com; 26 Th Takua Pa; dishes 180-480B; ☯ dinner Tue-Sun) Dining here is reason enough to come to town. Dripping Old Phuket charm and creaking under the weight of the owner's fabulous trinket collection, this atmospheric little eatery offers great food, top-notch music and – if you're lucky – some sensationally camp cabaret. Enjoy your dinner, sip some wine and then dance the night away.

La Gaetana (☎ 0 7625 0523; 352 Th Phuket; dishes 200-450B; ☽ lunch Mon, Tue & Fri, dinner Tue-Sun) An irresistibly intimate five-table restaurant, La Gaetana has black concrete floors, colourful walls and stemware, an open kitchen in the courtyard and a superb Italian menu. Think: duck breast carpaccio followed by osso bucco.

Drinking

This is where you can party like a local. Bars buzz until late, patronised almost exclusively by Thais and local expats. If you're tired of the sleazy, resort party scene, the vibe here will feel like a fresh ocean breeze, even if it is another sweaty, windless night in Old Town.

Bo(ok)hemian (☎ 0 7625 2854; 61 Th Thalang; ☽ 9am-10pm; ☎) Every town should have a coffee house this cool. The split-level open design feels both warm and leading edge. It has wi-fi, used DVDs and books for sale, gourmet coffee and tea, and damn good chocolate cake.

Glastnöst (☎ 08 4058 0288; 14 Soi Romanee) With the unusual moniker 'Law & Notary Public Bar', this place doubles as a law office but don't let that intimidate you. It's about as laid-back and intimate a setting as you could find, and spontaneous jazz jam sessions are the norm. Call three hours ahead to have an authentic Phuketian dinner for four prepared by the man who represents Greenpeace in Thailand.

our pick Saneha (☎ 08 1892 1001; Th Yaowarat; ☽ 6pm-late) An upscale bohemian joint lit by seashell chandeliers, with plenty of dark corners where you can sip, snuggle, snack, and dig that soulful acoustic crooner on stage.

Entertainment

Timber Hut (☎ 0 7621 1839; 118/1 Th Yaowarat; admission free; ☽ 6pm-2am) Thai and expat locals have been filling this old clubhouse every night for 18 years. They gather at long wooden tables on two floors, converge around thick timber columns, swill whiskey, and sway to live bands that swing from hard rock to funk to hip-hop with aplomb.

Shopping

There's some terrific shopping in the provincial capital.

Ban Boran Textiles (☎ 076 211 563; 51 Th Yaowarat; ☽ 10am-7pm) Simply put, this dusty hole-in-the-wall is the best shop on the island for silk, raw silk and cotton textiles and sarongs.

Day Market (Th Ranong) This market near the town centre traces its history back to the days

when pirates, Indians, Chinese, Malays and Europeans traded in Phuket. You might still find some fabrics from Southeast Asia, though it mostly sells food now.

Island Paradise (☎ 0 7625 6418; 8 Th Phang-Nga; ☽ 10am-9pm) Set in the same old relic as Siam Indigo, this lovely and expansive hippie-chic boutique features up-and-coming Thai designers, and has stylishly flowing dresses, silk skirts and blouses and exceptional jewellery.

Getting There & Around
TO/FROM THE AIRPORT

There is a minibus service at the airport that will take you into Phuket Town for 120B per person; Patong, Kata and Karon beaches cost 180B. If there aren't enough passengers to make the minibus run profitable, you may have to shell out for a taxi. Taxis between the airport and Phuket Town cost 500B; between the airport and beaches is 700B to 800B.

BUS

You'll find the **bus terminal** (☎ 0 7621 1977) just to the east of the town centre, within walking distance of the many hotels. Services from here include the following:

Destination	Bus type	Fare	Duration
Bangkok	2nd class	375B	15hr
	air-con	720B	13-14hr
	VIP	1120B	13hr
Chumphon	air-con	287B	6½hr
Hat Yai	air-con	600B	6-7hr
Ko Samui	air-con	370B	8hr (bus/boat)
Krabi	ordinary	95B	4hr
	air-con	150B	3½hr
Nakhon Si Thammarat	air-con	330B	7hr
Phang-Nga	ordinary	120B	2½hr
Ranong	ordinary	209B	6hr
	air-con	270B	5hr
Surat Thani	ordinary	210B	6hr
	air-con	240B	5hr
Takua Pa	air-con	120B	3hr
Trang	ordinary	215B	6hr
	air-con	275B	5hr

CAR

There are cheap car-rental agencies on Th Rasada near **Pure Car Rent** (☎ 0 7621 1002; www.purecarrent.com; 75 Th Rasada), which is a good choice in the centre of town. Suzuki jeeps go for about 1200B per day (including insurance), though in the low season the rates can go down to 750B. And if you rent for a week or more, you should get a discount.

The rates are always better at local places than at the better-known internationals, though you may be able to get deals with the familiar companies if you reserve in advance.

MOTORCYCLE

You can rent motorcycles on Th Rasada near Pure Car Rent, or from various places at the beaches. Costs are anywhere from 200B to 300B per day, and can vary depending on the season. Bigger bikes (over 125cc) can be rented at shops in Patong, Kata, Rawai and Karon.

SŎRNG TĂA OU & TÚK-TÚK

Large bus-sized sŏrng·tăa·ou run regularly from Th Ranong near the market to the various Phuket beaches (25B to 40B per person) – see the respective destinations for details. These run from around 7am to 5pm; outside these times you have to charter a túk-túk to the beaches, which will set you back 400B to Patong, 400B to Karon and Kata, 300B to 350B for Rawai and 450B to Kamala. You'll probably have to bargain. Beware of tales about the tourist office being 5km away, or that the only way to reach the beaches is by taxi, or even that you'll need a taxi to get from the bus terminal to the town centre (it is more or less in the town centre). For a ride around town, túk-túk drivers should charge 100B to 200B.

Motorcycle taxis around town cost 30B.

KO SIREH

เกาะสิเหร่

This tiny island, 4km east of the district capital and connected to the main island by a bridge, is known for its *chow lair* village and a hilltop reclining Buddha at **Wat Sireh**.

The largest settlement of *chow lair* in Thailand is little more than a poverty-stricken cluster of tin shacks on stilts, plus one seafood restaurant. The Urak Lawoi, the most sedentary of the three *chow lair* groups, are found only between the Mergui Archipelago and the Tarutao-Langkawi Archipelago, and speak a creolised mixture of Malay and Mon-Khmer.

A single road loops the island, passing a few residences, prawn farms, lots of rubber plantations and a bit of untouched forest. On the east coast there's a public beach called **Hat**

Teum Suk, as well as a terrific cooking school, the **Phuket Thai Cookery School** (p307); the school is set on a quiet seafront plot.

LAEM PHANWA

แหลมพันวา

Laem Phanwa is a gorgeous, wooded, elongated cape, jutting into the sea south of Phuket. At the tip of the cape, **Phuket Aquarium** (Map p303; ☎ 0 7639 1126; www.phuketaquarium.org; adult/child 100/50B; ⊙ 8.30am-4.30pm) displays a varied collection of tropical fish and other marine life. Experience it with a stroll along the walk-through tunnel.

The beaches and coves are rustic and protected by rocky headlands and mangroves. The sinuous coastal road is magic. If you just can't leave, check into the recently renovated Cape **Panwa Hotel** (☎ 0 7639 1123; www.capepanwa.com; 27 Moo 8, Th Sakdidej; r from 4950B), a four-star, family-friendly stunner perched on 400m of secluded white sand.

The seafood restaurants along the Laem Phanwa waterfront are a great place to hang out and watch the pleasure skiffs and painted fishing boats passing by.

To get to the cape, take Rte 4021 south and then turn down Rte 4023 just outside Phuket Town.

RAWAI

หาดราไวย

Now this is a place to live, which is exactly why Phuket's rapidly developing south coast is teeming with retirees, Thai and expat entrepreneurs, and a service sector that, for the most part, moved here from somewhere else.

The region is not just defined by its beautiful beaches but by the lush coastal hills that rise steeply and tumble into the Andaman Sea forming **Laem Promthep**, Phuket's southernmost point. These hills are home to pockets of development – neighbourhoods and cul de sacs that are knitted together by just a few roads. So even with the growth – there are dozens of housing developments and more than 60 restaurants here – you can feel nature, especially when you hit the beach.

Hat Nai Han, with its bobbing yachts, seafront temple Wat Nai Han and tremendous monsoon-season surf break, is the best beach in the area and one of the best in Phuket, but there are smaller, hidden beaches that are just as beautiful. **Hat Rawai** lacks Nai Han's good looks. It's just a rocky long-tail and speedboat harbour, which makes it the perfect place to open up a seafood grill. There are a string of them here. All are locally owned and equally delicious.

And there is another fantastic, albeit counterintuitive, reason to base here. Even though Rawai is on the southern edge, it's actually quite central. From here it's just 15 minutes to Phuket Town, five minutes to Kata and 20 minutes to Patong; most visitors book vacation homes and plan to stay a while.

If you do extend your stay (or even if you don't), drop into the **Ganesha Yoga Shala** (☎ 08 9868 2639; www.ganeshayogaphuket.com; Soi Salika; per class 300B). This quaint, Ashtanga-style studio is open to all levels and has a loyal following among longtime expats. Prepare to stretch, bend, flow and sweat before settling into sweet savasana.

Sleeping

Ao Sane Bungalows (☎ 0 7628 8306, 08 1326 1687; 11/2 Moo 1, Th Viset, Hat Nai Han; bungalows 600B; ✉) Rickety cold-water, fan-cooled wooden bungalows on a secluded beach, with million-dollar views of Ao Sane and Ao Nai Han. Yes, backpackers do have options on the south coast.

Baan Krating (☎ 0 7628 8264; www.baankrating .com; 11/3 Moo 1, Th Viset, Hat Nai Han; bungalows from 4000B; ✉ 🖵) Situated beautifully on the jungled northern bluff above Hat Nai Han, this property offers attractive, air-conditioned wooden cottages with bamboo ceilings and Thai art on the walls. It does make for a nice hideaway.

Evason Phuket Resort (☎ 0 7638 1010; www .sixsenses.com; 100 Th Viset, Hat Rawai; r 4992-12,935B; ✉ 🖵 ⚶) This spa-hotel extraordinaire offers copious amounts of luxury. And while the 'Six Senses Spa' experience (see p309) is usually rather indulgent and expensive, the prices at this four-star offering are downright reasonable.

Royal Phuket Yacht Club (☎ 0 7638 0200; www.royal phuketyachtclub.com; 23/3 Moo 1, Th Viset, Hat Nai Han; r from 6800B; ✉ 🖵 ⚶) Still a destination for many a transcontinental yachty, there's an air of old-world elegance here, especially in it's fabulous lobby-bar spinning with ceiling fans. Rooms feature large terraces – and stunning bay views – and there's every creature comfort you could

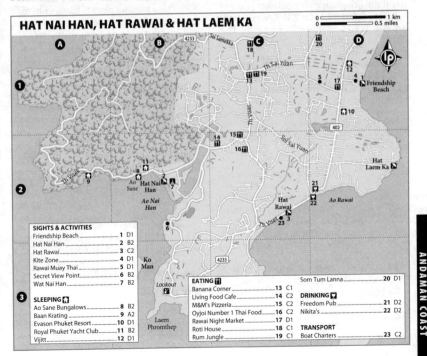

HAT NAI HAN, HAT RAWAI & HAT LAEM KA

SIGHTS & ACTIVITIES	
Friendship Beach	1 D1
Hat Nai Han	2 B2
Hat Rawai	3 C2
Kite Zone	4 D1
Rawai Muay Thai	5 D1
Secret View Point	6 B2
Wat Nai Han	7 B2

SLEEPING	
Ao Sane Bungalows	8 B2
Baan Krating	9 A2
Evason Phuket Resort	10 C2
Royal Phuket Yacht Club	11 B2
Vijitt	12 D1

EATING	
Banana Corner	13 C1
Living Food Cafe	14 C2
M&M's Pizzeria	15 C2
Oyjoi Number 1 Thai Food	16 C2
Rawai Night Market	17 D1
Roti House	18 C1
Rum Jungle	19 C1
Som Tum Lanna	20 D1

DRINKING	
Freedom Pub	21 D2
Nikita's	22 D2

TRANSPORT	
Boat Charters	23 C2

Friendship Beach

Hat Laem Ka

Ao Sane · Hat Nai Han

Ao Nai Han

Hat Rawai

Ao Rawai

Ko Man

Lookout

Laem Phromthep

imagine somewhere on site. If you can snag one of the low-season discounts, it really is excellent value.

Vijitt (☎ 0 7636 3600; 16 Moo 2, Th Viset; villas from 7600B; 🔋) Arguably the area's most elegant property is sprinkled with deluxe villas that boast limestone floors, large bathtubs, outdoor showers, and gorgeous sea views from private terraces. Its stunning, black-bottom infinity pool overlooks Friendship Beach.

Eating

Besides the restaurants listed here, there are a dozen tasty seafood grills roasting fresh catch along the roadside near Hat Rawai.

Som Tum Lanna (☎ 0 8659 32711; 2/16 Th Sai Yuan; dishes 50B; 🕑 breakfast & lunch, closed Mon) It has three dishes worth mentioning, the salted, grilled red snapper, grilled chicken and a paint-peelingly spicy *sôm đam* (green papaya salad). Now, the fish is good, but you can find its equal on Hat Rawai. The chicken on the other hand…well, let's just say it provoked some heartfelt, expletive-rich praise from the blissed-out, greasy-mouthed customer seated next to us. As for the *sôm đam*? Don't be a hero. Order it mild. It will still bring some serious heat.

Banana Corner (☎ 0 7628 9045; www.bananacorner.net; 43/47 Th Viset; dishes 80-150B) Exquisite Thai dishes and ample garden seating in private, thatched pagodas.

Roti House (81/6 Soi Samekka; meals 35B; 🕑 breakfast) If you like French toast or croissants in the morning, you'll love roti, Thailand's Muslim morning delicacy. You'll receive a plate of savoury crepes and a bowl of sweet breakfast curry. Dunk, munch, repeat.

Living Food Cafe (☎ 0 8167 74555; Th Viset; dishes 150-250B; 🕑 closed Mon & Tue) When a long-time American expat and 62-year-old naturopath extols the virtues of the raw vegan lifestyle and backs it up by showing off recent Triathlon trophies (he completed the fabled Ironman in 2008), you listen. When he serves smoothies, burgers, lasagne and cookies so tasty you almost forget how healthy it is, you demand seconds. Ask about his custom fasts and cleanses (per day US$300).

M&M's Pizzeria (☎ 08 1569 0244, 08 7272 3566; Th Viset; pizzas from 240B; 🕑 closed Mon) Simply put, this is the best pizzeria on the island. The slightly sour crust is thin but with ample integrity. Pizzas are tossed and wood-fired by the Italian chef-owners, and their pastas and salads are tasty, too.

Oyjoi Number 1 Thai Food (☎ 08 9908 8808; 83/40 Moo 2, Th Viset; dishes 50-100B) This delightful garden cafe run from the chef's front yard serves spicy *panang* curry clotted with coconut cream, and the tamarind prawns – sticky but not too sweet – are extraordinary.

ourpick Rum Jungle (☎ 0 7638 8153; 69/8 Th Sai Yuan; meals 300-500B; 🕑 dinner, closed Sun) The best restaurant in the area and one of the best in all of Phuket is family run and spearheaded by a terrific Aussie chef. The thatched dining room is patrolled by a fun Thai crew, and the food is dynamite. The New Zealand lamb shank is divine, as are the steamed clams and the pasta sauces are all made from scratch. Everything – including the Pampero rocks – is served to an exceptional world-beat soundtrack.

Drinking

Freedom Pub (☎ 0 7628 7402; Hat Rawai; 🕑 noon-2am) More watering hole than restaurant (dishes 80B to 200B), this Rawai boozer features outdoor seating, a pool table, and live music on the weekends.

Nikita's (☎ 0 7628 8703; Hat Rawai; 🕑 11am-late) Overlooking the sea on Phuket's south coast, Nikita's is a pleasant place to hang, with coffee drinks, green teas, a nice selection of shakes, and furniture carved from driftwood. The bamboo bar has good whiskey, and if you're hungry you can order from Baan Rimlay (dishes 80B to 225B) next door.

Getting There & Away

Rawai is about 18km from Phuket Town and getting there costs 30B by sŏrng·tǎa·ou from Phuket's fountain circle at Th Ranong. Túk-túk charters cost at least 300B to 350B from Phuket Town. The túk-túk trip from Rawai to Nai Han is a hefty 200B.

You can hire taxis (which are actually just chartered cars) from Rawai and Hat Nai Han to the airport (700B), Patong (500B) and Phuket Town (500B).

Long-tail and speedboat charters are available from Hat Rawai. Destinations include Ko Bon (long-tail/speedboat 800/2000B, Coral Island (1200/3000B) and Ko Kai (4000/8000B). Maximum six passengers.

HAT KATA
หาดกะตะ

Kata makes for a fun base to explore Phuket. The beach is stunning and alive with tourists of all ages. There's surfing in the shoulder and wet seasons, some terrific day spas and fantastic food. The beach is actually divided in two by a rocky headland, and the road between them is home to Phuket's original millionaire's row. Hat Kata Yai is on the north end, while the more secluded Hat Kata Noi unfurls to the south. Both offer soft golden sand and attract a bohemian (read: topless sunbathing) crowd. Not that there's anything wrong with that.

The main commercial street of Th Thai Na is perpendicular to the shore and has most of the restaurants and shops, along with some cheaper places to stay.

Information

There are plenty of ATMs along Kata's main drag.

Post office (Map p320; ☽ 9am-4.30pm Mon-Fri, to noon Sat) On Rte 4028, at the end of Th Thai Na.

Sights & Activities

The small island of **Ko Pu** is within swimming distance of the shore (if you're a strong swimmer); on the way are some OK coral reefs. Be careful of rip tides; heed the red flags and don't go past the breakers. Both Hat Kata Yai and Hat Kata Noi offer decent **surfing** from April to November. Board rental costs 100B to 150B for one hour or 300B to 600B for the whole day.

If you're looking for an alternative to the St Tropez-esque south Kata crush, make a left turn (west) just before the main road rises up and heads towards Karon, continue past the cluster of Thai-food joints and you'll find a gorgeous stretch of Kata beach in the secluded, rocky north end (ie Hat Kata Yai) where long-tails bob in the tide. There are beach chairs and umbrellas for rent along with snorkel gear. And cold beverages are just a lazy wave away.

Crave more heat? Consider a class at **Kata Hot Yoga** (Map p320; ☎ 0 7660 5950; www.katahotyoga .com; 217 Th Khoktanod; per class 420B). This new Bikram-style studio is heated to make your muscles pliable and de-humidified to keep your breath free and easy. Classes are held three times per day. Prepare to sweat!

Sleeping

These are average prices for the high season (May to October). Like Patong, it's getting harder and harder to find anything under 1000B during the high season, but prices drop radically when tourism is down.

BUDGET & MIDRANGE

In general, the less-expensive places tend to be off the beach between Kata Yai (to the north) and Kata Noi (to the south). The best deals in town can be found on Th Kata (aka: the new road).

Fantasy Hill Bungalow (Map p320; ☎ 0 7633 0106; fantasyhill@hotmail.com; 8/1 Th Patak; r with fan/air-con 400/800B; ✻) Sitting in a lush garden on a hill, the bungalows here are good value and of the type that's pretty much disappeared from this beach. Fantasy Hill isn't a fancy spot, but it's better than average for the price.

Kata Inn (Map p320; ☎ 08 4746 5151; www.katainn .com; 87/4-5 Th Thai Na; r 800-1200B; ✻) A three-year-old guesthouse offering 12 super-clean, good-value rooms with hot showers, a sun terrace, minifridge and cable TV. It's frequently booked, so reserve ahead.

Be My Guest (Map p320; ☎ 0 7633 0501; www.be myguestphuket.com; 100/62 Th Kata; r 1500B; ✻) The louvred mod facade will lure you in, the sparkling new rooms with high-quality tiled floors, wardrobe, satellite TV and hot water will entice you to stay awhile. Discounts for walk-ins are frequently available.

Kata Country Resort (Map p320; ☎ 0 7633 3210; www .katacountryhouse.com; 82 Th Kata; r 1600-2600B; ✻ ⬛) We can't tell if the retro '60s/70s kitsch is done on purpose here or if it's just a lovely accident. Whatever the case, it's authentic. Expect wagon-wheel railings on the terraces, a Tiki-style (Polynesian) lounge that plays everything from swing to country and western, and sculptures everywhere ranging from elephants to Native American chiefs. The staff seem to get as big a hoot out of the place as the guests. It's nothing luxurious but we give it five stars for character.

Caffe @ Caffe (Map p320; ☎ 0 7628 4005; www .caffeatcaffe.com; 100/60-61 Th Kata; r 2000B; ✻ ☎) A hip entry to this three-storey walk-up gives way to simple yet elegant rooms, with gold-papered walls, dark-wood wardrobes, tastefully tiled baths, flat screen TV and a private terrace.

Honey Resort (Map p320; ☎ 0 7633 0938; www .honeyresort.com; 100/69 Th Kata; r 2700-3200B; ✻ ☎) Spacious new rooms with (tasteful!) wood panelling to spare. All rooms have daybeds, built-in dressers, desks, bathtubs and marble washbasins. There's free wi-fi and flat screen TVs, too. Promotional rates (699B) were absurdly low at research time, but rack rates are affordable year-round.

MOM LUANG TRIDHOSYUTH DEVAKUL, AKA MOM TRI

Former Senator, Architect, Artist & Phuket Visionary

Do you remember your first trip to Phuket? It was in the early '70s. Only naked hippies were on the beach. Gibbons would howl in the forest, streams would empty into the bays and wild boar would forage for turtle eggs in the sand.

When did things begin to change? The early '80s; not long after we built Club Med on Kata, the Yacht Club on Nai Han, and convinced Thai Airways to begin flying here. The country was bankrupt, and the new prime minister, General Prem, wanted to promote tourism. Back then Patong was one big tin-mining concession, so I brought him there. He revoked the concession and that's when Phuket tourism really started.

So development got out of control fairly quickly? I asked the government to create a master plan, to protect the coastline but the answer I got was, 'It's still pristine, so why bother?' It was never a priority, and you can see how it turned out.

How did the Phuket metamorphosis change you? We started an international school in Chiang Mai and it's growing into a community. We are teaching three generations and over 50 nationalities how to grow organic food and reduce waste. Our motto is 'sustainable living through lifelong learning'. We want to teach people how to live with nature.

As told to Adam Skolnick.

Sugar Palm Resort (Map p320; ☎ 0 7628 4404; www.sugarpalmphuket.com; 20/10 Th Kata; r incl breakfast 2800-4200B; ☒ ☐ ☒) It's a 'chic chill-out world' at the Sugar Palm, as this Miami-meets-Thailand-style resort claims. Rooms, decorated in urban whites, blacks and lavender, are exceptional value and sublimely comfy, and all surround a black-bottomed, U-shaped pool. You feel a bit on stage going for a swim here, but the beach isn't far and you're in the heart of Kata's lively shopping and restaurant strip.

TOP END

Sugar Palm Grand Hillside (Map p320; ☎ 0 7633 0388; www.sugarpalmgrand.com; 1 Th Kkoktanod; r incl breakfast 3350-9900B; ☒ ☐ ☒) Mod glitz rambles up Kata hill thanks to this stark resort with a Sonny Crockett–vibe, and massive views of Kata's glorious horseshoe bay. Minimalist rooms are sweet with concrete floors, glass-box showers, a flat screen TV and a wide deck. Service isn't phenomenal.

Kata Palm Resort (Map p320; ☎ 0 7628 4334; www.katapalmresort.com; 60 Th Kata; r from 5500B; ☒ ☜ ☒) Given the abundance of ever-creeping modernism, it's nice to see some classic Thai kitsch at this old standby. Expect Thai art on the walls, silks on the beds, fine wood furnishings, and handpainted columns in the lobby. Great deals are frequently available through its website.

Sawasdee Village (Map p320; ☎ 0 7633 0979; www.phuketsawasdee.com; 38 Th Ked Kwan; bungalows 6500-8500B; ☒ ☐ ☜ ☒) A boutique resort with a lush, opulent, but compact footprint built in classic Thai style. Ornate, peaked-roof bungalows have wood floors, beamed ceilings and open onto a thick tropical landscape laced with *koi* (carp) canals, and gushing with waterfalls. Not to mention those Buddhist art installations. Throw in its quality spa and this place is unique and inviting in every way, but it will cost you in the high season.

Katathani Resort & Spa (Map p320; ☎ 0 7633 0124; www.katathani.com; 14 Th Kata Noi; r from 7500B; ☒ ☜ ☒) Down on quieter Hat Kata Noi, this glitzy spa resort offers all the usual trimmings in stylish surrounds. It features a spa, a handful of pools, a beauty salon and heaps of space. Excellent low-season deals are on offer if you haggle.

Mom Tri's Boathouse (Map p320; ☎ 0 7633 0015; www.boathousephuket.com; 2/2 Th Kata (Patak West); r 8000-25,000B; ☒ ☒) For Thai politicos, pop stars, artists and celebrity authors, the intimate boutique Boathouse is still the only place to stay on Phuket. Rooms are spacious and gorgeous, some sporting large breezy verandahs. Critics complain that the Boathouse is a bit stiff-lipped and old-fashioned for this century, but no-one can deny that the main reason to stay here is for the food. The on-site restaurant, Boathouse Wine & Grill (opposite), is among the best on the island. The Boathouse also provides cooking courses, see p307.

OUR PICK Mom Tri's Villa Royale (Map p320; ☎ 0 7633 3568; www.villaroyalephuket.com; ste incl breakfast from 11,500B; ☒ ☐ ☒) Tucked away in a secluded

Kata Noi location with the grandest of views, Villa Royale opened in 2006 to nearly instant acclaim. The romantic place with fabulous food offers fabulous rooms straight out of the pages of *Architectural Digest*. Guiltless pleasures include an attached spa and a saltwater pool if you prefer a tamer version of the real thing – which is just steps away.

Eating

There's some surprisingly classy food in Kata, though you'll be paying for it. For cheaper eats, head to Th Thai Na and to the cluster of affordable, casual seafood restaurants on Th Kata (Patak West) near the shore.

Kwong Shop Seafood (Map p320; ☎ 08 1273 3707; 66 Th Thai Na; mains 40-130B) This no-frills seafood joint displays fresh fish outside and pictures of its happy customers on the walls. It is cheap and very, very cheerful – a winning combination.

Thai Kitchen (Map p320; ThThai Na; meals 80B; ☙ breakfast, lunch & dinner) Good rule of thumb: if a humble, roadside cafe is packed with Thai people, you can be certain that the food will rock. Its green curry (warning: your nose will run) and glass-noodle dishes are superb. It's just down the road from, ahem, 'Pussy Bar'.

our pick **Capannina** (Map p320; ☎ 0 7628 4318; capannina@fastmail.fm; 30/9 Moo 2, Th Kata; mains 200-700B) The chefs at this hip, open-air bistro with moulded concrete booths and imported olive oil on the tables start prepping early. Everything here – from the pastas to the sauces – are made fresh. The ravioli and gnocchi are remarkable, the risotto comes highly recommended, and it has great pizzas, calzones and veal Milanese, too. It gets crowded during the high season, so you may want to reserve ahead.

Boathouse Wine & Grill (Map p320; ☎ 0 7633 0015; www.boathousephuket.com; Th Kotanod; mains 450-950B; ☙ breakfast, lunch & dinner) The perfect place to wow a fussy date, the Boathouse is the pick of the bunch for most local foodies. The atmosphere can be a little stuffy – this is the closest Phuket gets to old-school dining – but the Mediterranean fusion food is fabulous, the wine list expansive and the sea views sublime.

Oasis (Map p320; ☎ 0 7633 3423; Th Kotanod; meals 350-600B) Two restaurants in one, the top shelf is an Asian fusion tapas bar blessed with live jazz. The lower level is a candlelit fine-dining

patio restaurant where you can sample fresh barracuda fillet with a sun-dried herb crust while you watch the oblong paper lanterns swing in the trees.

Drinking

Kata's nightlife tends to be pretty mellow.

Ska Bar (Map p320; ☙ till late) At Kata's southernmost cove, tucked into the rocks and seemingly intertwined with the trunk of a grand old banyan tree, is our choice for oceanside sundowners. The Thai bartenders add to Ska's funky Rasta vibe, and the canopy dangles with buoys, paper lanterns and the flags of 10 countries.

Ratri Jazztaurant (Map p320; ☎ 0 7633 3538; Kata Hill; dishes 145-345B; ☙ 6pm-midnight) Hang out on the hillside terrace, listen to live jazz, watch the sun go down and enjoy delicious Thai food. Now *this* is a vacation.

Getting There & Around

Sŏrng·tăa·ou to both Kata and Karon (per person 25B) leave frequently from the day market on Th Ranong in Phuket from 7am to 5pm. The main sŏrng·tăa·ou stop is in front of Kata Beach Resort.

Taxis from Kata go to Phuket Town (500B), Patong (500B) and Karon (150B).

Motorbike rentals (per day 300B) are widely available.

HAT KARON

หาดกะรน

Even with two megaresorts and package tourists aplenty, Hat Karon has more sand space per capita than Patong or Kata. On the northernmost edge, accessible from a rutted road that extends past the vendors and food stalls, the beach tucks into a headland. That's Karon's sweet spot, and the water is like turquoise glass. From here, the beach extends south in a gentle arc before curling again into another turquoise and gold crescent. Within the inland network of streets and plazas you'll find a blend of good local food, more Scandinavian signage than seems reasonable and lovely Karon Park, with its artificial lake, mountain backdrop and a fine stretch of sand.

Sleeping

BUDGET & MIDRANGE

Hat Karon is lined with lodging options. Cheaper places will naturally be found off the beach. Ask for discounts in the low season (50% off the rack rate is standard), and if you stay more than a few days.

Pineapple Guesthouse (Map p320; ☎ 0 7639 6223; www.pineapplephuket.com; Karon Plaza; r with fan 300-700B, r with air-con 450B-1000B; ☒ ☜) Super-clean and brightly tiled rooms, some with air-con and queen-sized beds.

ourpick Kangaroo Guesthouse (Map p320; ☎ 0 7639 6517; 269/6-9 Karon Plaza; r 800B; ☒ ☜) Basic, but very clean, sunny tiled rooms with hot water, air-con, a cute breakfast nook, and balconies overlooking a narrow, palm-shaded soi.

Pachumas Mansion (Map p320; ☎ 0 7639 6737; 426 Th Patak; r 1000B; ☒) Brand new and spotless, this Ikea-chic budget inn is set in an attractive canary-yellow building on Karon's back road. Rooms all come with cable TV, hot water, air-con and access spacious, private decks.

Karon Sunshine Guesthouse (Map p320; ☎ 0 7628 6351; karonsunshineguesthouse.com; r 1200B; ☒ ☜) Large sunlight-flooded rooms with wardrobes, rattan furnishings, hot water, cable TV and Buddhist art on the walls. Nothing fancy, but very homey and nice value.

In On The Beach (off Map p320; ☎ 0 7639 8220; karon-inonthebeach.com; 695-697 Moo 1, Th Patak; r 3500B; ☒ 🖳 ☜ 🖵) A sweet, tasteful inn on Karon Park. The location is sublime, and the rooms – think: marble floors, wi-fi, air-con and ceiling fans – horseshoe the pool and come with sea views. With substantial low-season discounts, this is the perfect surf lair in the wet.

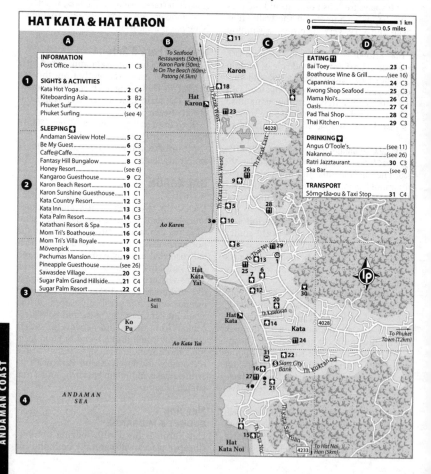

HAT KATA & HAT KARON

0 _____ 1 km
0 _____ 0.5 miles

INFORMATION		
Post Office	1	C3

SIGHTS & ACTIVITIES		
Kata Hot Yoga	2	C4
Kiteboarding Asia	3	B2
Phuket Surf	4	C4
Phuket Surfing	(see 4)	

SLEEPING		
Andaman Seaview Hotel	5	C2
Be My Guest	6	C3
Caffe@Caffe	7	C3
Fantasy Hill Bungalow	8	C3
Honey Resort	(see 6)	
Kangaroo Guesthouse	9	C2
Karon Beach Resort	10	C3
Karon Sunshine Guesthouse	11	C1
Kata Country Resort	12	C3
Kata Inn	13	C3
Kata Palm Resort	14	C3
Katathani Resort & Spa	15	C4
Mom Tri's Boathouse	16	C4
Mom Tri's Villa Royale	17	C4
Mövenpick	18	C1
Pachumas Mansion	19	C1
Pineapple Guesthouse	(see 26)	
Sawasdee Village	20	C3
Sugar Palm Grand Hillside	21	C4
Sugar Palm Resort	22	C4

EATING		
Bai Toey	23	C1
Boathouse Wine & Grill	(see 16)	
Capannina	24	C3
Kwong Shop Seafood	25	C3
Mama Noi's	26	C2
Oasis	27	C4
Pad Thai Shop	28	C2
Thai Kitchen	29	C3

DRINKING		
Angus O'Toole's	(see 11)	
Nakannoi	(see 26)	
Ratri Jazztaurant	30	C3
Ska Bar	(see 4)	

TRANSPORT		
Sŏrng·tăa·ou & Taxi Stop	31	C4

To Seafood Restaurants (50m); Karon Park (50m); In On The Beach (60m); Patong (4.5km)

TOP END

Many of the remaining places to stay in Karon are newer resort-type hotels with all the amenities. Posh spots tend to cluster around the northern and southern headlands. In the low season 50% discounts are common.

our pick **Andaman Seaview Hotel** (Map p320; ☎ 0 7639 8111; www.andamanphuket.com; 1 Soi Karon, Th Kata (Patak West); r from 4700B; ✖ ◻ ⧂ ⛀) With its sky-blue-and-white Cape Cod exterior and checkerboard marble floors in the lobby, this place has old-world charm to spare. Rooms keep the turn of the 20th-century Americana theme going with marble tables, antiquated ceiling fans, art deco-ish bathroom tiles and white-shutter cabinet doors. The rooms on the ground floor have access to the pool out the back door.

Karon Beach Resort (Map p320; ☎ 0 763 3006; 51 Th Kata (Patak West); r from 7900B; ✖ ⧂ ⛀) Perched on the south end of Hat Karon, there are some elegant touches here. From the Buddhist sculpture in the jasmine-scented halls to the crown mouldings, wood furnishings, ceramic tiles and cushy duvets in the rooms, to those luscious sea views from the balcony.

Mövenpick (Map p320; ☎ 0 7639 6139; www.moevenpick-hotels.com; 509 Th Kata (Patak West); r from 5040B, villas from 7650B; ✖ ⧂ ⛀) Grab a secluded villa and choose from a private plunge pool or outdoor rainforest shower; alternatively chill in the cubelike rooms with huge floor-to-ceiling glass windows (in some cases covering two entire walls) in the swank ultramodern hotel. Besides a prime location across the street from a pretty stretch of the beach, the Mövenpick offers artistic decor, top-end linen, a big pool with swim-up bar, a spa, and an alfresco restaurant and bar with a giant selection of wood-fired pizzas.

Eating & Drinking

As usual, almost every place to stay has a restaurant. There are a few cheap Thai and seafood places off the roundabout (including a number of beachside seafood houses under one louvred roof 100m north of it) and a similar group on the main road near the southern end of Hat Karon.

Bai Toey (Map p320; ☎ 08 1691 6202; Soi Old Phuket; meals 200B-250B) A charming Thai bistro with shaded outdoor patio and indoor seating. It has the traditional curry, stir-fry and noodle dishes, but you'd do well to sample its Thai-style grilled beef. It's a sliced fillet

> **DANGER: RIP TIDES**
>
> The seas are quite rough in the low season, and while this can translate to stellar waves for surfers, swimmers should not to venture out if there are red flags flying on Hat Karon. Flags signify heavy rip currents, which are frequent and claim dozens of lives every year. If you do get caught in a rip tide, and find yourself being carried out to sea, do not flail and fight against the current. That's a recipe for disaster. The best course of action is to stay calm and swim parallel to shore. After a time, you should be out of the current and out of harms way, though you'll probably have to walk a way back to your towel once you're back on dry ground.

brushed in oyster sauce, served with sticky rice (200B).

Mama Noi's (Map p320; ☎ 0 7628 6272; 291/1-2 Moo 3, Th Patak, Karon Plaza; meals 50-80B) Repeat visitors adore this place, which churns out fantastic Thai and Italian pasta dishes. It does a superb *gaeng som*, a southern Thai curry with fish and prawns; it bakes its own baguettes every morning; and has the best banana shake on the island.

Pad Thai Shop (Map p320; Th Patak East; dishes 40B; ⧖ breakfast, lunch & dinner) On the busy main road behind Karon, just north of the tacky Ping Pong Bar, is this glorified food stand where you can find rich and savoury chicken stew (worthy of rave reviews in its own right), and the best *pàt tai* on planet earth. Spicy and sweet, packed with prawns, tofu, egg and peanuts, and wrapped in a fresh banana leaf, you will be grateful.

Angus O'Tooles (Map p320; Th Patak, Centara Mall, ⧖ 10am-midnight) This proper Irish pub has all the cricket and rugby matches on the flat screen and Guinness and Kilkenny on tap.

Nakannoi (Map p320; ☎ 08 7898 5450; Karon Plaza; ⧖ 5pm-1am) A boho arthouse hideaway with original canvasses on the walls, found art (including antique motorcycles and bicycles) decor, a concrete island bar and a permanent bandstand, where the owner jams with his mates almost every night after 8pm.

Getting There & Away

For details on transport to Karon, see Getting There & Around, p319.

HAT PATONG

หาดป่าตอง

With its infinite procession of sun-scorched Scandinavians, beach-buzzing wave runners, complete disregard for managed development, and its penchant for turning the midlife crisis into a full-scale industry (sorry, Viagra and Cialis, Patong was here first), Patong is rampant with unintentional comedy. But for all the concrete and silicon, and moral and gender bending, there's something honest about this place.

Patong is a free for all. Anything, from a Starbucks 'venti latte' to an, ahem, companion for the evening is available for the right price. And while that's true about dozens of other, phonier, destinations, Patong doesn't try to hide it. Patong is what it is. And that's refreshing.

Of course, that doesn't mean you're going to like it. But even if you don't, if you land in Phuket, you will spend some time here (it's almost unavoidable). And when you arrive you'll take one look at the wide, white-sand beach and its magnificent crescent bay, and you'll understand how all this started.

Diving and spa options abound, as well as upscale dining, street-side fish grills, campy cabaret, Thai boxing, dusty antique shops and one of Asia's coolest shopping malls.

The pristine Trai-Trang and Freedom beaches to the south are soul soothing, and if you want a quiet patch of sand on Patong beach, you can head to the more serene northern end. The most insidious aspect of all this is that after a few days of Patong, even haters start to enjoy it.

Information

There are internet cafes, and banks with ATM and currency-exchange facilities across town.

Bookazine (☎ 0 7634 5834; 18 Th Bangla; ☼ 10am-11pm) For English-language books and magazines.

Post office (Th Thawiwong; ☼ 9am-4.30pm Mon-Fri, to noon Sat)

Tourist police (☎ 1699; Th Thawiwong)

Activities

Patong is a centre for diving on the island; see p305 for a list of established dive shops. Most Patong dive shops also book live-aboard trips to the Similan and Surin islands.

Motor yachts, sailboats and catamarans can sometimes be chartered with or without crew; see p306.

Sleeping

It's getting pretty difficult to find anything in Patong under 1000B from approximately November to April (the period that corresponds to the prices listed in this book), but outside this time rates drop by 40% to 60%.

BUDGET

On the beach there is nothing in the budget range, but on and off Th Rat Uthit there are several guesthouses with rooms that hover around 1200B in the high season and plummet to as low as 500B in the low season.

Casa Jip (☎ 0 7634 3019; www.casajip.com; 207/10 Th Rat Uthit; r from 700B; ✿) Italian run and great value, this place has very big, if simple, rooms with comfy beds and a taste of Thai style. You get cable TV and there's even a breakfast room service.

our pick Merrison Inn (☎ 0 7634 0383; www.merrisoninn.com; 5/35 Th Hat Patong; r 850B; ✿ ☎) The search for best Patong cheap sleep ends now. There are polished concrete floors, terrazzo bathrooms, wall-mounted flat screens, queen-sized beds and more than a little Asian kitsch.

Sawasdee Apartment (☎ 0 7634 1326; 108/15 Soi Patong Resort; r 1000-1200B; ✿ ☎) A terrific, albeit understated, cheapie. Rooms are large and very clean, with crown mouldings, built-in wardrobes, cable TV and flowers blooming over the railing on your private terrace. Long-term discounts are available.

MIDRANGE

You won't get beachfront for midrange prices but you will get cleanliness and comfort.

First Resort Albergo (☎ 0 7634 0980; firsthotel @hotmail.com; 19/12 Th Rat Uthit; r from 1200B; ✿ ☎ ✿) This solid, Italian-run spot offers simple, spotless rooms around a pool. There's TV, a terrace restaurant (expect pizza and bolognese made with Thai basil) and plenty of warm Mediterranean hospitality.

MVC Patong House (☎ 0 7634 3449; www.mvcpatonghouse.com; 94/10 Th Sai Namyen; r from 1400B; ✿ ☎ ✿) Small but sparkling new rooms with high-end tile floors, wood furnishings, cable TV and safety boxes. Offer terrific value at this price.

Baan Pronphateep (☎ 0 7634 3037; baanpronphateep.com; 168/1 Th Thawiwong; r 1500-1900B; ✿) Banyan tree shaded and nestled down a secluded little soi, this is a fine three-star choice. Rooms are spacious and come with a full-sized fridge and a private patio.

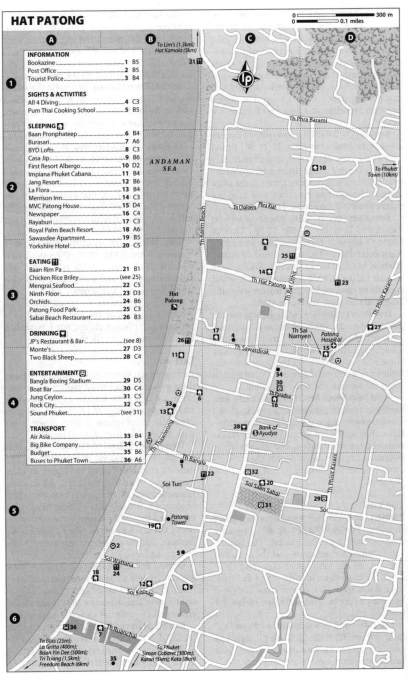

HAT PATONG

0 ———— 300 m
0 ———— 0.1 miles

Yorkshire Hotel (☎ 0 7634 0904; www.theyorkshire hotel.com; 169/16 Soi Saen Sabai; r 1800-2300; 🕲 🖭 🛜) About as Thai as a plate of Yorkshire pud, this is an unabashedly British outfit, courting visitors who insist on putting the home in their comforts. There's a flicker of homey B&B charm here, it's very well managed and can put together a mean fry-up. The rooms are sleek, spotless and come with cable TV and wi-fi.

Rayaburi (☎ 0 7629 7111; www.rayaburiphuket.com; 3/8-16 Th Sawatdirak; r from 2160B; 🕲 🛜 🐼) Brand new at the time of research and already fully booked. There's more decor and amenities available here compared to others in the price range. Though not everyone will love the rather loud take on classic Thai style.

Newspaper (☎ 0 7634 6276; www.newspaperphuket .com; 125/4-5 Th Paradise; r 2200B; 🕲 🛜) One of Patong's classiest three-star inns and easily the most stylish and sophisticated on this gay-friendly block of bars and cafes. Rooms have upscale tile floors, bedside lanterns, dark-wood furnishings and understated feature walls. It's frequently booked, so reserve ahead.

Jang Resort (☎ 0 7634 3122; www.jangresort.com; 210/23 Soi Kepsap; r 2400B; 🕲 🛜 🐼) Spacious, comfortable rooms are offered in kitschy Thai-style townhouses at this hidden-away three-star joint. You'll like the stone showers, built-in cabinetry and satellite TV, and you'll learn to live with the wood panelling.

Royal Palm Beach Resort (☎ 0 7629 2510; www .theroyalpalm.com; 66/2 Th Thawiwong; r 3700B; 🕲 🐼) Contemporary three-star comfort and amenities come with Thai accents like silk tapestries and throw cushions. The splashy lobby is misleading, but it's a decent choice with steep low-season discounts, just steps from the sand.

TOP END

Burasari (☎ 0 7629 2929; www.burasari.com; 18/110 Th Ruamchai; r 4000-9300B; 🕲 🛜 🐼) Arguably Patong's best four-star habitat. The beautifully landscaped grounds and those etched columns in the lobby ooze class and character. Rooms have blonde-wood furnishings, flat screen TVs, queen-sized beds and bamboo accents, and staff are warm yet professional.

BYD Lofts (☎ 0 7634 3024; www.bydlofts.com; 5/28 Th Rat Uthit; apt 5180-8750B; 🕲 🖭 🐼) If style and comfort are more important to you than beachfront (although it's only a minute's walk

to the beach), look no further. Urban-style apartments with lots of white (floors, walls, blinds) and sharp lines feel angelic compared with the seedy world of Patong on the streets below. There's a day spa, a rooftop pool and an excellent restaurant on the premises.

Impiana Phuket Cabana (☎ 0 7634 0138; www.impi ana.com; 41 Th Thawiwong; r from 6900B; 🕲 🐼) Cabana style and plumb on the best part of the beach, the rooms here are laden with chic and creature comforts and are close to all the action.

La Flora (☎ 0 7634 4241; www.lafloraphuket.com; 39 Th Thawiwong; r from 9500B; 🕲 🛜 🐼) Here's where clean lines and minimalist decor spill onto Patong beach. Rooms are large with wood furnishings (check out that floating desk), flat screen TV and DVD, bathtub and shower. The minibar is stocked with complimentary soft drinks, and there's a huge lap pool.

Bliss (☎ 0 7629 2098; www.theblissphuket.com; 40 Th Thawiwong; ste from 15,000B; 🕲 🛜 🐼) A sleek, new all-suite resort. Suites are 90 sq m with a full-sized living room and master bedroom with wood floors, two flat screens, a Jacuzzi and a blooming garden on the terrace. There's a common lap pool on the 2nd floor and wi-fi throughout. It's not cheap, but low-season discounts make it worth the splurge.

Eating

Patong has stacks of restaurants, some of them quite good. Patong's most glamorous restaurants are in a little huddle above the cliffs on the northern edge of town. Back in town, expect the usual spread of expat diners, filled with topless (the men, that is) tourists.

Chicken Rice Briley (☎ 0 7634 4079; Patong Food Park, Th Rat Uthit; meals 35-45B; ☺ breakfast & lunch) The only diner in the Patong food park to offer sustenance when the sun shines. All it serves is steamed and sliced chicken breast on a bed of steamed rice, bowls of chicken broth with crumbled bits of meat and bone, and roast pork. The chicken is best when dipped in its fantastic chilli sauce. There's a reason it's forever packed with locals.

Orchids (☎ 0 7634 0462; 78/3-4 Th Thawiwong; dishes from 80B; ☺ breakfast, lunch & dinner) Get your fantastic, cheap Thai food here. Its beef *lâhp* is scintillating and delicious, plus it has all the curries and noodle dishes you love so much.

Mengrai Seafood (☎ 08 7263 7070; Soi Tun; meals 120-300B) Located down a sweaty, dark soi off Th Bangla is a wonderful food court serving fresh, local food. The stalls towards the end serve daily curries that local expats swear by. This restaurant specialises in (very) fresh fish, prawns and mussels.

Sabai Beach Restaurant (☎ 08 1892 6158; 45 Th Thawiwong; dishes meals 200-400B; ☿ breakfast, lunch & dinner) If you prefer your fresh grilled seafood served beachfront, come here, pick your fresh catch and munch it on a sweet stretch of Patong beach.

our pick Baan Rim Pa (☎ 0 7634 4079; Th Kalim Beach; dishes 215-475B) Stunning Thai food is served with a side order of spectacular views at this institution. Standards are high, with prices to match, but romance is in the air, with candlelight and piano music aplenty. Book ahead and tuck in your shirt.

Lim's (☎ 0 7634 4834; www.lim-thailand.com; 28 Th Phrabaramee, Soi 7; meals 300-600B; ☿ 6pm-midnight) Lim's is 500m uphill from the coast road to Kamala. It's a modern, moulded-concrete dining room and lounge serving upscale Thai cuisine. When celebrities land in Phuket, most spend at least one evening here.

Ninth Floor (☎ 0 7634 4311; www.the9thfloor.com; 47 Th Rat Uthit; mains 290-1990B; ☿ dinner) To get some perspective on just how massive Patong has become, come on up to the 9th floor of the Sky Inn Condotel building where you can watch the sea of lights spread through sliding floor-to-ceiling glass doors. This is the highest open-air restaurant on the island, but its ridiculously tender, perfectly prepared steaks and chops are what made it a Patong institution.

Bargain seafood and noodle stalls pop up across town at night – try the lanes on and around Th Bangla, or venture over to the **Patong Food Park** (Th Rat Uthit; ☿ 4pm-midnight) once the sun drops.

Drinking

Some visitors may find that Patong's bar scene is enough to put them off their *pàt tai*, but if you're in the mood for plenty of beer, winking neon and short skirts, it is certainly worth sampling.

Th Bangla is Patong's beer and bar-girl mecca and features a number of spectacular, go-go extravaganzas, where you can expect the usual mix of gyrating Thai girls and often red-faced Western men. The music is loud (expect techno), the clothes are all but non-existent and the decor is typically slapstick with plenty of phallic imagery. That said, the atmosphere is more carnival than carnage and

you'll find plenty of Western women pushing their way through the throng to the bar.

JP's Restaurant & Bar (☎ 0 7634 3024; www.bydlofts .com; 5/28 Th Hat Patong; ☿ 10.30am-11.30pm) This hipster indoor-outdoor lounge definitely brings a touch of style and panache to Patong. There's a low-slung bar, the outdoor sofa booths are cush, happy hour (with free tapas) starts at 10pm and there are weekly DJ parties.

La Gritta (☎ 0 7634 0106; www.amari.com; 2 Th Meun-ngern; ☿ 10.30am-11.30pm) A spectacular, modern restaurant that doesn't fit in with the aging bones of this once-great property, but who cares? With tiered booths, massive yet muted light boxes and a deck that is just centimetres above the boulder-strewn shore, there is no better place for a sunset cocktail.

Monte's (Th Phisit Karani; ☿ 11am-midnight) Now this, my friends, is a tropical pub. There's a thatched roof, a natural-wood bar, dozens of orchids and a flat screen for ballgames. The barflies swarm on Fridays for Monte's famous Belgian-style mussels, and on the weekends he fires up the grill.

Two Black Sheep (☎ 0895 921 735; www.twoblack sheep.net; 172 Th Rat Uthit; ☿ 11am-2am) Owned by a fun Aussie couple (he's a musician, she's a chef), this old-school pub is a great find. It has good grub and live music nightly. From 8pm to 10pm there's an acoustic set, then Chilli Jam, the house band gets up and rocks till last call. Towards the wee hours local musicians, fresh off their gigs, filter in and spontaneous jams ensue. And it bans bar girls, which keeps everything PG-13.

Entertainment

Once you've done the go-go, there's plenty more to see. Cabaret and Thai boxing, in particular, are something of a speciality here.

Bangla Boxing Stadium (☎ 0 7282 2348; Th Phisit Karani; admission 1000-1500B; ☿ 9-11.30pm Tue, Wed, Fri & Sun) Old name, new stadium, same game: a packed line-up of competitive *moo·ay tai* (Thai boxing) bouts.

Phuket Simon Cabaret (☎ 0 7634 2011; www .phuket-simoncabaret.com; Th Sirirach; admission 700-800B; ☿ performances 7.30pm & 9.30pm nightly) About 300m south of town, this cabaret offers entertaining transvestite shows. The 600-seat theatre is grand, the costumes are gorgeous and the ladyboys are convincing. The house is often full – book ahead.

Rock City (Th Rat Uthit; www.rockcityphuket.com; ☿ 9pm-late) Let the grunge begin! This dark

GAY PRIDE IN PHUKET

Although there are big gay pride celebrations in Bangkok and Pattaya, the **Phuket Gay Pride Festival** is considered by many to be the best in Thailand, maybe even Southeast Asia.

The first Phuket Gay Pride Festival started as a small community project in November 1999, in response to plans for similar events in the capital and in Pattaya. When the festival proved to be very successful, the planners realised that Phuket would be competing with other cities' festivals, so it was moved from November to February – a drier month on Phuket. The date has changed several times, but it usually lands between February and April. Whenever it blooms, the whole island – but the town of Patong specifically – is packed with (mostly male) revellers from all over the world.

The main events of the four-day weekend party are a huge beach volleyball tournament and, of course, the Grand Parade, featuring floats, cheering crowds and beautiful costumes in the streets of Patong. In recent years, the festival has also included social-responsibility campaigns against child prostitution, substance abuse and for HIV awareness.

Any other time of year, the network of streets that link the Royal Paradise Hotel with Th Rat Uthit in Patong is where you'll find Phuket's gay pulse. The **Boat Bar** (☎ 0 7634 2206; www.boatbar .com; 125/20 Th Rat Uthit), Phuket's original gay nightspot and still its only disco, is usually jumping with a lively mostly gay crowd. Make sure to arrive before the midnight cabaret! For updates on future festivals, to sign up for the spectacular volleyball tournament or for more information about the scene in general, go to www.gaypatong.com.

den of rock lives on the glory of AC/DC, Metallica and Guns N' Roses tribute bands. On Tuesdays, Fridays and Sundays, rockers channel the Red Hot Chili Peppers, the Rolling Stones, U2 and Bon Jovi in one International Rock City Party (1000B) with free cocktails and beer before 11pm, so get there early and keep it rockin'.

Sound Phuket (☎ 0 7636 6163; www.soundphuket .com; Jung Ceylon, Unit 2303, 193 Th Rat Uthit; admission varies; ۞ 10pm-4am) When internationally re-nowned DJs come to Phuket these days, they are usually gigging amid the rounded, futur-istic environs of Patong's hottest (and least sleazy) nightclub. If top-shelf DJs are on the decks, expect to pay up to 300B entry fee.

Jung Ceylon (Th Rat Uthit) You can catch new Hollywood releases in pristine, amphitheatre-style cinemas at the shopping mall.

Getting There & Around

Air Asia (☎ 0 7634 1792; www.airasia.com; 39 Th Thawiwong; ۞ 9am-9pm) has an office in town.

Túk-túks circulate around Patong for 50B to 100B per ride. There are numerous places to rent 125cc motorbikes and jeeps. **Big Bike Company** (☎ 0 7634 5100; 106 Th Rat Uthit) rents proper motorcycles (500B to 1000B per day). Keep in mind that the mandatory helmet law is strictly enforced in Patong, where roadblocks/checkpoints can spring up at a moment's notice. **Budget** (☎ 0 7629 2389; 44

Th Thawiwong; ۞ 9am-4pm) has an office in the Patong Merlin Hotel.

Sŏrng·tăa·ou to Patong from Phuket Town leave from Th Ranong, near the day mar-ket and fountain circle; the fare is 25B. The after-hours charter fare is 400B. Sŏrng·tăa·ou then drop off and pick up passengers at the southern end of Patong beach. From here you can hop on a motorbike taxi (20B to 30B per ride), flag down a túk-túk (prices vary widely) or walk till your feet hurt.

HAT KAMALA

หาดกมลา

A chilled-out hybrid of Hat Karon and Hat Surin, calm but fun Kamala tends to lure a mixture of longer-term guests (some of which appear to suffer from adult-onset adolescence), a regular crop of Scandinavian families, and young couples. The bay is magnificent, tur-quoise and serene with shore breakers that lull you to sleep. Palms and pines mingle on the leafy and rocky northern end where the water is a rich emerald green and the snorkelling around the rock reef is pleasant, while new resorts are ploughed into the southern bluffs above the gathering long-tails. The entire beach is backed with lush rolling hills, which one can only hope are left alone…forever. And it's the only beach with a walking path lined with restaurants, resorts and shops. Ditch the motorbike and step into Kamala bliss.

Sights & Activities

Local beach boffins will tell you that **Laem Singh**, just north of Kamala, is one of the best capes on the island. Walled in by cliffs, there is no road access so you have to park your car on the headland and clamber down a narrow path, or you could charter a long-tail (1000B) from Hat Kamala.

Phuket Fantasea (Map p327; ☎ 0 7638 5000; www.phuket-fantasea.com; admission with/without dinner 1900/1500B; ⏰ 6-11.30pm Fri-Wed) is a US$60 million 'cultural theme park' located just east of Hat Kamala. Despite the billing, there aren't any rides, but there is a show that takes the colour and pageantry of traditional Thai dance and costumes and combines this with state-of-the-art light-and-sound techniques that rival anything found in Las Vegas (think 30 elephants). All of this takes place on a stage dominated by a full-scale replica of a Khmer temple reminiscent of Angkor Wat. Kids especially will be captivated by the spectacle but it is over-the-top cheesy, and cameras are forbidden.

Back in Kamala, you can scuba dive with **Scuba Quest** (Map p327; ☎ 0 7627 9016; www.scuba-quest-phuket.com).

Sleeping & Eating

Clear House (Map p327; ☎ 0 7638 5401; www.clearhousephuket.com; r 1300B; ⚡ 🌐) Shabby chic with a mod twist, white-washed rooms have pink feature walls, plush duvets, flat screen TVs, wi-fi and huge pebbled baths. This place just feels good.

ourpick Layalina Hotel (Map p327; ☎ 0 7638 5942; www.layalinahotel.com; r incl breakfast 5500-7700B; ⚡ 💻 🌐 📺) We loved this tiny beachfront boutique hotel, especially the split-level suites with very private rooftop terraces for romantic sunset views over white sand and blue sea. Decor is simple, Thai and chic, with fluffy white duvets and honey-toned wood furniture. This is a place that is ideal for honeymooners, simply dripping in intimacy and sophistication. Room rates include a one-hour couple's massage at the on-site spa. The only downside is that the pool is ridiculously small – but that turquoise ocean *is* only steps away.

Cape Sienna Hotel (Map p327; ☎ 0 7633 7300; www.capesienna.com; r 8500-10,130B; bungalows 4350-5600B; ⚡ 💻 🌐 📺) This new flash hotel dominates

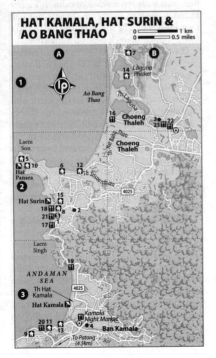

HAT KAMALA, HAT SURIN & AO BANG THAO

NORTHERN ANDAMAN COAST

the southern headland and offers magnificent azure bay views from the lobby, pool, and each and every room. Rooms are four-star quality with all the amenities.

Ma Ma Fati Ma (Map p327; Hat Kamala; dishes 50-150B; ✆ lunch & dinner) This beachfront snack shack is a real find. The family who owns and operates it could not be more welcoming. The tasty Thai food is exceptional, and if you forget your wallet, it will still feed you and trust that you'll pay later. Try that in the Western world.

Rockfish (☎ 0 7627 9732; www.rockfishrestaurant.com; 33/6 Th Kamala Beach; dishes 150-1000B; ✆ breakfast, lunch & dinner) Perched above the river mouth and the bobbing long-tails, with beach, bay and mountain views, is Kamala's best dining room. It rolls out gems like braised duck breast with kale, and prosciutto-wrapped scallops.

Getting There & Away

To catch a regular sŏrng·tăa·ou from Kamala to Patong costs 50B per person, while a sŏrng·tăa·ou charter (starting in the evenings) costs 250B.

HAT SURIN
หาดสุรินทร์

Like that hot boy or girl in school who also happens to have style, soul, a fun personality and wealthy parents, Surin beach is the kind of place that can inspire (travel) lust in anyone who meets her/him. With a wide, blonde beach, water that blends from pale turquoise in the shallows to a deep blue on the horizon and two lush, boulder-strewn headlands, Surin could easily attract tourists on looks alone. Ah, but there are stunning galleries, five-star spa resorts and wonderful beachfront dining options, too. So by the time you're done swimming, sunbathing, snacking at local fish grills and sipping cocktails at barefoot-chic beach clubs, don't be surprised if you've fallen in love.

Information

There is an ATM at Surin Plaza, just east of the beach on Rte 4025. Internet access is available at most hotels for 1B per minute.

Sleeping

There are a couple of midrangers, but luxury options dominate Hat Surin.

Surin Bay Inn (Map p327; ☎ 0 7627 1601; www.surin bayinn.com; r 2000-3000B; ✖ 🖳 🛜) Very clean, large

and homey rooms with rattan sitting areas, silk throw cushions on the bed and granite wash basins in the bathrooms. More expensive rooms have balconies with sea views.

Benyada Lodge (Map p327; ☎ 0 7627 1261; www .benyadalodge-phuket.com; r 2800-3500B; ✖ 🖳 🛜 🛒) Chic, modern rooms – with black louvred closets, terracotta-tiled bathrooms and silk, pastel-coloured throw pillows scattered in the lounging corner – are a great bargain for this area. Service is stellar and we loved the high-end details, such as ice-water service every time you sit anywhere in the lobby. Take in the sunset and have a dip in the pool at the rooftop bar. The hotel is right next to the Surin Bay Inn and only a few minutes' walk to the beach.

Twin Palms (Map p327; ☎ 0 7631 6500; www.twin palms-phuket.com; r 6100-38,800B; ✖ 🖳 🛒) This is the Audrey Hepburn of Phuket's hotels – it's classic yet completely contemporary. There's a pervasive feeling of space with minimalist, artsy swimming pools everywhere that are fringed by delicate white frangipani. Even the simplest rooms are extra spacious and have oversized bathrooms, sublimely comfortable beds and a supreme sense of calm. It's a few minutes' walk to the beach. Expats from all over Phuket can be found eating the island's most popular brunch here on Sundays.

Chava (Map p327; ☎ 0 7637 2600; www.thechavaresort .com; r 8000-35,000B; ✖ 🖳 🛒) Draped in flowering vines and blessed with gurgling fountains and shimmering reflection pools, this place is part hotel, part condo development and completely stylish. The massive two-, three- and four-bedroom apartments have fully stocked stylish, stainless-steel fridges in the kitchen, complete entertainment systems in the living room and another flat-screen TV in the master bedroom. It's privately owned, and available for rent by the night, week and month. Bring a group and it can be terrific value.

our pick **Chedi** (Map p327; ☎ 0 7662 1579; www.ghm hotels.com; r 17,000-58,000B; ✖ 🛒) Almost any place that was located on a private beach this quiet and stunning would have be a top pick. But Chedi's bungalows, with naturalistic wooden exteriors that hide beneath the foliage of the hillside, and earthy, luxurious interiors, make the site that much better. The restaurant has a dreamy, *Robinson Crusoe* feel and looks out over the water and an unexpectedly modern, six-sided pool. You'll have to be in decent shape for walking around the resort, since it can be quite a hoof up hills and over wooden walkways to get to many of the bungalows.

Amanpuri Resort (Map p327; ☎ 0 7632 4333; www.amanresorts.com; villas US$925-8050; 🔀 🖵 🕿) Phuket's number-one celebrity magnet, the Amanpuri offers lashings of glamour and palatial luxury – in fact, it was designed by the architect behind the former Shah of Iran's winter palace. With a staggering 3.5 staff members to every guest, this is exclusive service with bells on. Accommodation is in private villas and you can even book your own chef to cook for you.

Eating & Drinking
There are plenty of excellent restaurants in and around Surin. For cheap seafood, your first stop should be the numerous, fun and delicious seafront dining rooms.

Beach House (Map p327; ☎ 08 9651 1064; mains 150-250B) In addition to its popular cooking classes (1900B, four hours), it serves upscale Thai cuisine at reasonable prices on a beachfront deck beneath the trees.

our pick **Taste** (Map p327; ☎ 08 7886 6401; www .tastesurinbeach.com; tapas 160-225B) The best of a new breed of urban-meets-surf eateries along the beach. Its creative seafood tapas are among the best plates on Phuket.

Catch (Map p327; ☎ 0 7631 6500; mains 250-450B) Slip on your breeziest dress or a pair of linen trousers to dine at this draped, cabana-style eatery right on the beach. It's part of Twin Palms, even though it's not attached, and has all the same classy attributes as the hotel in both ambience and cuisine.

Stereo Lab (Map p327; ☎ 08 9218 0162; www.stereo labphuket.com; Hat Surin; ⏰ 11am-2am) The hottest new club on Phuket at the time of research. Its sliver of beach is decked out with cushy daybeds and lounges surrounding an outdoor bar and dance floor. The flash white 'interior' has another bar and dance floor, and unbroken sea views. Special events feature known international DJs.

Getting There & Away
A regular sŏrng·tăa·ou from Phuket Town's Th Ranong to Hat Surin costs 35B per person, and túk-túk or sŏrng·tăa·ou charters cost 450B.

Rent cars from **Andaman Car Rental** (Map p327; ☎ 0 7662 1600; www.andamancarrent.com; ⏰ 9am-9pm), opposite the entrance to Twin Palms. Vehicles can be rented from 1400B per day.

AO BANG THAO
อ่าวบางเทา
Almost as large and even more beautiful than Patong Bay, the stunning, 8km white-sand sweep of Ao Bang Thao is the glue that binds the region's disparate elements. The southern half is home to a sprinkling of three-star bungalow resorts. Further inland you'll find an old fishing village laced with canals along with a number of upstart villa subdivisions. Don't be alarmed if you see a herd of water buffalo grazing just 100m from a gigantic construction site. That's how fast Bang Thao is changing.

Smack in the centre of it all is the somewhat absurd Laguna Phuket complex – a network of five four- and five-star resort properties and an ageing shopping mall knitted together by an artificial lake, patrolled by tourist shuttle boats, and a paved nature trail. But in the north Mother Nature asserts herself once more, and a lonely stretch of powder white sand and tropical blue extends past all the bustle and change, and delivers the kind of peace you imagined when you booked your trip.

The **Hideaway Day Spa** (Map p327) has an excellent reputation. It offers traditional Thai massage, sauna and mud body wraps in a tranquil wooded setting at the edge of a lagoon. Treatments start at 1500B. The Hideaway also has its own line of spa products. See also p309.

Sleeping
Laguna Phuket is home to five luxury resorts, an 18-hole golf course and 30 restaurants (the gargantuan Sheraton Grande alone has eight restaurants). Guests at any one of the resorts can use the dining and recreation facilities at all of them. Frequent shuttle buses make the rounds of all the hotels, as do pontoon boats (via the linked lagoons).

Andaman Bangtao Bay Resort (Map p327; ☎ 0 7627 0246; www.andamanbangtaobayresort.com; bungalows incl breakfast 4900-7900B; 🔀 🕿) Every bungalow has a sea view and there's a summer-camp vibe at this pleasant little resort. The design is very Thai, with woodcarvings on the walls and coconuts hanging from the eaves of the roofs, but for this price we expected a little more luxury.

Dalar Resort (Map p327; ☎ 0 7631 4200; www.bang taodalarresort.com; r 6000-6800B; 🔀 🖵 🕿) The blocky exterior of this sprawling beachfront resort won't win any design awards, but rooms

---

TOP PHUKET RESORTS

Taking a Splurge

Amanpuri Resort (p329) Still Phuket's prime celeb magnet.

Anantara Phuket (p332) Soul-stirring luxury and natural beauty.

Chedi (p328) Location, location, location.

Indigo Pearl (opposite) Hardware meets high-style Tropicana.

Sala Resort & Spa (opposite) A modern take on art deco glam on Hat Mai Khao.

Without Breaking the Bank

Casa 104 (p311) Old Shanghai lives!

Layalina Hotel (p327) Boutique gem on a quiet beach.

Sino House (p311) *Mad Men*–chic.

---

are quite nice with built-in chocolate-wood wardrobes, granite wash basins and mosaic baths. The pool is massive and swarming with children.

Sheraton Grande Laguna Phuket (Map p327; ☎ 0 7632 4101; www.starwoodhotels.com; r from 7200B; ✄ ☐ ☎) Gated away in Laguna Phuket, the Sheraton will appeal to a lively, active crowd. It features a gigantic 323m-long pool, water-sports facilities galore, a kids' club and a whopping 423 rooms.

our pick **Banyan Tree Phuket** (Map p327; ☎ 0 7632 4374; www.banyantree.com; villas from 17,400B; ✄ ☐ ☎) One of Phuket's finest hotels, and the first to introduce bungalows with their own private pool, the Banyan Tree Phuket (in Laguna Phuket) is an oasis of sedate, understated luxury. Accommodation is in villas – and, as long as you're here, the on-site spa should not be missed.

Eating

Despite what some local hoteliers would have you believe, there is good food to be had outside the confines of Bang Thao's luxury hotels. You will find much of it just outside Laguna's main gate, and more at the seafood-oriented beach cafes south of the Banyan Tree Phuket.

Babylon Beach Club (Map p327; ☎ 08 1970 5302; www.babylonbeachclub.com; Hat Bang Thao; dishes 120–250B) Accessible by dirt road are the polished, whitewashed environs of the Babylon Beach Club. The food is nice, and all the Thai specialities are on offer, along with fresh grilled seafood and good burgers. Dishes are served on banana-leaf liners and four tables are set up with white tablecloths and umbrellas centimetres from the sea.

Tawai Restaurant (Map p327; ☎ 0 7632 5381; Moo 1, Laguna Resort Entrance; mains 180–300B) Set in a lovely

old house decorated with traditional art is this gem of a Thai kitchen, serving classics like roast duck curry and pork *lâhp*. Free shuttle service is available to and from the Laguna hotels.

Tatonka (Map p327; ☎ 0 7632 4349; Th Srisoonthorn; dishes 250–300B; ✄ dinner Thu-Tue) This is the home of 'globetrotter cuisine', which owner-chef Harold Schwarz developed by taking fresh local products and combining them with cooking and presentation techniques learned in Europe, Colorado and Hawaii. The eclectic, tapas-style selection includes creative vegetarian and seafood dishes and such delights as Peking duck pizza (220B). There's also a tasting menu (750B per person, minimum two people), which lets you try a little of everything. Call ahead during the high season.

Chaba (Map p327; ☎ 0 7627 1580; Moo 1, Laguna Resort Entrance; meals 400–800B) Upscale Thai served with flair on the lagoon just outside the Laguna gates. Just point, it will steam, grill or fry it.

Getting There & Away

A sŏrng·tăa·ou between Ao Bang Thao and Phuket Town's Th Ranong costs 25B per person. Túk-túk charters are 600B.

SIRINAT NATIONAL PARK

อุทยานแห่งชาติสิรินารถ

Comprising the beaches of Nai Thon, Nai Yang and Mai Khao, as well as the former Nai Yang National Park and Mai Khao wildlife reserve, **Sirinat National Park** (☎ 0 7632 8226; www.dnp .go.th; admission 200B; ✄ 8am-5pm) encompasses 22 sq km of coastal land, plus 68 sq km of sea. It runs from the western Phang-Nga provincial border south to the headland that separates Hat Nai Yang from Hat Nai Thon.

If you're after a lovely arc of fine golden sand, far from the buzz of Phuket busy-ness, **Hat Nai Thon** is your Eden. Accessed by a sinuous road through rubber plantations and banana groves, all you'll see here is a quiet main strip, a cosy turquoise bay and a few long-tails bobbing to the fish market on nearby Hat Nai Yang. Swimming is quite good here except at the height of the monsoon, and there is some coral near the headlands at either end of the bay. The remains of a wrecked 50m-long tin dredger lie off the coast near tiny **Ko Waew** at a depth of 16m. **Aqua Divers** (☎ 0 7620 5440; www .aquadivers.com; 23/26 Th Nai Thon Beach; dives from 1590B) can arrange dive trips in the area.

Hat Nai Yang's glassy bay is sheltered by a reef that slopes 20m below the surface – which makes for both good snorkelling in the dry season and fantastic surfing in the monsoon season. A string of local seafood restaurants and tiki bars line the main beach, which becomes pristine as it stretches north. It's hard to believe you can practically walk to the airport from here.

About 5km north of Hat Nai Yang is **Hat Mai Khao**, Phuket's longest beach. Sea turtles lay their eggs here between November and February. A visitors centre with toilets, showers and picnic tables is at Mai Khao, from where there are some short trails through the casuarinas to a steep beach. Take care when swimming, as there's a strong year-round undertow. Except on weekends and holidays you'll have this place almost to yourself; even during peak periods, peace and solitude are usually only a few steps away.

The whole area is mere minutes from Phuket International Airport, which makes it particularly convenient for a first stop after a long trip.

Sleeping & Eating
HAT NAI THON
Naithon Beach Resort (☎ 0 7620 5379; www.phuket -naithon.com; 23/31 Moo 4, Th Hat Nai Thon; cottages 3300B; ☼ Nov-May; ❄) Aka Woody's Paradise, small polished wood chalets with slate bathrooms are tucked into the south end of Hat Nai Thon, 10 steps from the sand.

Naithonburi (☎ 0 7620 5500; www.naithonburi. com; Moo 4, Th Hat Nai Thon; r 3500-4500B) A mellow megaresort if ever there was one. Yes, it has 222 rooms, but it rarely feels too crowded or busy. Rooms are spacious with terracotta tile floors, Thai silks on the bed and private balconies. The enormous pool is lined with lounges and daybeds. Its Chao Lay Bistro (mains from 180B) is as swank as Nai Thon gets.

Coconut Tree (34 Moo 4, Th Hat Nai Thon; meals 120-300B) A beach cafe serving fresh grilled fish in the evening, and outstanding curries served with coconut rice in sweet sugar bowls when the sun shines. Its beach bar is always a popular afternoon oasis.

HAT NAI YANG & HAT MAI KHAO
Along the dirt road at the very southern end of Hat Nai Yang is a seemingly endless strip of seafood restaurants and, oddly enough, tailor shops. There is also a small minimart near the entrance to the Indigo Pearl resort.

Sirinat National Park (☎ 0 7632 7152; reserve@dnp .go.th; campsites 30B, bungalows 1000-2000B) There are campsites (bring your own tent) and large bungalows at the park headquarters. Check in at the visitors centre or book online.

Nai Yang Beach Resort (☎ 0 7632 8300; www.nai yangbeachresort.com; 65/23-24 Th Hat Nai Yang; bungalows 2500-4300B; ❄) This resort is clean, quiet, near the beach and does a great barbecue at night. The lowest-end rooms are fan cooled, while higher-end ones sport modern Thai style and are quite chic.

our pick **Indigo Pearl** (☎ 0 7632 7006; www.indigo -pearl.com; r 5600-26,250B; ❄ ▢ ❄) One of the most unique and hip of Phuket's high-end resorts takes its design cues from the island's tin-mining history – although it sounds weird, this industrial theme melded with tropical luxe creates a spectacularly beautiful and soothing place to stay. Hardware, such as vices, scales and other mining tools, is used in the decor to the tiniest detail – even the toilet-paper rolls are big bolts – and the common lounge areas are infused with indigo light. The gardens are modern and lush and surround a pool that looks like an oasis with a big waterfall.

Sala Resort & Spa (☎ 0 7633 8888; www.salaphuket .com; 333 Moo 3, Tambon Maikhao; r from 11,550B, villas from 15,750B) This uberstylish, boutique property is a blend of Sino-Portuguese and art deco influences with mod flair. Even 2nd-storey rooms have outdoor bathrooms. The black-granite infinity pool at the beachfront is gorgeous, and the bar area includes cushy, circular sofa lounges. It's the kind of place that makes everyone feel like a celebrity. It also offers spa services (p309).

Anantara Phuket (☎ 0 7633 6100; www.phuket
.anantara.com; 888 Moo 3, Tumbon Mai Khao; villas from
35,000B) Phuket's newest all-villa property
opens onto a serene lotus-filled lagoon that
extends to the beach. Luxurious, classic Thai
pool villas are connected to the lobby, bars
and restaurants, and the beach, by old timber
boardwalks that wind beneath swaying palms.
It also offers the Bua Luang Spa (see p309).

Mr Kobi's Bar (Nai Yang Beach; dishes from 100B;
⏰ 11am-1am) The sign says, 'Broken English
spoken here perfect.' But, truthfully, the gregarious Mr Kobi speaks English very well
and has a fantastic wood bar on the beach.
When the other beach shacks close, Mr Kobi's
blender whirs on and his kitchen doesn't close
till the guests go home, or pass out.

Batik Seafood (88/3 Th Nai Yang Beach; dishes 150-
350B) This beautiful beach-garden restaurant,
nestled on the south end just after the road
turns to dust, sports tables beneath thatched
gazebos and surrounded by orchids. It specialises in fresh grilled fish, which it buys from the
fish market held just north of the restaurant
every afternoon.

Getting There & Away

If you're coming from the airport, a taxi costs
about 300B. There is no regular sŏrng·tăa·ou,
but a túk-túk charter from Phuket Town costs
about 700B.

KHAO PHRA TAEW ROYAL WILDLIFE & FOREST RESERVE

อุทยานสัตว์ป่าเขาพระแทว

It's not all sand and sea. In the north of the
island, this park protects 23 sq km of virgin
island rainforest (evergreen monsoon forest).
There are some pleasant hikes over the hills
and a couple of photogenic waterfalls: **Nam Tok
Ton Sai** and **Nam Tok Bang Pae**. The falls are best
seen in the rainy season between June and
November; in the dry months they slow to a
trickle. The highest point in the park is **Khao
Phara** (442m). Because of its royal status, the
reserve is better protected than the average
national park in Thailand.

A German botanist discovered a rare and
unique species of palm in Khao Phra Taew
about 50 years ago. Called the white-backed
palm or *langkow* palm, the fan-shaped plant
stands 3m to 5m tall and is found only here
and in Khao Sok National Park (p290).

Tigers, Malayan sun bears, rhinos and
elephants once roamed the forest here, but
nowadays resident mammals are limited to
humans, pigs, monkeys, slow loris, langur,
civets, flying foxes, squirrels, mousedeer and
other smaller animals. Watch out for cobras
and wild pigs.

The **Phuket Gibbon Rehabilitation Centre** (Map
p303; ☎ 0 7626 0492; www.gibbonproject.org; donations
encouraged; ⏰ 9am-4pm), in the park near Nam
Tok Bang Pae, is open to the public. Financed
by donations (1500B will care for a gibbon for
one year), the centre adopts gibbons that have
been kept in captivity in the hopes they can
be reintroduced to the wild.

If you're the thrill-seeking sort, harness
up at **Cable Jungle Adventure Phuket** (☎ 08 1977
4904; 232/17 Moo 8, Th Bansuanneramit; per person 1,950B;
⏰ 9am-6pm). Tucked into the hills is this maze
of eight zip lines linking cliffs to ancient trees.
The zips range from 6m to 23m above the
ground and the longest run is 100m long.
Closed-toe shoes are a must.

Park rangers may act as guides for hikes
in the park on request; payment for services
is negotiable.

To get to Khao Phra Taew from Phuket
Town, take Th Thepkasatri north about 20km
to Thalang District and turn right at the intersection for Nam Tok Ton Sai, which is 3km
down the road.

THALANG DISTRICT

อำเภอถลาง

A few hundred metres northeast of the famous
Heroines Monument in Thalang District on Rte
4027, and about 11km northwest of Phuket
Town, is **Thalang National Museum** (Map p303;
☎ 0 7631 1426; admission 30B; ⏰ 8.30am-4pm). The
museum contains five exhibition halls chroni-
cling southern themes such as the history of
Thalang-Phuket and the colonisation of the
Andaman Coast, and describing the various
ethnicities found in southern Thailand. The
legend of the 'two heroines' (memorialised
on the nearby monument), who supposedly
drove off an 18th-century Burmese invasion
force by convincing the island's women to
dress as men, is also recounted in detail. The
focal point of one hall is the impressive 2.3m-
tall statue of Vishnu, which dates to the 9th
century and was found in Takua Pa early in
the 20th century.

Also in Thalang District, just north of the
crossroads near Thalang town, is **Wat Phra
Thong** (Map p303; admission by donation; ⏰ dawn-dusk),
Phuket's 'Temple of the Gold Buddha'. The

image is half buried so that only the head and shoulders are visible. According to local legend, those who have tried to excavate the image have become very ill or encountered serious accidents. The temple is particularly revered by Thai-Chinese, many of whom believe the image hails from China. During Chinese New Year pilgrims descend from Phang-Nga, Takua Pa and Krabi. In addition to Phra Thong there are several other Buddha images, including seven representing the different days of the week, plus a Phra Praket (an unusual pose in which the Buddha is touching his own head with his right hand). Each promises a different virtue (success, health, wealth etc) to those who make offerings.

Some scenes in the movie *Good Morning Vietnam* were filmed on location in Thalang.

Southern Andaman Coast

Island hoppers, this is your dreamland. The south is the quieter half of the Andaman coast; even the regional star, Ko Phi-Phi, can't rival the glam and crowds of Phuket. Just slowly putter from white-sand isle to white-sand isle, and prepare for serious relaxation, outdoor fun and chummy nights at beachside bars.

Social seekers will love the developed beauties, such as Ko Phi-Phi and Ko Lanta, where you can party into the wee hours and meet plenty of fellow ramblers on the beach, yet still find a peaceful strip of sand. And roads less travelled are just next door: head down through the lightly developed Trang islands to the even-less-visited Satun Province to find powder-white beaches, outrageous snorkelling and plenty of spicy southern Thai culture. The entire region is made up of a spectacular undulating coastline pierced by sheer limestone formations, speckled with islands and cloaked in greenery.

Besides the phenomenal diving and snorkelling, some of the best rock climbing in the world can be found in Krabi and Trang Provinces. All that limestone means there are plenty of caves to explore; some house shrines while others require that you shimmy on your stomach or even swim to get through.

Much of this region shuts down in the April-to-November low season, but even at that time you can still get to most places with determined effort, and you'll be rewarded with nearly deserted beaches and large doses of serenity.

HIGHLIGHTS

- Zipping around in long-tail boats and oohing and aahing at monolithic rock formations and perfect beaches throughout the **Trang islands** (p371) or **Ko Tarutao Marine National Park** (p383)

- Scaling a limestone cliff then recuperating on the sparkling beaches and in the jade waters of **Railay** (p346)

- Trying to decide if **Ko Phi-Phi** (p351) is more beautiful above or below water

- Forgetting what day it is on **Ko Jum** (p366)

- Snorkelling or drift diving along pristine coral reefs by day and chilling at low-key reggae bars by night on **Ko Lipe** (p386)

★ Railay

★ Ko Jum

Ko Phi-Phi ★

Trang Islands ★

Ko Tarutao Marine National Park ★

Ko Lipe ★

■ DRY SEASON: NOVEMBER–MARCH | ■ WET SEASON: MAY–OCTOBER

SOUTHERN ANDAMAN COAST

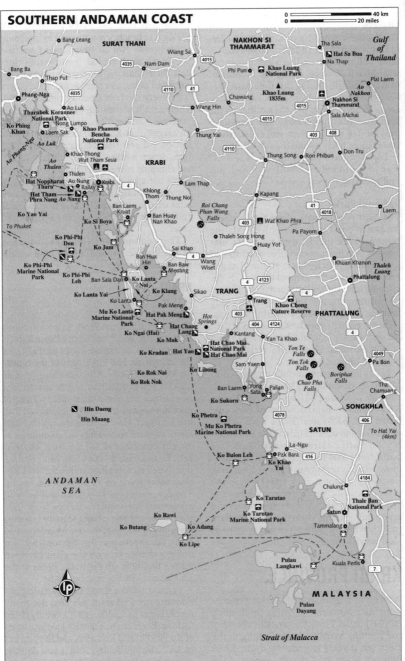

Climate

The weather can be a big concern for travellers in this region. The Andaman coast receives more rain than the southern gulf provinces, with May to October being the months of heaviest rainfall. During this time passenger boats to some islands, such as Ko Tarutao, are suspended. If you find the weather on the Andaman coast unpleasant, you can easily travel to the southwestern gulf coast, where you're more likely to find the sun shining.

Top daytime temperatures average 32°C year-round (it's always hot!), with high humidity during the wet season.

National Parks

The most popular park along the Southern Andaman coast is the Ko Phi-Phi Marine National Park (p351), with its spectacular lagoons, beaches, impenetrable sea cliffs and rock climbing. Mu Ko Lanta Marine National Park (p359) is in the south of the quickly developing island of Ko Lanta and includes pristine islands, fine coral reefs and long sandy beaches. In the far south, bordering Malaysia, is the increasingly popular Ko Tarutao Marine National Park (p383), which preserves a group of jungle-covered islands, coral reefs and immaculate tropical beaches.

Lesser known parks include tiny Hat Chao Mai National Park (p371) near Trang, which contains coral-fringed islands; mountainous Khao Phanom Bencha National Park (see boxed text, p339) near Krabi town, whose jungles are full of rare birds; Satun Province's Mu Ko Phetra Marine National Park (see boxed text, p385) featuring islands and mangrove wildlife, including dugongs; Tharnbok Korannee National Park (p341), near the town of Ao Luk, which preserves sprawling areas of mangroves full of limestone caves and cave paintings; and Thale Ban National Park (p382), which straddles the Malay border, ideal for visa runs.

KRABI PROVINCE

With mind-bogglingly beautiful karsts (limestone rock formations) jutting up through tangled jungles, lining the crystalline beaches and forming knobby islands floating in the green sea, it's easy to understand why Krabi Province is the most popular region of the Southern Andaman coast. There are over 150 islands here and many are lined with the sorts of beaches you thought existed only on postcards. Not far from Krabi town, the province's small capital, the towering cliffs cast their shadows on mainland beaches; some feel as lost as a remote isle while others have every modern amenity right at hand. There's really something for everyone in this province whether it's partying and lounging on magnificent Ko Phi-Phi, living out your lost-on-a-desert-island fantasies on quiet Ko Jum, or scrambling up some of the world's top climbing routes at Railay.

It's not all islands and beaches, however. The region's interior features tracts of primary rainforest home to a plethora of tropical birds and animals, waterfalls, swimming holes and caves.

The mainland has excellent links to the rest of Thailand year-round, and in high season the islands do, too.

KRABI

กระบี่

pop 30,882

Upon arrival in Krabi Town, as it is affectionately known, you'll first notice those impossibly angular limestone karsts jutting from the mangroves and looming over the brackish Mae Nam Krabi. After breathing in their majesty you're attention will be drawn to a more unnatural wonder: the sheer volume of guesthouses and travel agencies packed into this compact, easy to navigate, quirky little town. Western restaurants are ubiquitous, as are gift shops that all sell the same 'ole trinkets. Yet if you hang out a while, you'll also see that there's an appealing, authentic, working-class scene going on in between the cracks. The day market on Th Sukhon is filled with mysterious treats and few foreign faces, likewise in several restaurants scattered, almost invisibly, throughout the tourist centre. And really, can anyone pass through town without doing a double take on the giant cavemen statues that hold up the traffic lights at the Th Maharat–Th Vogue crossroads?

Because a dozen island and beach destinations are serviced from this city, not many people linger here, although it's awfully cheap to do so. Boats can be organised to the islands of Ko Phi-Phi and Ko Lanta, and the beaches of Ao Nang and Railay. And if you do stay, succumb to a languid, yet life-affirming, mangrove wildlife tour.

Orientation

Th Utarakit is the main road into and out of Krabi and most places of interest are on the soi (laneways) that branch off it. Ferries to Ko Phi-Phi, Ko Lanta and other islands leave from Khlong Chilat (Krabi passenger pier) about 4km southwest of town, while long-tail boats to Railay depart from Khong Kha (Chao Fa) pier on Th Khong Kha. The Krabi bus terminal is north of the town centre at Talat Kao, near the junction of Th Utarakit, while the airport is nearly 17km northeast on Hwy 4.

Information

IMMIGRATION

Immigration Office (☎ 0 7561 1350; Th Chamai Anuson; ⊙ 8.30am-4pm Mon-Fri) Just south of the post and telephone office; handles visa extensions.

INTERNET ACCESS

Almost all of Krabi's budget travel agencies and restaurants offer internet access (per hour 40B to 60B).
World Net (cnr Th Utarakit & Th Issara; ⊙ 8am-11pm) Fast computers and switched-on staff.

INTERNET RESOURCES

Krabi Directory (www.krabidir.com) Has lots of information on Krabi Province and links to most of the tourist-oriented businesses in the area.

MEDICAL SERVICES

Krabi Hospital (☎ 0 7561 1210; Th Utarakit) Located 1km north of the town centre.

MONEY

Along Th Utarakit, Bangkok Bank, Krung Thai Bank, Siam City Bank and Siam Commercial Bank all exchange cash and travellers cheques and have ATMs.

POST

Post office (Th Utarakit) Just south of the turn-off to Khong Kha pier; there's a separate poste-restante entrance at the side.

TELEPHONE

Communications Authority of Thailand (CAT; Th Utarakit) About 500m north of Krabi Hospital, offering international calls.

TOURIST INFORMATION

Krabi Tourist Association (☎ 0 7562 2163; tatkrabi@ tat.or.th; Th Utarakit) Provides a free map of Krabi with a smile, but the staff don't speak great English.

TRAVEL AGENCIES

Thamit & Krabi Holiday Travel (☎ 0 7562 2998; 177 Th Utarakit) Helpful staff arranges air, boat and bus tickets, tours and island accommodation booking.
Thepparat Travel (☎ 0 7562 2048, 08 7454 2555; Th Maharat) Terrific source of information, with great prices on regional tours and transport.

Sights

There are not many must-see sights in Krabi itself. On the edge of town, **Wat Kaew** (Th Issara) contains some interesting 19th- and early-20th-century teak buildings in the back of the compound.

It's possible to climb one of the two limestone massifs of **Khao Khanap Nam**, just north of the town centre. A number of human skeletons were found in the caves here, thought to be the remains of people trapped during an ancient flood. To get here, charter a long-tail boat from Khong Kha pier for about 400B.

When it comes to sheer volume of seafood, few places compare with Krabi's **Morning Market** (Th Hem; ⊙ 5-9am), set in the cavernous Krabi Fresh Market warehouse. Think huge buckets of prawns, oysters and clams, massive tuna, schools of pink snapper and barracuda – and don't be surprised to see a shark among the bounty. This is also the place to eat a Thai breakfast, which may include any or all of the following: fried chicken and fish, noodle soup, pork ribs and black tea. Or you could just stick to the deep-fried doughnuts.

Activities

Sea Kayak Krabi (☎ 0 7562 3395, 08 9724 8579; www .seakayak-krabi.com; 40 Th Ruen Rudee) offers a wide variety of sea-kayaking tours, including to Ao Thalen (half-/full day 900/1500B), which has looming sea cliffs; Ko Hong (full day 1800B), famed for its emerald lagoon; and Ban Bho Tho (half-/full day 1000/1700B), which has sea caves with 2000- to 3000-year-old cave paintings. All rates include guides, lunch, fruit and drinking water.

While many diving agencies have offices on the islands and beaches, **Blue Juice Divers** (☎ 0 7563 0679; www.bluejuicedivers.com; Th Chao Fah) is in town and has two-dive packages to local islands (2900B). It also runs PADI Open Water courses (13,900B) and it has a brand new guesthouse.

For rock climbing, boats go from Krabi to Railay (see p348). For more activities in the area, see p342.

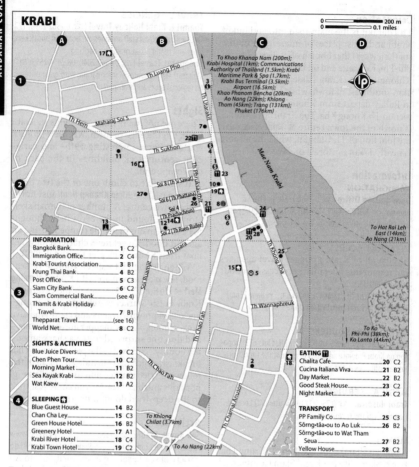

KRABI

0   200 m
0   0.1 miles

To Khao Khanap Nam (200m);
Krabi Hospital (1km); Communications
Authority of Thailand (1.5km); Krabi
Maritime Park & Spa (1.7km);
Krabi Bus Terminal (3.5km);
Airport (16.5km);
Khao Phanom Bencha (20km);
Ao Nang (22km); Khlong
Thom (45km); Trang (131km);
Phuket (176km)

To Hat Rai Leh
East (14km);
Ao Nang (21km)

To Ko
Phi-Phi (38km);
Ko Lanta (44km)

To Khlong
Chilat (3.7km)

To Ao Nang (22km)

INFORMATION	
Bangkok Bank	1 C2
Immigration Office	2 C4
Krabi Tourist Association	3 B1
Krung Thai Bank	4 B2
Post Office	5 C3
Siam City Bank	6 C2
Siam Commercial Bank	(see 4)
Thamit & Krabi Holiday Travel	7 B1
Thepparat Travel	(see 16)
World Net	8 C2

SIGHTS & ACTIVITIES	
Blue Juice Divers	9 C2
Chen Phen Tour	10 C2
Morning Market	11 B2
Sea Kayak Krabi	12 B2
Wat Kaew	13 A2

SLEEPING	
Blue Guest House	14 B2
Chan Cha Ley	15 C3
Green House Hotel	16 B2
Greenery Hotel	17 A1
Krabi River Hotel	18 C4
Krabi Town Hotel	19 C2

EATING	
Chalita Cafe	20 C2
Cucina Italiana Viva	21 B2
Day Market	22 B2
Good Steak House	23 C2
Night Market	24 C2

TRANSPORT	
PP Family Co	25 C3
Sŏrng·tǎa·ou to Ao Luk	26 B2
Sŏrng·tǎa·ou to Wat Tham Seua	27 B2
Yellow House	28 C2

Tours

Any travel agency in town can book tours with an environmental focus from Krabi. **Chen Phen Tour** (☎ 0 7561 2004; Th Utarakit) and others offer birdwatching tours in the mangroves around Krabi for about 500B per boat per hour (early morning is best); alternatively, you can hire a boat at Khong Kha pier for around 400B per hour. Keep an eye out for fiddler crabs and mudskippers on the exposed mud.

A number of companies offer day trips to **Khlong Thom**, about 45km southeast of Krabi on Hwy 4, taking in some nearby hot springs and freshwater pools. Expect to pay around 1050B, including transport, lunch and beverages; bring a swimsuit and good walking shoes. Various other 'jungle tour' itineraries are available.

Tours to surrounding islands are also deservedly popular.

Sleeping

New guesthouses (often named with a one or two letter initial) are appearing all over Krabi and most of them offer clean, tiled rooms with shared bathrooms. In the low season, prices plummet to as low as 150B. There are a few quality midrange options.

Blue Guest House (☎ 08 3640 8553; 35 Th Prachacheun; r 300-500B; 🅿 🛜) Yes, the dark halls are vaguely depressing, but the rooms are surprisingly clean and bright, if a bit basic. The more expensive rooms have air-con and hot water, along with satellite TV, and its well situated in the centre of town.

ourpick Chan Cha Lay (☎ 0 7562 0952; www.geo cities.com/chan_cha_lay; 55 Th Utarakit; r 200-650B; ❄) A superb choice and the top guesthouse in town. En suite rooms are decorated in Mediterranean blues and whites and have stylish, white-pebble and polished-concrete bathrooms. Shared-bathroom, fan-only rooms are plain, but spotless with firm beds.

Greenery Hotel (☎ 0 7562 3648; http://krabidir .com/thegreeneryhotel/index.htm; 167/2 Th Maharat; r 850B; ❄ ▯ ☎) Rooms here are modern with bright-coloured bedheads, cable TV and minifridges. The semi-outdoor hallways look out over the lush garden that lends a peaceful feel to the place. It's about a five- to 10-minute walk from the town centre.

Green House Hotel (☎ 0 7562 2960; 35 Th Maharat; r 1200B; ❄ ▯ ☎) Just opposite a narrow soi that leads to the morning market are four floors of superclean rooms with queen-sized beds, granite floors and wash basins, and satellite TV.

Krabi Maritime Park & Spa (☎ 0 7562 0028, in Bangkok 0 2719 0034; www.maritimeparkandspa.com; r from 3000B; ❄ ▯ ☒) On lovely riverside grounds and framed by those signature limestone karsts, this dated but swanky hotel is 2km from Krabi town proper. It sports a nightclub, stylish pool, fitness centre, spa and even a lake on which you can pedal swan-shaped boats. Rooms are classy and the balconies sport impressive views. Promotional rates of 1500B are often available. There are free shuttle buses to Krabi town and Ao Nang, and shuttle boats to Railay.

Krabi River Hotel (☎ 0 7561 2321; krabiriver@hot mail.com; 73/1 Th Khong Kha; r 700-1000B; ❄) Sure, it feels like a flashback from the early '80s, but rooms have newly tiled bathrooms and queen-sized beds, and offer terrific views of the dark river and misty mangroves.

Krabi Town Hotel (☎ 0 7561 1956; 9/11 Th Phattana; r 300-450B; ❄ ▯ ☎) Rooms are cramped, but clean with new bathroom tiles, glass-bowl sinks, wardrobes and flat screen TVs. More expensive rooms have hot water and air-con.

Eating

Night market (Th Khong Kha; meals 20-50B) The most popular and pleasant place for an evening meal is this market near the Khong Kha pier. The menus are in English but the food is authentic and excellent. Stalls here sell papaya salad, fried noodles, *dôm yam gûng* (prawn and lemon grass soup with mushrooms), grilled snapper, huge skillets of egg battered and fried oysters, all things satay, plus sweet milky Thai desserts.

Day Market (Th Sukhon; meals 20-60B) This market is even more authentic. Among the bouquets of flowers and weighty tropical-fruit stands are simmering curry pots, and banquet trays of steaming noodles with fried squid, sautéed beef, devilled eggs, fried fish and boiled corn. Eat daring.

Good Steak House (☎ 08 9724 7008; Th Utarakit; meals from 45B ⌚ breakfast, lunch & dinner) Airy and bright, with just a half-dozen tables and one large booth, the menu includes steaks and smoked sausage, but it's the wok stir-fried plates (from 45B) that merit mention here. Think sesame beef in oyster sauce, squid

---

DETOUR: KHAO PHANOM BENCHA NATIONAL PARK

This 50 sq km **park** (☎ 0 7566 0716; adult/child under 14yr 200/100B) protects a dramatic area of virgin rainforest along the spine of 1350m-high Khao Phanom Bencha, 20km north of Krabi. The park is full of well-signed trails to scenic waterfalls, including the 11-tiered **Huay To Falls**, 500m from the park headquarters. Nearby and almost as dramatic are Huay Sadeh Falls and Khlong Haeng Falls. On the way into the park you can visit **Tham Pheung**, a dramatic cave with shimmering mineral stalactites and stalagmites. The numerous trails that wend through the area are excellent for hiking.

The park is home to abundant wildlife – but only monkeys are commonly seen. Many bird-spotters come here to see white-crowned and helmeted hornbills, argus pheasants and the extremely rare Gurney's pitta. Local guides aren't absolutely necessary here, considering the well-marked trails. But visitors who hire guides tend to spot more wildlife, and have a deeper experience in general.

There is no public transport to the park, but it's easy to get here from Krabi by hired motorcycle; follow the sign-posted turn-off from Hwy 4. Park your motorcycle by the park headquarters and remember to apply the steering lock. Alternatively, you can hire a túk-túk (pronounced đúk đuk; motorised three-wheeled pedicab) for around 600B round-trip.

with hot basil, or prawns in chilli paste. Portions aren't huge, but at these prices who's complaining?

Chalita Cafe (☎ 08 1206 6299; Th Chao Fah; dishes 60-180B; ☾ dinner) Owned by a local Krabi woman whose family has lived here for generations, and set in an antiquated building, this is easily the most charming Thai restaurant in town. Burgundy and gold lanterns dangle from the teak rafters, black-and-white photos of old time Krabi are nailed to the teak walls, jazz wafts through the room like a welcome breeze and the Thai seafood dishes are as tasty as Billie Holiday's vibrato on a steamy tropical night.

Cucina Italiana Viva (☎ 0 7563 0517; 29 Th Phruksauthit; pizzas 160-260B) This is the place to sample tasty, thin-crust pizza, with a variety of cheeses and toppings to choose from. It has calzones, Italian wine, ice cream and coffee, and it delivers.

Getting There & Away

AIR

THAI Airways International (www.thaiairways.com), **Air Asia** (www.airasia.com), **Nok Air** (www.nokair.com), **Bangkok Air** (www.bangkokair.com) and **One 2 Go** (www.fly12go.com) all fly between Bangkok and Krabi (one-way around 1500B, 1¼ hours). Shop around – there are bargains to be had here.

Bangkok Air also has three weekly flights to Ko Samui (one-way 2300B).

BOAT

Boats to Ko Phi-Phi and Ko Lanta leave from the passenger pier at Khlong Chilat, about 4km southwest of Krabi. Travel agencies will arrange free transfers when you buy a boat ticket with them.

The largest boat operator is **PP Family Co** (☎ 0 7561 2463; www.phiphifamily.com; Th Khong Kha), which has a ticket office right beside the pier in town. All year round there are boats to Ko Phi-Phi (400B, 1½ hours) at 10am and 3pm.

From November to May, there is only one daily boat to Ko Lanta (400B, two hours) leaving Krabi at 11am. These can also stop at Ko Jum (one hour), where long-tails shuttle you to shore (though you'll pay the full 400B). During the wet season, you can only get to Ko Lanta by frequent air-con vans (300B, 2½ hours), which also run throughout the high season.

If you want to get to Railay, long-tail boats leave from Krabi's Khong Kha pier to Hat Rai Leh East (150B, 45 minutes) from 7.45am to

6pm. The boatmen will wait until they can fill a boat with 10 people before they leave; if you're antsy to go before then, you can charter the whole boat for 1500B.

BUS

Government Bus

With fewer touts and guaranteed departure times, taking a government bus from the **Krabi bus terminal** (cnr Th Utarakit & Hwy 4) in nearby Talat Kao, about 4km from Krabi, is an altogether more relaxing option than taking a private bus. Air-con government buses leave for Bangkok (700B, 12 hours) at 7am, 4pm and 5.30pm. There's a plush 24-seat VIP bus to Bangkok (1050B) departing at 5.30pm daily. From Bangkok's Southern Bus Terminal, buses leave at 7.30am and between 7pm and 8pm.

Other services for regular, air-con government buses:

Destination	Price	Duration	Frequency
Hat Yai	218B	5hr	frequent
Nakhon Si	89B	3hr	frequent
Phang-Nga	100B	2hr	hourly
Phuket	145B	3½hr	hourly
Ranong	270B	6hr	every 2hr
Surat Thani	130B	2½hr	frequent
Trang	90B	2hr	frequent

MINIVAN

Dozens of travel agencies in Krabi run air-con minivans and VIP buses to popular tourist centres throughout southern Thailand, but you may end up crammed cheek to jowl with other backpackers. Most travel agencies also offer combined minivan and boat tickets direct to Ko Samui (500B, 5½ hours) and Ko Pha-Ngan (550B, 7½ hours). Destinations from Krabi:

Destination	Price	Duration
Ao Luk	60B	1hr
Hat Yai	350B	3hr
Ko Lanta	250B	1½hr
Phuket	350B	2-3hr
Satun	550B	5hr
Trang	350B	2hr

SÖRNG·TÄA·OU

Sörng·tăa·ou run from the bus station to central Krabi and on to Hat Noppha Thara (40B), Ao Nang (60B) and the Shell Cemetery at Ao Nam Mao (70B; see p346). There are services from 6am to 6.30pm. In the high season there are less-frequent services until 10pm for a 10B surcharge. For Ao Luk (60B, one hour) there are frequent sŏrng·tăa·ou from the corner of Th Phattana and Th Phruksauthit; the last service leaves at around 3pm.

Getting Around

Central Krabi is easy to explore on foot, but the bus terminal and airport are both a long way from the town centre. A taxi from the airport to town will cost 350B. In the reverse direction, taxis cost 300B, while motorcycle taxis cost 250B. Agencies in town can arrange seats on the airport bus for 120B. Sŏrng·tăa·ou between the bus terminal and central Krabi cost 30B.

Hiring a vehicle is an excellent way to explore the countryside around Krabi. Most of the travel agencies and guesthouses in town can rent you a Yamaha motorbike for around 150B per day. **Yellow House** (☎ 0 7562 2809; Th Chao Fah) has a gleaming fleet of Yamahas and provides helmets. A few of the travel agencies along Th Utarakit rent out small 4WDs for 1200B to 1700B per day.

AROUND KRABI
Wat Tham Seua
วัดถ้ำเสือ

Thailand has a lot of wát (temples), but **Wat Tham Seua** (Tiger Cave Temple), 8km northwest of Krabi, is unique. The main wí·hăhn (hall) is built into a long, shallow limestone cave. On either side of the cave, dozens of gù·đì (monastic cells) are built into various cliffs and caves. You may see a troop of monkeys roaming the grounds.

The best part of the temple grounds can be found in a little valley behind the ridge where the bòht (central sanctuary) is located. Walk beyond the main temple building, keeping the cliff on your left, and you'll come to a pair of steep stairways leading to a 600m karst peak. The fit and fearless are rewarded with a Buddha statue, a gilded stupa and spectacular views; on a clear day you can see well out to sea.

The second stairway, next to a large statue of Kuan Yin (the Mahayana Buddhist Goddess of Mercy), leads over a gap in the ridge and into a valley of tall trees and limestone caves. Enter the caves on your left and look for light switches on the walls – walk chamber by chamber through the labyrinth until you rejoin the path on the other side.

If you go to the temple, please dress modestly: pants down to the ankles, shirts covering the shoulders and nothing too tight.

GETTING THERE & AWAY

A motorcycle taxi or túk-túk to Wat Tham Seua costs 200B while private taxis cost 250B. By sŏrng·tăa·ou, get on at Krabi's Th Maharat to the Talat Kao junction for 30B, then change to any bus or sŏrng·tăa·ou (20B) heading east on Hwy 4 towards Trang and tell the driver 'Wat Tham Seua' – these can be rather infrequent, though. Get off at the road on the left just past the small police station. Motorcycle taxis hang out here and drivers charge 25B to the wát, or you can walk the 2km straight up the road.

THARNBOK KORANNEE NATIONAL PARK
อุทยานแห่งชาติธารโบกขรณี

Close to the small town of Ao Luk, a stunning 46km drive northwest of Krabi, **Tharnbok Korannee National Park** (Than Bok; adult/child under 14yr 200/100B) protects a large area of islands, mangroves and limestone caves. The most important cave here is **Tham Pee Hua Toe** (Big-Headed Ghost Cave), reached by long-tail boat or sea kayak from the pier at Ban Bho Tho, 7km south of Ao Luk. Legend has it that a huge human skull was found in the cave, but the ghost story probably has more to do with the 2000- to 3000-year-old cave paintings that adorn the cave walls. Nearby **Tham Lot** (Tube Cave) can also be navigated by boat. Both caves are popular destinations for sea-kayaking tours from Krabi or Ao Nang, but you can also hire sea kayaks from local guides who grew up in the shadow of the Bho Tho pier. **Kayaking Bor Thor** (☎ 08 1273 9762) offers a three-hour tour, including lunch (1000B, 1500B including hotel pick up). Long-tails are available for 400B.

Just off the Bor Thor pier is a fabulous seafood restaurant. **Aree's Seafood** (☎ 08 1979 6389; dishes from 40B), with fresh fish at market prices, and lazy mangrove views. sprawls over a network of creaky piers.

There are at least seven other caves in the park, including **Tham Sa Yuan Thong**, a few kilometres southeast of Ao Luk, which has a natural spring bubbling into a pool. The national park also includes the uninhabited island of **Ko Hong**, with fine beaches, jungle-cloaked cliffs and a scenic hidden lagoon. Sea-kayak and long-tail tours come here from Ao Nang.

Just to the south of Ao Luk, the park headquarters is a popular picnic spot. There's an

1800m nature trail that links a series of babbling brooks and shady emerald pools linked by little waterfalls. The usual vendors sell noodles, fried chicken and *sôm·đam* (spicy green papaya salad). There's also a small **visitors centre** (6am-6pm; park admission 200B) that has displays in Thai and English.

Nearby Ao Them Lem is another stunning panorama of limestone and mangroves laced with concrete streets and sandy lanes. Day-trippers buzz in for long-tail trips to nearby *hôrng* (semisubmerged island caves) and lagoons, but otherwise this is a mellow, very local village with a few modest resorts.

Discovery Resort (08 1298 9533; 500 Moo 1 Kao Tong; bungalows 1300B;) is the tightest operation. The owner-operator speaks English and her attractive peaked-roof bungalows have cable TV and are almost brand new. She offers kayak tours and rentals, with the mangroves and looming limestone karsts a short drive away. The Ramshackle **Coconut Bungalows** (08 1537 0247; bungalows 500B) are a bit yellow at the edges, but they are clean, spacious and set in a gorgeous coconut grove, steps from the sea with views of *hôrng* and islands on the horizon.

Getting There & Away

The park headquarters is about 1.5km south of Ao Luk town along Rte 4039. Buses and sŏrng·tǎa·ou from Krabi stop on Hwy 4. Catch a government bus to Pha-Ngan or Phuket and ask to be let off at Ao Luk (80B, one hour), from where you can walk down to the park headquarters or take a motorcycle taxi for 15B. The easiest way to get to Tham Pee Hua Toe and Tham Lot is on a sea-kayaking tour from Krabi or Ao Nang.

To get to Ban Bho Tho from Ao Luk under your own steam, take a motorcycle taxi (70B) or a Laem Sak sŏrng·tǎa·ou (30B) to the Tham Pee Hua Toe turn-off on Rte 4039. From the junction it's about 2km to Ban Bho Tho along the first signposted road on the left.

Sŏrng·tǎa·ou from Krabi also travel directly to Ao Them Lem (60B).

AO NANG
อ่าวนาง
pop 12,400

Granted, you're not breaking ground, but there's still plenty to like about Ao Nang. It all starts with the beaches, framed by limestone headlands tied together by narrow strips of golden sand. In the dry season the sea glows a lovely turquoise hue, in the wet season riptides stir up the mocha shallows. If you're hankering for a swim in crystalline climes at any time of year, you can easily book a trip to the local islands that dot the horizon.

Ao Nang is compact, easy to navigate, and with the onrush of attractive, midrange development, accommodation standards are especially high, with substantial discounts possible. It's not as cheap (or as authentic) as Krabi town, but it's a lot cleaner and sunnier, and it's much better value than what you'll find in Railay and Phuket. There's plenty to do (mangrove tours? snorkelling trips?), it's only 40 minutes away from the Krabi airport, and a smooth 20-minute long-tail boat ride from stunning Railay. It's no wonder this beach is increasingly popular with travellers of every ilk.

Information

All the information offices, including **Ao Nang Visitor Center** (0 7562 8221), on the strip, are private tour agencies, and most offer international calls and internet access for around 1B per minute. Several banks have ATMs and foreign-exchange windows (open from 10am to 8pm) on the main drag.

Activities

Loads of activities are possible at Ao Nang and children under 12 years typically get a 50% discount.

KAYAKING

At least seven companies offer kayaking tours to mangroves and islands around Ao Nang. Popular destinations include the scenic sea lagoon at Ko Hong (1500B to 1800B), where you get to paddle inside the island and view collection points for sea swallow nests (spurred by demand for bird's-nest soup). There are also trips to the lofty sea cliffs and wildlife-filled mangroves at Ao Thalane (half-/full day 500/800B) and to the sea caves and 2000- to 3000-year-old paintings at Ban Bho Tho (half-/full day 700/900B; see p341) – the caves are also filled with layers of archaeological shell formations. Rates will vary slightly, but always include lunch, fruit, drinking water, sea kayaks and guides.

DIVING & SNORKELLING

Ao Nang has numerous dive schools offering trips to 15 local islands, including Ko Si, Ko Ha, Yava Bon and Yava Son. It costs about 3200B

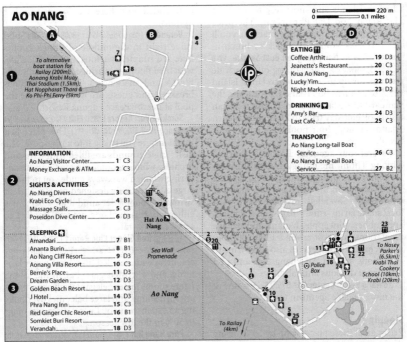

AO NANG

INFORMATION	
Ao Nang Visitor Center	1 C3
Money Exchange & ATM	2 C3

SIGHTS & ACTIVITIES	
Ao Nang Divers	3 C3
Krabi Eco Cycle	4 B1
Massage Stalls	5 C3
Poseidon Dive Center	6 D3

SLEEPING	
Amandari	7 B1
Ananta Burin	8 B1
Ao Nang Cliff Resort	9 C3
Aonang Villa Resort	10 C3
Bernie's Place	11 D3
Dream Garden	12 D3
Golden Beach Resort	13 C3
J Hotel	14 D3
Phra Nang Inn	15 C3
Red Ginger Chic Resort	16 B1
Somkiet Buri Resort	17 D3
Verandah	18 D3

EATING	
Coffee Arthit	19 D3
Jeanette's Restaurant	20 C3
Krua Ao Nang	21 B2
Lucky Yim	22 D3
Night Market	23 D2

DRINKING	
Amy's Bar	24 D3
Last Cafe	25 C3

TRANSPORT	
Ao Nang Long-tail Boat Service	26 C3
Ao Nang Long-tail Boat Service	27 B2

for two dives. Ko Mae Urai is one of the more unique local dives, with two submarine tunnels lined with soft and hard corals. Other trips run further afield to King Cruiser (three dives 4700B) and Ko Phi-Phi (two dives 3900B). A PADI Open Water course will set you back 14,900B to 16,000B. Reliable dive schools include **Ao Nang Divers** (☎ 0 7563 7244; www.aonang-divers.com) and **Poseidon Dive Center** (☎ 0 7563 7263; www.poseidon-diving.com). Most dive companies can also arrange snorkelling trips in the area.

ELEPHANT TREKKING
Several operators run elephant treks in the forest surrounding Ao Nang. **Nosey Parker's** (☎ 08 9291 0964; Rte 4202; adult/child 1hr trek 800/400B, half-day trek 1700/900B) is based about 7km from Ao Nang and offers forest treks where you can spot monkeys and exotic birds.

CYCLING
Take a Tour de Krabi by hooking up with **Krabi Eco Cycle** (☎ 0 7563 7250; www.krabiecocycle.com; 41/2 Muu 5; half-/full-day tour 800/1700B). The recommended full-day 15.5km pedal takes you through rubber plantations, small villages, hot

springs and, finally, a cooler dip at the aptly named Emerald Pool. Lunch is included on all tours except the half-day bike-only tour.

MASSAGE
Walk past the Golden Beach Resort and through those stone arches you'll enter Shangri-la for Thai massage lovers. Here are no less than 18 thatched, open-air massage stalls shaded by banyan trees with views of Ao Nang's finest stretch of sand. Massages are high quality, and cost just 100B to 200B per hour.

Courses
Krabi Thai Cookery School (☎ 0 7569 5133; www.thaicookeryschool.net; 269 Muu 2, Ao Nang, Rte 4204) is about 10km from Ao Nang between Wat Sai Thai and Ao Nam Mao and offers half-/one-day Thai-cooking courses for 1000/2200B; transfers are included in the price.

Tours
Any agency worth its salt can book you on one of the popular four-/five-island tours (about 2200B), which includes stops on Poda and

Chicken Islands and short respites on both Hat Railay and Hat Phra Nang. The price should include snorkelling gear but you'll need to pack your own snack or lunch in Railay. The **Ao Nang Long-tail Boat Service** (☎ 0 7569 5313; www.aonangboatco-op.com) offers private charters for up to six people to Hong Island (2500B) and Bamboo Island (3800B), and the standard five-island tour, of course. You can also book half-day trips to Poda and Chicken Islands (1700B, four hours) for up to four people.

Several tour agencies also offer tours to Khlong Thom, including visits to freshwater pools, hot springs and the Wat Khlong Thom Museum; the price is 1200/900B per adult/child. So-called 'mystery tours' visit local snake farms, rural villages, crystal pools, and rubber, pineapple, banana and papaya plantations and cost around 1300/600B per adult/child. Tour agencies also offer trips to attractions around Ao Phang-Nga and to a number of dubious animal shows.

Ao Nang Visitor Center (☎ 0 7562 8221) is one of the more reliable agents in town.

Sleeping

Prices at all these places drop by 50% during the low season.

BUDGET

Bernie's Place (☎ 0 7563 7093; r 400–700B; 🖳) Bernie's will excite the penniless in the high season – rooms max out at just 700B. You'll have to share a bathroom, but rooms are big and bright with ceiling fans, and some have sea views from a common verandah. The great downstairs bar offers protein-packed, backpacker-priced buffets (all you can eat for 190B).

J Hotel (☎ 0 7563 7878; j_hotelo@hotmail.com; r 400–1500B; 🖳 💻) J Hotel is an old standby. Large, bright rooms have new tiled floors, built-in desks, wardrobes and satellite TV, but some smell a bit musty. Sniff well before you commit.

Dream Garden (☎ 0 7563 7338; r 500–1200B; 🖳 💻) These large tiled rooms are cute and charming, with hot water, wood furnishings and a living area inside and out. The property is set back from the road down a long, narrow walkway.

MIDRANGE & TOP END

Most accommodation in Ao Nang falls into this bracket. The following places are rec-

ommended, but there are dozens of other options.

Verandah (☎ 0 7563 7454; r 1800B; 🖳 💻) Solid value right in the middle of things, rooms here are simple, spacious and immaculate, with tiled floors, minifridge, hot water, satellite TV and safety boxes. The price includes breakfast and guests are welcome to use the pool at nearby Peace Laguna Resort.

Somkiet Buri Resort (☎ 0 7563 7320; www.somkietburi.com; r 2850–3800B; 🖳 💻 🛜) This place just might inspire you to slip into a yoga pose. The lush jungle grounds are filled with ferns and orchids, while lagoons, streams and meandering wooden walkways guide you to the 26 large and creatively designed rooms. A great swimming pool is set amid it all – balconies either face this pool or a peaceful pond. The service is first-rate.

ourpick **Red Ginger Chic Resort** (☎ 0 7563 7777; 88 Moo 3; r 3000–5000B; 🖳 💻 🛜) Fashionable and colourful with detailed tiles, large paper lanterns, and a frosted glass bar in the lobby. Large rooms feature elegant wallpaper, modern furnishings and large balconies overlooking an expansive pool. Expect discounts of up to 50% in the low season.

Phra Nang Inn (☎ 0 7563 7130; vacationvillage.co.th; r incl breakfast from 3800B; 🖳 💻) An artistic explosion of rustic coconut wood, bright orange and purple paint and plenty of elaborate Thai tiles. There are two pools, and a second, similarly designed branch is across the road from the original.

Amandari (☎ 0 7563 7188; amandarikrabi.com; r 4000B; 🖳 💻 🛜) One of a handful of stylish new midrangers on Ao Nang's newest boulevard. Rooms have high-end tiled floors, built-in desks and wardrobes, and flat screen TVs. All rooms have balconies overlooking the lap pool. It's exceptional value in the low season.

Golden Beach Resort (☎ 0 7563 7870-74; www.krabigoldenbeach.com; r 4500–6000B, bungalows 6000–10,000B; 🖳 💻) This sprawling seven-year-old resort dominates the southernmost 400m of Ao Nang's beachfront. It's made up of large hotel blocks and stylish bungalows arranged in a tidy garden around a big pool. It's not hip but it most definitely feels good to be here.

Aonang Villa Resort (☎ 0 7563 7270; www.aonangvillaresort.com; r 4500–7500B; 🖳 💻) An understated yet swank, family-oriented seaside joint nestled in the shadow of a towering limestone bluff.

Ananta Burin (☎ 0 7566 1551; www.anantaburin resort.com; 166 Moo 3; r 5000-6000B; ✖ ♨ ☎) A new splashy boutique resort that horseshoes a pool and features nice design elements, including dark-wood built-in furnishings. First-floor rooms spill directly into the pool.

Ao Nang Cliff Resort (☎ 0 7562 6888; www.aonang cliffbeach.com; r from 8000B; ✖ ♨ ☎) Think sunken bedrooms, daybeds, duvets, and rain showers. The best-situated rooms have cliff and sea views, and the pool outside the lobby is stunning. If you come in the low season you can grab a room for 2500B.

Eating

At the western end of the beach is Soi Sunset, a narrow alley housing a number of seafood restaurants. They all have bamboo seating abutting the ocean, and model ice boats at the entrance showing off the day's catch.

Lucky Yim (meals 35-90B) If you're in the mood for a ramshackle local food joint, look no further. Ignore its Western dishes and dig into something tasty, spicy and authentic, like the fried squid with hot basil, seafood *đôm yam*, and massaman curry or vermicelli salad. it has plenty of vegie options, and serve complimentary fresh fruit with the bill. You'll smell it before you see it, and that's almost always a good sign.

Krua Ao Nang (☎ 0 7569 5260; Soi Sunset; dishes 60-400B; ☯ lunch & dinner) One of the best (and most popular) of the many options in Soi Sunset.

Coffee Arthit (☎ 0 7563 7847; breakfast from 100B; ☯ breakfast, lunch & dinner; ☎) Serves excellent all-day Western-style breakfasts (from continental to vegie and meaty fry-ups). It has tasty espresso, smoothies and protein shakes, too.

Jeanette's Restaurant (☎ 089474 6178; www.jeanette krabi.com; dishes 120-450B; ☯ breakfast, lunch & dinner) Always popular thanks to its signature bench seating, inkblot art on the walls and traditional Thai menu augmented with Swedish hits (that apple pie does sound good).

For meals on a budget, an informal night market serving *gài tôrt* (fried chicken), *pàt tai* (thin rice noodles fried with tofu, vegetables, egg and peanuts) and the like sets up along the road to Krabi (near McDonald's).

Drinking & Entertainment

Amy's Bar (☯ 11am-2am) Give Amy's points for its floral retro hippy design, which comes with flat screens streaming live football games, billiards and the ladies who love them. It's one of

several pubs on this soi, which runs perpendicular to the cliff.

Aonang Krabi Muay Thai Stadium (☎ 0 7562 1042; admission 800B, ringside 1200B) If you get tired of the beach-bars and video movies on the strip, this place has boisterous *moo·ay tai* (often spelt *muay thai*; Thai boxing) bouts every Friday and Monday from 8.45pm. A free sŏrng·tăa·ou runs along the strip at Ao Nang, collecting punters before the bouts.

Last Café (☯ 11am-7pm) At the far southern end of Hat Ao Nang is this barefoot beach cafe, with cold beer and cool breezes. Come here for a welcome blast of Ao Nang natural.

Getting There & Around

Ao Nang is served by regular sŏrng·tăa·ou from Krabi (50B, 20 minutes). These start at the Krabi bus terminal (add 10B to the fare) and then pass by the 7-Eleven on Th Maharat and the Khong Kha pier in Krabi, continuing on to Hat Noppharat Thara, Ao Nang and finally the Shell Cemetery. From Ao Nang to Hat Noppharat Thara or the Shell Cemetery it's 20B. Airport buses to and from Ao Nang cost 200B and leave throughout the day. Private taxis from the airport cost about 800B.

Dozens of places along the strip rent out small motorcycles for 150B to 200B. Budget Car Hire has desks at most of the big resort hotels and charges around 1600B per day for a dinky Suzuki micro-4WD.

Boats to Railay's Hat Rai Leh West are run by **Ao Nang Long-tail Boat Service** (☎ 0 7569 5313; www.aonangboatco-op.com) and rates are fixed at 100B per person or 800B for a private charter. It's a 15-minute journey – boats leave when full and operate between 8am and 4pm. During rough seas, boats leave from a sheltered cove about 200m west of Ao Nang – you can get here from Ao Nang by motorcycle taxi (30B), sŏrng·tăa·ou (10B) or on foot.

There are two boats a day to Ko Phi-Phi in the high season (450B, two hours, 9am and 1.30pm). Boats leave from nearby Hat Noppharat Thara (see p346). The morning boat makes the run year-round.

Tourist minibuses connect Ao Nang and Ko Lanta year-round (500B, two hours).

AROUND AO NANG
Hat Noppharat Thara

หาดนพรัตน์ธารา

North of Ao Nang, the golden beach goes a bit more au natural as it curves around a headland for 4km with limited development, until the sea eventually spills into a natural lagoon at the Ko Phi-Phi Marine National Park headquarters. Here scores of long-tails mingle with fishing boats and speedboats against a stunning limestone backdrop. The small visitors centre has displays on coral reefs and mangrove ecology, labelled in Thai and English.

The beach itself, with its hulking headlands, offshore islands, jade coves and lines of rollers rippling into shore is a popular local picnic spot on weekends.

SLEEPING & EATING

Laughing Gecko (☎ 08 1270 5028; www.laughinggecko99@hotmail.com; bungalows 400-700B) This island-style, bamboo-basic bungalow property has a great travellers' vibe, with frequent acoustic jam sessions, an artistically decorated restaurant with driftwood furniture and all-you-can-eat Thai buffets for 150B.

Government bungalows (☎ 0 7563 7200; bungalows 800B-1000B) These wooden, fan-cooled bungalows across the street from the beach are rustic yet well maintained and a terrific budget choice. Prices don't go up in the high season, but you'd better book ahead. Check in at national park headquarters near the harbour. Meals are no longer served on-site.

Sabai Resort (☎ 0 7563 7791; www.sabairesort.com; bungalows 1200-2200B; 🗶 🖭 🖳) The most professionally run of the area's bungalow properties. The tiled-roof bungalows are fan cooled with pebbled concrete patios overlooking a palm-shaded swimming pool, and a flower garden. It offers massage and accepts credit cards.

Sala Talay Resort & Spa (☎ 0 7581 0888; www.salatalay.com; r from 5800B; 🗶 🖭 🖳) Just around the bluff from Ao Nang proper, this intriguing new hotel is all moulded concrete, wood and stone. Architectural features include arched walls and frosted-glass awnings, and the property abuts the mangroves. Rooms have polished concrete floors, walls and washbasins, DVD players and flat screen TVs.

Around the national park headquarters there are several restaurants serving the usual Thai snacks, such as fried chicken and papaya salad, and there's a handful of dining stalls and seafood restaurants along the frontage road.

GETTING THERE & AWAY

Sŏrng·tăa·ou between Krabi and Ao Nang stop in Hat Noppharat Thara; the fare is 40B from Krabi or 10B from Ao Nang.

From November to May the *Ao Nang Princess* runs between Ko Phi-Phi Marine National Park headquarters and Ko Phi-Phi (400B, two hours). The boat leaves from the national park jetty at 10.30am, returning from Ko Phi-Phi at 3.30pm. It also stops at Railay's Hat Rai Leh West. This boat can also be used for day trips to Ko Phi-Phi. During the same high-season months there's also a direct boat to Phuket, leaving from the same pier at 3.30pm (400B) and to Ko Lanta at 10.30am (280B).

Shell Cemetery
สุสานหอย

About 9km east of Ao Nang at the western end of Ao Nam Mao is the **Shell Cemetery**, also known as Gastropod Fossil or Su-San Hoi. Here you can see giant slabs formed from millions of tiny 75-million-year-old fossil shells. There's a small **visitors centre** (admission 50B; ⏲ 8.30am-4.30pm), with geological displays and various stalls selling snacks. Sŏrng·tăa·ou from Ao Nang cost 30B.

RAILAY
ไร่เลย์

With Krabi Province's signature vertical limestone karsts framing cream-coloured beaches and luscious aquamarine sea, roadless Railay (also spelled Rai Leh) is the kind of place you wish you had to yourself – but it's no secret. With Ao Nang and Krabi just around the corner there's no stopping the flow of tourist traffic. Thankfully, impenetrable cliffs cut it off from the mainland hubbub. The only way to get here is by boat.

Although every beach has been filled in with resorts and bungalows, development is neatly (unless you count those, um, strategically placed electrical cords) tucked away in the coconut palms and lush gardens so it doesn't feel cramped. The beaches do get crowded in the high season but there is so much more to do here than tan and burn. Railay is best known for the hundreds of excellent rock-climbing routes afforded by the surrounding cliffs. Loads of climbing shops provide equipment rental and instruction for beginners and advanced climbers alike. If climbing isn't your thing, check out the local caves, go diving, join a snorkelling trip or rent a kayak.

Hat Rai Leh East is the most developed beach and is where boats from Krabi arrive. The shallow, muddy bay lined with mangroves

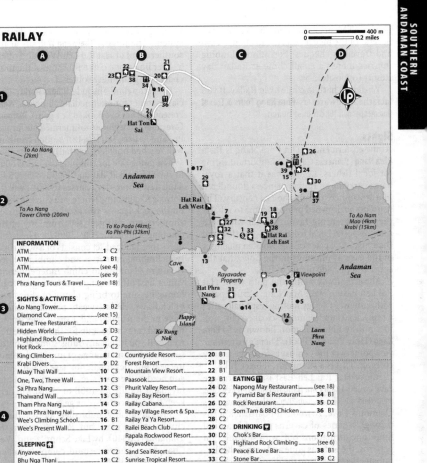

RAILAY

0   400 m
0   0.2 miles

INFORMATION
ATM	1 C2
ATM	2 B1
ATM	(see 4)
ATM	(see 9)
Phra Nang Tours & Travel	(see 18)

SIGHTS & ACTIVITIES
Ao Nang Tower	3 B2
Diamond Cave	(see 15)
Flame Tree Restaurant	4 C2
Hidden World	5 D3
Highland Rock Climbing	6 C2
Hot Rock	7 C2
King Climbers	8 C2
Krabi Divers	9 D2
Muay Thai Wall	10 C3
One, Two, Three Wall	11 C3
Sa Phra Nang	12 C3
Thaiwand Wall	13 C3
Tham Phra Nang	14 C3
Tham Phra Nang Nai	15 C2
Wee's Climbing School	16 B1
Wee's Present Wall	17 C2

SLEEPING
Anyavee	18 C2
Bhu Nga Thani	19 C2
Countryside Resort	20 B1
Forest Resort	21 B1
Mountain View Resort	22 B1
Paasook	23 B1
Phurit Valley Resort	24 D2
Railay Bay Resort	25 C2
Railay Cabana	26 D2
Railay Village Resort & Spa	27 C2
Railay Ya Ya Resort	28 C2
Railei Beach Club	29 C2
Rapala Rockwood Resort	30 D2
Rayavadee	31 C3
Sand Sea Resort	32 C2
Sunrise Tropical Resort	33 C2

EATING
Napong May Restaurant	(see 18)
Pyramid Bar & Restaurant	34 B1
Rock Restaurant	35 D2
Som Tam & BBQ Chicken	36 B1

DRINKING
Chok's Bar	37 D2
Highland Rock Climbing	(see 6)
Peace & Love Bar	38 B1
Stone Bar	39 C2

is not very appetising for swimming, but the beach is lined with hotels and guesthouses, and those headlands and limestone cliffs are miraculous – especially if you're roped in on the face. Plus, it's only a five-minute walk over the peninsula to the lounge-worthy sands of **Hat Rai Leh West**. This near-flawless, white wonder is the best place to swim, sunbathe, join an afternoon pick-up football game or just watch the sun go down when the cliffs are illuminated gold then red with falling light. Tastefully designed midrange resorts are sprinkled throughout, and long-tail boats make pick-ups and drop-offs from here to nearby Ao Nang. At the tip of the headland, **Hat Phra Nang** is quite possibly one of the world's most beautiful beaches, with a squeaky-clean cres-

cent of pale, golden sand, framed by karst cliffs carved with caves home to frolicking monkeys. Those distant limestone islets peeking out of the cerulean sea are Chicken (Ko Hua Khwan) and Poda islands. Rayavadee, the peninsula's most exclusive resort, is the only one on this beach but anyone can drop a beach towel. **Hat Ton Sai** is the grittier climbers' retreat and is reached by long-tail (either directly from Ao Nang or from Hat Rai Leh West) or by a sweaty 20-minute scramble from the northern end of Hat Rai Leh West.

Information

The website www.railay.com has lots of information about Railay. There are two ATMs along Hat Rai Leh East. On Hat Ton Sai there is one ATM near the Ton Sai Bay Resort. Several of the bigger resorts can change cash and travellers cheques. For minor climbing injuries there's a small clinic at Railay Bay Resort (opposite).

Wi-fi isn't hard to come by in Railay. If you lack the hardware, try **Phra Nang Tours & Travel** (internet per min 1B) on east beach.

Sights

At the eastern end of Hat Phra Nang is **Tham Phra Nang** (Princess Cave), an important shrine for local fishers. Legend has it that a royal barge carrying an Indian princess floundered in a storm here during the 3rd century. The spirit of the drowned princess came to inhabit the cave, granting favours to all who paid their respects. Local fishermen – Muslim and Buddhist – still place carved wooden phalluses in the cave as offerings in the hope that the spirit will provide plenty of fish.

About halfway along the path from Hat Rai Leh East to Hat Phra Nang, a crude path, with somewhat dodgy footing (especially after a rain), leads up the jungle-cloaked cliff wall to a murky hidden lagoon known as **Sa Phra Nang** (Holy Princess Pool). There's a dramatic viewpoint over the peninsula from the nearby cliff top. This is a strenuous, if brief, hike.

Above Hat Rai Leh East is another large cave called **Tham Phra Nang Nai** (Inner Princess Cave; adult/child 40/20B; ☽ 5am-8pm), also known as Diamond Cave. A wooden boardwalk leads through a series of caverns full of beautiful limestone formations but, with shifting rain patterns, the water is gone and with it the illuminati effects that won the diamond moniker. But even in monochrome conditions, it's still worth a stroll.

Activities

ROCK CLIMBING

With nearly 500 bolted routes, ranging from beginner to challenging advanced climbs, all with unparalleled cliff-top vistas, it's no surprise that Railay is among the top climbing spots in the world. You could spend months climbing and exploring – and many people do. The newest buzz is deep-water soloing where climbers free-climb ledges over deep water – if you fall you will most likely just get wet, so even daring beginners can give this a try.

Most climbers start off at **Muay Thai Wall** and **One, Two, Three Wall**, at the southern end of Hat Rai Leh East, which have at least 40 routes graded from 4b to 8b on the French system. The mighty **Thaiwand Wall** sits at the southern end of Hat Rai Leh West and offers a sheer limestone cliff with some of the most challenging climbing routes.

Other top climbs include: **Hidden World** (some classic routes for intermediate climbers), **Wee's Present Wall** (an overlooked 7c+ gem), **Diamond Cave** (another beginner-to-intermediate favourite) and **Ao Nang Tower** (a three-pitch climbing wall reached only by long-tail).

The going rate for climbing courses is 800B to 1000B for a half-day and 1500B to 2000B for a full day. Three-day courses (6000B) will involve lead climbing, where you clip into bolts on the rock face as you ascend. Experienced climbers can rent gear sets from any of the climbing schools for 800/1300B for a half-/full day – the standard set consists of a 60m rope, two climbing harnesses and climbing shoes. If you're planning to climb independently, you're best off bringing your own gear from home; be sure to bring plenty of slings and quickdraws, chalk (sweaty palms are inevitable in the tropics) and a small selection of nuts and cams as backup for thinly protected routes. If you forget anything, some climbing schools sell a small range of imported climbing gear but they might not have exactly what you need or the right size. A woven rattan mat (available locally for 100B to 150B) will help keep the sand out of your gear.

Several locally published books detail climbs in the area, but *Rock Climbing in Thailand* (US$40), by Elke Schmitz and Wee Changrua, is one of the more complete guides. Recommended climbing shops:

Highland Rock Climbing (☎ 08 0693 0374; chaow_9 @yahoo.com; Hat Rai Leh East) If you're bunking on the mountain, this is the man to climb with.

Hot Rock (☎ 0 7562 1771; www.railayadventure.com; Hat Rai Leh West) Has a very good reputation and is owned by one of the granddaddies of Railay climbing.

King Climbers (☎ 0 7563 7125; www.railay.com; Hat Rai Leh East) One of the biggest, oldest, most reputable and commercial schools.

Wee's Climbing School (☎ 08 1149 9745; www.tonsai basecamp; Hat Ton Sai) Arguably the most professional outfit in the area.

WATER SPORTS

Several **dive** operations in Railay run trips out to Ko Poda and other neighbouring dive sites. **Krabi Divers** (☎ 0 7562 1686/7; www.krabidivers.com; Hat Rai Leh East), at Railay Viewpoint Resort, charges

2000B for two local dives at outlying islands. A three- or four-day PADI Open Water dive course is 12,000B.

Full-day, multi-island **snorkelling** trips to Ko Poda, Chicken Island and beyond can be arranged through any of the resorts for about 1800B (maximum six people). If you just want to snorkel off Railay, most resorts can rent you a mask set and fins for 100B to 150B each.

Flame Tree Restaurant (Hat Rai Leh West) was under renovation when we visited, but it was still renting out **sea kayaks** for 200B per hour or 1000B per day. Overnight trips to deserted islands can be arranged with local boat owners, but you'll need to bring your own camping gear and food.

Sleeping & Eating
HAT RAI LEH WEST
It's all midrange and top-end options on this beach (where sunsets are fabulous), but rates often drop by 30% in the low season. All the resorts have decent restaurants.

Sand Sea Resort (☎ 0 7562 2608; www.krabisandsearesort.com; bungalows 1950-5950B; ✇ 🖳 ✇) The lowest-priced resort on this beach offers everything from ageing fan-only bungalows to newly remodelled cottages with every amenity. The grounds aren't as swank as the neighbours, but rooms are comfy enough and there's a peaceful karst-view, foliage-enclosed pool – if you're able to tear yourself away from that sublime beach out the front, that is. The restaurant here does a full buffet breakfast, which is included in the room rate.

Railei Beach Club (☎ 08 6685 9359; www.raileibeachclub.com; houses from 2800B) Hidden in forested grounds at the northern end of the beach, this is a collection of Thai-style homes, each unique in size and design, rented out on behalf of foreign owners. They come with patios, kitchens and amenities to make extended stays very comfortable. Some sleep up to eight people. It's a superb deal and location, so book well in advance for the high season.

our pick Railay Bay Resort (☎ 0 7562 2570-2; www.railaybayresort.com; bungalows 3700-16,800B; ✇) The amoeba-shaped blue pool here faces onto the best bit of the beach so you can switch between salt and fresh water. Elegant bungalows with big windows, white walls and rustic-chic timber terraces run right across the peninsula to Hat Rai Leh East via gorgeously planted grounds and a second pool. Bungalows on the east side are older, with dark-tinted windows,

and are the least expensive. The spa, which also overlooks the sea, offers a host of treatments at very reasonable prices.

Railay Village Resort & Spa (☎ 0 7563 7990; www.somkietburi.com; bungalows 7500-10,500B; ✇ ✇) A two-year-old villa property featuring posh bungalows with private hot tubs spread throughout gardens of lily ponds, tall palms and gurgling fountains, and alongside two pools. The open-air restaurant serves excellent green curry and particularly convincing Western-style pastas that are a boon if you're travelling with children.

HAT RAI LEH EAST
Often referred to as Sunrise Beach, it recedes to mud flats during low tide. The resorts on the hillside above the beach get sea breezes, but down on the beach it can feel like a sauna in the evenings. The best-value lodging is in the highlands. The following rates drop by half in the low season.

our pick Railay Cabana (☎ 0 7562 1733, 08 4057 7167; bungalows 350-600B) Superbly located high in the hills in a bowl of karst cliffs, this is your hippie tropical mountain hideaway. Simple, clean thatched-bamboo bungalows are surrounded by mango, banana and guava groves.

Railay Ya Ya Resort (☎ 0 7562 2593; www.railayyayaresort.com; r 1600-2000B) The large yet cosy wooden rooms are a bit dark, and some seem to shudder with every footstep, but the treehouse vibe works. Its on-site *sôm đam* cart, and low-season discounts (rooms 300B to 700B) make this place a steal.

Phurit Valley Resort (☎ 08 4096 4994; bungalows 650B, r 750-1100B) No other place on the peninsula has this combination of jungle, karst and sea views. The new rooms in the three-storey eyesore don't exactly blend in, but they are spotless and are easily the most comfy jungle rooms on offer. If you're in the mood for earthy grab a fan-cooled, cold-water bamboo bungalow.

Sunrise Tropical Resort (☎ 0 7562 2599; www.sunrisetropical.com; bungalows 2550-3700B; ✇ ✇) Bungalows here rival the better ones on Hat Rai Leh West but are priced for Hat Rai Leh East – it's only a five-minute walk to the west beach and even easier to access Hat Tham Phra Nang (the best beach), so we think this is one of the best deals in Railay.

Anyavee (☎ 0 7581 9437; www.anyavee.com; bungalows from 2600B; ✇ ✇) A quirky resort but one with more style than most on this beach. Bungalows here have lots of windows making them bright but not private. Interiors are country chic, with cream-and-beige plaid duvets and plenty of hardwoods.

Bhu Nga Thani (☎ 0 7581 9451; www.bhungathani.com; r 7500B, villas 25,000B) The newest, splashiest and easily the priciest spot on Railay East. The entry is elegant with louvred bridges over reflection pools. Rooms are exceptionally well built with high ceilings, limestone floors and all the amenities of a 4½ star joint, including wide terraces with magnificent karst views.

Rapala Rockwood Resort (☎ 08 4191 5326; bungalows 500-750B) Ramshackle bamboo bungalows have verandahs, bathrooms, mosquito nets and fans. The delightful location atop a hill means breezes and views of the sea (and your neighbours). The cushion-lined restaurant here is perfect for chilling – it serves Thai and Indian food and is run by a charming Thai grandma.

Napong May Restaurant (dishes 60-90B) This humble stall set just off east beach turns out all your spicy Thai faves for cheap. It has fried rice and noodles, curries and catfish, *sôm đam* and fried chicken. All praises be to the kitchen's matriarch. She means business, and her husband can turn a spoon just fine, too.

ourpick Rock Restaurant (meals 80-120B; ☟ breakfast, lunch & dinner) Amid dense jungle and karst cliffs, it's best to dine here during the day to appreciate the view. But the food (Thai and Western) is great anytime. Try to get one of the intimate shaded booths at the jungle's edge.

HAT THAM PHRA NANG

There's only one place to stay on this magnificent beach and it's a doozy.

Rayavadee (☎ 0 7562 0740-3; www.rayavadee.com; pavilions 22,300-38,000B; villas 72,000-128,000B) This exclusive colonial-style resort has sprawling, immaculate grounds navigated by golf buggies and dotted with meandering ponds. The two-storey, mushroom-domed pavilions are filled with antique furniture and every mod con you need in a home away from home. Classical music wafts throughout the lounge areas, and there are yoga classes for guests and a first-rate spa. Two restaurants grace Hat Tham Phra Nang and nonguests can stop in for pricey but divine Thai or Mediterranean meals.

HAT TON SAI

The beach here isn't spectacular, but with so many good climbs all around, most people don't mind. Bars and bungalows are nestled in the jungle behind the beach.

Paasook (☎ 08 9645 3013; bungalows 300-800B) Definitely the most stylish budget establishment on Ton Sai: wooden bungalows are huge, have elongated floor-to-ceiling windows and concrete floors. This place is at the far western end of the beach, right beneath Groove Tube. The gardens are lush, management is friendly and there's a rustic-chic outdoor restaurant, perfect for steamy evenings.

ourpick Countryside Resort (☎ 08 5473 9648; countryside-resort.com; cabins 850B; ☒ ▢ ☎) A UK-owned property with two rows of attractive, solar-powered cabins, which makes them the most ecologically sound in Railay. There are high ceilings, lace curtains and ceiling fans. Top row nests have insane karst views, and you'll love Ollie, the property mascot.

Forest Resort (☎ 08 0143 8261; bungalows 1000B) A collection of large, basic, thatched bungalows perched on a flowery hillside with typically amazing limestone views. They also have a groovy restaurant, made from sculpted wood, serving Indian food among other dishes.

Mountain View Resort (☎ 0 7562 2610-3; bungalows 1300-1900B; ☒) Bright, cheery and immaculate with mint green walls, tiled floors and crisp sheets in lodge-like environs. Some rooms are slightly musty, so sniff around.

Pyramid Bar & Restaurant (drinks from 30B, dishes from 60B) The most popular hangout in Ton Sai. They do fresh fruit lassis, shakes, ciabatta and baguette sandwiches with home-baked loaves, and tasty espresso drinks in thatched treehouse environs. Hit one of the hammocks or lounge on the floor cushions and stay a while.

Som Tam & BBQ Chicken (meals 60B) Look for the bamboo dining tables and smoking grills just back from the beach. They sell three dishes: grilled chicken, *sôm dam* and mango with sticky rice. Delicious!

Drinking

There's a bunch of places on the beaches where you can unwind and get nicely inebriated.

Chok's Bar (Hat Rai Leh East; ☟ 7pm-2am) A stylish, laid-back bamboo bar with live music almost nightly, decorated with bamboo mats and plenty of pillows to lean into. A popular hang when we came through.

Highland Rock Climbing (☎ 08 0693 0374; Hat Rai Leh East) Part climbing school, part cafe cobbled from driftwood and dangling with orchids. The owner, Chaow, sources his beans from sustainable farms in Chiang Rai, and serves the best coffee on the peninsula.

our pick Peace & Love Bar (☎ 08 9472 8379; Hat Ton Sai) The concrete bar is streaked with colourful, musical love murals. The bandstand is always set up for a jam and bongos are scattered throughout. Driftwood and lanterns dangle in the adjacent art studio, along with photos of Marley, Lennon and a prominent shot of the King blowing jazz with Benny Goodman.

Stone Bar (Hat Rai Leh East) Up the hill towards the Highland Resort, Stone Bar has an awesome setting under a massive climbing wall. It's enveloped by jungle and has a drinking gazebo perched atop a boulder. Bob Marley looms like a patron saint. Mojitos (160B) are poured liberally.

Getting There & Around

The only way to get to Railay is by long-tail boat, either from Khong Kha pier in Krabi or from the seafronts of Ao Nang and Ao Nam Mao. Boats between Krabi and Hat Rai Leh East leave every 1½ hours from 7.45am to 6pm when they have 10 people (150B, 45 minutes). Chartering a special trip will set you back 1500B.

Boats to Hat Rai Leh West or Hat Ton Sai leave from the eastern end of the promenade at Ao Nang. The fare is 100B (15 minutes), but the boats don't leave until eight people show up. Private charters cost 800B. If seas are rough, boats leave from a sheltered cove just west of Krabi Resort in Ao Nang. You can be dropped at Hat Phra Nang or Hat Ton Sai for the same fare.

During exceptionally high seas the boats from Ao Nang and Krabi stop running, but you may still be able to get from Hat Rai Leh East to Ao Nam Mao (100B, 15 minutes), where you can pick up a sŏrng·tăa·ou to Krabi or Ao Nang.

From October to May the *Ao Nang Princess* runs from Hat Noppharat Thara National Park headquarters to Ko Phi-Phi with a stop at Hat Rai Leh West. Long-tails run out to meet the boat at around 9.15am from in front of the Sand Sea Resort (p349). The fare to Ko Phi-Phi from Railay is 250B.

KO PHI-PHI DON
เกาะพีพีดอน

Oh, how beauty can be a burden. Like Marilyn Monroe, Phi-Phi Don's stunning looks have become its own demise. Everyone wants a piece of her. Though not exactly Hollywood, this is Thailand's Shangri-la: a hedonistic paradise where tourists cavort in azure seas and snap pictures of long-tails puttering between craggy cliffs. With its flashy, curvy, blonde beaches and bodacious jungles it's no wonder that Phi-Phi has become the darling of the Andaman coast. And, like any good starlet, this island can party hard all night and still look like a million bucks the next morning. Unfortunately, nothing can withstand this glamorous pace and unless limits are set, Phi-Phi is in for an ecological crash.

Although Ko Phi-Phi will seem expensive compared to the rest of Thailand (aside from Phuket and Ko Samui), if you compare it to other pin-up islands around the planet, we think you'll discover this 'paradise' comes pretty damn cheap.

Orientation & Information

Ko Phi-Phi Don (usually just referred to as Ko Phi-Phi) is part of the Ko Phi-Phi Marine National Park, which also includes uninhabited Ko Phi-Phi Leh. Development is forbidden on Phi-Phi Don's little sister, but it can be visited on popular day trips.

Phi-Phi Don is actually two islands joined by a narrow isthmus separating the prized beaches of Ao Ton Sai and Ao Lo Dalam. Boats dock at the large concrete pier at Ao Ton Sai and a sandy path, crammed full of rickety shacks housing tour operators, bungalows, restaurants, bars and souvenir shops, stretches along the beach towards Hat Hin Khom. The maze of small streets in the middle of this sand bar is equally packed, and is euphemistically called 'tourist village'. On the other side of the concrete scrum is breathtaking Ao Lo Dalam. The bay's narrow mouth shelters a placid turquoise bay, framed by jagged limestone cliffs. It's a screen saver. And if you come here at sunset you can take in its soul-soothing beauty, serenaded only by the gently lapping sea. After dark, on the other hand, this place rumbles with music until 4am every night of the week. So…there's that.

Hat Yao (Long Beach) faces south and has some of Phi-Phi Don's best coral reefs and one of its most impressive swimming beaches. The beautifully languid and long eastern bays of Hat Laem Thong and Ao Lo Bakao are reserved for top-end resorts, while the smaller bays of Hat Phak Nam, Hat Rantee and Ao Toh Ko play host to a few low-key bungalow affairs.

ATMs and internet shops (per minute 2B) are spread thickly throughout the tourist

SOUTHERN
ANDAMAN COAST

KO PHI-PHI DON

0 — 2 km
0 — 1 mile

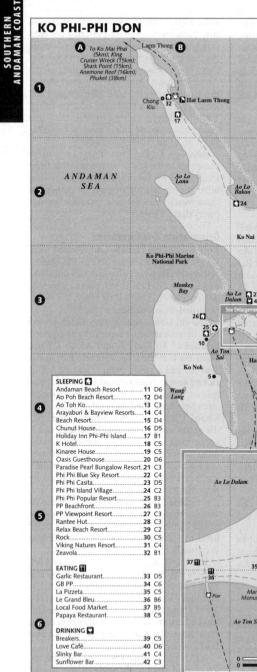

A To Ko Mai Phai
(5km); King
Cruiser Wreck (15km);
Shark Point (15km);
Anemone Reef (16km);
Phuket (38km)

Laem Thong

Chong
Klu

Hat Laem Thong

ANDAMAN
SEA

Ao Lo
Lana

Ao Lo
Bakao

Ko Phi-Phi Marine
National Park

Monkey
Bay

Ko Nai

Hat Phak Nam

Ao Lo
Dalam

Hat Rantee

Ao Toh
Ko

ANDAMAN
SEA

Ao Lo
Mu Di

See Enlargement

Ao Ton
Sai

Ko Nok

Hat Hin Khom

To Krabi (38km)

Wang
Long

Laem Hin

Hat Yao

Laem Phaw

To Ko Phi-Phi Leh (5km);
Ko Binda Nai & Ko Bida Nok (6km);
Hin Bida (8km); Ko Lanta (30km);
Hin:Daeng (70km);
Hin:Muang (70km)

To Phuket
(42km)

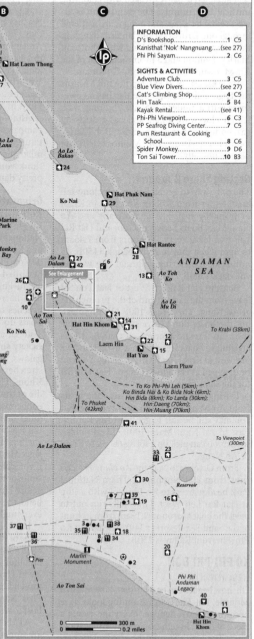

Ao Lo Dalam

To Viewpoint
(300m)

Reservoir

Ao Ton Sai

Pier

Marlin
Monument

Phi Phi
Andaman
Legacy

Hat Hin
Khom

0 — 300 m
0 — 0.2 miles

village but aren't available on the more remote eastern beaches. Wi-fi is available at **D's Bookshop** (7am-10pm) in the heart of the tourist village. It also sells new and used fiction, and pours a decent espresso (50B).

Phi-Phi Sayam (0 7560 1190; internet per min 2B; 8am-11pm) books boats to Phuket, Krabi, Ao Nang and Lanta. On the Dalam side, seek out **Kanisthat 'Nok' Nangnuang** (08 9195 0692; nokk-td@hotmail.com). Her full-service travel agency is set in front of Blue View Divers at the PP Viewpoint Resort.

Activities

The strenuous climb to the **Phi-Phi viewpoint** is a rewarding short hike. Follow the signs from the road heading east towards Ao Lo Dalam from the tourist village. The viewpoint is reached via a 300m vertical climb that includes hundreds of steep steps and narrow twisting paths. The views from the top are amazing – this is where you can see Phi-Phi's lush mountain butterfly brilliance in full bloom. From here you can head over the hill through the jungle to the peaceful eastern beaches for a DIY snorkelling tour.

Ao Lo Dalam is ripe for exploration. Stop at the **Kayak Rental** (per hr 200B, full day 600B) stall on the sand in front of Slinky Bar, paddle out to the headland and dive in.

DIVING & SNORKELLING

The combination of perfectly clear Andaman waters and abundant coral means that Ko Phi-Phi is home to some enjoyable dive sites. Dozens of shops compete for your business and tout PADI Open Water courses.

The shipwrecked car ferry *King Cruiser* lies only 12m below the surface and is visited by dive outfits from both Ko Phi-Phi and Phuket, as is **Shark Point** – which can have up to 20m visibility on a good day. Here you'll find resident leopard sharks, turtles and gardens of hard and soft corals with eye-popping purples, oranges and yellows.

All of Phi-Phi's dive shops charge the same price – an Open Water certification course costs 12,500B, while the standard two-dive trips cost 3200B, or 3900B if you want to visit Shark Point or the wreck of the *King Cruiser*.

You can also dive out at **Hin Daeng** and **Hin Muang**, stunning coral-crusted pinnacles that drop to 70m some 70km off Ko Phi-Phi (5500B for two dives). These are the best dive sites in the Phi-Phi orbit and arguably the best in the South Andaman, not least because of the frequent whale shark sightings. Local Phi-Phi dives generally max out at 18m, and are calming sheltered explorations with some nice soft corals, and an occasional migrating manta around the **Bida Islands**.

Adventure Club (08 1895 1334; www.phiphidivecamp.com), the longest tenured outfit, and **Blue View Divers** (0 7581 9395; www.blueviewdivers.com) are the most ecofriendly outfitters on the island. Adventure Club is working on reef rehabilitation along Phi-Phi Leh, while Blue View focuses on community involvement and beach clean-ups (its latest cleared up 700 tonnes of rubbish) and is the only shop to offer dives from a long-tail. **PP Seafrog Diving Center** (0 7560 1073, 08 7920 0680) is a boutique shop with a great wooden dive boat.

AFTER THE TSUNAMI

The tragic Boxing Day tsunami of 2004 wiped out nearly every standing structure on the densely populated twin bays of Ao Ton Sai and Ao Lo Dalam. In terms of loss of life and property, Ko Phi-Phi Don was second only to Khao Lak and Bang Niang in Phang-Nga Province. Following the tsunami it was hoped it could be used as an opportunity to rectify past development and tourism mistakes, but Ao Ton Sai today looks almost exactly as it did before 26 December 2004, and Ao Lo Dalam may be in even worse shape, with competing beach parties that rock until 4am keeping most of the island awake. On the resources front, a water-treatment plant, opened in 2006, has supposedly suspended water-supply issues and rubbish is starting to head into rubbish bins. Do your part in recycling – look for the rubbish bins and deposit as much garbage as you can find.

Reminders of the tsunami still linger on Phi-Phi through pictures of the volunteers that helped rebuild restaurants and guesthouses, memorials to those who died and a palpable air of thanks, both for being alive and to the tourist industry that helped bring this island back into business – this appreciation extends to all visitors, old and new, and you can't help but feel touched by it.

One popular snorkelling destination is **Ko Mai Phai** (Bamboo Island), north of Phi-Phi Don. There's a shallow area here where you may see small sharks. Snorkelling trips cost between 600B and 2400B, depending on whether you travel by long-tail or motorboat. There is also good snorkelling along the eastern coast of **Ko Nok**, near Ao Ton Sai, and along the eastern coast of **Ko Nai**. If you're going on your own, most bungalows and resorts rent out a snorkel, mask and fins for 150B to 200B per day.

ROCK CLIMBING
Yes, there are good limestone cliffs to climb on Ko Phi-Phi, and the views are spectacular. The main climbing areas are **Ton Sai Tower**, at the western edge of Ao Ton Sai, and **Hin Taak**, a short long-tail boat ride around the bay. There are some good climbing shops on the island and most places charge around 1000B for a half-day of climbing or 1500B to 2000B for a full day, including instruction and gear. **Spider Monkey** (☎ 07581 9384; www.spidermonkeyclimbing.com) is run by Soley, one of the most impressive climbers on Phi-Phi. One of the bigger outfits around is **Cat's Climbing Shop** (☎ 08 1787 5101; www.catclimbingshop.com) in the tourist village. Cat's gets good reports for safety and service.

Courses
Thai-food fans can take cooking courses at the recommended **Pum Restaurant & Cooking School** (☎ 08 1521 8904; www.pumthaifoodchain.com; classes 450-4650B) in the tourist village. You'll learn to make some of the excellent dishes that are served in its restaurant and go home with a great cookbook.

Tours
As well as the popular long-tail boat tours to Phi-Phi Leh and Ko Mai Phai (Bamboo Island), tour agencies can arrange sunset tours to Monkey Bay and the beach at Wang Long (600B). Adventure Club (see p353) is a green business that was instrumental in helping clean up Phi-Phi's underwater habitat after the tsunami. It runs educational, ecofocused tours and dive trips, including guaranteed shark-watching snorkelling trips, reef-restoration dive trips, and 007 trips that are shrouded in secrecy, always changing and often involving a mix of hiking, snorkelling, rappelling into limestone caves and copious amounts of natural beauty.

Sleeping
Finding accommodation on this ever-popular island has never been easy and you can expect serious room shortages at peak holiday times. Masses of touts meet incoming boats and, while often annoying, can make your life easier.

Be sure you lock the door while you sleep and close all the windows when you go out. Break-ins can be a problem.

AO TON SAI & AO LO DALAM
We hate to sound like your annoyed granny, but facts are facts and Phi-Phi noise pollution has never been worse. Nightlife rules to the point that you can often hear music from more than one sound system pound into your bedroom until 2am on the Ao Ton Sai side and until 4am on Ao Lo Dalam. The most peaceful accommodation can be found along

---

KO PHI-PHI DIVE SITES

The dive sites around Ko Phi-Phi are some of the best in Thailand, and leopard sharks and hawksbill turtles are very common. Whale sharks sometimes make cameo appearances around Hin Daeng, Hin Muang, Hin Bida and Ko Bida Nok in February and March. The top five dives at Ko Phi-Phi:

Dive site	Depth	Features
Anemone Reef	17-26m	Hard coral reef with plentiful anemones and clownfish.
Hin Bida Phi-Phi	5-30m	Submerged pinnacle with hard coral, turtles, leopard sharks and occasional mantas and whale sharks.
Hin Muang	19-24m	Submerged pinnacle with a few leopard sharks, grouper, barracuda, moray eels and occasional whale sharks.
Ko Bida Nok	18-22m	Karst massif with gorgonians, leopard sharks, barracuda and occasional whale sharks.
Phi-Phi Leh	5-18m	Island rim is covered in coral and oysters, with moray eels, octopus, seahorses and swim-throughs.

Phi-Phi's east coast, and on the back road that connects the southeast end of Ao Ton Sai with Ao Lo Dalam. Of course, the best option may be to simply grab a bucket and join the scrum.

Rock (☎ 08 1607 3897; dm 250B, r 400B) A proper hostel on the village hill, with clean dorms lined with bunk beds, tiny private rooms, an inviting restaurant-bar and a rugged, graffiti-scrawled exterior.

Phi-Phi Popular Beach Resort (☎ 08 4744 7665, 08 0698 7884; bungalows with fan 600-1200B, with air-con 3000B; 🔊) One of three like-minded properties tucked into the far edges of Hat Ton Sai. Its eight cabanas and bungalows are directly below majestic Ton Sai tower.

Oasis Guesthouse (☎ 0 7560 1207; r 900B; 🔊) It's worth the walk up the side road east of the village centre to find this cute guesthouse with wooden shutters surrounded by trees. The innkeeper can be surly, but he does offer freshly painted rooms with sparkling bathrooms. He won't take reservations. It's first come, first serve only.

K Hotel (☎ 0 7660 1048; r 900-1500B; 🔊 🖥) OK, it is in the middle of town, and the view is, well, not a selling point. Still, if you're looking for a cheap, clean room with minifridge, hot water and wood furnishings, this offers good value.

Kinaree House (☎ 0 7560 1139, 08 1854 5187; www .kinnareehouse.phiphiroom.com; r 1000B; 🔊) It's got more style than anywhere else in central Ton Sai (walls in shocking hues of orange, turquoise and purples, contemporary Thai art and so on) and its location can be great if tranquillity is an afterthought to shopping and partying. Rooms are small but reception is friendly.

our pick **Chunut House** (☎ 0 7560 1227; bungalows 1000-2000B; 🛜) On a quiet path away from the bazaar of the tourist village, this place is refreshingly tranquil. Spacious wooden and bamboo bungalows are dripping with naturalistic mobiles, planters and crafty touches, plus have clean tiled bathrooms.

PP Viewpoint Resort (☎ 0 7560 1200, 0 7561 8111; www.phiphiviewpoint.com; bungalows 1700-3500B; 🔊 🖥) At the far northeastern end of Ao Lo Dalam, wooden bungalows sit high on stilts and enjoy awesome views. There is a small swimming pool that practically drops into the ocean below and a glass-walled tower with 360-degree views where you can pamper yourself with a Thai massage.

PP Beachfront (☎ 08 3388 4847; r 2000B; 🔊) A cute peach-tinted, brick inn tucked into the headland at the northwest edge of Ao Lo Dalam. Rooms are laid with spotless tiled floors, have TVs, DVD players and glass-bowl sinks and are accented with silk flowers. Its common patio and romantic porch demands lengthy lounging sessions as you watch the water buzz with long-tails. Unfortunately you will have to deal with club noise till the wee small hours.

Phi-Phi Casita (☎ 0 7560 1214; www.phiphi-hotel.com; bungalows 2000-3500B; 🔊 🖥) A step back from Ao Lo Dalam beach, this place looks like a classy fisher village – tiny wooden bungalows hover on stilts over flower-planted mud flats. There's not much privacy, but the stylish infinity pool and proximity to the beach are major draws.

HAT HIN KHOM

The beach here was never Phi-Phi's best, but there's a bunch of abodes and the area is a short jungle walk from both the stunning Hat Yao and the Ao Ton Sai bustle, which unfortunately means you will hear whatever the DJs are spinning.

our pick **Viking Natures Resort** (☎ 08 3649 9492; www.vikingnaturesresort.com; bungalows 700-6500B; 🛜) Wood, thatch and bamboo bungalows here are exceptionally creative and stylish with lots of driftwood, shell mobiles and art all around. All bungalows have mosquito nets and balconies, but the cheaper rooms don't have their own bathrooms. That said, both shared and private bathrooms are exquisite and are always stocked with plenty of soaps, shampoos and fresh flowers. We say splurge for one of several wooden lodge rooms. They open onto exceptional verandahs, are well lit with funky lanterns and have huge bathrooms and high ceilings.

Andaman Beach Resort (☎ 0 7560 1077; www.and amanbeachresort.com; bungalows 1750-2050B; 🔊 🖥) A U-shape of neat, tiled huts sits around a large spartan lawn. The biggest attraction is the small pool at its epicentre – perfect for sleeping off nights spent at Hippies bar next door.

Arayaburi & Bayview Resorts (☎ 0 7560 1127; www .phiphibayview.com; bungalows incl breakfast 4100-5000B; 🞩 💷) These twin resorts under common management offer a cornucopia of concrete bungalows straddling one rocky headland. Most of the bungalows are modern in design, come stocked with amenities and have excellent ocean views from their front decks.

HAT YAO

You can either walk here in about 20 minutes from Ton Sai via Hat Him Khom beach or take a long-tail (100B to 150B) from Ton Sai pier. This long, stunning stretch of pure-white beach is perfect for swimming and well worth the walk. A trail leads from here over to beautiful and secluded Ao Lo Mu Di.

Paradise Pearl Bungalow Resort (☎ 0 7560 1246; www.paradise-pearl.com; bungalows 2900-3300B; 🞩 💷) Location is the key and families are the clientele at this attractive, well-managed property. Bungalows are dark wood, classic Thai, there's a beautiful stretch of beach in the foreground and a swathe of jungle behind for young lizard hunters.

Phi-Phi Blue Sky Resort (☎ 08 9881 7929; www .phiphibluesky.com; bungalows 2900-4300B; 🞩 💷) Spacious, whitewashed, concrete bungalows are strewn throughout a blooming, palm-shaded tropical garden. Digs are more comfortable than stylish. New wooden bungalows were set to be available by the time of this book's publication.

Beach Resort (☎ 0 7561 8268; phiphithebeach.com; bungalows 3950-5350B; 🞩 💷) An expanding class act with a good pool and chic bar, this place swarms with package tourists looking for (and finding) comfort, but it is a touch overpriced.

AO POH

This sliver of white sand, tucked between rocky outcrops, is where Phi-Phi's dreadlocked backpacker soul still lives and breathes. The best way in is by long-tail (200B) from Ton Sai pier.

Ao Poh Beach Resort (☎ 08 4186 1245; bungalows 700-2000B) A sweet collection of bamboo, thatched bungalows with wide wooden decks set on a secluded beach, with outstanding roots reggae on the stereo.

HAT RANTEE & AO TOH KO

Still fairly low-key, this series of small, remote bays is home to a few modest bungalow operations. The pretty beach here has rocky outcroppings and the snorkelling is excellent. You can either get here by long-tail from Ao Ton Sai pier (300B) or by making the strenuous 45-minute hike over the viewpoint.

Rantee Hut (☎ 08 9741 4846; bungalows 400-1000B) You're in with a lovely Thai family when you stay at these basic bamboo huts (complete with fans and on-deck hammocks). There's a tiny restaurant that serves inexpensive, relatively authentic Thai fare.

Ao Toh Ko Beach Resort (☎ 08 1537 0528; bungalows 800-1800B; 💷 🛜) All alone on white, mellow Ao Toh Ko, there's a summer-camp camaraderie here with several long-term guests and plenty of new ones who wish they were long term. Wooden, fan-cooled bungalows are perched on a hill and have stone baths and mosquito nets. There are also family rooms and a big, friendly restaurant right on the beach, where you'll find kayaks and snorkel gear for rent.

HAT PHAK NAM

This beach is nestled on the same bay as a small fishing hamlet. To get here, you can either charter a long-tail from Ao Ton Sai for around 500B (150B by shared taxi boat upon your return), or make the sweaty one-hour hike over the viewpoint (not recommended with roller luggage).

Relax Beach Resort (☎ 08 1083 0194, 08 9475 6536; bungalows 1600-2800B) There are 47 unpretentious but attractive Thai-style bungalows with wood floors, driftwood railings and mosaic baths in the newest nests. All are rimmed by lush jungle – there's a good restaurant and breezy bar, and it's worked by incredibly charming staff who greet and treat you like family. It's one of the best choices on the island, so reserve ahead.

AO LO BAKAO

This fine stretch of palm-backed sand is ringed by dramatic hills, offers offshore views of Bamboo and Mosquito Islands and is home to a single upmarket resort. From Ao Ton Sai, you will have to charter a long-tail to get here (800B). Phi-Phi Island Village also arranges transfers for guests.

Phi-Phi Island Village (☎ 0 7636 3700; www.ppisland .com; bungalows 6700-25,000B; 🞩 💷) This place really is a village unto itself: its whopping 100 bungalows take up much of the beachfront with palms swaying between them. Facilities vary from the family friendly and casual to romantic dining experiences and pampering spa treatments. It offers dozens of activities and excursions. The infinity pool blends seamlessly into the ocean, and fresh flowers are artfully arranged throughout the resort. Good living if you have the means.

HAT LAEM THONG

The beach here is long and sandy with a small *chow lair* (sea gypsy) settlement of corrugated metal shacks at the north end. A long-tail charter from Ao Ton Sai costs 800B. Operators can also arrange transfers. Look for troops of monkeys in the jungle behind Zeavola resort.

Holiday Inn Phi-Phi Island (☎ 0 7562 7300; www .phiphi.holidayinn.com; bungalows 8297–10,400B; 🅿 🅿 🛜) These handsome Thai-Malay–style bungalows are set on lovely grounds awash with grass and palm trees. You'll find tennis courts, beckoning hammocks, a spa and a dive centre. The restaurant allows you to dine alfresco or inside, buffet or à la carte.

Zeavola (☎ 0 7562 7000; www.zeavola.com; bungalows 16,900–26,900B; 🅿 🅿 🅿 🛜) Got money to burn? Let this be your pyre. Here's an outstanding top-end resort with gorgeous teak bungalows that incorporate a traditional Thai style with a simple, sleek modern design. Each comes with glass walls on three sides (with remote-controlled bamboo shutters for privacy), beautiful 1940s fixtures and antique furniture, a patio and impeccable service. Some villas come with a private pool and there's a fabulous couples-oriented spa.

Eating

Most of the resorts, hotels and bungalows around the island have their own restaurants. Ao Ton Sai is home to some reasonably priced restaurants but don't expect haute cuisine.

Local Food Market (Ao Ton Sai; 🕑 breakfast, lunch & dinner) The cheapest, and some of the best, eats are at the market. A handful of local stalls huddle on the narrowest sliver of the isthmus and serve up scrumchous *pàt tai*, fried rice, *som tam* and smoked cat fish. Walls are scrawled with the blessings of a thousand travellers.

Garlic Restaurant (☎ 08 3502 1426; dishes 45–95B; 🕑 breakfast, lunch & dinner) A dilapidated looking hut on the main path to Ao Lo Dalam serving cheap, terrific Thai food. It has all the usuals and an ice raft of fresh catch at supper.

TOP FIVE PHI-PHI RESORTS

- **Viking Natures Resort** (p355) No horned helmets but plenty of driftwood chic in the stunning lodge rooms.

- **Ao Poh Beach Resort** (opposite) Groovy travellers' scene on a near forgotten beach.

- **Relax Beach Resort** (opposite) The perfect blend of style, warmth and natural beauty.

- **Phi-Phi Island Village** (opposite) Luxe holiday central for all, from families to romantic hipsters.

- **Zeavola** (left) Indulgent and sleek Thai style.

---

our pick **Papaya Restaurant** (☎ 08 7280 1719; Tourist Village; dishes 80–300B) Cheap, tasty and spicy. Here's some real-deal Thai food served in heaping portions. It has your basil and chilli, all the curries and *dôm yam*, too.

La Piazzetta (dishes 130–210B; 🕑 lunch & dinner Tue-Sat) If you're in the mood for authentic, home-style Italian cuisine, come to this quaint bistro. It has the best Italian meats and cheeses on the island and exquisite pastas and pizzas. Save room for the tiramisu.

GB PP (☎ 08 2289 6820; burgers 165–195B) Damn good half-pound burgers come piled with bacon and avocado, slathered in barbecue sauce, brushed with pesto, coated in melted mozzarella or painted in red curry, and served with fresh cut, chunky fries. It also has vegie burgers and tender steaks.

Le Grand Bleu (☎ 08 1979 9739; mains 195–695B; 🕑 lunch & dinner) Thai-Euro fusion set in a charming wooden house just off the main pier. It serves French and Aussie wines, and you can get your duck wok-fried with basil or oven-roasted and caramelised with mango. It closes from 2pm to 6.30pm (between lunch and dinner).

Drinking

A rowdy nightlife saturates Phi-Phi. And while it is indeed strange to be beckoned into Thai bars by (somewhat) sexy-ish *farang* girls rather than comely Thai maidens, and drinking buckets of cheap whiskey, Coke and Red Bull is clearly the domain of spring break wannabes and a recipe for a hangover or worse, the truth is if you're nesting within earshot of the Phi-Phi wilds you may as well enjoy the chaos.

Breakers (Tourist Village; ☼ 11am-2am; 🛜) A proper sports bar with two flat screens, rock and roll on the sound system, eight draught beers (including Guinness), and an impressive list of top-shelf spirits like Don Julio and Macallan.

Love Café (☎ 08 7273 8738; www.lovephiphi.com; Ao Ton Sai; coffee drinks 80-110B, pots of tea 100-120B; ☼ 8am-7pm) A brand-new coffee and tea bar at Phi-Phi Villa Resort that specialises in organic craftsman black, green and oolong teas and terrific organic coffee all sourced from Chiang Rai.

Slinky Bar (Ao Lo Dalam) The beach-bar of the moment when we visited. Expect the standard fire show, buckets of souped-up candy juice and throngs of Thais, local expats and tourists mingling, flirting and flailing to throbbing, distorted bass.

our pick Sunflower Bar (Ao Lo Dalam) Poetically ramshackle, this driftwood gem is still the chillest bar in Phi-Phi. Destroyed in the tsunami, the owner rebuilt it with reclaimed wood. The long-tail booths are named for the four loved ones he lost in the flood.

Getting There & Away

Ko Phi-Phi can be reached from Krabi, Phuket, Ao Nang and Ko Lanta. Most boats moor at Ao Ton Sai, though a few from Phuket use the isolated northern pier at Laem Thong. The Phuket and Krabi boats operate year-round, while the Ko Lanta and Ao Nang boats only run in the October to April high season.

Boats depart from Krabi for Ko Phi-Phi (400B, 1½ hours) at 10am and 2pm. From Phuket, boats leave at 8.30am, 1.30pm and 2.30pm, and return from Ko Phi-Phi at 9am, 2.30pm and 3pm (400B, 1¾ to two hours). To Ko Lanta, boats leave Phi-Phi at 11.30am and 2pm and return from Ko Lanta at 8am and 1pm (350B, 1½ hours).

Getting Around

There are no roads on Phi-Phi Don so transport on the island is mostly by foot, although long-tails can be chartered at Ao Ton Sai for short hops around Ko Phi-Phi Don and Ko Phi-Phi Leh.

Long-tails leave from the Ao Ton Sai pier to Hat Yao (100B to 150B), Laem Thong (800B), Hat Rantee (500B) and Viking Cave (500B). Chartering speedboats for six hours costs around 6500B, while chartering a long-tail

boat costs 1200B for three hours or 2500B for the whole day.

KO PHI-PHI LEH
เกาะพีพีเล

Rugged Phi-Phi Leh is the smaller of the two islands and is protected on all sides by soaring cliffs. Coral reefs crawling with marine life lie beneath the crystal-clear waters and are hugely popular with day-tripping snorkellers. Two gorgeous lagoons await in the island's interior – **Pilah** on the eastern coast and **Ao Maya** on the western coast. In 1999 Ao Maya was controversially used as the setting for the filming of *The Beach*, based on the popular novel by Alex Garland. Visitor numbers soared in its wake.

At the northeastern tip of the island, **Viking Cave** (Tham Phaya Naak) is a big collection point for swifts' nests. Nimble collectors scamper up bamboo scaffolding to gather the nests. Before ascending, they pray and make offerings of tobacco, incense and liquor to the cavern spirits. This cave gets its misleading moniker from 400-year-old graffiti left by Chinese fishermen.

There are no places to stay on Phi-Phi Leh and most people come here on one of the ludicrously popular day trips out of Phi-Phi Don. Tours last about half a day and include snorkelling stops at various points around the island, with detours to Viking Cave and Ao Maya. Long-tail trips cost 800B; by motorboat you'll pay around 2400B. Expect to pay a 400B National Park day-use fee upon landing.

It is possible to camp on Phi-Phi Leh through **Maya Bay Camping** (☎ 08 6944 1623; www .mayabaycamping.com; per person 2100B). It offers action-packed overnight trips that include kayaking, snorkelling, lunch, dinner, and sleeping bags under the stars.

KO LANTA
เกาะลันตา
pop 20,000

It's still grasping at its reputation as a kick-back island where tired travellers can get away from the tourist hullabaloo, but Ko Lanta has quickly grown up into a midrange and very popular destination. Ferries shuttling people to Ko Phi-Phi and onto Phuket in one direction and to Krabi town, the Trang islands and even as far as Ko Lipe in the other, have helped turn this low-lying, beach-fringed island into a transportation hub as well as a major stop unto itself – especially for divers interested in exploring Hin Daeng and Hin Muang. The island doesn't have those stunning karst cliffs found all around Krabi Province, or even particularly good coral around the island proper; what it does promise is miles of sandy beaches and plenty to do – you can take cooking classes in the morning, ride elephants or visit the national park in the afternoon, and party till the wee hours at happening beach-bars.

Plus, Lanta's 20,000 local residents are mixed descendants of Muslim Malay and seafaring *chow lair* (see boxed text, p39), which gives the island a cultural identity missing in Ao Nang and Phi-Phi. The east coast remains their stronghold and aside from Ban Ko Lanta's charming, 100-year-old wharf district, development hasn't arrived…yet.

Orientation & Information

The Ko Lanta region is made up of 52 islands, but the term is most commonly used to refer to Ko Lanta Yai, the biggest and most popular of the lot. At the north of the island, Ban Sala Dan is the main port of entry to Ko Lanta It has lots of restaurants, tour agencies and dive shops, in addition to passenger- and vehicle-ferry piers. Ko Lanta's western coast has most of its best beaches. Hat Khlong Dao is the most occupied stretch of beach, while the main budget centre is Hat Phra Ae (Long Beach). At the far southern tip, surrounded by wonderful wild beaches, is the headquarters of Mu Ko Lanta National Park.

During the wet season, rain drenches Ko Lanta and the tide washes right up to the front of the resorts, bringing plenty of driftwood and rubbish (see p363) with it. Only a few resorts remain open and transport connections become thin on the ground.

There's no official tourist office but the websites www.ko-lanta.com and www.lantainfo.com have useful information on the area. Siam City Bank has a **foreign-exchange booth** (☼ 8.30am-4pm Mon-Fri low season) and ATMs are found all over Ban Sala Dan, and on Hat Phra Ae and Hat Klong Nin. **Ko Lanta Hospital** (☎ 0 7569 7017) is near Ban Ko Lanta on the east coast. Internet cafes dot the beaches and Ban Sala Dan charging 1B per minute.

Sights

Although Ko Lanta is primarily a beach destination, there are some worthwhile sights inland if you get tired of the sea and sand.

MU KO LANTA MARINE NATIONAL PARK
อุทยานแห่งชาติเกาะลันตา

Set up in 1990, this **marine national park** (adult/child 200/100B) protects 15 islands in the Ko Lanta group, including the southern tip of Ko Lanta Yai. However, the park is increasingly threatened by the runaway development on the western coast of Ko Lanta Yai. The other islands in the group have fared slightly better – **Ko Rok** is still very beautiful, with a crescent-shaped bay backed by cliffs, fine coral reefs and a sparkling white-sand beach. Camping is permitted on Ko Rok and nearby **Ko Ha**, with permission from the national park headquarters. On the eastern side of Ko Lanta Yai, **Ko Talabeng** has some dramatic limestone caves that you can visit on sea-kayaking tours. The national park fee applies if you visit any of these islands.

The park headquarters is at Laem Tanod, on the southern tip of Ko Lanta Yai, reached by a steep and corrugated 7km dirt track from Ao Nui. There are basic hiking trails, a **scenic lighthouse** with spectacular panoramas of the rugged cape and offshore islands, and two of Lanta's most picturesque and least-visited beaches.

BAN KO LANTA

Halfway down the eastern coast, **Ban Ko Lanta** (Lanta Old Town) was the original port and commercial centre for the island, and provided a safe harbour for Arabic and Chinese trading vessels sailing between the larger ports of Phuket, Penang and Singapore. Some of the gracious and well-kept wooden stilt houses and shopfronts here are over 100 years old and are a pleasure to stroll through. Pier restaurants offer up fresh catch and have prime views over the sea. There's a small afternoon market on Sundays, and if you're looking for sturdy, attractive handmade leather goods, stop by **Lanta Leather** (☎ 08 5046 6410; ☼ 8am-8pm).

A few kilometres past the hospital lies the **Gypsy House** (Ban Ko Lanta), a bohemian driftwood creation replete with ponds and traditional music, where artisans sell handicrafts and jewellery. There are a few pamphlets here on the *chow lair* of Ko Lanta, but it's mainly just a pleasant waterside chill-out space.

If you crave information on culture, stop by the **Chao Leh Museum** (Ban Sanghka-U), where you'll find a complex of traditionally lashed bamboo homes, engaging oil canvasses and exhibits detailing their myths, music and ceremonies. To find it look for the houseboat jutting from the hillside across the road from the sea.

SOUTHERN
ANDAMAN COAST

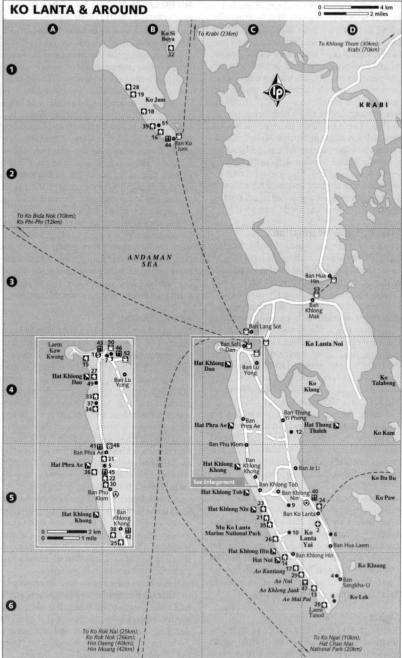

KO LANTA & AROUND

0 —————— 4 km
0 —————— 2 miles

Ⓐ Ⓑ Ko Si Boya To Krabi (23km) Ⓒ Ⓓ

To Khlong Thom (30km); Krabi (70km)

KRABI

32

28
19 Ko Jam
18

39 51
16
44 Ban Ko Jum

To Ko Bida Nok (10km); Ko Phi-Phi (12km)

ANDAMAN SEA

Ban Hua Hin
53
Ban Khlong Mak

Ban Lang Sot

Ban Sala Dan
Hat Khlong Dao
Ban Lu Yong

Ko Lanta Noi

Ko Klang

Ko Talabeng

Laem Kaw Kwang
43 50
46
18 7 3 52
15
27
Hat Khlong Dao 49
33
37
34
Ban Lu Yong

Hat Phra Ae
Ban Phra Ae
Ban Thung Yi Pheng
Hat Thung Thaleh
12

Ko Kam

41 48
31
Ban Phra Ae
5
Hat Phra Ae 45
36 22
30
Ban Phu Klom

Ban Phu Klom
Hat Khlong Khong
Ban Khlong Khong

Ban Je Li

Ko Bu Bu

Hat Khlong Khong
38
42
25

0 —— 2 km
0 —— 1 mile

See Enlargement

Ban Khlong Tob
Hat Khlong Tob
Ban Khlong Nin
40
9 24
Hat Khlong Nin
21
23
35
Ban Ko Lanta

Mu Ko Lanta Marine National Park
26
10
Ko Lanta Yai
2
6
Ban Hua Laem

Ko Paw

Hat Khlong Hin
Ban Khlong Hin
Hat Nui 14
Ao Kantiang 17
29
Ao Nui 47
Ao Khlong Jaak
Ao Mai Pai 13
8 Ko Lek
20
Laem Tanod

Ko Kluang
4 Ban Sangkha-U

To Ko Rok Nai (25km); Ko Rok Nok (26km); Hin Daeng (40km); Hin Muang (42km)

To Ko Ngai (10km); Hat Chao Mai National Park (20km)

THAM KHAO MAI KAEW
ถ้ำเขาไม้แก้ว

Monsoon rains pounding away at limestone cracks and crevices for millions of years have created this complex of forest caverns and tunnels. There are chambers as large as cathedrals, dripping with stalactites and stalagmites, and tiny passages that you have to squeeze through on hands and knees. There's even a subterranean pool you can take a chilly, creepy swim in. This is *Raiders of the Lost Ark* kind of fun that involves few safety precautions and a certain level of fitness. Total coverage in mud is almost guaranteed. It's a blast.

Tham Khao Mai Kaew is reached via a guided hike through the jungle. A local family offers guided hikes to the caves (with torches) for around 200B. Elephant treks to the caves (adult/child 900/450B) are also possible in the high season and are only really fun if you're with kids. The best way to get here is by rented motorcycle. Most resorts can arrange transport.

Close by, but reached by a separate track from the dirt road leading to the marine national park headquarters, **Tham Seua** (Tiger Cave) also has interesting tunnels to explore; elephant treks run up here from Hat Nui.

Activities
DIVING & SNORKELLING

Several shops run two-dive trips to local sights for 2900B to 3400B, while PADI Open Water courses are 13,900B to 15,600B. There are also trips to Ko Phi-Phi and the undersea pinnacles at **Hin Muang** and **Hin Daeng**, about 45 minutes from Ban Sala Dan by speedboat. These world-class dive sites have lone coral outcrops in the middle of the sea that are important feeding stations for large pelagic fish such as sharks and tunas and occasionally whale sharks and manta rays. These are the best dive sites in Krabi, and trips out here cost 3500B to 4400B for two dives. The sites around **Ko Ha** have consistently good diving conditions, depths of 18m to 34m, plenty of marine life and a cave known as 'The Cathedral'. Reliable dive companies include **Lanta Diver** (☎ 0 7568 4208; www.lantadiver.com; Ban Sala Dan), **Dive & Relax** (☎ 08 4842 2191; www.diveandrelax.com; Hat Phra Ae) and **Blue Planet Divers** (☎ 0 7566 2724; www.blueplanetdivers.net; Ban Sala Dan). Blue Planet is the only school that specialises in free diving instruction. November to April is the best time for diving at Ko Lanta; the rest of the year most dive shops close.

Numerous tour agencies along the strip can organise snorkelling trips out to Ko Rok Nok, Ko Phi-Phi and other nearby islands.

ELEPHANT TREKKING

There are elephant-trekking camps at Hat
Phra Ae (right), Hat Nui (above) – from where
you can visit Tham Seua – and Ao Khlong Jaak
(Waterfall Bay; p364). All charge 900/450B
per adult/child for a two-hour trek. If you
have your own transport, you can just show
up at any of these elephant-trekking camps,
otherwise most travel agencies or bungalow
operators can arrange treks and transfers. All
outings are slow, uneventful lumberings that
are best suited for families with children.

OTHER ACTIVITIES

There are several other activities available including: **sea kayaking** (adult/child 1000/600B)
around the mangroves near Ban Hua Hin and Ko
Pang; and **deep-sea fishing** (by long-tail/speedboat
3500/15,000B). All of these can be arranged
through resort tour desks or tour agencies
in Ban Sala Dan. If you're into community
tourism, check into the new mangrove tours
offered at **Tung Yee Peng** (☺ 8am-5pm). You can
walk the boardwalk through the bush (20B),
rent a kayak and paddle the canals with a guide
(500B per hour) or take a long-tail boat tour
(800B). Proceeds benefit a village community
learning centre.

Courses

Time for Lime (☎ 0 7568 4590; www.timeforlime.net), at
Hat Khlong Dao, has a huge, hip and professional moulded-concrete kitchen with plenty of
room to run amok. It offers excellent cooking
courses with a slightly more exciting selection of dishes than most cookery schools in
Thailand; half-day courses cost from 1500B to
1800B. There are also good bungalows here (see
below), and it serves a mean mojito, too.

Sleeping

Ko Lanta is home to many long stretches of
good-looking beach packed with accommodation. Some resorts close down for the May-to-
October low season, others drop their rates by
50% or even more. Resorts usually have their
own restaurants and tour-booking facilities
that can arrange island snorkelling, massages,
tours and motorcycle rental.

HAT KHLONG DAO

Also known as Long Beach, this is an outstanding 2km stretch of white sand with no
rocks, which makes it perfect for swimming.
Unfortunately garbage does accumulate when

the tides shift. Locals say it comes from Phi-
Phi. And they say it disdainfully.

Somewhere Else (☎ 08 1536 0858; bungalows 500-
1000B) Big octagonal bamboo huts grace a
shady lawn right on a very social and lounge-
worthy stretch of beach. Bathrooms are big
and clean, as is the beachfront restaurant that
serves Indian, Thai and European food. It's
not private but is a lot of fun and run by the
folks of Where Else? on Hat Khlong Khong.

Time For Lime (☎ 08 9967 5017; www.timeforlime
.net; bungalows 1000-1500B; 🖳) An ideal spot if
you're serious about Thai cooking (see left).
Inexpensive, clean bungalows with mini lofts
and front porches line up in a lovely flower garden behind the beachfront cooking school and
restaurant. The owner takes in stray dogs (with
plans to start a local animal shelter), so you'll
have plenty of friendly and furry company.

Ocean View Resort (☎ 0 7568 4089; bungalows 1800-
2900B; 🖳 🖳 🖳) Large, somewhat stylish, tiled
bungalows with queen-sized beds, cable TV,
hammocks on the porch and a seaside pool.
The fabulous Mrs Oh is here to help.

Maya Beach Resort (☎ 0 7568 4267; mayalanta
.com; r 4300B; 🖳 🖳 🖳) Ignore that Best
Western affiliation if you can, because this
place has attractive, large, Ikea-chic rooms on
two floors. There are louvred railings on the
terrace, Buddhist shrines on the sand and a
pool that blends with the nearby sea.

our pick **Costa Lanta** (☎ 0 7566 8168; www.costalanta
.com; r 6200B; 🖳 🖳 🖳 🛜) Incredibly Zen stand-
alone abodes nestled in a garden shaded by
coconut palms and laced with tidal canals at
the north end of Hat Khlong Dao. Everything
from the floors to walls to the washbasins
are polished concrete and the barn doors of
each cabana open on two sides to maximise
air flow. The restaurant is stunning, as is the
black spill-over pool on the edge of the sand.
Discounts are available if booked through its
website. Low-season rates are a steal.

Slow Down Villas (☎ 08 4999 6780; www.slowdown
lanta.se; villas per week 25,000B; 🖳 🖳 🖳 🛜) These
nine mod, two- and three-bedroom wood-
and-shingle villas are all about clean lines,
open spaces and comfy beach living. They are
privately owned by expats but rented out by
the week and month.

HAT PHRA AE

A large travellers' village has grown up at Hat
Phra Ae, with faràng-oriented restaurants,
beach-bars, internet cafes and tour offices.

FIVE GYRES

When you wander Hat Khlong Dao in the wet or shoulder season you can't help but notice how much garbage washes up on shore. Here are 1m high (or higher) piles of plastic bottles, bags and styrofoam tangled in seaweed and driftwood. Locals point to Ko Phi-Phi as the source of the plague, but it isn't quite that simple. In truth, plastic pollution in the marine environment is an enormous global issue.

Natural oceanic currents on the seven seas flow into what scientists call five 'oceanic gyres'. These gyres are fundamentally important to the marine system. In essence they are nutritious, oxygen-rich whirlpools historically attracting large pelagics and flocks of seabirds, which feed on smaller fish, which munch plankton as they spin in large schools.

But if you sail to the gyres today, you'll find areas larger than the state of Texas swirling with more plastic debris than marine life. Some of it was tossed overboard from boats, but the majority gets washed into the sea from rivers that carry waste from urban areas. Once in the ocean, the plastics eventually breakdown into the resin pellets that are used in industrial plastic production and are often ingested by seabirds, killing them and releasing toxic chemicals into the marine food chain. Even if Phi-Phi is the source of Lanta's garbage problem, think of how much more is spinning its way into the Indian Ocean gyre? The best thing you can do is to begin eliminating plastic from your life. Start by carrying a refillable, stainless-steel water bottle. For more information, check out **5GYRES** (www.5gyres.org).

Hutyee Boathouse (☎ 08 9645 1083; bungalows 300B) Groovy basic, fan-cooled, braided-bamboo bungalows with driftwood railings, nestled in a forest just back from the beach behind Nautilus. The owner is the happiest sultan on earth. This is your low-budget salvation.

Lanta Marina (☎ 0 7568 4168; www.lantamarina.com; bungalows 300-500B; ☉ Nov-Apr; ☎) For something really cool, try out these giant bungalows, which almost look like towering hay bales with wide porches. It has a tribal feel and is excellent value.

Sanctuary (☎ 08 1891 3055; sanctuary_93@yahoo .com; bungalows 700-1200B) The original Phra Ae resort is still a delightful place to stay. There are artistically designed wood-and-thatch bungalows with lots of grass and a hippyish atmosphere that's low-key and friendly. The restaurant offers Indian and vegetarian eats and the Thai usuals. It also holds yoga classes.

our pick **Relax Bay** (☎ 0 7568 4194; www.relaxbay .com; bungalows 700-3700B; ☉ Oct-Apr; ☎) This gorgeous French-run place is spread out over a tree-covered headland by a small beach. Its wooden bungalows sit on stilts with large decks overlooking the bay and stunning sunsets. And there's an incredibly stylish, open-air bar and restaurant.

Thai House Beach Resort (☎ 0 7568 4289; www .thaibeachhouseresort.net; bungalows 1500B; ☎) Stilted wooden bungalows with wrap-around decks, minifridge and TV and close to the beach. Not fabulous, but a solid, comfortable choice.

HAT KHLONG KHONG

Only the resorts at the northern end of this rather rocky beach are worth looking at. Most of the others are soulless concrete boxes. There is a travellers' vibe here with plenty of mellow little beach bars.

our pick **Where Else?** (☎ 08 1536 4870; www.lanta -where-else.com; bungalows 500-1500B) Make your way here for Ko Lanta's little slice of bohemia. The bungalows may be a bit shaky but there is great mojo and the place swarms with backpackers. The restaurant, a growing piece of art in itself, feels like an ever-expanding homage to Sigmund the Sea Monster. The pricier bungalows are all unique, multilevel abodes sleeping up to four people.

Lanta Pavilion (☎ 0 7566 7079; bungalows 1000-1600B; ☎ 🖥 ☎) Cosy, peach-tinted tin-roof bungalows, well maintained and laid out in a neatly manicured garden. As far as the Khlong Khong concrete boxes go, this is as good as they get.

Moonlight Bay Resort (☎ 0 7566 2590; moonlightre sort.com; bungalows 4000B; ☎ 🖥 ☎) A Scandinavian resort that plays up the ecoresort angle with natural materials, simple Nordic design and gorgeous bungalows either along a lush river, facing verdant greenery or right on the beach. It sits on a private rocky cove where most of the flora is labelled for your edification.

HAT KHLONG NIN

After Hat Khlong Tob, the main road heading south forks: head left for the inland road which runs to the east coast, go right and the country road hugs the coastline for 14km to the tip of Ko Lanta. The first beach here is lovely Hat Khlong Nin, which gets progressively nicer as you travel south.

Lanta Beach Paradise (☎ 0 7566 2569; www.lanta paradiseresort.com; bungalows 1200-2200B; ✕ 🖳 🖳) OK, it's a little cheesy, with Bambi in the garden and whatnot, but these tiled concrete bungalows are spotless, well maintained and managed by a sweet family, and they're right on the beach.

Sri Lanta (☎ 0 7566 2688; www.srilanta.com; cottages 2900B; ✕ 🖳 🖳) At the southern end of the beach, this sophisticated resort consists of minimalist, naturalistic wooden villas in wild gardens set back from the shore. There's a very stylish beachside area with a restaurant, infinity pool and private drapery-swathed massage pavilions.

Andalay Resort (☎ 0 7566 2699; www.andalay lanta.com; bungalows 5400B; ✕ 🖳 🛜) A stylish, new 12-room resort. Rooms open onto porches perched above a lotus pond, which blends into the pool and sea. Rooms have rose-coloured concrete floors, ceiling fan and air-con, built-in wood furnishings, satellite TV and wi-fi.

HAT NUI

There are several small, rocky beaches around here with upmarket places to stay.

Narima (☎ 0 7566 2668; www.narima-lanta.com; bungalows 2000-3500B; ✕ 🖳 🖳) The ever-so-slightly upscale bamboo bungalows have wood floors, queen-sized and twin beds, simple tiled baths and wide verandahs overlooking their own sheltered cove. Still, the bungalows are a touch overpriced.

AO KANTIANG

A superb sweep of sand backed by mountains is also its own self-contained little village. This is arguably the best base on Lanta. There are just three choices here and they all have their selling points. Internet access and motorbike rental are easy to find.

Kantiang Bay Resort (☎ 0 7566 5049; kantiang bay.net; bungalows 600-2000B; ✕ 🖳) Choose between the cheap, rickety, not-exactly-spotless wooden-and-bamboo bungalows or the more expensive, candy-coloured tiled rooms with minifridge. The restaurant serves decent, faràng-friendly Thai dishes.

ourpick Baan Laanta Resort & Spa (☎ 0 7566 5091; www.baanlaanta.com; bungalows from 5000B; ✕ 🖳 🖳) Fragrant, green, landscaped grounds wind around stylish wooden bungalows and a pool that drops off to a stretch of white sandy beach. The room's centrepiece is a futon-style bed on a raised wooden platform under a gauzy veil of mosquito netting. White bed linen and cream-coloured curtains complement the natural woods in the rooms, while bamboolined bathrooms are clean and bright.

Phra Nang Lanta (☎ 0 7566 5025; lanta@vacation village.co.th; studios 6000B; ✕ 🖳 🖳 🛜) Funky concrete 'studios' built adobe style are huge, with mosaic bathrooms and large bathtubs ,and there is complimentary motorbike rental. The pool is right on the beautiful beach as is the whimsical restaurant-bar (although it only serves breakfast).

AO KHLONG JAAK

There's a splendid beach here. The namesake waterfall is further inland.

Andalanta Resort (☎ 0 7566 5018; www.andalanta .com; bungalows 4500-6900B; ✕) You'll find beachstyle, modern air-con bungalows (some with loft) and simple fan-cooled ones facing the sea. The garden is a delight, there's an ambient restaurant and the waterfall is just a 30- to 40-minute walk away.

AO MAI PAI

ourpick La Lanta (☎ 0 7566 5066; www.lalanta.com; bungalows 6000B; ✕ 🖳 🖳) Barefoot elegance at it's finest. Owned and operated by a young, hip, English-speaking Thai-Vietnamese couple, this is the grooviest spot on the entire island. Thatched bungalows have polished-concrete floors, platform beds, floral-design motifs and decks overlooking a pitch of sand, which blends into a rocky fishermen's beach. Set down a rutted dirt road, it's also the closest resort to the marine national park.

LAEM TANOD

The road to the marine national park headquarters fords the *klong* (canal), which can get quite deep in the wet season.

Mu Ko Lanta Marine National Park Headquarters (☎ in Bangkok 0 2561 4292; camping with own tent per person 30B, with tent hire 300-400B) The secluded grounds of the national park headquarters are a wonderfully serene place to camp. The flat camping areas are covered in shade and sit in the wilds of the tropical jungle. Out the front lie craggy outcroppings and the sounds of the ocean lapping up the rocks. There are toilets and running water, but you should bring your own food. You can also get permission for camping on Ko Rok or Ko Ha here. National park entry fees apply (see p359).

BAN KO LANTA
There are three inns open for business on Lanta's oft-ignored, wonderfully dated and incredibly rich Old Town. The best choice:

Mango House (☎ 0 7569 7181; www.mangohouses .com; villas 1500B-2500B; ☀ Oct-April) These villas (really just large rooms) are set in a 100-year-old teak house and former opium den stilted over the harbour. The original time-worn wood floors are still intact, ceilings soar and rooms are decked out with satellite TVs, DVD players and ceiling fans. The restaurant is also terrific.

Eating
The best places to grab a bite are at the seafood restaurants along the northern edge of Ban Sala Dan. With tables on verandahs over water, they offer fresh seafood sold by weight (which includes cooking costs).

Lanta Seafood (☎ 0 7566 8411; Ban Sala Dan). The best option of the seafood-by-weight options. Order the *pla tod ka min* – it's white snapper rubbed with fresh, hand-ground turmeric and garlic then deep fried. It's not oily, but it is smoky, spicy and juicy. Its steamed mussels are also divine.

Bai Fern (☎ 0 7566 8173; Ban Sala Dan; mains 40-100B; ☀ breakfast, lunch & dinner) Cheap, tasty and authentic Thai salads, noodles and curry served over the water in its stilted dining room.

Green Leaf Cafe (282 Moo 2 Hat Khlong Khong; coffee 40-100B; breakfast 50-90B; baguettes 90-100B; ☀ breakfast & lunch) A pleasant little Thai-Brit-run cafe with tasty lattes, frappes, cappuccinos, full breakfasts and an array of baguettes. Yes, it has HP sauce.

Country Lao (☎ 08 5796 3024; Ban Phra Ae; mains 80-180B) A huddle of bamboo umbrellas and thatched pagodas on the main road, you'll endure the smooth jazz soundtrack for its house speciality: crispy papaya salad (150B). Green papaya shreds are battered and crispy fried to taste like sweet noodles. They are served in an indulgent heap alongside a bowl of lime dressing swimming with peanuts, green beans and juicy cherry tomatoes. Your job: combine, devour. Pair it with a green or Massaman curry.

Beautiful Restaurant (☎ 0 7569 7062; Ban Ko Lanta; mains 100-200B) The best of Old Town's seafood

houses. Tables are scattered on four piers that extend into the sea. Fish is fresh and exquisitely prepared.

Red Snapper (☎ 0 7885 6965; www.redsnapper-lanta .com; tapas/mains from 70/235B; ☀ dinner) A Dutch-run tapas restaurant on the roadside in Ao Phra Ae, the garden setting is romantic and the duck breast with shitake mushrooms comes highly recommended.

Drinking & Entertainment
During the high season Ko Lanta has some nightlife, but there are so many driftwood-style reggae bars along the west coast it can get diluted. Low season is beyond mellow.

Moonwalk (Hat Phra Ae; cocktails 180B; ☀ 7am-11pm) A sprawling, thatched bar and restaurant that brings a little Thai funk back to what is becoming an increasingly plotted, planned and international island. Expect tasty cocktails, Jack Johnson in stereo and seafood barbecue in the high season.

Opium (Hat Phra Ae; ☀ from 6pm) This chic club has live music some nights, guest DJs and a big dance floor. It's still the top party spot on Lanta.

our pick Same Same But Different (☎ 08 1787 8670; Ao Kantiang; cocktails 200B; ☀ 8am-11pm) In a sweet seaside setting, you can sample tasty Thai cuisine and sip terrific cocktails beneath massive trees, thatched pagodas or in a bamboo chair sunk into the sand.

Getting There & Away
Most people come to Ko Lanta by boat or aircon minivan. If you're coming under your own steam, you'll need to use the frequent **vehicle ferries** (motorcycle 20B, car/4WD 75/150B; ☀ 7am-8pm) between Ban Hua Hin and Ban Khlong Mak (Ko Lanta Noi) and on to Ko Lanta Yai.

BOAT
There are two piers at Ban Sala Dan. The passenger jetty is about 300m from the main strip of shops; vehicle ferries leave from a second jetty that's several kilometres further east.

There is one passenger ferry connecting Krabi's Khlong Chilat pier with Ko Lanta. It departs from Ko Lanta at 8am (400B, two hours) and returns from Krabi at 11am. It also stops at Ko Jum (for the full 400B fare).

Boats between Ko Lanta and Ko Phi-Phi technically run year-round, although service can peter out in the low season if there are too few passengers. Ferries usually leave Ko

Lanta at 8am and 1pm (350B, 1½ hours); in the opposite direction boats leave Ko Phi-Phi at 11.30am and 2pm.

From around 21 October through May, you can join a four-island snorkelling tour to the Trang Islands and hop off with your bags at any destination you choose, but they'll charge you the full fare (1700B). Boats stop on Ko Ngai (two hours), Ko Muk (three hours) and Ko Kradan (four hours) in Trang Province.

Tigerline (☎ 08 1092 8800; www.tigerlinetravel.com), a high-speed ferry, runs between Ban Sala Dan on Ko Lanta and Ko Lipe (1400B, four hours), stopping at Ko Ngai (500B, 30 minutes), Ko Kradan (750B, 1½ hours) and Ko Muk (750B, two hours). The service leaves at 1pm. The next day the same boat makes the return trip from Ko Lipe departing at 9am and arriving in Ban Sala Dan at noon. The **Satun-Pak Bara Speedboat Club** (☎ 0 7475 0389, 08 2433 0114; www.tarutaolipeisland.com), a slightly pricier and swifter Lipe service (1900B, three hours), had just launched at research time, stopping in the Trang islands along the way.

MINIVAN

This is the main way of getting to and from Ko Lanta: minivans run year-round. Daily minivans to Krabi airport (250B, 1½ hours) and Krabi Town (300B, 1½ hours) leave hourly between 7am and 3.30pm. From Krabi, minivans depart hourly from 8am till 4pm. Minivans to Phuket (480B, four hours) leave every two hours or so, but are more frequent in the high season. **P&P Lanta Travel** (☎ 0 7566 8271; Ban Sala Dan) books minivan and ferry tickets to all Lanta destinations. **KK Tour & Travel** (☎ in Trang 0 7521 1198) has several daily air-con minivans between Trang and Ko Lanta (250B, 2½ hours).

Getting Around

Most resorts send vehicles to meet the ferries – a free ride *to* your resort. In the opposite direction expect to pay 80B to 150B. Alternatively, you can take a motorcycle taxi from opposite the 7-Eleven in Ban Sala Dan; fares vary from 50B to 200B depending on distance.

Motorcycles (250B per day) can be rented all over. Unfortunately, very few places provide helmets and none provide insurance, so take extra care on the bumpy roads.

Several places rent out small 4WDs for around 1600B per day, including insurance. The best option on two or four weeks is **Lanta Car Rental** (☎ 0 7568 4411; Hat Khlong Dan).

KO JUM & KO SI BOYA

เกาะจำ(เกาะปู) /เกาะศรีบอยา

Just north of Ko Lanta, Ko Jum and its neighbour Ko Si Boya have surprisingly little development; what's there is tucked away in the trees making the islands look and feel nearly deserted. Although technically one island, the locals consider only the flatter southern part of Ko Jum to be Ko Jum; the northern hilly bit is called Ko Pu.

Once the exclusive domain of Lanta's *chow lair* people, ethnic Chinese began landing in Ko Jum after Chairman Mao rose up in the 1950s. At the time there were no Thai people living here at all, but eventually the three cultures merged into one, which is best sampled amid the warm, early morning, ramshackle poetry of **Ban Ko Jum**, the island's fishing village. It has a few restaurants, an **internet cafe** (per min 3B), **Blue Juice Divers** (☎ in Krabi 0 7563 0679; www.bluejuicedivers.com), the island's lone dive shop.

Sleeping & Eating

Accommodation on Ko Jum is spread out along the island's west coast. There are upwards of 20 properties to choose from these days. Some places rent out sea kayaks and most have a restaurant. Public transport to Ko Jum and Ko Si Boya is very limited in the low season so most resorts close down between May and October.

Joy Bungalow (☎ 0 7561 8199, 08 9875 2221; www.kohjum-joybungalow.com; Hat Yao; bungalows 500-1500B) On the southwestern coast of Ko Jum, Joy has some very attractive stilted, polished-wood cottages on a tremendous stretch of beach. The best are raised 2m high in the trees.

Koh Jum Lodge (☎ 0 7561 8275; www.kohjumlodge.com; Hat Yao; bungalows 4000-5000B; 🕑 May-Mar; ;) An ecolodge with style: imagine lots of hard woods and bamboo, gauzy mosquito netting, manicured grounds and a hammock-strewn curve of white sand out the front. Bliss.

our pick **Koh Jum Resort** (☎ 08 0221 4040; www.kohjumresort.com; Ko Pu; bungalows 1700-3000B; 🕑 May-Mar;) The most stylish spot on the island with five stunning two-storey and ranch-style teak chalets built with crooked, polished wood and designed with cylindrical turrets. Its five bamboo huts, attached to wide sun terraces stilted high above the sea, aren't bad either. Add in the excellent landscape design and it's no wonder guests laze around in wonder.

Oon Lee Bungalows (☎ 08 7200 8053; www.koh-jum-resort.com; bungalows 500-3800B) This Crusoe-chic,

Thai-French family-run resort is nestled on a deserted white beach on the Ko Pu part of Ko Jum. Wooden stilted bungalows are in a shady garden and plenty of activities, including some of the island's best hiking, are on offer. The fantastic fusion restaurant here is reason enough for a visit.

Ting Rai Bay Resort (☎ 08 7277 7379; www.tingrai .com; Ko Pu; bungalows 500-1300B; ♥ May-Mar; ☒) Next door to splashy Koh Jum Resort, this property is no slouch. Bungalows, which vary in size and comfort, are built in a horseshoe on a sloping landscaped hill, so they all have sea views.

our pick **Woodland Lodge** (☎ 08 1893 5330; www .woodland-koh-jum.com; Hat Yao; bungalows 500-1000B) Tasteful, clean bamboo huts with proper thatched roofs, shiny, polished wood floors and verandahs. The exceptionally friendly British-Thai owners can organise boat trips and fishing and have an excellent, sociable restaurant. This is one of two resorts open year-round.

Mama Cooking (Ban Ko Jum; dishes 10B; ♥ 4am-8am) Buzzing with fishermen and local families at breakfast, this is where you dunk Thai doughnuts into filtered coffee stirred with condensed milk, and follow it with tasty chicken satay and Chinese pandan leaf tea. Mama's was the first restaurant on the island and has been in business for 22 years.

Ko Jum Seafood (☎ 08 1893 6380; Ban Ko Jum; meals 100-400B) By all accounts the best fish kitchen on the island. Fresh catch is served on a stilted deck overlooking the narrow strait with a keyhole view of Ko Lanta.

KO SI BOYA

Low-lying, rural Ko Si Boya has yet to garner more than a trickle from the annual tourism stream, and that's just fine with repeat visitors – almost all of whom land at a single, exceptional bungalow compound.

Siboya Resort (☎ 0 7561 8026, 08 1979 3344; www .siboyabungalows.com; bungalows 200-1600B; 🖳 ☜) OK, the beach itself isn't spectacular. But the mangrove setting is wild, and full of life, and the wood bungalows are large, tasteful and affordable. The restaurant rocks and it's wired with high-speed internet. No wonder ever-smiling, secretive, European and Canadian 50-somethings flock here like it's the menopausal version of Alex Garland's *The Beach*.

Getting There & Around

From November to May, boats between Krabi and Ko Lanta can drop you at Ko Jum, but you'll pay full fare (400B, one hour) – see p340. In the fringe months of November and May only the early boat will drop you. There are also small boats to Ko Jum from Ban Laem Kruat, a village about 30km southeast of Krabi, at the end of Rte 4036, off Hwy 4. Boats leave at 1pm, 3pm, 4pm and 5pm. They return the following day at 7am, 8am, 1pm and 1.30pm. Most boats cost 50B, the swiftest and largest long-tail departs from Laem Kruat at 3pm and costs 70B.

If you plan to arrive in Ko Jum via Laem Kruat you should arrange a transfer to your guesthouse of choice ahead of time because there is no motorcycle-taxi armada awaiting your arrival. Guesthouses can arrange transfers, but you could also call **Kun Det** (☎ 08 7264 9185), a reliable taxi driver who speaks decent English and can arrange affordable long-tail charters around Ko Jum. **Phruksa Bungalows** (☎ 08 5299 3986), located on the main road, rents bicycles (100B), mountain bikes (130B to 150B) and motorbikes (250B) at standard rates.

Boats to Ko Si Boya (20B) make the 10-minute hop from **Laem Hin**, just north of Ban Laem Kruat throughout the day. Private charters are 150B. Call Siboya Resort to arrange transfer from the pier.

TRANG PROVINCE

Lining the Andaman Sea south of Krabi, Trang Province has an impressive limestone-covered coast with several sublime islands. For the adventurous, there's also plenty of big nature to explore in the lush interior, including dozens of scenic waterfalls and limestone caves. And it's nowhere near as popular as Krabi, which means you're more likely to see tall rubber plantations here than rows of vendors selling the same 'same same but different' T-shirts. Transport links are improving every year and during the high season it's now possible to island hop all the way to Malaysia.

TRANG

อ.เมืองตรัง

pop 77,200

Most visitors to Trang are in transit to nearby islands, but if you're an aficionado of culture, Thai food or markets, you really should plan to stay a day or more. It's an easy-to-manage town where you can get lost in wet markets by day and hawker markets and late-night

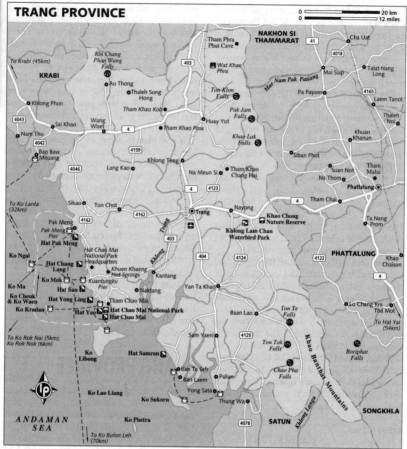

TRANG PROVINCE

Chinese coffee shops by night; at nearly any time of the year, there's likely to be some minor festival that oozes with local colour. Although there aren't any must-see attractions, there are lots of travel agencies in town dedicated to helping you hop to your island of choice as quickly as possible. Some Trang island resorts maintain satellite offices here that can assist with bookings and transfers.

Most of the tourist facilities lie along the main drag, Th Praram VI, between the clock tower and the train station.

Information

You'll find several internet cafes and various banks with ATMs and foreign-exchange booths on Th Praram VI.

My Friend (☎ 0 7522 5984; 25/17-20 Th Sathani; per hr 30B) Has the best 24-hour internet cafe in town.

Post office (cnr Th Praram VI & Th Kantang) Also sells CAT cards for international phone calls.

Sights

Trang is more of a business and market centre than a tourist town. **Wat Tantayaphirom** (Th Tha Klang) has a huge white *chedi* (stupa) enshrining a Buddha footprint, and the imposing Confucian **Kew Ong Yia Temple** is across the road. The Chinese **Meunram Temple**, between Soi 1 and Soi 3, sometimes sponsors performances of southern Thai shadow theatre. It's also recommended to stroll around the large **wet and dry markets** on Th Ratchadamnoen and Th Sathani.

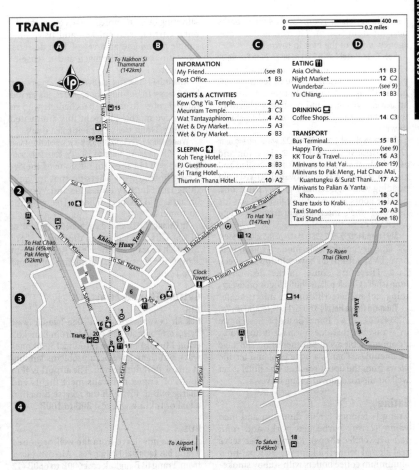

TRANG

0 ——— 400 m
0 ——— 0.2 miles

INFORMATION
My Friend....................................(see 8)
Post Office.....................................**1** B3

SIGHTS & ACTIVITIES
Kew Ong Yia Temple..................**2** A2
Meunram Temple........................**3** C3
Wat Tantayaphirom....................**4** A2
Wet & Dry Market.......................**5** A3
Wet & Dry Market.......................**6** B3

SLEEPING
Koh Teng Hotel...........................**7** B3
PJ Guesthouse.............................**8** B3
Sri Trang Hotel............................**9** A3
Thumrin Thana Hotel................**10** A2

EATING
Asia Ocha...................................**11** B3
Night Market.............................**12** C2
Wunderbar...............................(see 9)
Yu Chiang...................................**13** B3

DRINKING
Coffee Shops.............................**14** C3

TRANSPORT
Bus Terminal.............................**15** B1
Happy Trip................................(see 9)
KK Tour & Travel.......................**16** A3
Minivans to Hat Yai.................(see 19)
Minivans to Pak Meng, Hat Chao Mai,
   Kuantungku & Surat Thani...**17** A2
Minivans to Palian & Yanta
   Khao......................................**18** C4
Share taxis to Krabi..................**19** A2
Taxi Stand................................**20** A3
Taxi Stand...............................(see 18)

Activities

Tour agencies around the train station and along Th Praram VI offer various tours around Trang. **Boat trips** to Hat Chao Mai National Park start at 750B per person and take in Ko Muk, Ko Cheuk and Ko Kradan, with lunch and drinks thrown in. National park fees are extra. There are also **sea-kayaking** tours to Tham Chao Mai (650B), where you can explore mangrove forests and canoe under commanding stalactites. **Snorkelling** trips on private long-tails to Ko Rok (3500B, maximum four people) and trips to local **caves and waterfalls** (1800B, maximum three people) by private car can also be arranged by most agencies. For a cultural fix you can spend a day **hiking** in the Khao Banthat Mountains to visit villages of the Sa Kai mountain people (2500B, maximum two people). This includes a visit to waterfalls, lunch and a knowledgeable local guide.

Festivals & Events

Vegetarian Festival Trang's Chinese population celebrates this wonderful festival every October, coinciding with the similar festival in Phuket; for more about the latter festival, see boxed text, p21.

Sleeping

Trang has good budget options but midrange and top-end places leave much to be desired.

PJ Guesthouse (☎ 08 1374 6769; 25/12 Th Sathani; r 150B;) Named for the delightful English-speaking owners, Pong and Joy, they offer supercheap, clean rooms with shared baths near the train station. Their in-house travel agency is one of the best in town.

Koh Teng Hotel (☎ 0 7521 8148; 77-79 Th Praram VI; r 180-380B; ✖) The undisputed king of backpacker digs in Trang. If you're feeling optimistic, the huge, window-lit rooms here have an adventuresome kind of shabby charm to them; if not, the grunge factor might get you down.

Sri Trang Hotel (☎ 0 7521 8122; www.sritrang.com; 22-26 Th Praram VI; r 450-690B; ✖ �)) Hip, fun and affordable, there are a range of fan-cooled and air-con rooms in this renovated 60-year-old building with high ceilings, groovy paint jobs, new tile floors and wi-fi throughout. It was the hub of Trang's international traveller scene when we came through.

My Friend (☎ 0 7522 5984; 25/17-20 Th Sathani; r 550B; ✖ ⬚) Very comfortable, modern rooms here have TVs, but not all have windows – check first. There are some quirky decorative flourishes (Greek pillars, hotel logos on everything etc) and a terrific on-site internet cafe.

Thumrin Thana Hotel (☎ 0 7521 1211; 69/8 Th Huay Yot; r 1200-40,000B; ✖ ⬚) It may be the poshest choice in Trang, but that doesn't make it luxurious. Room are a bit aged, but there's no shortage of amenities. There's a huge pool and terrific views from the upper reaches. The hotel is set well off the road, down a long driveway.

Eating

Trang is famous for its dim sum and *mŏo yâhng* (crispy barbecued pork) and *ráhn goh·ƀêe* (coffee shops). *Ráhn goh·ƀêe* serve real filtered coffee (look for the charcoal-fired aluminium coffee boilers with stubby smokestacks) and you can find *mŏo yâhng* in the mornings at some coffee shops or by weight at the wet market on Th Ratchadamnoen. To really get into the local scene get to a dim sum depot early in the morning and stay out late at the coffee shops along Th Ratsada.

Ruen Thai (☎ 0 7521 9342; 63/5 Th Pluanphithak; dishes 15B; ✓ breakfast) This cavernous dim sum warehouse is packed most mornings because it has one of the few kitchens that make fresh dim sum from hand-rolled rice dough. There are deep-fried doughnuts, minced chicken and roast pork dumplings. The baskets are heated on a steam table just for you.

ourpick Night market (btwn Th Praram VI & Th Ratchadamnoen; meals around 30B) The best night market on the Andaman coast will have you

salivating over an impressive selection of bubbling curries, fried chicken and fish, some simple *pàt tai* and an array of Thai desserts. Go with an empty stomach and a sense of adventure.

Asia Ocha (Th Kantang; meals from 30B; ✓ breakfast, lunch & dinner) In business for 65 years, it's served filtered coffee to an all-Thai clientele who sit at vintage marble tables in this antiquated building. Don't sleep on their roast duck.

Wunderbar (☎ 0 7521 4563; www.wunderbar-trang .com; 24 Th Praram VI; mains 40-95B; ✓ breakfast, lunch & dinner; ⬚) On the ground floor of the Sri Trang hotel, this is a terrific spot for anything from buttery croissants and Western breakfasts to icy beer. There's free wi-fi for customers.

Yu Chiang (Th Praram VI; dishes from 50B; ✓ breakfast & lunch) This funky place on the corner of Soi 2 and Th Praram VI (there's no Roman script sign) is the classic stop for filtered coffee and *mŏo yâhng*.

Getting There & Away

AIR

Nok Air (www.nokair.com) and **One-Two-Go** (www .fly12go.com) operate daily flights from Bangkok (Don Muang) to Trang (around 1500B oneway), but there have been problems landing at this airport during rain. The airport is 4km south of Trang; minivans meet flights and charge 60B to town. In the reverse direction a taxi or túk-túk will cost 80B to 100B.

BUS

All buses now leave from the well-organised Trang **bus terminal** (Th Huay Yot). Air-con buses from Trang to Bangkok cost 600B to 650B (12 hours, morning and afternoon). More comfortable are the VIP 24-seater buses at 5pm and 5.30pm (1050B). From Bangkok, VIP/air-con buses leave between 6.30pm and 7pm.

Other services:

Destination	Price	Frequency	Duration
Hat Yai	100B	frequent	3hr
Krabi	150B	frequent	2hr
Phang-Nga	175B	hourly	3½hr
Phuket	240B	hourly	4hr
Satun	100B	frequent	3hr

MINIVAN & SHARE TAXI

There are shared taxis to Krabi (180B, two hours) and air-con minivans to Hat Yai (160B, two hours) from offices just west of the Trang bus terminal. Hourly vans heading to Surat

Thani (180B, 2½ hours), with connections to Ko Samui and Ko Pha-Ngan, leave from a **depot** (Th Tha Klang) just before Th Tha Klang crosses the railway tracks. **Happy Trip** (☎ 0 7522 2165; 22 Th Sathani) books all bus, boat and minivan tickets and offers several day tours, as well. **KK Tour & Travel** (☎ 0 7521 1198; 40 Th Sathani) runs several daily air-con minivans between Trang and Ko Lanta (250B, 2½ hours).

Local transport is mainly by air-con minivan rather than sǎorng·tǎa·ou. Minivans leave regularly from the depot on Th Tha Klang for Hat Pak Meng (70B, 45 minutes), Hat Chao Mai (80B, one hour) and Kuantungku pier (100B, one hour). To get to Ko Sukorn, sǎorng·tǎa·ou carrying market-going, Sukorn fishermen's wives leave the wet market on Th Ratchadamnoen at 10.30am to the jetty at Palian (60B), where you can charter (250B) or take a public long-tail (50B) to the island. Or you can book a private car to Ban Ta Seh (800B) and charter a boat (200B) from there. It's best to reserve this trip through Sukorn Beach Bungalows (p377).

TRAIN

Only two trains go all the way from Bangkok to Trang: the express 83, which leaves from Bangkok's Hualamphong station at 5.05pm and arrives in Trang at 7.55am the next day, and the rapid 167, which leaves from Hualamphong station at 6.20pm, arriving in Trang at 10.20am. From Trang, trains leave at 1.25pm and 5.20pm. Fares are 1480B/831B for a 1st-/2nd-class air-con sleeper and 285B for 3rd class.

Getting Around

Túk-túk mill around near the intersection of Th Praram VI and Th Kantang and charge 30B for local trips, 250B per hour. Motorbike taxis charge the same price. Motorcycles can be rented at travel agencies for about 200B per day. Most agencies can also help you arrange car rental for around 1400B per day.

TRANG BEACHES & ISLANDS

Think: luscious limestone karsts rising from steamy palm-studded valleys and swirling seas, white-sand beaches massaged by shallow tides, seagrass pastures home to resident dugong, a swim-through Emerald Cave suffused with pirate mythology, and snorkelling that rivals the best you'll find in Ko Phi-Phi and Ko Lipe. With all this easily accessible

by a network of ferries and private long-tails that can be chartered for a song, you can certainly understand why the Trang islands and beaches are no longer off-the-beaten-track. The beauty here is simply too deep, the island life too hypnotic, the seafood too tasty to be overlooked by the hordes descending in ever increasing numbers (upon Ko Muk in particular). Still, if you plan your trip for shoulder season when prices drop and crowds thin, and you make sure to include hidden gems like Ko Sukorn and Ko Libong, Trang will still feel just as wild and remote as ever.

Some islands in the chain are protected by the Hat Chao Mai National Park, including Ko Muk, Ko Kradan and Ko Cheuk. The beaches of Hat Pak Meng to Hat Chao Mai, which hosts an annual regatta in May for traditional wooden sailboats, also fall under its jurisdiction.

Hat Pak Meng & Hat Chang Lang
หาดปากเม็ง

Thirty-nine kilometres from Trang in Sikao District, Hat Pak Meng has been developed as the main jumping-off point for the nearby island of Ko Ngai. There's a wild-looking stretch of coastline here, and though the beach is scruffy, the backdrop – jutting limestone karsts on all sides that rival the best Railay and Phi-Phi have to offer – is absolutely spectacular. The main pier is at the northern end of the beach and there are several fresh seafood restaurants with deck chairs under casuarinas where Rte 4162 meets the coast.

Tour agencies at the jetty organise one-day boat tours to Ko Muk, Tham Morakot (Emerald Cave, on Ko Muk), Ko Cheuk, Ko Ma and Ko Kradan for 900B to 1000B per person (minimum three people), including lunch and beverages. There are also snorkelling day tours to Ko Ngai (750B) and Ko Rok (1200B to 1400B, plus national park fees). Mask and snorkel sets and fins can be rented by the pier for 50B each.

Hat Chang Lang is the next beach south from Hat Pak Meng and it continues the casuarina-backed beach motif. At the southern end of Hat Chang Lang, where the beachfront road turns inland, is the headquarters of **Hat Chao Mai National Park** (☎ 0 7521 3260; adult/child under 14yr 200/100B; ☽ 6am-6pm).

The 231 sq km park covers the shoreline from Hat Pak Meng to Laem Chao Mai and encompasses the islands of Ko Muk, Ko

Kradan and Ko Cheuk plus a host of small islets. In various parts of the park you may see endangered dugong and rare black-necked storks, as well as more common species such as sea otters, macaques, langurs, wild pigs, pangolins, little herons, Pacific reef egrets, white-bellied sea eagles and monitor lizards.

You usually only need to pay the national park fees if you visit the park headquarters, or Hat San and Hat Yong Ling (the next two beaches south of Hat Chang Lang).

SLEEPING

Anantara Sikao (☎ 0 7520 5888; www.sikao.anantara .com; r 8000-10,000B; ✖ ⬛ ⬛ ⬀) Set on the northern edge of Hat Chang Leng, Anantara's glamorous yet hip vibe has refreshed these old bones (it was once an Amari Resort). Deluxe oceanfront rooms have wood floors, floating desks, flat-screen TVs and amazing views of Pak Meng's signature karsts. There are impressive timber columns and Balinese wood furnishings in the lobby, and the view from its Acqua restaurant is jaw dropping. And if it's a turquoise sea and white sand you seek, take the free shuttle to its guests-only beach club on seductive Ko Kradan.

National park headquarters (☎ 0 7521 3260; www .dnp.go.th/index_eng.asp; camping with own tent free, with tent hire 300B, cabins 800-1000B) Simple cabins sleep up to six people and have fans. You can also camp under the casuarinas. There's a restaurant and a small shop here, too.

GETTING THERE & AWAY

There are several daily boats from Pak Meng to Ko Ngai (300B to 350B) at 10am, returning from Ko Ngai between 8am and 9am. A long-tail charter is 1000B to 1200B.

Regular air-con minivans from Th Kha Klang in Trang run to Hat Pak Meng (50B, 45 minutes) and Chao Mai (60B, one hour). Or you can charter a taxi from Trang for 650B to 800B.

The Chao Mai National Park headquarters is about 1km off this road, down a clearly signposted track.

Ko Ngai
เกาะไหง(ไห)

The long, blonde, wind-swept beach along the developed eastern coast of Ko Ngai (Ko Hai) extends into blue water with a sandy bottom (perfect for children) that ends at a reef drop-off with excellent snorkelling. Coral

and clear waters actually encircle the entire densely forested island – it's a stunning place. With no indigenous population living here, several spiffy resorts have the whole island to themselves. Mask and snorkel sets and fins can be rented from resorts for 60B each, sea kayaks for around 150B per hour, or you can take half-day snorkelling tours of nearby islands (850B per person). Trips to Ko Rok, 29km southwest of Ko Ngai, cost 1500B by speedboat (plus the marine national park fee). Internet at the big resorts is slow and cost 100B to 150B per hour.

Even though it's technically a part of Krabi Province, the island's mainland link is with Pak Meng.

SLEEPING

There's little here for budgetarians and most places are decidedly midrange, with their own restaurants and 24-hour electricity. The low-season boat pier is at Koh Ngai Resort, but if you book ahead resorts on the other beaches will arrange transfers.

Ko Hai Seafood (☎ 08 1367 8497; r 1000-1500B; ✖ ⬛ ⬛) These braided-bamboo bungalows are easily the most charming budget choice on the beach. The owners are fun and laid-back, they have one of the best kitchens on the island and offer good deals on long-tail charters.

Fantasy Resort & Spa (☎ 0 7520 6960; www.kohhai .com; r 1500-2800B; ✖ ⬛ ⬛ ⬀) Fantasy is a massive Angkor Wat–meets-cheesy-cruise-ship-style place that extends from the beach and up the hillside. The bungalows are comfy but a little gaudy (floral wallpaper matched with red Chinese art), with nice wooden decks, all mod cons and breakfast included. There are also plainer hotel-style rooms up the hill. Service is tip-top, there's an in-house dive shop and the restaurant serves excellent seafood.

Mayalay Resort (☎ 08 3530 7523; www.mayalay beachresort.com; r 2000-3500B; ✖ ⬛ ⬛) Another larger-than-life beach resort with a seafront spa, dive shop and charming, circular peaked-roof bamboo-and-wood bungalows that sleep three. So don't be scared off by the well-amplified easy listening tunes.

ourpick Coco Cottages (☎ 08 1693 6457, 08 9724 9225; www.coco-cottage.com; bungalows 2150-4700B; ✖ ⬀) Easily the best option and best value on the island. As the name suggests, cottages are thatched, coconut-wood pods lit with coconut-shell lanterns. There's a deck out the

---

REMARKABLE RUBBER TREES

If you ever wondered where the bounce in your rubber comes from, wonder no further: unlike money, it grows on trees. All over the Trang region, particularly on the islands floating off its coast, you are likely to come across tracts of these rubber-tree plantations.

Rubber trees produce the milky liquid known as latex in vessels that grow within the bark of the tree at a rakish 30-degree angle. It's a common misconception that latex is the actual sap of the tree. Once trees reach maturity after five to six years, collection begins. The trees are 'tapped' by making a thin incision into the bark at an angle parallel with the latex vessels. A small cup, usually made from a coconut shell, collects the latex as it drips down the tree. New scores are made every day – you can see these notched trees and collection cups throughout the region.

Latex from multiple trees is collected, poured into flat pans and mixed with formic acid, which serves as a coagulant. After a few hours, the very wet sheets of rubber are wrung out by squishing them through a press. They're then hung out to dry. You'll see these large, yellowish pancakes drying on bamboo poles wherever rubber trees are grown. The gooey ovals are then shipped to processing plants where they are turned into rubber as we know it.

---

front with lounge chairs, and they catch such a breeze, air-con isn't necessary. Grab a sea-view fan bungalow if you can. There are bamboo lounges on the beach, massage pavilions, and a terrific restaurant and beachfront bar.

Thanya Beach Resort (☎ 0 7520 6967; www.kohn gaithanyaresort.com; bungalows 3500-5000B; ✕ ▢) Bunk in one of two dozen attractive, spacious teak bungalows. Each one has indoor hot and outdoor country-style bucket showers (don't knock it till you've tried it). Dry in fine linens, then stroll to your seafront terrace and gaze at the palm-dappled lawn, which rolls towards the sea.

GETTING THERE & AWAY

The resorts provide daily boats from Hat Pak Meng to Ko Ngai at 10am, returning from Ko Ngai between 8am and 9am. Transfers cost 300B to 350B (30 minutes). You can also privately charter a long-tail to and from Pak Meng for 1000B, as well as Ko Muk (1200B) and Ko Kradan (1500B).

In the high season, the **Tigerline** (☎ 08 1092 8800; www.tigerlinetravel.com) high-speed ferry runs between Ban Sala Dan (500B, 30 minutes) on Ko Lanta and Ko Lipe (1400B, four hours) stopping at the pier on Ko Muk. **Lanta Garden Hill Speedboat** (☎ 0 7568 4042; www.lantaislandtours .com) is the more direct and comfortable choice from Ko Lanta (700B, 45 minutes). Or you can charter a long-tail to Lanta for 1500B.

Ko Muk

เกาะมุก

Motoring into Ko Muk is unforgettable. Whether you land on **Hat Sivalai**, the sugary-white triangular sand bar known for the four-star resort of the same name, or the spectacular **Hat Faràng** (aka Hat Sai Yao, aka Charlie's Beach) on the west coast where jade water kisses white sand and hulking, jungled limestone peaks hint at the location of the island's once-hidden, now-famous **Tham Morakot** (Emerald Cave). Unfortunately, the lodging options aren't tremendous, there's a steady stream of Speedo-clad package tourists tramping the beach, and even more in the speedboats that buzz to the cave from Ko Lanta. Still, the west-coast sunsets are glorious, it's easy to hop from here to any and every island in the province, and you may be shocked to feel Ko Muk's topography stir something deep and wild in your primordial soul.

Now, about that cave. It's actually a beautiful limestone tunnel that leads 80m into a *hôrng*. No wonder long-gone pirates buried treasure here. You have to swim or paddle through the tunnel, part of the way in pitch blackness, to a small concealed white-sand beach surrounded by the lofty limestone walls, with a chimney that lets in a piercing shaft of light around midday. The Emerald Cave features prominently on most tour itineraries, so it can get pretty crowded in the high season. If you can stomach early mornings, arrange a long-tail boat to zip you over to the cave just after daybreak and you'll have it to yourself.

Between Ko Muk and Ko Ngai are the small karst islets of **Ko Cheuk** and **Ko Waen**, both of which have good snorkelling and small sandy beaches.

SLEEPING & EATING
Hat Sivalai
The following places are a short walk from the pier on a shallow beach. Most are open year-round.

Coco Lodge (☎ 08 1387 4832; bungalows 400-800B) Just steps away from the main pier and scattered in a breezy coconut grove are these simple bamboo bungalows with braided walls, beamed ceilings, sweet outdoor baths and a sun terrace out the front.

Pawapi Resort (www.pawapi.com; bungalows 900-3000B) The intriguing wood-and-bamboo bungalows here were in being constructed when we visited but have since opened. Set on 350m of magnificent beach, they're worth looking into.

Sivalai (☎ 08 9723 3355; www.komooksivalai.com; bungalows incl breakfast 5000-8000B; ✷) Straddling an arrow-shaped peninsula of white sand and surrounded by views of karst islands and the mainland, you can't beat this new resort's location. Still, the cottages are more comfortable than fabulous, and the pool needs an upgrade.

Hat Farang
To stay on Hat Faràng on the west coast, you'll need to take a 10-minute motorbike taxi from the pier (80B). Don't let touts convince you there's only one resort to choose from over there. A few little restaurants serving Thai and Western food are popping up inland.

Sawasdee Resort (☎ 08 1508 0432; bungalows 500B) Simple, cleanish wooden bungalows with terraces overlooking the sea are set above the black rocks on the north end of Hat Farang.

Rubber Tree Bungalow (☎ 08 1270 4148; www.mookrubbertree.com; bungalows 600-1790B) Inland from the beach, there are cute, peach-tinted air-con cottages, cheaper bamboo bungalows and a large restaurant high up among rubber trees.

Charlie Beach Resort (☎ 0 7520 3281/3; www.kohmook.com; bungalows 1290-3150B; ✷ 🖵) There's a bunch of different bungalow options, ranging from basic beach shacks to three-star, air-con cottages at this sprawling resort, which dominates the beach and is linked by sandy paths. Skip the restaurant. Staff, although not always helpful, can organise snorkelling tours to Tham Morakot and other islands for around 1000B. Charlie's is open year-round.

ⓞⓤⓡⓟⓘⓒⓚ Ko Yao Restaurant (meals 100-200B; ☯ breakfast, lunch & dinner) Perched on the cliffs, with wood tables scattered beneath a string of lights, is this cute family-owned patio restaurant. The beer is cold, the fish is fresh and taurant. The beer is cold, the fish is fresh and steamed in a smouldering broth of chilli and lime. The red curry is tasty, and the friendly owner is happy to arrange long-tail charters at reasonable prices.

GETTING THERE & AWAY
Boats to Ko Muk leave from the pier at Kuantungku, a few kilometres south of the national park headquarters. There are several ferries to Ko Muk leaving around noon and returning at 8am (100B, 30 minutes). A chartered long-tail from Kuantungku to Ko Muk (600B, 30 minutes) and to either Pak Meng or Hat Yao is around 1200B (45 minutes to one hour). Air-con minivans run frequently from Trang to Kuantungku for 200B to 250B (one hour).

Long-tail charters to Ko Kradan (600B, 30 minutes) and Ko Ngai (1000B, one hour) are easily arranged on the pier or at Rubber Tree Bungalow or Ko Yao Restaurant on Hat Faràng.

From November to May, the **Tigerline** (☎ 08 1092 8800; www.tigerlinetravel.com) high-speed ferry runs between Ko Lanta (via Ko Ngai; 750B, two hours) and Ko Lipe (via Ko Bulon Leh; 1400B, 3½ hours), and stops on Ko Muk. **Lanta Garden Hill Speedboat** (☎ 0 7568 4042; www.lantaislandtours.com) is the swifter choice to Ko Lanta (800B, one hour).

Ko Kradan
เกาะกระดาน
Petite Kradan's beauty is plainly laid out. What you get are slender, silky white-sand beaches, bathtub-warm shallows and limestone karst views. There are pristine hard and soft corals, home to resident turtles and lionfish, just off the south coast and a small but lush tangle of remnant jungle inland. Care to slip into a lazy tropical trance? You've come to the right place. Ko Kradan is part of Hat Chao Mai National Park and for years had been spared major development, but slowly the number of resorts – including one new four-star choice – is rising. Anantara Sikao Resort (p372) has a beach club here for its mainland guests, and plenty of additional day-trippers pour onto the shore during the high season.

SLEEPING & EATING
Paradise Lost (☎ 08 9587 2409; bungalows 600-1200B) This groovy, inland American-owned bungalow property has easy access to the island's more remote beaches. Small bamboo nests

have solid wood floors and shared baths. Larger bungalows are all wood and have private facilities. Its kitchen (dishes 120B to 1800B) is the best on the island.

Ao Niang Beach Resort (☎ 08 1891 7379; bungalows 800B) Accessed by a narrow jungle track from Paradise Lost and a short wade away from some of the best snorkelling in the Trang Islands, these bungalows are quite basic. They are also spacious and clean, and the setting is magnificent nestled on a secluded sliver of white sand.

Koh Kradan Paradise Beach (☎ 0 7521 1391; www .kradanisland.com; bungalows 900-2500B; 🗙) The charm of the beachfront restaurant doesn't migrate to the rooms, which range from concrete-block and fan-cooled cheapies to larger brick bungalows with outdoor showers.

Seven Seas Resort (☎ 08 2490 2442; www.seven seasresorts.com; r 6600-7600B, bungalows 11,750-15,600B; 🗙 🗔 🛌 🛜) A stylish luxury resort with cushy lounges and shaded day beds on the sand next to an infinity pool. Lavender-brushed, palm-thatched bungalows have fine linens, terrazzo floors and cool antiquated plumbing fixtures – not to mention wide terraces with ample cushions. Rooms are slightly smaller, but still divine.

GETTING THERE & AWAY

A chartered long-tail from Kuantungku will cost around 800B one-way (45 minutes to one hour); you can also charter boats from Kradan to other islands within the archipelago. **Tigerline** (☎ 08 1092 8800; www.tigerlinetravel .com) connects Kradan with Ko Lanta (750B, 1½ hours) and Hat Yao (750B, one hour). **Lanta Garden Hill Speedboat** (☎ 0 7568 4042; www .lantaislandtours.com) is a quicker, more comfortable Lanta option (900B, one hour).

Hat Yao
หาดยาว

A rickety, scruffy fishing hamlet just south of Hat Yong Ling, Hat Yao is sandwiched between the sea and imposing limestone cliffs, and sits at the mouth of a thick mangrove estuary. A rocky headland at the southern end of Hat Yao is pockmarked with caves and there's good snorkelling around the island immediately offshore. The best beach in the area is the tiny **Hat Apo**, hidden away among the cliffs; you can get here by long-tail or wade around from the sandy spit in front of Sinchai's Chaomai Resort.

Tham Chao Mai is a vast cave full of crystal cascades and impressive stalactites and stalagmites that can be explored by boat. To visit it, you can charter a long-tail for 400B per hour from Yao pier. Haad Yao Nature Resort offers guided sea-kayaking trips to the cave, including lunch, for around 800B per person. You can also rent a kayak and self explore the cave for 600B (map included).

Just south of the headland is the Yao pier, the main departure point for Ko Libong and the midpoint in the *Tigerline* chain that connects Lipe to Lanta.

SLEEPING & EATING

Haad Yao Nature Resort (☎ 08 1894 6936; www.trangsea .com; r 500-1200B, bungalows 800B; 🗙 🗔) There are a few other choices in Hat Yao, but this is the only resort worth considering. Set in the harbour and run by the Lifelong Learning Foundation, an ecological and educational NGO led by enthusiastic naturalists, this place offers a variety of environmental-focused tours in the Hat Yao area. It has large cottages with wide terraces, TV and DVD, simpler motel-style rooms and a few over-water bungalows.

Along the beach, north of the limestone headland, is a collection of wooden seafood restaurants selling cheap Thai meals. There is also a handful of tasty harbour restaurants.

GETTING THERE & AROUND

From here, you can catch one of the regular long-tail boats to Ko Libong (50B, 20 minutes). You can also charter long-tail boats to Ko Libong (800B, 20 minutes) or to Ko Muk (1500B, one hour) each way. Sŏrng·tǎa·ou to Trang (100B, one hour) leave when full from the pier – your best bet is before 9am. **Tigerline** (☎ 08 1092 8800; www.tigerlinetravel.com) is the area's high-speed ferry service, which docks in Hat Yao for lunch on its way between Lanta (750B, 2½ hours) and Lipe (750B, 2½ hours).

Ko Libong
เกาะลิบง

Trang's largest island is just 15 minutes by long-tail from Hat Yao. Less visited than neighbouring isles, it's a peaked, mountainous jungle pearl, known for its captivating flora and fauna more than its thin reddish-brown beaches. The island is home to a small Muslim fishing community and has a few resorts on the west coast.

NICE DAY FOR A WET WEDDING

Every Valentine's Day (14 February), Ko Kradan is the setting for a rather unusual wedding ceremony. Around 35 brides and grooms don scuba gear and descend to an altar among the coral reefs, exchanging their vows in front of the Trang District Officer. How the couples manage to say 'I do' underwater has never been fully explained, but the ceremony has made it into *Guinness World Records* for the 'Most Couples Married Underwater'. Before and after the scuba ceremony, the couples are paraded along the coast in a flotilla of motorboats. If you think this might be right for your special day, visit www.underwaterwedding.com.

On the east coast of Ko Libong at **Laem Ju Hoi** is a large area of mangroves protected by the Botanical Department as the **Libong Archipelago Wildlife Reserve** (☎ 0 7525 1932). The sea channels here are one of the last habitats of the rare dugong, and around 40 of them graze on the sea grass that flourishes in the bay. The 'Nature Resorts' in Hat Yao and Ko Libong, both nonprofit NGOs that use funds to hire and train local fishermen in ecotourism and sustainable fishing practices, offer dugong-spotting tours by sea kayak, led by trained naturalists, for 1000B. Sea kayaks can also be rented at most resorts for 150B per hour.

Libong also has tremendous migrating bird life. Keep your eyes peeled for the crab plover, black-necked stork and the Eurasian curlew, which fly here all the way from Siberia each winter.

SLEEPING

Libong Beach Resort (☎ 0 7522 5205; www.libong beachresort.com; bungalows 500-800B; ❄ 💻) Right next door to Le Dugong Resort, this is the only place on the island that's open year-round – rates drop considerably in the low season. There are several options from bland slap-up shacks behind a murky stream to beachfront and very comfortable wood-and-thatch chalets. It offers dugong-spotting trips (1000B, three hours) and internet access (per hour 100B). There's also a dive centre (two dives 3500B) open during the high season.

Le Dugong Resort (☎ 08 7972 7228; www.libong resort.com; bungalows 500-900B) An intimate resort with rustic yet stylish wood-and-bamboo bungalows with terracotta sinks, braided walls and shuttered doors that open the whole room to the sea and setting sun. Motorbikes can be rented here for 400B per day.

Libong Nature Resort (☎ 08 1894 6936; www .trangsea.com; bungalows 600-1500B; ❄) Once a sacred site for *chow lair* shamen, this property is owned and run by the Lifelong Learning Foundation and managed by resident international volunteers. Bunk in one of a dozen concrete cottages set on a palm-shaded lawn that rolls to the best beach on the island. It runs excellent sea-kayaking tours of the mangroves and to the sea-grass mounds to spot dugong.

GETTING THERE & AWAY

Long-tail boats to Ban Ma Phrao on the eastern coast of Ko Libong leave regularly from Hat Yao (20 minutes) during daylight hours for 50B per person; the long-tail jetty at Hat Yao is just west of the newer Yao pier. On Ko Libong, motorcycle taxis run across to the resorts on the western coast for 80B. A chartered long-tail directly to the resorts will cost 800B each way.

Ko Lao Liang
เกาะเหลาเหลียง

Ko Lao Liang is actually two islands right next to each other: Ko Laoliang Nong, the smaller of the two where the only resort is found, and the larger Ko Laoliang Pi, where there's a small fishermen's settlement. The islands are karst formations with small white-sand beaches, clear water and plenty of coral close to shore.

The only place to stay is **Laoliang Island Resort** (☎ 08 4304 4077; www.laoliangresort.com; per person 1200-1500B). Lodging is in comfy tents equipped with mattresses and fans, right on the beach, and there are plenty of activities on offer, including snorkelling, climbing the islands' karst cliffs and sea kayaking. At night there's a small bar and the restaurant fires up its seafood barbecue regularly. Rates include all meals, snorkel gear and sea kayaks; you'll pay a bit more for a snorkel tour or climbing instruction.

Tigerline (☎ 08 1092 8800; www.tigerlinetravel .com) stops just off Ko Lao Liang between Lanta (1400B, 2½ hours) and Lipe (750B, 2½ hours).

Ko Sukorn

เกาะสุกร

Clichés be damned, there are places in this world that are more than the sum of their parts. Sukorn is one of them. The pleasant charcoal beaches, light-green sea, black-rock headlands shrouded in jungle, and stilted shack neighbourhoods home to about 2800 Muslim fisher folk – their rice fields, watermelon plots and rubber plantations unfurling on narrow concrete roads – are not spectacular in and of themselves. It's the way these rhythms converge that sucks the road angst from your soul. Here you will find a deep quiet and black nights. Like the sight of a single beached long-tail at sunset, Sukorn's simple stillness is breathtaking.

The best way to see the island is by renting a mountain bike for the day (150B) – with few hills, stunning panoramas, lots of shade and plenty of opportunities to meet locals. Covering up is an absolute must when you leave the beach.

SLEEPING

Sukorn Cabana (☎ 08 9724 2326; www.sukorncabana.com; bungalows 500–1800B; ✺) Sloping grounds dotted with large and clean bungalows meet interesting conglomerate rock formations on the shore. There are lots of places for lounging in the flower garden, and there is a good restaurant.

our pick **Sukorn Beach Bungalows** (☎ 0 7520 7707, 08 1647 5550; www.sukorn-island-trang.com; bungalows 750–2200B) Easily the most professionally run place on this island, the concrete-and-wood bungalows all have comfy verandahs and a long beach out the front from which you can watch the sun set over outlying islands. The friendly Dutch and Thai owners are chock-full of information, can arrange excellent tailor-made island-hopping tours throughout the region, and offer guided tours of Sukorn (per person 250B) that reveal its culture and natural beauty. Oh, and the food (fresh seafood meals 200B to 300B) absolutely rocks. Try the wild king prawns or the blah tôrt kamin (fish rubbed with a ground turmeric and garlic paste, then flash fried in a wok). The resort is open year-round (rates drop by 60% in the low season).

Ko Sukorn Paradise (☎ 08 3168 6630; www.sukorncabana.com; bungalows 1000–1200B) A lazy, lush beach resort where spider orchids grace the thatched-roof restaurant and a handful of comfy, thatched coconut-wood bungalows await.

GETTING THERE & AWAY

The easiest way to get to Sukorn is by private transfers from Trang available with the resorts for 1550B to 1950B per person. The more adventurous way is to catch one of the sŏrng·tăa·ou carrying market-going Sukorn villagers that leave the wet market on Th Ratchadamnoen in Trang for Palian (transfer in Yan Ta Khao; 100B, 1½ hours) at 10.30am. These trucks meet one public long-tail (50B, one hour) per day, which leaves the Palian pier at noon. The long-tail returns to Palian the following morning at 7.30am. Or you can charter a long-tail from here for 250B.

Otherwise book a private taxi or sŏrng·tăa·ou from Trang to Ban Ta Seh (800B), where you can charter a long-tail to Ban Saimai (250B), the main village on Ko Sukorn. The resorts are a 20-minute walk or 50B motorcycle taxi ride from Ban Saimai. You can also charter long-tails directly to the beach resorts (750B).

From Ko Sukorn you can charter long-tails to Ko Lao Liang (1750B) – where you can meet the high-speed **Tigerline** (☎ 08 1092 8800; www.tigerlinetravel.com) ferry that connects Lanta with Lipe and serves all islands inbetween – including Ko Kradan, Ko Ngai or Ko Muk (1400B).

AROUND TRANG PROVINCE

The eastern edge of Trang Province is lined with forested hills that are full of dramatic limestone caves and scenic waterfalls. Unfortunately, none of these can be reached by public transport, so you'll need to take a tour or rent a vehicle. If you want to explore the region under your own steam, travel agencies in Trang (see p369) can help you arrange either motorbike (200B per day) or car rental (around 1400B per day). These agencies can also arrange tours.

Waterfalls

Trang Province is famous for its waterfalls, particularly in the southeast, where the Trang and Palian Rivers meet the Khao Banthat Mountains. A scenic, paved road branches south from Hwy 4, near the Trang–Phattalung border, passing several cascades including the towering **Ton Te Falls**. A hiking trail leads 1km from here to **Ton Tok Falls**, which offers grand views back over Ton Te Falls. In the Palian District near Laem Som, **Chao Pha Falls** has about 25 stepped falls of 5m to 10m each, with pools at every level.

There's another cluster of falls between Trang and Huay Yot off Rte 4123, including **Ton Klon**, **Pak Jam** and **Khao Lak**. Perhaps the most unusual waterfall in the province is **Roi Chang Phan Wang** (Hundred Levels, Thousand Palaces), about 70km northwest of Trang in Wang Wiset District, a little-explored corner of the region. Surrounded by rubber groves, dozens of thin cascades of water tumble down limestone rock formations into pools below.

You'll need your own transport to reach most of these falls, but Trang travel agencies (see p369) can arrange tours in private cars to Ton Te for around 1800B.

Caves

Dramatic caves are another speciality of the Trang region. Close to the Trang River, near Wang Wiset in the north, **Tham Khao Kob** (Lay Cave) has scenic limestone formations and a 4km-long subterranean stream that you can explore by sea kayak. The local Tambon administration rents out boats for 50B per person. Nearby is **Tham Khao Pina**, off Hwy 4 at the Km43 marker, which contains a large, multilevel Buddhist shrine that's popular with Thai tourists.

North of Huay Yot at the very top of the province is **Tham Phra Phut**, a cave temple with a large Ayutthaya-period reclining Buddha. Nearby **Wat Khao Phra** is housed in a cave temple with mysterious red seals carved into the walls. About 15km northeast of Trang, near the weaving village of Na Meun Si on Rte 4123, is **Tham Khao Chang Hai**, another famous cavern with impressive limestone formations.

Travel agencies in Trang charge 1800B for tours in private cars (maximum three people) to Tham Khao Kob and Tham Khao Chang Hai, including a stop at Na Meun Si.

SATUN PROVINCE

Until recently, Satun was mostly overlooked, but that's all changed thanks to the dynamic white sands of Ko Lipe – a one-time backpacker secret turned mainstream beach getaway and the growing popularity (among Thais) of one of Thailand's true wild gems, the undeveloped Ko Tarutao Marine National Park. This phenomenal park encompasses some of the most pristine islands in the Andaman, all drenched in greenery and edged by tropical beaches; fortunately much of it is well protected. Beyond Ko Lipe the province still hardly rates a blink of the eye as visitors rush north to Ko Lanta or south to Pulau Langkawi, Malaysia. Which means, of course, that they miss the untrammelled beaches and sea caves on Ko Tarutao, the rugged trails and ribbon waterfalls of Ko Adang and the rustic beauty of Ko Bulon Leh.

Until 1813 Satun was a district of the Malay state of Kedah, but the region was ceded to Britain in 1909 under the Anglo-Siamese Treaty and became a province of Siam in 1925. Largely Muslim in make-up, Satun has seen little of the political turmoil that plagues the neighbouring regions of Yala, Pattani and Narathiwat (see boxed text, p258). Around 60% of people here speak Yawi or Malay as a first language, and the few *wát* in the region are quite humble and vastly outnumbered by mosques.

SATUN
อ.เมืองสตูล
pop 33,720

Lying in a steamy jungle valley surrounded by limestone cliffs, and framed by a murky river, isolated Satun is a relaxing coastal town where tourism is limited to visa-run traffic, which flows in both directions. Malay-based yachties, passing through for cheap repairs in Satun's acclaimed boat yard, are the only travellers who seem to hang around. The nearby Tammalang pier has boats to Kuala Perlis and Pulau Langkawi in Malaysia, but if you wander a bit before you leave, you'll see some interesting religious architecture, lots of friendly smiles and plenty of gritty charm.

Information

Bangkok Bank (Th Burivanich) Has a foreign-exchange desk and an ATM.

CAT office (Th Satun Thanee) Same location as the post office.

Immigration Office (☎ 0 7471 1080; Th Burivanich; ⏰ 8.30am-4.30pm Mon-Fri) Handles visa issues and extensions for long termers. It's easier and cheaper for tourists to exit Thailand via the border check post at Tammalang pier and immediately re-enter to obtain a new 15-day tourist visa. You will need to catch the boat and enter Malaysia before you come back, however. If you have wheels, hop to Malaysia via Thale Ban National Park (see p382).

Post office (cnr Th Satun Thanee & Th Samanta Prasit)

Siam Commercial Bank (Th Satun Thanee) Also has foreign exchange and an ATM.

Sinkiat Thanee Hotel (50 Th Burivanich; internet access per hr 30B; ⏰ 8am-11pm)

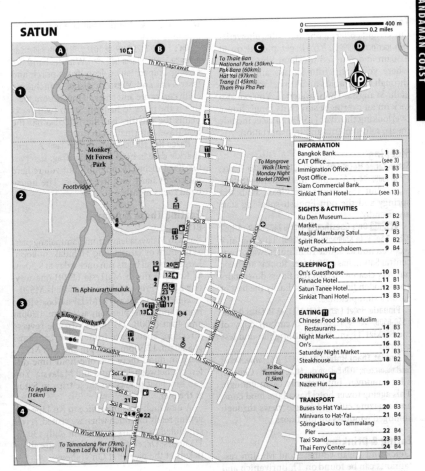

SATUN

0 — 400 m
0 — 0.2 miles

Sights

KU DEN MUSEUM

Housed in a lovely old Sino-Portuguese mansion just off Th Satun Thanee is the excellent **Ku Den Museum** (Satun National Museum; Soi 5, Th Satun Thanee; admission 20B; 8.30am-4.30pm Sun-Wed). The building was constructed to house King Rama V during a royal visit, but the governor of Satun took the house as his private residence when the king failed to show. The building has been lovingly restored and now has exhibits and dioramas with soundtracks in Thai and English, covering every aspect of southern Muslim life.

OTHER SIGHTS

Satun has an undeniable lazy beauty. You can access it by hiking **Monkey Mountain**, a jungled mound of limestone teeming with primates, by winding around **Spirit Rock**, a kitschy but locally beloved Buddhist shrine, or by walking over a bridge and strolling through a stilted fishing village that is just a kilometre from town but feels like another world. The new, self-guided **Mangrove Walk**, a boardwalk with a river viewpoint behind the football stadium, is especially popular at sunset.

There are lots of rivers and inlets to explore in the Satun region, your best bet is to head down to Tammalang pier, a 7km sörng·tăa·ou ride south of Satun, where you can hire longtail boats to visit **Tham Lod Pu Yu**, a picturesque limestone cave dripping with stalactites, right on the Malaysian border. Boat operators charge about 700B round-trip.

Tours

On's (right) offers a one-day **Satun Discoveries trip** (per person 990B). You'll get picked up at 8.30am and shuttled to Tham Phu Pha Pet, where you'll slip into kayaks and paddle through mini-rapids for 7km before relaxing at the Wang Sai Thong waterfall. You can also tack on an overnight stay in its jungle house overlooking the river (1500B). Prices include meals, refreshments and transportation.

Sleeping

Satun Tanee Hotel (☎ 0 7471 1010; 90 Th Satun Thanee; r 170-380B; 🛏) A rather institutional-feeling place, but the rooms are clean, beds are springy and the non-English-speaking staff are friendly.

our pick **On's Guesthouse** (☎ 0 7473 0469, 08 1097 9783; 1 Soi 1, Th Khuhaprawat; r 200B) This big airy wooden house, about 10 minutes' walk from central Satun, has a B&B feel. Rooms are basic but very clean with concrete floors downstairs and wooden floors upstairs. Easily the best of Satun's slim pickings.

Pinnacle Hotel (☎ 0 7471 1611; 43 Th Satun Thanee; r 550-650B; 🛏 🛜) Almost a carbon copy of the Sinkiat Thani, but a bit brighter and less central.

Sinkiat Thani Hotel (☎ 0 7472 1055; www.sinkiat hotel.thport.com; 50 Th Burivanich; r 680B; 🛏 🛜) Central, a bit rundown, but certainly clean enough. This ageing tower hotel has all the mod cons, and amazing city and jungle views through smudged windows on top floors.

Eating & Drinking

Quick and cheap Chinese and Muslim restaurants can be found on Th Burivanich and Th Samanta Prasit. The Chinese food stalls specialise in *kôw mǒo daang* (red pork with rice), while the Muslim restaurants offer roti with southern-style chicken curry (around 50B each).

Night markets (Th Satun Thanee) There are some excellent night markets in Satun. The daily market begins just north of Satun Tanee Hotel, comes to life around 5pm, and serves great fried fish, squid skewers and spicy, southern-style curries. There's also a much larger Saturday night market on Th Burivanich and a Monday night market 1km from town on Th Yatrasawat.

Steakhouse (☎ 0 7472 3777; 45/27 Th Satun Thanee; dishes 60-130B) A shiny new air-con place with rustic wood furnishings on the outdoor patio,

where tasty, authentic Thai fare is served by attentive staff.

On's (☎ 0 7473 0469, 08 1097 9783; 48 Th Burivanich; dishes 80-150B; 🕑 8am-late; 🛜) With its bamboo, sarong-draped tables, leafy front porch and tasty Thai and Western dishes – including chilli con carne and chicken mushroom pie – this is the place to hang in Satun (which explains the yachties bar flies). It also has the best travel information in town.

Nazee Hut (Th Burivanich; 🕑 6pm-1am) A ramshackle dive behind the main drag, it serves OK Thai dishes (from 50B), but you're here for cold Chang and live music. The house band rocks nightly.

Getting There & Away

BOAT

Boats to Malaysia leave from Tammalang pier, 7km south of Satun along Th Sulakanukoon. Large long-tail boats run once a day at 9.30am to Kuala Perlis in Malaysia (150B one-way, one hour). From Malaysia the fare is M$20.

For Pulau Langkawi in Malaysia, boats leave from Tammalang pier daily at 9.30am, 1.30pm and 4pm (300B, 1½ hours). In the reverse direction, boats leave from Pulau Langkawi at 8.30am, 12.30pm and 3pm and cost M$27. Keep in mind there is a one-hour time difference between Thailand and Malaysia. You can buy boat tickets for these trips in Satun at the pier.

A new high-season service to Ko Lipe was getting ready to launch when we visited. It was scheduled to depart at 10.30am daily (300B, 1½ hours; December to May). Enquire about tickets at the pier or at On's (above).

BUS

All buses now leave from the **bus terminal** (Th Samanta Prasit), 2km east of the town centre. Air-con services to Bangkok (800B to 1200B, 14 hours) leave at 7am, 7.30am, 3pm and 4pm. Ordinary and air-con buses to Trang (90B, 1½ hours) leave hourly. There are also a few daily buses to Krabi (221B, four hours) and Phuket (340B, seven hours). Buses to Hat Yai (70B, two hours) will stop and pick up passengers on Th Satun Thanee as they slowly make their way north.

MINIVAN & SHARE TAXI

There are regular minivans to the train station in Hat Yai (70B, one hour) from a depot south of Wat Chanathipchaloem on Th

Sulakanukoon. Occasional minivans run to Trang, but buses are much more frequent. If you're arriving by boat at Tammalang pier, there are direct air-con minivans to Hat Yai and Hat Yai airport (90B).

Share taxis can be hired from next to the Masjid Mambang Satun to Pak Bara (500B, 45 minutes), La-Ngu (400B, 30 minutes) or Hat Yai (450B, one hour).

There is no longer any public transport to Thale Ban National Park, but On's (opposite) can arrange chartered transport. Expect to pay roughly 1500B return.

Getting Around

Small orange sŏrng·tăa·ou to Tammalang pier (for boats to Malaysia) cost 40B and leave from the 7-Eleven on Th Sulakanukoon 40 minutes before ferry departure. A motorcycle taxi from the same area costs 60B.

AROUND SATUN
Pak Bara
ปากบารา

The small fishing community of Pak Bara is the main jumping-off point for the islands in the Mu Ko Phetra and Ko Tarutao Marine National Park. Tourist facilities are slowly improving as Pak Bara becomes increasingly busy with tourists discovering these dazzling isles. The peaceful town has some decent sleeping options and great seafood, but unless you arrive after the boats have gone there's no pressing reason to stick around.

The main road from La-Ngu terminates at the pier where there are several travel agencies, internet cafes, cheap restaurants and shops selling beach gear. There's a **visitors centre** (☎ 0 7478 3485) for Ko Tarutao Marine National Park just back from the pier, where you can book accommodation and obtain permission for camping. Travel agencies here can arrange tours to the islands in the national park.

TOURS

There are several travel agencies near the pier that will vie for your transport custom. **Adang Seatours** (☎ 0 7478 3338; www.adangseatour .com) is one of the more reliable agencies. Shop around for kayaking daytrips through the impressive caves at **Tham Chet Khok** (per person incl lunch 1800B).

During the high season, the **Satun Pakbara Speedboat Club** (☎ 0 7478 3643; www.tarutaolipeisland .com) runs speedboat tours to Ko Tarutao, Ko

Bulon Leh and Ko Lipe – visit the website for the latest details.

SLEEPING & EATING

Happy House (☎ 0 7478 3631; r 300-390B; 🖳) Well signed from the main road, but set down a gravel lane in a local fishing enclave. Rooms are bright, spacious and come with cable TV and blooming flower boxes on the 2nd-storey terrace.

Best House Resort (☎ 0 7478 3058; bungalows 590B; 🖳) One hundred metres inland from the pier, this place has tidy concrete bungalows around a murky pond. Management is superfriendly and helpful with travel tips.

Red Boat (☎ 0 7478 3498; dishes 60-150B; 🕔 7am-11pm) Stop here while waiting for your ferry for Western breakfasts, espresso drinks, cocktails or tremendous fried prawns in tamarind sauce.

There are several elementary restaurants and vendors near the Pak Bara pier that serve good Malay Muslim food for 20B to 50B. There's also a series of tasty seafood stalls along the coast south of town that get smoking just before sunset. They're a popular local hang-out on Sundays.

GETTING THERE & AWAY

There are hourly buses between 7am and 4pm from Hat Yai to the pier at Pak Bara (90B, 2½ hours). Coming from Satun, you can take an ordinary bus towards Trang and get off at La-Ngu (40B, 30 minutes), continuing by sŏrng·tăa·ou to Pak Bara (30B, 15 minutes). You can also charter a taxi to Pak Bara from Satun for 450B.

Air-con minivans leave hourly for Hat Yai (150B, two hours) from travel agencies near Pak Bara pier. There are also minivans to Trang (200B, 1½ hours), which connect to numerous destinations like Krabi (450B, four hours) and Phuket (650B, six hours). It's cheaper, although more complicated, to get a minibus to Trang and then organise your own transport from there.

The day of the large, belching wooden ferry appears to have passed in Satun province. From 21 October to the end of May there is nothing but speedboats to Ao Pante Malacca on Ko Tarutao and on to Ko Lipe. **Adang Seatours** (☎ 0 7478 3338; www.adangseatour.com) is one of several competent speedboat operators who make the run. Its boats depart from Pak Bara at 11am and 2pm (return 1200B, 1½ hours); in

---

DETOUR: THALE BAN NATIONAL PARK

Very few foreigners make it out to this park, which lies on the Malaysian border about 30km northeast of Satun. Its main feature is a freshwater lake that sits in the middle of the 196-sq-km park, a scenic area of upland rainforest with captivating wildlife and abundant birdlife, along with wet-season waterfalls and caverns. Next to the lake are 13 national park cottages, which can be rented for 600B per night. Contact **Thale Ban National Park** (☎ 08 3533 1710; www.dnp.go.th) for bookings. An interesting market unfurls on both sides of the border every Sunday morning.

There's no public transport to the park, but you can get here by hired taxi from Satun or Hat Yai. See p380 for more details.

---

the reverse direction boats leave at 9.30am and 1.30pm. From 16 November these boats also stop at Ko Adang for the same price. For Ko Bulon Leh, boats depart at 12.30pm, arriving in Ko Bulon Leh one hour later (return 800B), before buzzing on to Ko Lipe. If you miss the Bulon boat, you can easily charter a long-tail from local fishermen (1500B to 2000B, 1½ hours). During the wet season, services to Ko Lipe are weather and demand dependent, but usually cut back to three times per week.

Ko Bulon Leh
เกาะบุโหลนเล

This pretty island, 23km west of Pak Bara, is surrounded by the Andaman's signature clear waters and has its share of faultless beaches with swaying casuarinas. Gracious Ko Bulon Leh is in that perfect phase of being developed enough to offer comfortable facilities, yet not so popular that you have to book beach-time days in advance.

The exceptional white-sand **beach** extends along the east coast from Bulone resort, on the northeast cape, to Pansand. At times the beach narrows a bit, especially where it is buffered by gnarled mangroves and strewn with thick sun-bleached logs. But those nooks and crannies make it easy to find a secret shady spot with dreamy views.

Bulon's lush interior is interlaced with a few tracks and trails that are fun to explore – though the dense, jungled rock that makes up the western half remains inaccessible on foot. Bulon's wild beauty is accessible amid the rocky blue lagoon of **Panka Yai** on the southern coast. There's good snorkelling around the western headland, and if you follow the trails through remnant jungle and rubber plantations – with eyes wide lest you miss glimpsing one of Bulon's enormous resident monitor lizards – you'll wind your way to **Ao Muang** (Mango Bay), where you'll find an authentic

chow lair squid-fishing camp. Ramshackle and timeless it spills onto the golden sand and overlooks a jade lagoon sheltered by jungled black-granite headlands.

Resorts can arrange snorkelling trips (1500B, four hours) to other islands in the Ko Bulon group for a maximum of six people, and fishing trips for 300B per hour. Trips usually take in glassy emerald waters of **Ko Gai** and **Ko Ma**, gnarled rocks ravaged by wind and time. But the most stunning sight has to be **White Rock** – bird-blessed spires rising out of the open sea. Beneath the surface is a rock reef crusted with mussels and teeming with colourful fish. Snorkelling is best at low tide. The area's best coral reef is off Laem Son near Bulone Resort, where you can rent masks, snorkels (100B), fins (70B) and kayaks (150B).

Bulone Resort also offers internet (per minute 3B), and battery-charging services for laptops (50B) and digital cameras (10B).

SLEEPING & EATING
Most places here shut down in the low season. Those that persevere rent out bungalows at discount rates.

Chaolae Homestay (bungalows 400B) With simple yet tasteful log cabanas on the hill above Panka Yai, this *chow lair* family-owned and operated property is the island's best newcomer and arguably its best-value option. There's good snorkelling off the nearby beach.

our pick **Marina Resort** (☎ 08 1598 2420, 08 5078 1552; www.marina-kobulon.com; bungalows 500-1000B) Low slung and shaggy with stilted decks, louvred floors and high ceilings, thatched huts never looked or felt so good. The best huts on the island come with a tasty kitchen attached to an inviting patio restaurant with cushioned floor seating. The ever-gracious Max will be your wise-ass host. The resort arranges speedboat tickets and snorkelling tours.

Bulone Resort (☎ 08 6960 0468; www.bulone-resort .com; bungalows 1000-1200B) Perched on the north-east cape with access to two exquisite stretches of white sand, these cute wooden bungalows are among the best sleeping options on Bulon. Queen-sized beds come with iron frames and ocean breezes. It has electricity all night long and serves up a tremendous mango smoothie with honey, lime and fresh yoghurt.

Pansand Resort (☎ 07521 1010; www.pansand-resort .com; cottages 1200-1500B; ☐) Pansand sits on the south end of the island's gorgeous white-sand beach. Brick-and-braided bamboo bunga-lows are fan cooled and come with sea views. Cheaper wooden bungalows are set back in the trees. All have 24-hour electricity. It runs the speedboat concession that links Bulon to Lipe and Lanta.

There are a few local restaurants and a small shop in the Muslim village next to Bulon Viewpoint.

GETTING THERE & AWAY

The boat to Ko Bulon Leh (400B) leaves from Pak Bara at 12.30pm daily if there are enough takers. Ship-to-shore transfers to the beach by long-tail cost 30B. In the reverse direction, the boat moors in the bay in front of Pansand Resort at around 9am. You can charter a long-tail from Pak Bara for 1500B to 2000B.

The island is no longer served by ferry, but from November to May there are two daily speedboats (600B, one hour) from Ko Bulon Leh to Ko Lipe in Ko Tarutao Marine National Park. Boats, which originate in Ko Lanta and make stops in the Trang Islands, depart from in front of the Pansand resort at 1pm and 3pm.

KO TARUTAO MARINE NATIONAL PARK

อุทยานแห่งชาติหมู่เกาะตะรุเตา

Ko Tarutao Marine National Park (☎ 0 7478 1285; www .dnp.go.th/parkreserve; adult/child under 14yr 200/100B) is one of the most exquisite and unspoilt regions in all of Thailand. This massive park encom-passes 51 islands covered with well-preserved virgin rainforest teeming with fauna, as well as healthy coral reefs and radiant beaches.

One of the first marine national parks in Thailand, the main accommodation in the park are small, ecofriendly government-run cabins and longhouses. Pressure from big de-velopers to build resorts on the islands has so far (mostly) been mercifully ignored, though concessions were made for the filming of the American reality-TV series *Survivor* in 2001. And there is the minor issue of a private fish-ing resort on Ko Adang, which is supposed to be off-limits to developers. Originally slated to open in 2010, local environmentalists have appealed to the Thai courts to keep it shut.

Rubbish on the islands can be a problem – removal of beach rubbish as well as that gen-erated from visitors only happens sporadi-cally. Do your part and tread lightly out here. Within the park you can spot dusky langurs, crab-eating macaques, mouse deer, wild pigs, sea otters, fishing cats, tree pythons, water monitors, Brahminy kites, sea eagles, horn-bills and kingfishers.

Ko Tarutao is the biggest and most-visited island in the group and is home to the park headquarters and government accommoda-tion. Many travellers choose to stay on Ko Lipe, which has managed to evade the park's protection and is fast becoming a popular and increasingly paved resort island with tourist facilities and bungalows aplenty. Long-tail tours to outlying islands can be arranged through travel agencies in Satun or Pak Bara, through the national park headquarters on Ko Tarutao or through resorts and long-tail boat operators on Ko Lipe. Note that there are no foreign-exchange facilities at Ko Tarutao – you can change cash and travellers cheques at travel agencies in Pak Bara and there's an ATM at La-Ngu.

Ko Tarutao

เกาะตะรุเตา

Most of Ko Tarutao's whopping 152 sq km is covered in old-growth jungle, which rises sharply up to the park's 713m peak. Mangrove swamps and typically impressive limestone cliffs circle much of the island, and the west-ern coast is pocked with caves and lined with quiet white-sand beaches. This is one of Thailand's wildest islands.

Tarutao's sordid history partly explains its preservation. Between 1938 and 1948, more than 3000 Thai criminals and political pris-oners were incarcerated here, including in-teresting inmates such as So Setabutra, who compiled the first Thai-English dictionary while imprisoned on Tarutao, and Sittiporn Gridagon, son of Rama VII. During WWII, food and medical supplies from the main-land were severely depleted and hundreds of prisoners died from malaria. The prisoners and guards mutinied, taking to piracy in the

KO TARUTAO MARINE NATIONAL PARK & AROUND

INFORMATION
Mu Ko Phetra Marine National Park	
Headquarters..................................1	F1
Park Headquarters............................2	E2

SIGHTS & ACTIVITIES
Ao Molae Ranger Station....................3	E2
Ao Taloh Udang Ranger Station.........4	E3
Ao Taloh Waw Ranger Station............5	E3
Castaway Divers.........................(see 18)	
Chado Cliff.......................................6	B4
Forra Dive..7	D4
Islander Sea Sports...........................8	D4
Laem Son Ranger Station..................9	B4
Lu Du Falls.....................................10	E3
Lu Po Falls......................................11	E3
Pirate's Falls...................................12	B4
Sabaye Divers...........................(see 24)	
Tham Jara-Khe...............................13	E2
Toe-Boo Cliff..................................14	E2

SLEEPING
Ao Molae Bungalows & Camp	
Sites.......................................(see 3)	
Ao Taloh Waw Campsites...........(see 5)	
Bila Beach......................................15	D4
Blue Tribes.....................................16	D4
Bundhaya Resort.............................17	D4
Castaway Resort.............................18	D4

Daya Resort....................................19	D4
Forra Dive......................................20	D4
Idyllic...21	D4
Laem Son Bungalows & Camp	
Sites.......................................(see 9)	
Mountain Resort.............................22	D3
Paradise Bungalows.........................23	D4

EATING
Canteen...................................(see 2)	
Flour Power Bakery.........................24	D4
Kafair..25	D4
Nong Bank Restaurant.....................26	D4

DRINKING
Beachside Bar...........................(see 23)	
Pattaya Song..................................26	D4
Pooh's Bar.....................................27	D4

TRANSPORT
Travel Shop..............................(see 7)	

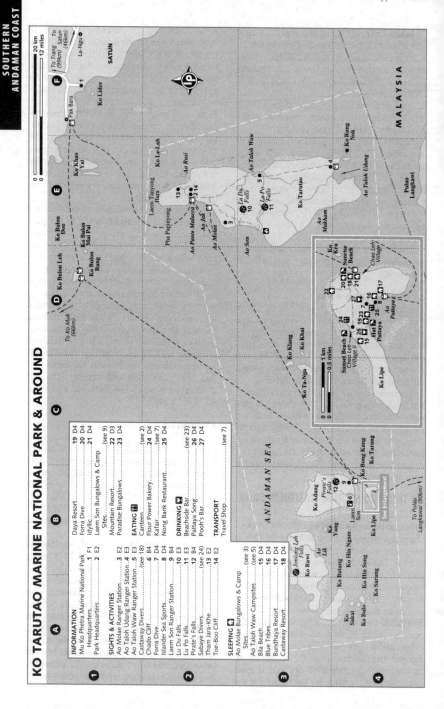

DETOUR: MU KO PHETRA MARINE NATIONAL PARK

A chain of smaller islands stretches north from Ko Tarutao, 22 of which are protected as **Mu Ko Phetra Marine National Park** (☎ 0 7478 3074, 0 7478 3504; adult/child under 14yr 200/100B). This little-visited park covers 495 sq km and includes the islands of the **Ko Bulon** group, as well as many uninhabited islands and islets. The largest island here is **Ko Khao Yai**, which has several pristine beaches suitable for swimming, snorkelling and camping, and a rock formation resembling a Gothic castle.

Nearby **Ko Lidee** features a number of beautiful coves with some shallow beaches and a large cave to which you can climb. The sea-grass beds around the island's Ao Jit support a small number of dugongs. Long-tail tours and sea-kayaking trips to Ko Lidee cost around 1500B per person and can be arranged at the national park headquarters on the mainland at Ao Nun, about 3km southeast of Pak Bara.

The park headquarters has a small visitors centre and a pleasing restaurant on stilts over the water, plus a nature trail through the forest. Bungalows here cost 800B to 1500B and sleep four to nine people, or there are longhouse rooms with fans for 600B. With permission, camping is possible on many of the uninhabited islands in the park. Park fees only apply if you visit the islands offshore. To get to the park headquarters, turn off Rte 4052 between the Km5 and Km6 distance markers, near the gold-domed mosque.

nearby Strait of Malacca until they were suppressed by British troops in 1944.

SIGHTS & ACTIVITIES

The main pier is on **Ao Pante Malacca** on the western coast, where you'll find a restaurant, and a lovely alabaster beach shaded by pandanus and casuarinas. If you follow the large stream flowing inland, you'll reach **Tham Jara-Khe** (Crocodile Cave), once home to deadly saltwater crocodiles. The cave is navigable for about 1km at low tide and can be visited on long-tail tours from the jetty. Next to the visitors centre at Ao Pante Malacca, a steep trail leads through the jungle to **Toe-Boo Cliff**, a dramatic rocky outcrop with fabulous views of Ko Adang and the surrounding islands.

The overgrown remains of the political prisoners' camp are a tough 12km jungle hike from the visitors centre to the southeast of the island at **Ao Taloh Udang**. The beach and bay here is absolutely pristine and makes for a superbly secluded campsite. If you don't want to hike you can get here by long-tail. The prison camp for civilian prisoners was on the eastern coast at **Ao Taloh Waw**. A concrete road runs across the island from Ao Taloh Waw to Ao Pante Malacca.

Immediately south of Ao Pante Malacca is **Ao Jak**, which has another fine sandy beach, and **Ao Molae**, which has more sugar-white sand and a ranger station with bungalows, a longhouse and campsite. A 30-minute boat ride or 8km walk south of Ao Pante you'll find

Ao Son, an isolated sandy bay where turtles nest between September and April. You can camp here but there are no facilities. Ao Son has decent snorkelling, as does **Ao Makham**, further south. From the ranger station at Ao Son you can walk inland to **Lu Du Falls** (about 1½ hours) and **Lu Po Falls** (about 2½ hours).

On the far northeast side of the island is **Ao Rusi** with a dramatic cave and good coral offshore, accessible by long-tail from Ao Pante Malacca. Nearby **Ko Le-Lah** is another good snorkelling spot. There are interesting sheer-sided rocky buttresses along the southeastern coast, including **Ko Rung Nok** (Bird-Nest Island), off Ao Taloh Udang, a treasure trove of valuable swallows' nests.

SLEEPING & EATING

All the formal park accommodation on Ko Tarutao is at Ao Molae. The accommodation (open mid-November to mid-May) is far more sensitive to the environment than the average Thai resort. Water is rationed, rubbish is (sporadically) transported back to the mainland, lighting is provided by power-saving lightbulbs and electricity is available between 6pm and 7am only.

Choose between recently constructed one- and two-room **bungalows** (r 600-1000B) and simple **longhouse rooms** (r 500B), which sleep up to four people. All rooms have mosquito nets, but bring some repellent as backup. Accommodation can be booked at the **park office** (☎ 0 7478 3485) in Pak Bara. National park entry fees can be paid at Ao Pante Malacca or Ao Taloh Waw.

Camping is permitted under casuarinas at Ao Molae and Ao Taloh Waw, where there are toilet and shower blocks, and on the wild beaches of Ao Son, Ao Makham and Ao Taloh Udang, where you will need to be self-sufficient. The cost is 30B per person with your own tent, or you can hire tents for 225B. Camping is also permitted on Ko Adang and other islands in the park.

The park authorities run **canteens** (dishes 40-120B; ☾ 7am-2pm & 5-9pm) at Ao Pante Malacca and Ao Molae. The food is satisfying and tasty and they even have cold beer.

GETTING THERE & AROUND
From Pak Bara (p381), boats stop at Ao Pante Malacca at noon and 3pm (400B, one hour) on their way to Ko Lipe (250B, one hour); in the reverse direction, boats arriving from Ko Lipe towards Pak Bara dock at 9.30am and 2pm. The island officially closes from the end of May to 15 September. Regular boats run from 21 October to the end of May; when the boats aren't running, you'll have to charter a long-tail from Pak Bara for 1500B. During the high season you can also come here on speedboat day tours from Pak Bara for 2000B, including national park fees, lunch, drinks and snorkelling.

You can take a park car (per person 60B) from the jetty at Ao Pante Malacca to the bungalows at Ao Molae. You can also charter a vehicle (per day 600B). Long-tails can be hired for trips to Ao Taloh Udang (2000B), Ao Taloh Wow (1500B), and Tham Jara-Khe or Ao Son for around 800B each.

If you're partial to self-propulsion, hire a kayak (per hour/day 100B/250B) or mountain bike (50/250B).

Ko Khai & Ko Klang
เกาะไข่/เกาะกลาง
Between Ko Tarutao and Ko Adang there's a cluster of three islands collectively known as **Muu Ko Klang** (Middle Island Group). Most interesting is **Ko Khai**, which has a neat white-sand beach and a scenic rock arch. The coral here has suffered a bit, but both Ko Khai and **Ko Klang** have crystal-clear water for swimming. Get here by chartered long-tail from Ao Pante Malacca on Ko Tarutao, or Ko Lipe; a round-trip will cost around 1500B from either end.

Ko Lipe
เกาะหลีเป๊ะ
In the distant past Lipe was a dreadlocked pirate hideaway. A place to bury treasure and wait out howling storms. More recently it became the dreadlocked travellers' waking dream. Blessed with two wide white-sand beaches separated by lush, jungled hills, and within spitting distance of protected coral reefs and massive islands thick with wildlife, this was where the backpacker trail led if you were lucky enough to hear the whispers after Phi-Phi broke your hippie heart. Unfortunately, whispers, when multiplied, become a buzz then a roar – you know, the kind generally associated with bulldozers. Yes, Lipe is changing, following the same path of development that has shifted (read: spoilt) places like Railay and Phi-Phi to some degree. Sandy trails have become concrete, dark nights have been banished by Phi-Phi Electric and slowly but surely the package tourists and their four-star nests have supplanted pirate lairs and humble huts. The biggest losers in Lipe's metamorphosis have been the 700-strong community of *chow lair* villagers who sold to a Thai developer.

Yet, given this upheaval, there is still plenty to love about Lipe, which remains a far cry from Phi-Phi – for now. The gorgeous white-sand crescent of **Hat Pattaya** on the southern coast has some stylish bamboo-and-wood bungalows, a few terrifically ramshackle beach bars, tremendous seafood and a party vibe during the high season. The one drawback is the preponderance of long-tails that crowd out swimmers. Windswept **Sunrise Beach** is even more spectacular with a long stretch of sand that juts to the north where you'll have spectacular Adang views. **Sunset Beach**, with its golden sand, gentle jungled hills and serene bay that spills into the Adang Strait, has an altogether different feel and retains Lipe's wild soul. In between there's an ever-expanding concrete maze of cafes, travel agencies, shops and salons, but with more resorts opting to stay open year-round there is definitely a way to find peace within the tumult if you don't mind a little wind in your eyes.

There are no banks or ATMs on the island, though several of the bigger resorts can change travellers cheques, cash or give advances on credit cards – all for a hefty fee. Internet is available along the cross-island path for 3B per minute.

SIGHTS & ACTIVITIES

There's good coral all along the southern coast and around **Ko Kra**, the little island opposite Sunrise Beach. Most resorts rent out mask and snorkel sets and fins for 50B each, and can arrange four-point long-tail snorkel trips to Ko Adang and other coral-fringed islands for around 1500B. The best way to see the archipelago is to hire a local *chow lair* captain. **Mr Rim** (☎ 08 9464 5289; Sunrise Beach), based just south of Idyllic, is a warm, welcoming and unrepentant seadog. **Islander Sea Sports** (☎ 08 7294 9770; per hr/day 100/600B) rents brand-new kayaks on Hat Pattaya.

While it would be a stretch to call the diving here world class, it's certainly very good with fun drift dives and two rock-star dive sites. **Eight Mile Rock** is a natural amphitheatre of coral-crusted boulders that attracts mantas and whale sharks. **Stonehenge** is popular because of its beautiful soft corals, resident seahorses, rare leopard and whale sharks, and also because it resembles that (possibly) alien-erected monstrosity that inspired Spinal Tap's greatest work. On Sunrise and Pattaya beaches, French-run **Forra Dive** (☎ 08 1479 5691, 08 4407 5691; www.forradiving.com), Lipe's least expensive choice, offers PADI Open Water dive courses for 12,600B, and day trips with two dives for 2600B. **Castaway Divers** (☎ 08 7478 1516; www.kohlipedivers.com), based on Sunrise Beach, offers PADI and SDI training, and more intimate dive trips (two dives 2800B) off longtail boats. **Sabaye Divers** (☎ 08 9464 5884; www.sabaye-sports.com) is the small Greenfins-certified shop on Sunset Beach owned by a long-time expat.

While it may look inviting, do not try to swim the narrow strait between Lipe and Adang at any time of year. Currents are swift and can be deadly.

SLEEPING & EATING

Most, but not all, resorts on Ko Lipe close from May to October, when the boats don't run as frequently. Many resorts offer water refills to ease rubbish problems – please, please take advantage of these services.

Forra Dive (☎ 08 1479 5691; www.forradiving.com; Sunrise Beach; bungalows 350-700B) Announced by 17 flags that whip in the eastward breeze, this is a monument to international beach-bungalow culture and the one place on the island that best captures Lipe's pirate spirit with a range of bamboo bungalows and lofts. The best are quite large with indoor-outdoor baths and breezy hammock-strung terraces. Plus, there's a rather inviting lounge with driftwood furnishings and plenty of cushions and hammocks. Divers get 25% off lodging.

Bila Beach (☎ 08 0589 2056; www.bilabeach.com; Sunset Beach; dm 400B, bungalow 800B) There's a killer bamboo bar and beachfront restaurant below stylish cliffside bungalows set on and above a private boulder-strewn cove on Sunset Beach. It's the perfect setting for your hippie honeymoon. It also has a cool bamboo dorm, and it's just over the hill from Pattaya.

Daya Resort (☎ 0 7472 8030; Hat Pattaya; bungalows 800B) A family-run place, the striped bungalows are your standard slap-up wooden affairs but the beach is fantastic, the back garden charming, and the restaurant has the absolute best and cheapest seafood grill on the island... and that's saying something.

Paradise Bungalows (☎ 08 0547 9475, 08 1479 3858; Hat Pattaya; bungalows 800B) These new bamboo bungalows don't look like much from the beach, but venture inside and you'll find tasteful lighting, lovely outdoor baths accented by wall-mounted orchids and creamy-lace mosquito netting. The bamboo terrace comes with ample cushions and sea views.

Mountain Resort (☎ 0 7472 8131; www.mountainresortkohlipe.com; Sunrise Beach; bungalows 1100-2600B; ✆ ❑) This big resort has views from its hillside location out over Ko Adang and winding wooden walkways lead down to the sublime beach on Sunrise Beach's northern sand bar. The huts are intricately designed from thatch and wood and come with verandahs. The restaurant has a huge menu as well as gargantuan views of the sea.

Bundhaya Resort (☎ 0 7475 0248; www.bundayaresort.com; Hat Pattaya; bungalows 1300-4000B; ✆ ❑ 🛜) It looks like a massive, cheesy three-star joint from the beach, but these wooden bungalows, with marbled-wood walls, dark-wood floors and indoor-outdoor baths aren't bad. The deluxe garden bungalows are the best value.

Blue Tribes (☎ 08 6285 2153; www.bluetribeslipe.com; Hat Pattaya; bungalows 1500-2500B; ✆ ❑) One of Pattaya's most attractive resorts, its best nests are the two-storey thatched wooden bungalows with a downstairs living room and top-floor bedrooms that have sliding doors opening to sea views. Its loungy, driftwood-studded restaurant twirls with ceiling fans and serves tasty northeast Italian cuisine.

KO LIPE'S METAMORPHOSIS

Ko Lipe began to change in earnest just three years ago. That's when the sandy cross-island trail was smothered in concrete. However, the seeds of change were planted more than a decade earlier when a Phi-Phi developer named Ko Kyiet approached local *chow lair* (sea gypsy) families about their ancestral land. Although deals were struck, they were never completed. Enter Ko Pi Tong, a Satun native who, according to Kun Pooh of Pooh's Bar and Pooh's Bungalows – a long-time local and one of Lipe's tourism leaders – made his money on the ecologically dubious and lucrative enterprise of collecting swift's nests.

'Pi Tong is like Robin Hood', said Pooh. 'He paid what Kyiet owed the locals plus interest.' Indeed, Tong went back to the *chow lair* families, most of who didn't have proper documentation for their land, and offered them lump sums of cash. They accepted, which means that technically this was all legal and that they participated in their own plight, but it isn't quite that simple.

When Kyiet negotiated the initial deals, he allowed the *chow lair* to keep a slice of their ancestral land. But Tong bought everything. Kun Pan, an elder, who lives in the new cordoned-off *chow lair* village on the hillside above Sunset Beach, explained the situation.

'Before, we had the whole island, we all lived on the beach', said Pan, a silver-haired fishermen with deep lines worn into his leathery brow. 'My brother and I, we not want to sell. The police come and take us to Satun. They said we had no land rights.'

Pooh disputes Pan's claim. He suggests the seaman is confused because 'Tong let [local people] live on the land he bought from them for years'. Tong evicted them relatively recently.

According to Pooh, Tong is now selling the land for many times the purchase price. Clearly, Tong has brought commerce, jobs, infrastructure and wealth into what once was a southern Thai backwater. Plus, some *chow lair* families held out, kept their land and launched successful businesses, such as Daya Resort, on their own – a fact that seems to contradict Pan's story. Still, it's hard not to notice that the vast majority of *chow lair* appear left out of the prosperity.

ourpick Castaway Resort (☎ 08 3138 7472; www .castaway-resorts.com; Sunrise Beach; bungalows 3000-4500B; 🖳 🛜) Understated hippie-chic elegance is yours on dreamy Sunrise Beach. The roomy wood bungalows have hammock-laden terraces, cushions everywhere, overhead fans and fabulous, modern-meets-naturalistic bathrooms are the most chic on Lipe. It's also one of the most environmentally friendly – with solar water heaters and lights. The candlelit restaurant here is pricey, but the food is excellent and the ambience divine. And it's open year-round.

Idyllic (☎ 08 1802 5453; www.idyllicresort.com; Sunrise Beach; bungalows 5950B; ♨ 🖳 🛜) High design has arrived on Lipe. With slanted roofs, concrete-and-glass walls, flat screen TVs, a shingled exterior and floating decks out the front, the digs are more like futuristic pods than beach bungalows. It's not for everyone, but it does have a certain presence.

Flour Power Bakery (☎ 08 6957 3101; Sunset Beach; dishes from 60B; ☯ breakfast, lunch & dinner) Its iced coffees, freshly baked banana bread and coconut brownies alone are worth the hike to Sunset Beach. Enjoy them on wood lounges in the shade.

Kafair (Tourist Village; dishes 70-190B; ☯ breakfast, lunch & dinner) If you hear good jazz filtering out onto the concrete tourist highway, follow it into this fine boho bakery and coffeehouse serving up scrumptious Western breakfasts.

Nong Bank Restaurant (Hat Pattaya; dishes 80-120B; ☯ breakfast, lunch & dinner) This place serves point-and-grill seafood and a superb yellow curry with crab (120B), with a half-dozen tables scattered beneath a tree on the white sand.

DRINKING

It's still a driftwood-clad Rasta bar scene on Ko Lipe. At least some things never change.

Beachside Bar (Hat Pattaya; ☯ 8am-late) With plenty of candlelit nooks, an eclectic soundtrack that bounces from the Eels to Manu Chao, and a consistently mixed crowd of Thai and faràng, this is one of the best.

Pooh's Bar (☎ 0 7472 8019; www.poohlipe.com) This massive complex was built by a Lipe pioneer and includes bungalows, a dive shop and several restaurants. It's a very popular local expat hang-out, especially in the low season. Each night it project films onto its big screen.

GETTING THERE & AWAY

From 21 October through until the end of May, several speedboat operators make the run from Pak Bara (see p381) to Ko Lipe via Ao Pante Malacca on Ko Tarutao and Ko Bulon Leh, at 11am, 12.30pm and 2pm (550B to 650B, 1½ hours); in the reverse direction it's inexplicably cheaper (500B) and boats leave at 9am, 11am and 1.30pm. Low-season transport depends on the weather but there are usually three boats per week. You always have the option of chartering a boat to Ko Lipe from Pak Bara for a hefty 4000B each way.

Tigerline (☎ 08 1092 8800; www.tigerlinetravel.com) offers the cheapest high-speed ferry service to Ko Lanta (1500B, 5½ hours), stopping at Ko Muk (1400B, 3½ hours), Ko Kradan (1400B, four hours) and Ko Ngai (1400B, 4½ hours). It departs from Ko Lipe at 9am.

The **Satun-Pak Bara Speedboat Club's** (☎ 0 7475 0389, 08 2433 0114; www.tarutaolipeisland.com) daily speedboat departs from Ko Lipe for Ko Lanta (1900B, three hours) at 9am stopping at Ko Bulon Leh (600B, one hour), Ko Muk (1400B, two hours) and Ko Ngai (1600B, 2½ hours). The same boat makes the return trip from Ko Lanta at 1pm.

It also offers two daily trips to Pulau Langkawi (1200B, one hour) in Malaysia; departure is at 10.30am and 4pm. Be at the immigration office at the Bundhaya Resort early to get stamped out. In reverse, boats leave from Pulau Langkawi for Ko Lipe at 9.30am and 2.30pm Malay time.

No matter which boat you end up deciding to use, you will have to take a long-tail shuttle (per person 50B) to and from the floating pier at the edge of the bay. You can buy tickets from any of the several travel agents and boat companies scattered on the beaches and inland paths. The most reliable and professional of these agencies is **Travel Shop** (☎ 08 9464 5854; www.kohlipethailand.com; Tourist Village).

Ko Adang & Ko Rawi

เกาะอาดัง/เกาะราวี

The island immediately north of Ko Lipe, **Ko Adang** has brooding, densely forested hills, white-sand beaches and healthy coral reefs. Lots of snorkelling tours make a stop here, and there are mooring buoys to prevent damage from anchors. Inland are jungle trails and tumbling waterfalls, including the creek-bed scramble up to **Pirate's Falls**, which is rumoured to have been a freshwater source for pirates. There are great views from **Chado Cliff**, above the main beach, where green turtles lay their eggs between September and December. The only accommodation is provided by the national park service, which maintains a ranger station at **Laem Son** in the southeast of the island.

Ko Rawi, a long rocky, jungled ellipse 11km west of Ko Adang, has first-rate beaches and large coral reefs offshore. Camping at Ao Lik is allowed, with permission from the national park authorities. Excellent snorkelling spots include the northern side of **Ko Yang** and tiny **Ko Hin Ngam**, which has underwater fields of giant clams, vibrant anemones and striped pebble beaches. Legend has it that the stones are cursed and anyone who takes one away will experience bad luck until the stone is returned to its source. There is a small restaurant here, but bring your lunch from Lipe, where it's cheaper and (much) tastier. Even a short stop on the island will cost you the park's entrance fee (adult/child 200/100B).

Park accommodation on Ko Adang is located near the ranger station at Laem Son. There are new and attractive **bungalows** (3-9 people 600B), scruffier **longhouses** (4-bed r 400B) and facilities for **camping** (sites per person 20B, with tent hire 200B). A small restaurant provides basic meals.

GETTING THERE & AWAY

You can get to Ko Adang on any of the boats that run to Ko Lipe for the same fare; just tell the driver that you want to go to Ko Adang. Longtails to and from Ko Lipe are 50B each way.

DIRECTORY

Directory

CONTENTS

ACCOMMODATION

The accommodation on Thailand's islands and beaches is astonishing both for its range of quality and design. From bare-bones bamboo shacks under swaying palms to vast resort complexes where every whim is taken into consideration, you won't need to look too hard to find a place to suit your sensibility and your budget.

Beach Bungalows

Simple beach huts used to make up most of the accommodation on Thailand's islands

---

> **BOOK YOUR STAY ONLINE**
>
> For more accommodation reviews and recommendations by Lonely Planet authors, check out the online booking service at www.lonelyplanet.com/hotels. You'll find the true, insider low-down on the best places to stay. Reviews are thorough and independent. Best of all, you can book online.

and beaches. But these old-style A-frames are quickly being replaced by sturdier concrete huts. They are universally known as bungalows, no matter what they look like or are made from.

The cheapest bungalows are still those made of palm thatch and woven bamboo, with or without simple tiled bathrooms attached. They may contain nothing more than a basic bed or mattress, a bare light bulb, and (if you're lucky) a mosquito net and fan. However, there is often a small balcony where you can dry your beach towel and swing in your hammock. Bungalows generally house two people. As wooden bungalows are replaced by concrete structures with facilities including air-con and satellite TV, rates rise two or three times higher.

Nightly rates vary greatly according to the popularity of the beach, the quality of the bungalows and the season. In the high season, wooden bungalows on the cheapest beaches start from 200B per night with shared bathroom, and upwards of 300B with private bathroom. Concrete bungalows usually have bathrooms and air-con; rates start from 400B in the low season and 1000B in the high season. Bungalows in upmarket resorts, such as Ko Samui's Hat Chaweng and Phuket's Hat Surin, can cost more than 3000B.

National Parks Accommodation

Some national parks provide accommodation in bungalows (sleeping up to 10 people) and reu·an tăa·ou (longhouses), which consist of small rooms with mattresses on the floor for three or four people. Bungalows and longhouses usually have lights and fans, but electricity is often only available from

6pm to midnight or 6pm to 6am. Parks with bungalows often have a basic restaurant and many have a simple provisions shop. Rooms in longhouses cost between 400B and 600B, while bungalows vary from 1000B to 2000B, depending on their size and condition.

Advance booking is advisable at the more popular parks; on holidays and weekends it's essential. The **National Park Office** (Map pp70-1; ☎ 0 2562 0760; www.dnp.go.th/parkreserve; 61 Th Phahonyothin, Chatuchak, Bangkok 10900) has a very convenient, easy-to-use online booking facility.

While few people bother carrying camping equipment in Thailand (the guesthouses are just too cheap), camping is possible at many parks. Expect to pay between 20B and 50B per person if you bring your own tent, and 200B to 450B if you hire one, plus 60B for bedding.

Most campsites will have toilets, running water, cold showers and sometimes a canteen serving authentic Thai meals. With permission from park authorities, you can camp in more remote locations, including some wonderful uninhabited islands and isolated beaches. However, you'll need to be totally self-sufficient, which includes bringing your own water and food.

Thai students get first preference for sites and equipment, so make reservations in advance or have a back-up plan.

Note that you'll usually be required to pay the national-park entry fee if you stay overnight – for foreigners this is usually 200B per adult or 100B for each child under 14, but in some parks it's double that. Hold on to your receipt as rangers randomly check visitors. Note also that securing a tent is obviously harder than locking a room.

Guesthouses

Apart from in some provincial capitals and island commercial centres, rooms in a converted family home are not common in southern Thailand, though Bangkok has plenty. By and large, most people refer to modest collections of beach bungalows as guesthouses, as a matter of habit, when referring to places where backpackers stay.

Traditionally, Thai guesthouses have featured tiny box rooms with a bed or mattress on the floor, a fan and not much else, but competition is forcing standards up. In general, rooms with shared bathroom range from 100B to all the way up to 1000B per night for trendier places in Bangkok. With a private bathroom, expect to pay from about 300B to 1700B. Many guesthouses are in old wooden Thai houses, so remove your shoes before entering and expect creaking floorboards at night. Once ubiquitous, squat toilets are an absolute rarity these days. Showers are often cold. Many guesthouses have an attached restaurant serving simple Thai meals.

Hotels

In provincial towns you can often find cheap hotels – often run by Thai-Chinese families – with basic box rooms, though in recent years many of these have been given a makeover. Expect to pay about 300B for a room with a fan and shared bathroom, and 500B to 1000B for more privacy and cool air. The cheaper places can be grim and noisy, especially when they are rented by the hour; not great for women travelling alone. The midrange options are more wholesome and good value, with private bathrooms, TVs, phones and air-con.

PRACTICALITIES

- Thailand uses an electrical current of 220V AC, 50Hz (cycles). Electrical plugs have two flat or two round pins; adapters and voltage converters are widely available.

- The main English-language daily newspapers are the *Bangkok Post* (www.bangkokpost.com) and the *Nation* (www.nationmultimedia.com), which usually reach beach destinations midmorning.

- Thailand has five VHF TV networks based in Bangkok and broadcasting in Thai, but not all are available in the south. Most midrange and top-end hotels have satellite or cable TV. The Thai video system is PAL and Thailand is in DVD Zone 3.

- Thailand has more than 400AM and FM radio stations, some with hourly newscasts in English.

- Thailand uses the metric system of measurements, with exceptions: gold and silver are weighed in *bàht* (15g), and land area is often measured in *râi* (equivalent to 1600 sq m).

DIRECTORY

Larger towns and tourist resorts have bigger, tidier business- or tourist-class hotels, which offer air-con, satellite TV and private bathrooms containing hot showers and Western-style toilets. Most also have attached restaurants or coffee shops. These hotels vary dramatically – some are old, some are brand new, some have pools, some have business centres, some have views. Most are centrally located and room rates fall between 800B and 3000B per room.

At the top of the market are the genuine luxury hotels run by Thai and international chains. Rates start at around 3000B and climb to thousands of US dollars per night. These places typically have several restaurants and bars plus a spa, sporting facilities and a business centre. Bangkok, Pattaya and Phuket have dozens of such hotels. There are also some very appealing independent boutique hotels, particularly in Bangkok (see p93), Ko Samui and Phuket.

Resorts

In most countries, 'resort' refers to hotels that offer substantial recreational facilities (eg tennis, golf, swimming, sailing, dive school, water sports) in addition to accommodation and dining. In Thai hotel lingo, however, the term simply refers to any hotel that isn't in an urban area. Hence a few thatched beach huts or a cluster of bungalows in a forest may be called a 'resort'.

However, in recent years many a beach-shack 'resort' has been transformed into the sort of genuine resort you dream of on wet winter's days. Indeed, the islands and beaches of southern Thailand are the new Caribbean, boasting some of the most-luxurious resorts on earth, with plenty more on the way. While all resorts were not created equal, many are simply stunning, with outlandish luxuries at rates that could go some way towards clearing the debts of small African nations. The better resorts have taken a refreshingly holistic approach to design, incorporating Thai themes to create a luxury experience that differs from international resorts elsewhere. Most of the major resorts are within striking distance of an airport, with Phuket, Ko Samui, Pattaya, Krabi and Ao Nang hosting the lion's share.

Along with the top-end places there are many more modest midrange affairs. You'll find everything from the TVs to the single infinity pool – via the bar tabs – is smaller, but when you're paying just a couple of thousand baht a night such privations are bearable. As one traveller we met put it: 'Is my

---

ROOM RATES & SEASONS

In this book, accommodation is arranged by budget and listed from cheapest to most expensive. The following categories are for a room with private bathroom in the high season:

Budget Up to 1000B.
Midrange 1000B to 3000B (4500B in Bangkok).
Top End More than 3000B (4500B in Bangkok).

Bangkok suffers from capital-city syndrome and while hotel quality is often higher, it comes at a significantly higher price; see the boxed text, p91, for details. Rates on the high-profile beaches on Ko Samui and Phuket are also much higher than elsewhere.

Be aware that for some listings in this book the cheapest price quoted for an establishment is often for a single cheap room, which is almost invariably booked out.

Thailand has a 7% value-added tax (VAT) on many goods and services. Many midrange lodgings and almost all top-end hotels (and restaurants) will add this and a 10% service tax to the bill. When the two are combined this becomes the 17% king hit known as 'plus plus', or '++'. Prices for listings in this book include the taxes.

Discounts of up to 50% can be found on the internet (see the boxed text, opposite) and, in the case of guesthouses, by just turning up during the low season. In general, Thailand's tourist high season runs from November to April, with prices peaking between mid-December and mid-January, and around Songkran (mid-April). Low season runs from May to October, with the biggest discounts usually in May and early June, and mid-September until the beginning of November.

Let us reemphasise that these dates are fairly general, as local weather variations also impact on prices. See p12 for more on the weather.

BOOKING ONLINE: JUST DO IT

'You know,' said the woman as she glanced conspiratorially around the reception of one of Bangkok's top hotels, 'if you book online the rates are much cheaper...about 30% usually'. We have been offered similar surprisingly honest advice several times while researching hotels in Thailand, with the general message being that for midrange and top-end hotels booking ahead gets you discounts you can't even contemplate when you walk in – even during the January peak season.

During the low season (May to October) rates can fall to less than half the listed tariff as hotels and resorts compete to fill rooms. The number of budget places bookable online is also rising, but for these and a lot of relatively cheaper midrange places that don't have the same economies of scale, old-style bargaining at reception remains a good plan. Indeed, for budget places this is the best option except at the busiest times. And if you're arriving by plane there is often a desk at the airport offering last-minute discounts; Phuket is particularly good for this.

So where should you look online? There are dozens of hotel booking websites but most allow the hotels to write their own reviews. As fellow Lonely Planet scribe Karla Zimmerman discovered after arriving in Bangkok to a place she'd booked online, the website's promised 'luxurious comfort' with 'teakwood decorations and cable TV' was actually located in a de facto brothel. The website had conveniently neglected to mention that 'easy access, 24 hours' meant more than just being near the Skytrain. As Karla put it: 'Despite the distraction of drinking one's beer and eating one's *pàt tai* in venues where most of the patrons were getting hand jobs, we appreciated our unplanned bite of this classic slice of Bangkok.' Mind you, she also said that she'll be more careful when booking online next time. Quite.

Fortunately there are websites that offer independent reviews rather than endless superlatives. **Lonely Planet's Hotels & Hostels** (www.lonelyplanet.com) features thorough author reviews of more places than listed in this book, plus traveller feedback. The website also has a booking facility. For a one-stop look at the sort of discounts available, the independent website **Travelfish** (www.travelfish.org) has a handy list of nothing more than the hotel name and current online price for the relevant island or beach.

US$70 bungalow really 10 times worse than that resort?'

While researching this guide the authors gave the resorts a good looking over and we've highlighted some of our favourites, both for people seeking value and those for whom money is no object. More reviews of these places, with more detail, can be found in the Hotels & Hostels section of www.lonelyplanet.com.

ACTIVITIES

Thailand is Asia's adventure capital and in the south the focus is on the marine world. There are hundreds of places you can go snorkelling and scuba diving. Sea kayaking around islands and mangroves is becoming increasingly popular, and you can go sailboarding at many of the bigger resorts. Back on dry land, rock climbing is a major drawcard in the area around Krabi, while hiking is possible in some national parks and elephant trekking is widely available.

For a full rundown of diving and other activities, see p281.

Diving

Below are some of the details you'll need to know before disappearing below the surface.

RESPONSIBLE DIVING

Lately, 'over-diving' is a common problem in Thailand. Many reefs see hundreds of divers per day, which puts a great strain on the environment that causes corals to wilt and die, and marine life to seek new feeding grounds. Many dive operators actively participate in reef rehabilitation programs; however, every diver should do their part to keep the sites pristine. Before diving below, make sure that you are properly weighted; buoyancy control is essential in ensuring that you don't bang against outcroppings and sea walls. Never stand on coral – if you must secure yourself to the reef, only hold fast to exposed rock or dead coral. Fin kicks often disturb reefs as well; heavy strokes can create tiny eddies and displace sand over delicate organisms. The rest is quite logical: don't bully the marine creatures and don't loot the sea. If you see unscrupulous activity underwater, report it when you get back to shore.

DIVE MEDICINE
For the amount of diving throughout Thailand, the kingdom has a surprising limited number of medical facilities dedicated to diving accidents.

Decompression (hyperbaric) chambers can be found at most major hubs, including Bangkok (p67), Ko Samui (p196), Pattaya (p130) and Phuket (p305). Ko Tao has an emergency chamber – most injuries are dealt with on Ko Samui. We advise you to ask your operator of choice about the nearest chamber before diving. Also, make sure that there is an emergency supply of oxygen on your dive boat.

DIVE SEASONS
Generally speaking, the Gulf of Thailand (Ko Tao, Ko Pha-Ngan and Ko Samui) has a year-round dive season, although tropical storms sometimes temporarily blow out visibility. The southwestern monsoon seems to affect the Ko Chang Archipelago more than other eastern gulf coast dive sites; hence, November to early May is the ideal season for those islands.

On the Andaman coast the best diving conditions (calm surf and good visibility) fall between December and April; from May to November monsoon conditions prevail and visibility is often poor. Many dive centres at Ko Lanta and the islands further south close down, but diving is still possible out of Phuket, Ao Nang and Ko Phi-Phi.

Manta ray sightings are more frequent on the Andaman side, while whale sharks usually make an appearance on the gulf side, particularly at Sail Rock. In the last two years the number of whale shark sightings has greatly increased. If you stick around long enough you are almost guaranteed to see one of these gentle beasts.

DIVE COURSES & TOURS
Most dive centres offer first-timers Open Water certification with PADI or SSI at a cost of around 9800B to 20,000B. Courses are three and half days, include several classroom sessions and four guided dives testing various skills. For detailed information about what to consider when choosing dive schools, see p235.

For experienced divers, most centres offer all-inclusive day or half-day trips featuring two dives, lunch, guides and taxi transfers for around 2000B to 6000B. Live-aboard tours are popular on the Andaman side, particularly around the Surin and Similan Islands; the most popular operators depart from Khao Lak (p293).

DIVING PACKING LIST

If you're planning to dive during your trip to Thailand, the following items will greatly ease your ability to hop right in and explore the deep.

- **Diving insurance** – check with your travel insurance provider to see if it offers extra insurance for divers, if not, check out www.daneurope.org for more information.

- **Doctor's note** – divers with any medical problem (including mild asthma) must have a doctor sign off on their ability to dive safely. Skip the unnecessary (and sometimes costly) trip to a local clinic and take care of this before you leave.

- **Dive log & certification** – you must bring proof of your previous experience, especially for deep dives and night dives.

- **Nondrowsy motion sickness pills** – it is technically illegal for dive operators to give out medicine, and purchasing your own in your native country will better assure unwanted side effects.

- **Electrolyte sachets** – diving can cause serious dehydration, so it is worth purchasing small sachets of electrolyte powder to mix into a bottle of water. These packets are available on virtually every island in Thailand that has a quorum of dive shops.

Hiking

For ideas of where to hike in southern Thailand, see p287.

When hiking in Thailand, take some basic precautions:

- Don't go hiking alone.
- Let someone in the local community know where you are going and for how long.
- Always take plenty of water and insect repellent.
- Take your rubbish back with you.
- Walk in sturdy shoes and long pants to ward off pesky leeches and snakes.

Meditation & Thai Massage

The isalnds and beaches of Thailand offer many opportunities for meditation and Thai massage. Places to try include Ko Chang (p155), Ko Tao (p239), Ko Samui (p200), Ko Pha-Ngan (p221) and Phuket (p309). Massages are also available in Bangkok (p86).

For information on courses, see p397.

BUSINESS HOURS

Most government offices are open from 8.30am to 4.30pm Monday to Friday, though the wheels grind to a halt during the noon to 1pm lunch hour. Banks are generally open from 8.30am to 3.30pm Monday to Friday, and sometimes until 4.30pm (usually on Friday). Many banks run foreign-exchange booths in Bangkok and at tourist resorts, and these are open from around 8am to 8pm daily. Note that government offices and banks are all closed on public holidays (see p403).

Commercial businesses usually operate between 8.30am and 5pm on weekdays and sometimes Saturday morning as well. Larger shops usually open from 10am to 6.30pm or 7pm, but the big Bangkok malls are open later (until 9pm or 10pm) and smaller shops may open earlier and close later. Hours for restaurants and cafes vary greatly. Some local Thai places open as early as 7am, while more formal restaurants usually open around 11am and still others are open in the evenings only. Local places might close as early as 5pm or 6pm, while in Bangkok restaurants often stay open to 10pm or 11pm. Bars, by law, can't open before 4pm and must close by 1am. Do note that shops operated by Muslims might close on Friday, the Islamic holy day. In the deep south restaurants tend to close earlier than elsewhere, so don't head out for dinner too late.

WILDLIFE CONSERVATION

- Do not engage in or encourage hunting. It is illegal in all parks and reserves.
- Don't buy items made from endangered species.
- Don't attempt to exterminate animals in huts. In wild places, they are likely to be protected native animals.
- Discourage the presence of wildlife by not leaving food scraps behind you. Place gear out of reach and tie packs to rafters or trees.
- Do not feed the wildlife as this can lead to animals becoming dependent on handouts, to unbalanced populations and to diseases.

CHILDREN

Thailand is a surprisingly easy place to travel with children and many former solo backpackers are returning to Thailand with their own families. Thais love children and in many instances will shower attention on your offspring, who will find ready playmates among their Thai counterparts.

Of course, travel with children in Thailand is still subject to the same obstacles that are faced by parents travelling with children anywhere, ie keeping the little 'uns healthy and entertained. Lonely Planet's *Travel with Children*, coauthored by Celeste Brash, who wrote the Eastern Gulf Coast chapter in this guide and has years of relevant experience, contains advice on how to cope with kids on the road, with special attention to travel in the developing world.

Practicalities

Transport is an important consideration for parents, as children will get bored quickly on long bus or boat rides. If you're heading to the far south, consider flying. There are cheap, direct flights from Bangkok to Ko Samui, Phuket, Krabi, Trang and Trat. Though not as fast, the train does offer sleeping compartments and room to explore and runs to Surat Thani (for boat transfer to Ko Samui), Trang and Hat Yai.

Bus companies charge full fare for children using a seat, but it's free for those who ride on their parent's lap. On the train children under

12 years pay half, while under-threes travel free if they don't take up a seat.

Thailand is one of the few tropical countries that doesn't require specific jabs, and malaria prophylaxis usually isn't necessary. Having said that, the incidence of dengue fever is on the rise, so protecting against mosquito bites (at any time of day) is very important – BYO good repellent. The biggest problem for children is keeping them hydrated and free of the bellyache. The Health chapter has details of good practices for keeping adults and children healthy.

A high-factor sunscreen is essential. Warn your children not to play with dogs and cats; pets in Thailand are typically more the guard dog or rubbish-eating variety than Mr Snuggles. Rabies is also a concern. Be particularly wary of aggressive monkeys.

Only in the best hotels will you find high chairs, and strollers are rarely seen outside top resort areas. Most Thais just carry their children in their arms and hold them at the dinner table. While strollers might be convenient on some of the more popular resort islands, Thai pavements are such that elsewhere it will feel more like off-roading than strolling. International-style beach resorts and upmarket hotels usually provide childcare facilities and crèches. Thai food is often a little too spicy for young palates, but fried rice, roti, pasta and especially fried noodles are widely available. Big supermarkets in large cities sell Western staples.

If you are travelling with very young children, public breast-feeding is far less frowned upon than in the West, but it's always done discreetly. However, breast-feeding is losing ground among Thais due to the relentless marketing of powdered milk formula, which is portrayed as a miracle tonic that will transform children into academically brilliant prodigies. It's widely available from shops and pharmacies.

Sights & Activities

Bangkok has plenty of attractions for kids, from shimmering gold and giant statues at Bangkok's wát (temples) to a world-class oceanarium (see p89). However, warn your children about touching religious objects such as shrines, offerings and spirit houses (which can look a lot like dolls' houses to a child). Hotels with swimming pools help work off city claustrophobia.

The vast majority of Thai beaches are well suited to swimmers, sandcastle builders and fish spotters, though be aware of seasonal strong currents off Phuket. Pattaya (p130), Phuket (p307) and Ko Samui (p201) have plenty of non-beach diversions that don't involve prostitutes or vodka shots.

Many of the fantastic range of activities available in Krabi (p337), including rock-climbing and sea-kayaking tours, are open to children. For more on outdoor activities see the chapter, p281.

CLIMATE CHARTS

The climate charts following give you a reasonable idea of what are the hottest and wettest months in the region. For more information on the best times to visit Thailand's islands and beaches, see p12. And for even more detail on when it's likely to rain where, and for how long, see the excellent interactive map on the website www.travelfish.org/weather_fish.php.

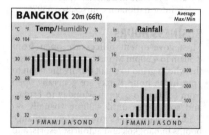

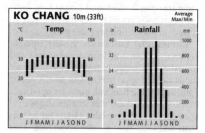

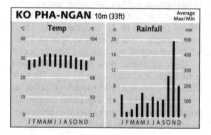

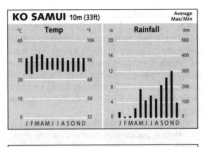

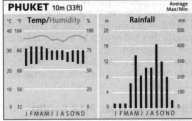

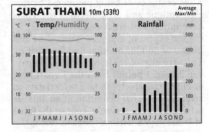

Two basic systems of meditation, *samatha* (calm) and *vipassana* (insight), are taught. Most places specialise in *vipassana*, which focuses on concentration to achieve personal insight – it's sometimes called 'mindfulness' meditation.

Foreigners who come to Thailand can choose from dozens of temples and meditation centres (*săm·nák wí·bàt·sà·nah*) and there is usually no charge, but you must attend daily prayers and make a daily contribution between 50B and 100B towards expenses. Most places teach in Thai, but there are a few English-speaking instructors. Contact the centres in advance before turning up on the doorstep. For even a brief visit, wear clean and neat clothing (ie long trousers or a skirt, and sleeves that cover the shoulders).

A one-month tourist visa is ample for most courses. If you formally ordain as a Buddhist monk or nun, you will be allowed to stay in Thailand as long as you remain in robes.

English-language meditation instruction is available in Bangkok; see p88. Elsewhere, meditation courses are available in Ko Si Chang (p119); Ko Chang (p155); outside Surat Thani (p252); on Ko Pha-Ngan (p220); and on Ko Samui (p200).

Useful online resources:

Dharma Thai (www.dhammathai.org)
House of Dhamma (www.houseofdhamma.com)
World Fellowship of Buddhists (www.wfb-hq.org)

COURSES

If you'll be staying in Thailand for a while, there are some good courses on offer. You can learn to speak Thai or study meditation, learn Thai cooking or Thai massage, or train as a scuba-diver or Thai boxer. For cooking courses, see p52; for dive courses, see p282.

Language

Bangkok has the largest concentration of formal language schools and tuition rates (see p88), but there are plenty of informal language schools in most places where foreigners congregate. The best way to find them is on notice boards (often outside grocery stores) and by just asking around.

Meditation

Thailand has long been a popular destination for Western students of Buddhism, particularly those interested in meditation.

Moo·ay Tai (Thai Boxing)

The martial art of *moo·ay tai* (also *muay thai*) is legendary around the world, but you'll need to be tough to last long at a traditional Thai *moo·ay tai* camp. As well as a rigorous training regimen, you may also have to adopt a special (often rudimentary) diet and learn the Thai language. Unlike most East Asian martial arts, *moo·ay tai* training features full-contact sparring.

As the sport's popularity has exploded, however, several schools have adapted their programs to better suit Westerners. Bangkok has several of these, with English-speaking trainers and better equipment, but which charge higher tuition fees; see p88.

Training periods can range from a one-day course to multiweek sessions. Do be aware that the potential for some camps to be interested only in tuition fees is a concern and it pays to do your research.

The website www.muaythai.com contains useful information, including the addresses of training camps.

Thai Massage

Described as a 'brutally pleasant experience', this ancient form of healing has been practised in Thailand for over 1000 years and was modified from ancient Indian meditation techniques. Unlike Western massage techniques, Thai massage (*nôo·at păan boh·rahn*) uses the elbows, forearms, knees and feet as well as the fingers and palms to apply pressure to traditional pressure points along various *sên* (meridians – lines of energy in the human body) in order to distribute energies evenly through the nervous system.

If you want to study Thai massage, Wat Pho in Bangkok (see p83) is the national authority on traditional healing and offers regular week-long massage training courses; see also p88.

CUSTOMS

The white-uniformed officers of Thai customs prohibit the import or export of the usual goods – porn, weapons and drugs. If you're caught with drugs, in particular, expect life never to be the same again. Otherwise, customs regulations are quite reasonable. The usual 200 cigarettes or 250g of tobacco are allowed in without duty, along with 1L of wine or spirits. Ditto for electronic goods as long as you don't look like you're planning to sell them – best to leave your third and fourth laptops at home.

There is no limit to the amount of Thai or foreign currency you can bring into the country, but you can only take out 50,000B per person without special authorisation. If you're going to one of Thailand's neighbouring countries, you can take as much as 500,000B per person. The exportation of foreign currencies is unrestricted.

Thailand has strict regulations on the export of antiques and some religious items (see right). For hours of fun reading other customs details, check out www.customs.go.th/Customs-Eng/indexEng.jsp.

Claiming Back VAT

Visitors to Thailand who depart by air and who haven't spent more than 180 days in Thailand during the previous calendar year can apply for a VAT refund on purchases made at approved stores; look for the blue and white VAT Refund sticker in store windows. Minimum purchases must add up to 2000B per store in a single day, with a minimum total of 5000B. You must get a VAT Refund form and tax invoice from the store. In Bangkok the major malls will probably direct you to a desk dealing with VAT refunds, but elsewhere you might need to ask.

At the airport, take the items (preferably in original packaging) to the customs desk, which will issue the paperwork. You can then check larger items in, but smaller items (such as watches and jewellery) must be carried by hand as they will need to be reinspected once past immigration. Either way, you actually get your money at a VAT Refund Tourist Office once you've passed through immigration. For all the details, see www.rd.go.th/vrt.

Exporting Antiques, Art & Buddha Images

After centuries of being plundered by foreign antique and art collectors, the Thais have introduced strict regulations governing the export of antiques, *objets d'art* and images of Buddha or other Buddhist deities. To carry any of these out of the country, you'll need a permit from the Department of Fine Arts, which can take several days to arrange. The Thai definition of an antique is fairly broad. If in doubt, contact the **Office of Archaeology & National Museums** (Map pp72-3; ☎ 0 2226 1661) at the Department of Fine Arts. Before you buy antiques or relics in Thailand, take a look at **Heritage Watch** (www.heritagewatchinternational.org).

DANGERS & ANNOYANCES

Although Thailand is generally a pretty safe place to visit, it's easy to get taken for a ride. It's wise to be a little cautious, particularly if you're travelling alone. For information on diseases and environmental dangers such as jellyfish stings, see p429. The following might help you stay out of trouble.

Drugging

It doesn't happen as much as it used to, but beware of friendly strangers offering cigarettes, drinks or sweets, especially in hostess bars or other houses of dubious repute. In some cases the food is drugged and the victim wakes up hours later without a wallet or valuables.

Drugs

Despite Thailand's party reputation, it is illegal to buy, sell or possess any of the good-times drugs in any quantity. There are severe penalties – they don't get much more severe than death – if caught. Even more than in most countries, drugs are a huge political issue in Thailand. The government of Thaksin Shinawatra was notoriously hardline on drugs (see boxed text, below) and popular for it, and the successor Peoples Power Party followed a similar line. At the time of research the policy was not quite so draconian, but crackdowns are frequent and a raid is never too far away.

Said raids usually take place in bars, saunas and nightclubs, particularly in Bangkok and Phuket, with everyone being held until they've been photographed and submitted a urine sample. All this makes you wonder how it is that every mind-altering substance known to man can be available at the Full Moon Parties on Ko Pha-Ngan – despite regular spot searches of people and vehicles heading to Hat Rin for the full moon.

As well as manufactured drugs, the ban extends to so-called 'natural' drugs, such as grà·tôrm (a leaf of the *Mitragyna speciosa* tree) and hallucinogenic 'magic mushrooms'. 'Special omelettes' containing magic mushrooms are a long-running tradition at Ko Pha-Ngan, but these have always been a risky proposition and hundreds of foreigners have ended up with severe mental-health problems over the years after taking hallucinogenic drugs in Thailand. A hallucinogenic plant called đôn lam·pong, which can cause permanent psychosis, is sometimes peddled on Ko Pha-Ngan.

Insurgent Activity

The far south of Thailand continues to be troubled by separatist violence, and travel

---

ADDICTED TO THE WAR ON DRUGS

In January 2003, as the world's attention was focused on the impending advance of the 'War on Terror' into Iraq, the Thai police embarked on a crackdown on drug dealers and users with the stated aim of declaring Thailand 'drug free' within months. In announcing the move, the words of then prime minister Thaksin Shinawatra were ominous: 'Because drug traders are ruthless to our children, so being ruthless back to them is not a bad thing... It may be necessary to have casualties... If there are deaths among traders, it's normal.'

Thailand's 'War on Drugs' was initially met with broad support from the public, which had become understandably frightened of the impact of growing methamphetamine use. But what followed was criticised by the UN Commission on Human Rights. In just three months more than 50,000 people were arrested and at least 2275 killed, according to figures released by the police. The government claimed most of the killings were carried out by rival drug gangs. The police claimed 51 of those killed had been shot by police in self-defence. But Human Rights Watch and several other nongovernment organisations claim many if not most of the dead had been summarily executed by the police themselves (for more detail read HRW's 2004 report Not Enough Graves; www.hrw.org/en/reports/2004/07/07/not-enough-graves). The dead included many who had some involvement in the drug trade, but a government report states that over a thousand probably had nothing to do with drugs whatsoever. Three months after the campaign began Shinawatra hastily declared 'mission accomplished'. Seven years later, the drugs trade shows no sign of having disappeared.

Not surprisingly, new kingpins rose up to meet the demand and the battle against methamphetamine (yah bâh; crazy medicine) continues in a more conventional manner. The Thai government's attempts to coordinate with poorly funded and poorly motivated police in Myanmar, Laos and Cambodia have resulted in some high-profile busts, but no killer blow. Because of this, and despite the public-relations disaster of the 2003 'War on Drugs', the government declared a second 'War on Drugs' in early 2008. This proved much less violent than the first 'war', but ultimately the outcome was the same – lots of publicity and a short-term interruption of the drug flow, this time without any clearly defined 'victory'. As the second 'war' was quietly petering out, the publicity lessened. The fight continues through seasonal crackdowns, yet for all the talk, action and blood, if you're on the islands, where drugs are so widely available, it's often hard to see any signs of their having any success at all.

THE WORLD-FAMOUS BANGKOK GEM SCAM! *Andrew Burke*

'Hello sir, where are you going?' asked the well-dressed man in his early 50s, 'Where are you from?' When I told him 'Australia' I could almost see the memory whirring into action. 'Ah, Australia! Sydney or Melbourne? My daughter is studying at university in Melbourne.' My new friend, acquired as I walked along a touristy Bangkok street, went on to correctly answer questions about Melbourne universities (he knew all the main schools) and Australian university holidays. It was only when he asked 'How long have you been in Bangkok?', and I told him 'two years', that his interest suddenly and dramatically waned.

My 'friend' was a scammer, a con artist expert in inveigling unsuspecting new arrivals into his trust and then subtly bullying them into buying something for way more than its real worth – usually gems. Every question or statement was designed to push emotional buttons. My 'friend' told me how expensive Australian universities were and how hard it was to pay for his daughter's education, and rising inflation was making it so hard to keep paying for the school she needed so she could have a better life.

So what should you do? The truth is that Thais don't usually act this way so, as much as it pains us to say this, if you're in a touristy area (not just in Bangkok) treat anyone who approaches you from out of the blue with suspicion. And look for the signs. Assume the scam is in gear when your new friend asks if you have a map (a major clue since most Thais can't be bothered with maps) and/or a túk-túk magically arrives. Don't believe people who claim major tourist sites are closed for renovations or government holidays unless you see it for yourself. It's just a ploy to give them an excuse to take you somewhere else – somewhere you don't want to go.

If I'd allowed it, my 'friend' would probably have taken me to a local wát (temple) or some other mildly interesting attraction as a means of building trust. We'd end up taking a convenient túk-túk (everyone in the scam gets a cut) to a gem shop where the scammers might tell me about a 'government gem sale' that will soon end, or some other unlikely scheme. The government doesn't do 'gem sales', nor does it have schemes for students to sell gems to raise money for education. Eventually I'd be talked into buying large amounts of gems either for cash or on my credit card, with assurances that I can resell the stones for a huge profit at home. At home I'd find the gems were real, but worth a fraction of the price paid in Bangkok. In a worst-case scenario my credit card would also be billed for extra items using forged credit-card imprints.

If you find yourself in any of these scenarios, remember that you can stop it at any time. A good countermeasure is to ask for a photo with your 'friend' – and as many of the maybe-scammers as possible – if they refuse, it's a scam. Even better, don't allow yourself to be tempted. The scammer will often play on your greed – don't be greedy.

That scams like this have been going on for years, by the same operators, is a sad indictment on the Thai government's legislative ability and on the credit-card companies that continue to do business with dodgy dealers. The names of the culprits are all over the internet – why can't they be stopped? For more on the gem scam (including lists of known operators) or to seek solace from the scammed, check out www.bangkokscams.com and www.2bangkok.com, which has an antiscam campaign.

in Yala, Pattani and Narathiwat Provinces can be dangerous. Many governments advise against nonessential travel to Thailand's deep south and it is worth checking your government's travel advisory before hitting the road. Having said that, a steady trickle of travellers passes through these provinces en route to or from Malaysia and most report no trouble.

For more on the long history of trouble between Muslims and Buddhists in the south, see the boxed text, p28. For details on travelling there, see the boxed text, p258. If you are thinking of heading to this part of Thailand be sure to check online for fresh information; the Thorn Tree bulletin board at www.lonely planet.com is a good place to start.

Physical Safety

Violent crime is rare in Thailand, but not unheard of. During the last few years several women travellers have been raped – and some murdered – on remote beaches, and men are often injured or killed in drunken skirmishes. For beach safety precautions for women, see p413.

Wherever you are in Thailand it makes sense to exercise the same street smarts you would anywhere else. These include the obvious, such as ensuring your room is securely locked and bolted and avoiding quiet, dark places at night. Women should also inspect cheap, thin-walled rooms for strategic peepholes.

Motorbikes, however, pose the greatest risk. Tourist motorcyclists are killed fairly regularly, and many others end up with a 'Thai tattoo' – burned inner right calf – or worse. See boxed text, p424, for more on motorcycle safety.

Scams

Well, just where do we start? Thailand has its fair share of scams that have been consistently separating tourists from their cash for years. Bangkok is the centre of Thai scamming, but islands such as Ko Samui and Phuket are doing their best to claim the title. Of the various scams, the gem scam (see boxed text, opposite) and the transit and lodging scams are those you're most likely to come across.

TRANSIT & LODGING SCAMS

In terms of infrastructure, it is a breeze getting from point A to point B in Thailand. But there are still the taxi and túk-túk drivers and bogus travel agents to dodge – nearly an Olympic event. Several well-established scams exist – see boxed text, p421, for details.

Don't believe anyone who tells you that a hotel or guesthouse is 'closed', 'full', 'dirty', 'haunted' or 'burnt down' (we're not making this up) until you see it for yourself. Săhm·lór and túk-túk drivers often offer free or low-cost rides to the place they're touting but you'll be paying for the ride later on, either in terms of cash or discomfort.

Theft & Fraud

People seem so friendly in Thailand that a visitor can forget to follow the basic precautions of travelling abroad.

While violent crime is rare, there are plenty of stories of bags being snatched and pockets picked, particularly in Bangkok's crowded markets; Chatuchak is probably the worst.

Use your common sense, however, and you should be fine; keep your bags in front of you and in sight at all times. On the islands, don't put your bag in the front basket of rented bicycles or motorbikes, as you might as well just put out a sign saying 'rob me'.

The best way to keep your money safe is to split the risk. Bring a mixture of cash and travellers cheques, and keep an emergency stash of money separate from your main finances. Credit cards are very useful in Thailand but keep them safe and have the emergency cancellation phone number on hand. If you have two cards, keep them in separate places. Money belts or pouches worn under clothing are much safer than wallets or purses.

We'd say keep your valuables, including credit cards, cash or travellers cheques, with you at all times, but clearly that's going to be a problem when you're lounging around the beach all day. At these times it's best to store them in the safety box at your hotel or guesthouse. In cheaper places, this means a locked drawer or a mysterious place behind the counter.

It pays to seal your valuables before you hand them over. A taped-up envelope with a signature over the top is the best way. If you can't do this, then at least make a show of counting and noting your money when you hand it over. This works for both parties as while most staff are trustworthy, there are exceptions and the same applies to foreigners. In the case of an alleged theft, the staff have as much reason to suspect you of fraud as you do them.

Never let vendors take your credit card out of sight to run it through the machine. Unscrupulous merchants have been known to run off multiple receipts with one credit-card purchase, forging your signature on the blanks after you have left the shop.

Finally, remember that a padlock on a bag doesn't turn it into Fort Knox, particularly on long-distance bus trips. See p421 for bus theft horror stories.

DISCOUNT CARDS

Apart from airlines and travel agents, youth discounts in Thailand are limited mainly to students in uniform, and discounts for seniors are almost unheard of. **Hostelling International** (HI; www.tyha.org) issues a membership card that will allow you to stay at the country's handful of associated hostels without having to pay the additional surcharge for nonmembers; membership can be bought for 200B at the relevant hostels.

The decades-old Th Khao San trade in fake student cards and press passes is still bubbling along, and the unsurprising consequence is that Bangkok institutions don't accept these cards as proof of anything.

EMBASSIES & CONSULATES
Thai Embassies & Consulates

Most nationalities can obtain a free one-month tourist visa on arrival in Thailand, but if your country is exempt or you want more time, contact a Thai embassy or consulate before your trip; for a full list see the website of the **Thai Ministry of Foreign Affairs** (www.mfa .go.th/web/886.php) and click through to Foreign Missions in Thailand, Diplomatic Consular List to get to the list under Diplomatic Missions.

Embassies & Consulates in Thailand

Bangkok is an excellent place to collect visas for onward travel. The visa sections of most embassies and consulates are open from 9am to noon Monday to Friday, but call first to be sure. For a full list, go to www.mfa.go.th/ web/12.php and click through to Thailand and the World, Diplomatic Corps Directory and Diplomatic Consular List to get to the list under Diplomatic Missions.

Australia (Map pp72-3; ☎ 02 344 6300; www.austem bassy.or.th; 37 Th Sathon Tai)

Cambodia (Map pp70-1; ☎ 0 2957 5851; 518/4 Th Pracha Uthit, aka Soi Ramkhamhaeng 39, Wangthong-lang)

Canada (Map pp72-3; ☎ 0 2636 0540; geo.international .gc.ca/asia/bangkok; 15th fl, Abdulrahim Bldg, 990 Th Phra Ram IV, Lumphini)

China (Map pp72-3; ☎ 0 2245 0088, 0 2245 7044; www .chinaembassy.or.th/eng; 57 Th Ratchadaphisek, Din Daeng)

France Embassy (Map pp78-9; ☎ 0 2266 8250-6; www .ambafrance-th.org; 35 Soi 36, Th Charoen Krung; Consu-late (Map pp72-3; ☎ 0 2287 1592; 29 Th Sathon Tai)

Germany (Map pp72-3; ☎ 0 2287 9000; www.bangkok .diplo.de; 9 Th Sathon Tai)

India Embassy (p82; ☎ 0 2258 0300-5; www.indian embassy.in.th; 46 Soi 23, Th Sukhumvit); Consulate (Indian Visa Application Center; Map p82; ☎ 0 2665 2968; www.ivac-th.com; 15th fl, Glas Haus Bldg, Soi 25, Th Sukhumvit)

Israel (Map p82; ☎ 0 2204 9200; http://bangkok.mfa .gov.il; 25th fl, Ocean Tower II, 75 Soi 19, Th Sukhumvit)

Indonesia (Map pp80-1; ☎ 0 2252 3135; 600-602 Th Phetburi, Ratchathewi)

Laos (Map pp70-1; ☎ 0 2539 6667; 520/1-3 Soi Sahakarnpramoon, Th Pracha Uthit, Wangthonglong)

Malaysia (pp72-3; ☎ 0 2629 6800; 33-35 Th Sathon Tai)

Myanmar (Map pp78-9; ☎ 0 2234 0278; 132 Th Sathon Neua)

Netherlands (Map pp80-1; ☎ 0 2309 5200; www .netherlandsembassy.in.th; 15 Soi Tonson, Ploenchit)

New Zealand (Map pp80-1; ☎ 0 2254 2530-3; www .nzembassy.com; 19th fl, M Thai Tower, All Seasons Pl, 87 Th Withayu)

Singapore (Map pp78-9; ☎ 0 2286 2111; www.mfa.gov .sg/bangkok; 9th & 18th fl, Rajanakam Bldg, 129 Th Sathon Tai)

South Africa (Map pp80-1; ☎ 0 2659 2900; www.saembbang kok.com; 12th fl, M-Thai Tower, All Seasons Pl, Th Witthaya)

Sweden (Map p82; ☎ 0 2263 7200; www.swedenabroad .com; 20th fl, One Pacific Pl, 140 Th Sukhumvit)

UK (Map pp80-1; ☎ 0 2305 8333; www.britishembassy .gov.uk; 14 Th Withayu, Ploenchit)

USA (Map pp80-1; ☎ 0 2205 4000; http://bangkok .usembassy.gov; 120/22 Th Withayu, Lumphini)

Vietnam (Map pp80-1; ☎ 0 2251 5836-8; 83/1 Th Withayu, Ploenchit)

FESTIVALS & EVENTS

Exact dates for many festivals vary each year. Some events, particularly Buddhist and Muslim ones, follow the lunar calendar, while others are changed by organisers or local au-thorities. Major festivals and their dates, where known, are listed in the Events Calendar on p20. Some smaller festivals are covered in the regional chapters.

The website of **Tourism Authority of Thailand** (www.tourismthailand.org) has dates for larger festi-vals occurring in the current year; for more on Buddhist festivals, see **Buddhanet** (www.buddhanet .net/thai_cal.htm).

Thailand's Muslim community has its own festivals, which are celebrated throughout the south. Like Buddhist religious festivals, these are linked to the lunar calendar so the dates come forward usually by 11 or 12 days every year. For example, the fasting month of Ramadan starts on about (it depends when the moon is sighted) 11 August 2010, 1 August 2011 and 20 July 2012. During Ramadan, which lasts one month, celebrants are barred from eating, drinking or smoking between sunrise and sunset. The end of Ramadan is Eid al-Fitr, probably the biggest party of the Islamic year.

For details of holidays, see opposite.

FOOD

Thai food is legendary around the world for its chilli heat and exotic spices. There is a huge variety of food on offer, and you can pay as much or as little as you like and still get a fantastic meal. Places to eat in this book have been arranged by location and then price.

The budget category includes street food, food courts, night markets and cheap local restaurants, with prices ranging up to 150B. Midrange eateries are mainly sit-down restaurants – most restaurants in this book fall into this bracket, except in Bangkok, which is amply stocked with upmarket restaurants. In midrange restaurants, you can expect to pay 150B to 500B, while meals at top-end restaurants start at about 500B and climb far beyond.

Prices given in the listings in regional chapters are typically for meals or main courses. Side orders, such as rice, salads and vegetables, cost extra, with prices reflecting the quality of the establishment. For the lowdown on food in Thailand, see the Food & Drink chapter, p45.

GAY & LESBIAN TRAVELLERS

While Thai culture may seem very tolerant of homosexuality, both male and female, there is a difference between tolerance and acceptance. Although there is little risk of being verbally or physically abused, Thais are quite conservative and it wasn't until early 2003 that the Department of Mental Health formally accepted that homosexuality was not a psychiatric disease.

The reasons for this ambiguous stance are rooted in the importance of the family in Thai society. Gays are often seen as being immature and selfish for refusing to get married and have children. As a result, many gay men live a double life: raising a family by day and having clandestine meetings by night. As in the West, people with a high-profile public life rarely admit they are gay, while entertainers and comedians often make a living out of their sexuality.

Bangkok is the undisputed gay capital of Southeast Asia – most probably the whole of Asia – with several streets dedicated to gay bars and clubs (see boxed text, p90). There is a well-established scene, but prostitution is endemic in bars where foreign gays hang out. On top of this, a Western boyfriend is perceived by many people as an easy route to money or emigration, so it can be very hard to meet Thai gays on an even footing. As is the case with straight relationships, many Thais are openly offended by Western gays who come to Thailand to pick up Thai boyfriends.

After Bangkok, the other main gay areas are Phuket and Pattaya. The scene is most relaxed and least commercial in Phuket, which has a huge and colourful **gay pride festival** (www.gaypatong.com), usually sometime between February and April. Bangkok has a gay festival every November or December (visit www.bangkokpride.org), while Pattaya has events virtually year-round (see www.pattayagayfestival.com).

For an idea of what's going on in the GLBT scene, see these websites:

Dreaded Ned (www.dreadedned.com) Listings, forums, personal ads.

Fridae (www.fridae.com) Listings of events across Asia; click through Agenda for Thailand.

Gay Guide in Thailand (www.gayguideinthailand.com) Exactly that – a gay tour guide.

Gay Patong (www.gaypatong.com) All things gay in Phuket.

Lesbian Guide to Bangkok (www.bangkoklesbian .com) The most active and useful site for lesbians in Bangkok, with helpful forums and news on events and venues.

Long Yang Club (www.longyangclub.org/thailand) A 'multicultural social group for male-oriented men who want to meet outside the gay scene', with branches all over the world. The Thailand chapter hosts occasional events.

Utopia (www.utopia-asia.com) Long-running website with lots of information and member reviews.

HOLIDAYS

Chinese New Year (held in February or early March) and Songkran (13–15 April) are the two holiday periods that most affect Thailand. For up to a week before and after these holidays public transport is packed full of people heading for their home towns to celebrate with family. This means all transport from Bangkok is full before the date but seats are available afterwards, when people are heading back to Bangkok and work. See the Events Calendar (p20) for more on individual festivals and holidays.

Public Holidays

Government offices and banks close down on the following public holidays. For the exact dates of lunar holidays, see the website of **TAT** (www.tourismthailand.or g/travel-information).

New Year's Day	1 January
Magha Puja Day	February/
(mah·ká boo·chah)	March (lunar)
Chakri Day	6 April
Songkran	13-15 April
Labour Day	1 May
Coronation Day	5 May
Visakha Puja Day	May/June
(wí·sǎh·kà boo·chah)	(lunar)
Khao Phansa	July/August
	(lunar)
Queen's Birthday	12 August
King Chulalongkorn Day	23 October
Ok Phansa	October/
	November (lunar)
King's Birthday	5 December
Constitution Day	10 December
New Year's Eve	31 December

School Holidays

As well as enjoying the main public holidays, children and staff get a day off on 16 January for Teachers' Day. The main school holidays fall during March and April and the end of May; exact dates vary from school to school.

INSURANCE

With travel anywhere, the golden rule about travel insurance is simple: get some! While Thailand is generally a safe country to travel in, sickness, accidents and theft are not uncommon. If you can't afford to pay for travel insurance, you certainly can't afford to cover the costs of theft or medical expenses if the worst happens. There is a wide variety of policies, all with varying prices, inclusions, terms and conditions. Your travel agent can advise or shop around on the web.

Always check the small print to see if the policy covers potentially dangerous sporting activities, such as diving, rock climbing, hiking and riding motorbikes (they often don't). Premiums tend to vary depending on the level of cover for theft (where most claims come from). But the most important factor is health cover: even if it's just a policy that covers emergency health (these are relatively cheap), be sure to have one. For more information, see p429.

Worldwide cover for travellers is available online: check under Travel Services at www .lonelyplanet.com.

WI-FI ACCESS

Wi-fi (wireless fidelity) is not hard to find in much of Thailand, and particularly in Bangkok. Many cafes now offer either free or paid wi-fi access, as do most top-end and midrange hotels. A growing number of guesthouses offer wi-fi, though it depends largely on where they are – the more remote, the less wired. Various websites list Bangkok wi-fi spots, including www .bkkpages.com, www.stickmanbangkok. com and www.jiwire.com; J! Wire also offers an iPhone app version of its listings, though it's not by any means comprehensive.

INTERNET ACCESS

Thailand is pretty well wired. In all but the most remote locales you'll find at least one internet cafe, and this includes many islands off the Thai coast. Connections are dependent on the local phone lines and how many computers are networked to the same connection.

Internet cafes usually charge 1B to 2B per minute in towns and 3B to 4B per minute on the islands and more remote beaches. There are also internet stations in shopping malls, at most airports and in an ever-growing number of hotels and guesthouses, where connections range from free to more than 700B an hour. Because internet cafes are so ubiquitous, in this book we've mainly provided directions to where they congregate rather than to individual businesses.

On any shared computer be very careful with your personal information. If you're banking online, always delete the cache (or 'cookies') and history on the web browser when you finish so no-one can access your account.

Laptops are becoming almost as common as backpacks on Thai islands and beaches, and the price you need to pay for a room that has internet is steadily falling.

If you need to plug in, Thailand uses RJ11 phone jacks; prepaid dial-up accounts are available from 7-Elevens. They come with a list of dial-up numbers for towns around the country, a user name and password, plus a number of free hours – a 20-hour card costs about 200B.

LEGAL MATTERS

In general Thai police don't hassle foreigners, especially tourists. The one major exception involves drugs, which are public enemy number one. While the enforcement of antidrug policies tends to ebb and flow according to whether a crackdown has been announced or not, it's not unusual for Thai police to sweep bars and clubs in search of offenders. If the music suddenly stops and men in brown shirts file into the room, expect to be there until you've been searched and tested (usually a urine test) for drugs. Resistance is futile – unless you know someone powerful. It's worth remembering that just being caught in possession of hard drugs (as opposed to trafficking) will likely mean your life is never the same again, and could possibly end much sooner.

If you are arrested for any offence, the police will allow you to make a phone call – if you don't know that powerful person then your embassy or consulate in Thailand is probably the best place to start. Once arrested, the time you can be held without charge depends on the police officers and, like anywhere, how much respect you show the arresting officers. Thai law does not presume an indicted detainee to be either 'guilty' or 'innocent' but rather a 'suspect' whose guilt or innocence will be decided in court. Trials are usually speedy and Thailand has plenty of private attorneys (preferable to the state-appointed counsels).

Smoking is banned in all indoor spaces, including bars and pubs. The ban extends to open-air public spaces, which means lighting up outside a shopping centre, in particular, might earn you a polite request to butt out. If you throw your cigarette butt on the ground, however, you could then be hit with a hefty littering fine.

Tourist Police Hotline

If you get into any kind of trouble, immediately contact the Tourist Police, who specialise in dealing with foreigners. The 24-hour Tourist Police hotline is ☎ 1155. The Tourist Police don't have all the powers of the regular

FINDING ADDRESSES

The Thai word thanŏn means road, street or avenue (it's shortened to 'Th' in addresses in this book). Hence Ratchadamnoen Rd or Ave is called Th Ratchadamnoen in Thai.

A soi is a small street or lane that runs off a larger street. An address referred to as 48/3-5 Soi 1, Th Sukhumvit will be located off Th Sukhumvit on Soi 1. The same address may be written as 48/3-5 Th Sukhumvit Soi 1, or even just 48/3-5 Sukhumvit 1.

Smaller than a soi is a ḍ̀ròrk (often spelt tràwk or trok) or alley.

Many street addresses show a string of numbers divided by slashes and dashes; for example, 48/3-5 Soi 1, Th Sukhumvit. The number before the slash is the original lot number; the numbers after the slash indicate buildings (or entrances) within that lot. These lot numbers are often useless, as they usually don't run sequentially. But don't worry, if you can find the main number (in this case 3-5), then you'll be fine.

In rural areas, along beaches and on most islands, addresses sometimes consist of a house number followed by a village number. For example, 34 Mòo 7 would be house 34 in village 7 (mòo, also spelt as muu, is short for 'mòo bâhn', Thai for 'village'). Villagers almost never display this address anywhere on their houses, as it is really only used by postal workers and other officials. Places such as guesthouses do sometimes display such an address, though you're more likely to spot a sign with the name of the guesthouse before you see the address. Further complicating matters, street and town names usually have variant spellings as there is no standard convention for transliterating Thai into English.

If it gets too confusing just ask a local, showing or telling them the address you're after. As most Thais have grown up in a world devoid of maps, asking for directions on a map will often lead to confusion.

DIRECTORY

police, but they can help with translation, contacting your embassy and arranging incident reports for insurance purposes.

MAPS

Periplus Travel Maps publishes a reliable map of *Thailand* (1:2,000,000), plus more detailed maps of Bangkok, Phuket and Ko Samui. The *Phuket Southern Thailand* and *Ko Samui Southern Thailand* maps have useful insets for places along the Andaman and gulf coasts respectively. **ThinkNet** (www.thinknet .co.th) produces a high-quality city and country series, including the large-scale *Bilingual Map of Southern Thailand* (1:500,000), which is widely available for 120B, and the *Islands in Thailand* sheet from the MapGuide series. Look for these in bookshops or 7-Elevens.

Popular resort destinations, including Ko Samui, Phuket and Pattaya, are well served by free maps and for most travellers these will be all you'll need; they're usually available at airports and tourist offices.

Anyone planning to drive should buy the Roads Association of Thailand's large-format, bilingual road atlas *Thailand Highway Map*.

MONEY

Most travellers rely on credit or debit cards to access cash in Thailand because they are convenient and ATMs are everywhere. The basic unit of Thai currency is the baht. There are 100 satang in one baht – though most goods are priced in whole baht numbers, so you rarely see them in change unless you're in a 7-Eleven. Coins come in denominations of 25 satang, 50 satang, 1B, 5B and 10B. Paper currency comes in denominations of 20B (green), 50B (blue), 100B (red), 500B (purple) and 1000B (brown).

Cash machines (ATMs) and foreign-currency exchanges typically dispense funds in 1000B notes, which can be difficult for the average vendor or taxi driver to change. It is not advisable to pull out a big note to pay a small bar tab; sometimes the change returned doesn't agree with both parties. Break big bills at 7-Elevens or when paying for a room, so you have small notes for everyday purchases. See the inside cover of this book for exchange rates at the time of publication.

ATMs

In most towns in Thailand you won't need a map to find an ATM – they're everywhere.

Most bank ATMs accept major international credit cards and many will also cough up cash (Thai baht only) if your savings/current account from home has a card affiliated with the Cirrus or Plus networks. You can withdraw up to 20,000B at a time from most ATMs, and 25,000B from some Bangkok Bank ATMs. Home banks will charge a fee for every international transaction, with Thai banks now adding a fee of their own, too.

Credit Cards

International credit cards such as Visa and MasterCard (and bank debit cards backed by these companies) can be used to withdraw local currency from ATMs. You can also use credit cards to purchase currency over the counter at many foreign-exchange booths; however, the commission can be astronomical, so ask first.

Credit cards and debit cards can also be used almost anywhere you'll spend enough to need one. The most commonly accepted cards are Visa and MasterCard, followed by American Express and JCB. Credit-card fraud does occur, particularly in the increasingly rare shops still using the old-fashioned card imprint system.

If your card is lost or stolen, contact the Tourist Police for a police report. To report a lost or stolen card, call the following telephone hotlines:
Amex (☎ 0 2273 5544)
MasterCard (☎ 001 800 11 887 0663)
Visa (☎ 001 800 11 535 0660, 0 2256 7324-9)

Moneychangers

There is no black market for baht. Banks or legal moneychangers offer the best exchange rates. US dollars and euros are the most readily accepted currencies, followed by UK pounds sterling and Australian dollars. Travellers cheques get better exchange rates than cash, and large banknotes are often worth more than small bills. There are exchange facilities at many branches of Bangkok Bank, Krung Thai Bank, Siam City Bank, Siam Commercial Bank and Kasikorn Bank; look for the 'Exchange' signs. Standard banking hours are 8.30am to 3.30pm Monday to Friday, though they will often stay open until 4.30pm Fridays. Some banks in popular tourist areas maintain foreign-exchange booths, which are usually open daily from around 10am until 8pm.

Many Thai banks refuse to exchange Malaysian ringgit, Indonesian rupiah, Nepali rupees, Cambodian riel, Lao kip, Vietnamese dong or Myanmar kyat – in other words, it's best to change your money at the border and bargain hard when you do it. If you need to buy or sell any of these currencies in Thailand the moneychangers along Th Charoen Krung and Th Silom in Bangkok are your best bet, though rates won't be great.

Money Transfers

International money-transfer companies such as **Western Union** (www.westernunion.com) and **Moneygram** (www.moneygram.com) have operations in Thailand. Western Union has offices worldwide where friends or family can transfer money to you instantly. Within Thailand, you can receive Western Union transfers at the Bank of Ayuthaya, Siam City Bank and Thailand Post offices. Moneygram offers similar services through branches of Siam Commercial Bank. The downside of these services is the cost, which is typically 5% to 10% of the value transferred. If you do get a bailout this way (or any other), be sure to send your saviour a thank you postcard.

Tipping

Tipping is uncommon in Thailand, except in big hotels and posh restaurants. Having said that, in tourist areas such as Bangkok and the islands and beaches of the south Thais are becoming increasingly familiar with tipping. Taxi drivers will automatically round the price up to the nearest 10B. For most places, however, tips remain appreciated rather than expected.

Travellers Cheques

All banks with foreign-exchange facilities and private foreign-exchange desks accept travellers cheques backed by Visa, MasterCard, Thomas Cook and American Express. Commonly accepted currencies of travellers cheques include the euro; UK pound sterling; Swedish, Danish and Norwegian Kroner; the Swiss franc; and the US, Canadian, New Zealand and Australian dollar. In practice, US dollars, UK pounds and euros are most useful. Banks charge a standard commission for each travellers cheque cashed, so you can save on commissions by using large denomination cheques. Some banks partner with certain providers of travellers cheques in commission-free exchanges. Remember to keep the receipts for your cheques separate from your main finances, so you can have the cheques replaced if they are stolen.

PHOTOGRAPHY & VIDEO

Thailand is a photographer's dream and there are myriad opportunities for still and video photography. The usual rules apply: ask permission before photographing or filming local people, particularly at religious sites. Thai Buddhists may be flattered to have their portraits taken, but this is less true with Thai Muslims. Either way, engaging your potential subject in even the briefest conversation before asking them, with a smile, will greatly improve your chances of an affirmative answer – it's also the polite thing to do. Never agree or promise to send a photo to your subject if you won't actually do that.

Thailand is humid (understatement alert!), so be sure to pack some silica gel with your lenses and camera to keep the mould away. A polarising filter is useful for cutting down tropical glare, particularly when taking photos around water and the shimmering gold at wát. In these conditions, bracketing (ie taking extra shots that are one stop overexposed and one stop underexposed) is also a good idea.

Thais have eagerly embraced digital photography and all but the common 100, 200 and 400ASA print film is hard to find outside of Bangkok. On the plus side, photo labs can print your digi shots fast and cheap, and most internet cafes can burn your memories onto CDs and/or DVDs. Camera batteries and Mini-DV tapes are widely available in Bangkok and tourist areas.

POST

Thailand Post (☎ call centre 1545; www.thailandpost.com) runs a reliable and highly efficient postal service and staff at Thai post offices almost always speak some English. Aside from Bangkok's main post office (p67), most post offices open from 8.30am to 4.30pm Monday to Friday and 9am to noon on Saturday; some open Sunday mornings, too. Some larger offices often have phone offices and offer poste restante, and most offer parcel services, with cardboard boxes for sale and tape and string provided free. Don't send valuables or money through the mail.

For courier packages, Thai Post EMS (available at post offices) is a good option and usually less than half the price of private courier companies. **DHL** (www.dhl.co.th) and **Fedex** (www.fedex.com/th) have offices in Bangkok and the major tourist centres.

DIRECTORY

Postal Rates

The rates for internal and international postage are very reasonable. Postcards to anywhere in the world cost 12B or 15B, depending on size. Airmail letters weighing 10g cost 12B to 20B to Western countries. Aerograms cost 15B regardless of the destination. Letters sent by registered mail cost 25B in addition to regular airmail postage.

By airmail, a parcel weighing 1/2/5kg will cost about 880/1230/2280B to Europe and take about two weeks.

Sea mail takes about three months to Europe or the US and is about 60% cheaper than airmail. Surface-air-lifted mail (by air and sea) takes about one month to most places and costs about double the sea-mail rate. Rates vary slightly by country; ask to see the post office's magic folder for every variable you can imagine.

You can insure a package's contents for 7B per US$20 of the goods' value.

Receiving Mail

You can receive mail while you are in Thailand through the poste-restante service, which is available at most post offices, including the main post office in Bangkok: Your Name (surname first), Poste Restante, General Post Office, Charoen Krung Rd, Bangrak, Bangkok, 10501.

SHOPPING

Thailand is a shopper's paradise and many travellers come home with their bags bulging with wooden carvings, sarongs, jewellery and clothes. Bangkok has the best selection of goods, from knock-offs to the real McCoy; see p107.

Many travellers come to Thailand intent on shopping for bespoke clothing at bargain prices. And while there are more tailors than public garbage cans in Thailand, it pays to shop around and, if you want something that will fit well, have it made in Bangkok where some tailor shops rely on repeat business from the diplomatic corps and expat community instead of tourist shops who don't depend on satisfied customers. For more on tailoring, see the boxed text, p108.

Genuine brand-name clothes are also a good buy for some. Bangkok has the most fashion-conscious shops and foreign sizes are available. Bangkok's high-end malls stock the real deal, while markets and the Mahboonkrong (MBK) shopping centre have the not-so-real deal.

Dive gear is supercheap in southern Thailand (if they have your size), and most dive centres have shops where you can buy scuba gear and prescription masks.

Almost all visitors to Thailand bring home some handicrafts. Silver jewellery is

---

WHAT A BARGAIN!

As a general rule in Thailand, if you have to ask the price then you can bargain. Markets are usually bargaining friendly and shopping centres are bargaining free. If you don't like to bargain, then shop at the shopping centres. On the other hand, for souvenir-type products, suits, jewellery and unmetered taxis, bargaining is essential.

Bargaining can be tough if you're not used to it, so here are a couple of pointers. First, when you find something you like be sure not to show too much interest. Vendors can smell desperation a mile away. Second, don't buy the first one you see; subtly check out a few alternatives to get an idea of the price and quality. With this knowledge, casually enquire as to the price and then make a counter-offer (usually half or less), thus beginning the bargaining process. The vendor will often beseech you to make a better offer: 'This is my first sale for the day' or 'I must feed my six children'. However, having looked at the competition you know the fair price so only edge up slowly. As you volley numbers back and forth remember to keep it good-natured; your smile is your best weapon and getting angry or upset while bargaining causes everyone to lose face and won't get you a better deal.

Remember that bargaining is not a life-and-death battle. A good bargain is when *both* parties are happy and doesn't necessarily require you to screw every last baht from the vendor. If you paid more than your travelling companion, don't worry. As long as you're happy, it was a good deal. Remember too that no-one is forcing you to buy anything. Your money will stay in your pocket until you decide to take it out.

extremely popular and portable, but unless you own a shop, do not get talked into buying bulk jewellery to sell back home. Gemstones are a particularly hazardous buy (see boxed text, p400). As a general rule, anything made from shells or endangered animals should be avoided. Lots of shops sell ivory, tortoiseshell and seashells poached from marine national parks.

Antiques and convincing reproductions of antiques are widely available, but note that genuine antiques and Buddha images may not be taken out of the kingdom without a permit – see p398.

Basketware is light to carry and is available all over the south, as is traditional Thai clothing, such as Thai fishermen's pants, sarongs and the like. Other popular handicrafts include hill-tribe jewellery, wooden chopsticks (sold only to the tourists), Thai axe pillows, Thai and Lao silk, lacquerware, stainless-steel Thai cutlery, wooden bowls and vases, and woodcarvings. The cheapest markets are those provincial markets off the tourist trail, such as in Trang. If you don't want to carry stuff around, most of these items can be obtained more cheaply in Bangkok before your flight home.

All over Thailand you'll find OTOP outlets. OTOP is the sanctioned local crafts centre.

SOLO TRAVELLERS

Thailand is one of the easiest countries in the world for solo travellers. Even the most timid traveller should be able to meet people in the guesthouses and beach-bars of southern Thailand, though resorts heavy with couples or sex workers can get lonely.

In Bangkok, Th Khao San is the world's greatest concentration of travellers, though oddly it can be such a fashion show that it's not as easy to meet people here as elsewhere; hanging around your guesthouse is the best idea. Wherever you meet your fellow wanderers, there's a pretty good chance you'll meet them again somewhere on the well-defined tourist circuit of Thailand's islands and beaches.

Thais might be a little bewildered that you would want to go out and about without friends, a reflection of their social nature. But many are impressed by Westerners', especially solo women's, courage to venture into the unknown. For more on women travellers, see p413.

TELEPHONE

The Thai telephone system is efficient enough that you should be able to direct-dial most major centres without trouble. Thailand's country code is ☎ 66.

Inside Thailand you must dial the area code no matter where you are. In effect, that means all numbers are nine digits; in Bangkok they begin with 02 then a seven-digit number. The only time you drop the initial 0 is when calling from outside Thailand. Calling the provinces usually involves a three-digit code beginning with 0, then a six-digit number. Mobile-phone numbers have 10 digits and begin with 08.

To direct-dial an international number from a private phone, you can first dial ☎ 001 then the country code. However, you wouldn't do that, because 001 is the most expensive way to call internationally and numerous other prefixes give you cheaper rates. These include ☎ 006, ☎ 007, ☎ 008 and ☎ 009, depending on which phone you're calling from. If you buy a local SIM card (see p410), which we recommend, the network provider will tell you which prefix to use; read the fine print.

For operator-assisted international calls, dial ☎ 100. For free local directory assistance, call ☎ 1133 inside Bangkok.

Payphones are common, though these days they stand forlornly waiting for people's mobile-phone batteries to go flat. If you need one, red phones are for local calls, blue are for local and long-distance calls (within Thailand), and the green phones are for use with phonecards. Calls start at 1B for three minutes; for mobile-phone numbers it's 3B per minute. Local calls from private phones cost 3B, with no time limit.

Internet Phone & Phonecards

The cheapest way to call internationally is via the internet, and many internet cafes are set up for phone calls. Some have Skype loaded and (assuming there's a working headset) you can use that for just the regular per-hour internet fee. Others might have their own Voice over Internet Protocol (VoIP) service at cheap international rates.

CAT offers the PhoneNet card, which comes in denominations of 200B, 300B, 500B and 1000B and allows you to call overseas via VoIP for less than regular rates. You can call from any phone; landline, your mobile phone etc. Quality is good and rates represent excellent value; refills are available.

DIRECTORY

Cards are available from any CAT office or online at www.thaitelephone.com, from which you get the necessary codes and numbers immediately. See www.thaitelephone.com/EN/RateTable for rates.

That table also displays rates for CAT's standard ThaiCard, a prepaid international calling card selling for 300B and 500B. You can use the ThaiCard codes from either end, eg calling the UK from Thailand or calling Thailand from the UK. These are better value than Lenso cards, which are used from payphones.

Skype aside, these options are all more expensive than the right prepaid SIM card...

Mobile Phones

If you have a GSM phone you will probably be able to use it on roaming in Thailand. If you have endless cash, or you only want to send text messages, you might be happy to do that. Otherwise, consider buying a local SIM card.

Buying a prepaid SIM is as difficult as finding a 7-Eleven. The market is supercompetitive and deals vary so check websites first, but expect to get a SIM for as little as 49B. More expensive SIMs might come with preloaded talk time; if not, recharge cards are sold at the same stores and range from 100B to 500B. Per-minute rates start at less than 50 satang. Calling internationally the network will have a promotional code (eg ☎ 006 instead of ☎ 001) that affords big discounts on the standard international rates. If you're using an iPhone then the number of open wi-fi connections in Bangkok should keep the costs down. The main networks:

AIS (www.12call.ais.co.th) Offers wide coverage across Thailand; One-2-Call is the prepaid option.

DTAC (www.dtac.co.th) Lots of options, including Happy (www.happy.co.th) for prepaid SIM.

True Move (www.truemove.com) Probably the cheapest of the lot, with the Inter SIM offering international calls to many countries for 1B per minute, and cheap local calls, too. The network is not as good outside Bangkok.

If your phone is locked, head to Bangkok's Mahboonkrong (MBK) shopping centre (p108) to get it unlocked or shop for a new or cheap used phone (they start at less than 2000B).

TIME

Thailand is seven hours ahead of GMT/UTC. Thus, noon in Bangkok is 9pm the previous day in Los Angeles, midnight the same day in New York, 5am in London, 6am in Paris, 1pm in Perth, and 3pm in Sydney and Melbourne. Thailand does not use daylight saving time.

The official year in Thailand is reckoned from the Western calendar year 543 BC, the beginning of the Buddhist Era, so that AD 2010 is 2553 BE, AD 2011 is 2554 BE etc. All dates in this book refer to the Western calendar.

TOILETS

Public toilets can be found at bus and train stations, in shopping malls and in fast-food restaurants. There is often an entrance charge of between 1B and 3B, and sometimes there are machines dispensing tissue paper (don't flush the paper, put it in the bin). In tourist areas, Western-style thrones are ubiquitous, but at cheaper guesthouses and at bus and train stations you can expect to squat. In the vast majority of squat toilets you'll need to BYO paper (widely available in convenience stores) or embrace another option. The most obvious of these is to go local and use the hose or jug and tap in your stall, which will result in you getting wet until you've acquired the skills. If you must have paper and don't have a stash, you could always use this page – though we won't vouch for its softness.

TOURIST INFORMATION

Tourism contributes a huge amount to the Thai economy, so it's little surprise that the government-run **Tourism Authority of Thailand** (TAT; ☎ tourist information line 1672; ; www.tourismthailand.org; ☉ 8am-8pm) is highly organised and has offices around the country and 20 more overseas; for the full list see www.tourismthailand.org/tat-oversea-office. TAT is also the main regulatory body for tourism in Thailand, and issues licences to businesses that pass its exacting standards. Be aware, however, that not all TATs are equal. A huge number of travel agencies have large 'T.A.T.' and 'Information' signs on their windows to lure in commissions. These places are not officially sanctioned information services, but just agencies registered with the TAT. So how can you tell the difference? Apparently it's all in the full stops – 'T.A.T.' means agency, 'TAT' is official.

Legit TAT offices produce a huge range of pamphlets and booklets, which are available at the addresses listed in the relevant chapters of this book. TAT has handy information counters in the international and domestic terminals of Suvarnabhumi International Airport.

Bangkok Metropolitan Administration runs the excellent **Bangkok Tourist Bureau** (☎ 0 2225 7612-4; www.bangkoktourist.com), which covers Bangkok and its environs in detail. Other private information organisations can be found in many provincial centres – see the regional chapters for details.

TOURS

Even if you're short on time, most of southern Thailand can be visited independently. Once you have reached your destination, there are plenty of local tour operators who will shuttle you to secluded beaches, on snorkelling tours, to visit waterfalls, ride elephants and whatever else you can imagine, all for less than you'd pay for an organised tour.

Most travellers do sign up for a jungle tour of Khao Sok National Park (p290), though, as reaching it via public transport is very time-consuming and touring is enhanced with a guide. On-the-ground recommendations for Khao Sok tour guides will be more accurate than a print endorsement. Elsewhere, the following tour operators are worth an investigation:

Barefoot Traveller (www.barefoot-traveller.com) Beaches and diving trips, including live-aboards.

Intrepid Travel (www.intrepidtravel.com) Big adventure tour company offering small, down-to-earth trips.

JYSK Rejsebureau (www.jysk-rejsebureau.dk) Low-budget trips with strong backpacker clientele; Ko Chang Archipelago by boat a highlight.

Paddle Asia (www.paddleasia.com) Kayaking tours to various southern Thailand destinations. Good choice.

Spice Roads (www.spiceroads.com) Cycling trips to southern Thailand and elsewhere.

TRAVELLERS WITH DISABILITIES

Travelling in Thailand can be challenging for the disabled. The government makes few infrastructure provisions and footpaths are often cracked and uneven, making them difficult to negotiate if you're in a wheelchair. But Thais are used to doing things for themselves in these matters and most people will lend a hand without fear or embarrassment.

Large international hotel chains usually have handicapped access to their properties, and home-grown luxury hotels use their high employee-to-guest ratios to help accommodate the mobility impaired. Elsewhere, you are pretty much left to your own resources.

Consider hiring a private car and driver for transport. Disabled travellers have reported

that túk-túk can carry two people and a wheelchair. Many activities in Thailand are open to the disabled, including snorkelling trips and elephant trekking.

For a developing country without a sophisticated social safety net, Thailand is pretty creative at incorporating the disabled into society. The disabled in poor families typically rely on family members for mobility as wheelchairs and other aides are prohibitively expensive. The blind are considered auspicious lottery-ticket sellers and regarded as adept at traditional massage because their sense of touch is more refined than the sighted. In Bangkok, an association of deaf vendors sells souvenirs in tourist areas.

However, it's not all positive. Many disabled people without family support migrate to Bangkok for marginal jobs as itinerant troubadours or beggars. Some of these beggars might be pocketing whatever meagre coinage comes their way, but many others – particularly Cambodian land-mine and burn victims – are little more than slaves to a callous begging mafia.

Organisations

Help & Care Travel Company Ltd (☎ 08 1375-0792; www .wheelchairtours.com) specialises in tours of Thailand for wheelchair users, the aged and deaf travellers using modified vehicles and trained guides. *Exotic Destinations for Wheelchair Travelers* by Ed Hansen and Bruce Gordon contains a useful chapter on Thailand. Other books of value include Rough Guides' *Able to Travel: True Stories by and for People with Disabilities*.

Other companies and resources worth checking out for travel to Thailand include the following:

Access-Able Travel Source (www.access-able.com)

Access Foundation (www.accessibility.com.au)

Accessible Journeys (www.disabilitytravel.com)

Asia Pacific Development Centre on Disability (www.apcdproject.org)

Routes International (www.routesinternational.com)

Society for Accessible Travel & Hospitality (www .sath.org)

Travelability Ltd (www.accessibletravel.co.uk)

Worldwide Dive & Sail (www.worldwidediveandsail .com)

VISAS

Thailand has developed a penchant for changing its immigration laws in recent years, ostensibly to get rid of illegal workers and 'bad

DIRECTORY

influences' such as sex tourists. At the time we went to press the citizens of 41 countries, including most Western European countries, Australia, Canada, Japan, New Zealand, Singapore and the USA (and also Hong Kong SAR) could still enter Thailand without a visa. If you arrive by air you can stay for up to 30 days, but coming overland you can only stay for 15 days. Either way, citizens of Brazil, Republic of Korea and Peru may enter without a visa for 90 days. For a full list of eligible countries and other visa matters, see the website of the Thai **Ministry of Foreign Affairs** (www .mfa.go.th/web/12.php).

The Thai authorities' penchant for cracking down on bludging faràng has meant periodic immigration offensives in recent years, with the once-ignored requirement of an onward ticket being more strictly enforced, usually by airline staff in the departing city. We've heard of several people who had to buy an onward ticket just to get onto the plane; it can be refunded later, with a penalty. Chances are this won't be a problem, but it's worth remembering that the better dressed you are, the less likely you are to be hassled.

What all this means is that if you're planning to stay longer than 30 days it's best to get a 60-day tourist visa or multiple-entry tourist visa before you arrive. These can then be extended by 30 days at any visa office; see right.

Other Visas

Thai embassies and consulates issue a variety of other visas for people on business, students, retirees or those with employment in Thailand. The Non-Immigrant Visa comes in several classifications and is good for 90 days. To stay longer without needing to constantly renew you need an education visa (minimum requirement four hours a week of Thai classes), an investment visa (minimum requirement 10 million baht – ka-ching!), or a work permit. If you plan to apply for a Thai work permit, you'll need a Non-Immigrant Visa first. Getting a Non-Immigrant Visa with the intention of working in Thailand can be difficult and involves a tedious amount of paperwork. If you get one, usually with the support of an employer, you'll likely end up at the **One-Stop Service Centre** (☎ 0 2937 1155; www .boi.go.th; 16th fl, Rasa Tower, 555 Th Phahonyothin, Bangkok) for several hours of paper pushing – get there early!

Note that Transit Visas no longer exist. For more information on all things visa, see the **Ministry of Foreign Affairs** (www.mfa.go.th/web/12. php) and **Bureau of Immigration** (www.immigration .go.th) websites; if you still have questions, seek help on www.thaivisa.com.

Visa Extensions & Visa Runs

The 60-day Tourist Visa can be extended by up to 30 days at the discretion of Thai immigration authorities. Rule changes aimed at preventing people on tourist visas staying longer than 90 days in any six-month period are no longer being enforced (though that situation could change at any time). This means you can, for now, do a visa run every 90 days and, if you can persuade the Thai officials in Vientiane, Phnom Penh or Penang to give you another 60-day visa, stay quite a while.

In Bangkok, extensions are handled by the **Immigration Bureau office** (Map pp70-1; ☎ 0 2141 9889, Call Center 1178; Bldg B, Government Center, Soi 7, Th Chaeng Watthana, Thung Hong Song, Laksi; ☺ 8.30am-noon & 1-4.30pm Mon-Fri); elsewhere any immigration office will do. A fee of 1900B will be charged, and you'll need the usual mug shots. Some travel agencies can also organise extensions.

The 15-day or 30-day no-visa stay can be extended for a maximum of seven days for 1900B. It's better to get a proper tourist visa. It is, however, possible to plan your itinerary so you leave the country after 15/30 days and get another 15/30 days when you return by land/air. Currently this can be done numerous times before officials start asking questions, but this could change at any time.

For a simple visa run (that is, to get a 15-/30-day stamp rather than a full visa) the borders at Hat Lek (see boxed text, p148) to Cambodia, Victoria Point (see boxed text, p276) to Myanmar, and via Satun (p380) to Malaysia are particularly handy. The visa run has been a well-used tool of travellers and residents for years, and several companies exist just to cater to this market.

If you overstay your visa the usual penalty is a fine of 500B for each extra day, with a 20,000B limit (after that, more trouble awaits). Fines can be paid at international airports and border crossings, or at an Immigration Bureau office in advance. Children under 14 years travelling with a parent do not have to pay the penalty.

VOLUNTEERING

Volunteering seems to be all the rage at the moment, and Thailand is one of the favourite destinations. Most volunteering positions are in rural Thailand, but there are also plenty of possibilities in Bangkok. Working in some capacity with people who need your help can make a difference and be rewarding both to you and them. But it's not all sweetness and light, and it's important to understand what you're getting yourself into. Unless you know the country, speak the language and have skills needed in a particular field (eg computing, health and teaching), what you can offer in a short period will largely be limited to manual labour – a commodity not in short supply in Thailand. Having said that, if you can match your skills to a project that needs them, this can be a great way to spend time in Thailand.

There are two main forms of volunteering. For those interested in a long-term commitment, typically two or three years, there are a few long-established organisations that will help you learn the language, place you in a position that will, hopefully, be appropriate to your skills and pay you (just barely). In Thailand, such organisations include the following:

Australian Volunteers International (www.australia nvolunteers.com)

US Peace Corps (www.peacecorps.gov)

Volunteer Service Abroad (VSO NZ) (www.vsa.org.nz)

Voluntary Service Overseas (VSO Canada; www .vsocanada.org)

VSO UK (www.vso.org.uk)

The more popular form of volunteering, sometimes called 'voluntourism', is something you actually pay to do. This is a fast-growing market, and a quick web search for 'Thailand volunteering' will turn up pages of companies offering to place you in a project in return for your hard-earned cash. With these companies you can be a volunteer for as little as a single week up to six months or longer. Fees vary, but start at about €500 for four weeks. The projects can be very good, ongoing affairs with a solid chance of success. But some are not. The list following is a starting point and should not be read as a recommendation. Do your own research and check out all the options before making a decision; consider phoning them to ask, among other things, where your money will go.

Locally focused organisations include **Volunthai** (www.volunthai.com) and **Thai Experience** (www.thai-experience.org). Other general volunteering sites worth looking at are the **Global Volunteer Network** (www.volunteer.org.nz), **Idealist** (www.idealist.org) and **Volunteer Abroad** (www.vo lunteerabroad.com), which lists available positions with a variety of companies. Multicountry organisations that sell volunteering trips include the following:

Cross Cultural Solutions (www.crossculturalsolutions.org)

Cultural Embrace (www.culturalembrace.com)

Global Crossroad (www.globalcrossroad.com)

Global Service Corps (www.globalservicecorps.org)

Institute for Field Research Expeditions (www. ifrevolunteers.org)

Open Mind Projects (www.openmindprojects.org)

Starfish Ventures (www.starfishventures.co.uk)

Thai Volunteer (www.thaivolunteer.org)

Transitions Abroad (www.transitionsabroad.com)

Travel to Teach (www.travel-to-teach.org)

WOMEN TRAVELLERS

Women travellers generally face few problems in Thailand, a fact that has made Thailand Asia's most popular destination for women independent travellers. But like anywhere there are cultural differences that, if respected, help to keep you safe and make your trip run smoother.

In the provincial towns, it is advisable to dress conservatively, covering shoulders, knees and belly buttons. Outside Bangkok, most Thai women cover up in the sun to avoid unnecessary exposure since white skin is considered more beautiful. That Westerners believe the opposite is an endless source of amusement and confusion.

Covering up isn't as much of an issue in Bangkok or in beach resorts where dress codes are looser. However, topless sunbathing is frowned upon by Thais. In some extreme cases (usually involving lone women on remote beaches) topless sunbathing has led directly or otherwise to violent attacks. Going topless is actually banned under the government guidelines for many national parks.

Codes of conduct are more conservative in the Muslim south, where local women cover their heads and bodies. In these areas you should also refrain from public displays of affection.

Attacks and rapes are less common in Thailand than in many Western countries, but incidents do occur, especially when an attacker observes a vulnerable target, a drunk or solo woman. Perhaps you went to the bar to find someone, but if you do return alone, be sure to have your wits about you. Full moon Parties at Ko Pha-Ngan are another trouble spot and we have heard from several women who were sexually assaulted during these parties. Avoid taking dodgy gypsy cabs or accepting rides from strangers late at night – common sense stuff that might escape your notice in a new environment filled with hospitable people. And remember there is safety in numbers – if you're going to collapse, do it near some friends. In cases of rape or other assault, the Thai police will investigate and prosecute the crime, but offer little in the way of counselling.

While Bangkok might be a men's paradise, foreign women are finding their own Romeos on Thai beaches. Women who aren't interested in romantic encounters should not presume that Thai men have equally platonic motives. Often, Thai men ignore their own culture's strictures when it comes to dealing with a foreign woman. There's usually no threat, rather misconceptions – the same sort of stuff that happens back home.

The hotels around the lower end of Th Sukhumvit in Bangkok, or on Hat Patong in Phuket, are the centres of Bangkok's sex tourism and are filled with what can be construed as demeaning attitudes towards women. Sex tourists can act nervously when a reminder from home encroaches on their naughty playground.

Sanitary napkins (*pâh à·nah·mai*) are widely available at minimarts and supermarkets throughout Thailand. Thai women generally don't use tampons (*taam·porn*) but minimarts and pharmacies in tourist areas usually stock a few local and imported brands. Bring your own supplies if you're heading to more remote islands.

WORK

Thailand's steady economic growth has provided a variety of work opportunities for foreigners, but obtaining permission to work in Thailand is harder than you might expect. Thailand is increasingly refusing to issue work permits if a Thai citizen can be found for

the job (as is the norm in most Western nations). One prominent exception is teaching English.

All work, whether paid or voluntary, officially requires a Thai work permit. Work permits must be obtained through an employer, who can apply before you enter Thailand, but the permit itself is not issued until you physically enter Thailand on a valid Non-Immigrant Visa. For information about work permits, contact any Thai embassy abroad or check the **Ministry of Foreign Affairs** (www.mfa .go.th/web/12.php) website. No joy? Seek solace and advice on the message boards of www .thaivisa.com.

For information on doing business in Thailand, see the website of the **Thai Board of Investment** (www.boi.go.th/english/).

Scuba Diving

PADI instructors and qualified dive masters often find work at major dive resorts, such as Ko Tao, Phuket, Ko Phi-Phi, Hat Khao Lak, Ao Nang and, increasingly, Ko Chang. A second language apart from English is an advantage. Some schools offer subsidised training to dive-master level, if you'll work for them when you complete your training. Technically, you must have a work permit for all these jobs.

Teaching English

Many foreigners come to Thailand to teach English, but generally you need academic credentials, such as a TEFL (teaching of English as a foreign language) certificate, to get the decent jobs. There may also be opportunities for private tutoring in the larger cities. Private language academies across Thailand sometimes hire nonqualified teachers by the hour. A work permit is almost always required.

A website maintained by a Bangkok-based English teacher, www.ajarn.com, has tips on finding jobs and pretty much everything else you need to know about getting into the teaching game in Thailand. A similarly popular forum is www.teakdoor.com. If you're more dedicated (or desperate), the **Yellow Pages** (www.yellow.co.th/Bangkok) has contact details for hundreds of schools, universities and language schools.

Transport

GETTING THERE & AWAY

ENTERING THE COUNTRY

Entry procedures for Thailand, by air or by land, are straightforward. You'll have to show your passport, with at least six months validity remaining. You may or may not require a visa; see p411 for details. You'll also need to present completed arrival and departure cards. These are usually distributed on the incoming flight or, if arriving by land or sea, can be picked up at the immigration counter. You do not have to fill in a customs form on arrival unless you have imported goods to declare: you can get the proper form from Thai customs officials at the point of entry (look for the white suits).

Periodic immigration crackdowns have seen some airlines refuse to allow passengers to board flights to Thailand unless they have an onward ticket; see p411 for details on this and other visa requirements.

Flights, tours and rail tickets can all be booked online at www.lonelyplanet.com/travelservices.

AIR

Bangkok is a major regional air hub and Thailand is well served by airlines from Europe, Australia, North America, the Middle East and pretty much every major airport in Asia. There is a 700B departure tax on all international flights, which is now included in the ticket price.

Airports & Airlines

Most international flights arrive in Bangkok and have connecting domestic services to Phuket, Krabi, Ko Samui, Hat Yai and other southern towns. Phuket and Ko Samui both receive some international flights from elsewhere in Asia and, in Phuket, charter flights from Europe. For details on Suvarnabhumi International Airport in Bangkok and transport into the city, see p110 .

Thailand's national carrier is **THAI Airways International** (THAI; www.thaiair.com), which also operates a number of domestic air routes. Some of the other airlines flying to Bangkok at the time of writing, and those that have offices there, are listed below, while the five airlines that fly Thai domestic routes, including those linking Bangkok to the south, are listed with their destinations on p419. Speak to a travel agent or search online for the latest information or take a look at the Suvarnabhumi airport Wikipedia page, which has a fairly up-to-date and complete list.

AIRLINES FLYING TO/FROM THAILAND

Details here include Bangkok phone numbers.

Air Asia (airline code AK; ☎ 0 2515 9999; www.airasia.com)
Air Canada (AC; ☎ 0 2670 0400; www.aircanada.ca)
Air France KLM (AF; ☎ 0 2635 1191; www.airfrance.com)
Air India (AI; ☎ 0 2653 2288; www.airindia.com)
Air New Zealand (NZ; ☎ 0 2235 8280; www.airnewzealand.com)

THINGS CHANGE...

The information in this chapter is particularly vulnerable to change. Check directly with the airline or a travel agent to make sure you understand how a fare (and ticket you may buy) works and be aware of the security requirements for international travel. Shop carefully. The details given in this chapter should be regarded as pointers and are not a substitute for your own careful, up-to-date research.

Bangkok Airways (PG; ☎ 1771 or 0 2265 5555; www
.bangkokair.com)
British Airways (BA; ☎ 0 2236 2800; www.ba.com)
Cathay Pacific Airways (CX; ☎ 0 2263 0606; www
.cathaypacific.com)
China Airlines (CI; ☎ 0 2250 9898; www.china-airlines
.com)
Emirates (EK; ☎ 0 2664 1040; www.emirates.com)
Japan Airlines (JL; ☎ 0 2649 9500; www.jal.co.jp/en)
Jetstar (3K; ☎ 0 2267 5125; www.jetstar.com)
Malaysia Airlines (MH; ☎ 0 2263 0565; www
.malaysiaairlines.com)
Qantas (QF; ☎ 0 2627 1701; www.qantas.com.au)
Singapore Airlines (SQ; ☎ 0 2353 6000; www
.singaporeair.com)
THAI Airways International (TG; ☎ 0 2232 8000;
www.thaiair.com)
United Airlines (UA; ☎ 0 2353 3900; www.united.com)

Tickets

Air tickets to Thailand can be purchased
cheaply online and work well if you are
doing a simple one-way or return trip on
specified dates. For more detailed itineraries, a good travel agent can find special deals
and incorporate them into strategies to avoid
layovers, and can offer advice on everything
from picking the airline with great vegetarian
food to the best travel insurance to bundle
with your ticket.

When you're looking for tickets, it's worth
remembering that the more circuitous the
route, the cheaper it will probably be. For
example, if you spend 24 hours flying from
Europe to Bangkok via Dhaka in Bangladesh,
you'll pay less than a direct flight with THAI
or your national carrier. However, it's also
worth remembering that your carbon footprint becomes bigger every time you take off
and land; see the boxed text, below, for more
on climate change.

In Thailand, domestic routes are increasingly booked online, with budget airlines including Air Asia and Nok Air (p419) dealing
almost exclusively with online and phone
bookings. Travel agents can book these flights
for you, but they will just make an online
booking and charge you 50B for it. Most international flights are booked through an agent.
Most firms are honest and solvent, but there
are some fly-by-night outfits around, particularly in the Th Khao San area. Paying by
credit card generally offers protection, as most
card issuers provide refunds if you can prove
you didn't get what you paid for. Agents who
accept only cash should hand over the tickets
straight away and not tell you to 'come back
tomorrow'. After you've made a booking or
paid your deposit, call the airline and confirm
that the booking was made.

CLIMATE CHANGE & TRAVEL

Climate change is a serious threat to the ecosystems that humans rely upon, and air travel is the
fastest-growing contributor to the problem. Lonely Planet regards travel, overall, as a global benefit, but believes we all have a responsibility to limit our personal impact on global warming.

Flying & Climate Change

Pretty much every form of motor travel generates CO_2 (the main cause of human-induced climate
change) but planes are far and away the worst offenders, not just because of the sheer distances
they allow us to travel, but because they release greenhouse gases high into the atmosphere.
The statistics are frightening: two people taking a return flight between Europe and the US will
contribute as much to climate change as an average household's gas and electricity consumption over a whole year.

Carbon Offset Schemes

Climatecare.org and other websites use 'carbon calculators' that allow jetsetters to offset the
greenhouse gases they are responsible for with contributions to energy-saving projects and
other climate-friendly initiatives in the developing world – including projects in India, Honduras,
Kazakhstan and Uganda.

Lonely Planet, together with Rough Guides and other concerned partners in the travel industry,
supports the carbon offset scheme run by climatecare.org. Lonely Planet offsets all of its staff
and author travel.

For more information check out our website: lonelyplanet.com

Booking flights in and out of Bangkok during the high season (December to March) can be difficult and expensive. For air travel during these months you should make your bookings as far in advance as possible.

ROUND-THE-WORLD (RTW) TICKETS

If you're travelling to multiple countries, then a round-the-world (RTW) ticket – where you pay a single discounted price for several connections – may be the most economical option.

Here are a few online companies to try:

Air Brokers International (www.airbrokers.com)
Airstop & Go (www.airstop.be)
Airtreks (www.airtreks.com)
Around the Worlds (www.aroundtheworlds.com)

Asia

There are regular flights to Suvarnabhumi International Airport from almost every major city in Asia. With the emergence of budget airlines, quick hops from, say, Bangkok to Kuala Lumpur, Singapore or Hong Kong are part of the Asian yuppie's weekend budget. Air Asia, Tiger Air and Jetstar are discount carriers that run frequent promotions. It's also worth asking your agent about cheap seats on airlines you might not expect, such as Emirates, Ethiopian or China Airlines between Bangkok and Hong Kong. Bangkok Airways flies direct to Ko Samui from Hong Kong and Singapore, and Air Asia links Phuket directly to Kuala Lumpur and Singapore.

Recommended booking agencies for reserving flights from Asia include **STA Travel** (www.statravel.com), which has offices in Bangkok, Hong Kong, Japan and Singapore. Another resource in Japan is **No1 Travel** (www.no1-travel.com); in Hong Kong try **Four Seas Tours** (www.fourseastravel.com). For India, try **STIC Travels** (www.stictravel.com), which has offices in dozens of Indian cities.

Australia

THAI, Qantas, British Airways, Jetstar and Emirates, among others, have direct flights to Bangkok, and Jetstar flies directly between Bangkok and Melbourne, and Phuket and Sydney. Garuda Indonesia, Singapore Airlines, Philippine Airlines, Malaysia Airlines and Royal Brunei Airlines also have frequent flights with stopovers to Bangkok.

Shop for cheap tickets from **STA Travel** (☎ 134 782; www.statravel.com.au) and **Flight Centre** (☎ 133 133; www.flightcentre.com.au), both of which have offices throughout Australia.

Canada

Air Canada, THAI, Cathay Pacific and several US-based airlines fly from different Canadian cities to Bangkok. **Travel Cuts** (☎ 800-667-2887; www.travelcuts.com) is Canada's national student travel agency. For online bookings try www.expedia.ca and www.travelocity.ca.

Continental Europe

Following are recommended agencies and websites across Europe.

FRANCE

Anyway (www.anyway.fr)
Lastminute (☎ 04 66 92 30 29; www.lastminute.fr)
Nouvelles Frontières (☎ 08 25 00 07 47; www.nouvelles-frontieres.fr)
Voyageurs du Monde (www.vdm.com)

GERMANY

Expedia (www.expedia.de)
Lastminute (www.lastminute.de)
STA Travel (☎ 0 697 430 3292; www.statravel.de) Good choice for travellers under the age of 26.

ITALY

CTS Viaggi (www.cts.it) Specialises in student and youth travel.

NETHERLANDS

Airfair (☎ 0 900 7717 717; www.airfair.nl)

SPAIN

Barcelo Viajes (☎ 902 200 400; www.barceloviajes.com)

New Zealand

Air New Zealand, British Airways, THAI and Australian-based airlines have direct flights to Bangkok. Malaysian Airlines, Qantas and Garuda International also have flights to Bangkok, with stopovers.

Both **Flight Centre** (☎ 0800 243 544; www.flightcentre.co.nz) and **STA Travel** (☎ 0800 474 400; www.statravel.co.nz) have branches throughout the country. The site www.goholidays.co.nz is recommended for online bookings.

UK

At least two dozen airlines fly between London and Bangkok, although only three of them – British Airways, Qantas and THAI – fly nonstop. Discount air-travel ads appear in *Time Out*, the *Evening Standard* and in the free magazine *TNT*.

Recommended travel agencies include the following:

Bridge the World (☎ 0800 082 5000; www.bridgetheworld.net)

Flight Centre (☎ 0870 499 0040; www.flightcentre.co.uk)

Flightbookers (☎ 0800 082 3000; www.ebookers.com)

North South Travel (www.northsouthtravel.com)
Part of this company's profit is donated to projects in the developing world.

Quest Travel (☎ 0871 423 0135; www.questtravel.com)

STA Travel (☎ 0871 230 0040; www.statravel.co.uk)
Has branches throughout the UK.

Trailfinders (☎ 0845 058 5858; www.trailfinders.co.uk)

Travel Bag (☎ 0800 082 5000; www.travelbag.co.uk)

USA

It's cheaper to fly to Bangkok from west-coast cities than from the east coast.

The airlines that generally offer the lowest fares include China Airlines, **EVA Airways** (www.evaair.com) and Korean Air. EVA Airways (Taiwan) offers the 'Evergreen Deluxe' class between the USA and Bangkok, via Taipei, which has business-class-sized seats and personal movie screens for about the same cost as regular economy fares on most other airlines.

One of the most reliable discounters is **Avia Travel** (☎ 800 950 2842, 510 558 2150; www.aviatravel.com), which specialises in custom-designed RTW fares.

The following agencies are recommended for online bookings:

CheapTickets (www.cheaptickets.com)

Lowestfare (www.lowestfare.com)

STA Travel (www.sta.com)

Travelocity (www.travelocity.com)

BORDER CROSSINGS

Thailand has borders with Myanmar, Laos, Cambodia and Malaysia. Border details are prone to unexpected change so ask around before you set off, check Lonely Planet's Thorn Tree bulletin board at lonelyplanet.com, or the dedicated border pages on **Travelfish** (www.travelfish.org/board/topic/visabordercrossings).

Cambodia

There is a land border crossing between Thailand and Cambodia at Poipet, the seedy frontier town 6km from the Thai town of Aranya Prathet. It is a long haul, but if you're going to Siem Reap and Angkor from Bangkok this is the route most people take. For details

on getting to Siem Reap from the eastern Gulf coast, see the boxed text, p147.

Catch an air-con bus from Bangkok's Northern and Northeastern (Mo Chit) station to Aranya Prathet (220B), then take a túk-túk (pronounced đúk đúk; motorised, open-sided cab) to the border. You can purchase a Cambodian visa on arrival. You can also reach Aranya Prathet from Bangkok's Hualamphong station (54B, 3rd class). A tourist shuttle bus outside the Cambodian immigration office delivers passengers free of charge to Poipet's taxi stand, where onward transport can be arranged to Siem Reap. The most important advice on this route is to steer clear of the agents on Th Khao San offering dirt-cheap trips; they're dodgy. And do some research on the Thorn Tree to be aware of the host of other scams. See Lonely Planet's *Cambodia* guidebook for details of less direct border crossings, and for a rundown of the scams.

More useful if you're coming from the coast is the crossing at Hat Lek, on the coast southeast of Trat. From here you can take direct buses to Sihanoukville or Phnom Penh along the newly sealed highway. The fast ferries that used to connect Ko Kong and Sihanoukville no longer run. For the details, see the boxed text, p148.

Malaysia

It is possible to cross by land from Thailand to Malaysia at several points but by far the most popular route is from Hat Yai to Alor Setar. Hat Yai can be reached from Bangkok by train or bus. Alternatively, you can book all the way from Bangkok to Butterworth (Malaysia) with a stop-off for border formalities. Entry permits for Thailand and Malaysia for most nationalities are available at the border crossings. See Hat Yai (p260) for more transport details. For details on doing a visa run from Hat Yai, see the boxed text on p261.

South of Hat Yai, the train separates into two spurs: one headed to the west coast of the Malay Peninsula and the other to the east coast. The border crossing in the east is at Sungai Kolok (p268). The border is 1km from the train station and most travellers walk across to the Malaysian side where they catch a train or share a taxi to Kota Bharu. This is also the most common route to Pulau Perhentian. Note that the Sungai Kolok train station has been targeted by bomb attacks in the past. Note too that Israeli passport-holders are prohibited from crossing from Thailand to Malaysia.

There are several ways of travelling between southern Thailand and Malaysia by sea. The easiest border crossing is from Satun to Kuala Perlis (Malaysia) or Pulau Langkawi (Malaysia); see p380 for details. Many nationalities can obtain an entry permit for either Thailand or Malaysia at the border.

Myanmar

The land crossings into Myanmar have peculiar restrictions that often don't allow full access to the country. For information on the current status of border crossings into Myanmar, contact the Myanmar embassy in Bangkok (p402).

The only crossing open to foreigners in the south is a crossing by boat from Ranong to Kawthoung (aka Victoria Point) via the Gulf of Martaban and Pakchan estuary. Many people cross on a day trip to renew their Thai visas; for day passes, no Myanmar visa is required. See the boxed text, p276, for details. If you plan to stay longer, or travel further, you'll need to arrange your visa and official permission in advance.

GETTING AROUND

AIR

Flying around Thailand is more affordable than ever and it's not unusual to find seats to cities in the south for less than 2000B, including extras (like, umm, fuel) that usually double the advertised fare. The exceptions are Ko Samui and Trat, where competition is less intense.

Bangkok is the primary hub for domestic flights, but you can also fly to some other Thai cities from Phuket and Ko Samui. If you are heading to northern Thailand from anywhere in the south, you'll usually have to connect through Bangkok. Remember that Bangkok has two airports and if you don't want to transfer be sure to book your domestic connection through Suvarnabhumi (that is, use any airline except Nok Air and One-Two-Go; see p110 for more details.

Thailand has several airlines flying domestic routes. THAI is the full-service carrier with the most-expensive tickets; Bangkok Airways is a good mid-market option with airport lounges open to everyone and prices higher than the budget airlines; while Air Asia and Nok Air are the low-cost airlines. The Airfares & Rail Tickets map (p420) offers an idea of average fares, but they can vary enormously even on the same day. Most airlines deal only in e-tickets, so there's no reason to schlep out to their distant offices to book a fare; use a travel agent, the internet or the phone. For last-minute fares, shop at the departures level in the relevant airport. If you have the choice, avoid flying out of Bangkok on a Friday or Sunday, when seats can cost double the weekday fares.

Airlines in Thailand

Reliable airlines flying to destinations in the south include the following:

Bangkok Airways (airline code PG; ☎ 1771, 0 2265 5555; www.bangkokair.com) From Bangkok (Suvarnabhumi) to Ko Samui, Phuket and Trat; from Ko Samui to Chiang Mai, Krabi, Pattaya, Phuket, Hong Kong and Singapore; and from Phuket to Pattaya.

Nok Air (OX; ☎ 1318; www.nokair.com) From Bangkok (Don Muang) to Hat Yai, Nakhon Si Thammarat, Phuket, Surat Thani and Trang.

Thai Air Asia (AK; ☎ 0 2515 9999; www.airasia.com) From Bangkok (Suvarnabhumi) to Hat Yai, Krabi, Phuket, Nakhon Si Thammarat, Surat Thani and Narathiwat. It also flies from Phuket to Chiang Mai and several regional capitals.

Thai Airways International (☎ 0 2232 8000; www.thaiair.com) From Bangkok (Suvarnabhumi) to Ko Samui, Krabi, Phuket, Hat Yai and Surat Thani. From Phuket to Hat Yai.

If you don't fancy taking the ferry around the Andaman islands, Phuket-based **Destination Air** (☎ 0 7632 8637-39; www.destinationair.com) has charter seaplane services from Patong to Ko Phi-Phi, Ko Lanta, Ao Nang, Ko Yao (Noi and Yai), the Similan Islands and Khao Lak, among others.

Air Passes

Most air passes available aren't particularly valuable if you are just visiting southern Thailand as most flights have to go through Bangkok. THAI and Bangkok Airways do offer passes, which change periodically, but a series of individually booked budget airline flights will probably still cost less.

BICYCLE

The quiet back roads in the low-lying south of Thailand are perfect for bicycle touring. Most roads are sealed and the hard shoulder

AIRFARES & RAIL TICKETS

Airfares
One-way fares, including tax and other charges.
These are mid-priced, mid-season fares,
cheaper seats are usually available.
Rail
2nd-class air-con sleeper,
lower-berth fares from Bangkok.
All fares in baht.

is kept deliberately wide to accommodate two-wheeled vehicles. The road surface is generally pretty good but punctures are common. There is also plenty of opportunity for off-road pedalling.

You can take bicycles on the train for about what you'd pay for a 3rd-class ticket. Buses charge a nominal fee for bikes (if they charge at all). On ordinary buses, your bike will probably be put on the roof; on air-con buses it will go in the cargo hold. Locals routinely carry their bikes on long-tail boats, so getting between islands shouldn't be a problem.

Thais tend to use their bikes for short journeys, so long-distance cyclists are still something of a novelty – expect to see plenty of smiles and surprised stares. Established in 1959, the **Thailand Cycling Club** (☎ 0 2612 5510-1; www.thaicycling.com; 849/53 Chulalongkorn 6, Th Bantadtong, Bangkok) serves as an information clearing house on bicycling tours and cycling clubs throughout the country; see also p411 for recommended companies.

Hire

Bicycles can be hired in many locations, including guesthouses in the south, and generally go for about 50B to 100B per day. Be sure to get the seat and handlebars adjusted to your size and take the bike for a quick spin before you hire – there are some real boneshakers out there. Some historical sites also offer rental bikes.

Purchase

Bangkok has a number of shops selling imported bicycles and their components. The biggest and most-respected store, if not the cheapest, is **Probike** (Map pp72-3; ☎ 0 2253 3384; www .probike.co.th; 237/2 Th Sarasin, Lumphini). Another good choice is **Velo Thailand** (Map pp74-5; ☎ 089 201 7782; www.velothailand.com; 88 Soi 2, Th Samsen, Banglamphu), a smaller operation that also rents and repairs bikes and runs cycling tours. Prices are comparable to Europe or the USA. Resale is possible, but you'll need to stick around long enough to find an interested traveller or expat. Bangkok and Phuket are the best places to sell your wheels; try putting up fliers in hostels and backpacker hotels.

BOAT

Private boat operators link the various islands and ports of the Andaman Sea and the Gulf of Thailand. Your floating conveyance could be anything from a simple wooden fishing boat with open deck to an air-conditioned jetfoil with hot food and video entertainment. Life jackets are usually provided but many boats have inadequate emergency exits, so opendecked boats are often safer than super-ferries. See the regional chapters for information on specific ferry routes to and between the Thai islands.

The waters off many Thai islands are too shallow for large boats, so long-tail boats are used to transfer passengers to the shore. There is usually a per-person charge for this service.

BUS

The bus network in Thailand is prolific and reliable and is a great way to see the countryside and sit among the locals. The Thai government subsidises the **Transport Company** (bò·rí·sàt kŏn sòng; ☎ 1490 or 0 2936 2841; www.transport .co.th), usually abbreviated to Baw Khaw Saw (BKS), and every city and town in Thailand linked by bus has a BKS station, even if it's just a patch of dirt by the side of the road. BKS buses are generally the safest and most reliable.

Government (BKS) Bus

The cheapest and slowest of the BKS buses are the orange 'ordinary' or 2nd-class buses (rót tam·má·dah). These tend to run regularly but they have no air-con and stop in every little town and hamlet along the way – indeed, you can flag these buses down wherever you see them. The faster, blue-and-white air-conditioned buses are called rót air, rót ʼbràp ah·gàht (air-conditioned bus) or rót too·a (tour bus) and typically run throughout the day. On the bottom rung of the air-con class is 2nd class, without a toilet, and 1st class with a toilet. VIP buses have 34 seats while 'Super VIP' buses have only 24 seats and all sorts of trimmings: plush reclining seats, Arctic air-con (bring something warm) and onboard entertainment. VIP buses are good options for long-haul routes, but there are typically only a few departures a day, usually in the evenings.

THERE'S A MAN IN MY LUGGAGE

Buying a bus ticket south through a travel agent on Th Khao San might seem convenient, but too often it ends in tears. Buses are often late, or they depart as scheduled only to drive around town for three hours picking up other passengers. Other common woes include buying a VIP ticket and then being picked up in a jalopy or buying a boat and ferry combination that no one will honour during the second leg of the trip.

But perhaps the worst scam is one that has been operating for years and which the Thai police seem totally incapable of stopping (ask yourself how hard it should be?). It's a crude but very effective scheme – while you are (hopefully) sleeping your way south on the overnight bus, a man is hiding in the luggage hold and slowly working his way through all the bags, stealing whatever takes his fancy. One traveller reported that his stolen credit card was used to pay for the trip's petrol. How generous! Locks are no great deterrent as these guys can pick one faster than you can tie your shoes. By the time you realise you've been robbed, you're far away and the thieves (and evidence) are long gone. If you do take these buses, pack anything valuable in your hand luggage and keep those bags with you at all times.

Of course, the best way to avoid these scams is to skip the tourist buses and deal with the official government bus stations. These buses are much safer, cheaper and you get to hang out with Thais instead of fuming foreigners.

There are ticket windows for the various bus companies at most bus stations. At popular tourist destinations, the schedule is often listed in English by the ticket window. If you're headed further south than Hua Hin, call the bus station in Bangkok (p110) as it can be worth buying your ticket the day before and to confirm departure times. See the regional chapters for detailed information on fares and trip duration.

Tourist Bus & Minivan

As well as government-run buses, numerous tourist bus companies ply between the various tourist centres in the south. These companies use large air-con buses typically painted with chintzy tropical scenes and have onboard toilets, reclining seats and some form of video entertainment. The latest trend is to adorn one's already gaudy-looking bus with about a million headlights, which is quite a sight at night. Unlike the BKS buses, private buses tend to leave from offices in the middle of town or near tourist centres such as Th Khao San in Bangkok. Tickets are sold through travel agents and hotel and guesthouse tour desks. Fares are usually more expensive than on BKS buses.

While tourist buses save you a trip to the bus station, there are countless tales of woe; see the boxed text, p421.

Minivans typically hang around the bus stations and pick up passengers who have missed their bus or tourists who don't know better. Typically the agent will tell you that the bus is leaving in five minutes, which really means you'll have to wait until more people show up to make it profitable enough to leave. Minibuses often cover shorter routes of an hour or two between larger towns. Once they get going, minibus drivers rarely spare the horses; we can think of several minibus trips we consider as near-death experiences.

In general, private bus companies that deal mostly with Thais are good, while those that deal predominantly with faràng (foreigners) – especially those connected with Th Khao San in Bangkok – are the worst. To minimise the chance of trouble, book bus tickets directly at the bus station rather than with an agency.

CAR & MOTORCYCLE

One look at the traffic in Bangkok may be enough to put you off driving in Thailand, but things are a little calmer in the countryside.

Nonetheless, driving in Asia will definitely take a little getting used to. If you keep your speed down and drive *very* defensively, you should be able to get by. However, driving a car in Thailand is never going to be a relaxing experience. If you feel up to the challenge, there are car-hire companies in Bangkok and most other tourist centres – see opposite.

Motorcycles are a great way to explore the Thai countryside but you must adapt to local riding rules. Most importantly, motorcyclists are 2nd-class citizens on Thai roads and are expected to give way to all larger vehicles.

Bringing Your Own Vehicle

Few people bother with their own vehicles if they're coming to see Thailand's islands and beaches. However, passenger vehicles (eg car, van, truck or motorcycle) can be brought into Thailand for tourist purposes for up to six months. Documents needed for the crossing are a valid International Driving Permit, passport, vehicle registration papers (in the case of a borrowed or hired vehicle you will need authorisation from the owner) and a cash or bank guarantee equal to the value of the vehicle plus 20%. For entry through Khlong Toey Port or Suvarnabhumi Airport, this means a letter of bank credit; for overland crossings via Malaysia, Cambodia or Laos a 'self-guarantee' filled in at the border should be sufficient. For more information, see the website of the **Customs Department** (www.customs.go.th) and click through the Personal Vehicles link; for news from others try the **Horizons Unlimited** (www.horizonsunlimited.com) bulletin board (the HUBB), **GT Rider** (www.gt-rider.com) or Lonely Planet's **Thorn Tree** (www.lonelyplanet.com/thorntree).

Driving Licence

Foreigners who want to drive motor vehicles (including motorcycles) in Thailand need either a Thai licence or a valid International Drivers Permit (with a motorcycle entitlement if applicable), though such bothersome details are often overlooked by small island operators. International Drivers Permits are available from driving associations in your home country.

If the police catch you driving without a licence, they may fine you or request an arbitrary cash 'fee' to let you go. If you find yourself in this situation, it's best to do as the locals do and pay up, though 'fees' can be negotiated. If you have an accident and

ROAD DISTANCES (KM)

	Aranya Prathet	Ayuthaya	Bangkok	Chumphon	Hat Yai	Hua Hin	Krabi	Nakhon Si Thammarat	Narathiwat	Pattani	Phuket	Prachinburi	Ranong	Rayong	Sungai Kolok	Surat Thani	Trang
Ayuthaya	246																
Bangkok	275	79															
Chumphon	727	531	452														
Hat Yai	1268	1072	993	555													
Hua Hin	458	262	183	269	810												
Krabi	1278	1082	1003	551	287	820											
Nakhon Si Thammarat	971	775	696	244	192	513	209										
Narathiwat	1495	1299	1220	782	227	1037	514	580									
Pattani	1402	1206	1127	689	134	944	421	487	93								
Phuket	1125	929	862	412	474	667	185	394	701	608							
Prachinburi	161	124	155	607	1148	338	1158	851	1375	1282	1017						
Ranong	855	659	580	128	368	397	882	789	287	735							
Rayong	321	279	200	652	1193	383	1203	1008	1420	1327	1062	248	780				
Sungai Kolok	1555	1359	1280	842	287	1097	576	640	60	153	761	1435	944	1480			
Surat Thani	927	731	652	214	401	469	318	151	731	638	286	807	315	852	791		
Trang	1417	1221	1142	690	147	959	139	142	374	281	324	1297	507	1342	437	234	
Trat	285	392	313	765	1306	496	1316	1009	1533	1440	1175	334	893	180	1593	965	1455

TRANSPORT

you don't have the appropriate licence, the penalties can be more severe.

Fuel & Spare Parts

As well as modern petrol (gasoline) stations with electric pumps, Thailand has roadside stands selling petrol (*ben·sin* or *nám·man rót yon*) from petrol drums and even smaller stalls selling petrol in recycled Coke bottles. All fuel is lead-free in Thailand.

Spare parts for the kinds of vehicles commonly hired out in Thailand are easy to come by in larger towns but can be hard to find in rural areas. If you get into mechanical trouble, it's best to let the hire company sort out the repairs. Be warned that many of the spare parts in motorcycle shops are pirate copies made from inferior materials. For news updates about fuel options and other car talk, see **BKK Auto** (www.bkkautos.com).

Hire

CAR

Big international car-hire companies, such as Avis and Budget, have offices in Bangkok and at large hotels and resorts around the country. All offer Japanese-made sedans, 12-seater minivans, miniature jeeps and luxury 4WD vehicles, usually with manual transmission. There are local car-hire companies in tourist centres such as Ko Lanta and Ko Samui that rent out small Suzuki jeeps from about 1000B a day. If you're heading south, fly or take a train or bus to your destination and hire a car on arrival. See regional chapters for details.

International company rates start at about 1500B per day and include unlimited mileage and tax with an extra 100B a day for insurance. Check the small print carefully to make sure you are fully insured. Drivers can usually be hired with a rental for an additional 600B to 1000B per day. Several companies offer cheap one-way rental between Bangkok and Phuket or Krabi.

MOTORCYCLE

Touring around the countryside on a rented motorcycle has become almost a rite of passage for travellers in Thailand and at most of the beaches and islands you'll find someone (or many people) renting bikes. It's different in Bangkok, where renting is not a good idea unless you are an adrenaline junkie or just enjoy the taste of smog.

The standard rental bike in Thailand is the Honda Dream or very similar no-frills 100cc to 150cc machines with automatic clutches and 'four down' gear configurations. The keys have a tendency to pop out of the ignition on bumpy roads so remember to use the string provided to secure them. In general, the 100cc and 110cc bikes are more comfortable than the 125cc wannabe racing bikes, as the rear pegs are much lower.

The going rate for a 100cc to 150cc bike is 150B to 300B for 24 hours. You'll be expected to leave your passport or driver's licence as a deposit and you should return with as much fuel as it had to start with. Insurance usually isn't provided, so drive with extra care. According to Thai law, all riders and passengers must wear a helmet, but not all hire com-

panies provide them. This is a pain as traffic police routinely stop foreigners who aren't wearing helmets and extract fines. Traffic cops may also ask to see your passport and charge a 'fine' if you can't provide it.

In some tourist centres, you can pick up larger imported bikes such as Harley Davidsons, Japanese road-bikes and 250cc dirt-bikes, though there's limited scope for touring on an island. Rates for these vary from 500B to 1500B and they are usually rented on a standard hire agreement, with insurance and a substantial credit-card deposit.

Insurance

If it's available, ensure you are fully insured before signing a rental contract. With the exception of a few companies that rent out large, imported road bikes, motorcycles are almost always rented without insurance. As

---

STAYING SAFE ON TWO WHEELS

While motorcycle touring is undoubtedly one of the most liberating and exciting ways to see Thailand, dozens of travellers are injured or killed on Thai roads every year. Inexperience is the main cause, so if you don't have much experience, think twice before renting. If you go ahead, take heed of the following to maximise your chances of getting home in one piece. Check your rental bike thoroughly before you hire it – pay particular attention to the brakes and tyre tread, look for oil leaks and make sure the lights and horn work and the engine starts cleanly from the kick-starter.

- Get insurance with your rental if at all possible, and be extra careful if you can't. If you crash or the bike is stolen you will be responsible for the full cost. Make sure that your travel health insurance covers you for motorcycles before you ride (many do not).

- Always wear a helmet, even if you're riding a small scooter on an empty dirt road.

- Cover your arms and legs. As well as protecting yourself from sunburn, you'll save some skin if you come off.

- If you have an open-fronted helmet (pretty likely), wear sunglasses, glasses or goggles to keep the dust and bugs out of your eyes, especially at sunset when crickets and their friends like to leap out at the oncoming light.

- When you get onto a bike, always do it from the left side to keep clear of the hot exhaust. Likewise, if you come off make sure you get away from the bike as quickly as possible, lest you end up with the 'Thai tattoo' – a burned inner right calf – seen festering on beaches across the country.

- Keep your speed down. Thai roads are often full of potholes and there are loads of unfamiliar obstacles to watch out for.

- Try to avoid riding alone in remote areas at night. A number of faràng bikers have been attacked while riding alone in rural areas.

- Motorcycles are always expected to give way to bigger vehicles. Do as local riders do and keep to the hard shoulder with your speed way down.

- Keep an eye on oil levels during long rides. For two-stroke bikes, add two-stroke engine oil in with the gasoline.

most travel insurance policies do not cover motorcycling (some will if you have a dedicated motorcyclist's licence), that means you can have all the fun you like but you must also take all the responsibility, both to yourself and anyone or anything you damage. Regardless of who actually caused the accident, foreigners are often forced to pay up for everything – if you do have an accident, get in contact with the **tourist police** (☎ 1155) immediately.

Road Rules & Conditions

Thailand has some of the best-maintained roads in the region and the traffic isn't too bad once you get away from the main highways. Main roads are well signed, often in Thai and English, but on small country roads most signs are in Thai script only. Large four-lane highways carry most of the long-distance traffic between major towns, but accidents are horribly common, especially during holiday periods such as Songkran. Back roads are quieter and safer, but carry a map as it's easy to get lost.

Size matters in the Darwinian world of Thai driving. And if you only remember two road rules, remember to give way to anyone bigger and to forget about lanes and drive with 180-degree vision. Cars share the road with buses, trucks, motorcycles, bicycles, bullock-carts and wandering buffalo and wildlife, and you never know when a young buffalo (or child!) is going to leap out in front of you. Expect the unexpected, especially at dusk when animals are heading home. Overtaking on hills or blind corners is common (see the boxed text, p427, to understand why) and the largest vehicle has the right of way in any situation.

Motorcycles are relegated to the hard shoulder, so watch out for them when you turn off any highways. Don't be too surprised if you see another vehicle coming towards you on the hard shoulder on your side of the road – it's the only way to get to some turn-offs.

Turn signals are often used to warn passing drivers about oncoming traffic. A left-turn signal means it's OK to pass, while a right-turn signal means someone is approaching from the other direction. However, do not rely entirely on these signals when making the decision to overtake.

The official maximum speed limits are 50km/h within city limits and 100km/h on most highways, though these are widely flouted. Military and police checkpoints are common and you should always slow down and behave courteously – the sentries will usually wave you through without any hassles.

HITCHHIKING

Hitching is never entirely safe in any country in the world and we don't recommend it. Travellers who decide to hitch should understand that they are taking a small but serious risk. On top of this, Thailand isn't a particularly easy place to hitch. Locals find it hard to comprehend why wealthy foreigners aren't willing to pay for public transport. Most of the vehicles that stop will be public buses or sŏrng·tǎa·ou (small pickup trucks), which you could have caught from the bus station anyway and which will ask for a fare.

If you do decide to hitch, never hitch alone, let someone know where you are planning to go, don't hitch at night and don't get into a car if you can smell alcohol on the driver. Be doubly cautious in the deep south, where foreigners may be perceived as a target for Islamic militants.

LOCAL TRANSPORT
Boat

Boats are used for public transport between the various islands and coastal villages of southern Thailand. The workhorse of inter-island transport is the charismatic, deafeningly noisy long-tail boat (reu·a hǎhng yow), which has a propeller mounted at the end of a long drive shaft. Passengers can get a drenching in rough seas (or heavy rain) so consider putting valuable items in plastic bags inside your rucksack. Long-tails either operate like sŏrng·tǎa·ou, leaving whenever there are enough passengers, or offer custom charters. The relevant destination chapters have more information.

Bangkok has its own network of urban boat transport, following the network of canals that radiate out from the Chao Phraya; see p111 for details.

Local Bus

Most larger cities have a local bus system. Bangkok has a comprehensive service with several classes; in smaller towns local transport is usually provided by sŏrng·tǎa·ou rather than buses. Provincial airports often provide a bus service into town whenever a flight arrives; however, you usually have to take a taxi in the other direction.

Motorcycle Taxi

Thais rely on motorcycle taxis for short journeys around town. Drivers wear coloured vests and hang around at bus stands and street corners waiting for passengers.

Within Bangkok, motorcycle taxis serve two purposes. Most commonly and popularly they run from the corner of a main thoroughfare, such as Th Sukhumvit, to the far ends of soi (lanes) that run off that thoroughfare, usually charging 10B to 20B for the trip. Their other purpose is as a means of beating the traffic. You tell your rider where you want to go, negotiate a price (from 20B for a short trip up to about 150B going across town), strap on the helmet (they will insist for longer trips) and say a prayer to whichever god you're into. Drivers range from responsible to kamikaze, but the average trip involves some time on the wrong side of the road and several near-death experiences. It's the sort of white-knuckle ride you'd pay good money for at Disneyland, but is all in a day's work for these riders. Comfort yourself with the knowledge that there are good hospitals nearby.

Women wearing skirts are expected to ride side-saddle; be sure to gather up loose material so that it doesn't get caught in the vehicle's drive chain.

Sähm-lór & Túk-Túk

Sähm-lór means 'three wheels', and that's just what they are – three-wheeled vehicles, usually without a motor. The motorised version is known as túk-túk from the noise they make. Most are powered by noisy two-stroke engines, usually running on LPG (liquid petroleum gas), and have open-sided cabs that let in all the noise, dust and traffic fumes.

Both provide taxi services in provincial towns and villages. You can flag them down anywhere but the fare must be established before you start the journey. In Bangkok, túk-túk are no cheaper than metered taxis and are roving scam artists. Away from the capital, túk-túk are the taxis.

Nonmotorised sähm-lór are basically bicycle rickshaws, of the kind seen all over Asia. The Thai version has the seat at the back, behind the driver, as in India. There are no bicycle sähm-lór in Bangkok but they are fairly common elsewhere in the country. Bicycle sähm-lór are cheaper than túk-túk, but far slower and can't go the same distances.

Sörng-täa-ou

A sörng-täa-ou (literally two rows) is a usually small truck with a row of bench seats down each side, similar to an Indonesian *bemo* or a Filipino *jeepney*. Sörng-täa-ou sometimes operate fixed routes, like buses, but can also be booked for special trips like a regular taxi. In rural towns, you can usually pick up sörng-täa-ou from the bus stand or main market to outlying villages and beaches. If you are the first passenger on an empty sörng-täa-ou, the driver may try and talk you into chartering the whole vehicle; stand firm if you want to wait for other passengers. Sörng-täa-ou are also used on the islands and on Phuket and Ko Samui, where they make a refreshingly cheap and local way to get between beaches and avoid the taxi mafia rip-off merchants. Fares are charged per person, with foreigners often charged a few baht more than Thais.

Taxi

Western-style taxis are only really common in Bangkok, Pattaya and touristy islands like Phuket and Ko Samui. In most places, you have to rely on túk-túk and motorcycle taxis. Where you do find taxis in provincial towns, you'll have to establish the fare before you start your journey as the meter is rarely used.

Taxis operate between some towns on a share basis, with the fare split between passengers. Elsewhere pretty much any taxi can be persuaded to take a long-distance trip with enough notes. Taxis regularly run for fixed fares between Bangkok and centres such as Pattaya (1500B), Hua Hin (2300B), Ban Phe (for Ko Samet, 2300B) and Phetchaburi (1700B); see www.taxiradio.co.th for other fares. Fares back to Bangkok are often significantly cheaper – bargain.

Train

The train system in Thailand is primarily used for intercity travel. The exception is Bangkok, which has the Skytrain (see p114) and the underground Metro (see p114).

TRAIN

The railway network in Thailand is run by the government-subsidised **State Railway of Thailand** (SRT; ☎ 1690; www.railway.co.th). Trains are slightly slower than buses, but the standard of service is good and this is certainly one of the most pleasant ways to get around the kingdom. Apart from being smoother, more social and

---

TAXI ALTARS: INSURANCE ON THE DASHBOARD

As your taxi races into Bangkok from the airport your delight at being able to do the 30km trip for less than US$10 is soon replaced by uneasiness, anxiety and eventually outright fear. Because 150km/h is fast, you're tailgating the car in front and there's no seatbelt. You can rest assured (or not), however, that your driver will share none of these concerns.

All of which makes the humble taxi trip an instructive introduction to Thai culture. Buddhists believe in karma and in turn that their fate is to a large extent predestined. Unlike Western ideas, which take a more scientific approach to road safety, many Thais believe factors such as speed, concentration, seatbelts and simple driver quality have no bearing whatsoever on your chances of being in a crash. Put simply, if you die a horrible death on the road, karma says you deserved it. The trouble is that when a passenger gets into a taxi they bring their karma and any bad spirits the passenger might have along for the ride. Which could upset the driver's own fate.

To counteract such bad influences most Bangkok taxi drivers turn the dashboard and ceiling into a sort of life insurance shrine. The ceiling will have a yantra diagram drawn in white powder by a monk as a form of spiritual protection. This will often be accompanied by portraits of notable royals. Below this a red box dangling red tassels, beads and amulets hangs from the rear vision mirror, while the dashboard is populated by Buddhist and royal statuettes, and quite possibly banknotes with the King's image prominent and more amulets. With luck (such as it exists in Thailand), the talismans will protect your driver from any bad karma you bring into their cab. Passengers must hope their driver's number is not up. If you feel like it might be, try saying *cháa cháa* soothingly – that is, ask your driver to slow down. For a look inside some of Bangkok's 100,000 or so taxis, check out **Still Life in Moving Vehicle** (www.lifeinmovingvehicle .blogspot.com).

---

spacious than buses, trains are also safer, both in terms of accidents and thefts from baggage. Some trains have dining cars and snack vendors so you don't have to wait for meal stops, and the scenery is usually better than that beside the highway.

The rail network covers 4500km and there are four main rail lines within the country – the northern, southern, northeastern and eastern lines. The line most island-bound travellers use is the southern route with stops at Hua Hin, Chumphon (for transfers to Ko Tao), Surat Thani (for transfers to Ko Samui), Hat Yai and the border with Malaysia. There are also a handful of branch lines, including the useful side route between Tung Song (on the main southern line) and Trang, terminating at Kantang. The southern line splits at Hat Yai; one branch follows the east coast to Sungai Kolok on the Malaysian border and the other heads west to Padang Besar, then over the Malaysian border to Butterworth. Almost all the long-distance trains originate from Bangkok's Hualamphong train station.

All train stations within Thailand offer baggage-storage services. Meals are available in dining cars on most trains, or at your seat if you travel 1st or 2nd class; quality varies widely, but is rarely great. Roving vendors also wander up and down some trains selling bottled water, soft drink and beer for significantly more than you'll pay in a 7-Eleven.

Classes

There are three classes on SRT trains – 1st, 2nd and 3rd – but the standard of facilities in each varies considerably depending on whether you're on an ordinary, rapid or express train. Third-class seats are cheaper than ordinary buses, while 2nd class costs about the same as the equivalent journey by VIP or private bus. First class costs quite a lot more, but the extra luxury may be worth it on long journeys.

FIRST CLASS

First-class cars have private double cabins with individually controlled air-con, an electric fan, a washbasin and mirror, a small table and a long bench seat that converts into two beds. Drinking water and towels are provided free of charge. First-class cars are available only on express and special express trains. Single 1st-class cabins are not available, so if you're travelling alone you may be paired with another passenger, although the SRT takes great care not to mix genders.

TRANSPORT

SECOND CLASS

There are two types of 2nd-class cars – seat cars and sleepers. Seat cars have padded seats that recline but aren't really comfortable enough for sleeping on overnight trips. In a 2nd-class sleeper car a central aisle is flanked by a series of open compartments, each containing two facing padded seats that convert into berths. The lower berths cost a little more as they are roomier. When the berths are folded away, a table can be set up between the two seats for meals. Fresh linen is provided and each car has a toilet and basin. Second-class cars are found only on rapid and express trains and can either be fan-cooled, which gets hot once you've closed the curtains, or air-conditioned, which is usually so cold you'll be wondering if you're on the Trans-Siberian.

THIRD CLASS

A typical 3rd-class carriage consists of two rows of bench seats divided into facing pairs. Each bench seat is designed to seat two or three passengers, but you can expect four or more. On ordinary trains, 3rd-class seats may have hard wooden benches, but on rapid trains there is usually some padding to keep your bottom from going numb. Express trains do not carry 3rd-class carriages at all.

Costs

Ticket prices are very reasonable and you can check the latest on www.thairailways .co.th or www.thailandbytrain.com. Fares are calculated with a base price (the price of an ordinary class ticket) plus a dizzying array of surcharges depending on class, means of cooling (fan or air-con) and distance. Surcharges range from 50B for short trips on a *rót re·hou* (rapid train), are usually between 100B and 200B for trips on *rót dòo·an* (express trains), and peak at 500B on long *rót dòo·an pí·sèht* (special-express trains).

If all this surcharge stuff sounds confusing, the good news is that at most stations someone will be able to tell you in English when the train leaves, how long it takes and how much it costs – which is all you really need to know. Or you can look it all up on the www .railway.co.th website.

Reservations

Advance bookings may be made one to 60 days before your intended date of departure. For holiday-period travel – especially the middle of April approaching the Songkran Festival, during Chinese New Year and during the peak tourist-season months of December and January – it is advised to book tickets as far in advance as possible, especially for popular routes such as Surat Thani and Hat Yai.

You can make bookings from any train station, where ticket offices are generally open 8.30am to 6pm on weekdays, and 8.30am to noon on weekends and public holidays. Tickets can also be purchased by telephone at ☎ 1690, or at travel agencies in Bangkok, which charge a 50B processing fee but save you the trip to the station.

Midweek departures are always easier to book than weekends; during some months you can easily book a sleeper even one day before departure, as long as it's on a Tuesday, Wednesday or Thursday. With the exception of those departing Surat Thani or Chiang Mai, booking trains back to Bangkok is generally not as difficult as booking trains out of Bangkok.

If you change your plans you can get an 80% refund up to three days before travel and a 50% refund up to one hour after the train departs.

Train Passes

If you plan on doing a lot of rail travel, the SRT offers a rail pass that allows unlimited 2nd- and 3rd-class travel on Thai trains for 20 days. It costs 1500B, or 3000B including all supplemental charges (air-con, rapid and express charges). Passes are only available in Thailand and may be purchased at the advance booking office at Hualamphong train station in Bangkok. If you're just travelling in southern Thailand, the rail pass probably won't save you much money, but it can be a good deal if you are also planning to visit the north.

Passes must be validated at a local station before boarding the first train and reservations are recommended for later journeys. The pass is valid for all trains leaving before midnight on the last day of the pass.

Health Dr Trish Bachelor

CONTENTS

Health issues and the quality of medical facilities vary enormously depending on where and how you travel in Thailand. Bangkok has excellent hospitals (p67) and major cities have well-developed healthcare facilities. However, travel to rural areas can expose you to a variety of health risks and inadequate medical care.

Travellers may worry about contracting infectious diseases, but these rarely cause serious illness or death in travellers. Pre-existing medical conditions and accidental injury, especially traffic accidents, account for most life-threatening problems. Becoming ill, however, is relatively common. Most common illnesses can be prevented with common-sense behaviour or be treated easily with a well-stocked medical kit.

The following advice is a general guide only and does not replace the advice of a doctor trained in travel medicine.

BEFORE YOU GO

Pack medications in their original, clearly labelled containers. A signed and dated letter from your physician describing your medical conditions and medications, including generic names, is also a good idea. If carrying syringes or needles be sure to have a physician's letter documenting their medical necessity. If you have a heart condition, bring a copy of your ECG taken just prior to travelling.

If you happen to take any regular medication, bring double your needs in case of loss or theft. In most of Thailand, you can buy many medications over the counter without a doctor's prescription, but it can be difficult to find some newer drugs, particularly the latest antidepressant drugs, blood pressure medications and contraceptive pills, outside of Bangkok.

INSURANCE

Even if you are fit and healthy, don't travel without health insurance – accidents and illnesses do happen. If you are uninsured, emergency evacuation can be expensive; bills of over US$100,000 are not uncommon. Declare any existing medical conditions you have – the insurance company *will* check whether your problem is pre-existing and will not cover you if it is undeclared. You may require extra cover for adventure activities such as rock climbing and inquire if the insurance covers accidents on a motorbike. If your health insurance doesn't cover you for medical expenses abroad, consider getting additional insurance.

Find out in advance if your insurance plan pays providers directly or reimburses you later for expenditures. Some providers offer various medical-expense options; the higher ones are generally for countries with extremely high medical costs, such as the USA. You may prefer a plan that pays hospitals directly rather than having you pay on the spot and claim later. If you have to claim later, keep all documentation. Some policies might ask you to call (reverse charges) a centre in your home country where an immediate assessment of your problem is made.

VACCINATIONS

Specialised travel-medicine clinics are your best source of information; they stock all available vaccines and will be able to make recommendations tailored specifically for you and your trip. The doctors there will take into account factors such as your vaccination history, the length of your trip, activities you may be undertaking while away, and any underlying medical conditions, such as pregnancy.

Most vaccines don't produce immunity until at least two weeks after they're given, so visit a doctor four to eight weeks before departure. Ask your doctor for an International Certificate of Vaccination (otherwise known as the yellow booklet), which will list all the vaccinations you've received.

MEDICAL CHECKLIST
Recommended items for a personal medical kit:

- Antibacterial cream, eg Muciprocin
- Antibiotic for skin infections, eg Amoxicillin (Clavulanate) or Cephalexin
- Antibiotics for diarrhoea, eg Norfloxacin or Ciprofloxacin; for bacterial diarrhoea Azithromycin; for giardiasis or amoebic dysentery Tinidazole
- Antifungal cream, eg Clotrimazole
- Antihistamine – there are many options, eg Cetrizine for daytime and Promethazine for night
- Antiseptic, eg Betadine
- Antispasmodic for stomach cramps, eg Buscopa
- Contraceptives
- Decongestant, eg Pseudoephedrine
- DEET-based insect repellent
- Diarrhoea relief – consider packing a diarrhoea 'stopper' (eg Loperamide), an antinausea medication (eg Prochlorperazine) and an oral rehydration solution (eg Gastrolyte)
- First-aid items such as scissors, Elastoplasts, bandages, gauze, safety pins and tweezers, thermometer (but not mercury), and sterile needles and syringes.
- Ibuprofen or another anti-inflammatory
- Indigestion medication, eg Quick Eze or Mylanta
- Iodine tablets (unless you are pregnant or have a thyroid problem) to purify water
- Laxative, eg Coloxyl
- Migraine medicine if prone to migraines
- Paracetamol
- Permethrin to impregnate clothing and mosquito nets
- Steroid cream for allergic/itchy rashes, eg 1% to 2% hydrocortisone

- Sunscreen and hat
- Throat lozenges
- Thrush (vaginal yeast infection) treatment, eg Clotrimazole pessaries or Diflucan tablet
- Ural or equivalent if you're prone to urine infections

INTERNET RESOURCES
There is a wealth of travel health advice on the internet. For further information, **Lonely Planet** (www.lonelyplanet.com) is a good place to start. The **World Health Organization** (WHO; www.who.int/ith/) publishes a superb book, *International Travel & Health*, which is revised annually and is available free online. Another website of general interest is **MD Travel Health** (www.mdtravelhealth .com), which provides complete travel health recommendations for every country and is updated daily. The **Centers for Disease Control and Prevention** (CDC; www.cdc.gov) website also has good general information.

FURTHER READING
Lonely Planet's *Healthy Travel – Asia & India* is a handy pocket-size book that is packed with useful information including pretrip planning, emergency first aid, immunisation and disease information, and what to do if you get sick on the road. Other recommended references include *Traveller's Health,* by Dr Richard Dawood, and *Travelling Well,* by Dr Deborah Mills – check out the website www .travellingwell.com.au.

IN TRANSIT

DEEP VEIN THROMBOSIS (DVT)
Deep vein thrombosis (DVT) occurs when blood clots form in the legs during plane flights, chiefly due to prolonged immobility. The longer the flight, the greater the risk of developing deep vein thrombosis. While most clots are reabsorbed uneventfully, occasionally some clots break off and travel through blood vessels to the lungs, where they may result in life-threatening complications.

The chief symptom of DVT is swelling of or pain in the foot, ankle or calf, usually, but not always, on just one side. If a blood clot travels to the lungs it may cause chest pain and/or you could experience difficulty breathing. Travellers with any of these

POSSIBLE VACCINATIONS

There are no required vaccines for entering Thailand. Proof of vaccination against yellow fever is required only if you have visited a country in a yellow-fever zone within the six days prior to entering the region. If you are travelling to Southeast Asia from Africa or South America you should check to see if you require proof of vaccination.

Recommended Vaccinations

The World Health Organization recommends the following vaccinations for travellers heading to Thailand.

Adult diphtheria & tetanus Single booster recommended if not had in the previous 10 years. Side effects include sore arm and fever.

Hepatitis A Provides almost 100% protection for up to a year; a booster after 12 months provides at least another 20 years protection. Mild side effects such as headache and sore arm occur in 5% to 10% of people.

Hepatitis B Now considered routine for most travellers, it is given as three injections over six months. A rapid schedule is also available, as is a combined vaccination with Hepatitis A. Side effects are mild and uncommon, usually headache and sore arm. Lifetime protection occurs in 95% of people.

Measles, mumps & rubella Two doses of MMR required unless you have had the diseases. Occasionally a rash and flulike illness can develop a week after receiving the vaccine. Many young adults require a booster.

Polio In 2005 Thailand had no reported cases of polio. Only one booster required as an adult for lifetime protection. Inactivated polio vaccine is safe during pregnancy.

Typhoid Recommended unless your trip is less than a week and only to developed cities. The vaccine offers around 70% protection, lasts for two to three years and comes as a single injection. Tablets are also available, however the injection is usually recommended as it has fewer side effects. Sore arm and fever may occur.

Varicella If you haven't had chickenpox, discuss this vaccination with your doctor.

The following immunisations are recommended for long-term travellers (more than one month) or those at special risk.

Japanese B Encephalitis Three injections in all. Booster recommended after two years. Sore arm and headache are the most common side effects. Rarely will an allergic reaction comprising hives and swelling occur up to 10 days after any of the three doses.

Meningitis Single injection. There are two types of vaccination: the quadrivalent vaccine gives two to three years protection; meningitis group C vaccine gives around 10 years protection. Recommended for long-term backpackers aged under 25.

Rabies Three injections in all. A booster after one year will provide 10 years protection. Side effects are rare – occasionally headache and sore arm.

Tuberculosis Adult long-term travellers are usually recommended to have a TB skin test before and after travel, rather than a vaccination. Only one vaccine given in a lifetime.

symptoms should immediately seek medical attention.

To prevent the development of DVT on long flights you should walk about the cabin, perform isometric compressions of the leg muscles (ie contract the leg muscles while sitting), drink plenty of fluids and avoid alcohol.

JET LAG & MOTION SICKNESS

Jet lag is common when crossing more than five time zones; it results in insomnia, fatigue, malaise or nausea. To avoid jet lag, drink plenty of nonalcoholic fluids and eat light meals during the flight. Upon arrival, expose yourself to natural sunlight and readjust your schedule (for meals, sleep etc) to that of the country you have arrived in as soon as possible.

Antihistamines such as dimenhydrinate (Dramamine) and meclizine (Antivert, Bonine) are usually the first choice for treating motion sickness. Their main side effect is drowsiness. A herbal alternative to antihistamines is ginger, which works like a charm for some people.

IN THAILAND

AVAILABILITY OF HEALTH CARE

Bangkok has become a medical centre for foreigners seeking cosmetic, elective and primary care. Hospitals geared towards these clients have internationally trained doctors, English-speaking staff and top-notch service, though, as in the whole of the country, over-prescription can be a problem. Other tourist areas, such as Phuket and Ko Samui, will have equally accessible hospital facilities. On the smaller islands, there will be rudimentary clinics for bumps, scrapes and minor infections. It is difficult to find reliable medical care in rural areas. Recommended hospitals in Bangkok are listed on p67. Your embassy and insurance company are also good contacts. Many pharmacies in Thailand are equipped to deal with minor health problems such as traveller's diarrhoea. If you think you may have a serious disease, especially malaria or dengue fever, do not waste time – travel to the nearest quality facility to receive attention. It is always better to be assessed by a doctor than to rely on self-treatment.

Do be aware that some medications in Thailand are either fake, poorly stored or out-of-date.

INFECTIOUS DISEASES
Cutaneous Larva Migrans

Cutaneous Larva Migrans, caused by dog hookworm, is particularly common on the beaches of Thailand. The rash starts as a small lump, then slowly spreads in a linear fashion. It is intensely itchy, especially at night. It is easily treated with medications and should not be cut out or frozen.

Dengue Fever

This mosquito-borne disease is becoming increasingly problematic throughout Southeast Asia, especially in the cities. As there is no vaccine available it can only be prevented by avoiding mosquito bites. The mosquito that carries dengue will bite day and night, so implement insect avoidance measures at all times. Symptoms include high fever, severe headache and body ache (dengue was previously known as 'breakbone fever'). Some people develop a rash and experience diarrhoea. The southern islands of Thailand are a particularly high risk. There is no specific treatment, just rest and paracetamol – do not take aspirin as it increases the likelihood of haemorrhaging. See a doctor to be diagnosed and monitored.

Filariasis

This is a mosquito-borne disease that is very common in the local population, yet very rare in travellers. Mosquito-avoidance measures are the best way to prevent this disease.

Hepatitis A

Hepatitis A is a problem throughout the region. This food- and water-borne virus infects the liver, causing jaundice (yellow skin and eyes), nausea and lethargy. There is no specific treatment for hepatitis A; you just need to allow the liver time to heal. All travellers to Southeast Asia should be vaccinated against hepatitis A.

Hepatitis B

The only sexually transmitted disease that can be prevented by vaccination, hepatitis B is spread by body fluids, including sexual contact. In some parts of Southeast Asia up to 20% of the population are carriers of hepatitis B, and usually are unaware of this. The long-term consequences can include liver cancer and cirrhosis.

Hepatitis E

Hepatitis E is transmitted through contaminated food and water and has symptoms similar to hepatitis A, but is far less common. It is a severe problem in pregnant women potentially resulting in the death of both mother and baby. There is currently no vaccine, and prevention is by following safe eating and drinking guidelines.

HIV

HIV is one of the most common causes of death in people under the age of 50 in Thailand. Heterosexual sex is the primary method of transmission both in Thailand and neighbouring countries, several of which have rising numbers of people living with HIV, and dying from AIDS. However, while more than 1% of Thais are infected with HIV, aggressive safe-sex campaigns in the 1990s have seen the incidence of new infections drop sharply, and made Thailand a global pin-up for effectively dealing with the disease.

Influenza

Present year-round in Thailand, influenza (flu) symptoms include a high fever, muscle aches, runny nose, cough and sore throat. It can be very severe in people over the age of 65 or in those with underlying medical conditions such as heart disease or diabetes; vaccination is recommended for these individuals. There is no specific treatment, just rest and paracetamol.

Japanese B Encephalitis

This viral disease is transmitted by mosquitoes. While rare in travellers, at least 50,000 locals are infected each year. Most cases occur in rural areas; travellers spending more than one month outside of cities should be vaccinated. There is no treatment, and one-third of infected people will die while another third will suffer permanent brain damage.

Leptospirosis

This is most commonly contracted after river rafting or canyoning. Early symptoms are very similar to the flu and include headache and fever. Severity can vary from very mild to a being fatal. Diagnosis is achieved through blood tests and it is easily treated with Doxycycline.

Malaria

For such a serious and potentially deadly disease, there is an enormous amount of misinformation concerning malaria. You must get expert advice as to whether your trip actually puts you at risk, particularly if you are pregnant. Many parts of Southeast Asia, particularly city and resort areas, have minimal to no risk of malaria, and the risk of side effects from taking prophylactics may outweigh the risk of getting the disease. For most rural areas, however, the risk of contracting the disease outweighs the risk of tablet side effects. Remember that malaria can be fatal. Before you travel, seek medical advice on the right medication and dosage for you.

Malaria is caused by a parasite transmitted by the bite of an infected mosquito. The most important symptom of malaria is fever, but general symptoms such as headache, diarrhoea, cough or chills may also occur. Diagnosis can only be made by taking a blood sample.

Two strategies should be combined to prevent malaria – mosquito avoidance and antimalarial medications. Most people who catch malaria are taking inadequate or no antimalarial medication.

Travellers are advised to prevent mosquito bites by taking these steps:

- Use insect repellent containing DEET on exposed skin. Wash this off at night, only if you are sleeping under a mosquito net. Natural repellents such as Citronella can be effective, but must be applied more frequently than products containing DEET.
- Sleep under a mosquito net impregnated with Permethrin.
- Choose accommodation with fans (if not air-conditioning) and screens.
- Impregnate clothing with Permethrin in high-risk areas.
- Wear long sleeves and trousers in light colours.
- Use mosquito coils.
- Spray your room with insect repellent before going out for your evening meal.

There are a variety of malaria medications available:

Artesunate Derivatives of Artesunate are not suitable as a preventive medication. They are useful treatments under medical supervision.

Chloroquine & Paludrine The effectiveness of this combination is now limited in most of Southeast Asia. Common side effects include nausea (40% of people) and mouth ulcers. Not recommended.

Doxycycline This daily tablet is a broad-spectrum antibiotic that has the added benefit of helping to prevent a variety of tropical diseases, including leptospirosis, tick-borne disease, typhus and melioidosis. The potential side effects include photosensitivity (a tendency to sunburn), thrush in women, indigestion, heartburn, nausea and interference with the contraceptive pill. More serious side effects include ulceration of the oesophagus – you can help prevent this by taking your tablet with a meal and a large glass of water, and never lying down within half an hour of taking it. Must be taken for an additional four weeks after leaving the risk area.

Lariam (Mefloquine) Lariam has received a lot of bad press, some of it justified, some not. This weekly tablet suits many people. Serious side effects are rare but include depression, anxiety, psychosis and having fits. Anyone with a history of depression, anxiety, other psychological disorders or epilepsy should not take Lariam. It is considered safe in the second and third trimesters of pregnancy. It is around 90% effective in most parts of Southeast Asia, but there is significant resistance in parts of northern Thailand, Laos and Cambodia. Tablets must be taken for four weeks after leaving the risk area.

Malarone This newer drug is a combination of Atovaquone and Proguanil. Side effects are uncommon and mild, most commonly nausea and headache. It is the best tablet for scuba divers and for those on short trips to high-risk areas. It must be taken for one week after leaving the risk area.

A final option is to take no preventive medication but to have a supply of emergency medication should you develop the symptoms of malaria. This is not ideal and you will need to get to a good medical facility within 24 hours of developing a fever. If you choose this option the most effective and safest treatment is Malarone (four tablets once daily for three days). Other options include Artesunate, Mefloquine and Quinine but the side effects of the latter two drugs at treatment doses make them less desirable. Fansidar is no longer recommended.

Measles

Measles remains a problem in some parts of Southeast Asia. This highly contagious bacterial infection is spread via coughing and sneezing. Most people born before 1966 are immune as they had measles in childhood. Measles starts with a high fever and rash and can be complicated by pneumonia and brain disease. There is no specific treatment.

Melioidosis

This infection is contracted by skin contact with soil. It is rare in travellers, but in some parts of northeast Thailand up to 30% of the local population are infected. The symptoms are very similar to those experienced by tuberculosis sufferers. There is no vaccine but it can be treated with medication.

Rabies

Rabies is still a common problem in most parts of Southeast Asia. This uniformly fatal disease is spread by the bite or lick of an infected animal – most commonly a dog or monkey. Seek medical advice immediately after any animal bite and commence post-exposure treatment. Having a pre-travel vaccination means the post-bite treatment is simplified. If an animal bites you, gently wash the wound with soap and water, and apply iodine-based antiseptic. If you are not pre-vaccinated you

will need to receive rabies immunoglobulin as soon as possible.

STDs

Sexually transmitted diseases most common in Southeast Asia include herpes, warts, syphilis, gonorrhoea and chlamydia. People carrying these diseases often have no signs of infection. Condoms will prevent gonorrhoea and chlamydia but not warts or herpes. If after a sexual encounter you develop any rash, lumps, discharge or pain when passing urine seek immediate medical attention. If you have been sexually active during your travels have an STD check on your return home.

Strongyloides

This parasite, transmitted by skin contact with soil, is common in Thailand but rarely affects travellers. It is characterised by an unusual skin rash called *larva currens* – a linear rash on the trunk which comes and goes. Most people don't have other symptoms until their immune system becomes severely suppressed, when the parasite can cause an overwhelming infection. It can be treated with medications.

Tuberculosis

While rare in short-term travellers, medical and aid workers, and long-term travellers who have significant contact with the local population should take precautions. Vaccination is usually only given to children under the age of five, but adults at risk are recommended to take pre- and post-travel tuberculosis testing. The main symptoms are fever, cough, weight loss, night sweats and tiredness.

Typhoid

This serious bacterial infection is spread via food and water. Symptoms include a high, slowly progressive fever and headache, and may be accompanied by a dry cough and stomach pain. It is diagnosed by blood tests and treated with antibiotics. Vaccination is recommended for all travellers spending more than a week in Southeast Asia, or travelling outside the major cities. Be aware that vaccination is not 100% effective so you must still be careful with what you eat and drink.

Typhus

Murine typhus is spread by the bite of a flea, whereas scrub typhus is spread via a mite.

HEALTH

These diseases are rare in travellers. Symptoms include fever, muscle pains and a rash. You can avoid these diseases by following general insect-avoidance measures. Doxycycline will also prevent them.

TRAVELLER'S DIARRHOEA

Traveller's diarrhoea is by far the most common problem affecting travellers – between 30% and 50% will suffer from it within two weeks of starting their trip. For the vast majority it won't be a huge problem. A change of diet can often loosen stools and when you add copious amounts of chilli to unfamiliar cuisine there's a good chance you'll end up scampering to the throne sooner or later. Recovery is usually swift. So if the symptoms are not major (ie there's no blood in your stool) then the usual advice is to…errr…sit on it for a day or two before you reach for the antibiotics.

Having said that, genuine traveller's diarrhoea is usually caused by bacteria and therefore can be treated with antibiotics. Traveller's diarrhoea is defined as the passage of more than three watery bowel-actions within 24 hours, plus at least one other symptom such as fever, cramps, nausea, vomiting or feeling generally unwell.

Treatment includes staying hydrated; rehydration solutions such as Gastrolyte are the best for this. Antibiotics such as Norfloxacin, Ciprofloxacin or Azithromycin will kill the bacteria quickly.

Loperamide is just a 'stopper' and doesn't get to the cause of the problem. It can be helpful, for example if you have to go on a long bus ride. Don't take Loperamide if you have blood in your stools or a fever. Seek medical attention quickly if you don't respond to an appropriate antibiotic.

Amoebic Dysentery

Amoebic dysentery is very rare in travellers but is often misdiagnosed by poor quality labs in Southeast Asia. Symptoms are similar to bacterial diarrhoea (ie fever, bloody diarrhoea and generally feeling unwell). You should always seek reliable medical care if you have blood in your diarrhoea. Treatment involves two drugs: Tinidazole or Metronidazole will kill the parasite in your gut and a second drug will kill the cysts. If left untreated, complications such as liver or gut abscesses can occur.

Giardiasis

Giardia lamblia is a parasite that is relatively common in travellers. Symptoms include nausea, bloating, excess gas, fatigue and intermittent diarrhoea. 'Eggy' burps are often attributed solely to giardiasis, but work in Nepal has shown that they are not specific to this infection. The parasite will eventually go away if left untreated but this can take months. The treatment of choice is Tinidazole, with Metronidazole being a second-line option.

ENVIRONMENTAL HAZARDS
Air Pollution

Air pollution, particularly from vehicles, is an increasing problem in most of Southeast Asia's major cities. If you have severe respiratory problems speak with your doctor before travelling to any heavily polluted urban centres. This pollution also causes minor respiratory problems such as sinusitis, dry throat and irritated eyes. If troubled by the pollution, leave the city for a few days and get some fresh air.

Diving

Divers and surfers should seek specialised advice before they travel to ensure their medical kit contains treatment for coral cuts and tropical ear infections, as well as the standard problems. Divers should ensure their insurance covers them for decompression illness – get specialised dive insurance through an organisation such as **Divers Alert Network** (DAN; www.danseap.org). Have a dive medical before you leave your home country – there are medical conditions that are incompatible with diving, and economic considerations may override health considerations for some Thai dive operators.

Food

Eating in restaurants is the biggest risk factor for contracting traveller's diarrhoea. Ways to avoid it include eating only freshly cooked food, and avoiding shellfish and food that has been sitting around in buffets. Peel all fruit, cook vegetables and soak salads in iodine water for at least 20 minutes. Eat in busy restaurants with a high turnover of customers.

Heat

Many parts of Thailand are hot and humid throughout the year. For most people it takes at least two weeks to adapt to the hot climate. Swelling of the feet and ankles is common, as are muscle cramps caused by excessive sweating. Prevent these by avoiding dehydration and excessive activity in the heat. Take it easy when you first arrive. Don't eat salt tablets (they aggravate the gut) but drinking rehydration solution or eating salty food helps. Treat cramps by stopping activity, resting, rehydrating with double-strength rehydration solution and gently stretching.

Dehydration is the main contributor to heat exhaustion. Symptoms include feeling weak, headache, irritability, nausea or vomiting, sweaty skin, a fast, weak pulse and normal or slightly elevated body temperature. Treatment involves getting out of the heat and/or sun, fanning the victim and applying cool wet cloths to the skin, laying the victim flat with their legs raised and rehydrating with water containing ¼ teaspoon of salt per litre. Recovery from dehydration is usually rapid and it is common to feel weak for some days afterwards.

Heatstroke is a serious medical emergency. Symptoms come on suddenly and include weakness, nausea, a hot dry body, a body temperature of over 41°C, dizziness, confusion, loss of coordination, fits and eventually collapse and loss of consciousness. Seek medical help and commence cooling by getting the person out of the heat, removing their clothes, fanning them and applying cool wet cloths or ice to their body, especially the groin and armpits.

Prickly heat is a common skin rash in the tropics, caused by sweat being trapped under the skin. The result is an itchy rash of tiny lumps. Treat by moving out of the heat and into an air-conditioned area for a few hours and by having cool showers. Creams and ointments clog the skin so they should be avoided. Locally bought prickly-heat powder can be helpful.

Tropical fatigue is common in long-term expats based in the tropics. It's rarely due to disease and is caused by the climate, inadequate mental rest, excessive alcohol intake and the demands of daily work.

Insect Bites & Stings

Bedbugs don't carry disease but their bites are very itchy. They live in the cracks of furniture and walls and then migrate to the bed at night to feed on you. You can treat the itch with an antihistamine. Lice inhabit various parts of your body but most commonly your head and pubic area. Transmission is via close contact with an infected person. They can be difficult to treat and you may need numerous applications of an anti-lice shampoo such as Permethrin.

Ticks are contracted after walking in rural areas. Ticks are commonly found behind the ears, on the belly and in armpits. If you have had a tick bite and experience symptoms such as a rash at the site of the bite or elsewhere, fever or muscle aches, you should see a doctor. Doxycycline prevents tick-borne diseases.

Leeches are found in humid rainforest areas. They do not transmit any disease but their bites are often intensely itchy for weeks afterwards and can become infected. Apply an iodine-based antiseptic to any leech bite to help prevent infection.

Bee and wasp stings mainly cause problems for people who are allergic to them. Anyone with a major bee or wasp allergy should carry an injection of adrenaline (eg an Epipen) for emergency treatment. For others, to ease the pain, apply ice to the sting and take painkillers.

Jellyfish

Most jellyfish in Southeast Asian waters are not dangerous, just irritating; however, there have been incidents of serious (and in rare cases, fatal) stings by box jellyfish on both the Andaman and Gulf coasts. First-aid for jellyfish stings involves pouring vinegar onto the affected area to neutralise the poison. Do not rub sand or water onto the stings. Take painkillers if necessary, and for box jellyfish stings in particular seek immediate medical attention. Be sure to heed advice from local authorities, dive shops and your hotel about seasonal water conditions, and if there are dangerous jellyfish around keep out of the water.

Parasites

Numerous parasites are common in local populations in Southeast Asia; however, most of these are rare in travellers. The two rules to follow if you wish to avoid parasitic infections are to wear shoes and to avoid eating raw food, especially fish, pork and vegetables. A number of parasites, including strongyloides, hookworm and *cutaneous larva mi-*

grans, are transmitted via the skin by walking barefoot.

Skin Problems

Fungal rashes are common in humid climates. There are two fungal rashes that commonly affect travellers. The first occurs in moist areas that get less air such as the groin, armpits and between the toes. It starts as a red patch that slowly spreads and is usually itchy. Treatment involves keeping the skin dry, avoiding chafing and using an antifungal cream such as Clotrimazole or Lamisil. *Tinea versicolor* is also common. This fungus causes small, light-coloured patches, most commonly on the back, chest and shoulders. Consult a doctor.

Cuts and scratches can become easily infected in humid climates. Take meticulous care of any cuts and scratches to prevent complications such as abscesses. Immediately wash all wounds in clean water and apply antiseptic. If you develop signs of infection (increasing pain and redness) see a doctor. Divers and surfers should be particularly careful with coral cuts as they become easily infected.

Snakes

Thailand is home to many species of both poisonous and harmless snakes. Assume all snakes are poisonous and never try to catch one. Always wear boots and long pants if walking in an area that may have snakes. First-aid in the event of a snakebite involves pressure immobilisation via an elastic bandage firmly wrapped around the affected limb, starting at the bite site and working up towards the chest. The bandage should not be so tight that the circulation is cut off, and the fingers or toes should be kept free so the circulation can be checked. Immobilise the limb with a splint and carry the victim to medical attention. Do not use tourniquets or try to suck the venom out. Antivenom is available for most species.

Sunburn

Even on a cloudy day sunburn occurs rapidly. Use a strong sunscreen (factor 30), reapply after a swim, and always wear a wide-brimmed hat and sunglasses outdoors. Avoid lying in the sun during the hottest part of the day (10am to 2pm). If you become sunburnt, stay out of the sun until you have recovered, apply cool compresses and take painkillers for the discomfort and apply a 1% hydrocortisone cream.

WOMEN'S HEALTH

In the urban areas of Thailand, supplies of sanitary products are readily available. Birth control is cheap but not all options are widely available so it's safest to bring adequate supplies of your own form of contraception. Heat, humidity and taking antibiotics can all contribute to thrush. Treatment is with antifungal creams and pessaries such as Clotrimazole. A practical alternative is a single tablet of Fluconazole (Diflucan). Urinary tract infections can be precipitated by dehydration or long bus journeys without toilet stops; bring suitable antibiotics.

Pregnant women should receive specialised advice before travelling. The ideal time to travel is in the second trimester (between 16 and 28 weeks), when the risk of pregnancy-related problems is lowest and pregnant women generally feel at their best. During the first trimester there is a risk of miscarriage and in the third trimester complications such as premature labour and high blood pressure are possible. It's wise to travel with a companion. Always carry a list of quality medical facilities at your destination and ensure you continue your standard antenatal care at these facilities. Avoid rural travel in areas with poor transport and medical facilities. Most of all, ensure travel insurance covers all pregnancy-related possibilities, including premature labour.

Malaria is a high-risk disease during pregnancy. WHO recommends that pregnant women do *not* travel to areas with Chloroquine-resistant malaria. None of the more effective antimalarial drugs are completely safe during pregnancy.

Traveller's diarrhoea can quickly lead to dehydration and result in inadequate blood flow to the placenta. Many of the drugs used to treat various diarrhoea bugs are not recommended during pregnancy. Azithromycin is considered safe.

TRADITIONAL MEDICINE

Throughout Thailand traditional medical systems are widely practised. There is a big difference between traditional healing systems and 'folk' medicine. Folk remedies should be avoided, as they often involve rather dubious procedures with potential medical complica-

HEALTH

tions. On the other hand, healing systems, such as traditional Chinese medicine, are well respected and aspects of them are being increasingly utilised by medical practitioners throughout the West.

All traditional Asian medical systems identify a vital life force, and see blockage or imbalance as the cause of disease. Techniques such as herbal medicines, massage and acupuncture are utilised to bring the vital force back into balance, or to maintain balance.

These therapies are best used for treating chronic disease such as chronic fatigue, arthritis and some chronic skin conditions. Traditional medicines should be avoided for treating acute infections such as malaria.

Be aware that 'natural' doesn't always mean 'safe', and there can be drug interactions between herbal medicines and Western medicines. If you are utilising both systems, ensure you inform both practitioners what the other has prescribed.

Language

Learning some Thai is indispensable for travel in the kingdom; naturally, the more you pick up, the closer you get to Thailand's culture and people. Even if your first attempts to speak Thai meet with mixed success, keep trying. Listen closely to the way the Thais themselves use the various tones – you'll catch on quickly. Don't let laughter at your linguistic forays discourage you; this apparent amusement is really an expression of appreciation. Making the effort to meet Thai college and university students in particular, might be worthwile. Thai students are, by and large, eager to meet foreign visitors. They will often know some English, so communication isn't as difficult as it may be with shop owners, civil servants etc, and they're generally willing to teach you useful Thai phrases.

DIALECTS

Thailand's official language is effectively the dialect spoken and written in central Thailand, which has successfully become the lingua franca of all Thai and non-Thai ethnic groups in the kingdom.

All Thai dialects are members of the Thai half of the Thai-Kadai family of languages. As such, they're closely related to languages spoken in Laos (Lao, northern Thai, Thai Lü), northern Myanmar (Shan, northern Thai), northwestern Vietnam (Nung, Tho), Assam (Ahom) and pockets of south China (Zhuang, Thai Lü).

Modern Thai linguists recognise four basic dialects within Thailand: Central Thai (spoken as a first dialect through central Thailand and throughout the country as a second dialect); Northern Thai (spoken from Tak Province north to the Myanmar border); Northeastern Thai (northeastern provinces towards the Lao and Cambodian borders); and Southern Thai (from Chumphon Province south to the Malaysian border). There are also a number of Thai minority dialects such as those spoken by the Phu Thai, Thai Dam, Thai Daeng, Phu Noi, Phuan and other ethnic groups, most of whom reside in the north and northeast.

VOCABULARY DIFFERENCES

Like most languages, Thai distinguishes between 'polite' and 'informal' vocabulary, eg *tahn* is a more polite everyday word for 'eat' than *gin*, and *sěe-sà* is more polite than *hŏo-a* for 'head'. When given a choice, it's better to use the polite terms, since these are less likely to lead to unintentional offence.

SCRIPT

The Thai script, a fairly recent development in comparison with the spoken language, consists of 44 consonants (but only 21 separate sounds) and 48 vowel and vowel combination possibilities (32 separate symbols). Though learning the alphabet is not difficult, the writing system itself is fairly complex, so unless you're planning a lengthy stay in Thailand you may want to stick to learning the spoken language. The names of major places and food items included in this book are given in both Thai script and the Roman writing (or 'transliteration') system, so that you can 'read' the names of destinations or dishes, or point if needed.

For a food and drink glossary, see p000. For a more comprehensive guide to the language, get a copy of Lonely Planet's *Thai* phrasebook.

TONES

In Thai the meaning of a single syllable may be altered by means of different tones. In standard Central Thai there are five tones: low, mid, falling, high and rising tone. For example, depending on the tone, the syllable *mai* can mean 'new', 'burn', 'wood', 'not?' or 'not' – ponder the phrase *mái mài mâi mâi măi* (New wood doesn't burn, does it?) and you begin to appreciate the importance of tones in spoken Thai. Even when we 'know' what the correct tone in Thai should be, our tendency to denote emotion, verbal stress, the interrogative etc through tone modulation often interferes with producing the correct tone. Therefore the first rule in learning to speak Thai is to divorce emotions from your speech, at least until you've learned the Thai way to express them without changing essential tone value.

The following is visual representation in chart form to show relative tone values:

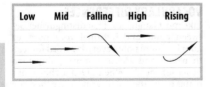

The list below is a brief attempt to explain the tones. The only way to really understand the differences is by listening to a native or fluent non-native speaker. The range of all five tones is relative to each speaker's vocal range, so there is no fixed 'pitch' intrinsic to the language.

low tone – pronounced 'flat', at the relative bottom of one's vocal range. It is low, level and has no inflection, eg *bàht* (baht – the Thai currency).

mid tone – pronounced 'flat', at the relative middle of the speaker's vocal range, eg *dee* (good); no tone mark is used.

falling tone – starting high and falling sharply, this tone is similar to the change in pitch in English when you are emphasising a word, or calling someone's name from afar, eg *mâi* (no/not).

high tone – usually the most difficult to learn. It's pronounced near the relative top of the vocal range, as level as possible, eg *máh* (horse).

rising tone – starting low and gradually rising, sounds like the inflection used by English speakers to imply a question – 'Yes?', eg *săhm* (three).

TRANSLITERATION

No wholly satisfactory system of writing Thai in Roman script has yet been devised to assure both consistency and readability. The Thai government uses the RTGS (Royal Thai General System of Transcription) transcription for official government documents in English and for most highway signs. However, local variations crop up on hotel signs, city street signs, menus and so on in such a way that visitors often become confused. Added to this is the fact that even the government system has its flaws.

Generally, names in this book follow the most common practice or simply copy their Roman script name, no matter what process was used in its transliteration. When this transliteration is markedly different from actual pronunciation, the pronunciation is included (according to the system outlined below) in parentheses after the transliteration. Where no Roman model was available, names have been transliterated phonetically, directly from Thai.

PRONUNCIATION

The following is a guide to the pronunciation system that's been used for the words and phrases in this chapter (and throughout the rest of the book when transcribing from Thai). The dots indicate syllable breaks within words, including compound vowels.

Consonants

Most consonants are close to their English counterparts. Here are a few exceptions:

b	a hard 'p' sound, almost like a 'b'; similar to the sound made when you say 'hi**p-b**ag'
d	a hard 't' sound, like a sharp 'd'; similar to the sound made when you say 'mi**d-t**one'
g	similar to the 'g' in 'good'
k	as in 'kite'
ng	as the 'ng' in 'singing'; can occur as an initial consonant
p	as in 'pie'

| r | similar to the 'r' in 'run' but flapped (ie the tongue touches palate); in everyday speech it's often pronounced like 'l' |
| t | as in 'tip' |

Vowels
The accent marks above the vowels indicate the tones (see previous page).

a	as in 'about'; half as long as **ah**
aa	as the 'a' in 'tab'
ah	as the 'a' in 'father'
ai	as in 'aisle'
air	as in English 'hair' but with no final 'r' sound
aa·ou	like the 'a' in 'cat' followed by a short 'u' as in 'put'
e	as in 'hen'
ee	as in 'feet'
ee·a	sounds like 'ee-ya'
ee·o	as the 'io' in 'Rio'
eh·ou	like the 'e' in 'bed', followed by a short 'u' as in 'put'
eu	as the 'er' in 'fern' (without the 'r')
eu·a	a combination of **eu** and **a**
ew	as in 'new'
i	as in 'bit'
o	as in 'hot'
oh	as the 'o' in 'toe'
oo	as in 'food'
oo·a	as the 'our' in 'tour'
oo·ay	sounds like 'oo-way'
or	as in 'torn' (without the 'r')
ow	as in 'now'
oy	as the 'oi' in 'coin'
u	as in 'put'

GENDER
The word for the pronoun 'I' changes in Thai depending on the gender of the speaker – so a man will refer to himself as *pŏm*, while a woman will refer to herself as *dì·chăn*. Similarly, when being polite, the speaker ends his or her sentence with *kráp* (for men) or *kâ* (for women). It is the gender of the speaker that is being expressed here; it is also the common way to answer 'yes' to a question or show agreement.

ACCOMMODATION
Where is a cheap hotel?

โรงแรมที่ราคา   *rohng raam têe rah·kah*
ถูกอยู่ที่ไหน   *tòok yòo têe năi*

I'm looking for a ...	ผม/ดิฉัน กำลังหา...	*pŏm/dì·chăn gam·lang hăh ...*
guesthouse	บ้านพัก/ เกสต์เฮาส์	*bâhn pák/ gèt hów*
hotel	โรงแรม	*rohng raam*
youth hostel	บ้าน เยาวชน	*bâhn yow·wá·chon*

Do you have any rooms available?
มีห้องว่างไหม   *mee hôrng wâhng măi*
May I see the room?
ดูห้องได้ไหม   *doo hôrng dâi măi*
Where is the bathroom?
ห้องน้ำอยู่ที่ไหน   *hôrng nám yòo têe năi*

I'd like (a) ...	ต้องการ...	*đôrng gahn ...*
bed	เตียงนอน	*đee·ang norn*
double room	ห้องคู่	*hôrng kôo*
ordinary room	ห้อง	*hôrng*
(with fan)	ธรรมดา (มีพัดลม)	*tam·má dah (mee pát lom)*
room with a	ห้องที่มี	*hôrng têe mee*
bathroom	ห้องน้ำ	*hôrng nám*
room with	ห้องที่มี	*hôrng têe mee*
two beds	เตียง สองตัว	*đee·ang sŏrng đoo·a*
single room	ห้องเดี่ยว	*hôrng dèe·o*
to share a dorm	พักใน หอพัก	*pák nai hŏr pák*

How much is it ...?	...เท่าไร	*... tôw rai*
per night	คืนละ	*keun lá*
per person	คนละ	*kon lá*

bath/shower	อาบน้ำ	*àhp nám*
cold	เย็น	*yen*
hot	ร้อน	*rórn*
room	ห้อง	*hôrng*
toilet	ห้องส้วม	*hôrng sôo·am*
towel	ผ้าเช็ดตัว	*pâh chét đoo·a*

I'm/We're leaving today.
ฉัน/พวกเรา   *chăn/pôo·ak row*
จะออกวันนี้   *jà òrk wan née*

CONVERSATION & ESSENTIALS

Hello.
สวัสดี(ครับ/ค่ะ) sà·wàt·dee (kráp/kâ)
Goodbye.
ลาก่อน lah gòrn
Yes.
ใช่ châi
No.
ไม่ใช่ mâi châi
Please.
กรุณา gà·rú·nah
Thank you.
ขอบคุณ kòrp kun
That's fine. (You're welcome)
ไม่เป็นไร/ยินดี mâi ben rai/yin·dee
Excuse me.
ขออภัย kŏr à·pai
Sorry. (Forgive me)
ขอโทษ kŏr tôht
How are you?
สบายดีหรือ sà·bai dee rĕu
I'm fine, thanks.
สบายดี sà·bai dee
What's your name?
คุณชื่ออะไร kun chêu à·rai
My name is ...
ผม/ดิฉันชื่อ... pŏm/dì·chăn chêu ...
Where are you from?
มาจากที่ไหน mah jàhk têe năi
I'm from ...
มาจาก... mah jàhk ...
See you soon.
เดี๋ยวเจอกันนะ dĕe·o jeu gan ná
I like ...
ชอบ... chôrp ...
I don't like ...
ไม่ชอบ... mâi chôrp ...
Just a minute.
รอเดี๋ยว ror dĕe·o
I/me (men/women)
ผม/ดิฉัน pŏm/dì·chăn
I/me (informal, men and women)
ฉัน chăn
You (for peers)
คุณ kun
Do you have ...?
มี...ไหม/ mee ... măi/
...มีไหม ... mee măi

I would like ... (+ verb)
อยากจะ... yàhk jà ...
I would like ... (+ noun)
อยากได้... yàhk dâi ...

DIRECTIONS

Where is ...?
...อยู่ที่ไหน ... yòo têe năi
What is the address?
ที่อยู่คืออะไร têe yòo keu à·rai
Can you write the address, please?
เขียนที่อยู่ kĕe·an têe yòo
ให้ได้ไหม hâi dâi măi
Can you show me (on the map)?
ให้ดู(ในแผนที่) hâi doo (nai păn têe)
ได้ไหม dâi măi
(Go) Straight ahead.
ตรงไป đrong bai
Turn left.
เลี้ยวซ้าย lée·o sái
Turn right.
เลี้ยวขวา lée·o kwăh
At the corner.
ตรงมุม đrong mum
At the traffic lights.
ตรงไฟแดง đrong fai daang

behind	ข้างหลัง	kâhng lăng
far	ไกล	glai
in front of	ตรงหน้า	đrong nâh
left	ซ้าย	sái
near	ใกล้	glâi
right	ขวา	kwăh

beach	ชายหาด	chai hàht
bridge	สะพาน	sà·pahn
canal	คลอง	klorng
countryside	ชนบท	chon·ná·bòt
hill	เขา	kŏw
island	เกาะ	gò
lake	ทะเลสาบ	tá·leh sàhp
mountain	ภูเขา	poo kŏw
paddy (field)	(ทุ่ง) นา	(tûng) nah
palace	วัง	wang
pond	หนอง/บึง	nŏrng/beung
river	แม่น้ำ	mâa nám
sea	ทะเล	tá·leh
temple	วัด	wát
town	เมือง	meu·ang
track	ทาง	tahng
village	(หมู่) บ้าน	(mòo) bâhn
waterfall	น้ำตก	nám đòk

EATING OUT

restaurant	ร้านอาหาร	ráhn ah·hăhn
I'd like ...	ขอ...	kŏr ...
What is that?	นั่นอะไร	nân à·rai

Can I see the menu, please?
ขอดูรายการ   kŏr doo rai gahn
อาหารได้ไหม   ah·hăhn dâi măi

Do you have a menu in English?
มีรายการอาหาร   mee rai gahn ah·hăhn
เป็นภาษา   ben pah·săh
อังกฤษไหม   ang·grìt măi

Not too spicy, please.
ขอไม่เผ็ดมาก   kŏr mâi pèt mâhk

Does it contain ...?
นี่ใส่...ไหม   nêe sài ... măi

I'm allergic to ...
ผม/ดิฉันแพ้...   pŏm/dì·chăn páa ...

Can I have a (beer), please?
ขอ(เบียร์) หน่อย   kŏr (bee·a) nòy

Please bring the bill.
ขอบิลหน่อย   kŏr bin nòy

EMERGENCIES

Help!	ช่วยด้วย	chôo·ay dôo·ay
There's been an accident.	มีอุบัติเหตุ	mee ù·bàt·đi·hèt
I'm lost.	ฉันหลงทาง	chăn lŏng tahng
Go away!	ไปซิ	bai sí
Stop!	หยุด	yùt
Call ...!	เรียก...	rêe·ak ...
	หน่อย	nòy
a doctor	หมอ	mŏr
the police	ตำรวจ	đam·ròo·at

I don't eat ...	ผม/ดิฉันกิน	pŏm/dì·chăn gin
	...ไม่ได้	... mâi dâi
chicken	ไก่	gài
fish	ปลา	blah
meat	เนื้อสัตว์	néu·a sàt
pork	หมู	mŏo
seafood	อาหาร	ah·hăhn
	ทะเล	tá·lair

Can you please bring me (a) ...?	ขอ...	kŏr ...
	ได้ไหม	dâi măi
fork	ส้อม	sôrm
glass	แก้ว	gâa·ou
knife	มีด	mêet
napkin	กระดาษ	grà·dàht
	เช็ดปาก	chét bàhk
plate	จานเปล่า	jahn blòw
some rice	ข้าวหน่อย	kôw nòy
some water	น้ำหน่อย	nám nòy
spoon	ช้อน	chórn

This food is ...	อาหารนี้...	ah·hăhn née ...
cold	เย็น	yen
delicious	อร่อย	a·ròy
undercooked	ไม่สุก	mâi sùk

HEALTH

I need a (doctor).
ต้องการ(หมอ)   đôrng gahn (mŏr)

I'm ill.
ฉันป่วย — *chăn bòo·ay*

It hurts here.
เจ็บตรงนี้ — *jèp đrong née*

I'm pregnant.
ตั้งครรภ์แล้ว — *đâng kan láa·ou*

I feel nauseous.
รู้สึกคลื่นไส้ — *róo·sèuk klêun sâi*

I have a fever.
เป็นไข้ — *ben kâi*

I have diarrhoea.
ท้องเสีย — *tórng sěe·a*

I'm ... ผม/ดิฉัน... — *pŏm/đi·chăn ...*

asthmatic	เป็นโรค	*ben rôhk*
	หืด	*hèut*
diabetic	เป็นโรค	*ben rôhk*
	เบาหวาน	*bow wăhn*
epileptic	เป็นโรค	*ben rôhk*
	ลมบ้าหมู	*lom bâh mŏo*

I'm allergic ผม/ดิฉัน — *pŏm/đi·chăn*
to ... แพ้... — *páa ...*

antibiotics	ยา	*yah*
	ปฏิชีวนะ	*bà·đi·chee·wá·ná*
aspirin	ยา	*yah*
	แอสไพริน	*àat·sà·pai·rin*
bees	ตัวผึ้ง	*đoo·a pêung*
peanuts	ถั่วลิสง	*tòo·a lí·sŏng*
penicillin	ยา	*yah*
	เพนิซิลลิน	*pair·ní·sin·lin*

antiseptic
ยาม่าเชื้อ — *yah kâh chéu·a*

aspirin
ยาแอสไพริน — *yah àat·sà·pai·rin*

chemist/pharmacy
ร้านขายยา — *ráhn kăi yah*

condoms
ถุงยางอนามัย — *tŭng yahng a·nah·mai*

contraceptive
การคุมกำเนิด — *gahn kum gam·nèut*

dentist
หมอฟัน — *mŏr fan*

hospital
โรงพยาบาล — *rohng pá·yah·bahn*

medicine
ยา — *yah*

mosquito coil
ยากันยุงแบบจุด — *yah gan yung bàap jùt*

mosquito repellent
ยากันยุง — *yaa gan yung*

painkiller
ยาแก้ปวด — *yaa gâe bòo·at*

sunblock cream
ครีมกันแดด — *kreem gan dàat*

tampons
แทมพอน — *taam·porn*

LANGUAGE DIFFICULTIES

Do you speak English?
คุณพูดภาษา — *kun pôot pah·săh*
อังกฤษได้ไหม — *ang·grìt dâi măi*

Does anyone here speak English?
ที่นี่มีใคร — *têe née mee krai*
พูดภาษา — *pôot pah·săh*
อังกฤษได้ไหม — *ang·grìt dâi măi*

How do you say ... in Thai?
...ว่าอย่างไร — *... wâh yàhng rai*
ภาษาไทย — *pah·săh tai*

What do you call this in Thai?
นี่ภาษาไทย — *nêe pah·săh tai*
เรียกว่าอะไร — *rêe·ak wâh à·rai*

Please write it down.
กรุณาเขียน — *gà·rú·nah kěe·an*
ให้หน่อย — *hâi nòy*

What does ... mean?
...แปลว่าอะไร — *... plaa wâh à·rai*

Do you understand?
เข้าใจไหม — *kôw jai măi*

A little.
นิดหน่อย — *nít nòy*

I understand.
เข้าใจ — *kôw jai*

I don't understand.
ไม่เข้าใจ — *mâi kôw jai*

NUMBERS

0	ศูนย์	sŏon
1	หนึ่ง	nèung
2	สอง	sŏrng
3	สาม	săhm
4	สี่	sèe
5	ห้า	hâh
6	หก	hòk
7	เจ็ด	jèt
8	แปด	bàat
9	เก้า	gôw
10	สิบ	sìp
11	สิบเอ็ด	sìp-èt
12	สิบสอง	sìp-sŏrng
13	สิบสาม	sìp-săhm
14	สิบสี่	sìp-sèe
15	สิบห้า	sìp-hâh
16	สิบหก	sìp-hòk
17	สิบเจ็ด	sìp-jèt
18	สิบแปด	sìp-bàat
19	สิบเก้า	sìp-gôw
20	ยี่สิบ	yêe-sìp
21	ยี่สิบเอ็ด	yêe-sìp-èt
22	ยี่สิบสอง	yêe-sìp-sŏrng
30	สามสิบ	săhm-sìp
40	สี่สิบ	sèe-sìp
50	ห้าสิบ	hâh-sìp
60	หกสิบ	hòk-sìp
70	เจ็ดสิบ	jèt-sìp
80	แปดสิบ	bàat-sìp
90	เก้าสิบ	gôw-sìp
100	หนึ่งร้อย	nèung róy
200	สองร้อย	sŏrng róy
300	สามร้อย	săhm róy
1000	หนึ่งพัน	nèung pan
2000	สองพัน	sŏrng pan
10,000	หนึ่งหมื่น	nèung mèun
100,000	หนึ่งแสน	nèung săan
one million	หนึ่งล้าน	nèung láhn
one billion	พันล้าน	pan láhn

PAPERWORK

name	ชื่อ	chêu
nationality	สัญชาติ	săn·châht
date of birth	เกิดวันที่	gèut wan têe
place of birth	เกิดที่	gèut têe
sex (gender)	เพศ	pêt
passport	หนังสือ	năng·sěu
	เดินทาง	deun tahng
visa	วีซ่า	wee·sâh

SHOPPING & SERVICES

I'd like to buy …
อยากจะซื้อ…   yàhk jà séu …

I'm just looking.
ดูเฉยๆ   doo chěr·i chěr·i

May I look at it?
ดูได้ไหม   doo dâi mǎi

I don't like it.
ไม่ชอบ   mâi chôrp

How much?
เท่าไร   tôw raí

How much is this?
นี่เท่าไร/   nêe tôw rai/
กี่บาท   gèe bàht

It's cheap.
ราคาถูก   rah·kah tòok

I'll take it.
เอา   ow

It's too expensive.
แพงเกินไป   paang geun bai

Do you have something cheaper?
มีถูกกว่านี้ไหม   mee tòok gwàh née mǎi

Can you reduce the price a little?
ลดราคาหน่อย   lót rah·kah nòy
ได้ไหม   dâi mǎi

Can you lower it more?
ลดอีกได้ไหม   lót èek dâi mǎi

How about … baht?
…บาทได้ไหม   … bàht dâi mǎi

I won't give more than … baht.
จะให้ไม่เกิน   jà hâi mâi geun
…บาท   … bàht

LANGUAGE

Do you accept ...?	รับ...ไหม	ráp ... mǎi
credit cards	บัตรเครดิต	bàt krair·đìt
travellers cheques	เช็คเดินทาง	chék deun tahng

more	อีก	èek
less	น้อยลง	nóy long
bigger	ใหญ่กว่า	yài gwàh
smaller	เล็กกว่า	lék gwàh
too expensive	แพงไป	paang bai
inexpensive	ราคา	rah·kah
	ประหยัด	brà·yàt

I'm looking for a/the ...	ผม/ดิฉัน กำลังหา...	pǒm/dì·chǎn gam·lang hǎh ...
bank	ธนาคาร	tá·nah·kahn
city centre	ใจกลาง เมือง	jai glahng meu·ang
... embassy	สถานทูต...	sà·tǎhn tôot ...
market	ตลาด	đà·làht
museum	พิพิธภัณฑ์	pí·pít·tá·pan
post office	ไปรษณีย์	brai·sà·nee
public toilet	ห้องน้ำ สาธารณะ	hôrng nám sǎh·tah·rá·ná
temple	วัด	wát
telephone centre	ศูนย์ โทรศัพท์	sǒon toh·rá·sàp
tourist office	สำนักงาน ท่องเที่ยว	sǎm·nák ngahn tôrng têe·o

I want to change ...	ต้องการ แลก...	đôrng gahn lâak ...
money	เงิน	ngeun
travellers cheques	เช็คเดินทาง	chék deun tahng

What time does it open?
เปิดกี่โมง
bèut gèe mohng

What time does it close?
ปิดกี่โมง
bìt gèe mohng

Can I/we change money here?
แลกเงินที่นี่ได้ไหม lâak ngeun têe née dâi mǎi

TIME & DATES

While the 12-hour clock divides the day between two time periods (am and pm), the Thai system has four periods. The 24-hour clock is also commonly used by government and the media. The list below shows each hour of the 12-hour clock translated into the Thai system.

What time is it?	กี่โมงแล้ว	gèe mohng láa·ou
12 midnight	หกทุ่ม/ เที่ยงคืน	hòk tûm/ têe·ang keun
1am	ตีหนึ่ง	đee nèung
2am	ตีสอง	đee sǒrng
3am	ตีสาม	đee sǎhm
4am	ตีสี่	đee sèe
5am	ตีห้า	đee hâh
6am	หกโมงเช้า	hòk mohng chów
7am	หนึ่งโมงเช้า	nèung mohng chów
11am	ห้าโมงเช้า	hâh mohng chów
12 noon	เที่ยง	têe·ang
1pm	บ่ายโมง	bài mohng
2pm	บ่ายสองโมง	bài sǒrng mohng
3pm	บ่ายสามโมง	bài sǎhm mohng
4pm	บ่ายสี่โมง	bài sèe mohng
	(lit: afternoon four hours)	
	สี่โมงเย็น	sèe mohng yen
	(lit: four hours evening)	
5pm	ห้าโมงเย็น	hâh mohng yen
6pm	หกโมงเย็น	hòk mohng yen
7pm	หนึ่งทุ่ม	nèung tûm
8pm	สองทุ่ม	sǒrng tûm
9pm	สามทุ่ม	sǎhm tûm
10pm	สี่ทุ่ม	sèe tûm
11pm	ห้าทุ่ม	hâh tûm

For times after the hour, just add the number of minutes following the hour:

4.30pm
บ่ายสี่โมงครึ่ง
bài sèe mohng krêung (lit: four afternoon hours half)

4.15pm
บ่ายสี่โมงสิบห้า
bài sèe mohng sìp·hâh (lit: four afternoon hours 15)

For times before the hour, add the number of minutes beforehand:

3.45pm

อีกสิบห้านาทีบ่ายสี่โมง
èek sìp·hâh nah·tee bài sèe mohng
(lit: another 15 minutes four afternoon hours)

When?	เมื่อไร	*mêu·a·rai*
today	วันนี้	*wan née*
tomorrow	พรุ่งนี้	*prûng née*
yesterday	เมื่อวาน	*mêu·a wahn*

Monday	วันจันทร์	*wan jan*
Tuesday	วันอังคาร	*wan ang·kahn*
Wednesday	วันพุธ	*wan pút*
Thursday	วันพฤหัสฯ	*wan pá·réu·hàt*
Friday	วันศุกร์	*wan sùk*
Saturday	วันเสาร์	*wan sŏw*
Sunday	วันอาทิตย์	*wan ah·tít*

January	มกราคม	*má·ga·rah·kom*
February	กุมภาพันธ์	*gum·pah·pan*
March	มีนาคม	*mee·naa·kom*
April	เมษายน	*mair·săh·yon*
May	พฤษภาคม	*préut·sà·pah·kom*
June	มิถุนายน	*mí·tù·nah·yon*
July	กรกฎาคม	*ga·rák·gà·đah·kom*
August	สิงหาคม	*sĭng·hăh·kom*
September	กันยายน	*gan·yah·yon*
October	ตุลาคม	*đù·lah·kom*
November	พฤศจิกายน	*préut·sà·jì·gah·yon*
December	ธันวาคม	*tan·wah·kom*

TRANSPORT
Public Transport

I'd like a ticket.
อยากได้ตั๋ว   *yàhk dâi đŏo·a*

I want to go to …
อยากจะไป…   *yàhk jà bai …*

The train has been cancelled.
รถไฟถูกยก   *rót fai tùk yók*
เลิกแล้ว   *léuk láa·ou*

The train has been delayed.
รถไฟช้าเวลา   *rót fai cháh wair·lah*

When does	…จะออก	… *jà òrk*
the … leave?	กี่โมง	*gèe mohng*
When does	…จะถึง	… *jà tĕung*
the … arrive?	กี่โมง	*gèe mohng*
boat	เรือ	*reu·a*
bus	รถบัส	*rót bát*
city bus	รถเมล์	*rót mair*
intercity bus	รถทัวร์	*rót too·a*
plane	เครื่องบิน	*krêu·ang bin*
train	รถไฟ	*rót fai*

I'd like (a) …	ผม/ดิฉัน	*pŏm/dì·chăn*
	อยากได้…	*yàhk dâi …*
1st class	ชั้นหนึ่ง	*chán nèung*
2nd class	ชั้นสอง	*chán sŏrng*
one-way	ตั๋วเที่ยว	*đŏo·a têe·o*
ticket	เดียว	*dee·o*
return ticket	ตั๋วไปกลับ	*đŏo·a bai glàp*
two tickets	ตั๋วสองใบ	*đŏo·a sŏrng bai*

airport	สนามบิน	*sa·năhm bin*
bus station	สถานีขนส่ง	*sa·tăh·nee kŏn sòng*
bus stop	ป้ายรถเมล์	*bâi rót mair*
platform	ชานชาลาที่	*chahn·chah·lah têe*
number		
taxi stand	ที่จอด	*têe jòrt*
	รถแท็กซี่	*rót táak·sêe*
ticket office	ตู้ขายตั๋ว	*đôo kăi đŏo·a*
timetable	ตารางเวลา	*đah·rahng wair·lah*
the first	ที่แรก	*têe râak*
the last	สุดท้าย	*sùt tái*
train station	สถานีรถไฟ	*sa·tăh·nee rót fai*

Private Transport

I'd like to	ผม/ดิฉัน	*pŏm/dì·chăn*
hire a/an …	อยากเช่า…	*yàhk chôw …*
4WD	รถโฟร์วีล	*rót foh ween*
car	รถยนต์	*rót yon*
bicycle	รถจักรยาน	*rót jàk·gà·yahn*
motorbike	รถ	*rót*
	มอเตอร์ไซค์	*mor·đeu·sai*

Is this the road to ...?
ทางนี้ไป...ไหม · *tahng née bai ... măi*

Where's a service station?
ปั๊มน้ำมันอยู่ที่ไหน · *bâm nám man yòo têe năi*

Please fill it up.
ขอเติมให้เต็ม · *kŏr đeum hâi đem*

I'd like (30) litres.
เอา(สามสิบ)ลิตร · *ow (săhm sìp) lít*

diesel
น้ำมันโซล่า · *nám man soh·lâh*

unleaded petrol
น้ำมันไร้สารตะกั่ว · *nám man rái săhn đà·gòo·a*

Can I park here?
จอดที่นี่ได้ไหม · *jòrt têe née dâi măi*

How long can I park here?
จอดที่นี่ได้
นานเท่าไร · *jòrt têe née dâi / nahn tôw·rai*

Where do I pay?
จ่ายเงินที่ไหน · *jài ngeun têe năi*

I need a mechanic.
ต้องการช่าง · *đôrng gahn châhng*

I have a flat tyre.
ยางแบน · *yahng baan*

I've run out of petrol.
หมดน้ำมัน · *mòt nám man*

I've had an accident.
มีอุบัติเหตุ · *mee ù·bàt·đì·hèt*

The car/motorbike has broken down at ...
รถ/มอเตอร์ไซค์ · *rót/mor·đeu·sai*
เสียที่... · *sĕe·a têe ...*

The car/motorbike won't start.
รถ/มอเตอร์ไซค์ · *rót/mor·đeu·sai*
สตาร์ทไม่ติด · *sa·đáht mâi đit*

Also available from Lonely Planet:
Thai phrasebook

TRAVEL WITH CHILDREN

Is there a ...? มี...ไหม · *mee ... măi*

baby change room	ห้องเปลี่ยน ผ้าเด็ก	*hông blèe·an pâh dèk*
(English-speaking) babysitter	พี่เลี้ยงเด็ก (ที่พูดภาษา อังกฤษได้)	*pêe lée·ang dèk (têe pôot pah·săh ang·grìt dâi)*
car seat for babies	เบาะนั่ง ในรถ สำหรับเด็ก	*bò nâng nai rót săm·ràp dèk*
child-minding service	บริการ เลี้ยงเด็ก	*bor·rí·gahn lée·ang dèk*
children's menu	รายการ อาหาร สำหรับเด็ก	*rai gahn ah·hăhn săm·ràp dèk*
highchair	เก้าอี้สูง	*gôw·êe sŏong*
milk formula	นมผง สำหรับเด็ก	*nom pŏng săm·ràp dèk*
(disposable) nappies/ diapers	ผ้าอ้อม (แบบใช้ แล้วทิ้ง)	*pâh ôrm (bàap chái láo·ou tíng)*
potty	กระโถน	*grà·tŏhn*
stroller	รถเข็นเด็ก	*rót kĕn dèk*

Glossary

See the Food Glossary, p52, for culinary terms and Thai dishes. See the Language chapter, p439, for some other useful words and phrases.

ah·hǎhn – food
ah·hǎhn jeh – vegetarian food
ah·hǎhn ʾbàh – 'jungle food'; usually refers to dishes made with wild game
ah·hǎhn ʾbàk ôâi – also spelt *ah·hǎhn pàk tâi;* southern Thai food
amphoe – also *amphur;* district, the next subdivision down from province
amphoe meu·ang – provincial capital
ao – also *ow;* bay or gulf

bâhn – also *ban;* house or village
bàht – traditional measure for gold and silver, equivalent to 15g
BMA – Bangkok Metropolitan Authority
bòht – central sanctuary or chapel in a Thai temple
BTS – Bangkok Mass Transit System (Skytrain)

CAT – Communications Authority of Thailand
chao leh – also *chow lair* or *chow nám;* sea gypsies
chedi – stupa; monument erected to house a Buddha relic
chow lair – also *chao leh* or *chow nám;* sea gypsies
chow samǔi – 'Samui folk'; rural people on Ko Samui

đa·làht – also *tàlàat;* market
đa·làht nám – also *tàlàat náam;* floating market
dhamma – right behaviour and truth according to Buddhist doctrine
đròrk – also *trok* or *tràwk;* alley, smaller than a soi
ôrù ò jeen – also *trùt jiin;* Chinese New Year

Eid al-Fitr – feasting at the end of the Muslim festival of Ramadan

faràng – foreigner of European descent

gâa·ou – also *kâew;* crystal, jewel, glass or gem
ga·teu·i – also *kàthoey;* 'ladyboy'; transvestites and transsexuals
gò – also *ko* or *koh;* island
gow·low – also *kaw·lae;* traditional fishing boats of southern Thailand
grà·tôrm – also *kràthâwm;* 'natural' drug, from the leaf of the Mitragyna speciosa tree
gù·ôi – also *kùti;* monk's hut or living quarters

hàht – also *hat;* beach
hôrng – also *hâwng* or *hong;* room or chamber; island caves semisubmerged in the sea

ìsǎhn – also *ìsan;* general term for northeastern Thailand

jang·wàt – province
jataka – stories of the Buddha's previous lives
jeen – also *jiin;* Chinese

kâew – also *gâa·ou;* crystal, jewel, glass or gem
kàthoey – also *ga·teu·i;* 'ladyboy'; transvestites and transsexuals
kaw·lae – also *gow·low;* traditional fishing boats of southern Thailand
klong – also *khlong* or *khlawng;* canal
ko – also *gò* or *koh;* island
kǒw – also *khao;* hill or mountain
krêu·ang tom – nielloware; a silver-and-black alloy/enamel jewellery technique borrowed from China many centuries ago
krút – mythical creature, half-man and half-bird (known as Garuda in Pali), a symbol of Thai Brahminism and royal patronage
kràthâwm – also *grà·tôrm;* 'natural' drug, from the leaf of the Mitragyna speciosa tree
Kun – also *Khun;* honorific used before first name
kùti – also *gù·ôi;* monk's hut or living quarters

lǎam – also *laem;* geographical cape
lá·kon – classical Thai dance-drama
lí·gair ʾbàh – also *lí·keh pàa* or *lí·gair bòk;* Thai folk dance-drama
longyi – Burmese sarong

mâa nám – river
masjid – also *mátsàyít;* mosque
meu·ang – also *muang;* city
mòo – also *mǔu;* short for *mòo bâhn;* village
moo·ay tai – also *muay thai;* Thai boxing
MRT – Metropolitan Rapid Transit (Metro); the underground railway in Bangkok
muay thai – also *moo·ay tai;* Thai boxing

ná·kon – also *nakhorn;* city
nám – water or juice
nám ôòk – also *náam tòk;* waterfall
nǎng ôà·lung – Thai shadow theatre; movies
nibbana – nirvana; the 'blowing out' or extinction of all desire and thus of all suffering

nôo·at pǎan boh·rahn – also *nûat paen boh-raan;* Thai massage

nóy – also *noi;* small

ow – also *ao;* bay or gulf

pàk tâi – also *bàk ðâi;* southern Thailand

Pali – language derived from Sanskrit, in which the Buddhist scriptures are written

pěe – also *phǐi;* spirits

pìi-phâat – also *bèe·pâht;* classical Thai orchestra

pôo nóy – also *phûu náwy;* 'little people'; those yet to attain social standing in the Thai system of deference and respect

pôo yài – also *phûu yài;* 'big people'; those who have higher social standing, expected to sponsor and provide for *pôo nóy*

prá – also *phrà;* monk or Buddha image

prang – also *brang;* Khmer-style tower on temples

ráhn goh·ʼbêe – also *ráhn ko-pǐi;* coffee shops (southern Thailand)

râi – an area of land measurement equal to 1600 sq m

Ramakian – Thai version of India's epic literary piece, the Ramayana

reu·a gow·low – also *reua kaw-lae;* large painted fishing boats, peculiar to Narathiwat and Pattani

reu·a hǎhng yow – also *reua hǎang yao;* long-tail taxi boat

reu·an tǎa·ou – a longhouse

reu·sěe – also *reusǐi;* Hindu rishi or sage

rót aa – blue-and-white air-conditioned buses

rót dòo·an – express trains

rót tam·má·dah – ordinary bus (no air-con) or ordinary train (not rapid or express)

sǎamláw – also *sǎhm·lór;* three-wheeled pedicab

sǎh·lah – also *sala* or *saalaa;* open-sided, covered meeting hall or resting place

sǎhm·lór – also *sǎamláw;* three-wheeled pedicab

sǎhn jôw – also *sǎan jâo;* Chinese shrine or joss house

sà·lěung – old system of Thai currency (one sà·lěung equals 25 satang)

samatha – meditation practice aimed at developing refined states of concentration

sǎm·nák wí·ʼbàt·sà·nah – meditation centre

sangha – brotherhood of Buddhist monks; temple inhabitants (monks, nuns and lay residents)

sà·nùk – fun

sà·pahn – bridge

sǎwngthǎew – also *sǒrng·tǎa·ou;* small pickup truck with two benches in the back, used as bus/taxi

soi – lane or small street

Songkhran – Thai New Year, held in mid-April

sǒrng·tǎa·ou – also *sǎwngthǎew;* small pickup truck with two benches in the back, used as bus/taxi

SRT – State Railway of Thailand

stupa – domed edifice housing Buddhist relics

suttas – discourses of the Buddha

tâh – also *tha* or *thâa;* pier, landing

tàlàat – also *ða-làht;* market

tàlàat náam – also *ða-làht nám;* floating market

TAT – Tourism Authority of Thailand

tha – also *tâh* or *thâa;* pier, landing

Thai ʼbàk ðâi – also *Thai pàk tâi;* southern Thais

tâm – also *thâm;* cave

thànǒn – street, road, avenue (we use the abbreviation 'Th' in this book)

Tripitaka – Theravada Buddhist scriptures

trok – also *ðròrk* or *tràwk;* alley, smaller than a soi

Trùt Jeen – also *ðrù̀ð jeen;* Chinese New Year

túk-túk – motorised sǎhm·lór

Ummah – the Muslim community

vipassana – Buddhist insight meditation

wâi – palms-together Thai greeting

wan prá – Buddhist holy days, falling on the days of the main phases of the moon (full, new and half) each month

wang – palace

wát – temple, monastery

wí·hǎhn – also *wihan* or *viharn;* counterpart to *bòht* in Thai temple, containing Buddha images but not circumscribed by sema stones

WFT – Wildlife Fund Thailand

yah bâh – 'crazy medicine'; methamphetamine

yài – big

ʼbàk ðâi – also *pàk tâi;* southern Thailand

ʼbèe·pâht – also *pìi-phâat;* classical Thai orchestra

ʼbrang – also *prang;* Khmer-style tower on temples

The Authors

ANDREW BURKE Coordinating Author, Destination, Getting Started, Itineraries, Events Calendar, Bangkok (coauthor), Directory, Transport

Andrew has been coming to Thailand for long enough to remember when there was only one full moon party a month on Ko Pha-Ngan and very little neon on Khao San Rd. Since then he's spent almost 20 years travelling through, photographing and writing about Asia, the Middle East and Africa, and the past 10 living in Hong Kong, Phnom Penh and Bangkok. Andrew writes and photographs for publications including *Travel+Leisure*, *National Geographic Traveler* and the *Australian Financial Review*, and contributes occasional television reporting to Channel 4 UK and CNN International. He has written or contributed to more than 20 books for Lonely Planet, including guides to Bangkok, Laos, China and Iran.

CELESTE BRASH Eastern Gulf Coast

Celeste first arrived in Thailand as a student of Thai language, history and culture at Chiang Mai University. She's come back several times since and has done the gamut from wild nights on Ko Pha-Ngan to weeks of silence at Wat Suan Mokkhaphalaram. Her award-winning travel stories have appeared in *Travelers' Tales* books and her travel articles have appeared in publications including the *LA Times* and *Islands* magazine. She's lost count of how many Lonely Planet guides she's contributed to, but her heart is irrevocably stuck on Southeast Asia. When not dragging her husband and two children to exotic places, she and her family live on the island of Tahiti in French Polynesia.

AUSTIN BUSH History, The Culture, Food & Drink, Bangkok (coauthor), Southwestern Gulf Coast (Deep South section)

After graduating from the University of Oregon with a degree in linguistics, Austin received a scholarship to study Thai at Chiang Mai University and has remained in Thailand ever since. After working several years at a stable job, he made the questionable decision to pursue a career as a freelance photographer/writer. This choice has since taken him as far as northern Pakistan and as near as Bangkok's Or Tor Kor Market. He enjoys writing and taking photos about food most of all because it's delicious. His work can be seen at www.austinbushphotography.com.

LONELY PLANET AUTHORS

Why is our travel information the best in the world? It's simple: our authors are passionate, dedicated travellers. They don't take freebies in exchange for positive coverage so you can be sure the advice you're given is impartial. They travel widely to all the popular spots, and off the beaten track. They don't research using just the internet or phone. They discover new places not included in any other guidebook. They personally visit thousands of hotels, restaurants, palaces, trails, galleries, temples and more. They speak with dozens of locals every day to make sure you get the kind of insider knowledge only a local could tell you. They take pride in getting all the details right, and in telling it how it is. Think you can do it? Find out how at **lonelyplanet.com**.

BRANDON PRESSER   Diving & Other Activities, Northwestern Gulf Coast, Southwestern Gulf Coast

Growing up in a land where bear hugs are taken literally, this wanderlusty Canadian always craved swaying palms and golden sand. A trek across Southeast Asia as a teenager was the clincher – he was hooked, returning year after year to scuba dive, suntan, and savour spoonfuls of spicy *sôm-đam* (papaya salad). After giving up his job at the Louvre, Brandon picked up his pen and rucksack and became a full-time freelance travel writer. These days he spends most of his time on the road authoring Lonely Planet books to far-flung destinations such as Iceland and Borneo. This is his fifth guide to Southeast Asia.

ADAM SKOLNICK   Northern Andaman Coast, Southern Andaman Coast

Adam became travel obsessed while working as an environmental activist in the mid '90s. A freelance journalist, he writes about travel, culture, health, sports and the environment for Lonely Planet, *Men's Health*, *Outside*, *Travel & Leisure*, and *Spa*. He has coauthored seven previous Lonely Planet guidebooks, including *Southeast Asia on a Shoestring*, *East Timor*, *Bali & Lombok* and *Indonesia*. He's also the author of *Phuket Encounter*. On this research trip he drove more than 3000km in his rented and extremely masculine blue bunny, made four visa runs and chartered or hitched 47 long-tails. You can read more of his work at www.adamskolnick.com.

CONTRIBUTING AUTHORS

Dr Trish Bachelor wrote the Health chapter. She is a general practitioner and travel-medicine specialist who works at the Ciwec Clinic in Kathmandu, Nepal, as well as being a Medical Advisor to the Travel Doctor New Zealand clinics. Trish teaches travel medicine through the University of Otago, and is interested in underwater and high-altitude medicine, and in the impact of tourism on host countries. She has travelled extensively through Southeast and East Asia and particularly loves high-altitude trekking in the Himalayas.

David Lukas wrote the Environment chapter. David is a professional naturalist who lives on the border of Yosemite National Park, where he conducts research and writes about the natural world. His many travels include spending a year in western Borneo studying the ecology of Southeast Asian rainforests. He is the author of environment chapters for about 20 Lonely Planet guides ranging from *Nova Scotia* to *Costa Rica*.

Behind the Scenes

THIS BOOK

This 7th edition of *Thailand's Islands & Beaches* was researched and updated by Andrew Burke, Celeste Brash, Austin Bush, Brandon Presser and Adam Skolnick, with contributions by David Lukas and Dr Trish Bachelor. This guidebook was commissioned in Lonely Planet's Melbourne office, and produced by the following:

Commissioning Editors Shawn Low, Tashi Wheeler
Coordinating Editor David Carroll
Coordinating Cartographer Jacqueline Nguyen
Coordinating Layout Designer Jim Hsu
Managing Editor Brigitte Ellemor
Managing Cartographers Shahara Ahmed, David Connolly
Managing Layout Designer Sally Darmody
Assisting Editors Monique Choy, Jessica Crouch, Andrea Dobbin, Melanie Dankel, Charlotte Harrison, Katie Lynch, Kristin Odijk, Gina Tsarouhas
Assisting Cartographer Hunor Csutoros
Cover Research Naomi Parker, lonelyplanetimages.com
Internal Image Research Aude Vauconsant, lonely planetimages.com
Project Manager Chris Girdler
Language Content Branislava Vladisavljevic

Thanks to Lucy Birchley, Bruce Evans, Corey Hutchison, Lisa Knights, Annelies Mertens, Trent Paton

THANKS
ANDREW BURKE

A heartfelt *khàwp khun khráp* to my wife Anne and daughter Ava for making Bangkok life so rewarding. Thanks to Mason Florence, Stuart McDonald, Jennifer Chen, Gun Aramwit, Karen Percy, Norm Hermant and Nisha Rai for tips, guidance and company discovering more of Bangkok, to May and Ae for making MeMay Café so welcoming, and to Raul Gallego Abellan for riding to Kanchanaburi and beyond. Special thanks to my diligent coauthor Austin Bush and, at Lonely Planet, Tashi Wheeler, Shawn Low, David Connolly, Chris Girdler, David Carroll and the editors and cartographers for their patience and determination to make this a better book.

CELESTE BRASH

Infinite thanks to my husband and kids for coping with my absences and supporting me through them. Fellow Lonely Planet author Mark Beales helped heaps with Pattaya and Sri Racha. Huge thanks to Jacob, Ton and Nok on Ko Kood, Canadians Kelly and Mike for good company, the wonderful people at Baan Zen, Yan at Baan Rim Nan and Pittaya – all on Ko Chang – and Morn in Trat. Brandon Presser provided excellent base text, set me up with contacts and offered all-time phone support

THE LONELY PLANET STORY

Fresh from an epic journey across Europe, Asia and Australia in 1972, Tony and Maureen Wheeler sat at their kitchen table stapling together notes. The first Lonely Planet guidebook, *Across Asia on the Cheap*, was born.

Travellers snapped up the guides. Inspired by their success, the Wheelers began publishing books to Southeast Asia, India and beyond. Demand was prodigious, and the Wheelers expanded the business rapidly to keep up. Over the years, Lonely Planet extended its coverage to every country and into the virtual world via lonelyplanet.com and the Thorn Tree message board.

As Lonely Planet became a globally loved brand, Tony and Maureen received several offers for the company. But it wasn't until 2007 that they found a partner whom they trusted to remain true to the company's principles of travelling widely, treading lightly and giving sustainably. In October of that year, BBC Worldwide acquired a 75% share in the company, pledging to uphold Lonely Planet's commitment to independent travel, trustworthy advice and editorial independence.

Today, Lonely Planet has offices in Melbourne, London and Oakland, with over 500 staff members and 300 authors. Tony and Maureen are still actively involved with Lonely Planet. They're travelling more often than ever, and they're devoting their spare time to charitable projects. And the company is still driven by the philosophy of *Across Asia on the Cheap*: 'All you've got to do is decide to go and the hardest part is over. So go!'

BEHIND THE SCENES

throughout. Thanks also to Catherine Bodry and Andrew Burke. And Tashi (sob) I'll miss you!

AUSTIN BUSH
I'd like to thank the book's previous authors, China Williams and Joe Cummings, for their excellent work, much of which still survives, my patient and helpful coordinating author Andrew Burke and commissioning editor Tashi Wheeler, map guru David Connolly and the rest of the Lonely Planet staff in Melbourne, my local experts Gregoire Glachant, Steven Pettifor and Kong Rithdee, as well as those who introduced me to new places and joined me at the old, including Yuthika Charoenrungruang, Ron Diaz, Nick Grossman, Richard Hermes, Yaowalak Itthichaiwarakom, Wes and Ann Hsu, Paul Hutt and Maylee Thavat.

BRANDON PRESSER
A heartfelt thank you to my dear friends the Bambridges for their generosity, hospitality and good company. Also, a very special thanks to Crystal. At Lonely Planet I would like to thank the following people for their dedication, teamwork and kind support: Tashi Wheeler, Chris Girdler, Andrew Burke and Chris Love. Additional thanks to Watcharin Fasiriporn, Matt, Hans, Stiof, Justin, Brian, and to my distinguished coauthor Celeste: Heads! Finally, thank you pesky mosquito for giving me dengue fever and thwarting my research plans...

ADAM SKOLNICK
Thanks to Paul at Wicked Diving, Mama in Khao Lak, Kun Mam on Yao Noi, Celine at Siam Indigo, Claude at Cape Panwa Hotel, the ingenious Old Town/Patong/Bangkok Lek, and to travel buds Steve & Catharine, Pete & Rosie, Kid Pablo, and Carrie & Noah. *Ko kun kaaaaaap* to the great and hairy John Gray, my friends at German Bakery and Rum Jungle, Diana at Rawai Muay Thai, Lisa at Mom Tri, Julie, Pan and the dog pound at Villa G, Austin, Celeste, Andrew and the entire Lonely Planet squad, and to the always lovely Georgiana Johnson.

OUR READERS
Many thanks to the travellers who used the last edition and wrote to us with helpful hints, useful advice and interesting anecdotes:

Reinier Bakels, Gavin Bartle, Andy Betts, Ian Bunton, Anne Fahey, Idoia Iturbe, Esther Jackson, Roozbeh Kaboli, Luke Kenyon Kenyon, Anique Landre, Ben Ogden, William Seager, Lisa Smieja, Christer Steffensen, Susan Wiltshire, Jennifer Yuill

ACKNOWLEDGMENTS
Many thanks to the following for the use of their content:

Globe on title page ©Mountain High Maps 1993 Digital Wisdom, Inc.

SEND US YOUR FEEDBACK
We love to hear from travellers – your comments keep us on our toes and help make our books better. Our well-travelled team reads every word on what you loved or loathed about this book. Although we cannot reply individually to postal submissions, we always guarantee that your feedback goes straight to the appropriate authors, in time for the next edition. Each person who sends us information is thanked in the next edition and the most useful submissions are rewarded with a free book.

To send us your updates – and find out about Lonely Planet events, newsletters and travel news – visit our award-winning website: **lonelyplanet.com/contact**.

Note: we may edit, reproduce and incorporate your comments in Lonely Planet products such as guidebooks, websites and digital products, so let us know if you don't want your comments reproduced or your name acknowledged. For a copy of our privacy policy visit lonelyplanet .com/privacy.

Index

INDEX

INDEX

INDEX

000 Map pages
0 Photograph pages

INDEX

GREENDEX

Many businesses catering to tourism in Thailand have made an effort to minimise their negative impacts. Some have invested in clean energy, while others support local food producers and minimise waste. Those listed here were chosen by the authors because they show real commitment to operating more sustainably. We are keen to expand this list and appreciate your feedback at lonelyplanet.com/feedback. For additional useful information on sustainable travel, see lonelyplanet.com/responsibletravel.

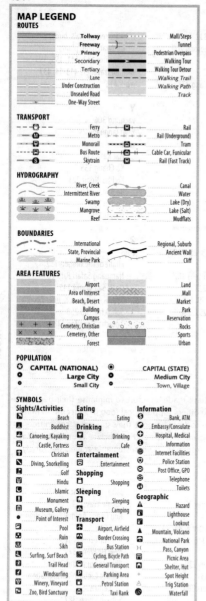

MAP LEGEND

ROUTES

Tollway	Mall/Steps
Freeway	Tunnel
Primary	Pedestrian Overpass
Secondary	Walking Tour
Tertiary	Walking Tour Detour
Lane	Walking Trail
Under Construction	Walking Path
Unsealed Road	Track
One-Way Street	

TRANSPORT

Ferry	Rail
Metro	Rail (Underground)
Monorail	Tram
Bus Route	Cable Car, Funicular
Skytrain	Rail (Fast Track)

HYDROGRAPHY

River, Creek	Canal
Intermittent River	Water
Swamp	Lake (Dry)
Mangrove	Lake (Salt)
Reef	Mudflats

BOUNDARIES

International	Regional, Suburb
State, Provincial	Ancient Wall
Marine Park	Cliff

AREA FEATURES

Airport	Land
Area of Interest	Mall
Beach, Desert	Market
Building	Park
Campus	Reservation
Cemetery, Christian	Rocks
Cemetery, Other	Sports
Forest	Urban

POPULATION

◎ CAPITAL (NATIONAL)	◉ CAPITAL (STATE)
● Large City	● Medium City
● Small City	● Town, Village

SYMBOLS

Sights/Activities
- Beach
- Buddhist
- Canoeing, Kayaking
- Castle, Fortress
- Christian
- Diving, Snorkelling
- Golf
- Hindu
- Islamic
- Monument
- Museum, Gallery
- Point of Interest
- Pool
- Ruin
- Sikh
- Surfing, Surf Beach
- Trail Head
- Windsurfing
- Winery, Vineyard
- Zoo, Bird Sanctuary

Eating
- Eating

Drinking
- Drinking
- Cafe

Entertainment
- Entertainment

Shopping
- Shopping

Sleeping
- Sleeping
- Camping

Transport
- Airport, Airfield
- Border Crossing
- Bus Station
- Cycling, Bicycle Path
- General Transport
- Parking Area
- Petrol Station
- Taxi Rank

Information
- Bank, ATM
- Embassy/Consulate
- Hospital, Medical
- Information
- Internet Facilities
- Police Station
- Post Office, GPO
- Telephone
- Toilets

Geographic
- Hazard
- Lighthouse
- Lookout
- Mountain, Volcano
- National Park
- Pass, Canyon
- Picnic Area
- Shelter, Hut
- Spot Height
- Trig Station
- Waterfall

LONELY PLANET OFFICES

Australia (Head Office)
Locked Bag 1, Footscray, Victoria 3011
☎ 03 8379 8000, fax 03 8379 8111
talk2us@lonelyplanet.com.au

USA
150 Linden St, Oakland, CA 94607
☎ 510 250 6400, toll free 800 275 8555
fax 510 893 8572
info@lonelyplanet.com

UK
2nd fl, 186 City Rd,
London EC1V 2NT
☎ 020 7106 2100, fax 020 7106 2101
go@lonelyplanet.co.uk

Published by Lonely Planet
ABN 36 005 607 983

© Lonely Planet 2010

© photographers as indicated 2010

Cover photograph: Beach on Ko Hong, Jose Fuste Raga/Corbis. Many of the images in this guide are available for licensing from Lonely Planet Images: lonelyplanetimages.com.

Printed through Colorcraft Ltd, Hong Kong
Printed in China

Mixed Sources
Product group from well-managed forests and other controlled sources
www.fsc.org Cert no. SGS-COC-005002
© 1996 Forest Stewardship Council